Frommer's®

P9-EKJ-162

San Francisco
from $70 a Day

5th Edition

by Matthew Richard Poole

Here's what the critics say about Frommer's:

"Amazingly easy to use. Very portable, very complete."

—*Booklist*

"Detailed, accurate, and easy-to-read information for all price ranges."
—*Glamour Magazine*

"Hotel information is close to encyclopedic."

—*Des Moines Sunday Register*

"Frommer's Guides have a way of giving you a real feel for a place."
—*Knight Ridder Newspapers*

WILEY

Wiley Publishing, Inc.

Published by:

Wiley Publishing, Inc.

111 River St.
Hoboken, NJ 07030-5774

ISBN-13: 978-0-471-76979-8
ISBN-10: 0-471-76979-7

Editor: Jennifer Reilly
Production Editor: Jana M. Stefanciosa
Cartographer: Elizabeth Puhl
Photo Editor: Richard Fox
Production by Wiley Indianapolis Composition Services

Front cover photo: Skyline through the Golden Gate Bridge
Back cover photo: Room at the Hotel des Arts

For information on our other products and services or to obtain technical support, please contact our Customer Care Department within the U.S. at 800/762-2974, outside the U.S. at 317/572-3993 or fax 317/572-4002.

Wiley also publishes its books in a variety of electronic formats. Some content that appears in print may not be available in electronic formats.

Manufactured in the United States of America

5   4   3   2   1

Contents

List of Maps   vi

What's New in San Francisco   1

1 The Best of San Francisco   4

1 Frommer's Favorite (& Mostly Free)   2 Best Low-Cost Hotel Bets 9
  San Francisco Experiences 4   3 Best Low-Cost Dining Bets 10

2 Planning an Affordable Trip to San Francisco   13

1 The San Francisco from   6 Travel Insurance 25
  $70 a Day Premise 13   7 Health & Safety 26
2 42 Money-Saving Tips 13   8 Specialized Travel Resources 26
  CityPass: The Budget   9 Planning Your Trip Online 29
  Traveler's Bonanza 18   Online Traveler's Toolbox 31
3 Visitor Information 19   10 Getting There 32
4 Money 19   11 Packages for the Independent
5 When to Go 20   Traveler 36
  San Francisco Calendar   12 Recommended Books & Films 37
  of Events 21

3 For International Visitors   39

1 Preparing for Your Trip 39   Fast Facts: For the International
2 Getting to the U.S. 45   Traveler 47
3 Getting Around the U.S. 46

4 Suggested San Francisco Itineraries   52

1 The Best of San Francisco   3 The Best of San Francisco
  in 1 Day 52   in 3 Days 56
2 The Best of San Francisco
  in 2 Days 55

5 Getting to Know San Francisco   59

1 Orientation .59   2 Getting Around 63
  Neighborhoods in Brief 60   Fast Facts: San Francisco 69

6 Accommodations You Can Afford   73

1 Union Square/Nob Hill 75

*Affordable Family-Friendly
Hotels* 80

*Accommodations with
Free Parking* 83

2 South of Market (SoMa) 84

*Four Great Reasons to
Stay with the Renesons* 85

3 North Beach/Fisherman's Wharf 88

4 Marina District/Cow Hollow 89

5 Pacific Heights 92

6 Civic Center & Environs 93

7 Haight-Ashbury 94

8 Richmond District 94

9 The Castro 95

10 Near the Airport 96

7 Great Deals on Dining   98

1 Restaurants by Cuisine 99

2 Union Square 102

3 Financial District 108

*The Sun on Your Face
at Belden Place* 108

4 Nob Hill/Russian Hill 110

5 South of Market (SoMa) 110

6 Chinatown 115

7 North Beach 118

8 Fisherman's Wharf 123

*The Best of San Francisco's
Family-Friendly Restaurants* 125

9 Marina District/Cow Hollow 126

10 Pacific Heights 130

11 Japantown 131

12 Civic Center & Environs 132

Hidden Treasures 133

13 Haight-Ashbury 134

14 Richmond District 136

15 Sunset District 138

16 The Castro 139

17 Mission District 141

8 Exploring San Francisco   146

1 San Francisco's Top Attractions 146

*Funky Favorites at Fisherman's
Wharf* 154

*Cheap Thrills: My Favorite Things
to See & Do for Free (or Almost)
in San Francisco* 156

2 Other Attractions 159

*San Francisco's Old-Fashioned
Arcade Museum* 160

Free Culture 165

3 Neighborhoods Worth a Visit 166

4 Golden Gate Park 171

5 The Presidio & Golden Gate National
Recreation Area 174

6 Religious Buildings Worth
Checking Out 178

7 Architectural Highlights 179

Especially for Kids 180

8 Self-Guided & Organized Tours 182

9 Outdoor Pursuits 185

10 Spectator Sports 188

9 City Strolls 190

Walking Tour 1: Chinatown:
History, Culture, Dim Sum &
Then Some 190

Walking Tour 2: Getting to Know
North Beach 197

10 Shopping 203

1 The Shopping Scene 203
2 Shopping A to Z 205

Discount Shopping 206
Amazing Grazing 212

11 San Francisco After Dark 219

1 The Performing Arts 220
2 Comedy & Cabaret 222
3 The Club & Music Scene 223
4 The Bar Scene 228

Midnight (or Midday) Mochas 231
5 Gay & Lesbian Bars & Clubs 234
6 Film 235

12 Side Trips from San Francisco 237

1 Berkeley .237
2 Oakland .242
3 Angel Island & Tiburon 245
4 Sausalito 248

5 Muir Woods, Mount Tamalpais
& Stinson Beach 250
6 Point Reyes National Seashore 251
Johnson Drake's Oyster Farm 254

13 The Wine Country 257

1 Napa Valley 257
The Ins & Outs of Shipping
Wine Home 267
Enjoying Art & Nature 268
Where to Stock Up for
a Gourmet Picnic 277

2 Sonoma Valley 279
Touring the Sonoma
Valley by Bike 283

Appendix: San Francisco in Depth 290

1 History 101 290
Dateline .291

2 San Francisco Today 299

Index 300

General Index 300
Accommodations Index 308

Restaurant Index 309

List of Maps

San Francisco at a Glance   6

The Best of San Francisco
   in 1 & 2 Days   53

The Best of San Francisco
   in 3 Days   57

San Francisco Mass Transit   64

Union Square & Nob Hill
   Accommodations   77

San Francisco Accommodations   86

Union Square & Financial
   District Dining   103

San Francisco Dining   112

Chinatown & North Beach
   Dining   117

Mission District Dining   143

Major San Francisco Sights   148

Fisherman's Wharf Area Sights   151

Yerba Buena Gardens   161

Haight-Ashbury & the Castro   167

Golden Gate Park   172

The Presidio & Golden Gate National
   Recreation Area   176

The Civic Center Area   181

Walking Tour 1: Chinatown   191

Walking Tour 2: North Beach   199

Berkeley   239

Marin Headlands   247

The Wine Country   259

An Invitation to the Reader

In researching this book, we discovered many wonderful places—hotels, restaurants, shops, and more. We're sure you'll find others. Please tell us about them, so we can share the information with your fellow travelers in upcoming editions. If you were disappointed with a recommendation, we'd love to know that, too. Please write to:

Frommer's San Francisco from $70 a Day, 5th Edition
Wiley Publishing, Inc. • 111 River St. • Hoboken, NJ 07030-5774

An Additional Note

About the Author

Matthew Richard Poole, a native Californian, has authored more than two dozen travel guides to California, Hawaii, and abroad, and is a regular contributor to radio and TV travel programs, including guest appearances on the award-winning *Bay Area Backroads* show. Before becoming a full-time travel writer and photographer, he worked as an English tutor in Prague, ski instructor in the Swiss Alps, and scuba instructor in Maui and Thailand. Highly allergic to office buildings, he spends most of his time traveling the globe and searching for new adventures. He is also the author of *Frommer's Irreverent Guide to San Francisco* and *Frommer's Los Angeles.*

Other Great Guides for Your Trip:

Frommer's Irreverent Guide to San Francisco
Frommer's Memorable Walks in San Francisco
Frommer's Portable San Francisco
Frommer's San Francisco
San Francisco For Dummies
The Unofficial Guide to San Francisco

Frommer's Star Ratings, Icons & Abbreviations

Every hotel, restaurant, and attraction listing in this guide has been ranked for quality, value, service, amenities, and special features using a **star-rating system.** In country, state, and regional guides, we also rate towns and regions to help you narrow down your choices and budget your time accordingly. Hotels and restaurants are rated on a scale of zero (recommended) to three stars (exceptional). Attractions, shopping, nightlife, towns, and regions are rated according to the following scale: zero stars (recommended), one star (highly recommended), two stars (very highly recommended), and three stars (must-see).

In addition to the star-rating system, we also use **seven feature icons** that point you to the great deals, in-the-know advice, and unique experiences that separate travelers from tourists. Throughout the book, look for:

Finds	Special finds—those places only insiders know about
Fun Fact	Fun facts—details that make travelers more informed and their trips more fun
Kids	Best bets for kids and advice for the whole family
Moments	Special moments—those experiences that memories are made of
Overrated	Places or experiences not worth your time or money
Tips	Insider tips—great ways to save time and money
Value	Great values—where to get the best deals

The following **abbreviations** are used for credit cards:

AE American Express	DISC Discover	V Visa
DC Diners Club	MC MasterCard	

Frommers.com

Now that you have the guidebook to a great trip, visit our website at **www.frommers.com** for travel information on more than 3,000 destinations. With features updated regularly, we give you instant access to the most current trip-planning information available. At Frommers.com, you'll also find the best prices on airfares, accommodations, and car rentals—and you can even book travel online through our travel booking partners. At Frommers.com, you'll also find the following:

- Online updates to our most popular guidebooks
- Vacation sweepstakes and contest giveaways
- Newsletter highlighting the hottest travel trends
- Online travel message boards with featured travel discussions

What's New in San Francisco

San Francisco—a city that is always in a state of flux. This section highlights the latest trends, attractions, and openings. There's some great stuff here, so be sure to add the below to your to-do list while exploring the city.

PLANNING A TRIP   New this year is the Go San Francisco Card, a sort of money-saving e-ticket that gets you unlimited pre-paid entry to about 45 attractions in the city and Bay Area, including museums, walking tours, bike rentals, sightseeing tours, and Six Flags Marine World. Prices range from $49 for one adult for 1 day, with lower costs per day for multiday cards and children's cards. See chapter 2, "Planning an Affordable Trip to San Francisco," for complete details.

SUGGESTED ITINERARIES IN SAN FRANCISCO   I've added this new chapter to help you make the most of your time while vacationing in San Francisco. Think of it as an insiders' guide on how to spend 3 memorable days in the city, complete with detailed maps and recommended restaurants along the route.

ACCOMMODATIONS   When the whole dot-com craze raised the rates for everything in San Francisco—especially hotel rooms—even the inevitable crash didn't make much of a dent in the cost of living or visiting, because once the rates are raised they rarely go down.

As such, several hotels in the previous edition have priced themselves out of this book, but I've replaced them with eight great lodgings I've ferreted out, ranging from a hip Mission District hostel to a sexy Union Square splurge called the Savoy. There's too many to list them all in this chapter, but I'll include three of my favorites.

On the lower end of the spending spectrum is **Elements Hotel,** 2524 Mission St. (© **866/327-8407**), the Mission District's new and very stylish youth hostel that's as vibrant and colorful as the nightlife and restaurants surrounding it. See chapter 6.

Hotel Carlton, 1075 Sutter St. (© **800/ 922-7586** or 415/673-0242) made the cut because, though it's located a wee bit off the tourist trail (in the rather ho-hum dreary outskirts of Union Square and Civic Center), it's an attractive and extremely well-priced option. See chapter 6.

I also highly recommend **Hotel des Arts,** formerly called the Alisa Hotel, at 447 Bush St. (© **800/956-4322** or 415/ 956-3232), near Union Square. It's cleverly designed by local artists and priced to house them, with rooms starting at $60. See chapter 6.

DINING   There are plenty of great new restaurants in the city, but most of them would nuke your budget, so instead I've added 15 more of my favorite places to enjoy an inexpensive dining experience. See chapter 7 for a description of each. A few of my favorites include **Bocadillos,** 710 Montgomery St. (© **415/982-2622**), yet another home run by Basque chef Girald Hirigoyen, where outstanding tapas are served in a casual Financial District setting.

Another favorite is **Levende Lounge,** 1710 Mission St. (© **415/864-5585**) in the Mission District. It's currently one of the hot new restaurants in the city, where superb small plates are served in a setting that combines DJ music and a lively bar scene.

Other new additions cover cuisines from across the globe: Moroccan, Vietnamese (three of them), Burmese, Belgian, Italian, French, Japanese, and my favorite place in the city to get a good ol' American burger—**Barney's Gourmet Hamburgers,** 3344 Steiner St. (© **415/563-0307**).

ATTRACTIONS   There's all kinds of exciting new stuff to see and do in San Francisco in this edition.

Over at Fisherman's Wharf is the gargantuan new **Boudin at the Wharf,** 160 Jefferson St. (© **415/928-1849**), a 26,000-square-foot baking emporium that's nearly half a block long and houses not only their signature demonstration bakery (strangely mesmerizing) but also a museum, gourmet marketplace, cafe, espresso bar, and restaurant. See chapter 8.

After closing for several years so a completely new building could be constructed, the **de Young Museum,** 50 Hagiwara Tea Garden Dr. (© **415/682-2481**), reopened in October 2005. The museum's collection includes American paintings, African arts, sculptural and decorative arts, and textiles. See "Everything Old is New Again," in chapter 8, for more.

I've also included a new tour run by **San Francisco Electric Tour Company** (© **415/474-3130**) where you can ride around on Segway Human Transporters, those weird-looking upright scooters you've probably seen on TV. After a 40-minute lesson you'll tool around Fisherman's

Wharf on a fun and informative guided tour (*way* better than a tour bus). See "San Francisco Segway Tours," in chapter 8, for more details.

But wait, there's more. Be sure to check out the new talking **GoCar**s, 2715 Hyde St. (© **800/91-GoCar** or 415/441-5695). I see them all over town now—tiny yellow 3-wheeled convertible cars that are cleverly guided by a talking GPS (Global Positioning System) and give computer-guided tours of the city's highlights. As you drive, the talking car tells you where to turn and what landmarks you're passing. Very cool. Read more in chapter 8, "GoCar Tours of San Francisco."

SHOPPING   As if San Francisco didn't already offer enough reasons to beg your credit-card company to up your spending limit, consider the latest additions to the shopping scene: France's **Diptyque,** 171 Maiden Lane (© **415/402-0600**), opened a downtown boutique where you can buy their to-die-for candles (if you're into that sort of thing). In Hayes Valley, which continues to expand as the epicenter of cool clothing and furnishings, **True Sake,** 560 Hayes St. (© **415/355-9555**), is America's first shop dedicated to rice wines ranging from cheap and quaffable to fancy stuff with gold flecks and rare finds at triple-digit prices. Around the corner, **RAG,** 541 Octavia St. (© **415/621-7718**), is where to go if you want to snag one-of-a-kind and rarely found female fashions, all of which are made by up-and-coming local designers and are very affordable. Speaking of one of a kind, San Francisco's hot new perfumer, Julie Elliott, opened a small boutique downtown called **Showroom by In Fiore,** 868 Post St. (© **415/840-1726**). Make an appointment, and see why her body balms, oils, and facial serums garner loyal celebrity fans such as Julia Roberts, Britney Spears, and Steven Tyler. For these and other recommendations, see chapter 10.

NIGHTLIFE There's an entirely new section to this chapter (chapter 11) called "Destination Bars with DJ Grooves," the latest nightlife trend in the city. With hip names like **Bambuddha Lounge,** 601 Eddy St. (© **415/885-5088**), and **The Monkey Club,** 2730 21st St. (© **415/ 647-6546**), these trendy new clubs have DJs spinning house, jazz, and world music till 2a.m. The cocktails tend to be pricey, but the entertainment—great music and major eye candy—is free.

I've also added my favorite cabaret and jazz venue, the **Empire Plush Room,** 940 Sutter St. (© **415/885-2800**), a swanky little club that lures national talent (be sure to check their website and see who's in town), and two new wine bars: **First Crush,** 101 Cyril Magnin St. (© **415/982-7874**) and **Nectar Wine Lounge,** 3330 Steiner St. (© **415/345-1377**). Both are sleek and chic places to sample California wines and snack on small plates.

SIDE TRIPS FROM SAN FRANCISCO There's a fantastic new restaurant in Oakland that's included in this edition. **À Côté,** 5478 College Ave. (© **510/655-6469**), serves superb small plates of Mediterranean-inspired cuisine in a festive setting.

Another great find I've added is the **Steep Ravine Environmental Cabins** at Mount Tamalpais State Park on the Marin County coast (© **415/388-2070**). For only $75, you and four of your best friends can stay the night in a rustic redwood cabin that's perched on a bluff overlooking the ocean.

Also new to Marin is the **Bear Valley Inn Bed & Breakfast** at Point Reyes National Seashore, 88 Bear Valley Rd. (© **415/663-1777**). You'll be hardpressed to find a better B&B for the price in Point Reyes than this cute two-story 1919 farmhouse. Read more about these side trips, and others, in chapter 12.

WINE COUNTRY It may be expensive to stay at a B&B in the Wine Country, but it's a bargain to dine well here. I've added six newcomers to the budget dining scene, ranging from **Bouchon Bakery** (6528 Washington St., © **707/ 944-2253**), a new French-style bakery in Yountville run by one of the top chefs in the nation, Thomas Keller, to a gourmet roadhouse in Napa that serves killer beer-battered onion rings, a gourmet pizzeria in St. Helena, a bear-themed diner in Sonoma that welcomes kids, and a new Thai restaurant in downtown Sonoma. See chapter 13 for all of them.

1

The Best of San Francisco

I know what you're thinking: How could anyone possibly enjoy a vacation in San Francisco for as little as $70 a day? After all, the average room rate alone is about $170 a night, not including taxes, tipping, and taxi fare.

But if there's one thing we underpaid travel writers know how to do, it's how to live large and spend little. As a San Francisco local for 14 years, I've perfected the art of having a lot of fun without spending loads of cash. Some of my advice is obvious (skip the Ritz Carlton brunch), some more comes from experience (dine off the fancy restaurant bar menus for the best deals), and all of it is geared to making sure that you will have a fantastic vacation in the city, regardless of your tax bracket.

Yes, ultra-luxury $400-per-night hotel rooms and eye-poppingly expensive restaurants are plentiful in the city, but that's not where the locals hang out or dine. Traveling on a budget in San Francisco means doing what most of its denizens do every day: eating at the city's many affordable restaurants, enjoying the wonderful parks and neighborhoods, and taking advantage of its wide variety of free or inexpensive attractions. If you do as the locals do, you're far more likely to experience the hidden secrets of San Francisco, which high-end travelers, lounging in their reclusive suites, will never see.

But the best advice I can give you about San Francisco is to just *go.* Enjoy the cool blast of salty air as you stroll across the Golden Gate. Stuff yourself with cheap dim sum in Chinatown. Browse the vintage clothing shops along Haight Street. Walk along the beach, pierce your nose, skate through Golden Gate Park, ride the cable cars: it's all happening every day in San Francisco, and everyone, whether filthy rich or in the red, is invited. All you have to do is arrive with an open mind and a sense of adventure—the rest is waiting for you.

1 Frommer's Favorite (& Mostly Free) San Francisco Experiences

- **Walking Across the Golden Gate Bridge.** Don your windbreaker and walking shoes and prepare for a wind-blasted, exhilarating walk across San Francisco's most famous landmark. It's one of those things you have to do at least once in your life, and it's free. See p. 156.
- **Touring Alcatraz.** Even if you loathe tourist attractions, you'll enjoy a tour of The Rock. The National Park Service has done a fantastic job of

preserving the venerable prison—enough to give you the heebie-jeebies just looking at it—and NPS rangers and volunteers give excellent guided tours. Even the boat ride across the bay is worth the price. You shouldn't miss this one, so be sure to reserve tickets far in advance. Day trips (with audio tour) run around $16. See p. 146.

- **Strolling Through Chinatown.** I've been through Chinatown at least 100 times, and it has never failed to entertain. Skip the crummy camera and luggage stores along Grant Street and wander around the funky side streets where a cornucopia of the bizarre, unbelievable, and just plain weird is on display. (*Tip:* Go very early in the morning, before the tourist throngs show up, to watch the merchants setting up their wares—you'd swear you're in a Beijing marketplace.) While you're there, take one of Shirley's **Wok Wiz** tours of Chinatown (© **415/981-8989;** www.wokwiz.com) for the full effect. See chapter 8.

- **Watching a Major League Baseball Game at SBC Park.** If it's baseball season, then you *must* spend an afternoon or evening watching the National League's Giants play at one of the finest ballparks in America. For only $10 you can buy a bleacher-seat ticket on the day of a game. Even if the season's over, you can still take a guided tour of the stadium. See p. 158.

- **Waking Up with North Beach Coffee.** One of the most pleasurable smells of San Francisco is the aroma of roasted coffee beans wafting down Columbus Avenue in the early morning. Start the day with a cup of Viennese at **Caffè Trieste** (a haven for true San Francisco characters; see p. 231), followed by a walk up and down Columbus Avenue, stopping for lunch at **Mario's Bohemian Cigar Store** (great focaccia sandwiches; see p. 121) and dinner at **L'Osteria del Forno** (p. 120). Finish off the day with a brandy cappuccino nightcap accompanied by Enrico Caruso on the jukebox at **Tosca's.** I've even included a walking tour of North Beach in chapter 9, "City Strolls."

- **Browsing the Haight.** Though the power of the flower has wilted, the Haight is still, more or less, the Haight: a sort of resting home for aging hippies, dazed ex-deadheads, skate punks, and an eclectic assortment of rather pathetic young panhandlers. Think of it as visiting a people zoo as you walk down the rows of used-clothing stores, hip boutiques, and leather shops, trying hard not to stare at that girl (at least I *think* it's a girl) with the pierced eyebrows and shaved head. End the mystery tour with a pitcher of sangria and a plate of mussels at **Cha Cha Cha** (p. 134), one of San Francisco's top ethnic restaurants, and a bargain to boot.

- **Getting Back to Nature at the Marin Headlands.** San Francisco's backyard of sorts, the Marin Headlands (located just across the Golden Gate Bridge to the west) offer not only the best views of the city, but also a wealth of outdoor activities. Bird-watching, hiking, mountain biking, horseback riding—the list goes on—are all fair game at this glorious national park. See chapter 12, "Side Trips from San Francisco."

- **Cruising the Castro.** The most populated and festive street in the city isn't just for gays and lesbians (though you'll find the best boy-toy cruising in town here). There are some great shops and inexpensive cafes—particularly **Café Flore** (p. 139) for lunch—but it's the people-watching that makes the trip to the legendary Castro District a must. And, *please,* make time to catch a flick (any flick, doesn't matter) at the **Castro Theatre** (p. 236), a beautiful 1930s Spanish-colonial movie palace that puts all those ugly multiplexes to shame.

- **Soaking Up the Sun in Golden Gate Park.** A sunny day walking through Golden Gate Park is a day well spent. Its arboreal paths stretch from the Haight all the way to Ocean Beach, offering dozens of fun things

San Francisco at a Glance

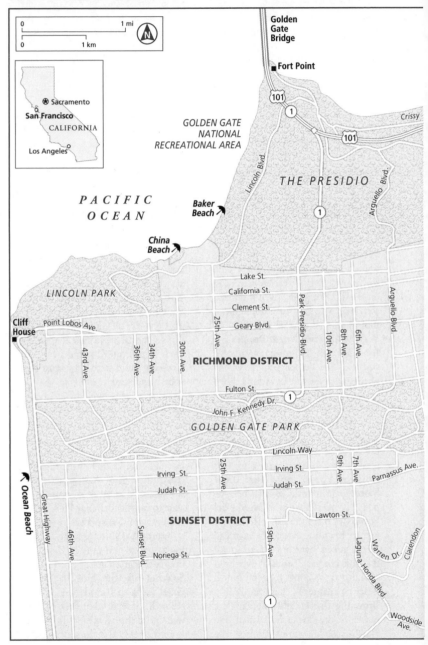

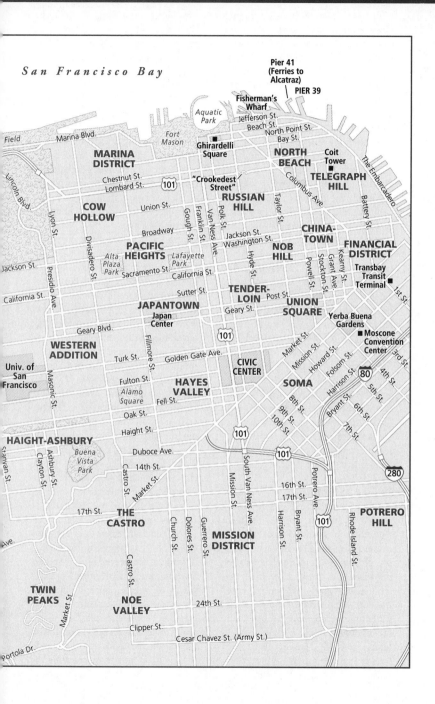

to do along the way. Top sites are the **Conservancy of Flowers, Japanese Tea Garden,** and **Stow Lake,** where you can rent paddleboats and feed the ducks. The best time to go is on Sunday, when portions of the park are closed to traffic (rent skates or a bike for the full effect). Toward the end of the day, head west to the beach and watch the sunset. See section 4, "Golden Gate Park," in chapter 8, "Exploring San Francisco."

- **Catching an Early-Morning Cable Car.** Skip the boring California line and take the Powell-Hyde cable car down to Fisherman's Wharf—the ride is worth the wait. When you reach the top of Nob Hill, grab the rail in one hand and hold the camera with the other, because you're about to see a view of the bay that'll make you a believer. *Insider tip:* Don't call it a trolley or a local might beat you over the head with a loaf of stale sourdough.

- **Dining on Dungeness Crab at San Francisco's Fisherman's Wharf:** Eating fresh Dungeness crabmeat straight from the seafood vendors' boiling pots at the corner of Jefferson and Taylor streets is a quintessential San Francisco experience. True crab gastronomes treasure the edible organs (crab butter) inside the carapace. See chapter 8.

- **Visiting the Museum of Modern Art.** Ever since the SFMOMA (p. 164) opened in 1995, it has been the best place to go for a quick dose of culture. If you go on the first Tuesday of the month, admission is free. There's also no admission charge after 6pm on Thursdays. Start by touring the museum, then head for the gift shop (oftentimes more entertaining than the rotating exhibits). Have a light lunch at **Caffè Museo,** where the food is a vast improvement over most museums' mush, and then finish the trip with a stroll through the **Yerba Buena Gardens** across from the museum (the Martin Luther King, Jr. memorial is particularly inspiring).

- **Spending a Soul-Stirring Sunday Morning at Glide Church.** The high-spirited singers and hand-clapping worshipers at Glide (p. 178) turn churchgoing into a spiritual party that leaves you feeling elated, hopeful, and at one with mankind. All walks of life attend the service, which focuses not on any particular religion but on what we all have in common. It's great fun, with plenty of singing, whooping, and roof-raising.

- **Golfing at Lincoln Park.** The only problem with playing this course is that the views are so stunning they may distract your game. For about $35, you can tee off with the Golden Gate Bridge as a backdrop. If you want to get in a few holes before sunset, nearby is the 9-hole Golden Gate Park Course, where you can play a round for about $15. See p. 187.

- **Walking the Coastal Trail.** Walk the forested coastal trail from the Cliff House to the Golden Gate Bridge, and you'll see why San Franciscans put up with living on a foggy fault line. Start at the parking lot just above Cliff House and head north. On a clear day, you'll have incredible views of the Marin Headlands, but even on foggy days, it's worth the trek to scamper over old bunkers and relish the crisp, cool air. Dress warmly. See chapter 8, "Exploring San Francisco."

- **Taking a Drive to Muir Woods, Stinson Beach, and Point Reyes.** If you have wheels, reserve a day for a trip across the Golden Gate. Take the Stinson Beach exit off U.S. 101, spend a few hours gawking at the monolithic redwoods at Muir Woods (this place is amazing), continue on to Stinson Beach for lunch at the

Parkside Café, and then head up the coast to the spectacular Point Reyes National Seashore. Rain or shine, it's a day trip you'll never forget. See chapter 12, "Side Trips from San Francisco."

• **Grazing at the Ferry Plaza Farmers' Market:** We San Franciscans take our farmers' markets very seriously. Arrive hungry at the Ferry Building (Embarcadero at Market St.) on Saturday, Sunday, Tuesday and Thursday and join the locals as they shop for America's finest organic produce and nosh on free samples from the complimentary cooking classes hosted by the city's top chefs. See chapter 8.

2 Best Low-Cost Hotel Bets

• **Best Overall Value:** This is a tough choice. The **Marina Inn,** 3110 Octavia St. (© **800/274-1420**), p. 90, is, without question, the best low-priced hotel in San Francisco, but its Marina location puts it far from the downtown scene. **The San Remo Hotel,** 2237 Mason St. (© **800/352-REMO**), p. 88, has an ideal North Beach location, friendly staff, and low prices, but the bathrooms are all shared. The best downtown deals are the **Hotel des Arts,** 447 Bush St. (© **800/956-4322**), p. 81, and the groovy **Mosser,** 54 Fourth St. (© **800/227-3804**), p. 85.

• **Best Place to Stay on a Shoestring:** I'd stay at either **The San Remo Hotel,** 2237 Mason St. (© **800/352-REMO**), p. 88, in North Beach or the **Hotel des Arts,** 447 Bush St. (© **800/956-4322**), p. 81, near Union Square. Both hotels are in excellent locations and have rooms with shared bathrooms for as low as $60.

• **Best Romantic Splurge:** The hopelessly romantic **Hotel Bohème,** 444 Columbus Ave. (© **415/433-9111**), p. 88, is the perfect mixture of art, style, class, and location—steps from the sidewalk cafes of North Beach. If Bette Davis were alive today, this is where she'd stay.

• **Best Hotel with Free Parking:** The **Laurel Inn,** 444 Presidio Ave., Pacific Heights (© **800/552-8735** or 415/567-8467), p. 91, may be off the beaten track, but it's one of the most affordable, fashionable hotels in the city—and it has free parking. Just outside of the southern entrance to the Presidio in the midst of residential Presidio Heights, it's a chic motel with soothing, contemporary decor and equally calming prices.

• **Best for Conventioneers:** My first choice is **The Mosser,** 54 Fourth St. (© **800/227-3804**), p. 85, a Victorian-chic hotel right around the corner from the Moscone Convention Center. **The Stratford Hotel,** 242 Powell St. (© **888/504-6835**), p. 83, may be a few blocks north of the Convention Center, but it's close enough. Both hotels are in the right location for heading out for the downtown happy-hour action.

• **Best for Long-Term Stays:** If you're planning to make yourself at home, you'll find all the necessary comforts—and a very affordable price tag—at **The Halcyon Hotel,** 649 Jones St. (© **800/627-2396**). See p. 79.

• **Best Views:** One would think that a city surrounded on three sides by water would have a slew of oceanview hotels, but, oddly enough, it doesn't. The **Seal Rock Inn,** 545 Point Lobos Ave. (© **415/752-8000**), p. 94, in the Richmond District, is the only budget hotel to offer a view of the ocean. You'll be lulled to sleep by the sound of the surf and distant foghorns.

- **Best for Families:** At **The Wharf Inn,** 2601 Mason St. (✆ 800/548-9918), p. 88, kids are within skipping distance of the famous Fisherman's Wharf, and mom and dad don't have to sweat parking the minivan, because there's plenty of free parking here. Less expensive—but a long walk to the wharf—is the **Hotel Del Sol,** 3100 Webster St. (✆ 877/433-5765), p. 91, where kids can play in the heated courtyard pool with lots of pool toys. They even provide free kites, beach balls, and sunglasses for playing on the Marina.

- **Best for a Budget Romantic Rendezvous:** The best place to get all lovey-dovey without spending big bucks is at the **Nob Hill Hotel,** 835 Hyde St. (✆ 877/662-4455), p. 81, a beautiful 1900s-era Victorian-style hotel with original marble flooring, high ceilings, and authentic antique furnishings—including heavy brass beds that don't squeak.

- **Best Service for a Budget Hotel:** This is an easy one: Any of the four family-owned **Reneson hotels** (✆ 800/736-3766) on Seventh Street will make you feel like you're a valued customer (as it should be). See p. 85.

- **Best Moderately Priced Hotel:** Ever since we've included **The Golden Gate Hotel,** 775 Bush St. (✆ 800/835-1118), in our lodging lineup, we've received nothing but kudos from satisfied guests. Just 2 blocks from Union Square, this 1913 Edwardian hotel is a real charmer and a fantastic value. See p. 78.

- **Best Budget B&B:** It may not be the most centrally located place, but if you want a slice of old-style San Francisco, the quaint **Monte Cristo Bed and Breakfast,** 600 Presidio Ave. (✆ 415/931-1875), will do the trick. Prices start at $83 a night (including a full breakfast buffet), but the manager has been known to negotiate when his beds are empty. See p. 92.

- **Best Funky/Groovy Hotel:** Former flower children will fall in love with the 1960s-nostalgic **Red Victorian Bed, Breakfast & Art,** 1665 Haight St. (✆ 415/864-1978), p. 94. Owner Sami Sunchild has retained an aura of peace, love, and happiness that radiates throughout her colorful inn. Then there's the retro 1950s-style **Phoenix Hotel,** 601 Eddy St. (✆ 800/248-9466), p. 93, a favorite with film and music stars (the Red Hot Chili Peppers usually stay here). If you're into contemporary art, some of the city's best local artists display their work on the guest room walls of **Hotel des Arts,** 447 Bush St. (✆ 800/956-4322), p. 81.

- **Best Public Space in a Historic Hotel:** You may not be staying the night, but you can certainly feel like a million bucks in the public rooms at **The Palace Hotel,** 2 New Montgomery St. (✆ 800/325-3535). The extravagant creation of banker "Bonanza King" Will Ralston in 1875, the Palace Hotel has one of the grandest rooms in the city: the **Garden Court.** Running a close second is the magnificent lobby at Nob Hill's **Fairmont Hotel & Tower,** 950 Mason St. (✆ 800/441-1414).

3 Best Low-Cost Dining Bets

- **Best Value:** Crepes. Yes, crepes. Cheap crepes that are bigger than your head and filled with everything from cheddar cheese and onions to spinach, ham, eggplant, pesto, tomatoes, roasted peppers, smoked salmon, mushrooms, sausage, and even scallops. **Crepes on Cole,** 100

Carl St. (© **415/664-1800**), p. 136, in the Haight, makes them for about $7, including a side of home fries. **Ti Couz,** 3108 16th St. (© **415/252-7373**), p. 144, in the Mission, makes even better crepes, but they are a bit more expensive.

- **Best Classic San Francisco Dining Experience:** The lovable loudmouths working behind the narrow counter of the **Swan Oyster Depot,** 1517 Polk St. (© **415/673-1101**), p. 110, have been satisfying patrons with fresh crab, shrimp, oysters, and clam chowder since 1912. My dad doesn't care much for visiting San Francisco ("Too crowded!") but he loves having lunch at this beloved seafood institution.

- **Best Splurge Choice:** Nancy Oaks' high-energy **Boulevard,** 1 Mission St. (© **415/543-6084**), p. 114, is a visual and gastronomical delight. For years it's been ranked as the city's most popular restaurant. Also worth the cash is a meal at **Kokkari,** 200 Jackson St. (© **415/981-0983**), p. 109, where French chef Jean Alberti creates masterpieces of Aegean cuisine.

- **Best Grease Pit:** Anyone who's a connoisseur of funky little ethnic eateries will love **Tú Lan,** 8 Sixth St. (© **415/626-0927**), p. 114, one of the greasiest little holes-in-the-wall in the city. But even Julia Child was a fan of their Vietnamese imperial rolls. For late-night noshing on tomato beef with noodles and house-special chow mein, **Sam Wo,** 813 Washington St. (© **415/982-0596**), is my favorite Chinatown dive. See p. 118.

- **Best Budget Dinner Show:** The gender-bending waitresses—mostly Asian men dressed *very* convincingly as hot-to-trot women—will blow your mind with their lip-synced show tunes, which take place every night at **AsiaSF,** 201 Ninth St. (© **415/255-2742**).

Bring the parents—they'll love it. See p. 110.

- **Best Dim Sum:** Downtown and Chinatown dim sum restaurants may be more centrally located, but that's all they have on the Richmond District's **Ton Kiang,** 5821 Geary Blvd. (© **415/387-8273**), p. 137, which serves up the best seafood dumplings and stuffed crab claws this side of China. For downtown dim sum, the venerable **Yank Sing,** 101 Spear St. (© **415/957-9300**), offers a superb dim sum surprise on every cart wheeled to your table. See p. 108.

- **Best Party Scene:** Throw back a few glasses of sangria with your tapas at **Cha Cha Cha,** 1801 Haight St. (© **415/386-5758**), p. 134, and you'll start swinging with the rest of the crowd.

- **Best Pizza:** Has **Pauline's,** 260 Valencia St. (© **415/552-2050**), p. 142, perfected pizza? Quite possibly. At least it's the best we've ever had. Pauline's only does two things—pizzas and salads—but does them both better than any other restaurant in the city. The best by-the-slice is North Beach's **Golden Boy Pizza,** 542 Green St. (© **415/982-9738**); everyone will watch with envy as you stroll down the sidewalk while savoring this doughy square of deliciousness. See p. 123.

- **Best Burritos:** It's impossible to deem one burrito the king in this town, but there's a reason why people come from across town to line up at **Taquerias La Cumbre,** 515 Valencia St. (© **415/863-8205**), in the Mission. See p. 144.

- **Best Place for Picnic Supplies:** If you're anywhere near North Beach, head to San Francisco's legendary **Molinari Delicatessen,** 373 Columbus Ave. (© **415/421-2337**), p. 201, which offers an eye-popping selection of cold salads, cheeses, and sandwiches packaged and priced to go (the Italian subs are big enough for two hearty appetites). Another good sunny-day option is a picnic on Marina Green, but first stop by the **Marina Safeway,** 15 Marina Blvd. (℃ **415/563-4946**), p. 126, to pick up fresh-baked breads, gourmet cheeses, and other foodstuffs (including fresh cracked crab when in season).

- **Best Coffee Shop or Cafe:** With all the wonderfully unique coffee shops throughout this cafe town, there can be no one winner. We do, however, love the authentic atmosphere at **Mario's Bohemian Cigar Store,** p. 121, 566 Columbus Ave. (℃ **415/ 362-0536**), and **Caffe Trieste,** 601 Vallejo Ave. (℃ **415/392-6739**). See p. 231.

- **Best Happy-Hour Spread:** At the top of Nob Hill inside the Fairmont Hotel is the beloved **Tonga Room,** 950 Mason St. (℃ **415/772-5278**). Every weekday, from 5 to 7pm, both locals and tourists rub elbows while getting stuffed at the all-you-can-eat buffet (chicken wings, chow mein, pot stickers, and much more) for a mere $7. See p. 230.

- **Best Desserts:** Okay, so maybe you can't afford a five-course meal here, but you can saunter into the **Grand Café,** 501 Geary Blvd. (℃ **415/292- 0101**), p. 107, near closing time for a decadent dessert, such as the devil's food chocolate pudding gateau with coffee caramel sauce and cashew toffee ice cream. Besides, it's a good excuse to check out one of the most beautiful dining rooms you'll ever see.

- **Best Breakfast:** We have a tie: **Dottie's True Blue Café,** 522 Jones St.

(℃ **415/885-2767**), p. 104, has taken the classic American breakfast to a new level—maybe the best I've ever had. Crummy neighborhood, superb food. **Ella's,** 500 Presidio Ave. (℃ **415/441-5669**), is far more yuppie, equally as divine, and in a much better neighborhood, but it's so popular that the wait on weekend mornings is brutal. See p. 127.

- **Best Funky Atmosphere:** That's an easy one: **Tommy's Joynt,** 1101 Geary Blvd. (℃ **415/775-4216**). The interior looks like a Buffalo Bill museum that imploded, the exterior paint job looks like a circus tent on acid, and the huge trays of hofbrau classics will make your arteries harden just looking at them. In short, you'll love this place. See p. 132.

- **Best Family-Style Restaurant:** Giant platters of classic Italian food and carafes filled with table wine are placed on long wooden tables by motherly waitresses while Sinatra classics play to the festive crowd of contented diners. Welcome to North Beach–style family dining at **Capp's Corner,** 1600 Powell St. (℃ **415/ 989-2589**). See p. 119.

- **Best Burger:** Another easy one: **Mo's Gourmet Burgers,** 1322 Grant Ave. (℃ **415/788-3779**). Consider yourself warned, however—no other burger will ever taste as good. See p. 121.

- **Best Surreal Dining Experience:** Sitting cross-legged on a pillow, shoes off, smoking apricot tobacco out of a hookah, eating baba ghanouj, and drinking spiced wine in an exotic Middle Eastern setting while beautiful, sensuous belly dancers glide across the dining room. Unwind your mind at **Kan Zaman,** 1793 Haight St. (℃ **415/751-9656**). See p. 135.

2

Planning an Affordable Trip to San Francisco

As expensive as San Francisco is, there are infinite ways to enjoy the city on a tight budget. But to get the most for your money, you'll need to do plenty of advance planning. Airfare and lodging will take the largest bites out of your travel budget, so either shop for the best bargains and secure them well in advance (especially during high season), or pay the consequences—literally.

1 The San Francisco from $70 a Day Premise

This chapter offers lots of useful information to help you plan a great trip to San Francisco without going broke. It's devoted to insider advice, money-saving tips, and ways to stretch your budget so you keep your accommodation costs and three meals a day to as little as $70 a day. (We assume that two adults are traveling together and that, between the two of you, you have at least $140 to spend.) The cost of transportation, activities, sightseeing, and entertainment are extra, but we have plenty of insider tips to save you money on those activities as well.

While planning your trip, don't get discouraged if you've spent almost your entire vacation budget on hotels before you've even packed. San Francisco is one of the most popular destinations in the world, and because of all the tourist and convention traffic, hotels can and do charge steep tariffs. But there's good news, too: Once you get here, pay for your room, and head out to explore, you'll find that many of the city's best activities and attractions won't cost you a dime.

2 42 Money-Saving Tips

The following tips can help keep your traveling costs to a minimum:

WHEN TO GO

1. **Try to travel in the off season,** roughly October through April. Most room rates at the smaller hotels decrease by as much as 50% from November through February, and 10% to 15% from March through May. Some hotels also offer slightly lower rates Sunday through Thursday. Case in point: A room at the Marina Inn on a summer Saturday is about $120. The same room on a weekday in February is less than $80. Ironically, because San Francisco's weather is so screwy, you'll have a much better chance of a sunny vacation during the winter months. When you're looking for a room, also inquire about special packages that a lodging might offer, ranging from a reduced rate for a multinight stay, to packages that may include a number of meals and attractions.

AIRFARES

2. **Surf the Internet for bargains.** There are lots of sites and online services designed to find you discounted airfares, accommodations, and car rentals. For more information and helpful hints, see "Flying for Less" later in this chapter. *Note:* Jet Blue (© 800/528-2583; www.jetblue.com) often offers particularly good deals from various U.S. cities into Oakland.

3. Even in the age of computers, you won't find bargains if you don't know where to look. Especially if you're not particularly Net savvy, it can be a good idea to call or **visit a travel agent** before your trip and see what can be arranged in the way of low airfares, room rates, cheap car rentals, and package deals that you don't have access to independently.

4. When calling the airlines directly, **be sure to ask for the lowest fare.** (And don't forget to inquire about discounts for seniors, children, and students, and any promotional fares.) Note, though, that the lowest-priced fares will often be nonrefundable, require an advance purchase of 1 to 3 weeks and a certain length of stay, and carry penalties for changing dates of travel. If you can be flexible, ask if you can secure a cheaper fare by staying an extra day or by flying midweek. Many airlines won't volunteer this information. Although you might find a slightly better rate by flying into Oakland International Airport, taxis and shuttles from Oakland to downtown San Francisco are far more expensive than the cheap ($5) and convenient BART train from SFO (San Francisco International Airport) to the city. It's only worth it if you save about $50 or more on airfare. And forget San Jose's airport—it's way too far south, and the traffic is horrible on Hwy 101.

5. Check the advertisements in newspaper travel sections, which often feature **special promotional fares and packages.** You'll rarely see a sale during the peak summer months of July and August, or during the Thanksgiving or Christmas seasons; but in periods of low-volume travel, you should pay no more than $400 to $500 for a round-trip cross-country flight.

6. Always check the Sunday travel section of your newspaper for **consolidators** ("bucket shops") **and charter flights.** Though tickets are usually heavily restricted (ask about all the details), you're likely to save a bundle—usually 20% to 35%. This can really be a great way to go if you're buying at the last minute. There are lots of fly-by-night consolidators, though, and problems can range from disputing never-received tickets to finding you have no seat booked when you get to the airport. Play it safe by going with a reputable business. For more information and helpful hints, as well as some recommended companies, see section 9, "Planning Your Trip Online," later in this chapter.

Discounted fares have pared the number of **charters,** but they're still available. Most charter operators advertise and sell their seats through travel agents, thus making these local professionals your best source of information for available flights. Before deciding to take a charter flight, check the restrictions on the ticket: You may be asked to purchase a tour package, to pay in advance, to be amenable if the day of departure is changed, to pay a service charge, to fly on an airline you're not familiar with (this usually is not the case), and to pay harsh penalties if you cancel, but to be understanding if the charter doesn't fill up and is canceled up to 10 days before departure. Summer charters fill up more quickly than others and are almost sure to fly, but if you decide on a charter, consider trip-cancellation and baggage insurance.

7. **Don't take a taxi from the airport into the city.** The fare from SFO to the downtown area will run $30 to $35 plus tip, so unless you're with a group who can split the fare, you're far better off taking BART or a shuttle. Both SFO and the Oakland International Airport (OAK), the two major airports serving the city, have convenient shuttle services that will take you directly to your hotel for far less money than a cab, and the BART line from SFO to the city is only $5. See section 10, "Getting There," for more information.

CAR RENTALS

8. If you plan to spend all your time in San Francisco, **don't rent a car.** Parking's a nightmare, most hotels charge a hefty parking fee, and the city is so condensed that you can easily bus, cab, cable car, or walk it.

9. The only reason you'd really need a car is if you're planning to do any road trips to the Wine Country or other surrounding areas. If that's the case, be sure to call all the major car-rental companies (use toll-free numbers listed in "Getting Around" in chapter 5) to **compare rates,** preferably before you arrive in San Francisco. I've always had a good experience renting through Priceline.com.

10. **Don't book a rental car through an airline's partner when you purchase your ticket without doing some research first.** Airlines may not offer the best deals; you may do better calling the chains directly, or going through a major Internet travel site.

11. In addition to the big chains, **consider renting from one of the dozens of regional rental places** in San Francisco for your getaway, many

of which offer lower rates. A good choice is **A-One Rent-A-Car,** 434 O'Farrell St. (between Jones and Taylor sts.; ℂ **800/238-2663** or 415/771-3977). Even after you've made your reservations, call again and check rates a few days or weeks later—you may stumble upon a lower rate.

12. Be sure to **check whether your credit card or personal auto-insurance policy covers you when you rent a car.** If you're covered by one or the other, you'll be able to avoid the cost of collision-damage waivers (usually an additional $10–$12 a day) that the car-rental agencies are eager to sell you.

13. Whether you're driving or not, it's a good idea to be a member of the **American Automobile Association (AAA),** which charges $40 to $60 per year (with an additional one-time joining fee) depending on where you join. Members (only those who carry their cards with them) not only receive free roadside assistance, but also have access to a wealth of free travel information (detailed maps and guidebooks). Also, many hotels and attractions in San Francisco offer discounts to AAA members—always inquire. Call ℂ **800/922-8228** or your local branch for membership information. **Amoco Motor Club** (ℂ **800/334-3300**) is another recommended choice.

14. **Fill the tank before you return the rental car** or you'll end up paying $3 or more a gallon to have the rental company fill it for you.

PUBLIC TRANSPORTATION

15. San Francisco's public transportation system—known as Muni—is both an easy and affordable way to get around (but certainly not the fastest or most reliable). **Muni discount passes,** called Passports, entitle holders to unlimited rides on buses, Metro

streetcars, and cable cars (see the box on p. 18 for details). An even better deal, however, is the new **CityPass** package, which includes free public transportation for a week and admission to several of the city's major attractions. See the "CityPass: The Budget Traveler's Bonanza" box on p. 18 for more information.

ACCOMMODATIONS

16. In addition to airfare, you'll also have better luck saving on room rates if you **visit in the off season.** In winter, when hotels have a low occupancy level, they slash rates by as much as 40%; be sure to call as far in advance as possible to get these discounts.

17. **The sooner you book a room, the better.** The cheapest accommodations are always the first to go, so the farther in advance you commit, the better your chances of scoring a bargain. You might score a great room at the last minute with a service like Priceline.com, but you have more control over the whole process if you book well in advance.

18. Whether you make a reservation or arrive on the spot, **ask for the cheapest room** and about any promotions, package deals, or discounted rates for students, seniors, military personnel, or government employees—whatever applies. Also, inquire about what makes a room worth less than other options (such as shared versus private bathrooms) and be sure that the downsides are acceptable to you.

19. When booking your hotel, **find out if there's an extra charge for parking** if you're going to have a car in the city. In downtown San Francisco, stashing your car can cost up to $35 per day *without* in-and-out privileges. If there's a charge, be sure to ask about the availability of street parking; hotel employees are usually more than happy to give you the lowdown on the local parking scene. Also consider staying at one of the city's few hotels offering free parking (see the "Accommodations with Free Parking" box in chapter 6).

20. **Bargain at the front desk.** A hotel makes zero dollars per night on an empty room. Hence, most hotels are willing to bargain on rates. Haggling probably won't work too well during the high season, when hotels are almost 100% booked, but if you're traveling off season and the answer is "no," try politely speaking with a manager, with whom you might be able to negotiate a better deal. An especially advantageous time to haggle for lower rates is late afternoon or early evening on the day of your arrival, when a hotel's likelihood of filling up with full-price bookings is remote.

21. **If you think "B&B" refers to "bargain and budget," think again.** You're likely to pay higher prices to stay at one of these homey little spots than you are at many hotels and motels. But if your heart is set on a bed-and-breakfast, we've sprinkled a few of the best B&B bargains throughout chapter 6.

22. If you're traveling with kids, try to **book a room at a hotel where children stay in your room for free.** Families may also wish to book rooms or suites with kitchenettes to save money on meals.

23. Some hotels, particularly more affordable choices, charge **lower rates for singles,** so inquire about them if you are traveling alone.

24. At hotels, if the first room you see is disappointing (all right, dismal), don't storm out. **Ask to see other rooms;** they often vary considerably, and if you're polite, the management might upgrade you to a better room for free just to keep you happy.

25. If you can avoid it, **don't make local phone calls from your hotel room.** Hotels often charge $1 or more for local calls, as well as inflated rates for long-distance calls. Even if you use a calling card for long-distance calls, you're often charged a fee for access. Use your cellphone, or get a calling card and call from your hotel lobby.

26. In a fiercely competitive market, more and more hotels are offering **free continental breakfast** with coffee as an enticement. Find out from your hotel or travel agent if this is available at your hotel. The savings can really add up, especially if you're staying for a longer period of time. But beware: Sometimes continental breakfast means nothing but so-so coffee and processed pastries.

DINING

27. San Francisco boasts some of the world's finest dining. If you want to try a place that's beyond your budget, **consider going for lunch instead of dinner.** Often the lunch menu is served until 4 or 5pm, and main courses usually cost 30% less than the same dishes do at dinner. You probably won't be hungry for the rest of the day, and will avoid spending big bucks for dinner.

28. Keep an eye out for **happy hours** at the bars and lounges throughout the city. Aside from cheap drink specials, many establishments provide a free snack spread that can easily replace dinner. The city's best happy hour is at the **Tonga Room,** 950 Mason St., at California Street (℃ **415/772-5278**). From 5 to 7pm Monday through Friday you can pull an all-you-can-eat binge for $7.

29. Pick up the *San Francisco Bay Guardian,* one of the city's free alternative newspapers, and look for **"two-for-one"** and other discount coupons for restaurants around town.

30. **Fixed-price menus** and **early-bird dinners** are big money-savers. Look for restaurants that offer them. If you're traveling with children, find restaurants that offer reduced-price children's menus.

31. San Francisco is an outdoor, sporty kind of place. If weather permits, instead of dining in restaurants, **consider putting together a picnic breakfast, lunch, or dinner.** There are myriad idyllic outdoor dining spots, and hundreds of phenomenal takeout joints that will help you create a cheap feast to go; even a gourmet spread can cost less than a meal in a restaurant.

32. Sure, there's plenty of hype about California-inspired cuisine; but if you follow the locals' lead to any of the city's **fantastic ethnic restaurants,** you'll find that, while few of them are locally influenced, they're definitely world-class—not to mention a heck of a lot cheaper than California-style restaurants. Two of my favorites are: **Thep Phanom,** 400 Waller St. (℃ **415/431-2526**), for exceptional Thai (p. 135); and **Taquerias La Cumbre,** 515 Valencia St. (℃ **415/863-8205**), which cranks out hefty fresh burritos, tacos, and combination plates for less than $7 (p. 144).

SIGHTSEEING

33. The **San Francisco Visitor Information Center,** on the lower level of Hallidie Plaza, 900 Market St., at Powell Street (℃ **415/391-2000;** www.sfvisitor.org), offers money-saving **coupons** for restaurants, shops, and attractions in the area. To get your hands on some, call or stop by.

34. **Most museums are open to the public free 1 day per month** (sometimes 1 day per week). Call the museum of your choice to find out

which day is free day or see the "Free Culture" box in chapter 8. Some museums also offer free admission later in the day at least 1 day a week.

35. **Check out local alternative and tourist newspapers,** many of which regularly run discounts for attractions and activities in San Francisco. The *San Francisco Bay Guardian* is free and is your best bet—it's widely distributed in street-corner boxes and at cafes and restaurants throughout the city. Another good one is the *San Francisco Weekly.*

36. **Many attractions offer discounts** to seniors, students, or military personnel. Inquire before paying full admission, and be sure to bring your ID.

37. **Skip the pricey guided tours and do it yourself** by putting together your own sightseeing itinerary based on the information included in this book. But if you'd still rather have someone lead you around town, you can take one of the free neighborhood tours offered by **City Guides,** an affiliate of the San Francisco Library (see p. 190 for details).

SHOPPING

38. If you live out of state and make a substantial purchase while in town, it may be wise to **have the store ship it to your home.** You'll have to pay a shipping charge, but you won't have to pay California sales tax—or lug it along the rest of your trip.

39. San Francisco is saturated with **secondhand stores,** and the selection is phenomenal. Two good haunts for pre-owned goods are **Polk Street** and **Haight Street,** though thrift stores abound everywhere, including ones that offer high-quality merchandise.

NIGHTLIFE

40. **Avoid clubs with high cover charges.** There are plenty of bars and dance clubs with cover charges of just a few dollars, and some with no admission fees at all; see our recommendations in chapter 11, "San Francisco After Dark."

41. Keep your eyes peeled for bars and clubs advertising **happy-hour specials, discounted covers, ladies' nights,** and other money-saving theme nights.

(*Value*) CityPass: The Budget Traveler's Bonanza

If you're going to be visiting San Francisco for a week or more, or you plan on doing a lot of sightseeing in the city, you might want to consider purchasing a **San Francisco CityPass.** Not only does it include 7 days of unlimited public transportation (including cable cars, Metro streetcars, and the entire bus system), it also gets you into six of the city's major attractions: the California Palace of the Legion of Honor art museum, the California Academy of Sciences and Steinhart Aquarium, the Asian Art Museum, the San Francisco Museum of Modern Art (SFMOMA), the Exploratorium, and a Blue & Gold Fleet bay cruise.

You can buy a CityPass at any of the above attractions or online at www.citypass.net. Current rates are $42 for adults and $34 for kids ages 5 to 17. For more information, visit the CityPass website at **www.citypass.net** or send an e-mail to info@citypass.com. For recorded information, call (*C*) **888/ 330-5008.**

42. If you want to see a musical or theatrical performance, contact the **TIX Bay Area** box office (© 415/433-7827; www.theatrebayarea.org) to inquire about discounted or matinee shows. Also, some theaters and companies offer same-day reduced tickets, student discounts, and standing-room rates; see chapter 11 for details.

3 Visitor Information

Visitors from outside the United States should also see chapter 3, "For International Visitors," for entry requirements and other pertinent information.

The **San Francisco Convention and Visitors Bureau,** 900 Market St. (at Powell St.), Hallidie Plaza, Lower Level, San Francisco, CA 94102 (© 415/391-2000; www.sfvisitor.org), is the best source of specialized information about the city. Even if you don't have a specific question, you might want to request the free "Visitors Planning Guide" and the "San Francisco Visitors' Kit." The kit includes a 6-month calendar of events, a city history, shopping and dining information, and several good, clear maps, plus lodging information. If you need specific information faxed to you, you can call © 800/220-5747; follow the prompts to receive information by fax only. The bureau highlights only its members' establishments, so if it doesn't have what you're looking for, that doesn't mean it's nonexistent.

You can also get the latest on San Francisco at the following online addresses:

- The *Bay Guardian,* the city's free weekly paper: **www.sfbg.com;**
- Hotel reservations: **www.hotelres.com;**
- *SF Gate,* the city's *Chronicle* newspaper: **www.sfgate.com;** and
- CitySearch: **www.citysearch.com.**

4 Money

See chapter 3, "For International Visitors," for more information.

ATMS

All over San Francisco, you'll find ATMs (automated teller machines) linked to a national network that most likely includes your bank at home. Withdrawing cash as you need it is the easiest way to deal with money while you're on the road. Cirrus (© 800/424-7787; www.mastercard.com) and PLUS (© 800/843-7587; www.visa.com) are the two most popular networks. Look at the back of your bankcard to see which network you're on, and then call or check online for ATM locations at your destination. Be sure you know your personal identification number (PIN) before you leave home, and be sure to find out your daily withdrawal limit before you depart. Also keep in mind that many banks impose a fee (approximately $3) every time a card is used at a different bank's ATM. On top of this, the bank from which you withdraw cash may charge its own fee. To compare banks' ATM fees within the U.S., use www.bankrate.com.

TRAVELER'S CHECKS

Traveler's checks are something of an anachronism from the days before the ATM made cash accessible at any time. Given the fees you'll pay for ATM use at banks other than your own, however, you might be better off with traveler's checks if you're withdrawing money often.

You can get traveler's checks at almost any bank. **American Express** offers denominations of $20, $50, $100, $500, and (for cardholders only) $1,000. You'll pay a service charge ranging from 1% to 4%. You can also get American Express traveler's checks over the phone by calling ℂ **800/221-7282;** Amex gold and platinum cardholders who use this number are exempt from the 1% fee.

Visa offers traveler's checks at Citibank locations nationwide, as well as at several other banks. The service charge ranges between 1.5% and 2%; checks come in denominations of $20, $50, $100, $500, and $1,000. Call ℂ **800/732-1322** for information. AAA members can obtain Visa checks for a $9.95 fee (for checks up to $1,500) at most AAA offices or by calling ℂ **866/339-3378. MasterCard** also offers traveler's checks. Call ℂ **800/223-9920** for a location near you.

If you do choose to carry traveler's checks, keep a record of their serial numbers separate from your checks in the event that they are stolen or lost. You'll get a refund faster if you know the numbers.

CREDIT CARDS

Credit cards are a safe way to carry money: They also provide a convenient record of all your expenses, and they generally offer relatively good exchange rates. You can also withdraw cash advances from your credit cards at banks or ATMs (though there are added fees for this), provided you know your PIN. If you've forgotten yours, or didn't even know you had one, call the number on the back of your credit card and ask the bank to send it to you. It usually takes 5 to 7 business days, though some banks will provide the number over the phone if you tell them your mother's maiden name or some other personal information.

5 When to Go

If you're dreaming of convertibles, Frisbee on the beach, and tank-topped evenings, change your reservations and head to Los Angeles. Contrary to California's sunshine-and-bikini image, San Francisco's weather is "mild" (to put it nicely) and can often be downright bone-chilling because of the wet, foggy air and cool winds—it's nothing like that of Southern California. Summer, the most popular time to visit, is often characterized by damp, foggy days; cold, windy nights; and crowded tourist destinations. A good bet is to visit in spring or, better yet, autumn. Every September, right about the time San Franciscans mourn being cheated (or fogged) out of another summer, something wonderful happens: The thermometer rises, the skies clear, and the locals call in sick to work and head for the beach. It's what residents call "Indian summer." The city is also delightful during winter, when the opera and ballet seasons are in full swing; there are fewer tourists, many hotel prices are lower, and downtown bustles with holiday cheer.

CLIMATE

San Francisco's temperate, marine climate usually means relatively mild weather year-round. In summer, chilling fog rolls in most mornings and evenings, and if temperatures top 70°F (21°C), the city is ready to throw a celebration. Even when autumn's heat occasionally stretches into the 80s (upper 20s Celsius) and 90s (lower 30s Celsius), you should still dress in layers, or by early evening, you'll learn firsthand why sweatshirt sales are a great business at Fisherman's Wharf. In winter, the mercury seldom falls below freezing and snow is almost unheard of, but that doesn't mean you won't be whimpering if you forget your coat. Still, compared to most of the states' weather conditions, San Francisco's is consistently pleasant.

It's that beautifully fluffy, chilly, wet, heavy, sweeping fog that makes the city's weather so precarious. A rare combination of water, wind, and topography creates Northern California's summer fog bank. It lies off the coast, and rising air currents pull it in when the land heats up.

Held back by coastal mountains along a 600-mile front, the low clouds seek out any passage they can find. The easiest access is the slot where the Pacific Ocean penetrates the continental wall—the Golden Gate.

San Francisco's Average Temperatures & Rainfall

	Jan	Feb	Mar	Apr	May	June	July	Aug	Sept	Oct	Nov	Dec
High °F	56	59	61	64	67	70	71	72	73	70	62	56
Low °F	43	46	47	48	51	53	55	56	55	52	48	43
High °C	13	15	16	18	19	21	22	22	23	21	17	13
Low °C	6	8	8	9	11	12	13	13	13	11	9	6
Rain (in.)	4.5	4.0	3.3	1.2	0.4	0.1	0.1	0.1	0.2	1.0	2.5	2.9
Rain (mm)	113.0	101.9	82.8	30.0	9.7	2.8	0.8	1.8	5.1	26.4	63.2	73.4

SAN FRANCISCO CALENDAR OF EVENTS

For more information, visit www.sfvisitor.org for an annual calendar of local events.

February

Chinese New Year, Chinatown. In 2006, public celebrations will again spill onto every street in Chinatown. Festivities begin with the "Miss Chinatown USA" pageant parade, and climax a week later with a celebratory parade of marching bands, rolling floats, barrages of fireworks, and a block-long dragon writhing in and out of the crowds. The revelry runs for several weeks and wraps up with a memorable parade through Chinatown that starts at Market and Second streets and ends at Kearny Street. Arrive early for a good viewing spot on Grant Avenue. Make your hotel reservations early. For dates and information, call © **415/982-3000** or visit www.chineseparade.com.

March

St. Patrick's Day Parade, Union Square and Civic Center. Everyone's an honorary Irish person at this festive affair, which starts at 11:30am at Market and Second streets and continues to City Hall. But the party doesn't stop there. Head down to the Civic Center for the post-party, or venture to The Embarcadero's **Harrington's Bar & Grill** (245 Front St.; © **415/392-7595**) and celebrate with hundreds of the Irish-for-a-day revelers as they gallivant around the closed-off streets and numerous pubs. No contact information. Sunday before March 17.

April

Cherry Blossom Festival, Japantown. Meander through the arts-and-crafts and food booths lining the blocked-off streets around Japan Center and watch traditional drumming, flower arranging, origami making, or a parade celebrating the cherry blossom and Japanese culture. Call © **415/563-2313** for information. Mid- to late April.

San Francisco International Film Festival, around San Francisco with screenings at the AMC Kabuki 8 Cinemas (Fillmore and Post sts.), and at many other locations. Begun in 1957, this is America's oldest film festival. It features more than 200 films and videos from more than 50 countries, as well as awards ceremonies in which renowned honorees join the festivities. Tickets are relatively inexpensive, and screenings are accessible to the public. Entries include new films by beginning and established directors. For a schedule or information, call © **415/561-5000** or visit www.sffs.org. Mid-April to early May.

May

Cinco de Mayo Celebration, Mission District. This is when the Latino community celebrates the victory of the

Mexicans over the French at Puebla in 1862; mariachi bands, dancers, food, and a parade fill the streets of the Mission. The parade starts at 10am at 24th and Bryant streets and ends at the Civic Center. No contact information. The first Sunday in May.

Bay to Breakers Foot Race, The Embarcadero through Golden Gate Park to Ocean Beach. Even if you don't participate, you can't avoid this run from downtown to Ocean Beach, which stops morning traffic throughout the city. More than 60,000 entrants gather—many dressed in wacky, innovative, and sometimes X-rated costumes—for the approximately 7½-mile run. If you don't want to run, join the throng of spectators who line the route. Sidewalk parties, bands, and cheerleaders of all ages provide a good dose of true San Francisco fun. The *San Francisco Examiner* (© **415/359-2800**; www.baytobreakers.com) sponsors the event. Third Sunday of May.

Carnaval, Mission District, Mission Street between 14th and 24th streets, and Harrison Street between 16th and 21st streets. The Mission District's largest annual event is a day of festivities that culminates in a parade on Mission Street. For one of San Franciscans' favorite events, more than half a million spectators line the route, and samba musicians and dancers continue to entertain on 14th Street, near Harrison, at the end of the march. Call the hot line at © **415/920-0125** for information or go to www.carnavalsf.com. The Sunday of Memorial Day weekend.

June

Union Street Art Festival, Pacific Heights, along Union Street from Steiner to Gough streets. This outdoor fair celebrates San Francisco with gourmet food booths, music, entertainment, and a juried art show featuring works by more than 250 artists. Call the **Union Street Association** (© **415/441-7055**) for more information or see www.unionstreetfestival.com. First weekend of June.

Haight Street Fair, Haight-Ashbury. A far cry from the froufrou Union Street Fair, this grittier fair features alternative crafts, ethnic foods, rock bands, and a healthy number of hippies and street kids whooping it up and slamming beers in front of the blaring rock-'n'-roll stage. The fair usually extends along Haight between Stanyan and Ashbury streets. For details and the exact date, call © **415/863-3489** or visit www.haightstreetfair.org.

North Beach Festival, Grant Avenue, North Beach. In 2004, this party celebrated its 50th anniversary; organizers claim it's the oldest urban street fair in the country. Close to 75,000 city folk meander along Grant Avenue, between Vallejo and Union streets, to eat, drink, and browse the arts-and-crafts booths, poetry readings, swing-dancing venue, and *arte di gesso* (sidewalk chalk art). But the most enjoyable part of the event is listening to music and people-watching. Call © **415/989-2220** or visit www.sfnorthbeach.org for details. Usually Father's Day weekend, but call to confirm.

Stern Grove Midsummer Music Festival, Sunset District. Pack a picnic and head out early to join the thousands who come here to lie in the grass and enjoy classical, jazz, and ethnic music and dance in the grove, at 19th Avenue and Sloat Boulevard. The free concerts take place every Sunday at 2pm between mid-June and August. Show up with a lawn chair or blanket at least an hour before the event to grab a spot. There are food booths if you forget snacks, but you'll be dying to leave if you don't bring warm clothes—the Sunset District can be one of the coldest parts of the city. Call ℭ **415/252-6252** for listings. Sundays, mid-June through August.

San Francisco Lesbian, Gay, Bisexual, Transgender Pride Parade & Celebration, downtown's Market Street. This prideful event draws up to half a million participants who celebrate all of the above—and then some. The parade proceeds west on Market Street until it gets to Market and Eighth Street, where hundreds of food, art, and information booths are set up around several soundstages. Call ℭ 415/864-3733 or visit www.sfpride. org for information. Usually the third or last weekend of June.

July

Fillmore Street Jazz Festival, Pacific Heights. July starts with a bang, when the upscale portion of Fillmore closes to traffic and several blocks of arts and crafts, gourmet food, and live jazz fill the street. (The blocked-off section is changing, so call for details.) Call ℭ **510/970-3217** for more information. First weekend in July.

Fourth of July Celebration & Fireworks, Fisherman's Wharf. This event can be something of a joke—more often than not, fog, like everyone else, comes into the city to join in the festivities. Sometimes it's almost impossible to view the million-dollar pyrotechnics from PIER 39 on the northern waterfront. Still, it's a party, and if the skies are clear, it's a darn good show. No contact information.

San Francisco Marathon, San Francisco and beyond. This is one of the largest marathons in the world. For entry information, contact West End Management, the event organizer (ℭ **800/698-8699;** www.runsfm.com). Usually the last weekend in July.

September

A La Carte, A La Park, Sharon Meadow, Golden Gate Park. You probably won't get to go to all the restaurants you'd like while you're visiting the city, but you can get a good sampling at this annual event. More than 40 of the town's favorite restaurants, accompanied by 20 microbreweries and 20 wineries, offer tastings in San Francisco's favorite park. There's entertainment as well, and proceeds benefit the Friends of Recreation & Parks. Though rates haven't been set yet, admission is likely to be higher than the previous fee of $10 adults in advance and $12 on-site, $8 seniors in advance and $10 on-site, free for children under 12. Call ℭ **415/458-1988** or visit www.events westca.com for 2006 prices. Labor Day weekend.

Sausalito Art Festival, Sausalito. A juried exhibit of more than 180 to 250 artists, this festival includes music— provided by jazz, rock, and blues performers from the Bay Area and beyond—and international cuisine, enhanced by wines from some 50 Napa and Sonoma producers. Parking is impossible; take the **Blue & Gold Fleet ferry** (ℭ **415/705-5555**) from Fisherman's Wharf to the festival site. For more information, call ℭ **415/332-3555** or go online to www.sausalitoart festival.org. Labor Day weekend.

Opera in the Park, usually in Sharon Meadow, Golden Gate Park. Each year the San Francisco Opera launches its season with a free concert featuring a selection of arias. Call ℭ **415/861-4008** to confirm the location and date. Usually the Sunday after Labor Day.

San Francisco Blues Festival, on the grounds of Fort Mason, The Marina. The largest outdoor, blues-music event on the West Coast was 30 years old in 2002 and continues to feature local and national musicians performing back-to-back during the 3-day extravaganza. You can charge tickets by phone at ℂ **415/421-8497** or online at www.ticketmaster.com. For schedule information, call ℂ **415/826-6837;** for recorded information, call ℂ **415/979-5588** or visit www.sfblues.com. Usually in late September.

Folsom Street Fair, along Folsom Street between 7th and 12th streets, SoMa. This is a local favorite for its kinky, outrageous, leather-and-skin gay-centric blowout celebration. It's hard-core, so only open-minded and adventurous types need head into the leather-clad and partially dressed crowds. Call ℂ **415/861-3247** or visit www.folsomstreetfair.org for the date, which is usually at the end of September.

October

Fleet Week, Marina and Fisherman's Wharf. Residents gather along the Marina Green, The Embarcadero, Fisherman's Wharf, and other great vantage points to watch incredible aerial performances by the Blue Angels, flown in tribute to our nation's marines. Call ℂ **415/705-5500** or visit www.fleetweek.com for details and dates.

Artspan Open Studios, various San Francisco locations. Find an original piece of art to commemorate your trip, or just see what local artists are up to by grabbing a map to over 700 artists' studios that are open to the public during weekends in October. Call ℂ **415/861-9838** or visit www.artspan.org for more information.

Castro Street Fair, The Castro. Celebrate life in the city's most famous gay neighborhood. Call ℂ **415/841-1824** or visit www.castrostreetfair.org for information. First Sunday in October.

Reggae in the Park, Sharon Meadow, Golden Gate Park. This event draws thousands to the park to dance and celebrate the soulful sounds of reggae. Big-name reggae and world-beat bands play all weekend, and ethnic arts-and-crafts and food booths line the stage's periphery. Tickets are about $22 in advance, $27 on-site, $12 for children ages 6 through 12, free for children younger than 5. Two-day discounted passes are available (only in advance) for $40 for adults and $20 for children ages 6 through 12. Call ℂ **415/458-1988** or visit www.eventswestca.com for more details. First weekend in October.

Italian Heritage Parade, North Beach and Fisherman's Wharf. The city's Italian community leads the festivities around Fisherman's Wharf, celebrating Columbus's landing in America. The festival includes a parade along Columbus Avenue; but, for the most part, it's a great excuse to hang out in North Beach and people-watch. For information and the exact date, call ℂ **415/703-9888** or visit www.sfcolumbusday.org. Sunday near October 12.

Exotic Erotic Halloween Ball, The Cow Palace, on the southern outskirts of San Francisco. Thousands come here dressed in costume, lingerie, and sometimes even less than that. It's a wild fantasy affair with bands, dancing, and costume contests. *Beware:* It can be somewhat cheesy. Tickets cost approximately $75 per person. For information, call ℂ **415/567-BALL** or visit www.exoticeroticball.com. One or two Friday or Saturday nights before Halloween.

Halloween, The Castro. This is a huge night in San Francisco. Though it's not an organized event, if you head to Castro and Market you'll find the street shut down and filled with a mixed gay/straight crowd reveling in extraordinary costumes. No contact information. October 31.

San Francisco Jazz Festival, various San Francisco locations. This festival presents eclectic programming in an array of fabulous jazz venues throughout the city. With close to 3 weeks of nightly entertainment and dozens of performers, the jazz festival is a hot ticket. Past events have featured Herbie Hancock, Dave Brubeck, the Modern Jazz Quartet, Wayne Shorter, and Bill

Frisell. For information, call ℃ **800/ 850-SFJF** or 415/788-7353; or visit www.sfjazz.org. Also check the website for other events throughout the year. Late October and early November.

December

The Nutcracker, War Memorial Opera House, Civic Center. The San Francisco Ballet (℃ 415/865-2000) performs this holiday classic annually. Be sure to order tickets, through the website or box office, well in advance.

6 Travel Insurance

Check your existing insurance policies and credit-card coverage before you buy travel insurance. You may already be covered for lost luggage, cancelled tickets, or medical expenses.

The cost of travel insurance varies widely, depending on the cost and length of your trip, your age and health, and the type of trip you're taking, but expect to pay between 5% and 8% of the vacation itself.

TRIP-CANCELLATION INSURANCE

Trip-cancellation insurance helps you get your money back if you have to back out of a trip, if you have to go home early, or if your travel supplier goes bankrupt. Allowed reasons for cancellation can range from sickness to natural disasters to the State Department declaring your destination unsafe for travel. (Insurers usually won't cover vague fears, though, as many travelers discovered who tried to cancel their trips in Oct 2001 because they were wary of flying.) In this unstable world, trip-cancellation insurance is a good buy if you're getting tickets well in advance—who knows what the state of the world, or of your airline, will be in 9 months? Insurance policy details vary, so read the fine print—and make sure that your airline or cruise line is on the list of carriers covered in case of bankruptcy. A good resource is **"Travel Guard Alerts,"** a list of companies considered high-risk by Travel Guard

International (see website below). Protect yourself further by paying for the insurance with a credit card—by law, consumers can get their money back on goods and services not received if they report the loss within 60 days after the charge is listed on their credit card statement.

For more information, contact one of the following recommended insurers: **Access America** (℃ 866/807-3982; www. accessamerica.com); **Travel Guard International** (℃ 800/826-4919; www.travel guard.com); **Travel Insured International** (℃ 800/243-3174; www.travel insured.com); and **Travelex Insurance Services** (℃ 888/457-4602; www.travelex-insurance.com).

MEDICAL INSURANCE   Most health insurance policies cover you if you get sick away from home—but check, particularly if you're insured by an HMO.

LOST-LUGGAGE INSURANCE   On domestic flights, checked baggage is covered up to $2,500 per ticketed passenger. On international flights (including U.S. portions of international trips), baggage coverage is limited to approximately $9.07 per pound, up to approximately $635 per checked bag. If you plan to check items more valuable than the standard liability, see if your valuables are covered by your homeowner's policy, get baggage insurance as part of your comprehensive travel-insurance package, or buy Travel Guard's "Bag-Trak" product. Don't buy insurance at the airport, because it's usually overpriced. Be sure to take any valuables or irreplaceable items with you in your carry-on luggage, because many valuables (including books, money, and electronics) aren't covered by airline policies.

If your luggage is lost, immediately file a lost-luggage claim at the airport, detailing the luggage contents. For most airlines, you must report delayed, damaged, or lost baggage within 4 hours of arrival. The airlines are required to deliver luggage, once found, directly to your house or destination free of charge.

7 Health & Safety

STAYING HEALTHY

No worries about staying healthy in San Francisco. The water's okay to drink, food's fresh—and tasty—and we tend to be a fit bunch. That said, you can spend your vacation in your hotel room if you wear shoes impractical for hiking the city's hills, or if you catch a cold because you don't dress for winter, spring, and summer—which often occur all in 1 day. Also, consider bringing pants with expandable waistbands, because you'll probably overindulge in San Francisco's restaurants.

WHAT TO DO IF YOU GET SICK AWAY FROM HOME

In most cases, your existing health plan will provide the coverage you need. But double-check; you may want to buy **travel medical insurance** instead. (See the section on insurance, above.) Bring your insurance ID card with you when you travel.

If you suffer from a chronic illness, consult your doctor before your departure. For conditions like epilepsy, diabetes, or heart problems, wear a

MedicAlert identification tag (✆ 888/633-4298; www.medicalert.org), which will immediately alert doctors to your condition and give them access to your records through MedicAlert's 24-hour hot line.

Pack **prescription medications** in your carry-on luggage and keep them in their original containers, with pharmacy labels—otherwise, they won't make it through airport security. Also bring along copies of your prescriptions in case you lose your pills or run out, and don't forget an extra pair of contact lenses or prescription glasses.

STAYING SAFE

San Francisco is as safe as any big city, and requires only that you use common sense (for example, don't leave the new video camera on the seat of your parked car). However, in neighborhoods such as Lower Haight, the Mission, the Tenderloin (a few blocks west of Union Square), and Fisherman's Wharf (at night especially), it's a good idea to pay particular attention to your surroundings.

8 Specialized Travel Resources

TRAVELERS WITH DISABILITIES

Most disabilities shouldn't stop anyone from traveling. There are more options and resources out there than ever before.

Many of San Francisco's major museums and tourist attractions have wheelchair ramps. A number of hotels offer special accommodations and services for wheelchair users and other visitors with

disabilities. As well as the ramps, they include extra large bathrooms and telecommunication devices for hearing-impaired travelers. The San Francisco Convention and Visitors Bureau (p. 19) should have the most up-to-date information.

Travelers in wheelchairs can request special ramped taxis by calling **Yellow**

Cab (© 415/626-2345), which charges regular rates for the service. Travelers with disabilities can also get a free copy of the *Muni Access Guide,* published by the San Francisco Municipal Railway, Accessible Services Program, 949 Presidio Ave. (© 415/923-6142), which is staffed weekdays from 8am to 5pm. Many of the major car-rental companies offer hand-controlled cars for drivers with disabilities. **Alamo** (© 800/651-1223), **Avis** (© 800/331-1212, ext. 7305), and **Budget** (© 800/314-3932) have special hot lines that help provide such a vehicle at any of its U.S. locations with 48 hours' advance notice; **Hertz** (© 800/654-3131) requires between 24 and 72 hours' advance notice at most locations.

Many travel agencies offer customized tours and itineraries for travelers with disabilities. **Flying Wheels Travel** (© 507/451-5005; www.flyingwheelstravel.com) offers escorted tours and cruises as well as private tours in minivans with lifts. **Access-Able Travel Source** (© 303/232-2979; www.access-able.com) offers extensive access information and advice for traveling around the world with disabilities. **Accessible Journeys** (© 800/846-4537 or 610/521-0339; www.accessible journeys.com) caters specifically to slow walkers and wheelchair travelers and their families and friends.

Organizations that offer assistance to travelers with disabilities include **MossRehab** (www.mossresourcenet.org), which provides a library of accessible-travel resources online; **SATH** (**Society for Accessible Travel & Hospitality;** © 212/447-7284; www.sath.org; annual membership fees: $45 adults, $30 seniors and students), which offers a wealth of travel resources for people with all types of disabilities and informed recommendations on destinations, access guides, travel agents, tour operators, vehicle rentals, and companion services; and the **American Foundation for the Blind** (**AFB;** © 800/232-5463; www.afb.org), a referral resource for the blind or visually impaired that includes information on traveling with Seeing Eye dogs.

For more information specifically targeted to travelers with disabilities, the community website **iCan** (www.ican online.net/channels/travel/index.cfm) has destination guides and several regular columns on accessible travel, though they don't appear to be updated very often. Also check out the quarterly magazine **Emerging Horizons** ($14.95 per year, $19.95 outside the U.S.; www.emerging horizons.com); and *Open World* magazine, published by SATH (see above; subscription $13 per year, $21 outside the U.S.).

GAY & LESBIAN TRAVELERS

If you head down to the Castro—an area surrounding Castro Street near Market Street—you'll understand why the city is a mecca for gay and lesbian travelers. Since the 1970s, this unique part of town has remained a colorfully festive neighborhood, teeming with "outed" city folk who meander the streets shopping, eating, partying, or cruising. If anyone feels like an outsider in this part of town, it's heterosexuals, who, although warmly welcomed in the community, may feel uncomfortable or downright threatened if they harbor any homophobia or aversion to being "cruised." For many San Franciscans, it's just a fun area (especially on Halloween) with some wonderful shops.

Gays and lesbians make up a good deal of San Francisco's population, so it's no surprise that clubs and bars all over town cater to them. Although lesbian interests are concentrated primarily in the East Bay (especially Oakland), a significant community resides in the Mission District, around 16th and Valencia streets.

Several local publications concentrate on in-depth coverage of news, information, and listings of goings-on around town for gays and lesbians. The *Bay Area Reporter* has the most comprehensive listings, including a weekly calendar of events. Distributed free on Thursday, it can be found stacked at the corner of 18th and Castro streets and at Ninth and Harrison streets, as well as in bars, bookshops, and stores around town. It may also be available in gay and lesbian bookstores elsewhere in the country.

GUIDES & PUBLICATIONS For a good book selection, contact **Giovanni's Room,** 345 S. 12th St., Philadelphia, PA 19107 (© **215/923-2960;** www.giovannis room.com), and **A Different Light Bookstore,** 489 Castro St., San Francisco, CA 94114 (© **415/431-0891;** www. adlbooks.com). There's another Different Light location in Los Angeles (© **310/ 854-6601**).

For other guides, try the *Spartacus International Gay Guide* and *Odysseus,* both are good, annual, English-language guidebooks focused on gay men; and the *Damron* guides (www.damron.com), with separate, annual books for gay men and lesbians.

You can also get lowdown on the best gay or gay-friendly hotels, restaurants, clubs, and other places in San Francisco or around the world by subscribing to Gay.com, which costs $10 for 1 month, $20 for additional months, or $89 for a year.

ORGANIZATIONS The **International Gay and Lesbian Travel Association (IGLTA;** © **800/448-8550** or 954/776-2626; www.iglta.org) is the trade association for the gay and lesbian travel industry, and offers an online directory of gay- and lesbian-friendly travel businesses; go to their website and click on "Members."

TRAVEL AGENCIES Many agencies offer tours and travel itineraries specifically for gay and lesbian travelers. **Now, Voyager** (© **800/255-6951;** www.nowvoyager. com) is a well-known San Francisco–based, gay-owned and -operated travel service. You might also want to try **Skylink Women's Travel,** 1455 N. Dutton Ave, Suite A, Santa Rosa, CA 95401 (© **800/ 225-5759** or 707/546-1212).

SENIOR TRAVEL

Mention the fact that you're a senior when you make your travel reservations. Although all of the major U.S. airlines except America West have canceled their senior discount and coupon book programs, many hotels still offer discounts for seniors. If you're a senior, don't be shy about asking for discounts; in most cities, people over the age of 60 qualify for reduced admission to theaters, museums, and other attractions, as well as discounted fares on public transportation. Always carry some kind of identification, such as a driver's license, that shows your date of birth.

The **Senior Citizen Information Line** (© **415/626-1033**) offers advice, referrals, and information on city services. The **Friendship Line for the Elderly** (© **415/752-3778**) is a support, referral, and crisis-intervention service.

Members of **AARP** (formerly known as the American Association of Retired Persons), 601 E St. NW, Washington, DC 20049 (© **888/687-2277;** www. aarp.org), get discounts on hotels, airfares, and car rentals. AARP offers members a wide range of benefits, including *AARP: The Magazine* and a monthly newsletter. Anyone over 50 can join.

Many reliable agencies and organizations target the 50-plus market. **Elderhostel** (© **877/426-8056;** www.elder hostel.org) arranges study programs for those ages 55 and over (and a spouse or companion of any age) in the U.S. and in more than 100 countries around the world. Most courses last 5 to 7 days in the U.S. (2–4 weeks abroad), and many include hotel accommodations, meals, and tuition.

Recommended publications offering travel resources and discounts for seniors include: the quarterly magazine *Travel 50 & Beyond* (www.travel50andbeyond. com); *Travel Unlimited: Uncommon Adventures for the Mature Traveler* (Avalon); *101 Tips for Mature Travelers,* available from Grand Circle Travel (℡ **800/221-2610** or 617/350-7500; www.gct.com); and *Unbelievably Good Deals and Great Adventures That You Absolutely Can't Get Unless You're Over 50* (McGraw-Hill), by Joann Rattner Heilman.

FAMILY TRAVEL

If you have enough trouble getting your kids out of the house in the morning, dragging them thousands of miles away may seem like an insurmountable challenge. But family travel can be immensely rewarding, giving you new ways of seeing the world through smaller pairs of eyes.

San Francisco is full of sightseeing opportunities and special activities geared toward children. See "Especially for Kids," in chapter 8, beginning on p. 180 for information and ideas for families.

Recommended family-travel Internet sites include **Family Travel Forum** (www. familytravelforum.com), a comprehensive site that offers customized trip planning; **Family Travel Network** (www. familytravelnetwork.com), an award-winning site that offers travel features, deals, and tips; **Traveling Internationally with Your Kids** (www.travelwithyourkids.com), a comprehensive site offering sound advice for long-distance and international travel with children; and **Family Travel Files** (www.thefamilytravelfiles.com), which offers an online magazine and a directory of off-the-beaten-path tours and tour operators for families.

PUBLICATIONS *Frommer's San Francisco with Kids* (Wiley Publishing, Inc.) is a good source of kid-specific information for your trip.

9 Planning Your Trip Online

SURFING FOR AIRFARES

The "big three" online travel agencies— **Expedia** (www.expedia.com), **Travelocity** (http://travelocity.com), and **Orbitz** (www.orbitz.com)—sell most of the air tickets bought on the Internet. (Canadian travelers should try www.expedia.ca and http://travelocity.ca; U.K. residents can go for www.expedia.co.uk and http:// opodo.co.uk.). Each has different business deals with the airlines and may offer different fares on the same flights, so it's wise to shop around. Of the smaller travel-agency websites, **SideStep** (www. sidestep.com) has gotten the best reviews from Frommer's authors. It purports to "search 140 sites at once," but in reality beats competitors' fares only as often as other sites do.

Also remember to check **airline websites,** especially those for low-fare carriers such as Southwest, JetBlue, AirTran, WestJet, or Ryanair, whose fares are often misreported or simply missing from travel-agency websites. Even with major airlines, you can often shave a few bucks from a fare by booking directly through the airline and avoiding a travel agency's transaction fee. But you'll get these discounts only by **booking online:** Most airlines now offer online-only fares that even their phone agents know nothing about. For the websites of airlines that fly to and from your destination, go to "Getting There," p. 32.

Great **last-minute deals** are available through free weekly e-mail services provided directly by the airlines. Most of these are announced on Tuesday or Wednesday and must be purchased online. Most are valid for travel that weekend only, but some (such as Southwest's) can be booked weeks or months in advance. Sign up for weekly e-mail alerts at airline websites or check megasites that compile comprehensive lists of last-minute specials, such as **Smarter Travel** (http://smartertravel.com). For last-minute trips, **site59.com** (www.site59.com) and **lastminutetravel.com** (http://lastminutetravel.com) in the U.S. and **lastminute.com** (http://us.lastminute.com) in Europe often have better air-and-hotel package deals than the major-label sites. A website listing numerous bargain sites and airlines around the world is **www.itravelnet.com**.

If you're willing to give up some control over your flight details, use what is called an **"opaque" fare service** like **Priceline** (www.priceline.com; www.priceline.co.uk for Europeans) or its smaller competitor **Hotwire** (www.hotwirecom). Both offer rock-bottom prices in exchange for travel on a "mystery airline" at a mysterious time of day, often with a mysterious change of planes en route. The mystery airlines are all major, well-known carriers—and the possibility of being sent from Philadelphia to Chicago via Tampa is remote; the airlines' routing computers have gotten a lot better than they used to be. But your chances of getting a 6am or 11pm flight are pretty high. Hotwire tells you flight prices before you buy; Priceline usually has better deals than Hotwire, but you have to play their "name our price" game. If you're new at this, the helpful folks at **BiddingForTravel** (www.biddingfortravel.com) do a good job of demystifying Priceline's prices and strategies. Priceline and Hotwire are great for flights within North America and between the U.S. and Europe. But for flights to other parts of the world, consolidators will almost always beat their fares. *Note:* In 2004, Priceline added nonopaque service to its roster. You now have the option to pick exact flights, times, and airlines from a

list of offers—or opt to bid on opaque fares as before.

SURFING FOR HOTELS

Shopping online for hotels is generally done one of two ways: by booking through the hotel's own website or through an independent booking agency (or a fare-service agency like Priceline; see below). These Internet hotel agencies have multiplied in mind-boggling numbers of late, competing for the business of millions of consumers surfing for accommodations around the world. This competitiveness can be a boon to consumers who have the patience and time to shop and compare the online sites for good deals—but shop they must, for prices can vary considerably from site to site. And keep in mind that hotels at the top of a site's listing may be there for no other reason than that they paid money to get the placement.

Of the "big three" sites, **Expedia** offers a long list of special deals and "virtual tours" or photos of available rooms so you can see what you're paying for (a feature that helps counter the claims that the best rooms are often held back from bargain booking websites). **Travelocity** posts unvarnished customer reviews and ranks its properties according to the AAA rating system. Also reliable are **TripAdvisor** (www.tripadvisor.com; love that one!), **Hotels.com** (www.hotels.com) and **Quikbook.com** (http://quikbook.com). An excellent free program, **TravelAxe** (www.travelaxe.net), can help you search multiple hotel sites at once, even ones you may never have heard of—and conveniently lists the total price of the room, including the taxes and service charges. Another booking site, **Travelweb** (www.travelweb.com), is partly owned by the hotels it represents (including the Hilton, Hyatt, and Starwood chains) and is therefore plugged directly into the hotels' reservations systems—unlike independent

Online Traveler's Toolbox

Veteran travelers usually carry some essential items to make their trips easier. The following is a selection of online tools to bookmark and use.

- **Visa ATM Locator** (www.visa.com), for locations of PLUS ATMs worldwide; or **MasterCard ATM Locator** (www.mastercard.com), for locations of Cirrus ATMs worldwide.
- **Intellicast** (www.intellicast.com) and **Weather.com** (www.weather.com). Both give weather forecasts for all 50 states and for cities around the world.
- **Mapquest** (www.mapquest.com). This best of the mapping sites lets you choose a specific address or destination and, in seconds, it will return a map and detailed directions.
- **Airplane Seating and Food.** Find out which seats to reserve and which to avoid (and more) on all major domestic airlines at www.seatguru.com. And check out the type of meal (with photos) you'll likely be served on airlines around the world at www.airlinemeals.net.
- **Universal Currency Converter** (www.xe.com/ucc). See what your dollar or pound is worth in more than 100 other countries.
- **TripAdvisor** (www.tripadvisor.com). Read honest reviews on San Francisco and Bay Area hotels.
- **OpenTable.com** (www.opentable.com). Book San Francisco restaurant reservations without being put on hold.
- **SF Gate** (www.sfgate.com). The *San Francisco Chronicle* posts all the latest news and happenings, along with a food section that includes The Inside Scoop, a weekly column with in-depth restaurant reviews.
- **City Search** (www.citysearch.com). Get the dirt on everything city-specific from hotel and restaurant reviews to movie showings, spas, bars, and nightclubs.
- **San Francisco Convention and Visitors Bureau** (www.sfvisitor.org). Cruise the pages for a calendar of events, dining and attractions discounts, and basic travel information on San Francisco.
- **Chowhound** (www.chowhound.com). Food fiends peruse this site for insider info on the latest restaurants. Its message board makes for tasty restaurant-related chats

online agencies, which have to fax or e-mail reservation requests to the hotel, a good portion of which get misplaced in the shuffle. More than once, travelers have arrived at the hotel, only to be told that they have no reservation. To be fair, many of the major sites are undergoing improvements in service and ease of use, and Expedia will soon be able to plug directly into the reservations systems of many hotel chains—none of which can be bad news for consumers. In the meantime, it's a good idea to **get a confirmation number** and **make a printout** of any online booking transaction.

In the opaque website category, **Priceline** and **Hotwire** are even better for hotels than for airfares; with both, you're

neighborhood and
tel before offering
he's hotel product
Asia, though it's
five-star lodging
at finding any-
e scale. On the
many hotels stick Priceline
guests in their least desirable rooms. Be
sure to go to the BiddingForTravel website

(see above) before bidding on a hotel
room on Priceline; it features a fairly up-
to-date list of hotels that Priceline uses in
major cities. For both Priceline and
Hotwire, you pay upfront, and the fee is
nonrefundable. *Note:* Some hotels do not
provide loyalty program credits or points
or other frequent-stay amenities when
you book a room through opaque online
services.

10 Getting There

BY PLANE

The northern Bay Area has two major airports: San Francisco International and
Oakland International.

**SAN FRANCISCO INTERNATIONAL
AIRPORT** Almost four dozen major
scheduled carriers serve **San Francisco
International Airport** (© 650/821-8211;
www.flysfo.com), 14 miles directly south
of downtown on U.S. 101. Travel time to
downtown during commuter rush hour is
about 40 minutes; at other times, it's
about 20 to 25 minutes.

The airport offers a **hot line** (© 415/
817-1717) for information on ground
transportation. It gives you a rundown of
all your options for getting into the city
from the airport (also see below for this
information). Each of the three main terminals has a desk where you can get the
same information.

GETTING INTO TOWN
FROM SAN FRANCISCO
INTERNATIONAL AIRPORT

Great news for the budget traveler: **BART
(Bay Area Rapid Transit;** © 510/464-
6000 or 415/989-2278; www.bart.gov)
began running from SFO to numerous
stops within downtown San Francisco in
June 2003. This new route, which takes
about 35 minutes, avoids gnarly traffic on
the way, and costs a heck of a lot less
(around $5 each way, depending on
exactly where you're going) than taxis or
shuttles. Just jump on the airport's free

shuttle bus to the International terminal,
enter the BART station there, and you're
on your way to San Francisco. Trains
leave approximately every 15 minutes.

A **cab** from the airport to downtown
costs $30 to $35, plus tip, and takes
about 30 minutes, traffic permitting.

SFO Airporter buses (© 650/246-
8942; www.sfoairporter.com) depart from
outside the lower-level baggage-claim
area for downtown San Francisco every
30 minutes from 5:35am to 10:05pm.
Shuttles on the 30-minute circuit stop at
several Union Square–area hotels, including the Westin St. Francis, Hilton,
Nikko, Renaissance Parc 55, and downtown Marriott. Those on longer circuits
also stop at the Palace Hotel and Crowne
Plaza Hyatt Regency and Grand Hyatt.
No reservations are needed. For the
return trip, SFO Airporter picks up at
hotels as early as 4:45am. The cost per
person is $15 one-way, $22 round-trip;
children younger than 3 ride free.

Other private shuttle companies offer
door-to-door airport service, in which
you share a van with a few other passengers. **SuperShuttle** (© 415/558-8500;
www.supershuttle.com) takes you anywhere in the city, charging $15 to a resi-
dence or business. Add $8 for each
additional person. It costs $65 to charter
an entire van for up to seven people. The
shuttle stops at least every 20 minutes,
sometimes sooner, and picks up passengers from the marked areas outside the

terminals' upper levels. Reservations are required for the return trip to the airport only and should be made 1 day before departure. These shuttles often demand they pick you up 2 hours before your domestic flight and 3 hours before international flights and during holidays. Keep in mind that you could be the first one on and the last one off, so this trip could take a while; you might want to ask before getting in.

The San Mateo County Transit system, **SamTrans** (© **800/660-4287** in Northern California, or 650/508-6200; www. samtrans.com), runs two buses between the San Francisco Airport and the Transbay Terminal at First and Mission streets. Bus no. 292 costs $1.25 and makes the trip in about 55 minutes. The KX bus costs $3.50 and takes just 35 minutes but permits only one carry-on bag. Both buses run daily—call for schedules.

OAKLAND INTERNATIONAL AIRPORT About 5 miles south of downtown Oakland, at the Hegenberger Road exit of Calif. 17 (U.S. 880; if coming from south, take 98th Ave.) **Oakland International Airport** (© **510/563-3300;** www.oaklandairport.com) primarily serves passengers with East Bay destinations. Some San Franciscans prefer this less-crowded, accessible airport during busy periods—especially because by car it takes around half an hour to get there from downtown San Francisco (traffic permitting). Also, the airport is accessible by BART, which is not influenced by traffic because it travels on its own tracks (see below for more information).

GETTING INTO TOWN FROM OAKLAND INTERNATIONAL AIRPORT

Taxis from the Oakland Airport to downtown San Francisco are expensive—approximately $50, plus tip.

Bayporter Express (© **877/467-1800** in the Bay Area, or 415/467-1800 elsewhere; www.bayporter.com) is a shuttle service that charges $26 for the first person and $12 for each additional person for the ride from the Oakland Airport to downtown San Francisco. Children younger than 12 pay $7. The fare for outer areas of San Francisco is higher. The service accepts advance reservations. To the right of the Oakland Airport exit, there are usually shuttles that take you to San Francisco for around $20 per person. The shuttles in this fleet are independently owned and prices vary.

The cheapest way to reach downtown San Francisco is to take the shuttle bus from the Oakland Airport to **BART** (Bay Area Rapid Transit; © **510/464-6000;** www.bart.gov). The AirBART shuttle bus runs about every 15 minutes Monday through Saturday from 6am to 11:30pm and Sunday from 8:30am to 11:30pm. It makes pickups in front of Terminals 1 and 2 near the ground transportation signs. Tickets must be purchased at the Oakland Airport's vending machines prior to boarding. The cost is $2 for the 10-minute ride to BART's Coliseum station in Oakland. BART fares vary, depending on your destination; the trip to downtown San Francisco costs $3.15 and takes 15 minutes once you're on board.

AIRLINES

Dozens of carriers serve San Francisco International Airport and Oakland International Airport, including the following major domestic airlines: **Alaska Airlines** (© 800/252-7522; www.alaskaair.com), **America West Airlines** (© 800/2FLY-AWA; www.americawest.com), **American Airlines** (© 800/433-7300; www.aa.com), **Continental Airlines** (© 800/523-3273; www.continental.com), **Delta Air Lines** (© 800/221-1212; www.delta.com), **Hawaiian Airlines** (© 800/367-5320; www.hawaiianair.com), **JetBlue** (© 800/538-2583; www.jetblue.com), **Northwest Airlines** (© 800/225-2525; www.nwa.com); **Southwest Airlines** (© 800/

I-FLY-SWA; www.southwest.com), **United Airlines** (© 800/864-8331; www.united.com), and **US Airways** (© 800/428-4322; www.usairways.com).

If you're coming from outside the United States, refer to chapter 3, which lists the major international carriers.

GETTING THROUGH THE AIRPORT

With the federalization of airport security, security procedures at U.S. airports are more stable and consistent than ever. Generally, you'll be fine if you arrive at the airport 1½ **hours** before a domestic flight and 2½ **hours** before an international flight; if you show up late, tell an airline employee and she'll probably whisk you to the front of the line.

Bring a **current, government-issued photo ID** such as a driver's license or passport. Keep your ID at the ready to show at check-in, the security checkpoint, and sometimes even the gate. (Children under 18 do not need government-issued photo IDs for domestic flights, but they do for international flights to most countries.)

In 2003, the Transportation Security Administration (TSA) phased out **gate check-in** at all U.S. airports. And **e-tickets** have made paper tickets nearly obsolete. Passengers with e-tickets can beat the ticket-counter lines by using airport **electronic kiosks** or even **online check-in** from their home computer. Online check-in involves logging on to your airlines' website, accessing your reservation, and printing out your boarding pass—and the airline may even offer you bonus miles to do so! If you're using a kiosk at the airport, bring a credit card or your frequent-flier card. Print out your boarding pass from the kiosk and simply proceed to the security checkpoint with your pass and a photo ID. If you're checking bags or looking to snag an exit-row seat, you will be able to do so using most airline kiosks. Even the smaller airlines are employing the kiosk system, but always call your airline to make sure these alternatives are available. **Curbside check-in** is also a good way to avoid lines, although a few airlines still ban curbside check-in; call before you go.

Security checkpoint lines are getting shorter than they were during 2001 and 2002, but some doozies remain. If you have trouble standing for long periods of time, tell an airline employee; the airline will provide a wheelchair. Speed up security by **not wearing metal objects** such as big belt buckles. If you've got metallic body parts, a note from your doctor can prevent a long chat with the security screeners. Keep in mind that only **ticketed passengers** are allowed past security, except for folks escorting passengers with disabilities or unaccompanied children.

Federalization has stabilized **what you can carry on** and **what you can't.** The general rule is that sharp things are out, nail clippers are okay, and food and beverages must be passed through the X-ray machine—but security screeners can't make you drink from your coffee cup. Bring food in your carry-on rather than checking it, as explosive-detection machines used on checked luggage have been known to mistake food (especially chocolate, for some reason) for bombs. Travelers in the U.S. are allowed one carry-on bag, plus a "personal item" such as a purse, briefcase, or laptop bag. Carry-on hoarders can stuff all sorts of things into a laptop bag; as long as it has a laptop in it, it's still considered a personal item. The TSA has issued a list of restricted items; check its website (www.tsa.gov/public/index.jsp) for details.

Airport screeners may decide that your checked luggage needs to be searched by hand. You can now purchase luggage locks that allow screeners to open and relock a checked bag if hand-searching is necessary. Look for Travel Sentry certified locks at luggage or travel shops and

Brookstone stores (you can buy them online at www.brookstone.com). These locks, approved by the TSA, can be opened by luggage inspectors with a special code or key. For more information on the locks, visit www.travelsentry.org. If you use something other than TSA-approved locks, your lock will be cut off your suitcase if a TSA agent needs to hand-search your luggage.

FLYING FOR LESS: TIPS FOR GETTING THE BEST AIRFARE

Passengers sharing the same airplane cabin rarely pay the same fare. Travelers who need to purchase tickets at the last minute, change their itinerary at a moment's notice, or fly one-way often get stuck paying the premium rate. Here are some ways to keep your airfare costs down.

- Passengers who can book their ticket **long in advance,** who can **stay over Saturday night,** or who **fly midweek** or **at less-trafficked hours** may pay a fraction of the full fare. If your schedule is flexible, say so, and ask if you can secure a cheaper fare by changing your flight plans.

- You can also save on airfares by keeping an eye out in local newspapers for **promotional specials** or **fare wars,** when airlines lower prices on their most popular routes. You rarely see fare wars offered for peak travel times, but if you can travel in the off months, you may snag a bargain.

- Search the **Internet** for cheap fares (see "Planning Your Trip Online," earlier in this chapter).

- **Consolidators,** also known as bucket shops, are great sources for international tickets, although they usually can't beat the Internet on fares within North America—including San Francisco. Start by looking in Sunday newspaper travel sections; U.S. travelers should focus on the *New York Times, Los Angeles Times,* and *Miami Herald.* For less-developed destinations, small

travel agents who cater to immigrant communities in large cities often have the best deals. *Beware:* Bucket-shop tickets are usually nonrefundable or rigged with stiff cancellation penalties, often as high as 50% to 75% of the ticket price, and some put you on charter airlines, which may leave at inconvenient times and experience delays. Several reliable consolidators are worldwide and available on the Net. **STA Travel** (© **800/781-4040;** www.statravel.com) is now the world's leader in student travel, thanks to its purchase of Council Travel. It also offers good fares for travelers of all ages. **FlyCheap** (© **800/FLY-CHEAP;** www.1800flycheap.com) is owned by package-holiday megalith MyTravel and has especially good access to fares for sunny destinations. **Air Tickets Direct** (© **800/778-3447;** www.air ticketsdirect.com) is based in Montreal and leverages the currently weak Canadian dollar for low fares; it'll also book trips to places that U.S. travel agents won't touch, such as Cuba.

- Join **frequent-flier clubs.** Accrue enough miles, and you'll be rewarded with free flights and elite status. It's free, and you'll get the best choice of seats, faster response to phone inquiries, and prompter service if your luggage is stolen, your flight is canceled or delayed, or if you want to change your seat. You don't need to fly to build frequent-flier miles—**frequent-flier credit cards** can provide thousands of miles for doing your everyday shopping.

BY CAR

San Francisco is easily accessible by major highways: **Interstate 5,** from the north, and **U.S. 101,** which cuts south-north through the peninsula from San Jose and across the Golden Gate Bridge to points north. If you drive from Los Angeles, you can take the longer coastal route (437 miles and 11 hr.) or the inland route (389 miles and 8 hr.). From Mendocino, it's 156 miles and 4 hours; from Sacramento, 88 miles and 1½ hours; from Yosemite, 210 miles and 4 hours.

If you are driving and aren't already a member, it's worth joining the **American Automobile Association** (© **800/922-8228;** www.aaa.com). It charges $49 to $79 per year (with an additional one-time joining fee), depending on where you join, and provides roadside and other services to motorists. **Amoco Motor Club** (© **800/334-3300**) is another recommended choice.

For information about renting a car, see the "Car Rentals" section (beginning on p. 67) of chapter 5, "Getting to Know San Francisco."

BY TRAIN

Traveling by train takes a long time and usually costs as much as, or more than, flying. Still, if you want to take a leisurely ride across America, rail may be a good option for getting to San Francisco.

San Francisco–bound **Amtrak** (© **800/ 872-7245** or 800/USA-RAIL; www.amtrak.com) trains leave from New York and cross the country via Chicago. The journey takes about 3½ days, and seats sell quickly. At this writing, the lowest round-trip fare cost $268 from New York and $245 from Chicago. Round-trip tickets from Los Angeles cost as little as $100 or as much as $200. Wherever you're arriving from, trains lead to Emeryville, just north of Oakland, and connect with regularly scheduled buses to San Francisco's Ferry Building and Cal-Train station in downtown San Francisco.

CalTrain (© **800/660-4287** or 415/ 546-4461; www.caltrain.com) operates train service between San Francisco and the peninsula towns. The city depot is at 700 Fourth St., at Townsend Street.

11 Packages for the Independent Traveler

Before you start your search for the lowest airfare, you may want to consider booking your flight as part of a travel package. Package tours are not the same thing as escorted tours. Package tours are simply a way to buy the airfare, accommodations, and other elements of your trip (such as car rentals, airport transfers, and sometimes even activities) at the same time and often at discounted prices—kind of like one-stop shopping. Packages are sold in bulk to tour operators—who resell them to the public at a cost that usually undercuts standard rates.

Frommers.com regularly covers the latest package deals for destinations all around the world; new stories are posted every Monday, Wednesday, and Friday. Another good source of package deals is the airlines themselves. Most major airlines offer air/land packages, including **American Airlines Vacations** (© 800/ 321-2121; www.aavacations.com), **Delta Vacations** (© 800/221-6666; www.deltavacations.com), **Continental Airlines Vacations** (© 800/301-3800; www.covacations.com), and **United Vacations** (© 888/854-3899; www.unitedvacations.com). Several big **online travel agencies**— Expedia, Travelocity, Orbitz, Site59, and Lastminute.com—also do a brisk business in packages. It's wise to check the quality of the lead hotel through **Trip-Advisor**'s (www.tripadvisor.com) unbiased reader reviews. It may be worthwhile to pay a little extra for one of the better hotels included in a package. If you're unsure about the pedigree of a smaller packager, check with the Better Business Bureau in the city where the company is based, or go online at www.bbb.org. If a packager won't tell you where they're based, don't fly with them.

Travel packages are also listed in the travel section of your local Sunday newspaper. Or check ads in the national travel magazines such as *Arthur Frommer's Budget Travel Magazine, Travel & Leisure, National Geographic Traveler,* and *Condé Nast Traveler.*

Package tours can vary by leaps and bounds. Some offer a better class of hotels than others, and some offer the same hotels for lower prices. Some offer flights on scheduled airlines, while others book charters. Some limit your choice of accommodations and travel days. You are often required to make a large payment up front. On the plus side, packages can save you money, offering group prices but allowing for independent travel. Some even let you add on a few guided excursions or escorted day trips (also at prices lower than if you booked them yourself)

without booking an entirely escorted tour.

Before you invest in a package tour, get some answers. Ask about the **accommodations choices** and prices for each. Then look up the hotels' reviews in a Frommer's guide and check their rates online for your specific dates of travel online. You'll also want to find out what **type of room** you get. If you need a certain type of room, ask for it; don't take whatever is thrown your way. Request a nonsmoking room, a quiet room, a room with a view, or whatever you fancy.

Finally, look for **hidden expenses.** Ask whether airport departure fees and taxes, for example, are included in the total cost.

12 Recommended Books & Films

San Francisco was a popular setting for many early literary works, including Mark Twain's *San Francisco* (Heyday Books, 2003), a collection of articles originally published in the 19th century that glorified "the liveliest, heartiest community on our continent." It was also the birthplace of Jack London, who wrote several short stories of his days as an oyster pirate on the San Francisco Bay, as well as *Martin Eden* (Penguin USA, 1994), his semiautobiographical account of life along the Oakland shores.

For mystery buffs, two must-reads include Frank Norris's *McTeague: A Story of San Francisco* (Signet, 2003), a violent tale of love and greed set at the turn of the 20th century, and Dashiell Hammett's *The Maltese Falcon* (Vintage Books, 1992), a steamy detective novel that captures the seedier side of San Francisco in the 1920s (you can even take a walking tour of Hammett's famous haunts). The novel was made into a classic 1941 film by John Huston, starring Humphrey Bogart and Mary Astor.

California has always been a hotbed for alternative—and, more often than not,

controversial—literary styles. Joan Didion, in her novel *Slouching Toward Bethlehem* (Noonday Press, 1990), and Hunter S. Thompson, in his columns for the *San Francisco Examiner* (brought together in the collection *Generation of Swine,* Vintage Books, 1989), both used a "new journalistic" approach in their studies of San Francisco in the 1960s. Tom Wolfe's early work *The Electric Kool-Aid Acid Test* (Doubleday, 1999) follows the Hell's Angels, the Grateful Dead, and Ken Kesey's Merry Pranksters as they ride through the hallucinogenic 1960s. Meanwhile, Beat writers Allen Ginsberg and Jack Kerouac were penning protests against political conservatism—and promoting their bohemian lifestyle—in the former's controversial poem "Howl" (daringly published by Lawrence Ferlinghetti, poet and owner of City Lights bookstore in North Beach) and the latter's famous tale of American adventure, *On the Road.*

Among Wallace Stegner's many other works of contemporary fiction and nonfiction about the West is his novel *All the Little Live Things* (Penguin USA, 1993), which explores the conflicts faced by retired literary agent Joe Allston; the book is set in the San Francisco Bay Area of the 1960s. *The Spectator Bird* (winner of the 1976 National Book Award) revisits Allston's character as he reflects on his life and his memories.

For a more recent look at San Francisco, check out Dave Eggers' memoir *A Heartbreaking Work of Staggering Genius* (Vintage Books, 2001), which offers a highly ironic account of the 1990s dot-com boom. Eggers is also an editor at the snarky literary magazine *McSweeney's,* which is based in San Francisco.

To get advice on San Francisco–based literature, head to North Beach and chat with the staff at **City Lights Booksellers & Publishers,** owned by Lawrence Ferlinghetti, the renowned Beat Generation poet. It's at 261 Columbus Ave. at Broadway (© **415/362-8193;** www.citylights.com).

3

For International Visitors

Whether it's your first visit or your tenth, a trip to the United States may require an additional degree of planning. This chapter will provide you with essential information, helpful tips, and advice for the more common problems that some visitors encounter.

1 Preparing for Your Trip

ENTRY REQUIREMENTS

Check at any U.S. embassy or consulate for current information and requirements. You can also obtain a visa application and other information online at the **U.S. State Department**'s website, at **www.travel.state.gov**.

VISAS The U.S. State Department has a **Visa Waiver Program** allowing citizens of certain countries to enter the United States, without a visa, for stays of up to 90 days. At press time these included Andorra, Australia, Austria, Belgium, Brunei, Denmark, Finland, France, Germany, Iceland, Ireland, Italy, Japan, Liechtenstein, Luxembourg, Monaco, the Netherlands, New Zealand, Norway, Portugal, San Marino, Singapore, Slovenia, Spain, Sweden, Switzerland, and the United Kingdom. Citizens of these countries need only a valid passport and a round-trip air or cruise ticket in their possession upon arrival. If they first enter the United States, they may also visit Mexico, Canada, Bermuda, and/or the Caribbean Islands and return to the United States without a visa. Further information is available from any U.S. embassy or consulate. Canadian citizens may enter the United States without visas; they need only proof of residence.

Citizens of all other countries must have (1) a valid passport that expires at least 6 months later than the scheduled end of their visit to the United States, and (2) a tourist visa, which may be obtained without charge from any U.S. consulate.

To obtain a visa, the traveler must submit a completed application form (either in person or by mail) with a 2-inch-square photo, and must demonstrate binding ties to a residence abroad. Usually you can obtain a visa at once or within 24 hours, but it may take longer during the summer rush from June through August. If you cannot go in person, contact the nearest U.S. embassy or consulate for directions on applying by mail. Your travel agent or airline office may also be able to provide you with visa applications and instructions. The U.S. consulate or embassy that issues your visa will determine whether you will be issued a multiple- or single-entry visa and any restrictions regarding the length of your stay.

British subjects can obtain up-to-date visa information by calling the **U.S. Embassy Visa Information Line** (© 0891/200-290) or by visiting the "Visa Services" section of the American Embassy London's website at www.usembassy.org.uk.

Irish citizens can obtain up-to-date visa information through the **Embassy of the USA Dublin,** 42 Elgin Rd., Dublin 4, Ireland (© 353/1-668-8777); or by checking the "Visas to the U.S." section of the website at http://dublin.usembassy.gov.

Australian citizens can obtain up-to-date visa information by contacting the **U.S. Embassy Canberra,** Moonah Place, Yarralumla, ACT 2600 (© 02/6214-5600), or by checking the U.S. Diplomatic Mission's website at http://usembassy-australia.state.gov/consular.

Citizens of **New Zealand** can obtain up-to-date visa information by contacting the **U.S. Embassy New Zealand,** 29 Fitzherbert Terrace, Thorndon, Wellington (© 644/472-2068), or get the information directly from the "For New Zealanders" section of the website at http://usembassy.org.nz.

MEDICAL REQUIREMENTS   Unless you're arriving from an area known to be suffering from an epidemic (particularly cholera or yellow fever), inoculations or vaccinations are not required for entry into the United States. If you have a medical condition that requires **syringe-administered medications,** carry a valid signed prescription from your physician—the Federal Aviation Administration (FAA) no longer allows airline passengers to pack syringes in their carry-on baggage without documented proof of medical need. If you have a disease that requires treatment with **narcotics,** you should also carry documented proof with you—smuggling narcotics aboard a plane is a serious offense that carries severe penalties in the U.S.

For **HIV-positive visitors,** requirements for entering the United States are somewhat vague and change frequently. According to the latest publication of *HIV and Immigrants: A Manual for AIDS Service Providers,* the Immigration and Naturalization Service (INS) doesn't require a medical exam for entry into the

United States, but INS officials may stop individuals because they look sick or because they are carrying AIDS/HIV medicine.

If an HIV-positive noncitizen applies for a nonimmigrant visa, the question on the application regarding communicable diseases is tricky no matter which way it's answered. If the applicant checks "no," INS may deny the visa on the grounds that the applicant committed fraud. If the applicant checks "yes" or if INS suspects the person is HIV-positive, it will deny the visa unless the applicant asks for a special waiver for visitors. This waiver is for people visiting the United States for a short time—to attend a conference, for instance, to visit close relatives, or to receive medical treatment. It can be a confusing situation. For up-to-the-minute information, contact **AIDSinfo** (© 800/448-0440 or 301/519-6616 outside the U.S.; www.aidsinfo.nih.gov) or the **Gay Men's Health Crisis** (© 212/367-1000; www.gmhc.org).

DRIVER'S LICENSES   Foreign driver's licenses are mostly recognized in the U.S., although you may want to get an international driver's license if your home license is not written in English.

PASSPORT INFORMATION

Safeguard your passport in an inconspicuous, inaccessible place such as a money belt. Make a copy of the critical pages, including the passport number, and store it in a safe place, separate from the passport itself. If you lose your passport, visit the nearest consulate of your native country as soon as possible for a replacement. Passport applications are downloadable from the websites listed below.

Note: The International Civil Aviation Organization has advocated a policy requiring that *every* individual who travels by air have a passport. In response, many countries are now requiring that children must be issued their own passport to travel internationally, where before, those under 16 or so may have been allowed to travel on a parent or guardian's passport.

FOR RESIDENTS OF CANADA

You can pick up a passport application at one of 28 regional passport offices or most travel agencies. Canadian children who travel must have their own passport. However, if you hold a valid Canadian passport, issued before December 11, 2001, bearing the name of your child, the passport remains valid for you and your child until it expires or until the child turns 16 years old. Passports cost C$87 for those 16 years and older (valid 5 years), C$37 children 3 to 15 (valid 5 years), and C$22 for children younger than 3 (valid 3 years). Applications, which must be accompanied by two identical passport-size photographs and proof of Canadian citizenship, are available at travel agencies throughout Canada or from the central **Passport Office,** Department of Foreign Affairs and International Trade, Ottawa, ON K1A 0G3 (© **800/567-6868;** www.dfait-maeci.gc.ca/passport). Processing takes 5 to 10 days if you apply in person, or about 3 weeks by mail.

FOR RESIDENTS OF THE UNITED KINGDOM

To pick up an application for a standard 10-year passport (5-year passport for children younger than 16), visit the nearest Passport Office, major post office, or travel agency. You can also contact the **United Kingdom Passport Service** at © **0870/571-0410,** or visit its website at www.passport.gov.uk. Passports are £42 for adults and £25 for children younger than 16, with another £30 fee if you apply in person at a Passport Office. Processing takes about 3 weeks (1 week if you apply at the Passport Office).

FOR RESIDENTS OF IRELAND

You can apply for a 10-year passport, costing €75 at the **Passport Office,** Setanta Centre, Molesworth Street, Dublin 2 (© **01/671-1633;** www.irlgov.ie/iveagh). Those under age 18 and older than 3 must apply for a €25 5-year passport; those 3 and younger need a €15 3-year passport. You can also apply at 1A South Mall, Cork (© **021/272-5252**) or over the counter at most main post offices and Garda stations.

FOR RESIDENTS OF AUSTRALIA

You can get an application from your local post office or any branch of Passports Australia, but you must schedule an interview at the passport office to present your application materials. Call the **Australian Passport Information Service** at © **131-232,** or visit the government website at www.passports.gov.au. Passports for adults are A$150 and A$75 for those younger than 18.

FOR RESIDENTS OF NEW ZEALAND

You can pick up a passport application at any New Zealand Passports Office or download one from its website. Contact the **Passports Office** at © **0800/225-050** in New Zealand or 04/474-8100, or go online to www.passports.govt.nz. Passports for adults are NZ$71 and are NZ$36 for children younger than 16.

CUSTOMS
WHAT YOU CAN BRING IN

Every visitor older than 21 years of age may bring in, free of duty, the following: (1) 1 liter of wine or hard liquor; (2) 200 cigarettes, 100 cigars (but not from Cuba), or 3 pounds of smoking tobacco; and (3) $100 worth of gifts. These exemptions are offered to travelers who spend at least 72 hours in the United States and who have not claimed them within the preceding 6 months. It is altogether forbidden to bring into the country foodstuffs (particularly fruit, cooked meats, and canned goods) and plants (vegetables, seeds, tropical plants, and the like). Foreign tourists may bring in or take out up to $10,000 in U.S. or foreign currency with no formalities; larger sums must be declared to U.S. Customs on entering or leaving, which includes filing form FinCEN 105. For more specific information regarding U.S. Customs and Border Protection, contact your nearest U.S. embassy or consulate, or the **U.S. Customs** office (© **202/282-8000** or www.customs.ustreas.gov).

WHAT YOU CAN TAKE HOME

U.K. citizens returning from a non-E.U. country have a customs allowance of: 200 cigarettes; 50 cigars; 250g of smoking tobacco; 2 liters of still table wine; 1 liter of spirits or strong liqueurs (over 22% volume); 2 liters of fortified wine, sparkling wine, or other liqueurs; 60cc (ml) perfume; 250cc (ml) of toilet water; and £145 worth of all other goods, including gifts and souvenirs. People younger than 17 cannot have the tobacco or alcohol allowance. For more information, contact **HM Customs & Excise** at © **0845/010-9000** (from outside the U.K., © **020/8929-0152**), or consult its website at http://customs.hmrc.gov.uk.

For a clear summary of **Canadian** rules, request the booklet *I Declare,* issued by the **Canada Customs and Revenue Agency** (© **800/461-9999** in Canada, or 204/983-3500; www.cra-arc.gc.ca). Canada allows its citizens a C$750 exemption, and you're allowed to bring back duty-free one carton of cigarettes, 200 grams of tobacco, 1.5 liters of wine, 1.14 liters of liquor, and 50 cigars. Canadian citizens younger than 18 or 19, depending on their province, cannot have the tobacco or alcohol allowance. In addition, you're allowed to mail gifts to Canada valued at less than C$60 a day, provided they're unsolicited and don't contain alcohol or tobacco (write on the package "Unsolicited gift, under $60 value"). All valuables should be declared on the Y-38 form

before departure from Canada, including serial numbers of valuables you already own, such as expensive foreign cameras. *Note:* The C$750 exemption can be used only once a year and only after an absence of 7 days.

The duty-free allowance in **Australia** is A$900 or, for those younger than 18, A$450. Citizens age 18 and older can bring in 250 cigarettes or 250 grams of loose tobacco, and 2.25 liters of alcohol. If you're returning with valuables you already own, such as foreign-made cameras, you should file form B263. A helpful brochure available from Australian consulates or Customs offices is *Know Before You Go.* For more information, call the **Australian Customs Service** at © **1300/363-263,** or go online to www.customs.gov.au.

The duty-free allowance for **New Zealand** is NZ$700. Citizens over 17 can bring in 200 cigarettes, 50 cigars, or 250 grams of tobacco (or a mixture of all three, if their combined weight doesn't exceed 250g); plus 4.5 liters of wine and beer, or 1.125 liters of liquor. New Zealand currency does not carry import or export restrictions, although you will need to fill out a Border Cash Report if you bring in more than NZ$10,000 or the foreign cash equivalent. Fill out a certificate of export, listing the valuables you are taking out of the country; that way, you can bring them back without paying duty. Most questions are answered in a free pamphlet available at New Zealand consulates and Customs offices: *New Zealand Customs Advice to Travellers.* For more information, contact **New Zealand Customs,** The Customhouse, 17–21 Whitmore St., Box 2218, Wellington (© **0800/428-786** or 04/473-6099; www.customs.govt.nz).

HEALTH INSURANCE

Although it's not required of travelers, health insurance is highly recommended.

Unlike many European countries, the United States does not usually offer free or low-cost medical care to its citizens or visitors. Doctors and hospitals are expensive, and, in most cases, require advance payment or proof of coverage before they render their services. Good policies cover the costs of an accident, repatriation, or death. See "Travel Insurance" in chapter 2 for more information. Packages such as **Europ Assistance's "Worldwide Healthcare Plan"** are sold by European automobile clubs and travel agencies at attractive rates. **Worldwide Assistance Services, Inc.** (© 800/777-8710; www.worldwide assistance.com) is the agent for Europ Assistance in the United States.

Though lack of health insurance may prevent you from being admitted to a hospital in nonemergencies, don't worry about being left on a street corner to die: The American way is to fix you now and bill the living daylights out of you later.

INSURANCE FOR BRITISH TRAVELERS
Most big travel agents offer their own insurance and will probably try to sell you their package when you book a holiday. Think before you sign. **Britain's Consumers' Association** recommends that you insist on seeing the policy and reading the fine print before buying insurance. **The Association of British Insurers** (© 020/7600-3333; www.abi.org.uk) gives advice by phone and publishes *Holiday Insurance,* a free guide to policy provisions and prices. You might also shop around for better deals: Try **Columbus Direct** (© 0870/033-9988; www.columbusdirect.com).

INSURANCE FOR CANADIAN TRAVELERS
Canadians should check with their provincial health plan offices or call **Health Canada** (© 866/225-0709; www.hc-sc.gc.ca) to find out the extent of their coverage and what documentation and receipts they must take home in case they are treated in the United States.

MONEY
CURRENCY The U.S. monetary system is very simple: The most common **bills** are the $1 (colloquially, a "buck"), $5, $10, and $20 denominations. There are also $2 bills (seldom encountered), $50 bills, and $100 bills (the last two are usually not welcome as payment for small purchases). All the paper money was recently redesigned, making the famous faces adorning them disproportionately large. The old-style bills are still legal tender.

There are seven denominations of coins: 1¢ (1 cent, or a penny); 5¢ (5 cents, or a nickel); 10¢ (10 cents, or a dime); 25¢ (25 cents, or a quarter); 50¢ (50 cents, or a half-dollar); the new gold-colored "Sacagawea" coin worth $1; and, prized by collectors, the rare, older silver-dollar coin.

Note: The "foreign-exchange bureaus" so common in Europe are rare, even at airports, in the United States, and nonexistent outside major cities. It's best not to change foreign money (or traveler's checks denominated in a currency other than U.S. dollars) at a small-town bank, or even a branch in a big city; in fact, leave any currency other than U.S. dollars at home—it may prove a greater nuisance to you than it's worth.

TRAVELER'S CHECKS Though traveler's checks are widely accepted, make sure that they're denominated in U.S. dollars, because foreign-currency checks are often difficult to exchange. The three traveler's checks that are most widely recognized—and least likely to be denied—are **Visa, American Express,** and **Thomas Cook.** Be sure to record the numbers of the checks, and keep that information in a separate place in case the checks get lost or stolen. Most businesses are pretty good about taking traveler's checks, but you're better off cashing them in at a bank (in small amounts, of course) and paying in cash. *Note*: You'll need identification, such as a driver's license or passport, to change a traveler's check.

Travel Tip

Be sure to keep a copy of all your travel papers separate from your wallet or purse, and leave a copy with someone at home should you need it faxed in an emergency.

CREDIT CARDS & ATMS Credit cards are the most widely used form of payment in the United States: **Visa** (Barclaycard in Britain), **MasterCard** (Euro-Card in Europe, Access in Britain, Chargex in Canada), **American Express, Diners Club,** and **Discover.** There are, however, a handful of stores and restaurants that do not take credit cards, so be sure to ask in advance. Most businesses display a sticker near their entrance to let you know which cards they accept. (*Note*: Businesses may require a minimum purchase, usually around $10, to use a credit card.)

It is strongly recommended that you bring at least one major credit card. You must have a credit or charge card to rent a car. Hotels and airlines usually require a credit card imprint as a deposit against expenses, and in an emergency, a credit card can be priceless.

You'll find **automated teller machines (ATMs)** on just about every block—at least in almost every town—across the country. Some ATMs will allow you to draw U.S. currency against your bank and credit cards. Check with your bank before leaving home, and remember that you will need your personal identification number (PIN) to do so. Most accept Visa, MasterCard, and American Express, as well as ATM cards from other U.S. banks. Expect to be charged up to $3 per transaction, however, if you're not using your own bank's ATM.

One way around these fees is to ask for cash back at grocery stores that accept ATM cards and don't charge usage fees. Of course, you'll have to purchase something first.

ATM cards with major credit card backing, known as "debit cards," are now a commonly accepted form of payment in most stores and restaurants. Debit cards draw money directly from your checking account. Some stores enable you to receive "cash back" on your debit-card purchases as well.

SAFETY

GENERAL SUGGESTIONS Although tourist areas are generally safe, U.S. urban areas tend to be less safe than those in Europe or Japan. You should always stay alert. This is particularly true of large American cities. If you're in doubt about which neighborhoods are safe, don't hesitate to make inquiries with the hotel front-desk staff or the local tourist office.

Avoid deserted areas, especially at night, and don't go into public parks after dark unless there's a concert or similar occasion that will attract a crowd.

Avoid carrying valuables with you on the street, and keep expensive cameras or electronic equipment bagged up or covered when not in use. If you're using a map, try to consult it inconspicuously—or better yet, study it before you leave your room. Hold onto your pocketbook, and place your billfold in an inside pocket. In theaters, restaurants, and other public places, keep your possessions in sight.

Always lock your room door—don't assume that once you're inside the hotel, you are automatically safe and no longer need to be aware of your surroundings. Hotels are open to the public, and in a large hotel, security may not be able to screen everyone who enters.

Yes, this advice is a little paranoid. San Francisco tends to be a relatively safe city. But it never hurts to be careful—especially if you're wandering at night through areas of the Mission, Tenderloin (a few blocks west of Union Square), Hunter's Point, SoMa, and Lower Haight.

DRIVING SAFETY Driving safety is important too, and carjacking is not unprecedented in San Francisco. Question your rental agency about personal safety and ask for a traveler-safety brochure when you pick up your car. Obtain written directions—or a map with the route clearly marked—from the agency showing how to get to your destination. (Many agencies now offer the option of renting a cellphone for the duration of your car rental; check with the rental agent when you pick up the car. Otherwise, contact **InTouch USA** at © **800/872-7626** or www.intouchusa.com for short-term cellphone rental.) And, if possible, arrive and depart during daylight hours.

If you drive off a highway and end up in a dodgy-looking neighborhood, leave the area as quickly as possible. If you have an accident, even on the highway, stay in your car with the doors locked until you assess the situation or until the police arrive. If you're bumped from behind on the street or are involved in a minor accident with no injuries, and the situation appears to be suspicious, motion to the other driver to follow you. Never get out of your car in such situations. Go directly to the nearest police precinct, well-lit service station, or 24-hour store.

Park in well-lit and well-traveled areas whenever possible. Always keep your car doors locked, whether the vehicle is attended or unattended. Never leave any packages or valuables in sight. If someone attempts to rob you or steal your car, don't try to resist the thief/carjacker. Report the incident to the police department immediately by calling © **911.**

2 Getting to the U.S.

AIRLINE DISCOUNTS The smart traveler can find numerous ways to reduce the price of a plane ticket simply by taking time to shop around. For example, overseas visitors can take advantage of the APEX (Advance Purchase Excursion) reductions offered by all major U.S. and European carriers. For more money-saving airline advice, see "Getting There," in chapter 2. For the best rates, compare fares and be flexible with the dates and times of travel.

IMMIGRATION & CUSTOMS CLEARANCE Visitors arriving by air, no matter what the port of entry, should cultivate patience and resignation before setting foot on U.S. soil. Getting through immigration control can take as long as 2

Tips **Prepare to Be Fingerprinted**

Starting in January 2004, many international visitors traveling on visas to the United States will be photographed and fingerprinted at Customs in a new program created by the Department of Homeland Security called **US-VISIT.** Non-U.S. citizens arriving at airports and on cruise ships must undergo an instant background check as part of the government's ongoing efforts to deter terrorism by verifying the identity of incoming and outgoing visitors. For more information, go to the Homeland Security website at **www.dhs.gov/dhspublic.**

hours on some days, especially on summer weekends, so be sure to carry this guidebook or something else to read. This is especially true in the aftermath of the World Trade Center attacks, when security clearances have been considerably beefed up at U.S. airports.

People traveling by air from Canada, Bermuda, and certain countries in the Caribbean can sometimes clear Customs and Immigration at the point of departure, which is much quicker.

3 Getting Around the U.S.

BY PLANE Some large airlines (for example, Northwest and Delta) offer travelers on their transatlantic or transpacific flights special discount tickets under the name **Visit USA,** allowing mostly one-way travel from one U.S. destination to another at very low prices. These discount tickets are not on sale in the United States and must be purchased abroad in conjunction with your international ticket. This system is the best, easiest, and fastest way to see the United States at low cost. You should obtain information well in advance from your travel agent or the office of the airline concerned, since the conditions attached to these discount tickets can be changed without advance notice.

BY TRAIN International visitors (excluding Canada) can also buy a **USA Rail Pass,** good for 15 or 30 days of unlimited travel on Amtrak (© **800/USA-RAIL;** www.amtrak.com). The pass is available through many overseas travel agents. Prices valid for travel across the United States in 2005 for a 15-day pass were $295 off-peak, $440 peak; a 30-day pass costs $385 off-peak, $550 peak. Fares are significantly cheaper, however, within particular regions. See Amtrak's website for the cost of travel within the western, eastern, or northwestern United States. With a foreign passport, you can also buy passes at some Amtrak offices in the United States, including locations in San Francisco, Los Angeles, Chicago, New York, Miami, Boston, and Washington, D.C. Reservations are generally required

and should be made for each part of your trip as early as possible. Regional rail passes are also available.

BY BUS Although bus travel is often the most economical form of public transit for short hops between U.S. cities, it can also be slow and uncomfortable—certainly not an option for everyone (particularly when Amtrak, which is far more luxurious, offers similar rates). **Greyhound/Trailways** (© **800/231-2222** or 214/849-8100; www.greyhound.com), the sole nationwide bus line, offers an **International Ameripass** that must be purchased before coming to the United States, or by phone through the Greyhound International Office at the Port Authority Bus Terminal in New York City (© **212/971-0492**). The pass can be obtained from foreign travel agents or through Greyhound's website (order at least 21 days before your departure to the U.S.) and costs less than the domestic version. 2005 passes cost as follows: 7 days ($239), 10 days ($289), 15 days ($349), 21 days ($419), 30 days ($479), 45 days ($529), or 60 days ($639). You can get more info on the pass at the website, or by calling © **402/330-8552.** In addition, special rates are available for seniors, students, and children.

BY CAR Unless you plan to spend the bulk of your vacation time in San Francisco proper, where walking or public transportation is the easiest way to get around (mostly due to the lack of parking and expensive lot fees), the most cost-effective, convenient, and comfortable way to travel around the United States, and Northern California, is by car. The interstate highway system connects cities and towns all over the country; in addition to these high-speed, limited-access roadways, there's an extensive network of federal, state, and local highways and roads. Some of the national car-rental companies include **Alamo** (© 800/462-5266; www.alamo.com), **Avis** (© 800/230-4898; www.avis.com), **Budget** (© 800/527-0700; www.budget.com), **Dollar** (© 800/800-4000; www.dollar.com), **Hertz** (© 800/654-3131; www.hertz.com), **National** (© 800/227-7368; www.nationalcar.com), and **Thrifty** (© 800/847-4389; www.thrifty.com).

If you plan to rent a car in the United States, you probably won't need the services of an additional automobile organization. If you're planning to buy or borrow a car, automobile-association membership is recommended. **AAA, the American Automobile Association** (© **800/222-4357;** http://travel.aaa.com), is the country's largest auto club and supplies its members with maps, insurance, and, most important, emergency road service. The cost of joining runs from $63 for singles to $87 for two members, but if you're a member of a foreign auto club with reciprocal arrangements, you can enjoy free AAA service in America. See "Getting There" in **chapter 2** for more information.

FAST FACTS: For the International Traveler

Automobile Organizations Auto clubs will supply maps, suggested routes, guidebooks, accident and bail-bond insurance, and emergency road service. The **American Automobile Association (AAA)** is the major auto club in the United States. If you belong to an auto club in your home country, inquire about AAA reciprocity before you leave. You may be able to join AAA even if you're not a member of a reciprocal club; to inquire, call AAA (© **800/564-6222**). AAA is actually an organization of regional auto clubs; so look under "AAA Automobile Club" in the White Pages of the telephone directory. AAA has a nationwide emergency-road-service telephone number (© **800/AAA-HELP**).

Business Hours Offices are usually open weekdays from 8am to 5pm. Banks are open weekdays from 9am to 3pm or later and sometimes Saturday mornings. Stores typically open between 9 and 10am and close between 5 and 6pm from Monday through Saturday. Stores in shopping complexes or malls tend to stay open late: until about 9pm on weekdays and weekends, and many malls and larger department stores are open on Sundays.

Currency & Currency Exchange See "Entry Requirements" and "Money" under "Preparing for Your Trip," earlier.

Drinking Laws The legal age for purchase and consumption of alcoholic beverages is 21; proof of age is required and often requested at bars, nightclubs, and restaurants, so it's always a good idea to bring ID when you go out. In San Francisco, supermarkets and grocery and liquor stores sell liquor daily from 6am to 2am. Licensed restaurants are permitted to sell alcohol during the same hours. Note that many restaurants are licensed only for beer and wine.

Do not carry open containers of alcohol in your car or any public area that isn't zoned for alcohol consumption. The police can fine you on the spot. And nothing will ruin your trip faster than getting a citation for DUI ("driving under the influence"), so don't even think about driving while intoxicated.

Electricity Like Canada, the United States uses 110 to 120 volts AC (60 cycles), compared to 220 to 240 volts AC (50 cycles) in most of Europe, Australia, and New Zealand. If your small appliances use 220 to 240 volts, you'll need a 110-volt transformer and a plug adapter with two flat parallel pins to operate them here. Downward converters that change 220 to 240 volts to 110 to 120 volts are difficult to find in the United States, so bring one with you.

Embassies & Consulates All embassies are located in the nation's capital, Washington, D.C. Some consulates are located in major U.S. cities, and most nations have a mission to the United Nations in New York City. If your country isn't listed below, call for directory information in Washington, D.C. (© **202/555-1212**) or go online to **www.embassy.org/embassies**.

The embassy of **Australia** is at 1601 Massachusetts Ave. NW, Washington, DC 20036 (© **202/797-3000**; www.austemb.org). There are consulates in New York, Honolulu, Atlanta, Chicago, Los Angeles, and San Francisco.

The embassy of **Canada** is at 501 Pennsylvania Ave. NW, Washington, DC 20001 (© **202/682-1740**; www.canadianembassy.org). Other Canadian consulates are in Buffalo (NY), Detroit, Los Angeles, New York, and Seattle.

The embassy of **Ireland** is at 2234 Massachusetts Ave. NW, Washington, DC 20008 (© **202/462-3939**; www.irelandemb.org). Irish consulates are in Boston, Chicago, New York, San Francisco, and other cities. See the website for complete listings.

The embassy of **New Zealand** is at 37 Observatory Circle NW, Washington, DC 20008 (© **202/328-4800**; www.nzemb.org). New Zealand consulates are in Los Angeles, Salt Lake City, San Francisco, New York, and Seattle.

The embassy of the **United Kingdom** is at 3100 Massachusetts Ave. NW, Washington, DC 20008 (© **202/588-7800**; www.britainusa.com). Other British consulates are in Atlanta, Boston, Chicago, Cleveland, Houston, Los Angeles, New York, San Francisco, and Seattle.

Emergencies Call © **911** to report a fire, call the police, or get an ambulance anywhere in the United States. This is a toll-free call. (No coins are required at public telephones.)

If you encounter serious problems, contact **Traveler's Aid International** (© **650/821-2730**; www.travelersaid.org) to help direct you to a local branch. This nationwide, nonprofit, social-service organization geared to helping travelers in difficult straits offers services that might include reuniting families separated while traveling, providing food and/or shelter to people stranded without cash, or even emotional counseling. If you're in trouble, seek them out.

Gasoline (Petrol) Petrol is known as gasoline (or simply "gas") in the United States, and petrol stations are known as both gas stations and service stations. At press time, the cost of gasoline in the U.S. is abnormally high ($3 a gallon) and fluctuating drastically. Taxes are already included in the printed price. One U.S. gallon equals 3.8 liters or .85 imperial gallons.

Holidays Banks, government offices, post offices, and many stores, restaurants, and museums are closed on the following legal national holidays: January 1 (New Year's Day), the third Monday in January (Martin Luther King, Jr. Day), the third Monday in February (Presidents' Day, Washington and Lincoln's Birthdays), the last Monday in May (Memorial Day), July 4 (Independence Day), the first Monday in September (Labor Day), the second Monday in October (Columbus Day), November 11 (Veterans' Day/Armistice Day), the fourth Thursday in November (Thanksgiving Day), and December 25 (Christmas). Also, the Tuesday following the first Monday in November is Election Day and is a federal government holiday in presidential-election years (held every 4 years, and next in 2008).

Legal Aid If you are "pulled over" for a minor infraction (such as speeding), never attempt to pay the fine directly to a police officer; this could be construed as attempted bribery, a much more serious crime. Pay fines by mail, or directly into the hands of the clerk of the court. If accused of a more serious offense, say and do nothing before consulting a lawyer. Here, the burden is on the state to prove a person's guilt beyond a reasonable doubt, and everyone has the right to remain silent, whether he or she is suspected of a crime or actually arrested. Once arrested, a person can make one telephone call to a party of his or her choice. Call your embassy or consulate.

Mail If you aren't sure what your address will be in the United States, mail can be sent to you, in your name, c/o General Delivery at the main post office of the city or region where you expect to be. (Call © **800/275-8777** for information on the nearest post office.) The addressee must pick up mail in person and must produce proof of identity (driver's license, passport, and the like). Most post offices will hold your mail for up to 1 month, and are open Monday to Friday from 8am to 6pm, and Saturday from 9am to 3pm.

Generally found at intersections, mailboxes are blue with a red-and-white stripe and carry the inscription U.S. Mail. If your mail is addressed to a U.S. destination, don't forget to add the five-digit postal code (or zip code), after the two-letter abbreviation of the state to which the mail is addressed. This is essential for prompt delivery.

At press time, domestic postage rates were 37¢ for a large postcard, 23¢ for a small postcard, and 37¢ for a letter. For international mail, a first-class letter of up to 1 ounce costs 80¢ (60¢ to Canada and Mexico); a first-class postcard costs 70¢ (50¢ to Canada and Mexico); and a preprinted postal aerogramme costs 70¢. For more information, see http://pe.usps.gov.

Taxes The United States has no value-added tax (VAT) or other indirect tax at the national level. Every state, county, and city has the right to levy its own local tax on all purchases, including hotel and restaurant checks, airline tickets, and so on.

Telephone, Telegraph, Telex & Fax The telephone system in the United States is run by private corporations, so rates, especially for long-distance service and operator-assisted calls, can vary widely. Generally, hotel surcharges on long-distance and local calls are astronomical, so you're usually better off using a **public pay telephone**, which you'll find clearly marked in most public buildings and private establishments as well as on the street. Convenience grocery stores and gas stations always have them. Many convenience groceries and packaging services sell **prepaid calling cards** in denominations up to $50; these can be the least expensive way to call home. Many public phones at airports now accept American Express, MasterCard, and Visa credit cards. **Local calls** made from public pay phones in most locales cost about 50¢. Pay phones do not accept pennies, and few will take anything larger than a quarter.

Most long-distance and international calls can be dialed directly from any phone. **For calls within the United States and to Canada,** dial 1 followed by the area code and the seven-digit number. **For other international calls,** dial 011 followed by the country code, city code, and the telephone number of the person you are calling.

Calls to area codes **800, 888, 877,** and **866** are toll-free. However, calls to numbers in area codes **700** and **900** (chat lines, bulletin boards, "dating" services, and so on) can be very expensive—usually a charge of 95¢ to $3 or more per minute, and they sometimes have minimum charges that can run as high as $15 or more.

For **reversed-charge or collect calls,** and for person-to-person calls, dial 0 (zero, not the letter O) followed by the area code and number you want; an operator will then come on the line, and you should specify that you are calling collect, or person-to-person, or both. If your operator-assisted call is international, ask for the overseas operator.

For **local directory assistance** ("information"), dial 𝄐 **411**; for long-distance information, dial 1 and then the appropriate area code and 𝄐 **555-1212.**

Most hotels have **fax machines** available for guest use (be sure to ask about the charge to use it). Many hotel rooms are even wired for guests' fax machines. A less-expensive way to send and receive faxes may be at stores such as **The UPS Store** (formerly Mail Boxes Etc.), a national chain of retail packing-service shops. (Look in the Yellow Pages directory under "Packing Services.")

There are two kinds of telephone directories in the United States. The so-called **White Pages** list private households and business subscribers in alphabetical order. The inside front cover lists emergency numbers for police, fire, ambulance, the Coast Guard, poison-control center, crime-victims hot line, and so on. The first few pages will tell you how to make long-distance and international calls, complete with country codes and area codes. Government numbers are usually printed on blue paper within the White Pages. Printed on yellow paper, the so-called **Yellow Pages** list all local services, businesses, industries, and houses of worship according to activity with an index at the front or back. (Drugstores/pharmacies and restaurants are also listed by geographic location.) The Yellow Pages also include city plans or detailed area maps, postal zip codes, and public transportation routes.

Time The continental United States is divided into **four time zones:** Eastern Standard Time (EST), Central Standard Time (CST), Mountain Standard Time (MST), and Pacific Standard Time (PST). Alaska and Hawaii have their own zones. For example, noon in New York City (EST) is 11am in Chicago (CST), 10am in Denver (MST), 9am in Los Angeles (PST), 8am in Anchorage (AST), and 7am in Honolulu (HST).

Daylight saving time is in effect at 2am on the first Sunday in April until 2am on the last Sunday in October, except in Arizona, Hawaii, most of Indiana, the U.S. Virgin Islands, and Puerto Rico. (Indiana will begin observing daylight saving time in April 2006 and a new law will extend daylight saving in 2007; clocks will change the second Sunday in March and the first Sunday in November.)

Tipping Tips are a very important part of certain workers' income, and gratuities are the standard way of showing appreciation for services provided. (Tipping is certainly not compulsory if the service is poor!) In hotels, tip **bellhops** at least $1 per bag ($1–$2 per bag at upscale hotels), and tip the **chamber staff** $2 to $3 per day (more if you've left a disaster area for him or her to clean up). Tip the **doorman** or **concierge** only if he or she has provided you with some specific service (for example, calling a cab for you or obtaining difficult-to-get theater tickets). Tip the **valet-parking attendant** $2 to $3 every time you get your car.

In restaurants, bars, and nightclubs, tip **service staff** 15% to 20% of the check, tip **bartenders** 10% to 15%, tip **checkroom attendants** $1 to $2 per garment, and tip **valet-parking attendants** $1 per vehicle.

As for other service personnel, tip **cab drivers** 15% of the fare; tip **skycaps** at airports at least $1 per bag ($2–$3 if you have a lot of luggage); and tip **hairdressers** and **barbers** 15% to 20%.

Toilets Public toilets can be hard to find in San Francisco. A handful of fancy French stalls (which look like spacious green cylinders with pocket doors) are strategically placed on high-volume streets, and a few small stores may allow you access to their facilities. You can almost always find a toilet in museums, department stores, railway and bus stations, service stations, and restaurants and bars; note, however, a growing practice in some restaurants and bars of displaying a notice that toilets are for the use of patrons only. You can ignore this sign or, better yet, avoid arguments by paying for a cup of coffee or soft drink, which qualifies you as a patron. If possible, avoid the toilets at parks and beaches, which tend to be dirty and may even be unsafe.

4

Suggested San Francisco Itineraries

If you've left your brain at the office and want someone else to make all the tough decisions during your vacation, you'll love this chapter. It's where I tell you exactly what I think you should see and do during your vacation in San Francisco. It's broken down into 1-day, 2-day, and 3-day itineraries, depending on how long you're in town. If you've already made your way through "The Best of San Francisco in 1 Day," the 2-day tour starts where the 1-day schedule left off, and so on. But if you really want to enjoy even a fraction of what San Francisco has to offer, you should plan on staying at least 3 days, preferably a week. And because renting a car in the city is an expensive hassle (and driving in the city is insane), all the itineraries below can be done via foot, cable car, bus, and bike.

1 The Best of San Francisco in 1 Day

If you have only 1 day to explore the city, put on your walking shoes and start early. You'll have a lot of ground to cover just to get to the must-sees; but, luckily, condensed geography (and hopefully weather) is in your favor. The whirlwind tour starts with a scenic ride on a cable car followed by a tour of Alcatraz Island. Next you'll hoof it up to two of the city's most colorful neighborhoods—Chinatown and North Beach—for lunch, shopping, browsing, cocktails, dinner, and cappuccino. Get an early start, because you're about to have a long, yet wonderful, day in the city by the bay. **Start:** *Buses: 2, 3, 4, 30, 45, or 76 to Union Square.*

❶ Union Square
Union Square—which was named for a series of pro-union mass demonstrations staged here on the eve of the Civil War—isn't an attraction in itself, but it's the epicenter of the city's shopping district. Macy's, Saks, Tiffany's, Neiman Marcus, Victoria's Secret, and others are located here, and are surrounded by blocks crammed with hundreds of other high-end boutiques. There are very few shopping bargains here, but it's fun for looking. Just 3 blocks down, at Powell and Market streets, is the cable car turnaround

where you'll embark on a ride on the nation's only moving National Historic Landmark. See p. 203.

❷ Cable Cars and Lombard Street 𝒜𝒜𝒜
Don't be intimidated by the line of people waiting to board at the cable car turnaround at Market and Powell streets—it's worth the wait. The $3 thrill ride starts with a steep climb up Nob Hill, then passes through Chinatown and Russian Hill before plummeting down Hyde Street to Fisherman's Wharf. It's an experience you'll never forget. (**Note:** If you

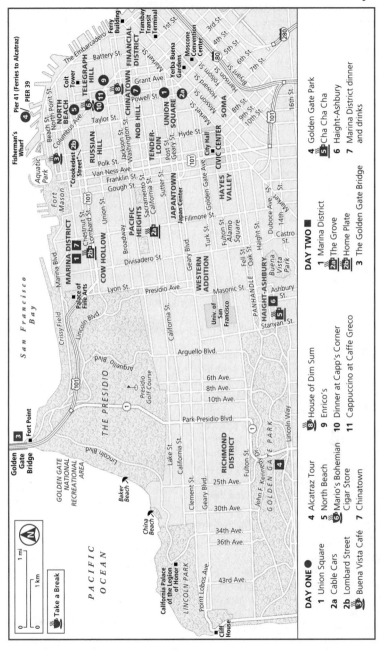

DAY ONE ●
1 Union Square
2a Cable Cars
2b Lombard Street
3 Buena Vista Café
4 Alcatraz Tour
5 North Beach
6 Mario's Bohemian Cigar Store
7 Chinatown
8 House of Dim Sum
9 Enrico's
10 Dinner at Capp's Corner
11 Cappuccino at Caffe Greco

DAY TWO ■
1 Marina District
2a The Grove
2b Home Plate
3 The Golden Gate Bridge
4 Golden Gate Park
5 Cha Cha Cha
6 Haight-Ashbury
7 Marina District dinner and drinks

Take a Break

want to check out the famous winding stretch of Lombard Street, hop off the cable car at the intersection of Hyde and Lombard sts. and, when you've seen enough, either walk the rest of the way down to Fisherman's Wharf or take the next cable car that comes along.) For maximum thrillage, stand up during the ride and hold onto the brass rail.

3 BUENA VISTA CAFE
After you've completed your first Powell-Hyde cable car ride, it's a San Francisco tradition to celebrate with an Irish coffee at the Buena Vista Café, located at 2765 Hyde St. across from the cable car turnaround (② 415/474-5044). The first Irish coffees served in America were mixed here in 1952, and they're still the best in the Bay Area. See p. 228.

4 Alcatraz Tour ☆☆☆
To tour "The Rock," the Bay Area's famous abandoned prison on its own island, you must first get there, and that's half the fun. The brief, but beautiful, ferry ride offers captivating views of the Golden Gate Bridge, Marin Headlands, and the city. Once inside, an excellent audio tour guides you through cellblocks and offers a colorful look at the prison's historic past as well as its most infamous inmates. Book well in advance because these tours consistently sell out in the summer, and bring snacks and beverages—the ferry's pickings are slim and expensive, and there's nothing available on the island. See p. 146.

5 North Beach ☆☆☆
One of the best ways to get the San Francisco vibe is to mingle with the locals, and one of my favorite places to do so is in San Francisco's "Little Italy." Dozens of Italian restaurants and coffeehouses continue to flourish in what is still the center of the city's Italian community. A stroll along Columbus Avenue will take you

past dozens of eclectic little cafes, delis, bookstores, bakeries, and coffee shops that give North Beach its Italian-bohemian character. See p. 168.

Tip: Be sure to see chapter 9, "City Strolls," for highlights about North Beach and Chinatown.

6 MARIO'S BOHEMIAN CIGAR STORE
Okay, so the menu's limited to coffee drinks and a few sandwiches (the meatball is my favorite), but the convivial atmosphere and large windows, which are perfect for people-watching, make this tiny, pie-shaped cafe a favorite, even with locals. 566 Columbus Ave.; ② 415/362-0536. See p. 121.

7 Chinatown ☆☆
One block from North Beach is a whole other world: Chinatown. San Francisco has one of the largest communities of Chinese people in the United States, with more than 80,000 people condensed around Grant Avenue and Stockton Street. Although frequented by tourists, the area caters mostly to the Chinese community, who crowd the vegetable and herb markets, restaurants, and shops carrying those ubiquitous pink plastic bags.

8 HOUSE OF DIM SUM
You can't visit Chinatown and not sample some dim sum. Walk to 735 Jackson St. to the House of Dim Sum (② 415/399-0888) and order shrimp dumplings, pork dumplings, sweet buns, turnip cake, and the sweet rice with chicken wrapped in a lotus leaf. Find an empty table, pour a side of soy sauce, and dig in.

After your light lunch, stroll through Chinatown, making sure to check out the Stockton Street markets, hawking live frogs, armadillos, turtles, and odd sea creatures destined for tonight's dinner table. *Tip:* The dozens of knickknack shops here are a great source for cheap souvenirs. See p. 190.

❾ Enrico's Mohitos to the Rescue ★

After touring Chinatown, your feet are probably killing you, so walk over to Enrico's at 504 Broadway (at Kearny St.; ☎ 415/982-6223) in North Beach, request an outside table overlooking bustling Broadway, and order a mojito—an addictive mix of rum, soda, sugar, and mint that really takes the edge off. See p. 119.

❿ Capp's Corner ★

What I love about North Beach are its old-school restaurants—those dusty, frumpy, loud, and over-sauced bastions of bacchanalia. **Capp's Corner** (1600 Powell St; ☎ **415/989-2589**) is one of my favorites, where patrons sit at long tables and dine family-style via huge platters of Italian comfort food, served by brusque waitresses, all while Frank croons his classics on the jukebox. See p. 119.

⓫ Cappuccino at Caffè Greco ★

By now you should be stuffed and exhausted. Good. End the night with a cappuccino at **Caffè Greco** (423 Columbus Ave.; ☎ **415/397-6261**). Sit at one of the sidewalk tables and reminisce on what a great day you had in San Francisco.

---

2 The Best of San Francisco in 2 Days

On your second day, get familiar with other famous landmarks around the city. Start with breakfast, a science lesson, and a pleasant bayside stroll in the Marina District. Next, cross the famed Golden Gate Bridge on foot, then take a bus to Golden Gate Park. After a stroll through the city's beloved park, it's time for lunch and power shopping on Haight Street, followed by dinner and cocktails back in the Marina District. **Start:** *Buses 22, 28, 30, 30X, 43, 76, or 82X.*

❶ Good Morning Marina District

The area that became famous for its destruction during the 1989 earthquake has long been one of the most picturesque and coveted patches of local real estate. Here, along the northern edge of the city, multimillion-dollar homes back up against the bay-front Marina, where a flotilla of sailboats and the mighty Golden Gate Bridge make for a magnificent backdrop for a morning stroll.

Start the day with a good cup of coffee (see "Take a Break" below), then walk to the Palace of Fine Arts building, built for the Panama-Pacific Exhibition of 1915 and home of the Exploratorium (p. 162). Spend a few hours being thoroughly entertained at the "best science museum in the world" (kids *love* this place) then walk over to Crissy Field (p. 176), where restored wetlands and a beachfront path lead to historic Fort Point (p. 176) and the footpath that will take you up to the southern end of the Golden Gate Bridge.

> **2ᴬ BREAKFAST IN SAN FRANCISCO**
> If you can't jumpstart your brain properly without a good cup of coffee, then begin your day at **2ᴬ The Grove** (2016 Fillmore St.; ☎ 415/474-4843; p. 129)—it's as cozy as an old leather couch. If you want a more substantial breakfast, walk over to **2ᴮ Home Plate** (2274 Lombard St.; ☎ 415/922-HOME; p. 129) for a hefty omelet and freshly baked scones. It's one of my favorite breakfast places in the city.

❸ The Golden Gate Bridge ★★★

It's one of those things you have to do at least once in you life—walk across the fabled Golden Gate Bridge (p. 156), the most photographed manmade structure in the world. As you would expect, the views along the span are spectacular and the wind is a wee bit chilly, so bring a light jacket. It takes at least an hour to walk northward to the vista point and back. When you return to the southern end, board either MUNI bus nos. 28 or 29 (be sure to ask the driver if the bus is headed toward Golden Gate Park).

❹ Golden Gate Park 🍿🍿🍿

Stretching from the middle of the city to the Pacific Ocean and comprised of 1,017 acres, Golden Gate Park is one of the city's greatest attributes. Since its development in the late 1880s, it has provided San Franciscans with urban respite via dozens of well-tended gardens, museums, and great grassy expanses prime for picnicking, lounging, or tossing a Frisbee.

Have the bus driver drop you off near John F. Kennedy Drive. Walking eastward on JFK Drive you'll pass three of the park's most popular attractions: **Stow Lake,** the newly renovated **de Young Museum,** and the wonderful **Conservatory of Flowers** (a must-visit).

---

5 CHA CHA CHA 🍿🍿

By now you're probably starving, so walk out of the park and into the Haight to Cha Cha Cha (1801 Haight St.; ✆ 415/386-7670; p. 134.), one of my favorite restaurants in the city. Order plenty of dishes from the tapas-style menu and dine family-style. Oh, and don't forget a pitcher of sangria—you've earned it.

---

❻ Exploring the Haight-Ashbury District 🍿🍿🍿

Ah, the Haight. Birthplace of the Summer of Love and Flower Power, shrine to the Grateful Dead, and where America's nonconformists still congregate over beers, bongos, and buds. Spend at least an hour strolling up Haight Street (p. 170), browsing the cornucopia of used clothes stores, leather shops, head shops, and poster stores. There are some great bargains to be found here, especially for vintage clothing. When you get to the intersection of Haight and Masonic street, take the MUNI no. 43 bus heading north, which will take you through the Presidio and back to the Marina District, for:

❼ Marina District Dinner and Drinks

You've had a full day, so rest your weary bones at the back patio at **Isa** (3324 Steiner St.; ✆ 415/567-9588; p. 128), a fantastic and surprisingly affordable French restaurant in the Marina. If you're energized after dinner, walk over to the **Balboa Café** (3199 Fillmore St.; ✆ 415/921-3944; p. 126) and practice your pick-up lines among the young-and-restless that practically live here.

---

3 The Best of San Francisco in 3 Days

If we weren't on a tight budget I'd have you rent a car and head to the Wine Country for a day of wine tasting, but that would probably blow your budget (if not, skip to the Wine Country chapter; see p. 257). Instead, we're going to carry out one of my all-time favorite things to do on my day off—bike riding from Fisherman's Wharf to Sam's Anchor Café in Tiburon (that small peninsula just north of Alcatraz Island). It's a beautiful and exhilarating ride that takes you over the Golden Gate Bridge, through the heart of Sausalito, along the scenic North Bay bike path, and ends with a frosty

The Best of San Francisco in 3 Days

1 Bike rental from Blazing Saddles
2 The Warming Hut
3 Bike across the Golden Gate Bridge
4 Sausalito Tour
5 Horizons
6 North Bay Tour
7 Lunch at Sam's Anchor Café
8 Ferry from Tiburon to San Francisco (Pier 39)

☕ Take a Break

beer and lunch at the best outdoor cafe in the Bay Area. And here's the best part: You don't have to ride back. After lunch, you can take the passenger ferry across the bay to Fisherman's Wharf—right back to where you started. Brilliant. *Start: Cable car: Powell-Hyde line. Buses: 10, 19, 30, 47.*

---

❶ Rent a Bicycle

Walk, take a bus, or ride the Powell-Hyde cable car (which goes right by it) to the **Blazing Saddles** bicycle rental shop at 2715 Hyde St, between Beach and North Point streets near Ghirardelli Square. (© **415/202-8888;** p. 186). Rent a single or tandem bike for a full day, and be sure to ask for 1) a free map pointing out the route to Sam's in Tiburon, 2) ferry tickets, 3) a bicycle lock, and 4) a bottle of water. Bring your own sunscreen, a hat (for the deck at Sam's), and a light jacket—no

matter how warm it might seem, the weather here can change in minutes. The bikes have a small pouch hooked to the handlebar where you can stuff all this stuff.

Fun Tip: While you're here, ask about the GoCar rentals (see the GoCar sidebar on p. 155 for more info).

❷ The Warming Hut

Start pedaling along the map route to Golden Gate Bridge. You'll encounter one short, steep hill right from the start at

Aquatic Park, but it's okay to walk your bike (hey, you haven't had your coffee fix yet). Keep riding westward through Fort Point and the Marina Green to Crissy Field. At the west end of Crissy Field right alongside the bike path is The Warming Hut, a white barnlike building where you can fuel up with a light snack and coffee drinks (don't eat too much). There are several picnic tables nearby with beautiful views of the bay.

❸ Biking the Golden Gate

After your break, there's one more steep hill up to the bridge. Follow the bike path to the west side of the bridge (pedestrians must stay on the east side), cross the bridge, and take the road to your left heading downhill and crossing underneath Highway 101. Coast all the way to Sausalito.

❹ Exploring Sausalito

You'll love Sausalito. Coasting your bike onto Bridgeway, the main strip here, is like being transported to one of those seaside towns on the French Riviera (see p. 248 for more info). After locking up your bike in town, mosey around on foot for a while, browsing through the shops and admiring the gorgeous view of San Francisco across the bay.

---

❺ HORIZONS

If you're thirsty, ask for a table on the bayside deck at Horizons (558 Bridgeway; ✆ 415/331-3232; p. 250) and order a bloody mary, but don't eat yet. (You'll want to save room for one of the last suggestions on this itinerary.)

---

❻ North Bay Tour

Back on your bike, head north again on the bike path that winds along the bay shore. When you reach the Mill Valley

Car Wash at the end of this path, turn right onto East Blithedale Avenue, which will cross over Highway 101 and turn into Tiburon Boulevard (this is the only part of the ride where you'll encounter traffic). About a mile past Highway 101 you'll enter a small park called Blackie's Pasture (look for the life-size bronze statue erected in 1995 to honor Tiburon's beloved "mascot," Blackie). Now it's an easy cruise on the bike path to Sam's.

❼ Lunch at Sam's Anchor Café

Ride your bike all the way to the south end of Tiburon and lock your bike at the bike rack near the ferry dock. Walk over to the ferry loading dock and check the ferry departure schedule for "Tiburon to Pier 39/Fisherman's Wharf." Then walk over to Sam's Anchor Café (27 Main St.; ✆ 415/435-4527; p. 248), request a table on the back patio overlooking the harbor, and relax with a cool drink—you've earned it.

❽ Ferry Ride Back to San Francisco

When it's time to leave, board the ferry with your bike (bike riders board first, so don't stand in line) and enjoy the ride from Tiburon to San Francisco, with a short stop at Angel Island State Park. From Pier 39 it's a short ride back to the rental shop.

After all this adventuring, it's time to reenergize your body and spirit with an Irish whiskey at the **Buena Vista Café** (2765 Hyde St., across from the cable car turnaround), a short walk from the bike rental shop. After libations, take the cable car back to your hotel for some rest, and then spend the rest of the evening enjoying dinner.

If this isn't one of the best days you've had on your vacation, send me this book and I'll eat it.

5

Getting to Know San Francisco

This chapter offers useful information on how to become better acquainted with San Francisco, even though half the fun of becoming familiar with this city is wandering around and haphazardly stumbling upon great shops, restaurants, and vistas that even locals might not know about. You'll find that although the city is metropolitan, San Francisco is still a small town—one where you won't feel like a stranger for long.

If you get disoriented, just remember that downtown is east and the Golden Gate Bridge is north—and even if you do get lost, you probably won't go too far, since water surrounds three sides of the city. The most difficult challenge you'll have, if you're traveling by car (which I suggest you avoid), is mastering the maze of one-way streets.

1 Orientation

VISITOR INFORMATION

The **San Francisco Visitor Information Center,** on the lower level of Hallidie Plaza, 900 Market St., at Powell Street (© **415/283-0177;** fax 415/362-7323; www.sfvisitor. org), has information, brochures, discount coupons, and advice on restaurants, sights, and events in the city. The staff can provide answers in German, Japanese, French, Italian, and Spanish (as well as English, of course). To find the office, descend the escalator at the cable car turnaround. The office is open Monday through Friday from 8:30am to 5pm, Saturday and Sunday from 9am to 3pm. However, it is closed on Sundays during winter, January 1, Thanksgiving Day, and December 25.

Dial © **415/283-0176** any time, day or night, for a recorded message about current cultural events, theater, music, sports, and other special happenings. This information is also available in German, French, Japanese, and Spanish. Keep in mind that this service recommends only businesses that are members of the Convention and Visitors Bureau and is very tourist oriented. While there is a ton of information available at this number, it's not representative of all that the city has to offer.

Pick up a copy of the *Bay Guardian* or the *S.F. Weekly,* the city's free alternative papers, to get listings of all city happenings. You'll find them in kiosks throughout the city and in most coffee shops. For information on Chinatown's shops and services, and on the city's Chinese community in general, contact the **Chinese Chamber of Commerce,** 730 Sacramento St. (© **415/982-3000**), open daily from 9am to 5pm.

CITY LAYOUT

San Francisco occupies the tip of a 32-mile peninsula between San Francisco Bay and the Pacific Ocean. Its land area measures about 46 square miles, although the city is often referred to as being 7 square miles. At more than 900 feet high, the towering

Twin Peaks marks the geographic center of the city and is a killer place to take in a vista of San Francisco.

With lots of one-way streets and plenty of nooks and crannies, San Francisco might seem confusing at first, but it'll quickly become easy to navigate. The city's downtown streets are arranged in a simple grid pattern, with the exceptions of Market Street and Columbus Avenue, which cut across the grid at right angles to each other. Hills appear to distort this pattern, however, and can disorient you. As you learn your way around, the hills will become your landmarks and reference points. But even if you get lost, it's no big deal: San Francisco's a small town—so much so, in fact that I've run from one end to the other (during the Bay to Breakers Foot Race) in an hour flat.

MAIN ARTERIES & STREETS   **Market Street** is San Francisco's main thoroughfare. Most of the city's buses travel this route on their way to the Financial District from the outer neighborhoods to the west and south. The tall office buildings clustered downtown are at the northeast end of Market; 1 block beyond lies The Embarcadero and the bay.

The Embarcadero *☞*—an excellent strolling, skating, and biking route (thanks to recent renovations)—curves along San Francisco Bay from south of the Bay Bridge to the northeast perimeter of the city. It terminates at Fisherman's Wharf, the famous tourist-oriented pier. Aquatic Park, Fort Mason, and the Golden Gate National Recreation Area are on the northernmost point of the peninsula.

From the eastern perimeter of Fort Mason, **Van Ness Avenue** runs due south, back to Market Street. The area just described forms a rough triangle, with Market Street as its southeastern boundary, the waterfront as its northern boundary, and Van Ness Avenue as its western boundary. Within this triangle lie most of the city's main tourist sights.

FINDING AN ADDRESS   Since most of the city's streets are laid out in a grid pattern, finding an address is easy when you know the nearest cross street. Numbers start with 1 at the beginning of the street and proceed at the rate of 100 per block. When asking for directions, find out the nearest cross street and the neighborhood where your destination is located, but be careful not to confuse numerical avenues with numerical streets. Numerical avenues (Third Ave. and so on) are in the Richmond and Sunset Districts in the western part of the city. Numerical streets (Third St. and so on) are south of Market Street in the east and south parts of town.

NEIGHBORHOODS IN BRIEF

For further discussion of some of the neighborhoods below, see the "Neighborhoods Worth a Visit" section of chapter 8, beginning on p. 166. For a map of the neighborhoods below, see the "San Francisco at a Glance" map on p. 6.

Union Square   Union Square is the commercial hub of San Francisco. Most major hotels and department stores are crammed into the area surrounding the actual square, which was named for a series of violent pro-union mass demonstrations staged here on the eve of the Civil War. A plethora of upscale boutiques, restaurants, and galleries occupy the spaces tucked between the larger buildings. A few blocks west is the **Tenderloin** neighborhood, a patch of poverty and blight where you should keep your wits about you. The **Theater District** is 3 blocks west of Union Square.

The Financial District   East of Union Square, this area, bordered by The

Embarcadero and by Market, Third, Kearny, and Washington streets, is the city's business district and the stamping grounds for many major corporations. The pointy TransAmerica Pyramid, at Montgomery and Clay streets, is one of the district's most conspicuous architectural features. To its east sprawls the Embarcadero Center, an 8½-acre complex housing offices, shops, and restaurants. Farther east still is the old Ferry Building, the city's pre-bridge transportation hub. Ferries to Sausalito and Larkspur still leave from this point. However, in 2003, the building became an attraction in itself when it was completely renovated, jam packed with outstanding restaurant and gourmet food- and wine-related shops, and surrounded by a farmers market a few days a week, making it one of San Franciscan residents' favorite places to grace.

Nob Hill & Russian Hill Bounded by Bush, Larkin, Pacific, and Stockton streets, Nob Hill is a genteel, well-heeled district still occupied by the city's major power brokers and the neighborhood businesses they frequent. Russian Hill extends from Pacific to Bay and from Polk to Mason. It contains steep streets, lush gardens, and high-rises occupied by both the moneyed and the more bohemian.

Chinatown A large red-and-green gate on Grant Avenue at Bush Street marks the official entrance to Chinatown. Beyond lies a 24-block labyrinth, bordered by Broadway, Bush, Kearny, and Stockton streets, filled with restaurants, markets, temples, shops, and, of course, a substantial percentage of San Francisco's Chinese residents. Chinatown is a great place for exploration all along Stockton and Grant streets, Portsmouth Square, and the alleys that lead off them, like Ross and Waverly. This area is crammed, so don't even think about driving here.

North Beach This Italian neighborhood, which stretches from Montgomery and Jackson to Bay Street, is one of the best places in the city to grab a coffee, pull up a cafe chair, and do some serious people-watching. Nightlife is equally happening in North Beach; restaurants, bars, and clubs along Columbus and Grant avenues attract folks from all over the Bay Area, who fight for a parking place and romp through the festive neighborhood. Down Columbus toward the Financial District are the remains of the city's Beat Generation landmarks, including Ferlinghetti's City Lights Bookstore and Vesuvio's Bar. Broadway—a short strip of sex joints—cuts through the heart of the district. **Telegraph Hill** looms over the east side of North Beach, topped by Coit Tower, one of San Francisco's best vantage points.

Fisherman's Wharf North Beach runs into Fisherman's Wharf, which was once the busy heart of the city's great harbor and waterfront industries. Today, it is a tacky but interesting tourist area with little, if any, authentic waterfront life, except for recreational boating and some friendly sea lions.

The Marina District Created on landfill for the Pan Pacific Exposition of 1915, the Marina District boasts some of the best views of the Golden Gate, as well as plenty of grassy fields alongside San Francisco Bay. Elegant Mediterranean-style homes and apartments, inhabited by the city's well-to-do singles and wealthy families, line the streets. Here, too, are the Palace of Fine Arts, the Exploratorium, and Fort Mason Center. The main street is Chestnut, between Franklin and Lyon, which abounds with shops, cafes, and boutiques. Because of its landfill foundation, the Marina was one of the hardest-hit districts in the 1989 quake.

Cow Hollow Located west of Van Ness Avenue, between Russian Hill and the Presidio, this flat, grazeable area supported 30 dairy farms in 1861. Today, Cow Hollow is largely residential and largely yuppie. Its two primary commercial thoroughfares are Lombard Street, known for its many relatively inexpensive motels, and Union Street, a flourishing shopping sector filled with restaurants, pubs, cafes, and shops.

Pacific Heights The ultra-elite, such as the Gettys and Danielle Steel—and those lucky enough to buy before the real-estate boom—reside in the mansions and homes in this neighborhood. When the rich meander out of their fortresses, they wander down to Union Street and join the yuppies and the young who frequent the street's long stretch of chic boutiques and lively neighborhood restaurants, cafes, and bars.

Japantown Bounded by Octavia, Fillmore, California, and Geary, Japantown shelters only a small percentage of the city's Japanese population, but exploring these few square blocks and the shops and restaurants within them is still a cultural experience.

Civic Center Although millions of dollars have gone toward brick sidewalks, ornate lampposts, and elaborate street plantings, the southwestern section of Market Street remains somewhat dilapidated. The Civic Center, at the "bottom" of Market Street, is an exception. This large complex of buildings includes the domed and dapper City Hall, the Opera House, Davies Symphony Hall, and the Asian Art Museum. The landscaped plaza connecting the buildings is the staging area

for San Francisco's frequent demonstrations for or against just about everything.

SoMa No part of San Francisco has been more affected by recent development than the area south of Market Street (dubbed "SoMa"), the area within the triangle of the Embarcadero, Highway 101, and Market Street. Until a decade ago it was a district of old warehouses and industrial spaces, with a few scattered underground nightclubs, restaurants, and shoddy residential areas. But when it became the hub of dot-commercialization and half-million-dollar-plus lofts, its fate changed forever. Today, though dot-coms don't occupy much of the commercial space, the area is jumping thanks to fancy loft residents, the baseball stadium, and surrounding businesses, restaurants, and nightclubs in addition to urban entertainment a la the Museum of Modern Art, Yerba Buena Gardens, Sony Metreon, and a slew of big-bucks hotels that make tons of money from businesspeople. Though still gritty in some areas, it's growing more glittery by the year.

Mission District This is another area that was greatly affected by the city's dot-com wealth. The Mexican and Latin American populations here, with their cuisine, traditions, and art, make the Mission District a vibrant area to visit. Some parts of the neighborhood are still poor and sprinkled with the homeless, gangs, and drug addicts, but young urbanites have also settled in the area, attracted by its "reasonably" (a relative term) priced rentals and endless oh-so-hot restaurants and bars that stretch from 16th and Valencia streets to 25th and Mission streets. Less adventurous tourists may just want to duck into Mission Dolores, cruise by a few of the 200-plus amazing murals, and head back downtown. But anyone who's interested in hanging with the hipsters and experiencing the hottest restaurant and bar nightlife should definitely beeline it here. Don't be afraid to visit this area, but do use caution at night.

The Castro One of the liveliest streets in town, the Castro is practically synonymous with San Francisco's gay community (even though it is technically a street in the Noe Valley District). Located at the very end of Market Street, between 17th and 18th streets, the Castro has dozens of shops, restaurants, and bars catering to the gay community. Open-minded straight people are welcome, too.

Haight-Ashbury Part trendy, part nostalgic, part funky, the Haight, as it's most commonly known, was the soul of the psychedelic, free-loving 1960s and the center of the counterculture movement. Now, visitors to this neighborhood straddling upper Haight Street on the eastern border of Golden Gate Park will probably be a bit saddened by how

touristy and commercial it's become, but at least it's still too radical for the Marina-type DINKS to settle here en mass. Leftover aging hippies mingle with grungy, begging street kids outside Ben & Jerry's Ice Cream Store (where they might still be talking about Jerry Garcia), nondescript marijuana dealers whisper "Buds" as shoppers pass, and many people walking down the street have Day-Glo hair. But you don't need to be a freak or wear tie-dye to enjoy the Haight—the food, shops, and bars cover all tastes. From Haight Street, walk south on Cole Street for a more peaceful and quaint neighborhood experience.

Richmond & Sunset Districts San Francisco's suburbs of sorts, these are the city's largest and most populous neighborhoods, consisting mainly of small (but expensive) homes, shops, and neighborhood restaurants. Although they border Golden Gate Park and Ocean Beach, few tourists venture into "The Avenues," as these areas are referred to locally.

2 Getting Around

BY PUBLIC TRANSPORTATION

The **San Francisco Municipal Railway,** 401 Van Ness Ave., better known as "Muni" (© **415/673-6864;** www.sfmuni.com), operates the city's cable cars, buses, and streetcars. Together, these three services crisscross the entire city. Fares for buses and streetcars are $1.50 for adults, 50¢ for seniors over 65 and children 5 to 17. Cable cars, which run from 6:30am to 12:50am, cost a whopping $5 for all people over 5 ($1 for seniors before 7am and after 9pm). Needless to say, they're packed primarily with tourists. Exact change is required on all vehicles except cable cars. Fares are subject to change.

For detailed route information, phone Muni or consult the Muni map at the front of the San Francisco Yellow Pages. If you plan to use public transportation extensively, you might want to invest in a comprehensive transit and city map ($2), sold at the San Francisco Visitor Information Center (p. 59), Powell/Market cable car booth, and many downtown retail outlets. Also, see the "Muni Discounts" box for more information.

CABLE CAR San Francisco's cable cars might not be the most practical means of transport, but the rolling historic landmarks are a fun ride. The three lines are concentrated in the downtown area. The most scenic, and exciting, is the **Powell-Hyde line,**

San Francisco Mass Transit

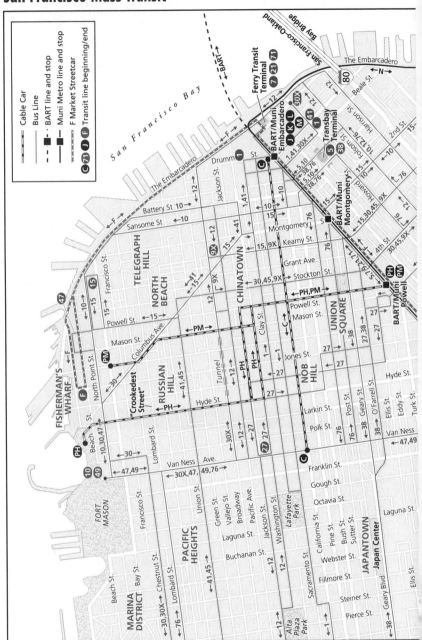

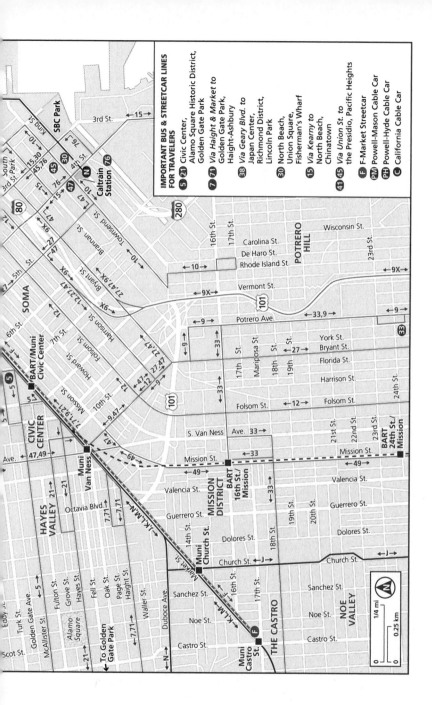

IMPORTANT BUS & STREETCAR LINES FOR TRAVELERS

5 **21** Civic Center, Alamo Square Historic District, Golden Gate Park

7 **71** Via Haight & Market to Golden Gate Park, Haight-Ashbury

38 Via Geary Blvd. to Japan Center, Richmond District, Lincoln Park

30 North Beach, Union Square, Fisherman's Wharf

15 Via Kearny to North Beach, Chinatown

41 **45** Via Union St. to the Presidio, Pacific Heights

F F-Market Streetcar

PM Powell-Mason Cable Car

PH Powell-Hyde Cable Car

C California Cable Car

(Value Muni Discounts

Muni discount passes, called **Passports,** entitle holders to unlimited rides on buses, streetcars, and cable cars. A Passport costs $11 for 1 day, $18 for 3 days, and $24 for 7 consecutive days. Muni's **City Pass,** which costs $42 for adults and $34 for kids 5 to 17, entitles you to unlimited rides for 7 days, plus admission to the California Academy of Sciences, Palace of the Legion of Honor, Steinhart Aquarium, Museum of Modern Art, Exploratorium, Asian Art Museum, and Blue & Gold Fleet Bay or Alcatraz cruises for 9 days. You can buy a Passport or City Pass at the San Francisco Visitor Information Center, Powell/Market cable car booth, Holiday Inn Civic Center, and TIX Bay Area booth at Union Square, among other outlets. But to include the Blue & Gold Fleet tour, you must purchase tickets through them by calling Blue & Gold Fleet at ✆ **415/705-5555.** A $2.25 fee applies when you get your tickets through this phone service.

---

which follows a zigzag route from the corner of Powell and Market streets, over both Nob Hill and Russian Hill, to a turntable at gaslit Victorian Square in front of Aquatic Park. The **Powell-Mason line** starts at the same intersection and climbs Nob Hill before descending to Bay Street, just 3 blocks from Fisherman's Wharf. The least scenic is the **California Street line,** which begins at the foot of Market Street and runs a straight course through Chinatown and over Nob Hill to Van Ness Avenue. All riders must exit at the last stop and wait in line for the return trip. The cable car system operates from approximately 6:30am to 12:50am, and each ride costs $5 (there are reduced rates for children and seniors).

BUS   Buses reach almost every corner of San Francisco and beyond—they even travel over the bridges to Marin County and Oakland. Overhead electric cables power some buses; others use conventional gas engines. All are numbered and display their destinations on the front. Signs, curb markings, and yellow bands on adjacent utility poles designate stops, and most bus shelters exhibit Muni's transportation map and schedule. Many buses travel along Market Street or pass near Union Square and run from about 6am to midnight. After midnight, there is infrequent all-night "Owl" service. For safety, avoid taking buses late at night.

Popular tourist routes include bus nos. 5, 7, and 71, all of which run to Golden Gate Park; 41 and 45, which travel along Union Street; and 30, which runs between Union Square and Ghirardelli Square. A bus ride costs $1.50 for adults and 50¢ for seniors over 65 and children 5 to 17.

STREETCAR   Five of Muni's six streetcar lines, designated J, K, L, M, and N, run underground downtown and on the streets in the outer neighborhoods. The sleek rail cars make the same stops as BART (see below) along Market Street, including Embarcadero Station (in the Financial District), Montgomery and Powell streets (both near Union Square), and the Civic Center (near City Hall). Past the Civic Center, the routes branch off: The J line takes you to Mission Dolores; the K, L, and M lines run to Castro Street; and the N line parallels Golden Gate Park and extends all the way to The Embarcadero and SBC Park. Streetcars run about every 15 minutes, more frequently during rush hours. They operate Monday through Friday from 5am to 12:45am, Saturday from 6am to 12:45am, and Sunday from 8am to 12:20am. The L and N lines operate 24 hours a day, 7 days a week, but late at night, regular buses trace the L and N routes, which are normally underground, from atop the city streets. Because the operation is part of Muni, the fares are the same as for buses, and passes are accepted.

The most recent new line to this system is not a newcomer at all, but is, in fact, an encore performance of San Francisco's beloved rejuvenated 1930s streetcar. The beautiful, retro multicolored F-Market streetcar runs from 17th and Castro streets to Beach and Jones streets; every other streetcar continues to Jones and Beach streets in Fisherman's Wharf. This is a quick and charming way to get up- and downtown without any hassle.

BART   BART, an acronym for **Bay Area Rapid Transit** (© **415/989-2278;** www. bart.gov), is a futuristic-looking, high-speed rail network that connects San Francisco with the East Bay—Oakland, Richmond, Concord, and Fremont. Four stations are on Market Street (see "Streetcar," above). Fares range from $1.25 to $7.45, depending on how far you go. Machines in the stations dispense tickets that are magnetically encoded with a dollar amount. Computerized exits automatically deduct the correct fare. Children 4 and under ride free. Trains run every 15 to 20 minutes, Monday through Friday from 4am to midnight, Saturday from 6am to midnight, and Sunday from 8am to midnight.

The 33-mile BART extension, which extends all the way to San Francisco International Airport, opened in June 2003. See the "Getting There" section in chapter 2, beginning on p. 32 for information on getting into town from the airport.

BY CAR

You don't need a car to explore downtown San Francisco. In fact, with the city becoming more crowded by the minute, a car can be your worst nightmare—you're likely to end up stuck in traffic with lots of aggressive and frustrated drivers, pay upward of $30 a day to park, and spend a good portion of your vacation looking for a parking space. Don't bother. However, if you want to venture outside the city, driving is the best way to go.

Before heading outside the city, especially in winter, call the CalTrans highway information network at © **800/427-7623** for California **road conditions.**

CAR RENTALS   All the major rental companies operate in the city and have desks at the airports. When I last checked, you could get a compact car for a week for anywhere from $165 to $315, including all taxes and other charges, but prices change dramatically on a daily basis and depend on which company you rent from.

Some of the national car-rental companies operating in San Francisco include **Alamo** (© 800/327-9633; www.alamo.com), **Avis** (© 800/331-1212; www.avis.com), **Budget** (© 800/527-0700; www.budget.com), **Dollar** (© 800/800-4000; www.dollar. com), **Enterprise** (© 800/325-8007; www.enterprise.com), **Hertz** (© 800/654-3131; www.hertz.com), **National** (© 800/227-7368; www.nationalcar.com), and **Thrifty** (© 800/367-2277; www.thrifty.com).

Car-rental rates vary even more than airline fares. Prices depend on the size of the car, where and when you pick it up and drop it off, the length of the rental period, where and how far you drive it, whether you buy insurance, and a host of other factors. A few key questions can save you hundreds of dollars, but you have to ask—reservations agents don't often volunteer money-saving information:

- Are weekend rates lower than weekday rates? Ask if the rate is the same for pickup Friday morning, for instance, as it is for Thursday night. Reservations agents won't volunteer this information, so don't be shy about asking.
- Does the agency assess a drop-off charge if you don't return the car to the same location where you picked it up?
- Are special promotional rates available? If you see an advertised price in your local newspaper, be sure to ask for that specific rate; otherwise, you could be charged the standard rate. Terms change constantly.
- Are discounts available for members of AARP, AAA, frequent-flier programs, or trade unions? If you belong to any of these organizations, you may be entitled to discounts of up to 30%.
- How much tax will be added to the rental bill? Will there be local tax and state tax?
- How much does the rental company charge to refill your gas tank if you return with the tank less than full? Most rental companies claim their prices are "competitive," but fuel is almost always cheaper in town, so you should try to allow enough time to refuel the car before returning it.

Some companies offer "refueling packages," in which you pay for an entire tank of gas upfront. The cost is usually fairly competitive with local prices, but you don't get credit for any gas remaining in the tank. If a stop at a gas station on the way to the airport will make you miss your plane, then by all means take advantage of the fuel purchase option. Otherwise, skip it.

Most agencies enforce a minimum-age requirement—usually 25. Some also have a maximum-age limit. If you're concerned that these limits might affect you, ask about rental requirements at the time of booking to avoid problems later.

Make sure you're insured. Hasty assumptions about your personal auto insurance or a rental agency's additional coverage could end up costing you tens of thousands of dollars, even if you are involved in an accident that is clearly the fault of another driver.

If you already have your own car insurance, you are most likely covered in the United States for loss of or damage to a rental car and liability in case of injury to any other party involved in an accident. Be sure to check your policy before you spend extra money (around $10 or more per day) on the **collision damage waiver (CDW),** offered by all agencies.

Most major credit cards (especially gold and platinum cards) provide some degree of coverage as well—if they were used to pay for the rental. Terms vary widely, however, so be sure to call your credit card company directly before you rent and rely on the card for coverage. If you are uninsured, your credit card may provide primary coverage as long as you decline the rental agency's insurance. If you already have insurance, your credit card may provide secondary coverage, which basically covers your deductible. However, note that *credit cards will not cover liability,* which is the cost of injury to an outside party and/or damage to an outside party's vehicle. If you do not hold an insurance policy, you should seriously consider buying additional liability insurance from your rental company, even if you decline the CDW.

PARKING   If you want to have a relaxing vacation, don't even attempt to find street parking on Nob Hill, in North Beach, in Chinatown, by Fisherman's Wharf, or on Telegraph Hill. Park in a garage or take a cab or a bus. If you do find street parking, pay attention to street signs that explain when you can park and for how long. Be especially careful not to park in zones that are tow areas during rush hours.

Curb colors also indicate parking regulations. *Red* means no stopping or parking; *blue* is reserved for drivers with disabilities who have a California-issued disabled plate or placard; *white* means there's a 5-minute limit; *green* indicates a 10-minute limit; and *yellow* and *yellow-and-black* curbs are for commercial vehicles only. Also, don't park at a bus stop or in front of a fire hydrant, and watch out for street-cleaning signs. If you violate the law, you might get a hefty ticket or your car might be towed; to get your car back, you'll have to get a release from the nearest district police department and then go to the towing company to pick up the vehicle.

When parking on a hill, apply the hand brake, put the car in gear, and *curb your wheels*—toward the curb when facing downhill, away from the curb when facing uphill. Curbing your wheels not only prevents a possible "runaway" but also keeps you from getting a ticket—an expensive fine that is aggressively enforced.

BY TAXI

This isn't New York, so don't expect a taxi to appear whenever you need one—if at all. If you're downtown during rush hour or leaving a major hotel, it won't be hard to hail a cab; just look for the lighted sign on the roof that indicates the vehicle is free. Otherwise, it's a good idea to call one of the following companies to arrange a ride; even then, there's been more than one time when the cab never came for me. What to do? Call back if your cab is late and insist on attention, but don't expect prompt results on weekends, no matter how nicely you ask. Here are the companies: **Veteran's Cab** (© 415/552-1300), **Luxor Cabs** (© 415/282-4141), and **Yellow Cab** (© 415/626-2345). Rates are approximately $2.85 for the first mile and 45¢ each fifth of a mile thereafter.

BY FERRY

TO/FROM SAUSALITO OR LARKSPUR The **Golden Gate Ferry Service** fleet (© 415/923-2000; www.goldengateferry.org) shuttles passengers daily between the San Francisco Ferry Building, at the foot of Market Street, and downtown Sausalito and Larkspur. Service is frequent, departing at reasonable intervals every day of the year except January 1, Thanksgiving Day, and December 25. Phone for an exact schedule. The ride takes half an hour, and one-way fares are $6.45 for adults and $4.85 for kids 6 to 12. Seniors and passengers with disabilities ride for $3.20. Up to two children under 6 with paying adults ride free on weekdays; on weekends, up to two children under 12 ride free with paying adults. Family rates are available on weekends.

Blue & Gold Fleet ferries (© 415/773-1188 for recorded info, or © 415/705-5555 for tickets; www.blueandgoldfleet.com) also provide round-trip service to downtown Sausalito and Larkspur, leaving from Fisherman's Wharf at Pier 41. The one-way cost is $8.00 for adults, $5.00 for kids 5 to 11. Boats run on a seasonal schedule; phone for departure information. Tickets can be purchased at Pier 41.

FAST FACTS: San Francisco

Airports See the "Getting There" section, in chapter 2, beginning on p. 32.

American Express For travel arrangements, traveler's checks, currency exchange, and other member services, an office is at 455 Market St., at First Street (© 415/536-2600), in the Financial District, open Monday through Friday from 9am to 5:30pm and Saturday from 10am to 2pm. To report lost or stolen traveler's checks, call ✆ **800/221-7282.** For American Express Global Assist, call ✆ **800/554-2639.**

Area Code The area code for San Francisco is **415**; for Oakland, Berkeley, and much of the East Bay, **510**; for the peninsula, generally **650.** Napa and Sonoma are **707.** Most phone numbers in this book are in San Francisco's 415 area code, but there's no need to dial it if you're within city limits. See the inside front cover of this book for more information on phoning in San Francisco.

Business Hours Most banks are open Monday through Friday from 9am to 5pm. Many banks also have ATMs for 24-hour banking (see the "Money" section, in chapter 2, beginning on p. 19).

Most stores are open Monday through Saturday from 10 or 11am to at least 6pm, with shorter hours on Sunday. But there are exceptions: Stores in Chinatown, Ghirardelli Square, and PIER 39 stay open much later during the tourist season, and large department stores, including Macy's and Nordstrom, keep late hours.

Most restaurants serve lunch from about 11:30am to 2:30pm and dinner from about 5:30 to 10pm. They sometimes serve later on weekends. Nightclubs and bars are usually open daily until 2am, when they are legally bound to stop serving alcohol.

Car Rentals See "Getting Around," earlier in this chapter.

Climate See the "When to Go" section in chapter 2, beginning on p. 20.

Dentists In the event of a dental emergency, see your hotel concierge or contact the **San Francisco Dental Office,** 131 Steuart St., Suite 323 (✆ **415/777-5115**), between Mission and Howard streets, which offers emergency service and comprehensive dental care Monday and Tuesday from 8am to 4:30pm, Wednesday and Thursday from 10:30am to 6:30pm, and Friday from 8am to 4:30pm.

Doctors **Saint Francis Memorial Hospital,** 900 Hyde St., between Bush and Pine streets on Nob Hill (✆ **415/353-6000**), provides emergency service 24 hours a day; no appointment is necessary. The hospital also operates a **physician-referral service** (✆ **800/333-1355** or 415/353-6566).

Drugstores **Walgreens** pharmacies are all over town, including one at 135 Powell St. (✆ **415/391-4433**). The store is open Monday through Friday from 7am to midnight and Saturday and Sunday from 8am to midnight; the pharmacy is open Monday through Friday from 8am to 9pm, Saturday from 9am to 5pm; it's closed on Sunday. The branch on Divisadero Street at Lombard (✆ **415/931-6415**) has a 24-hour pharmacy.

Earthquakes There will always be earthquakes in California, most of which you'll never notice. However, in case of a significant shaker, there are a few basic precautionary measures you should know. When you are inside a building, seek cover; do not run outside. Stand under a doorway or against a wall, and stay away from windows. If you exit a building after a substantial quake, use stairwells, not elevators. If you are in your car, pull over to the side of the road and stop—but not until you are away from bridges, overpasses, telephone poles, and power lines. Stay in your car. If you're out walking, stay outside and away from trees, power lines, and the sides of buildings. If you're in an area with tall buildings, find a doorway in which to stand.

Emergencies Dial ℂ **911** for police, an ambulance, or the fire department; no coins are needed from a public phone.

Internet Access Surprisingly, San Francisco has very few Internet cafes. However, there are locations around town where you can get online access, perhaps with a sandwich and a cup o' joe. You can do your laundry, listen to music, dine, and check your stocks online at SoMa's **Brainwash,** 1122 Folsom St., between Seventh and Eighth streets (ℂ **415/861-FOOD**). It's open Monday through Friday from 7am to 11pm and Saturday and Sunday from 7:30am to noon; rates are $3 for 20 minutes. For access without the ambience, try **Copy Central,** 110 Sutter St., at Montgomery Street (ℂ **415/392-6470**), which provides access cards costing 20¢ per minute. It's open Monday through Thursday from 8am to 8pm and Friday from 8am to 7pm. Ditto **Kinko's,** 1967 Market St., near Gough Street (ℂ **415/252-0864**), which charges 25¢ per minute. Both of these companies have numerous locations around town. If you've got wireless access, you're in luck. Most major hotels have wireless access in their lobbies as well as their rooms, so if you stroll into a hotel lobby and pull up a sofa, you can almost always get instantly connected.

Laundry Most hotels offer laundry service. But if you want to save money you can easily tote your gear to a local Laundromat or dry cleaner. Ask your hotel for the nearest location—they're all over town. Or for a scene with your suds, go to SoMa's **Brainwash,** 1122 Folsom St., between Seventh and Eighth streets (ℂ **415/861-FOOD**). It's open Monday through Friday from 7am to 11pm and Saturday and Sunday from 7:30am to noon and also offers music, food, and online access.

Liquor Laws Liquor stores and grocery stores, as well as some drugstores, can sell packaged alcoholic beverages between 6am and 2am daily. Most restaurants, nightclubs, and bars are licensed to serve alcoholic beverages during the same hours. The legal age for purchase and consumption of alcohol is 21; proof of age is required.

Newspapers & Magazines The city's main daily is the *San Francisco Chronicle,* which is distributed throughout the city. Check out the *Chronicle's* massive Sunday edition that includes a pink "Datebook" section—an excellent preview of the week's upcoming events. The free weekly *San Francisco Bay Guardian* and *San Francisco Weekly,* tabloids of news and listings, are indispensable for nightlife information; they're widely distributed through street-corner kiosks and at city cafes and restaurants. Of the many free tourist-oriented publications, the most widely read are *Key, San Francisco Guide,* and *Where San Francisco.* The first two are handbook-size weeklies containing maps and information on current events. The latter is a glossy regular format monthly magazine. You can find them in most hotels, shops, and restaurants in the major tourist areas.

Police For emergencies, dial ℂ **911** from any phone; no coins are needed. For other matters, call ℂ **415/553-0123**.

Post Office Dozens of post offices are located around the city. The closest to Union Square is inside the Macy's department store at 170 O'Farrell St. (① **800/275-8777** or 415/956-0131; zip code 94102). You can pick up mail addressed to you and marked "General Delivery" (Poste Restante) at the **Civic Center Post Office Box Unit,** "General Delivery," San Francisco, CA 94142-9991 (① **800/275-8777** or 415/563-7284). The street address is 101 Hyde St.

Safety San Francisco, like any other large city, has its fair share of crime, but most folks luckily don't have firsthand horror stories. In some areas, you need to exercise extra caution, particularly at night—notably the Tenderloin, the Western Addition (south of Japantown), the Mission District (especially around 16th and Mission sts.), the lower Fillmore area (also south of Japantown), around lower Haight Street, and around the Civic Center. In addition, there are a substantial number of homeless people throughout the city, with concentrations in and around Union Square, the Theater District (3 blocks west of Union Square), the Tenderloin, and Haight Street, so don't be alarmed if you're approached for spare change. Just use common sense.

For additional crime-prevention information, phone **San Francisco SAFE** (① **415/553-1984**).

Smoking If San Francisco is California's most European city in looks and style, the comparison stops when it comes to smoking in public. Each year, smoking laws in the city become stricter. Since 1998, smoking has been prohibited in restaurants and bars. Hotels are also offering more nonsmoking rooms, which often leaves those who like to puff out in the cold—sometimes literally.

Taxes An 8.5% sales tax is added at the register for all goods and services purchased in San Francisco. The city hotel tax is a whopping 14%. There is no airport tax.

Taxis See "By Taxi," on p. 69 of this chapter.

Time Zone San Francisco is in the Pacific Standard Time zone, which is 8 hours behind Greenwich Mean Time and 3 hours behind Eastern Standard Time. To find out what time it is in San Francisco, call ① **415/767-8900.**

Transit Information The San Francisco Municipal Railway, better known as **Muni,** operates the city's cable cars, buses, and streetcars. For customer service, call ① **415/673-6864** weekdays from 6am to 8pm, weekends from 8am to 6pm. At other times, you can call this number to get recorded information. Also see the "Getting Around" section earlier in this chapter, beginning on p. 63 for information on all of San Francisco's transit options.

Weather For a daily forecast while in town, check out the *San Francisco Chronicle* or visit www.weatherpages.com. Also call the National Weather Service at ① **831/656-1725** or visit www.nws.noaa.gov.

Accommodations You Can Afford

Although the implosion of the dot-com era put a cramp in my plans for early retirement, it's resulted in a boon for budget-conscious visitors. When the price of San Francisco real estate skyrocketed in the late '90s, all those frumpy old hotels throughout the downtown and South of Market districts were gussied up to accommodate the droves of stock-crazy newcomers. When the bubble burst, everyone went back to their crummy old jobs, and the hotel owners were forced to drastically lower their rates. Even a half-decade later, the average hotel rate has remained pretty much the same, but now the reasons have more to do with the repercussions of 9/11, when tourism hit an all-time low. The city's hotel industry is still reeling from that major blow.

Ergo, you can score some amazing lodging bargains in the heart of the city. With a little research and a lot of walking around, I managed to find numerous lodgings that are both inexpensive enough to be included in this guidebook and respectable enough that even a snob like me would be willing to stay there.

Of course, you can kiss mints-on-your-pillow luxuries goodbye, because most budget hotels keep their prices down by offering the bare essentials—phone, TV, bed, and bathroom—and in the Union Square district, even a private bathroom is considered an upgrade. One option is to avoid the heavily touristed areas such as Union Square and Fisherman's Wharf, and instead, park your bags at the city's outlying districts, such as the Marina, and take a bus into town. Not only are the room rates far lower (and the chances of having your own bathroom doubled), but also the clientele is usually more, shall we say, "polished" as well.

TIPS ON FINDING REASONABLE RATES Hunting for hotels in San Francisco can be tricky, particularly if you're not a seasoned traveler. What you don't know—and the reservations agent may not tell you—may very well ruin your vacation, so keep the following pointers in mind when it comes time to book a room:

- The prices below do not include the city's 14% hotel tax. Other hidden extras may include parking fees and surcharges—up to $1 per local call—for telephone use.
- Some hotels entice you with a free continental breakfast, which can be a real money saver. But beware: Sometimes a big promise translates to just coffee and a croissant.
- If a hotel is listed as "Super-Cheap," don't be surprised if your room is on the funky side (though I eighty-sixed the real dives). Nothing's free, mate.

- San Francisco is convention city, so if you wish to secure rooms at a particular hotel during high season—roughly April to September—book well in advance.
- Be sure to have a credit card in hand when making a reservation, and don't be surprised if you're asked to pay for at least 1 night in advance (this doesn't happen often, though).
- Reservations are usually held until 6pm. If you don't tell the hotel you'll be arriving late, you may lose your room.
- Almost every hotel in San Francisco requires a credit card imprint for "incidentals" (and to prevent walkouts). If you don't have a credit card, be sure to make arrangements with the management before you hang up the phone, and take down names.

Before you book your room, turn to "Money-Saving Tips" in chapter 2; tips 16 to 26 offer valuable information on getting the best hotel rates. Many hotels also offer rooms at rates above and below the price category that they have been assigned in this guidebook. All rooms have private bathrooms unless otherwise noted.

HOW I'VE ORGANIZED THIS CHAPTER   The hotels listed here are classified first by area and then by price. Most of our recommendations range in price from a bit under $60 per night to $110 a night for a basic hotel room for two. **Super-Cheap Sleeps** are classified as those under $40 a night (essentially hostels), while the **Worth a Splurge** category features hotels that cost more than $140 per night. These categories reflect the price of an average double room—*not including the 14% hotel tax*—during the high season, which runs approximately from April to September. Keep in mind that prices listed are the hotel's "rack rates" (the published rates for walk-ins) and you should *always* ask for discounts or, even better, vacation packages. It's possible that you could get the room you want for $20 to $40 a night less than what's quoted here, except in summer when the hotels are packed and bargaining is close to impossible. Also note that I don't list rates for singles. However, some hotels, particularly more budget-oriented establishments, do offer lower rates for singles, so be sure to ask about these if you're traveling alone. And if you're a AAA member, be sure to order the free guide to California's hotels and motels, which not only supplies readers with further options, but also ranks them from one to five diamonds. It also has discount coupons and quotes special member rates.

In general, hotel rates in San Francisco don't vary much during the year because the city is so popular year-round. You should always ask about weekend discounts, corporate rates, and family plans; most larger hotels offer them, but many don't mention

---

Tips Reservation Services

Having reservations about your reservations? Leave it up to the pros: **San Francisco Reservations,** 360 22nd St., Suite 300, Oakland, CA 94612 (© **800/677-1500** or 510/628-4450; www.hotelres.com), arranges reservations for more than 150 of San Francisco's hotels and often offers discounted rates. Their nifty website allows Internet users to make reservations online.

Other good online sites with discounted rates include www.hotels.com and www.placestostay.com.

Tips **Dial Direct**

When booking a room in a chain hotel, call the hotel's local line, as well as the toll-free number, and see where you'll get the best deal. A hotel makes nothing on a room that stays empty. The clerk who runs the place is more likely to know about vacancies and will often grant deep discounts in order to fill up rooms.

---

these discounts unless you make a specific inquiry. You'll find nonsmoking rooms in all the larger hotels and many of the smaller hotels; establishments that are entirely nonsmoking are listed as such. Nowadays, the best advice for smokers is to confirm a smoking-permitted room in advance.

While you'll find most accommodations have an abundance of amenities (including phones unless otherwise noted), don't be alarmed by the lack of air-conditioned guest rooms. San Francisco weather is so mild you'll rarely miss it.

Most of the larger hotels can accommodate guests with wheelchairs or those who have other special needs. Ask when you make a reservation to ensure that your hotel of choice will be able to accommodate your needs, especially if you're interested in a bed-and-breakfast or boutique hotel.

Pay close attention to the hotels that have one or more star icons. These are the exceptional ones, the ones that offer above-average accommodations at below-average rates.

AFFORDABLE HOTEL CHAINS   The reason I avoid reviewing chain hotels and motels is probably the very same reason you may want to consider staying in one: Every outpost is a veritable clone, hence you always know what you're going to get. But if all our recommendations in your price range are booked or if you don't mind going generic, you can always try one of the following chains, which all have hotels either in the city or nearby: **Best Western** (© 800/528-1234), **Comfort Inn** (© 800/228-5150), **Days Inn** (© 800/325-2525), **Doubletree Hotels** (© 800/222-TREE), **Econo Lodges** (© 800/55-ECONO), **Holiday Inn** (© 800/HOLIDAY), **Howard Johnson** (© 800/654-2000), **La Quinta Motor Inns** (© 800/531-5900), **Motel 6** (© 800/466-8356), **Ramada** (© 800/2-RAMADA), **Rodeway Inns** (© 800/228-2000), **Super 8** (© 800/800-8000), and **Travelodge** (© 800/255-3050).

1 Union Square/Nob Hill

The Andrews Hotel ⭐   For the location and price, the Andrews is a safe bet for an enjoyable stay. Two blocks west of Union Square, the Andrews was a Turkish bath before its conversion in 1981. As is typical in Euro-style hotels, the rooms are small but well maintained and comfortable, with nice touches like white lace curtains and fresh flowers. Continued upgrades help keep things fresh. But large bathroom lovers beware: Though they were painted in 2003, the facilities are forever tiny. A bonus is the adjoining Fino Bar and Ristorante, which offers respectable Italian fare and free wine to hotel guests in the evening.

624 Post St. (between Jones and Taylor sts.), San Francisco, CA 94109. © **800/926-3739** or 415/563-6877. Fax 415/928-6919. www.andrewshotel.com. 48 units (some with shower only). $109–$139 double; $139–$179 superior rooms. Rates include continental breakfast, coffee in lobby, and evening wine. AE, DC, MC, V. Valet parking $25. Bus: 2, 3, 4, 30, 38, or 45. Cable car: Powell-Hyde and Powell-Mason lines (3 blocks east). **Amenities:** Restaurant; access to nearby health club;

concierge; limited room service; babysitting; nearby self-service laundromat; laundry service; dry cleaning. *In room:* TV/VCR w/video library, dataport, fridge, hair dryer (on request), iron, CD player (suites only), wireless Internet access ($10 per day).

The Cartwright Hotel ⚥⚥   Diametrically opposed to the hip-hop, happenin' Hotel Triton down the street, the Cartwright Hotel is geared toward the more mature traveler. Management takes pride in its reputation for offering comfortable rooms at fair prices, which explains why most guests have been repeat customers for a long time. Remarkably quiet, despite its convenient location near one of the busiest downtown corners, the eight-story hotel looks not unlike it did when it opened some 80 years ago. Antiques collected during its decades of faithful service furnish the lobby and the individually decorated (and sometimes very small) rooms, all of which underwent a complete restoration in 2004 (think new paint and new furniture finishes). A nice perk usually reserved for fancier hotels are the fully equipped bathrooms, all of which have tubs, rainfall shower heads, and Aveda products, terry robes (in deluxe rooms), and thick fluffy towels. *Tip:* Request a room with a view of the backyard; they're the quietest. Complimentary wine is served in the small library each night, and afternoon tea and fresh-baked cookies are a daily treat, as are the apples and hot beverages in the lobby 'round the clock. A breakfast room added in 2004 serves a complimentary expanded continental breakfast with a make-your-own-waffle station.

524 Sutter St. (at Powell St.), San Francisco, CA 94102. ⓒ **800/919-9779** or 415/421-2865. Fax 415/398-6345. www.cartwrighthotel.com. 114 units. $99–$159 double; $189–$259 family/business suite (sleeps 4). Rates include continental breakfast, 24-hr. tea, coffee, and apples in the lobby, nightly wine hour, weekday newspapers, and afternoon cookies. AE, DC, DISC, MC, V. Valet parking $35; self-parking $25. Bus: 2, 3, 4, 30, or 45. Cable car: Powell-Hyde and Powell-Mason lines (direct stop). **Amenities:** Access to nearby health club for $15; concierge. *In room:* TV, dataport, fridge (upon request), hair dryer, iron, free Wi-Fi.

The Cornell Hotel de France ⚥   Its quirks make this old hotel more charming than many others in its price range. Resident pooch, Noel, greets you when you enter the small French-style hotel. Pass the office, where a few faces will glance in your direction and smile, and embark on a ride in the old-fashioned elevator (we're talking seriously old-school here) to get to your very basic room with either a standard or queen-size bed. Each floor is dedicated to a French painter and decorated with reproductions. Rooms are all plain and comfortable, with desks and chairs, and are individually and simply decorated. Smoking is not allowed. The full American breakfast included in the rate is served in the very cool, cavernlike provincial basement restaurant, Jeanne d'Arc. Union Square is just a few blocks away.

715 Bush St. (between Powell and Mason sts.), San Francisco, CA 94108. ⓒ **800/232-9698** or 415/421-3154. Fax 415/399-1442. www.cornellhotel.com. 55 units. $85–$130 double. Rates include full American breakfast. Package including 7 breakfasts and 5 dinners: $1,085 double per week for deluxe room, $925 for medium room. AE, DC, DISC, MC, V. Parking across the street $17. Bus: 2, 3, 4, 30, or 45. Cable car: Powell-Hyde and Powell-Mason lines. **Amenities:** Restaurant; free Internet in lobby. *In room:* TV, dataport, hair dryer.

Fitzgerald Hotel Union Square ⚥   Some of the rooms may be outfitted with half-canopy beds, fresh prints, and Victorian decor, but most of them are really small. (One

---

Fun Fact **Hotel Rendezvous**

For nearly a century, the most popular place for visitors to rendezvous in San Francisco has been under the magnificent hand-carved grandfather clock in the lobby of the Westin St. Francis hotel on Union Square.

Union Square & Nob Hill Accommodations

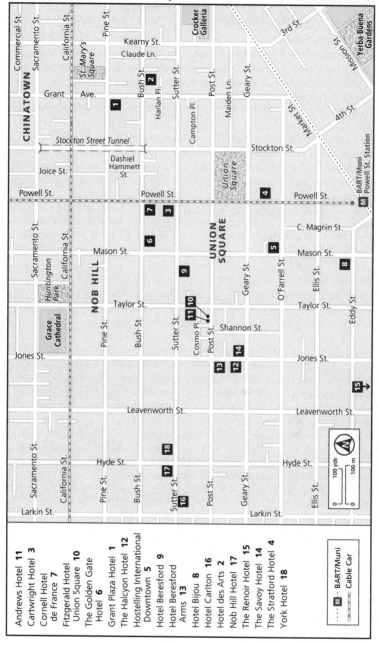

Andrews Hotel **11**
Cartwright Hotel **3**
Cornell Hotel
de France **7**
Fitzgerald Hotel
Union Square **10**
The Golden Gate
Hotel **6**
Grant Plaza Hotel **1**
The Halcyon Hotel **12**
Hostelling International
Downtown **5**
Hotel Beresford **9**
Hotel Beresford
Arms **13**
Hotel Bijou **8**
Hotel Carlton **16**
Hotel des Arts **2**
Nob Hill Hotel **17**
The Renoir Hotel **15**
The Savoy Hotel **14**
The Stratford Hotel **4**
York Hotel **18**

- **M** - BART/Muni
- Cable Car

Fun Fact A Living Legend

Tom Sweeny, the head doorman at the Sir Francis Drake hotel on Union Square, is a San Francisco living historical monument. Dressed in traditional Beefeaters attire (you can't miss those $1,400 duds), he's been the subject of countless snapshots—an average 200 per day for the past 20 years—and has shaken hands with every president since Gerry Ford.

---

that I saw had a dresser less than a foot from the bed.) Of course, at $80 per night, there's no room for complaining. But do ask for a larger room—and a quieter one. If you can live without a sizable closet, you'll find that the price, breakfast (home-baked breads, scones, muffins, juice, tea, and coffee), and cleanliness of this hotel make it a good value.

620 Post St. (between Jones and Taylor sts.), San Francisco, CA 94109. © **800/334-6835** or 415/775-8100. Fax 415/775-1278. www.fitzgeraldhotel.com. 47 units. $65–$125 double. Rates include continental breakfast. Lower rates in winter. AE, DC, DISC, MC, V. Valet parking $34; self-parking $24. Bus: 2, 3, 4, or 27. Cable car: Powell-Hyde and Powell-Mason lines. **Amenities:** Free access to a nearby health club; same-day dry cleaning; Internet access in lobby (for a fee). *In room:* TV, dataport, hair dryer.

The Golden Gate Hotel 🐾🐾 *Value*   San Francisco's stock of small hotels in historic turn-of-the-20th-century buildings includes some real gems, and The Golden Gate Hotel is one of them. It's 2 blocks north of Union Square and 2 blocks down (literally) from the crest of Nob Hill, with cable car stops at the corner for easy access to Fisherman's Wharf and Chinatown. The city's theaters and best restaurants are also within walking distance. But the best thing about the 1913 Edwardian hotel is that it's family run: John and Renate Kenaston and daughter Gabriele are hospitable innkeepers who take obvious pleasure in making their guests comfortable. Each individually decorated room has handsome antique furnishings (plenty of wicker) from the early 1900s, quilted bedspreads, fresh flowers, and recently updated carpeting. Request a room with a clawfoot tub if you enjoy a good, hot soak. Afternoon tea is served daily from 4 to 7pm, and guests are welcome to use the house fax and computer with wireless DSL free of charge.

775 Bush St. (between Powell and Mason sts.), San Francisco, CA 94108. © **800/835-1118** or 415/392-3702. Fax 415/392-6202. www.goldengatehotel.com. 25 units, 14 with bathroom. $85 double (shared bathroom); $130 double (private bathroom). Rates include continental breakfast and afternoon tea. AE, DC, MC, V. Self-parking $16. Bus: 2, 4, 30, 38, or 45. Cable car: Powell-Hyde and Powell-Mason lines (1 block east). BART: Powell and Market. **Amenities:** Access to nearby health club; tour desk; office equipment available; nearby laundry service; dry cleaning. *In room:* TV, dataport, hair dryer, iron (upon request).

Grant Plaza Hotel   You definitely won't find any mints on your pillow at this budget hotel. What you will find, however, are cheap rates and basic—and I mean basic—rooms right in the middle of the Union Square/Chinatown action. The six-story building overlooks Chinatown's main street, so you're right in the thick of the tourist action. You can pretty much count on your guest room to be rather petite, with minuscule bathrooms with small showers. Rooms do, however, come with satellite TVs, hair dryers, desks, and dataports. *Note:* Ask for a room on the top floor—they're the newest and are substantially nicer than the older rooms. If those aren't available, ask for one of the larger and brighter corner rooms.

465 Grant Ave. (at Pine St.), San Francisco, CA 94108. © **800/472-6899** or 415/434-3883. Fax 415/434-3886. www.grantplaza.com. 72 units, most with shower only. $59–$89 double. AE, DC, DISC, MC, V. Nearby parking $18. Cable

car: Powell-Hyde, Powell-Mason, and California–Van Ness lines. **Amenities:** Access to nearby health club ($8 per day); concierge; Internet stations in lobby (for a fee). *In room:* Dataport, hairdryer.

The Halcyon Hotel ℛ *Value*

Inside this small, four-story brick building is a penny-pincher's dream come true, the kind of place where you'll find everything you need yet won't have to pay through the nose to get. The small but very clean studio guest rooms are equipped with microwave ovens, refrigerators, flatware and utensils, toasters, alarm clocks, phones with free local calls, and voice mail—all the comforts of home in the heart of Union Square. A coin-operated washer and dryer are located in the basement, along with free laundry soap and irons. You also get your own individual doorbell and mailbox. The owners are usually on hand to offer friendly, personal service, making this option all in all an unbeatable deal. Be sure to ask about special rates for weekly stays.

649 Jones St. (between Geary and Post sts.), San Francisco, CA 94102. ✆ **800/627-2396** or 415/929-8033. Fax 415/441-8033. www.halcyonsf.com. 25 units. $79–$129 double year-round; $510–$590 weekly. Minimum length of stay Oct–Apr is 7 days. AE, DC, DISC, MC, V. Parking garage nearby $14–$16 per day. BART: Powell. Bus: 2, 3, 4, 9, 27, or 38. **Amenities:** Access to nearby health club; concierge; tour desk; laundry facilities; free fax available in lobby. *In room:* TV, dataport, kitchen, fridge, coffeemaker, hair dryer, iron, safe, voice mail.

Hotel Beresford ℛ

The small and friendly sister property of the Hotel Beresford Arms (see below), the seven-floor Hotel Beresford is another good, moderately priced choice near Union Square. Perks are the same: $5 video rentals for the VCR, clock radios, a mishmash of furniture, and stocked fridges. Everything's well kept and modest renovations in 2005—paint, wallpaper, and the like—promise fresh-looking, but, still, very modest surroundings. The on-site White Horse Tavern, an attractive and quaint replica of an old English pub, serves dinner Tuesday through Saturday and is a favorite for folks who like less trendy hullabaloo with their meals.

635 Sutter St. (near Mason St.), San Francisco, CA 94102. ✆ **800/533-6533** or 415/673-9900. Fax 415/474-0449. www.beresford.com. 114 units. $89–$165 double. Extra person $10. Rates include continental breakfast. Children under 12 stay free in parent's room. AE, DC, DISC, MC, V. Self parking and valet parking $20. Bus: 2, 3, 4, 30, 38, or 45. Cable car: Powell-Hyde line (1 block east). **Amenities:** Restaurant/pub; access to nearby health club ($10 per day); laundry service; free Internet access in lobby. *In room:* TV/VCR, dataport, minibar, hair dryer (upon request), iron.

Hotel Beresford Arms ℛℛ *Value*

The bargain prices are the main reason I recommend this dependable, though slightly unfashionable, hotel. On the plus side, suites have bidets and Jacuzzi bathtubs and junior suites offer a wet bar or fully equipped kitchenette—an advantage for families—and continental breakfast is included in the rock-bottom price of all rooms. All accommodations include plenty of in-room perks, including clock radios and $5 video rentals for the VCR, and there's a "Manager's Social Hour" (included in the room rates) with wine, tea, and snacks. The downsides are minimal: a few funky furnishings, small bathrooms, and the occasional old mattress. The location, between the Theater District and Union Square, in a quieter section of San Francisco, is ideal for visitors without cars, and the price for what you get is hard to beat. *Tip:* Rooms that face Post Street might be a bit noisier than others, but they're also larger and sunnier, and some have window seats.

701 Post St. (at Jones St.), San Francisco, CA 94109. ✆ **800/533-6533** or 415/673-2600. Fax 415/929-1535. www.beresford.com. 95 units. $99 double; $129 Jacuzzi suite; $169 parlor suite. Extra person $10. Rates include continental breakfast and afternoon wine and tea. Children under 12 stay free in parent's room. Senior and AAA discounts available. AE, DC, DISC, MC, V. Self parking and valet parking $20. Bus: 2, 3, 4, 27, or 38. Cable car: Powell-Hyde line (3 blocks east). **Amenities:** Access to nearby health club ($10 per day); laundry service; free Internet access in lobby. *In room:* TV/VCR, dataport, minibar, hair dryer (upon request), iron.

Hotel Bijou 🅚 ⓥⓐⓛⓤⓔ   Three words sum up this hotel: clean, colorful, and cheap. Although it's on the periphery of the gritty Tenderloin (just 3 blocks off Union Square), once inside this gussied-up 1911 hotel, all's cheery, bright, and perfect for budget travelers who want a little style with their savings. Joie de Vivre hotel group has disguised the hotel's age with lively decor, a Deco theater theme, and a heck of a lot of vibrant paint. To the left of the small lobby is a "theater" where guests can watch San Francisco–based double features nightly (there's cute old-fashioned theater seating, though it's just a basic TV showing videos). Upstairs, rooms named after locally made films are small, clean, and colorful (think buttercup, burgundy, and purple), and have all the basics from clock radios, dressers, and small desks to tiny bathrooms (one of which is so small you have to close the door to access the toilet). Alas, a few mattresses could be firmer, and there's only one small and slow elevator. But considering the price, and perks like the continental breakfast and friendly service, you can't go wrong here.

111 Mason St., San Francisco, CA 94102. ⓒ **800/771-1022** or 415/771-1200. www.hotelbijou.com. 65 units. $95–$139 double. Rates include continental breakfast. AE, DC, DISC, MC, V. Valet parking $25. Bus: All Market St. buses. Streetcar: Powell St. station. **Amenities:** Concierge; limited room service; same-day laundry service; dry cleaning; Internet access in lobby ($4 for 20 min.). *In room:* TV, dataport, hair dryer, iron.

Hotel Carlton ⓥⓐⓛⓤⓔ   If you're looking for wonderfully cheap, attractive, and clean accommodations and don't mind being in the middle of the city and simultaneously in the middle of nowhere, book a room here. The Joie de Vivre hotel group is behind this

---

(Kids) Affordable Family-Friendly Hotels

Comfort Suites (p. 96)   Enough pay cable channels to keep you and your kids glued to the TV set for an entire day, and a sleeper sofa in addition to a king-size bed make this an attractive airport option for families.

Cow Hollow Motor Inn & Suites (p. 89)   Inexpensive two-bedroom suites with full kitchens, dining areas, free local phone calls, and complimentary covered parking are just what the family needs for a holiday in the city.

Hotel Del Sol (p. 91)   Cheery colors, a heated courtyard pool with lots of pool toys, and beach balls and sunglasses for playing on the Marina beach make the Del Sol our top pick for entertaining the tots.

The Halcyon Hotel (p. 79)   Not only is this one of the city's best budget hotels, it's also a great place for families; rooms come with microwaves, refrigerators, and other lifesaving amenities, and weekly rentals are available.

San Francisco Airport North Travelodge (p. 97)   There's a heated outdoor pool, a laundromat, and a 24-hour IHOP on the premises. Deluxe rooms and suites have a refrigerator and microwave. There's free parking if you drive, and a free airport shuttle if you fly in.

The Wharf Inn (p. 88)   No whining about when you'll get there 'cause you're already there—right smack dab in the middle of Fisherman's Wharf. Parking is free, and there's no charge for packing along an extra pint-size munchkin.

163-room 1927 hotel revamped in May 2004 in "global vintage" decor. The interior boasts travel photographs from the American Himalayan Foundation, tribal figurines, Oriental rugs, a vibrant sarilike color scheme, and imported hand-painted Moroccan tables and cool Lucite-beaded table lamps in guest rooms. The surrounding neighborhood is drab, but it's only a seven-block walk to Union Square and with doubles starting at a mere $99, you can splurge for a taxi with the money saved.

1075 Sutter St. (between Larkin and Hyde sts.), San Francisco, CA 94109. ℂ 800/922-7586 or 415/673-0242. Fax 415/6734904. www.hotelcarltonsf.com. 163 units. $99–$119 double. Rates include evening wine hour. AE, MC, V. Valet parking $25; self parking $20. Bus: 2, 3, 4, 19, or 76. **Amenities:** Restaurant; concierge; laundry service; dry cleaning. *In room:* TV, dataports (in deluxe rooms), coffeemaker, hair dryer, iron, safe.

Hotel des Arts 𝒢★★ *Value*   You wouldn't believe how many crummy "European-style" hotels I've had to slog through, but the five-story Hotel del Arts is one of the gems. While it has the same floor plan as San Francisco's numerous other Euro-style hotels—small lobby, narrow hallways, cramped rooms—the owners of the des Arts have made an obvious effort to distance themselves from the competition by including a visually stimulating dose of artistic license throughout the hotel. The lobby, for example, hosts a rotating art gallery featuring contemporary works by emerging local artists and is outfitted with groovy furnishings, while the guest rooms are soothingly situated with quality furnishings and tasteful accoutrements. There's one suite that can sleep up to four persons at no additional charge. You'll love the lively location as well: right across the street from the entrance to Chinatown and 2 blocks from Union Square. There's even a French brasserie right downstairs. Considering the price (rooms with a very clean shared bathroom start at $49), quality, and location, it's quite possibly the best budget hotel in the city. *Note:* Ask for the Frommer's Weekly Special, at $294 a week for a double occupancy standard queen room; three people can share the room for an additional charge of $10 per night. This rate is based on availability and does not include tax.

447 Bush St. (at Grant St.), San Francisco, CA 94108. ℂ 800/956-4322 or 415/956-3232. Fax 415/956-0399. www.sf hoteldesarts.com. 51 units, 26 with private bathroom. $79–$159 (private bathroom); $59–$79 double (shared bathroom). Rates include continental breakfast. AE, DC, MC, V. Nearby parking $18. Cable car: Powell-Hyde and Powell-Mason lines. **Amenities:** 24-hour concierge; basic business services; laundry service; valet service. *In room:* TV, dataport, minifridge (some rooms), hair dryer, iron/ironing board, microwave (some rooms), voice mail.

Nob Hill Hotel 𝒢★★ *Value*   The Nob Hill Hotel is an amazing deal for such a ritzy inn, with rates starting at $109 during peak season. Located in a quiet area of Nob Hill, it was built in 1906 and fully restored in 1998, and whoever renovated the lobby did a smashing job restoring it to its original "Old San Francisco Victorian" splendor, complete with original marble flooring, high ceilings with decorative moldings, and stained-glass panels and alabaster dating from about 1892. Though the rooms are somewhat small, they are all handsomely decorated with old-fashioned furnishings such as Victorian antique armoires, rich carpeting, marble bathrooms, brass beds with comforters, and carved-wood nightstands. A pleasant oxymoron: All the rooms are equipped with a plethora of high-tech amenities such as Internet access and personal voice mail. Complimentary pastries and coffee are served each morning, and there's even a free evening wine tasting. The adjacent **Il Bacio** restaurant is a good place to refuel on regional Italian cuisine before venturing down the street to Union Square. *Tip:* The hotel's website offers a Priceline-style "Name Your Own Rate" option that might save you big bucks on your hotel room.

835 Hyde St. (between Bush and Sutter sts.), San Francisco, CA 94109. ℂ 877/662-4455 or 415/885-2987. Fax 415/921-1648. www.nobhillhotel.com. 53 units. $109–$299 double. Rates include continental breakfast. DC, DISC, MC, V. Parking $24. Bus: 2, 3, or 4. **Amenities:** Adjoining restaurant (Italian); Access to nearby 24-hr. health club;

basic business services; laundry service. *In room:* TV w/pay movies, fax, fax, dataport, hair dryer, iron, CD player; suites have Jacuzzi tubs, and English-style garden, microwave.

Nob Hill Motor Inn   If it weren't for the slightly inconvenient location, this well-tended motel would be our top choice for visitors with cars. It's a bit of a hike to most major tourist destinations—Fisherman's Wharf, Union Square, North Beach—but a very short bus or cab ride to everywhere in the city. It's obvious from the moment you pull into the covered parking area that the owners have put a lot of money and effort into maintaining the property. The spacious guest rooms—all with large TVs, big closets, and modern furnishings—have been completely renovated and are quite comfortable. You'll like the friendly staff as well. All in all, if you don't mind long walks, I highly recommend basing your vacation from Nob Hill Motor Inn.

1630 Pacific Ave. (between Van Ness Ave. and Polk St.), San Francisco, CA 94109. © **800/343-6900** or 415/775-8160. Fax 415/673-8842. www.staysf.com. 29 units. $85–$165 double. $10 extra person. Rates include continental breakfast. AE, DC, DISC, MC, V. Free covered parking. Bus: 12, 19, 42, 47, 49, or 83. *In room:* A/C, TV w/HBO, dataport, fridge, coffeemaker, hair dryer, iron, free wireless Internet access, microwave.

Renoir Hotel 🎇   Housed in a majestic 1909 Flatiron-style brick building, the Renoir is one of the few low-priced hotels in the downtown area whose guest rooms have pleasing views and direct sunlight. On the corner of Market and McAllister streets and within walking distance to most of the city's main attractions, the privately owned, family-run hotel was completely renovated in 2001 with a European-style, turn-of-the-20th-century theme—the high-ceiling lobby is replete with ornate columns, gilded elevators doors, chandeliers, antique furnishings, and spiffily dressed staff. Of course, such ostentation comes to a screeching halt once you enter your guest room; each is simply furnished with modern dark-wood furnishings, flower-patterned bedspreads and matching drapes, and those ubiquitous awful prints screwed into the wall above the bed. No matter: The hotel is in such a great location that you'll probably spend very little time supine. The hotel's restaurant, **Café do Brasil,** is San Francisco's first (and only) Brazilian "Churrasco Rodizio," the classic eat-until-you-say-"Uncle" Brazilian style of barbecue. *Tip:* Request a room overlooking Market Street that receives the morning sun.

45 McAllister St. (at Market St.), San Francisco, CA 94102. © **800/576-3388** or 415/626-5200. Fax 415/626-0916. www.renoirhotel.com. 135 units. $89–$159 standard double; $139–$169 superior; $175–$350 suite. Rates include coffee and tea each morning. AE, DC, MC, V. Valet parking $35. Streetcar: F, and all underground Muni and BART lines. Cable car: Union Sq. Children 12 and under stay free. **Amenities:** Restaurant (Brazilian); lounge; access to nearby YMCA gym and pool; basic business services; Internet access in lobby (for a fee); laundry service; dry cleaning. *In room:* TV, dataport, hair dryer, iron/ironing board (upon request), safe, voice mail.

The Savoy Hotel 🎇🎇 *Value*   A European-style hotel through and through, the Savoy is one of my favorite moderately priced downtown hotels. With a nice cozy apartmentlike feel to each guest room, old well-cleaned bathrooms with original tiles, newly painted rooms as of 2005, classic furnishings, and 400-thread-count sheets; it's easy to relax here. Not all rooms are alike—they can be small, but each has beautiful, white-wood shutters, large mirrors, and two-line telephones. Guests also enjoy access to the newly relocated Millennium, San Francisco's only gourmet vegan restaurant, as well as a wine and cheese reception each afternoon.

580 Geary St. (between Taylor and Jones sts.), San Francisco, CA 94102. © **800/227-4223** or 415/441-2700. Fax 415/441-0124. www.thesavoyhotel.com. 82 units. $119–$169 double; $149–$169 suite. Complimentary wine and cheese 4–6pm daily. Ask about packages; continental breakfast $5. AE, DC, DISC, MC, V. Valet parking $30. Bus: 2, 3,

Accommodations with Free Parking

Despite our exhortations to leave the driving to locals and use the public transportation system to get around, I know that some of you will still want to drive the crazy streets of San Francisco, or at least arrive by car. But with parking fees averaging $30 a night at most hotels, the extra charges can add up for visitors with wheels. So if you're going to rent a car or bring your own, you might want to consider staying at one of the following affordable choices, which all offer free parking:

- Americania, SoMa, p. 85
- Bay Bridge Inn, SoMa, p. 84
- Beck's Motor Lodge, the Castro, p. 95
- Chelsea Motor Inn, Marina District/Cow Hollow, p. 89
- Cow Hollow Motor Inn & Suites, Marina District/Cow Hollow, p. 89
- Flamingo Inn, SoMa, p. 85
- Hostelling International San Francisco—Downtown and Fisherman's Wharf, p. 91
- Hotel Del Sol, Marina District/Cow Hollow, p. 91
- The Laurel Inn, Marina District/Cow Hollow, p. 91
- Lombard Motor Inn, Marina District/Cow Hollow, p. 90
- Marina Motel, Marina District/Cow Hollow, p. 90
- Motel Capri, Marina District/Cow Hollow, p. 91
- Nob Hill Motor Inn, Marina District/Cow Hollow, p. 82
- Phoenix Hotel, Civic Center & Environs, p. 93
- San Francisco Airport North Travelodge, Near the Airport, p. 97
- Seal Rock Inn, Richmond District, p. 94
- The Wharf Inn, North Beach/Fisherman's Wharf, p. 88

4, 27, or 38. **Amenities:** Restaurant; 24 hr. concierge; laundry service; dry cleaning; free Internet in lobby. *In room:* TV, dataport, hair dryer, iron, safe.

The Stratford Hotel ☞   Renovation fever has hit the ever-touristy downtown, and the Stratford is the latest to get the bug. Until recently, no one ever noticed there are actually hotels along the noisiest, most densely tourist-populated section of Union Square. But the Stratford's colorful face-lift is drawing interested looks—and hotel reservations—to the southern corner of the area. The resurrection of this eight-story 1907 building includes the addition of colorfully painted hallways and brightly painted rooms done in a slightly tattered Euro-chic decor. Accommodations vary tremendously, so be sure to request what you want (and don't want); those that face Powell have more noise (clanging cable cars are far less cute when you're trying to sleep) but more sunlight and a great view; double-paned windows block much of the noise, however.

242 Powell St. (between Geary Blvd. and O'Farrell St.), San Francisco, CA 94102. ☎ **888/504-6835** or 415/397-7080. Fax 415/397-7087. www.hotelstratford.com. 100 units. $79–$139 double. Rates include continental breakfast. AE, MC, V. Garage parking nearby for $20 per day. Bus: 2, 3, 4, 27, 30, 38, 76, and all Market St. buses and streetcars;

Cable car: Powell-Hyde line; BART: Powell. **Amenities:** Babysitting; same-day laundry service; dry cleaning. *In room:* TV, dataport, hair dryer.

York Hotel 👍👍   Even as a local, I drop by the York frequently because it's home to the Empire Plush Room (p. 226), the city's best jazz and cabaret club, now featuring a new vaudeville show. But for the visitor, the hotel, built in 1922 and boasting a role in Hitchcock's *Vertigo,* is a boon because it's a hell of a deal. Awarded two and a half diamonds by AAA, the hotel has ridiculously helpful staff, a workout room, and promotional rates, which include a continental breakfast served in the spacious lobby. Rooms swathed in terra cotta and green are abundantly cheery and come loaded with nice touches like dark-wood writing desks, newly upholstered and comfy chairs, alarm clocks, tub/shower combinations, and walk-in closets. New to the room lineup is the Superior King room, which includes a flatscreen TV, free wireless Internet access, and new textiles.

940 Sutter St. (between Leavenworth and Hyde sts.), San Francisco, CA 94109. (✆ **800/808-9675** or 415/885-6800. Fax 415/885-2115. www.yorkhotel.com. 96 units. $119–$149 double. Rates include continental breakfast. AE, DISC, MC, V. Valet parking $35; self parking $25. Bus: 2, 3, or 4. **Amenities:** Jazz club; bar; health club, laundry. *In room:* TV w/pay movies, coffeemaker, hair dryer, iron (on request), safe, free wireless Internet access (Superior King rooms).

SUPER-CHEAP SLEEPS

Hostelling International San Francisco–Downtown   For just over $20 per night (with a notarized ID), you can relive college-dorm life in an old San Francisco–style building right in the heart of Union Square. Occupying five sparsely decorated floors—each with its own pay phone—rooms here are simple and clean. Each has two or three bunk beds with linens, its own sink, a closet, and lockers (bring your own lock or buy one at the front desk). Although most private rooms share hallway bathrooms, a few have private facilities. Laminated posters adorn the hallways, and there are several common rooms, including a reading room and a large kitchen with lots of tables, chairs, and refrigerator space. There are laundry facilities in the building and a helpful information desk where you can book tours and sightseeing trips. The hostel is open 24 hours, and reservations are essential, especially during the summer. Persons younger than 18 must be accompanied by an adult or have a signed guardian release form, which is available from their website.

312 Mason St. (between Geary and O'Farrell sts.), San Francisco, CA 94102. (✆ **888/GOHIUSA** or 415/788-5604. Fax 415/788-3023. www.sfhostels.com. 105 units (39 private, 241 dorm beds). Hostelling members $22–$25 per person in dorm; nonmembers $25–$29 per person in dorm; $55–$69 per private room. Children younger than 12 $12 when accompanied by a parent. Maximum stay 21 nights per month. Free limited parking. DC, MC, V. Bus: 7 or 38. Cable car: Powell-Mason line. BART: Powell St. **Amenities:** TV lounge; tour desk; kitchen; Internet access at kiosks (for a fee); laundry facilities. *In room:* Lockers, no phone.

2 South of Market (SoMa)

Bay Bridge Inn   The South of Market region is woefully short on budget accommodations, which is why I give the Bay Bridge Inn only a nominal recommendation. The only reason you might want to stay in this part of town is if you're here for a convention (the Moscone Convention Center and the San Francisco Museum of Modern Art are a few blocks away), you're a major Giants fan (SBC Park is just down the street), or you're a serious party hound who prefers to stay within stumbling distance of SoMa's club scene. The rooms score zero points for character, but they're quite clean and in good condition (think of it as a privately owned Motel 6). Queen-size beds are standard, and rooms with king-size beds run an extra $20. Parking is free (there's $20 a night saved), as is wireless Internet access, local calls, pastries, and coffee; and buses to nearly every corner of the city depart from the nearby Transbay Terminal.

966 Harrison St. (between Fifth and Sixth sts.), San Francisco, CA 94107. ✆ 415/397-0657. www.baybridgeinn.com. Fax 415/495-5117. 22 units. $65–$150 double. Light continental breakfast included in rates. AE, DC, DISC, MC, V. Free parking. Bus: 10, 20, 30, 42, 45, 50, 60, 70, or 80. *In room:* A/C, TV, free wireless Internet access.

The Mosser 🖈🖈 *Value* "Hip on the Cheap" might best sum up The Mosser, a highly atypical budget hotel that incorporates Victorian architecture with modern interior design. It originally opened in 1913 as a luxury hotel only to be dwarfed by the far more modern sky-rise hotels that surround it. But a major multimillion-dollar renovation in the fall of 2001 transformed this aging charmer into a sophisticated, stylish, and surprisingly affordable SoMa lodging. Guest rooms are replete with original Victorian flourishes—bay windows and hand-carved moldings—that juxtapose

---

Tips **Four Great Reasons to Stay with the Renesons**

When you're staying at a $500-per-night hotel, it's not the fancy Frette linens you're paying for, it's the service. The staff at four-star hotels are trained to do whatever it takes to make each guest feel special, so imagine my surprise when I discovered a quartet of low-key hotels just south of Market Street that offered four-star friendliness at one-star rates.

For four generations the family-owned Reneson Hotel Group has managed four small Best Western hotels along Seventh Street, between Mission and Howard streets, in addition to the Civic Center Inn, and the Renesons' dedication to hospitality is immediately evident as soon as you check in. The always-smiling and well-trained staff welcome the mostly repeat customers like old friends, offering a level of service rarely encountered at nonluxury hotels.

Each inn has its own geographical theme—the Mediterranean-style **Americania,** the Victorian-style **Carriage Inn,** the Spanish-style **Flamingo Inn,** and the European-style **Hotel Britton**—to suit a guest's particular taste. Your grandmother would probably prefer the boutique-style Hotel Britton, while young couples may prefer the more flamboyant and colorful Flamingo Inn. Me, I'm all about the heated outdoor swimming pool, fitness center, and on-site bar at the Americania. Rates start at about $120, but seasonal specials, such as their "Breakfast in San Francisco," bring the price down to $99 plus tax for two persons, including a full American breakfast, free parking, and complimentary shuttle service to and from Union Square.

Perks vary from inn to inn, ranging from free parking to complimentary continental breakfast, evening wine bar, Jacuzzis, fireplaces, and a business center. If, after visiting the Reneson website, you still can't decide which inn is best for you, just call their toll-free number and a staff member will help you choose. Regardless of your decision, you'll invariably be treated like an extended member of the Reneson family. For more information or reservations call ✆ **800/ 444-5816** or 415/864-7861 ext. 485, or log on to www.renesonhotels.com.

San Francisco Accommodations

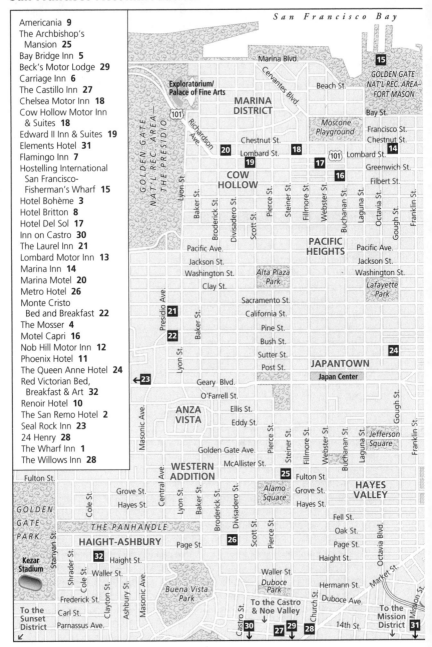

Americania **9**
The Archbishop's
  Mansion **25**
Bay Bridge Inn **5**
Beck's Motor Lodge **29**
Carriage Inn **6**
The Castillo Inn **27**
Chelsea Motor Inn **18**
Cow Hollow Motor Inn
  & Suites **18**
Edward II Inn & Suites **19**
Elements Hotel **31**
Flamingo Inn **7**
Hostelling International
  San Francisco-
  Fisherman's Wharf **15**
Hotel Bohème **3**
Hotel Britton **8**
Hotel Del Sol **17**
Inn on Castro **30**
The Laurel Inn **21**
Lombard Motor Inn **13**
Marina Inn **14**
Marina Motel **20**
Metro Hotel **26**
Monte Cristo
  Bed and Breakfast **22**
The Mosser **4**
Motel Capri **16**
Nob Hill Motor Inn **12**
Phoenix Hotel **11**
The Queen Anne Hotel **24**
Red Victorian Bed,
  Breakfast & Art **32**
Renoir Hotel **10**
The San Remo Hotel **2**
Seal Rock Inn **23**
24 Henry **28**
The Wharf Inn **1**
The Willows Inn **28**

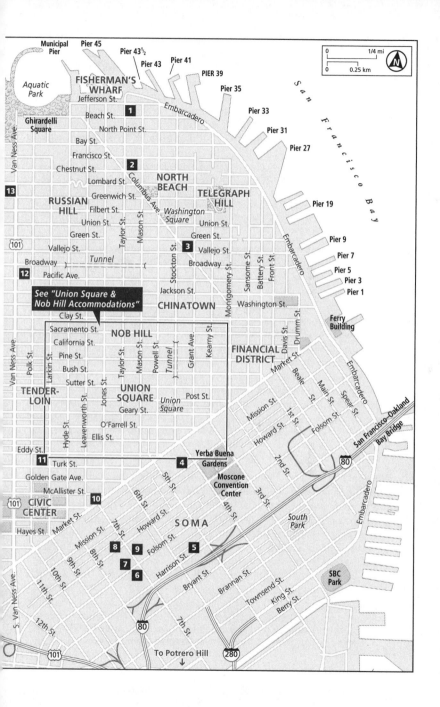

Municipal
Pier

Pier 45

Pier 43½

Pier 43

Pier 41

PIER 39

Pier 35

Aquatic
Park

FISHERMAN'S
WHARF

Jefferson St.

Embarcadero

Pier 33

Pier 31

Ghirardelli
Square

Beach St.   **1**

North Point St.

Bay St.

Pier 27

Francisco St.

Chestnut St.   **2**

NORTH
BEACH

Lombard St.

13

RUSSIAN
HILL

Greenwich St.

TELEGRAPH
HILL

Pier 19

Filbert St.

Union St.

Washington
Square

Union St.

Green St.

Green St.

Pier 9

Vallejo St.   **3**

Vallejo St.

Pier 7

Broadway

Tunnel

Broadway

Pier 5

12

Pacific Ave.

Pier 3

Pier 1

See "Union Square &
Nob Hill Accommodations"

Jackson St.

CHINATOWN

Washington St.

Clay St.

Ferry
Building

Sacramento St.

NOB HILL

California St.

FINANCIAL
DISTRICT

Pine St.

Bush St.

Tunnel

Sutter St.

TENDER-
LOIN

UNION
SQUARE

Union
Square

Post St.

Market St.

Geary St.

O'Farrell St.

Ellis St.

Mission St.

Howard St.

Folsom St.

Eddy St.

11

Turk St.

4

Yerba Buena
Gardens

Golden Gate Ave.

Moscone
Convention
Center

McAllister St.   **10**

101

CIVIC
CENTER

Market St.

Hayes St.

SOMA

South
Park

8   **9**

5

7

6

Harrison St.

Bryant St.

SBC
Park

Brannan St.

Townsend St.

King St.

Berry St.

80

To Potrero Hill

280

San Francisco Bay

San Francisco-Oakland Bay Bridge

well with the contemporary custom-designed furnishings, granite showers, stainless steel fixtures, ceiling fans, Frette linens, and modern electronics. The least expensive rooms share a bathroom but are an incredible deal with rates starting at $69. The hotel's restaurant, Annabelle's Bar and Bistro, serves continental breakfast, lunch, and dinner, and The Mosser even houses Studio Paradiso, a state-of-the-art recording studio. The location is excellent as well—3 blocks from Union Square, 2 blocks from the MOMA and Moscone Convention Center, and half a block from the cable car turnaround. It also borders on a "sketchy" street, but then again, so do most hotels a few blocks west of Union Square.

54 Fourth St. (at Market St.), San Francisco, CA 94103. ℂ 800/227-3804 or 415/986-4400. Fax 415/495-7653. www. themosser.com. 166 units, 112 with private bathroom. $159–$249 double (private bathroom); $69–$89 (shared bathroom). Rates include safe deposit boxes and mail services. AE, DC, DISC, MC, V. Parking $29 plus $10 for oversize vehicles. Streetcar: F, and all underground Muni and BART lines. **Amenities:** Restaurant; bar; 24-hr. concierge; same-day laundry service; dry cleaning. *In room:* TV, dataport, hair dryer, iron/ironing board, ceiling fan, CD player, voice mail, DSL Internet for $9.95 per day.

3 North Beach/Fisherman's Wharf

The San Remo Hotel 🏃🏃 *Value*   This small, European-style *pensione* is one of the best budget hotels in San Francisco. In a quiet North Beach neighborhood, within walking distance of Fisherman's Wharf, the Italianate Victorian structure originally served as a boardinghouse for dockworkers displaced by the great fire of 1906. As a result, the rooms are small and bathrooms are shared, but all is forgiven when it comes time to pay the bill. Rooms are decorated in cozy country style, with brass and iron beds; oak, maple, or pine armoires; and wicker furnishings. The immaculate shared bathrooms feature tubs and brass–pull-chain toilets with oak tanks and brass fixtures. If the penthouse is available, book it: You won't find a more romantic place to stay in San Francisco for so little money. It has its own bathroom, TV, fridge, and patio.

2237 Mason St. (at Chestnut St.), San Francisco, CA 94133. ℂ 800/352-REMO or 415/776-8688. Fax 415/776-2811. www.sanremohotel.com. 62 units, 61 with shared bathroom. $55–$95 double; $155–$175 penthouse suite. AE, DC, MC, V. Self-parking $10–$14. Bus: 10, 15, 30, or 47. Cable car: Powell-Mason line. Streetcar: F. **Amenities:** Access to nearby health club; chair massage; self-service laundry; TV lounge. *In room:* Ceiling fan.

The Wharf Inn 🏃🏃 *Value*   My top choice for good-value lodging at Fisherman's Wharf, the Wharf Inn offers above-average accommodations at one of the most popular tourist attractions in the world. Completely refurbished from 2002 through 2004 with new carpets debuting in 2005, rooms are done in handsome earth tones—muted greens, burnt orange, and sandy colors—and come well stocked. But more important, they are smack-dab in the middle of the wharf, 2 blocks from PIER 39 and the cable car turnaround, and they're within walking distance of The Embarcadero and North Beach. The inn is ideal for car-bound families because parking is free (that saves at least $25 a day right off the bat).

2601 Mason St. (at Beach St.), San Francisco, CA 94133. ℂ 800/548-9918 or 415/673-7411. Fax 415/776-2181. www.wharfinn.com. 51 units. $95–$199 double; $299–$449 penthouse. AE, DC, DISC, MC, V. Free parking. Bus: 10, 15, 39, or 47. Cable car: Powell-Mason and Powell-Hyde lines. Streetcar: F. **Amenities:** Access to nearby health club ($10 per day); concierge; tour desk; complimentary coffee/tea, and newspapers. *In room:* TV, dataport, hair dryer (on request), iron (on request).

WORTH A SPLURGE

Hotel Bohème 🏃🏃 *Finds*   Romance awaits at the intimate Bohème. Although it's located on the busiest strip in the neighborhood, once you climb the staircase to this narrow second-floor boutique hotel, you'll discover a style and demeanor reminiscent of a home in upscale Nob Hill. Alas, there are no common areas other than a little booth for check-in and a concierge, but rooms, lining a skinny corridor, though small, are truly sweet, with gauze-draped canopies, stylish decor such as ornate parasols shading ceiling lights, and walls dramatically colored with lavender, sage green, black, and pumpkin. *Note:* While the bathrooms are spiffy, they're also absolutely tiny and have showers only. The staff is ultra hospitable, and bonuses include sherry in the lobby each afternoon. Some fabulous cafes, restaurants, bars, and shops are just a few steps away, and Chinatown and Union Square are within walking distance. *Tip:* Request a room off the street side; these rooms are quieter.

444 Columbus Ave. (between Vallejo and Green sts.), San Francisco, CA 94133. © **415/433-9111.** Fax 415/362-6292. www.hotelboheme.com. 15 units. $149–$169 double. Rates include afternoon sherry. AE, DC, DISC, MC, V. Parking $12–$31 at nearby public garages. Bus: 12, 15, 30, 41, 45, or 83. Cable car: Powell-Mason line. **Amenities:** Concierge. *In room:* TV, dataport, hair dryer, iron, free wireless Internet access.

4 Marina District/Cow Hollow

Chelsea Motor Inn   This member of the "motel strip" that stretches from the Golden Gate Bridge to Van Ness Avenue is perfectly located for a stroll along Union Street or along the seaside Marina Green and Golden Gate Promenade (a great walk or jog). While the exterior is done in faux English Tudor style complete with an antique slate roof, the rooms are your generic motel type—large, clean, and unremarkable, but with a large bathroom, a Serta Perfect Sleeper queen-size bed, and a comfy seating area. The staff is extremely friendly and helpful; be sure to ask them for a room in the back, if available, to avoid traffic noise. If the Chelsea is full, try its sister property, the **Lombard Motor Inn** or **Cow Hollow Motor Inn & Suites** (see reviews below).

2095 Lombard St. (between Fillmore and Webster sts.), San Francisco, CA 94123. © **415/563-5600.** Fax 415/567-6475. www.chelseamotorinn.com. 60 units. $86–$135 double. $10 extra person. AE, DC, MC, V. Free parking. Bus: 22, 28, 30, or 76. *In room:* A/C, TV, fax, coffeemaker, hair dryer, iron, dataport, free wireless Internet access.

Cow Hollow Motor Inn & Suites ⚓ *(Kids)*   If you're less interested in being downtown than in playing in and around the beautiful bayfront Marina, check out this modest brick hotel on busy Lombard Street. There's no fancy theme, but each room, which was completely renovated in 2004, has cable TV, free local phone calls, free covered parking, and Internet access. Families will appreciate the one- and two-bedroom suites, which have full kitchens and dining areas as well as antique furnishings and surprisingly tasteful decor.

2190 Lombard St. (between Steiner and Fillmore sts.), San Francisco, CA 94123. © **415/921-5800.** Fax 415/922-8515. www.cowhollowmotorinn.com. 129 units. $86–$135 double; from $225 suite. Extra person $10. AE, DC, MC, V. Free parking. Bus: 28, 30, 43, or 76. **Amenities:** Access to nearby laundry; dry cleaning services. *In room:* A/C, TV, dataport, kitchens (in suites), coffeemaker, hair dryer, free wireless Internet access.

Edward II Inn & Suites ⚓⚓   This three-story "English country" inn has a room for almost anyone's budget, ranging from *pensione* units with shared bathrooms to luxuriously appointed suites and cottages with living rooms, kitchens, and whirlpool bathtubs. Originally built to house guests who attended the 1915 Pan-Pacific Exposition, it's still a good place to shack up in spotless and comfortably appointed rooms with cozy antique furnishings. Room prices even include a standard continental breakfast. Nearby Chestnut and Union streets offer some of the best shopping and dining in the city. The adjoining pub serves evening drinks daily. The only caveat is that the hotel's Lombard Street location is usually congested with traffic.

3155 Scott St. (at Lombard St.), San Francisco, CA 94123. ℂ 800/473-2846 or 415/922-3000. Fax 415/931-5784. www.edwardii.com. 32 units, 21 with private bathroom. $83–$89 double (shared bathroom); $115–$129 double (private bathroom); $185–$249 suite. Extra person $25. Rates include continental breakfast and evening sherry. AE, DISC, MC, V. Self-parking $12 per day nearby. Bus: 28, 30, 43, or 76. **Amenities:** Pub, Internet computer station (for nominal fee). *In room:* TV, dataport, hair dryer (on request), iron (on request), free Wi-Fi.

Lombard Motor Inn   The Lombard Motor Inn is one of the many big motels along Highway 101's approach to the Golden Gate Bridge, and a fine option if you're looking for a clean, decent-size room in the beautiful Marina District. Accommodations are spacious and a step above standard motel style—"with three-star AAA ratings," the manager reminds me. The immediate vicinity is not exactly charming, but with the neighborhoods of Pacific Heights and Cow Hollow, as well as the Palace of Fine Arts and the Marina promenade nearby, you'll be one of the lucky few who can park and meander around this crowded and popular area. Bonuses include free parking, free local calls, free wireless Internet, and baby cribs on request. Upon arrival, ask for a room in the back, if available, to avoid traffic noise.

1475 Lombard St. (at Franklin St.), San Francisco, CA 94123. ℂ 415/441-6000. Fax 415/441-4291. www.lombard motorinn.com. 48 units. $86–$125 double. $10 extra person. AE, DC, MC, V. Free parking. Bus: 42, 47, 49, 76, or 82X. *In room:* A/C, TV, fax, dataport, coffeemaker, iron, free wireless Internet access.

Marina Inn 𝔉𝔉 (Value)   Marina Inn is one of the best low-priced hotels in San Francisco. How it offers so much for so little is mystifying. Each guest room in the 1924 four-story Victorian looks like something from a country furnishings catalog, complete with rustic pinewood furniture, a four-poster bed with silky-soft comforter, pretty wallpaper, and soothing tones of rose, hunter green, and pale yellow. You also get remote-control televisions discreetly hidden in pine cabinetry—all for as little as *$65 a night!* Combine that with continental breakfast, friendly service, and an armada of shops and restaurants within easy walking distance, and there you have it: the top choice for best overall value. (*Note:* Traffic can be a bit noisy here, so the hotel added double panes on windows facing the street.)

3110 Octavia St. (at Lombard St.), San Francisco, CA 94123. ℂ 800/274-1420 or 415/928-1000. Fax 415/928-5909. www.marinainn.com. 40 units. Nov–Feb $65–$105 double; Mar–May $75–$125 double; June–Oct $85–$135 double. Rates include continental breakfast. AE, DC, DISC, MC, V. Self parking nearby (generally $20 per night).Bus: 28, 30, 43, or 76. *In room:* TV, hair dryer (on request), iron (on request).

Marina Motel 𝔉   Established in 1939, the Marina Motel is one of San Francisco's first motels, built for the opening of the Golden Gate Bridge. The same family has owned this peach-colored, Spanish-style stucco building for three generations, and they've taken exquisite care of it. All rooms look out onto an inner courtyard, which is awash with beautiful flowering plants and wall paintings by local artists. Though the rooms show minor signs of wear and tear, they're all quite clean, bright, quiet, and pleasantly decorated with framed lithographs of old San Francisco—a thoughtful touch that adds to the motel's old-fashioned character and which makes this budget accommodation stand out from all the rest along busy Lombard Street. Two-bedroom suites with fully equipped kitchens are also available. Location-wise, the Presidio and Marina Green are mere blocks away, and you can easily catch a bus downtown. Bonus: All rooms include a breakfast coupon valid for two entrees for the price of one at **Judy's Restaurant,** a short walk from the motel.

2576 Lombard St. (between Divisadero and Broderick sts.), San Francisco, CA 94123. ℂ **800/346-6118** or 415/921-9406. Fax 415/921-0364. www.marinamotel.com. 38 units. $89–$159 double; $199 suite. Lower rates in winter. Rates include 2-for-1 breakfast coupon at nearby cafe. AE, DISC, MC, V. Free covered parking. Bus: 28, 29, 30, 43, or 45. Pets accepted with $10 nightly fee. *In room:* Dataport, fridge, coffeemaker, hair dryer, iron.

Motel Capri   Of the Marina's motel selections, being a block off Lombard (Hwy. 101) makes all the difference when it comes to a quiet night's rest. Here the decor is anything but up-to-date (read: unintentionally retro, circa 1970s), but the place is squeaky clean and the beds are comfy. Plus you get free parking (a valuable commodity in the crowded Marina District) and complimentary coffee, tea, and hot chocolate in the lobby. A few bucks extra will get you a more modern hotel along Lombard; but if all you require is a quiet crash pad, this is the place. Families should consider a suite, which has four beds (2 doubles and 2 singles) and a kitchenette.

2015 Greenwich St. (at Buchanan St.), San Francisco, CA 94123. ℂ **415/346-4667.** Fax 415/346-3256. 46 units. $74–$109 double; $120–$160 suite. Complimentary hot beverages in the lobby. AE, DISC, MC, V. Free parking. Bus: 22, 41, or 45. *In room:* A/C, TV, dataport; kitchenette (in suites).

WORTH A SPLURGE

Hotel Del Sol 🄯🄯 *(Kids* *(Value*   The cheeriest motel in town is located just 2 blocks off the Marina District's bustling section of Lombard. Three-level Hotel del Sol is all about festive flair and luxury touches. The sunshine theme extends from the Miami Beach–style use of vibrant color, as in the yellow, red, orange, and blue exterior, to the heated courtyard pool, which beckons the youngish clientele as they head for their cars parked (for free!) in cabanalike spaces. (The great pool with pool toys can keep the tots busy all day.) Fair-weather fun doesn't stop at the front door of the hotel, which boasts 57 spacious rooms (updated in 2005) with equally perky interior decor (read: loud and very colorful) as well as unexpected extras like CD players, Aveda products, and tips on the town's happenings and shopping meccas. Suites also include mini fridges and DVD players.

3100 Webster St. (at Greenwich St.), San Francisco, CA 94123. ℂ **877/433-5765** or 415/921-5520. Fax 415/931-4137. www.thehoteldelsol.com. 57 units. $119–$189 double; $169–$229 suite. Rates include continental breakfast and complimentary newspapers in the lobby. AE, DC, DISC, MC, V. Free parking. Bus: 22, 28, 41, 43, 45, or 76. **Amenities:** Heated outdoor pool; same-day dry cleaning. *In room:* TV/VCR (DVD in suites), dataport, kitchenettes (in 3 units), fridge (in suites), iron, CD player, wireless Internet access ($10 per day).

The Laurel Inn 🄯🄯   If you don't mind being out of the downtown area, this lovely hotel, renovated in 1999, is one of the city's most tranquil, affordable places to rest your head. Tucked just beyond the southernmost tip of the Presidio and Pacific Heights, the outside is nothing impressive—just another motor inn. And that's what it was until the hotel group Joie de Vivre breathed new life into the place. Now decor is *très* chic and modern, with Zenlike influences (think W Hotel at half the price). Some rooms have excellent city views; all have spiffy bathrooms. The continental breakfast is fine, but why bother when you're across the street from Ella's (p. 127), which serves San Francisco's best breakfast? Other thoughtful touches: 24-hour coffee and tea service, pet-friendly rooms, and free parking. Add the great shopping 1 block away at Sacramento Street and the new and very hip bar, G, which serves libations and a surprisingly active slice of glamorous young Pacific Heights–style revelry, and there are plenty of reasons to stay here.

444 Presidio Ave. (at California Ave.), San Francisco, CA 94115. ℂ **800/552-8735** or 415/567-8467. Fax 415/928-1866. www.thelaurelinn.com. 49 units. $155–$190 double. Rates include continental breakfast and afternoon lemonade

and cookies. AE, DC, DISC, MC, V. Free parking. Bus: 1, 3, 4, or 43. Pets accepted. **Amenities:** Adjoining bar; concierge; same-day laundry; dry cleaning services; access to nearby mind-blowing JCC gym ($10 per day). *In room:* TV/VCR, dataport, kitchenette (in some units), hair dryer, iron, CD player, free Wi-Fi.

SUPER-CHEAP SLEEPS

Hostelling International San Francisco—Fisherman's Wharf ☆ *(Finds)*   Unbelievable but true—you can get front-row bay views for a mere $22 nightly. This hostel, on national park property, provides dorm-style accommodations and offers easy access to the Marina's shops and restaurants. Rooms sleep 2 to 12 people; communal space includes a fireplace, kitchen, dining room, coffee bar, and foosball. The breakfast alone practically makes this place worth the price. Make reservations well in advance because this place books up quickly.

Fort Mason, Building 240, San Francisco, CA 94123. © **800/909-4776** or 415/771-7277. Fax 415/771-1468. www.sf hostel.org. 170 beds. $22–$29 per person per night; kids $15–$17 per night. Rates include breakfast. MC, V. Free limited parking. Bus: 28, 30, 47, or 49. **Amenities:** Free wireless Internet access; computer stations (for small fee); self-service laundry and kitchen; meeting room; baggage storage; secure lockers.

5 Pacific Heights

Monte Cristo Bed and Breakfast ☆ *(Finds)*   Built in 1875, the Monte Cristo was once a bordello, a refuge after the 1906 earthquake, and a speakeasy; it's now one of the coolest old-style B&Bs in town. Located near Sacramento Street's boutique-shopping stretch—but far from Union Square and North Beach—the Monte Cristo seems a colorful mirage in a desert of gray concrete. Its elegant exterior (richly painted red, black, and cream) encloses equally exuberant accommodations. Every nook of the inn is adorned with period furnishings, antique wallpaper, cozy sitting areas, and sweet touches, such as the velvet curtains that frame each guest room's door. Heck, even the payphone booth is so attractive that you'll think of someone to call just to hang out in it. Bathrobes, stacks of newspapers, an engaging breakfast room—even the fact that some of the tasteful furniture is worn—make this place feel more like a stay at an old relative's house than at a hotel. *Note:* The front rooms are noisier, but the street quiets down at night; also, several rooms share the small, clean bathrooms.

600 Presidio (at Pine St.), San Francisco, CA 94115. © **415/931-1875.** Fax 415/931-6005. 14 units, 11 with private bathroom; 1 suite. $83 double (shared bathroom); $88–$98 double (private bathroom); $118 suite. Rates include buffet breakfast. AE, DC, DISC, MC, V. Limited street parking. Bus: 1, 2, 4, 31BX, or 43. *In room:* TV, no phone (in some rooms).

The Queen Anne Hotel ☆☆ *(Value)*   This majestic 1890 Victorian building, which was once a grooming school for upper-class young women, is today a stunning hotel. Restored in 1980 and most recently renovated in 2003, the four-story building recalls San Francisco's golden days. Walk under rich red draperies to the lavish "grand salon" lobby, complete with English oak wainscoting and period antiques. Guest rooms also contain antiques—armoires, marble-top dressers, and other Victorian pieces. Some have corner turret bay windows that look out on tree-lined streets, as well as separate parlor areas and wet bars; others have cozy reading nooks and fireplaces. All rooms have a telephone and nice bath amenities in their marble-tiled bathroom. Guests can relax in the parlor, with an impressive floor-to-ceiling fireplace, or in the hotel library. If you don't mind staying outside the downtown area, this hotel is highly recommended and very historic San Francisco in feel.

1590 Sutter St. (between Gough and Octavia sts.), San Francisco, CA 94109. © **800/227-3970** or 415/441-2828. Fax 415/775-5212. www.queenanne.com. 48 units. $99–$199 double; $169–$350 suite. Extra person $10. Rates include continental breakfast on weekday mornings, local complimentary limousine service, afternoon tea and sherry, and morning newspaper. AE, DC, DISC, MC, V. Parking $14. Bus: 2, 3, or 4. **Amenities:** Access to nearby health club ($15 daily); 24-hr. concierge; business center; same-day dry cleaning; front desk safe. *In room:* TV, dataport, hair dryer, iron, free wireless Internet access.

6 Civic Center & Environs

WORTH A SPLURGE

The Archbishop's Mansion ✦✦ *Finds*   One thing is certain: The archbishop who built this 1904 Belle Epoque beauty was no Puritan. Though the hotel isn't world-class, it is drippingly romantic, tucked away in a very residential but central neighborhood, and likely to be the most opulently decorated B&B you could possibly imagine. Here, within the uniquely adorned rooms, it's all about whimsy and drama. The Don Giovanni suite—larger than many San Francisco houses—holds a huge, French four-poster bed with cherubs carved into it, a grand fireplace, elaborate linens, and a shower with seven heads that you'll never want to leave. Slightly closer to Earth is the Carmen suite, which has a deadly romantic combination of a claw-foot bathtub fronting a wood-burning fireplace. In the morning, breakfast is delivered to the guest rooms, and in the evening, wine is served in the elegant parlor. With a CD player in every room and a video and CD library accessible to every guest, this is one hotel that is enticing enough to make you linger in your room.

1000 Fulton St. (at Steiner St.), San Francisco, CA 94117. © **800/543-5820** or 415/563-7872. Fax 415/885-3193. www.thearchbishopsmansion.com. 15 units. $149–$499 double. Rates include continental breakfast and evening wine. AE, DC, MC, V. Limited free parking. Bus: 5, 22, or 24. **Amenities:** Access to nearby health club ($20 daily); concierge; room service (snacks and alcohol only); same-day laundry; dry cleaning services. *In room:* TV/VCR, dataport, hair dryer, iron, CD player, free Wi-Fi.

Phoenix Hotel ✦✦ *Kids*   If you'd like to tell your friends back home that you stayed in the same hotel as Linda Ronstadt, Arlo Guthrie, Moby, and the Red Hot Chili Peppers, this is the place. On the fringes of San Francisco's less-than-pleasant Tenderloin District, this retro 1950s-style hotel is a gathering place for visiting rock musicians, writers, and filmmakers who crave a dose of Southern California—hence the palm trees and pastel colors. The focal point of the Palm Springs–style hotel is a small,

---

Finds **Hip Hostel**

Good news for hip hostellers: There's finally a budget option in the heart of the Mission District's trendy shopping and hopping nightlife. Opened in 2004, the **Elements Hotel** is a brightly painted crash pad that announces itself from the outside with orange and yellow squares. Inside, options include private rooms, shared dorms, and double-bed and twin-bunk rooms, all with private bathrooms. Add to that Wi-Fi Internet access throughout the hotel, a free high-speed Internet lounge, rooftop parties, lockers, luggage storage and laundry facilities, free linens, TVs (in private rooms), and all the neighboring restaurants and bars, and you've got it made, provided you don't mind the Mission's grit and are up for hunkering down with traveling party people. The hostel is at 2524 Mission St. (between 21st and 22nd sts.; © **866/327-8407** or 415/647-4100; www.elementssf.com). Rates per person are between $25 and $30; expect higher rates and minimum stays during holidays.

heated outdoor pool adorned with a mural by artist Francis Forlenza and ensconced in a modern-sculpture garden.

The rooms, while more pop than plush, were updated in 2005 and are comfortably equipped with bright festive furnishings and original local art. In addition to the usual amenities, the hotel offers VCRs and movies on request and a party vibe that's not part of the package at most city hotels. Some big bonuses: free parking and the hotel's hot new restaurant and club, the very groovy and very hip Bambuddha Lounge (© **415/ 885-5088**), which serves Southeast Asian cuisine with cocktail-lounge flair.

601 Eddy St. (at Larkin St.), San Francisco, CA 94109. © **800/248-9466** or 415/776-1380. Fax 415/885-3109. www.thephoenixhotel.com. 44 units. $149–$169 double; $219–$279 suite. Rates include continental breakfast. AE, DC, MC, V. Free parking. Bus: 19, 31, 38, or 47. **Amenities:** Bar; heated outdoor pool; concierge; tour desk; massage; same-day laundry; dry cleaning services. *In room:* TV, VCR (on request), dataport, fridge (some rooms), hair dryer, iron, microwave (some rooms), wireless Internet access (for a fee).

7 Haight-Ashbury

Metro Hotel   It's not exactly in the heart of the Haight, but from this remodeled Victorian you can walk to the Castro, Golden Gate Park, or upper or lower Haight in under 30 minutes. Buses stop a block away and blast downtown and to the Haight every few minutes (it's a 10-minute trip once you're on board). The neighborhood isn't the best in town, but it beats Civic Center by a long shot and has plenty of cheap restaurants nearby. The high-ceilinged hotel is reminiscent of a European *pensione*— smallish rooms, nothing too fancy, but clean and friendly with everything you need to get by. There's a garden out back, too. *Note:* Parking is free in the evenings, but you'll have to find your own during the day.

319 Divisadero St. (between Oak and Page sts.), San Francisco, CA 94117. © **415/861-5364.** Fax 415/863-1970. www.metrohotelsf.com. 24 units. $66 double (double bed); $77 double (queen-size bed); $99–$120 suite. AE, DC, DISC, MC, V. Free overnight parking 6pm–9am. Bus: 6, 7, 16, 24, 66, or 71. **Amenities:** Restaurant (French bistro); bar. *In room:* TV.

Red Victorian Bed, Breakfast & Art ⊛ *Finds*   Still having flashbacks from the 1960s? Or want to? No problem. A room at the Red Vic, in the heart of the Haight, will throw you right back into the Summer of Love (minus, of course, the free-flowing LSD). Owner Sami Sunchild has re-created this historic hotel and "Peace Center" as a living museum honoring the bygone era. The rooms are inspired by San Francisco's sights and history, and are decorated accordingly. The Flower Child Room has a sun on the ceiling and a rainbow on the wall, while the bed sports a hand-crocheted shawl headboard. The Peacock Suite, though pricey, is one funky room, with red beads, a canopy bed, and multicolored patterns throughout. The clincher is its bedroom bathtub, which has a circular pass-through looking into the sitting area. Four guest rooms have private bathrooms; the rest share four bathrooms down the hall. In general, the rooms and bathrooms are clean and the furnishings lighthearted. Rates for longer stays are a great deal. A family-style continental breakfast is a gathering place for a worldly array of guests, and there's a gift shop called the Meditation Room and Peace Center. Be sure to check out Sami's website to get a sneak peek at the weird and wonderful guest rooms.

1665 Haight St. (between Cole and Belvedere sts.), San Francisco, CA 94117. © **415/864-1978.** Fax 415/863-3293. www.redvic.com. 18 units, 4 with private bathroom. $86–$110 double (shared bathroom); $120–$126 double (private bathroom); $200 suite. Rates include continental breakfast and afternoon tea. Lower rates for stays of 3 days or more. Guarded parking lot nearby for $12 daily. AE, DISC, MC, V. Bus: 7, 66, 71, or 73. Streetcar: N.

8 Richmond District

Seal Rock Inn ⚑ *Finds*   You would think that a city surrounded on three sides by water would have a slew of seaside hotels. Oddly enough, it has very few, one of which is the Seal Rock Inn. It's about as far from Union Square and Fisherman's Wharf as you can place a hotel in San Francisco, but that just makes it all the more unique. The motel fronts Sutro Heights Park, which faces Ocean Beach. Most rooms in the four-story structure have at least partial views of the ocean; at night, the sounds of the surf and distant foghorns lull guests to sleep. The rooms, although large and spotless, are basic, with rose and teal floral accents. Only some rooms have kitchenettes, but phones, TVs, fridges, covered parking, and use of the enclosed patio and pool area are standard. On the ground floor of the inn is a small old-fashioned restaurant serving breakfast and lunch. Golden Gate Park and the Presidio are both nearby, and the Geary bus—which snails its way to Union Square and Market Street—stops right out front.

545 Point Lobos Ave. (at 48th Ave.), San Francisco, CA 94121. ℂ **888/732-5762** or 415/752-8000. www.sealrock inn.com. Fax 415/752-6034. 27 units. $105–$143 double. AE, MC, V. Free parking. Bus: 38 or 38L. **Amenities:** Outdoor pool (heated in summer only). *In room:* TV, dataport, kitchenette (in some rooms), fridge, coffeemaker, hair dryer, iron.

9 The Castro

Though everyone is welcome, hotels in the Castro mainly cater to a gay and lesbian clientele. The options listed below are safe choices in the heart of the Castro, but the location is the real reason to stay here—pick any of the following choices and you'll be in the center of one of the most liberated gay environments in the world.

Beck's Motor Lodge ⚑   In a town where DINK (double income, no kids) tourists happily spend fistfuls of money, you'd think someone would create a gay luxury hotel—or even a moderate hotel, for that matter. But absurdly, the most commercial and modern accommodations in the touristy Castro is this run-of-the-mill motel. Standard but contemporary, the ultra tidy rooms include motel furnishings updated within the last year, a sun deck overlooking upper Market Street's action, and free parking. Unless you're into homey B&Bs, this is really your only choice in the area—fortunately, it's very well maintained.

2222 Market St. (at 15th St.), San Francisco, CA 94114. ℂ **800/227-4360** in the U.S., except Calif., 800/955-2325 within CA or 415/621-8212. Fax 415/241-0435. 58 units. $104–$145 double. AE, DC, DISC, MC, V. Free parking. Bus: 8 or 37. Streetcar: F. **Amenities:** Coin-operated washer/dryers. *In room:* TV, dataport, fridge, coffeemaker.

The Castillo Inn ⚑   Just 2 minutes from the heart of the Castro, this charming little house provides a safe, quiet environment. Catering mostly to gay men (although anyone is welcome), the Castillo makes its clientele feel at home. Hardwood floors decorated with throw rugs aid in the warmth. Rooms are small yet cozy, and the front desk uses voice mail to collect phone messages. The Castillo also offers the shared use of a large refrigerator and microwave oven in the kitchen.

48 Henry St., San Francisco, CA 94114. ℂ **800/865-5112** or 415/864-5111. Fax 415/641-1321. 4 units, all with shared bathroom. $80 double. Rates include continental breakfast. AE, MC, V. Bus: 8, 22, 24, or 37. Streetcar: F, J, K, L, or M. **Amenities:** Shared kitchen with fridge and microwave. *In room:* No phone.

Inn on Castro ⚑   One of the better choices in the Castro, half a block from all the action, is this Edwardian-style inn decorated with contemporary furnishings, original modern art, and fresh flowers throughout. It definitely feels more like a home than an inn, so if you like less commercial abodes, this place is for you. Most rooms share a small back patio, and the suite has a private entrance and outdoor sitting area. The inn also offers access to four individual nearby apartments ($85–$160, with discounts on stays of more than 4 nights) with complete kitchens.

321 Castro St. (at Market St.), San Francisco, CA 94114. © **415/861-0321.** Fax 415/861-0321. www.innoncastro.com. 8 units (2 with shared bathroom across the hall), 4 apts. $85–$155 double; $125–$160 suite. Rates include full breakfast and evening brandy. AE, DC, MC, V. Self parking $20 daily. Streetcar: F, K, L, or M. **Amenities:** Hall fridges stocked with complimentary sodas and water. *In room:* TV, dataport, free wireless Internet access, hair dryer.

24 Henry Its Castro location is not the only thing that makes 24 Henry a good choice for gay travelers. The building, an 1870s Victorian on a serene side street, is quite charming. The 10 guest rooms have high ceilings, period furniture, and voice mail. Guests tired of tromping around the neighborhood can watch TV or read in the double parlor (where breakfast is served). All rooms are nonsmoking.

24 Henry St. (near Sanchez St.), San Francisco, CA 94114. © **800/900-5686** or 415/864-5686. Fax 415/864-0406. www.24henry.com. 10 units, 3 with private bathroom. $45–$70 double (shared bathroom); $89–$109 double (private bathroom). Extra person $20. Rates include continental breakfast. AE, MC, V. Self parking $20 daily. Bus: 8, 22, 24, or 37. Streetcar: F, J, K, L, M, or N. *In room:* free Wi-Fi.

The Willows Inn ★ Right in the heart of the Castro, the all-nonsmoking Willows Inn employs a staff eager to greet and attend to visitors. The country and antique willow furnishings don't strictly suit a 1903 Edwardian home, but everything's quite comfortable—especially considering the extras, which include an expanded continental breakfast (fresh fruit, yogurt, baked goods, gourmet coffee, eggs, assorted teas, and orange juice), the morning paper, nightly cocktails, a sitting room, and a pantry with limited kitchen facilities. The homey rooms vary in size from large (queen-size bed) to smaller (double bed) and are priced accordingly. Each room has a vanity sink, and all the rooms share eight bathrooms and shower rooms.

710 14th St. (near Church and Market sts.), San Francisco, CA 94114. © **800/431-0277** or 415/431-4770. Fax 415/431-5295. www.willowssf.com. 12 units, all with shared bathroom. $99–$109 double; $139–$159 suite. Rates include continental breakfast, complimentary newspaper and evening coctails. AE, DC, DISC, MC, V. Self parking for $18 to $20 daily. Bus: 22 or 37. Streetcar: Church St. station (across the street) or F. **Amenities:** Sitting room, shared pantry with limited kitchen facilities. *In room:* TV/VCR, free Wi-Fi, fridge.

10 Near the Airport

Comfort Suites *(Kids)* Two miles north of the airport, well outside the heart of the city, Comfort Suites is a well-appointed option for travelers on the way into or out of town. Each studio-suite has a king-size bed, queen-size sleeper sofa (great for the kids), and all the basic amenities for weary travelers. There are also enough pay cable channels to keep you glued to your TV set for an entire day. Rooms are fine, but the freebies are the most attractive part of this hotel: continental breakfast, an airport shuttle, and use of the outdoor hot tub.

121 E. Grand Ave., South San Francisco, CA 94080. © **800/293-1794** or 650/589-7100. Fax 650/589-7796. www.csusfo.com. 168 units. $109 double. Rates include continental breakfast. AE, DC, DISC, MC, V. Free parking. **Amenities:** Outdoor Jacuzzi; free airport shuttle. *In room:* A/C, TV, dataport (in some rooms), fridge, coffeemaker, hair dryer, iron, microwave.

Embassy Suites ★ If you've stayed at an Embassy Suites before, you know the drill. But this hotel is one of the best airport options, if only for the fact that every room is a suite. But there is more: The property has an indoor pool, whirlpool, courtyard with fountain, palm trees, and a bar/restaurant. Plus, each tastefully decorated two-room suite was updated in 2005 and has nice additions such as two TVs. Additionally, a complimentary breakfast of your choice is available before you're whisked to the airport on the free shuttle—all that and the price is still right.

250 Gateway Blvd., South San Francisco, CA 94080. ℂ **800/EMBASSY** or 650/589-3400. Fax 650/589-1183. www. embassysf.com. 312 units. $109–$159 double. Rates include breakfast and complimentary evening cocktails. AE, DC, MC, V. Free self parking. **Amenities:** Restaurant; bar; indoor pool; Jacuzzi; complimentary airport shuttle. *In room:* A/C, TV, Wi-Fi ($9.95/day), fridge, coffeemaker, hair dryer, iron, microwave.

Holiday Inn   Considering all the free amenities—movie channels, 24-hour airport shuttle, free guest parking—a room at this Holiday Inn is surprisingly reasonable. Granted, there's nary a thing to see or do within a 10-mile radius, but as a stop before a morning flight, the Holiday Inn is always a safe bet: The airport is a mere 5 minutes away on the hotel's complimentary shuttle. The rooms are classic Holiday Inn: large, clean, and inoffensively dull, with the usual amenities.

San Francisco International Airport North, 275 S. Airport Blvd. (off Hwy. 101), South San Francisco, CA 94080. ℂ **800/ HOLIDAY** or 650/873-3550. Fax 650/873-4524. www.holidayinnssf.com. 224 units. $90–$195 double. Free parking. AE, DC, DISC, MC, V. **Amenities:** Restaurant (American/Barbeque); bar; health club; complimentary airport shuttle. *In room:* A/C, TV w/pay movies, dataport, coffeemaker, hair dryer, iron.

San Francisco Airport North Travelodge *(Kids*   The Travelodge is a good choice for families, mainly because of the hotel's large heated pool. The rooms are as ordinary as you'd expect from a Travelodge. Still they're comfortable and come with plenty of perks like Showtime and free toll-free and credit-card calls. Each junior suite has a microwave and refrigerator. The clincher is the 24-hour complimentary shuttle, which makes the 2-mile trip to the airport in 5 minutes.

326 S. Airport Blvd. (off Hwy. 101), South San Francisco, CA 94080. ℂ **800/578-7878** or 650/583-9600. Fax 650/873-9392. www.sfotravelodge.com. 199 units. $79–$129 double. Free parking. AE, DC, DISC, MC, V. **Amenities:** Restaurant; heated outdoor pool; complimentary airport shuttle; basic business services; dry cleaning; Internet access at computer station (for fee). *In room:* A/C, TV w/pay movies, coffeemaker, hair dryer, iron, safe, microwaves (in some rooms).

7

Great Deals on Dining

Afghan, Burmese, Cambodian, Cajun, Moroccan, Persian, Ethiopian—whatever cuisine you're in the mood for, this city serves it. With more than 3,300 reasons to avoid cooking at home, more San Franciscans eat out than any other city's citizens in the U.S. And all you need to join the dinner party is a little money and an adventurous palate, because half the fun of visiting San Francisco is the opportunity to sample the flavors of the world in one fell swoop. Best of all, much of the city's greatest eating experiences are its small, affordable neighborhood haunts, the kind you'll never find unless someone (that would be me) lets you in on San Francisco's dining secrets.

To help you decide where to dine I've categorized the restaurants by area and by price (for a dinner). The majority of restaurants fall into the $8 to $15 range; everything below or above this range is placed into either the **Super-Cheap Eats** (most main courses are $9 or less) or **Worth a Splurge** (most main courses are more than $15) categories. These categories reflect the cost per person for a main course and a beverage—which means you *can* get away with spending that amount, but you can also blow your budget if you go crazy on appetizers, cocktails, coffee, and dessert.

While dining in San Francisco is almost always a hassle-free experience, there are a few things you should keep in mind the next time you eat out:

- If there's a long wait for a table, ask if you can order at the bar, which is often faster, more affordable, and more fun.
- Don't leave *anything* valuable in your car while dining, particularly in or near high-crime areas such as the Mission, downtown, or—believe it or not—Fisherman's Wharf (thieves know tourists with nice cameras and a trunkful of mementos are headed there). Also, it's best to give the parking valet only the key to your car, *not* your hotel room or house key.
- ***Remember:*** It is against the law to smoke in any restaurant in San Francisco, even if it has a separate bar or lounge. You're welcome to smoke outside, however.
- When choosing a restaurant, keep in mind that there are ways to eat in places beyond your budget. Many high-end restaurants offer a bar and lounge menu of equal quality as the main menu (in fact, I prefer eating at the bar). Also consider heading to the pricier restaurants for lunch.
- If you want a table at the more expensive "Worth a Splurge" restaurants with the best reputations, you should book at least 6 weeks ahead for weekends and several weeks ahead for a table during the week.
- This ain't New York: Plan on dining early. Most restaurants close their kitchens around 10pm.
- If you're driving to a restaurant, add extra time into your itinerary to find parking, which can be an especially infuriating exercise in areas like the

---

Tips Reservations Tip

To make reservations online, visit **www.opentable.com**, where you can save seats in San Francisco and the Bay Area in real time.

Mission, Downtown, the Marina, and most everywhere else for that matter. And expect to pay around $10 for valet parking if the restaurant offers it.

1 Restaurants by Cuisine

AMERICAN

Balboa Café ✿ (Marina District/ Cow Hollow, p. 126)

Barney's Gourmet Hamburgers ✿ (Marina District/Cow Hollow, p. 129)

Beach Chalet Brewery & Restaurant ✿ (Sunset District, p. 138)

Boulevard ✿✿ (South of Market [SoMa], p. 114)

Café de la Presse (Union Square, p. 104)

Chow ✿✿ (The Castro, p. 140)

Dottie's True Blue Café ✿✿ (Union Square, p. 104)

Ella's ✿✿ (Marina District/ Cow Hollow, p. 127)

Firewood Café ✿✿ (The Castro, p. 140)

Fog City Diner ✿ (Fisherman's Wharf, p. 123)

Hard Rock Cafe (Fisherman's Wharf, p. 124)

Levende Lounge ✿✿ (Mission District, p. 142)

Mecca ✿ (The Castro, p. 141)

Mel's Drive-In ✿ (Marina District/Cow Hollow, p. 128)

Mo's Gourmet Burgers ✿✿ (North Beach, p. 121)

Postrio ✿✿ (Union Square, p. 108)

RNM ✿ (Haight-Ashbury, p. 135)

San Francisco Art Institute Café ✿ (North Beach, p. 123)

Sears Fine Foods ✿ (Union Square, p. 107)

Tommy's Joynt (Civic Center & Environs, p. 132)

ASIAN

AsiaSF ✿ (South of Market [SoMa], p. 110)

BASQUE/BASQUE TAPAS

Bocadillos ✿✿ (Union Square, p. 102)

BELGIAN

Frjtz Fries ✿ (Civic Center & Environs, p. 132)

BREAKFAST

Dottie's True Blue Café ✿✿ (Union Square, p. 104)

Ella's ✿✿ (Marina District/ Cow Hollow, p. 127)

Home Plate ✿ (Marina District/ Cow Hollow, p. 129)

BURGERS

Barney's Gourmet Hamburgers ✿ (Marina District/Cow Hollow, p. 129)

Mo's Gourmet Burgers ✿✿ (North Beach, p. 121)

BURMESE

Burma Superstar ✿✿ (Richmond District, p. 136)

CAFES
Caffe Centro ❀ (South of Market
[SoMa], p. 114)
The Grove ❀ (Marina District/
Cow Hollow, p. 129)

CAJUN
Lou's Pier 47 (Fisherman's Wharf,
p. 124)

CALIFORNIA
AsiaSF ❀ (South of Market [SoMa],
p. 110)
Café Flore (The Castro, p. 139)
Cafe Kati ❀❀ (Pacific Heights,
p. 130)
Café Metropol (Union Square,
p. 104)
Caffé Luna Piena ❀ (The Castro,
p. 139)
Enrico's ❀ (North Beach, p. 119)
Gordon Biersch Brewery Restaurant
❀ (South of Market [SoMa],
p. 111)
Levende Lounge ❀❀ (Mission
District, p. 142)
Pluto's ❀ (Marina District/
Cow Hollow, p. 129)

CARIBBEAN
Cha Cha Cha ❀❀ (Haight-Ashbury,
p. 134)

CHINESE/DIM SUM
Brandy Ho's Hunan Food ❀
(Chinatown, p. 115)
Eliza's ❀❀ (Civic Center & Environs,
p. 132)
Gold Mountain ❀ (Chinatown,
p. 115)
Great Eastern ❀ (Chinatown, p. 116)
House of Nanking ❀ (Chinatown,
p. 116)
Hunan Home's ❀❀ (Chinatown,
p. 116)
Oriental Pearl ❀ (Chinatown, p. 116)
R&G Lounge ❀❀ (Chinatown,
p. 118)
Sam Wo (Chinatown, p. 118)

Ton Kiang ❀❀ (Richmond District,
p. 137)
Yank Sing ❀❀ (Financial District,
p. 108)

CREPES
Crepes on Cole (Haight-Ashbury,
p. 136)
Ti Couz ❀ (Mission District, p. 144)

DELIS
Boudin Sourdough Bakery & Café
(Fisherman's Wharf, p. 124)
Mocca ❀ (Union Square, p. 106)

EAST-WEST FUSION
Cafe Kati ❀❀ (Pacific Heights,
p. 130)

FRENCH
Café Claude ❀ (Union Square,
p. 102)
Café de la Presse (Union Square,
p. 104)
Chez Nous ❀❀ (Pacific Heights,
p. 130)
Forbes Island ❀ (Fisherman's Wharf,
p. 126)
Grand Café ❀❀ (Union Square,
p. 107)
Isa ❀❀ (Marina District/
Cow Hollow, p. 128)

GREEK
Kokkari ❀❀❀ (Financial District,
p. 109)

ITALIAN
A16 ❀❀ (Marina District/
Cow Hollow, p. 130)
Café Metropol (Union Square,
p. 104)
Cafe Pescatore ❀ (Fisherman's Wharf,
p. 123)
Caffè Macaroni ❀❀ (North Beach,
p. 118)
Caffè Sport ❀ (North Beach, p. 119)
Capp's Corner ❀ (North Beach,
p. 119)

Delfina (Mission District, p. 141)

E'Angelo Restaurant (Marina District/Cow Hollow, p. 127)

Emporio Armani Cafe (Union Square, p. 105)

Firewood Café (The Castro, p. 140)

Gira Polli (North Beach, p. 119)

Golden Boy Pizza (North Beach, p. 123)

The Gold Spike (North Beach, p. 120)

Il Pollaio (North Beach, p. 120)

Kuleto's (Union Square, p. 105)

L'Osteria del Forno (North Beach, p. 120)

Mario's Bohemian Cigar Store (North Beach, p. 121)

Mocca (Union Square, p. 106)

Nob Hill Café (Nob Hill/Russian Hill, p. 110)

North Beach Pizza (North Beach, p. 121)

Pasta Pomodoro (North Beach, p. 121)

Puccini & Pinetti (Union Square, p. 106)

Sodini's Green Valley Restaurant (North Beach, p. 122)

The Stinking Rose (North Beach, p. 122)

Tommaso's (North Beach, p. 122)

JAPANESE

Ace Wasabi's Rock 'n' Roll Sushi (Marina District/Cow Hollow, p. 126)

Hana Zen (Union Square, p. 105)

Kabuto A&S (Richmond District, p. 136)

Mifune (Japantown, p. 131)

Sanppo (Japantown, p. 131)

Sanraku (Union Square, p. 106)

MEDITERRANEAN

Caffé Luna Piena (The Castro, p. 139)

Foreign Cinema (Mission District, p. 145)

Kokkari (Financial District, p. 109)

La Méditerranée (Pacific Heights, p. 130)

Truly Mediterranean (Mission District, p. 145)

Zuni Café (Civic Center & Environs, p. 133)

MEXICAN

Andalé Taqueria (Marina District/Cow Hollow, p. 128)

Puerto Alegre Restaurant (Mission District, p. 144)

Taquerias La Cumbre (Mission District, p. 144)

Zona Rosa (Haight-Ashbury, p. 136)

MIDDLE EASTERN

Kan Zaman (Haight-Ashbury, p. 135)

MOROCCAN

Aziza (Richmond District, p. 138)

NOODLES

Citrus Club (Haight-Ashbury, p. 134)

PIZZA

Golden Boy Pizza (North Beach, p. 123)

Little Star Pizza (Western Addition, p. 133)

L'Osteria del Forno (North Beach, p. 120)

Marcello's Pizza (The Castro, p. 141)

Nob Hill Café (Nob Hill/Russian Hill, p. 110)

North Beach Pizza (North Beach, p. 121)

Pauline's (Mission District, p. 142)

SEAFOOD

Lou's Pier 47 (Fisherman's Wharf, p. 124)

Swan Oyster Depot 𝕣𝕣 (Nob Hill/Russian Hill, p. 110)

SINGAPOREAN

Straits Café 𝕣 (Richmond District, p. 137)

SOUTHEAST ASIAN

Betelnut 𝕣 (Marina District/ Cow Hollow, p. 127)

SPANISH

ThirstyBear Brewing Company 𝕣 (South of Market [SoMa], p. 114)

STEAK

Lou's Pier 47 (Fisherman's Wharf, p. 124)

SUSHI

Ace Wasabi's Rock 'n' Roll Sushi 𝕣𝕣 (Marina District/Cow Hollow, p. 126)

Isobune 𝕣 (Japantown, p. 131)

Kabuto A&S 𝕣𝕣 (Richmond District, p. 136)

Nippon Sushi (The Castro, p. 140)

Sanraku 𝕣 (Union Square, p. 106)

Yum Yum Fish 𝕣 (Sunset District, p. 139)

THAI

Cha Am Thai 𝕣 (South of Market [SoMa], p. 111)

Khan Toke Thai House 𝕣𝕣 (Richmond District, p. 137)

Manora's 𝕣 (South of Market [SoMa], p. 111)

Neecha Thai 𝕣 (Japantown, p. 131)

Thep Phanom 𝕣𝕣 (Haight-Ashbury, p. 135)

VIETNAMESE

Pho Hóa 𝕣 (Union Square, p. 106)

Saigon Saigon (Mission District, p. 144)

The Slanted Door 𝕣𝕣 (Financial District, p. 109)

Thanh Long 𝕣 (Sunset District, p. 133)

Tú Lan 𝕣 (South of Market [SoMa], p. 114)

2 Union Square

Bocadillos 𝕣𝕣 *Finds* BASQUE/BASQUE TAPAS   The latest restaurant from Piperade chef and owner Gerald Hirigoyen is flat-out fabulous if you're in the mood for tapas or Spanish-influenced small plates. Hirigoyen celebrates his Basque roots with outstanding calamari with creamy tomato-and-garlic romesco sauce, scallops "mole cortado" with sherry and orange, caramelized quail, sautéed hot peppers, tuna carpaccio, decadent foie gras sushi rolls, and oh-my-is-this-good warm chocolate cake with sautéed bananas. In fact, there are so many tasty snacks on the menu you might find yourself returning to this small, casual Financial District space with orange-painted brick walls to pull up a chair at the wine bar, tall tables, or centerpiece "community table" to snack your way to heaven—especially since prices range from $3 to $12 per plate. But don't come anticipating a formal dining environment—or a strong cocktail. This place is cafe-casual and beer-and-wine only.

710 Montgomery St. (at Washington St.). ☎ **415/982-2622.** www.bocasf.com. Breakfast $2–$5.25, lunch and dinner small items $3–$12. AE, MC, V. Mon–Fri 7am–11pm; Sat 5–11pm. Closed Sun. Bus: 15, 30X, or 41.

Café Claude 𝕣 FRENCH   Euro transplants love Café Claude, a crowded and lively restaurant tucked into a narrow (and very European feeling) side street near Union Square. Seemingly everything—every table, spoon, saltshaker, and waiter—is imported from France. With prices topping out at about $20 for classic fare like steak tartare; steamed mussels; duck confit; escargot; and steak with spinach gratin and crisp potatoes, Café Claude offers an affordable slice of Paris in San Francisco. There is live

Union Square & Financial District Dining

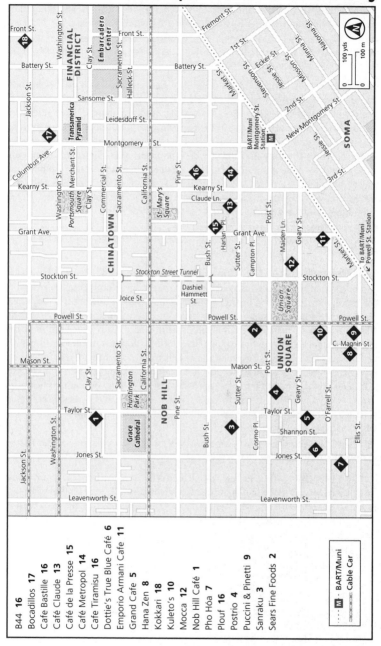

B44 **16**
Bocadillos **17**
Café Bastille **16**
Café Claude **13**
Café de la Presse **15**
Café Metropol **14**
Café Tiramisu **16**
Dottie's True Blue Café **6**
Emporio Armani Cafe **11**
Grand Cafe **5**
Hana Zen **8**
Kokkari **18**
Kuleto's **10**
Mocca **12**
Nob Hill Café **1**
Pho Hóa **7**
Plouf **16**
Postrio **4**
Puccini & Pinetti **9**
Sanraku **3**
Sears Fine Foods **2**

M – BART/Muni
Cable Car

jazz on Thursdays, Fridays, and Saturdays from 7:30 to 10:30pm, and atmospheric sidewalk seating for 30 diners is available when the weather permits.

7 Claude Lane (off Sutter St.). ℂ 415/392-3515. www.cafeclaude.com. Reservations recommended. Main courses $8–$12 lunch, $14–$20 dinner. AE, DC, DISC, MC, V. Mon 11:30am–5:30pm; Tues–Wed 11:30am–10pm; Thurs–Sat 11:30am–10:30pm. Bus: 30. Cable car: Powell-Mason line.

Café de la Presse AMERICAN/FRENCH Europeans will find this bright corner cafe and international newsstand familiarly comforting. But you needn't hail from the Continent to enjoy the flashy foreign magazines, children's books, travel guides, coffee drinks, sidewalk seating, and French-speaking staff. Its location, directly across from the Chinatown gates, makes it one of the best places in the Union Square area to sit and enjoy the busy downtown vibe. The menu offers light fare at somewhat inflated prices—eggs, sandwiches, burgers, quiches, pastas, and salads—and the main courses get a little too pricey as well (around $17 for salmon or lamb). But the main reason to come here isn't to indulge your appetite, it's to rest your weary feet, nurse a cappuccino, nosh on a pastry, and soak up the streetside scene.

352 Grant Ave. (at Bush St.). ℂ 415/398-2680. Breakfast $6.25–$10; lunch and dinner main courses (other than fish and meat) $9–$13; fish and meat main courses $15–$20. AE, DC, DISC, MC, V. Daily 7am–11pm. Bus: 9X, 15, 30, or 45.

Café Metropol CALIFORNIA/ITALIAN It's the colorful, flavorful, fresh salads and other healthy, produce-oriented dishes that keep loyal locals coming back to the Metropol, a stylish cafe and bar in the heart of the Financial District. The bean salad, for example, is no plain old green, garbanzo, and kidney mix, but rather black and whites tossed with mango, tomatoes, and cilantro. Beet salads have been in fashion recently, so you can bet on finding one here, too—with pears, red onions, herbs, and lemon vinaigrette. Sandwiches are of the gourmet variety: roast pork loin, grilled eggplant, and roast beef on brioche with horseradish sauce and pickled onions. Most dishes are available in half portions—great for grazers. But if you must go hearty, the rosemary chicken with goat-cheese mashed potatoes or one of the pasta dishes will do you right. There's also a tempting selection of house-made sweets. *Tip:* Come for lunch, when the place is at its liveliest.

168 Sutter St. (between Montgomery and Kearny sts.). ℂ 415/732-7777. Salads and sandwiches $6.50–$8; main courses $9–$13. AE, DC, MC, V. Mon–Fri 7:30am–9pm; Sat noon–4pm. Bus: 2, 3, 4, 9X, 15, 30, or 45.

Dottie's True Blue Café ★★ Kids AMERICAN/BREAKFAST This family-owned breakfast restaurant is one of my favorite downtown diners. It's the kind of place you'd expect to see off Route 66, where most customers are on a first-name basis with the staff and everyone is welcomed with a hearty hello and steaming mug of coffee. Dottie's serves above-average American morning fare (big portions of French toast, pancakes, bacon and eggs, omelets, and the like), delivered to tables laminated with old

---

ⓘ Tips Food Lover's Guide

Want more insider secrets on where to dine? Pick up Patricia Unterman's latest edition of *Patricia Unterman's San Francisco Food Lover's Guide,* third edition (Ten Speed Press, May 2004). Not only is Patty one of the best food writers in the States, she's also a chef and a local who noshes her way through the city's best-known and most obscure culinary must-visits.

---

movie star photos on rugged, diner-quality plates. Whatever you order arrives with delicious homemade bread, muffins, or scones, as well as homemade jelly. There are also daily specials and vegetarian dishes.

In the Pacific Bay Inn, 522 Jones St. (at O'Farrell St.). ℂ 415/885-2767. Reservations not accepted. Breakfast $5–$11. DISC, MC, V. Wed–Mon 7:30am–3pm. Bus: 2, 3, 4, 27, or 38. Cable car: Powell-Mason line.

Emporio Armani Cafe ⊛ ITALIAN   All the hobnobbing of an elite luncheon comes at a moderate price at the Armani Cafe. It's nothing more than a circular counter in the middle of Armani's ever-fashionable (and expensive) clothing store, a few tables on a mezzanine, and some crowded sidewalk seats when the weather's right. But the fare and upscale casual atmosphere are enough to lure folks who have only lunch, not a new designer suit, on their minds. Local favorites include the homemade antipasto *misto*, panini, salads, and daily pizza specials. There's also a nice variety of pricey lunch entrees, such as pasta specials, and in case you need a stiff drink after swallowing the steep shopping prices, the bar stays open until 7pm.

1 Grant Ave. (at O'Farrell St., off Market St.). ℂ 415/677-9010. Reservations accepted. Main courses $9–$17. AE, DC, DISC, MC, V. Mon–Sat 11:30am–4:30pm; Sun noon–4:30pm. Bus: All Union Square buses.

Hana Zen ⊛ *Finds* JAPANESE   Even most locals don't know about this Japanese restaurant, mistaking it for just another touristy sushi bar. Sure, they serve good sushi, but what makes this place special is the yakitori bar, which cranks out savory skewered and grilled meats and veggies that I can never seem to get enough of. It's all prepared Benihana style, with acrobatic chefs whirling knives around and making lots of "*Hai!*" "ahhh," and "ooohh" sounds. My favorites are the asparagus spears wrapped in thinly sliced pork, and the grilled marinated shiitake mushrooms. A few tables are perched beside windows overlooking downtown San Francisco, but the best seats are at the long, arched yakitori bar, where the deft chefs spear together nearly 30 versions of the meal-on-a-stick. You can order either one pair at a time if you like the show, or all at once for a feast; about a half dozen make a meal. The terminally indecisive can opt for the Yakitori Dinner Set for $20, which makes an interesting light meal for two.

115 Cyril Magnin St. (at Ellis St.). ℂ 415/421-2101. Sushi/yakitori items $4–$6. AE, DC, MC, V. Mon–Thurs 11:30am–2pm and 5–10:30pm; Fri 11:30am–2pm and 5–11:30pm; Sat–Sun 5–11:30pm. Bus: 27 or 38.

Kuleto's ⊛ ITALIAN   After systematic retrofitting and a face-lift in spring 2002, Kuleto's reclaimed its mark as one of downtown's Italian darlings. Muscle a seat at the antipasto bar or at the chef's counter overlooking the kitchen, and fill up on Italian specialties and selections from the wine list featuring 30 by-the-glass options. Or partake in the likes of penne pasta drenched in tangy lamb-sausage marinara sauce, clam linguine (generously overloaded with fresh clams), or any of the fresh-fish specials grilled over hardwoods in the casually refined dining room. If you don't arrive by 6pm, expect to wait—this place fills up fast. Not to worry though, you can always cross the hotel lobby to the wine bar, which also serves the full menu and is open from 6 to 10pm daily. Don't have time to sit down? Try Cafe Kuleto's, which is located just outside and serves paninis, pastries, salads, and espresso to go, and is open daily from 7am to 8pm.

In the Villa Florence Hotel, 221 Powell St. (between Geary and O'Farrell sts.). ℂ 415/397-7720. www.kuletos.com. Reservations recommended. Breakfast $5–$15; main courses $12–$25. AE, DC, DISC, MC, V. Mon–Fri 7–10:30am; Sat–Sun 8–10:30am; daily 11:30am–11pm. Bus: 2, 3, 4, or 38. Cable car: Powell-Mason and Powell-Hyde lines. Streetcar: All streetcars.

Mocca 🅡 DELI/ITALIAN   If you're like me and can't be bothered with a long lunch when there's serious shopping to be done, head to this classic Italian deli on foot-traffic-only Maiden Lane. Here it's counter service and cash only for sandwiches, caprese (Italian tomato and mozzarella salad), and big leafy salads. You can enjoy them at the few indoor tables or the pedestrian-only street-front tables shaded by umbrellas, which look onto Union Square.

175 Maiden Lane (at Stockton St.). ✆ **415/956-1188.** Reservations not accepted. Main courses $7–$13. No credit cards. Pastry and coffee daily 10:30am–5:30pm; lunch daily 11am–5:30pm. Bus: All Union Square buses.

Pho Hóa 🅡 🅥🅐🅛🅤🅔 VIETNAMESE   Although it's only a few blocks off Union Square, the walk to this simple Vietnamese restaurant in the downtrodden Tenderloin District is quite an adventure, often characterized by crack-smoking loiterers (literally) and plenty of people down on their luck. Thing is, the folks along the way are usually friendly enough and the arrival promises huge, killer bowls of Vietnamese soup with all the classic fixings (basil, bean sprouts, and so on) at absurdly low prices. Any of the dozens of selections is a meal in itself, be it my favorite—the seafood soup with rice noodles—or those with beef, chicken, shrimp, or flank steak. There are also plenty of rice dishes—with beef, vegetables, deep-fried egg rolls, or barbecued pork, and intensely strong iced coffee. For a cheap, hearty, but light meal, this is my favorite downtown option, and could be yours, too, provided you can overlook the fact that they use MSG and that the atmosphere is nothing more than clean cafeteria-style.

431 Jones St. (between O'Farrell and Ellis sts.). ✆ **415/673-3163.** Reservations accepted. Soups and main courses $5–$8. No credit cards. Daily 8am–7pm. Bus: 27, 31, or 38.

Puccini & Pinetti 🅡 ITALIAN   It takes some *buco bravado* to open yet another Italian restaurant in San Francisco, but partners Bob Puccini and Steve Pinetti obviously did their homework—this trendy little trattoria has been packed since it opened in 1998. The formula isn't exactly unique: good food at fair prices. What really makes it work, though, are the upbeat yet casual ambience, the colorful decor, a good location, and a very "in" crowd. The menu doesn't take any chances. Italian standbys—pastas, salads, thin-crust wood-fired-oven pizzas, grilled meats—dominate the menu. The fresh-baked focaccia sandwiches do well during lunch, as does the grilled portobello mushrooms with fresh mozzarella, roasted peppers, and baby mixed greens. The creamy tiramisu and devil's food cake both make for a proper finish. ***Budget tip:*** The Happy Hour "Pizza of the Day" and a glass of wine or champagne costs only $3 each every Monday to Friday from 4 to 6pm.

129 Ellis St. (at Cyril Magnin St.). ✆ **415/392-5500.** www.pucciniandpinetti.com. Reservations recommended. Main courses $7.95–$20. AE, DC, DISC, MC, V. Mon–Thurs 11:30am–10pm; Fri–Sat 11am–11pm; Sun 5–10pm. Bus: 27 or 38. Cable car: Powell-Mason line.

Sanraku 🅡 🅥🅐🅛🅤🅔 JAPANESE/SUSHI   A perfect combination of great cooked dishes and sushi at bargain prices makes this straightforward, bright, and busy restaurant the best choice for folks hankering for Japanese food. The friendly, hardworking staff does its best to keep up with diners' demands, but the restaurant gets quite busy during lunch when a special box lunch of the likes of a California roll, soup, salad, deep-fried salmon roll, and beef with noodles with steamed rice comes at a very digestible $8.25. The main menu, which is always available, features truly irresistible sesame chicken with teriyaki sauce and rice; tempura; a vast selection of *nigiri* (raw fish sushi) and rolls; and delicious combination plates of sushi, sashimi, and teriyaki. Dinner sees brisk business, too, but magically, there always seems to be an available table.

(Value) Haute Cuisine for Half the Price

So, you want to dine in high San Francisco style but can't afford the experience? Well, my fellow cognoscenti, here's the inside scoop: Both **Postrio** and the **Grand Cafe** (see reviews above and below), two of the city's primo restaurants, have small "open kitchens" in their stylish cocktail lounges, serving cuisine on par with their main menu at about half the price (and the tip). What's more, you don't need a reservation.

704 Sutter St. (at Taylor St.). ✆ **415/771-0803**. www.sanraku.com. Main courses $7.25–$13 lunch, $10–$23 dinner, 7-course fixed-price dinner $55. AE, DC, DISC, MC, V. Mon–Fri lunch 11am–4pm and dinner 4–10pm; Sat 11am–10pm; Sun 4–10pm. Bus: 2, 3, 4, 27, or 38. Cable car: Powell-Mason line.

Sears Fine Foods 🥢 Kids AMERICAN   Sears is not just another downtown diner run by motherly matrons—it's an old-fashioned institution, famous for its crispy, dark-brown waffles, light sourdough French toast, and silver dollar–size Swedish pancakes served with lingonberry jam. As the story goes, Ben Sears, a retired clown, founded the diner in 1938. His Swedish wife, Hilbur, was responsible for the legendary pancakes, which are still whipped up according to her family's secret recipe. Sears also offers classic lunch and dinner fare—try the Reuben for lunch and cod fish-n-chips for dinner, followed by a big slice of pie for dessert. Expect a brief wait to be seated on weekends.

439 Powell St. (between Post and Sutter sts.). ✆ **415/986-0700**. www.searsfinefood.com. Reservations accepted for parties of 6 or more. Breakfast $3–$8; salads and soups $3–$8; main courses $6–$10. AE, DC, MC, V Daily 6:30am–10pm (breakfast until 3pm). Bus: 2, 3, 4, or 38. Cable car: Powell-Mason and Powell-Hyde lines.

WORTH A SPLURGE

Grand Café 🥢🥢 FRENCH   If you aren't interested in exploring restaurants beyond those in Union Square and want a huge dose of atmosphere with your seared salmon, Grand Café is your best bet. Its claims to fame? The most *grand* dining room in San Francisco, an enormous turn-of-the-20th-century grand-ballroom–like dining oasis that's a magnificent combination of old Europe and Art Nouveau; and a festive (read: crowded) cocktail area. No matter where you sit while dining on the French-inspired, California-based cuisine, you'll see playful sculptures, original murals, and a cadre of dazzling Deco chandeliers.

To match the surroundings, newly appointed Chef Fabrice Roux serves up dressed-up dishes such as Dungeness crab salad with celery and apple rémoulade and vanilla-infused foie gras with pineapple-mango chutney and toasted brioche. However, since it's too soon to tell whether his food will be worthy and there are lots of great restaurants nearby, I'd recommend dropping in for cocktails and perhaps a snack at the bar area—known as the Petit Café, which offers a raw bar and similar dishes for about half the price. Sit at the cherrywood bar or at a cocktail table for food from $3 to $12 (including stuffed piquillo peppers with feta cheese; steak tartare; pizzas from the wood-burning oven; and an onion and gruyere tart). Libation lovers stop here for the great selection of small-batch American whiskies and single-malt Scotches.

501 Geary St. (at Taylor St., adjacent to the Hotel Monaco). ✆ **415/292-0101**. Reservations recommended. Main courses $15–$25. AE, DC, DISC, MC, V. Mon–Fri 7–10:30am and 11:30am–2:30pm; Sat 8am–2:30pm; Sun 9am–2:30pm; Sun–Thurs 5:30–10pm; Fri–Sat 5:30–11pm. Valet parking complimentary at lunch, $10 for 3 hr. at dinner, $3 each additional ½ hr. Bus: 2, 3, 4, 27, or 38.

Postrio *&&* AMERICAN   Eating is only part of the reason you come to this Wolf-gang Puck–owned glamorous downtown restaurant. After squeezing through the perpetually swinging bar—which dishes out excellent pizzas from a wood-burning oven and is a great place to grab an affordable bite at lunch or dinner—guests are forced to make a grand entrance down the antebellum staircase to the cavernous dining room below (it's everyone's 15 seconds of fame, so make sure your fly is zipped). Pure Hollywood, for sure, but it's fun.

The menu, by brother executive chefs, Mitchell and Steven Rosenthal, who also run SoMa's Town Hall combines Italian, Asian, French, and California styles with mixed results—sometimes the kitchen is on, other evenings it's way off. The nightly changing menu might include grilled chicken breast with potato sausage, onion purée, and walnut vinaigrette; or roasted salmon with potato eggplant ravioli, Thai basil mint salad, and orange coconut-milk cream. If you're up for a fancy dinner, there are better options around town, but for a bar bite or a scene with your supper, this is a prime pick. *Note:* Lunch is served in the bar only.

In the Prescott Hotel, 545 Post St. (between Mason and Taylor sts.). © 415/776-7825. www.postrio.com. Reservations recommended. Main courses $12–$16 lunch, $26–$39 dinner. AE, DC, DISC, MC, V. Sun–Wed 5:30–10pm; Thurs–Sat 5:30–10:30pm. Bar menu daily 11:30am–11:30pm. Valet parking $12 at lunch for 3 hr., $14 at dinner for 6 hr. Bus: 2, 3, 4, or 38. Cable car: Powell-Mason and Powell-Hyde lines.

3 Financial District

Finding cheap eats (particularly for dinner) in the Financial District can be challenging, since most diners in this neighborhood are footing the bill with corporate credit cards or expense accounts. Nevertheless, I've scouted out some affordable options.

Yank Sing *&&* CHINESE/DIM SUM   Loosely translated as "a delight of the heart," cavernous Yank Sing is the best dim sum restaurant in the downtown area. Confident,

---

Finds **The Sun on Your Face at Belden Place**

San Francisco has always been woefully lacking in the alfresco dining department. One exception is **Belden Place,** an adorable little brick alley in the heart of the Financial District that is open only to foot traffic. When the weather is agreeable, the restaurants that line the alley break out the big umbrellas, tables, and chairs, and voilà—a bit of Paris just off Pine Street.

A handful of adorable cafes line Belden Place and offer a variety of cuisines all at a moderate price. There's **Cafe Bastille,** 22 Belden Place (© **415/986-5673**), a classic French bistro and fun speakeasy basement serving excellent crepes, mussels, and French onion soup; it schedules live jazz on Fridays. **Cafe Tiramisu,** 28 Belden Place (© **415/421-7044**), is a stylish Italian hot spot serving addictive risottos and gnocchi. **Plouf,** 40 Belden Place (© **415/986-6491**), specializes in big bowls of mussels slathered in a choice of seven sauces, as well as fresh seafood. **B44,** 44 Belden Place (© **415/986-6287**), serves up revered paella and other seriously zesty Spanish dishes. (Come at night for a Euro-speakeasy vibe with your dinner.)

Tips Fast Food from Around the World

Catering to the dense population of downtown white-collar workers, the **Rincon Center's Food Court** ✦, 101 Spear St. at Mission Street (© 415/777-4100), has about a dozen to-go places serving cheap, respectable fare running the gastronomic gamut: Korean, American, Mexican, pizza, coffee and cookies, Indian, Thai, sandwiches, Middle Eastern, and Chinese. Seat-yourself tables are dispersed throughout the indoor courtyard. Most of the restaurants are open Monday through Friday from 11am to 3pm, but some remain open until early evening.

Similar eats, though not as good or as cheap, can be found at the base of **Embarcadero Four's Justin Herman Plaza,** at the foot of Market Street at the Embarcadero. It's a great place to catch a few rays when the sun is shining.

---

experienced servers take the nervousness out of novices—they're good at guessing your gastric threshold as they wheel carts carrying small plates of exotic dishes past each table. Most dim sum dishes are dumplings, filled with tasty concoctions of pork, beef, fish, or vegetables. *Congees* (porridges), spare ribs, stuffed crab claws, scallion pancakes, shrimp balls, pork buns, and other palate-pleasers complete the menu. While the food is delicious, the location makes this a popular tourist spot and weekday lunch spot; at other times, residents generally head to Ton Kiang (p. 137), the undisputed top choice for these Chinese delicacies. A second location, open during weekdays for lunch only, is at 49 Stevenson St., off First Street (© **415/541-4949**).

101 Spear St. (at Mission St. at Rincon Center). © **415/957-9300.** Dim sum $3.50–$8 for 2–4 pieces. AE, DC, MC, V. Mon–Fri 11am–3pm; Sat–Sun and holidays 10am–4pm. Validated parking in Rincon Center Garage. BART: Embarcadero. Bus: 1, 12, 14, or 41. Cable car: California St. line. Streetcar: F.

WORTH A SPLURGE

Kokkari ✦✦✦ *Finds* GREEK/MEDITERRANEAN   It figures that it would take a French chef to make Greek food fabulous, and executive chef Jean Alberti (the mastermind behind the moussaka) who departed in early 2004, did exactly that. Thankfully, he left his secret recipes behind, and Kokkari (Ko-*car*-ee) is still fashionable and flavorful under new executive chef, Erik Cosselmon, previously at Half Moon Bay's beloved Cetrella. The love affair starts with the setting: a beautifully rustic living room–like dining area with a commanding fireplace and oversize furnishings. Past the tiny bar, the other main room is pure rustic revelry with exposed wood beams, pretty standing lamps, and a view of the glass-enclosed private dining room. Then there are the traditional Aegean dishes. Start with *pikilia* (a sampling of traditional Greek spreads served with dolmades) or fabulous baby octopus salad. Try not to overindulge before the main courses, which include grilled whole petrale sole with lemon, olive oil, and braised greens; to-die-for moussaka (eggplant, lamb, potato, and béchamel); and braised lamb shank over orzo. Also keep an eye out for Cosselman's rotisserie specialties, such as a rotisserie-roasted pork loin.

200 Jackson St. (at Front St.). © **415/981-0983.** www.kokkari.com. Reservations recommended. Main courses $14–$23 lunch, $19–$35 dinner. AE, DC, DISC, MC, V. Lunch Mon–Fri 11:30am–2:30pm; bar menu 2:30–5:30pm; dinner Mon–Thurs 5:30–10pm, Fri 5:30–11pm, Sat 5–11pm. Valet parking (dinner only) $8. Bus: 12, 15, 41, or 83.

The Slanted Door ✦✦ *Finds* VIETNAMESE   This restaurant is so popular that Mick Jagger and former President Clinton made stopovers at its previous location in the Mission District when they hit town. It's even more of a hot spot since its April 2004 relocation to its beautiful bay-inspired custom-designed space in the Ferry Building Marketplace. Why all the hype? The restaurant serves incredibly fresh and flavorful (albeit relatively expensive) Vietnamese food. Pull up a chair and order anything from clay-pot catfish or amazing green papaya salad to one of the lunch rice dishes, which come in a large ceramic bowl and are topped with such options as grilled shrimp and stir-fried eggplant. Dinner items, which change seasonally, might include beef with garlic and organic onions, grapefruit, and jicama salad. Whatever you order, it's bound to be wholesome, flavorful, and outstanding. There's also an eclectic collection of teas, which come by the pot for $4 to $6.

1 Ferry Plaza (at the Embarcadero and Market). © 415/861-8032. www.slanteddoor.com. Reservations recommended. Lunch main courses $8.50–$17, 7-item fixed-price lunch $38, most dinner dishes $15–$27, 7-item fixed-price dinner $45 (parties of 8 or more only). AE, MC, V. Mon–Sat 11am–2:30pm; Mon–Thurs 5:30–10pm; Fri–Sat 5:30–10:30pm. Bus: All Market Street buses. Streetcar: F, N.

4 Nob Hill/Russian Hill

Nob Hill Café *Finds* ITALIAN/PIZZA   Considering the cost and formality of most meals on ultra-elite Nob Hill, it's no wonder that neighborhood residents don't mind waiting around for a table to open up at the Nob Hill Café. This is the kind of place where you can come wearing jeans, relax over a large bowl of pasta and a glass of merlot, and leave fulfilled without blowing a wad of dough. The dining room is split into two small, simple rooms, with windows looking onto Taylor Street and bright local art on the walls. Service is friendly, and one of the owners is almost always on hand to make sure everyone's content. When the kitchen is "on," expect hearty Tuscan comfort fare worth at least twice its price; on off days, it's still decent. Start with a salad or the decadent polenta with pesto and parmigiano, then fill up on the veal picatta, any of the pastas or pizzas, or *petrale* sole. They also serve some of the best french fries I've ever had.

1152 Taylor St. (between Sacramento and Clay sts.). © 415/776-6500. www.nobhillcafe.com. Reservations not accepted. Main courses $7–$16. DC, MC, V. Daily 11:30am–3pm and 5–10pm. Bus: 1.

Swan Oyster Depot *Finds* SEAFOOD   Turning 94 years old in 2006, Swan Oyster Depot is a classic San Francisco dining experience you shouldn't miss. Opened in 1912, this tiny hole-in-the-wall, run by the city's friendliest servers, is little more than a narrow fish market that decided to slap down some bar stools. There are only 20 or so seats here, jammed cheek-by-jowl along a long marble bar. Most patrons come for a quick cup of chowder or a plate of oysters on the half shell that arrive chilling on crushed ice. The menu is limited to fresh crab, shrimp, oyster, clam cocktails, a few types of smoked fish, Maine lobster, and Boston-style clam chowder, all of which are exceedingly fresh. *Note:* Don't let the lunchtime line dissuade you—it moves fast.

1517 Polk St. (between California and Sacramento sts.). © 415/673-1101. Reservations not accepted. Seafood cocktails $7–$15, clams and oysters on the half shell $7.50 per half-dozen. No credit cards. Mon–Sat 8am–5:30pm. Bus: 1, 19, 47, or 49.

5 South of Market (SoMa)

AsiaSF *Finds* ASIAN/CALIFORNIA   Part restaurant, part gender-illusionist musical revue, AsiaSF manages to be completely entertaining and extremely high-quality. As you're entertained by mostly Asian men—dressed as women—who lip-sync show tunes, you can nibble on excellent grilled shrimp and herb salad; baby-back pork ribs with honey tamarind glaze, pickled carrots, and sweet-potato crisps; or filet mignon with Korean dipping sauce, miso eggplant, and fried potato stars. The full bar, *Wine Spectator* award–winning wine list, and sake list add to the festivities. Fortunately, the food and the atmosphere are as colorful as the staff, which means a night here is more than a meal—it's a very happening event.

201 Ninth St. (at Howard St.). ⓒ 415/255-2742. www.asiasf.com. Reservations recommended. Main courses $9–$19, 3-course fixed-price menu Sun–Thurs $32, Fri–Sat $37 (Mon–Wed $25 minimum). AE, DISC, MC, V. Sun–Thurs 6–10pm; Fri–Sat 5–10pm. BART: Civic Center. Bus: 9, 12, or 47. Streetcar: Civic Center on underground streetcar.

Cha Am Thai ⓕ (Finds) THAI   Cha Am Thai—named after the province in the southwestern part of Thailand famous for its beaches—is one of those sleeper restaurants you'd never find unless someone told you about it. Hidden behind the Moscone Convention Center, this pleasant little Thai restaurant does a brisk lunch business when large conventions are in town. A good opener is the Cha Am prawn appetizer: stuffed, grilled prawns layered with a spicy tamarind sauce. Other favorites are *mu yang* (marinated sweet-and-sour pork chops) and *pla sam rod,* a whole striped bass that's deboned and deep fried until crispy, then topped with a spicy sweet-and-sour sauce. Service is efficient and friendly (be sure to ask about the daily specials), and prices are surprisingly reasonable.

701 Folsom St. (at Third St.). ⓒ 415/546-9711. www.chaamthaisf.com. Reservations recommended for parties of 3 or more. Main courses $5.95–$6.95 lunch, $6.95–$15 dinner. AE, DC, MC, V. Mon–Sat 11am–3pm and 5–10pm; Sun 5–10pm. Bus: 9 or 15.

Gordon Biersch Brewery Restaurant ⓕ CALIFORNIA   Popular with the young Republican crowd (loose ties and tight skirts dominate), this modern, two-tiered brewery and restaurant eschews traditional brewpub fare—no spicy chicken wings on this menu—in an attempt to attract a more upscale clientele. And it works. Goat cheese ravioli is a bestseller, followed by the herb-roasted half-chicken with garlic mashed potatoes. Start with the delicate and crunchy fried calamari appetizer or, if you're a garlic hound, the tangy Caesar salad. Most dishes can be paired with one of the brewery's lagers. Couples bent on a quiet, romantic dinner can skip this place; when the lower-level bar fills up, you practically have to shout to be heard. Beer-lovers who want to pair their suds with decent grub, however, will be quite content.

2 Harrison St. (on the Embarcadero). ⓒ 415/243-8246. www.gordonbiersch.com. Reservations recommended. Main courses $10–$23. AE, DC, DISC, MC, V. Sun–Thurs 11:30am–midnight; Fri–Sat 11:30am–2am. Bus: 32.

Manora's ⓕ THAI   Manora's cranks out some of the best Thai food in town and is well worth a jaunt to SoMa. But this is no relaxed affair: It's perpetually packed (unless you come early), and you'll be seated sardinelike at one of the cramped but well-appointed tables. During the dinner rush, the noise level can make conversation among larger parties almost impossible, but the food is so darned good, you'll probably prefer to turn toward your plate and stuff your face anyway. Start with a Thai iced tea or coffee and tangy soup or chicken satay, which comes with decadent peanut sauce. Follow these with any of the wonderful dinner dishes—which should be shared—and a side of rice. There are endless options, including a vast array of vegetarian plates. Every remarkably flavorful dish arrives seemingly seconds after you order it, which is great if you're hungry, a bummer if you were planning a long, leisurely dinner. *Tip:* Come before 7pm or after 9pm if you don't want a loud, rushed meal.

San Francisco Dining

Ace Wasabi's
  Rock 'n' Roll Sushi **8**
A16 **1**
Andalé Taqueria **7**
Asia SF **61**
Aziza **17**
Balboa Café **11**
Barney's Gourmet
  Hamburgers **9**
Beach Chalet Brewery
  & Restaurant **24**
Betelnut **12**
Boudin Sourdough
  Bakery & Café **46**
Boulevard **53**
Burma Superstar **15**
Café Flore **40**
Cafe Kati **20**
Cafe Pescatore **47**
Caffe Centro **58**
Caffe Luna Piena **40**
Cha Am Thai **57**
Cha Cha Cha **28**
Chez Nous **18**
Chow **38**
Citrus Club **25**
Crepes on Cole **29**
E'Angelo Restaurant **3**
Ebisu **30**
Eliza's **13**
Ella's **16**
Embarcadero Four's
  Justin Herman Plaza **51**
Firewood Café **40**
Frjtz Fries **22**
Fog City Diner **50**
Forbes Island **48**
Gordon Biersch Brewery
  Restaurant **55**
The Grove **4**
Hard Rock Cafe **49**
Home Plate **5**
Isa **6**
Isobune **21**

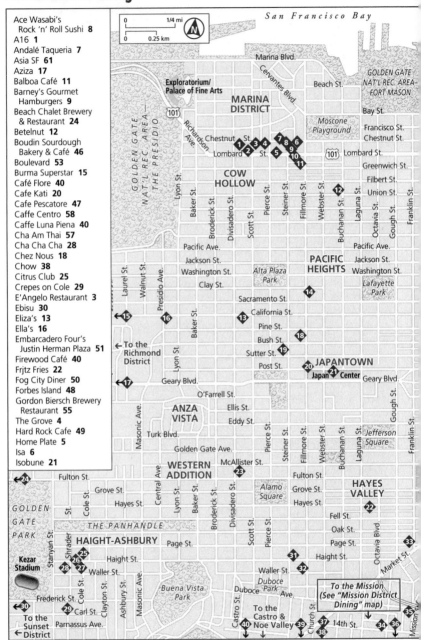

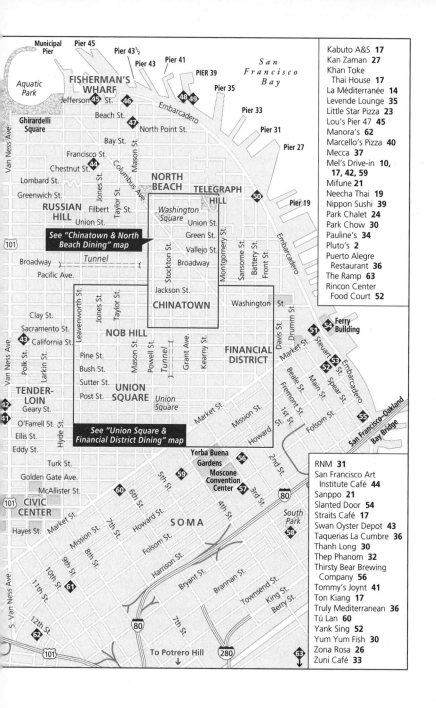

Municipal Pier
Pier 45
Pier 43½
Pier 43
Pier 41
PIER 39
Pier 35
Pier 33
Pier 31
Pier 27
San Francisco Bay

Aquatic Park

FISHERMAN'S WHARF
Jefferson St. 45 46
Beach St. 47
North Point St.
Bay St.
Ghirardelli Square
Francisco St.
Chestnut St. 44
Lombard St.
Greenwich St.
Filbert St.
Union St.
Washington Square
Union St.
Green St.
Vallejo St.
Broadway
Jackson St.

48 49

Embarcadero

Pier 19 50

RUSSIAN HILL

NORTH BEACH
TELEGRAPH HILL

See "Chinatown & North Beach Dining" map

Broadway
Tunnel
Pacific Ave.

CHINATOWN
Washington St.

Clay St.
Sacramento St.
43 California St.
Pine St.
Bush St.
Sutter St.
Post St.

NOB HILL

FINANCIAL DISTRICT

Ferry Building
51 54
53
52

TENDER-LOIN
42
41
Geary St.
O'Farrell St.
Ellis St.
Eddy St.

UNION SQUARE
Union Square

See "Union Square & Financial District Dining" map

San Francisco–Oakland Bay Bridge
55

Mission St.
Howard St.

Turk St.
Golden Gate Ave.
McAllister St.
101 CIVIC CENTER
Hayes St.

Yerba Buena Gardens 56
Moscone Convention Center 57
59
60

80

SOMA

South Park
58

To Potrero Hill
↓
280
63 ↓

Kabuto A&S **17**
Kan Zaman **27**
Khan Toke
  Thai House **17**
La Méditerranée **14**
Levende Lounge **35**
Little Star Pizza **23**
Lou's Pier 47 **45**
Manora's **62**
Marcello's Pizza **40**
Mecca **37**
Mel's Drive-in **10,
  17, 42, 59**
Mifune **18**
Neecha Thai **19**
Nippon Sushi **39**
Park Chalet **24**
Park Chow **30**
Pauline's **34**
Pluto's **2**
Puerto Alegre
  Restaurant **36**
The Ramp **63**
Rincon Center
  Food Court **52**

RNM **31**
San Francisco Art
  Institute Café **44**
Sanppo **21**
Slanted Door **54**
Straits Café **17**
Swan Oyster Depot **43**
Taquerias La Cumbre **36**
Thanh Long **30**
Thep Phanom **32**
Thirsty Bear Brewing
  Company **56**
Tommy's Joynt **41**
Ton Kiang **17**
Truly Mediterranean **36**
Tú Lan **60**
Yank Sing **52**
Yum Yum Fish **30**
Zona Rosa **26**
Zuni Café **33**

1600 Folsom St. (at 12th St.). © 415/861-6224. Reservations recommended for 4 or more. Main courses $7–$12. MC, V. Mon–Fri 11:30am–2:30pm; Mon–Sat 5:30–10:30pm; Sun 5–10pm. Bus: 9, 12, or 47.

ThirstyBear Brewing Company ℱ SPANISH   Despite the dumb name, Thirsty-Bear Brewing Company is a favorite of the Financial District/SoMa crowd, who come for the excellent house-made brews and Spanish food. Paella Valenciana—a sizzling combo of chicken, shrimp, sausage, shellfish, and saffron-laden rice served in a cast-iron skillet—is a must. Upscale pub grub includes a variety of hot and cold tapas, a few winners being *tortilla Española,* the classic potato & onion omelet with aioli and salsa verde, and *gambas al ajillo* (shrimp sautéed in garlic and olive oil). Ask the waiter which brews best accompany the dishes or wash them down with sangria. Almost as impressive as the food is the architecture—a costly conversion from a high-ceilinged brick warehouse to a two-level industrial-chic brewpub complete with pool tables and dartboards.

661 Howard St. (½ block east of the Moscone Center). © 415/974-0905. www.thirstybear.com. Reservations recommended. Tapas $4–$11; main courses $12–$18. AE, DC, MC, V. Mon–Thurs 11:30am–10pm; Fri–Sat 11:30am–midnight; Sun 5–10pm. Parking at garage at Howard and Third sts. Bus: 12, 15, 30, 45, or 76.

SUPER-CHEAP EATS

Caffe Centro ℱ CAFE   If it's a sunny day and you're in the mood for a little SoMa adventure, you'll find no place as relaxing as this hidden cafe retreat. Caffe Centro's limited kitchen and dining room inhibits it from becoming a destination restaurant, but its simple, cozy space, too-quaint sidewalk seating, and view of a grassy minipark and Old San Francisco–style homes make it the perfect place to catch a few rays, read the paper, and relax. The only reminder that you're in a big city is the dwindling cadre of dot-commers who come in for a dose of high-octane java and a salad or sandwiches for lunch. In the morning, stop in for a breakfast of pastries, fruit, granola, and poached eggs.

102 South Park (between Second and Third sts. and Bryant and Brannan sts.). © 415/882-1500. Main courses under $7. AE, DISC, MC, V. Mon–Fri 7am–6:30pm; Sat 8am–4:30pm. Bus: 9, 15, 30, 45, 76, or 81X.

Tú Lan ℱ VIETNAMESE   Only adventurous foodies interested in a cheap, midday snack need to read this review. You'll have to brave the winos, weirdos, and street stench to get to this total dive in an unsavory neighborhood bordering Union Square and SoMa, but I do it happily to get my hands on the best imperial rolls on the planet. Alas, the atmosphere inside isn't much better—it's about as greasy as greasy spoons get, and if you head to the upstairs bathroom you might even catch an unsavory glimpse of kitchen staff hovering over mounds of ground meat meant for tonight's dinner piled high on a banquet table. But once I get a bite of the crisp, thick imperial rolls, which are served over rice noodles and accompanied by lettuce, mint, peanuts, and a delicious dipping sauce, I could care less. There's also a good selection of stir-fried rice plates—including awesome barbecued pork, which can be washed down with intense iced coffee. In any case, you'll feel brave just eating here; I have, on one occasion, shared my table with a cockroach.

8 Sixth St. (at Market St.). © 415/626-0927. Reservations not accepted. Main courses $4–$7.50. No credit cards. Mon–Sat 11am–9pm. Bus: 6, 7, 27, 31, 66, or 71. Cable car: Powell-Mason and Powell-Hyde lines. Streetcar: All streetcars.

WORTH A SPLURGE

Boulevard ℱℱ AMERICAN   Master restaurant designer Pat Kuleto and chef Nancy Oakes teamed up to create one of San Francisco's most revered restaurants, and although it made its debut in 1993, it's still one of my—and the city's—all-time favorites.

The dramatically artistic Belle Epoque interior, with vaulted brick ceilings, floral banquettes, a mosaic floor, and tulip-shaped lamps, is the setting for Oakes's equally impressive sculptural and mouthwatering dishes. Starters alone could make a perfect meal, especially if you indulge in pan-seared day boat sea scallops with sautéed fresh hearts of palm, pomelo, basil, toasted shallots, and macadamia nuts; pan-seared foie gras with rhubarb syrup, whole grain toast, cara cara, tangelo, and blood orange salad; or Hawaiian ahi tuna tartare with habanero-chile tobiko, yellow tomato, tequila cream, guacamole and tortilla chips. The nine or so main courses are equally creative and might include grilled Pacific sea bass with fresh gulf prawns, grilled artichoke, spring asparagus, and green garlic purée; or fire roasted Angus filet with crispy Yukon gold potatoes, béarnaise sauce, sautéed spinach and crimini mushrooms, and red wine jus. Finish with warm chocolate cake with a chocolate caramel center, caramel corn, and butterscotch ice cream. Three levels of formality—bar, open kitchen, and main dining room—keep things from getting too snobby. Although steep prices prevent most from making Boulevard a regular gig, you'd be hard-pressed to find a better place for a special, fun-filled occasion. Cocktailers: Ask the bartender about the special martinis—they're some of the best in town.

1 Mission St. (between the Embarcadero and Steuart sts.). © 415/543-6084. www.boulevardrestaurant.com. Reservations recommended. Main courses $14–$22 lunch, $28–$39 dinner. AE, DC, DISC, MC, V. Mon–Fri 11:30am–2:15pm; Sun–Thurs 5:30–9:30pm; Fri–Sat 5:30–10:00pm. Valet parking $12 lunch, $10 dinner. BART: Embarcadero. Bus: 12, 15, 30, 32, or 41.

6 Chinatown

Brandy Ho's Hunan Food 🌟 (Kids) CHINESE/DIM SUM   Fancy black-and-white granite tabletops and a large, open kitchen give you the first clue that the food at this casual and fun restaurant is a cut above the usual Hunan fare. Take my advice and start immediately with fried dumplings (in sweet-and-sour sauce) or cold chicken salad and then move on to fish-ball soup with spinach, bamboo shoots, noodles, and other goodies. The best main course is Three Delicacies, a combination of scallops, shrimp, and chicken with onion, bell pepper, and bamboo shoots, seasoned with ginger, garlic, and wine, and served with black-bean sauce. Most dishes are quite hot and spicy, but the kitchen will adjust the level to meet your specifications. A full bar includes Asian-food–friendly libations like plum wine and sake from 11:30am to 11pm.

217 Columbus Ave. (at Pacific Ave.). © **415/788-7527.** www.brandyhos.com. Reservations recommended. Main courses $8–$13. AE, DC, DISC, MC, V. Sun–Thurs 11:30am–11pm; Fri–Sat 11:30am–midnight. Paid parking available at 170 Columbus Ave. Bus: 15 or 41.

Gold Mountain 🌟 (Finds) (Kids) CHINESE/DIM SUM   This gymnasium-size restaurant is a must-visit for anyone who's never experienced what it's like to dine with hundreds of Chinese-speaking patrons conversing loudly at enormous round tables among glittering chandeliers and gilded dragons while dozens of white-shirted wait staff push around stainless steel carts filled with small plates of exotic-looking edible adventures: chicken feet, pork buns, shrimp dumplings (yum), whole salted prawns, the ubiquitous chicken-in-foil, and myriad other quasi-recognizable concoctions that range from appealing to revolting (never ate beef tripe, never will). I remember coming here as a little kid on late Saturday mornings and being infatuated with the entire cacophonous event. And even if you eat until you're ill, you'll never put down more than $20 worth of food, making Gold Mountain a real bargain as well, especially for large groups.

Don't even bother with the regular menu: it's the dim sum service from 8am and 3pm on weekends and 10:30am to 3pm on weekdays that you want.

664 Broadway (between Grant Ave. and Stockton St.). ℂ 415/296-7733. Main courses $3-$9. AE, MC, V. Mon–Fri 10:30am–3pm and 5–9:30pm; Sat–Sun 8am–3pm and 5–9:30pm. Bus: 12, 15, 30, or 83.

Great Eastern ⓐ (finds) CHINESE/DIM SUM   If you like seafood and Chinese food and have an adventurous palate, you're going to love Great Eastern, which is well known for serving fresh and hard-to-find seafood, pulled straight from the myriad of tanks that line the walls. Rock cod, steelhead, sea conch, sea bass, shrimp, frogs, soft-shell turtle, abalone—if it's even remotely aquatic and edible, it's on the menu at this popular Hong Kong–style dinner house. The day's catch, sold by the pound, is listed on a board. Both upper- and lower-level dining rooms are stylish in a Chinatown sort of way, with shiny black and emerald furnishings. *Tip:* Unless you can translate an authentic Hong Kong menu, order a set dinner (the crab version is fantastic) or point to another table and say, "I want that."

649 Jackson St. (between Kearny St. and Grant Ave.). ℂ 415/986-2500. Most main courses $8–$13. AE, MC, V. Daily 10am–1am. Bus: 15, 30, 41, or 45.

House of Nanking ⓐ CHINESE/DIM SUM   This place would be strictly a tourist joint if it weren't for the die-hard fans who happily wait—sometimes up to an hour—for a coveted seat at this inconspicuous little restaurant serving Shanghai-style cuisine. Order the requisite pot stickers, green-onion-and-shrimp pancakes with peanut sauce, or any number of pork, rice, beef, seafood, chicken, or vegetable dishes from the menu, but I suggest you trust the waiter when he recommends a special. Even with an expansion that doubled the available space, seating is tight, so prepare to be bumped around a bit and don't expect perky or attentive service—it's all part of the Nanking experience.

919 Kearny St. (at Columbus Ave.). ℂ 415/421-1429. Reservations accepted for groups of 8 or more. Main courses $6–$12. MC, V. Mon–Fri 11am–10pm; Sat–Sun noon–10pm. Bus: 9, 12, 15, or 30.

Hunan Home's ⓐⓐ CHINESE/DIM SUM   One of Chinatown's best restaurants, Hunan Home's is a feast for the eyes—ubiquitous pink-and-white walls lined with big wall-to-wall mirrors that reflect armies of fish tanks and tacky chandeliers—as well as the palate. The rule of thumb here is not to put anything in your mouth until you're armed with a glass of water, because most every dish is *ooooweeeee* hot! Start with Home's excellent hot-and-sour soup (the acid test of every Chinese restaurant) or wonton soup (chock-full of shrimp, chicken, barbecued pork, squid, and vegetables), followed by the Succulent Bread appetizer, a platter of prawns with honeyed walnuts, and the scallops a la Hunan (sautéed along with snow peas, baby corn, celery, and mushrooms). Photographs of the more popular dishes are posted out front, though it's hard to tell which ones will singe your nose hairs.

622 Jackson St. (between Kearny St. and Grant Ave.). ℂ 415/982-2844. Main courses $7.95–$12. AE, DC, DISC, MC, V. Daily 11:30am–9:30pm. Bus: 15, 30, 41, or 45.

Oriental Pearl ⓐ CHINESE/DIM SUM   Wherever the Chiu Chow region in southern China is, one thing's for sure: They're eating well there! Oriental Pearl specializes in regional Chiu Chow cuisine, a variation of Cantonese that's unlike anything you've ever seen or tasted, such as the house special chicken meatball—a delicate mix of shrimp, chicken, water chestnuts, and ham wrapped in a thin veneer of egg whites. Other recommended choices are the *pei pa* tofu with shrimp, seafood chow mein, and

Chinatown & North Beach Dining

Brandy Ho's
Hunan Food **18**
Caffè Macaroni **21**
Caffè Sport **9**
Capp's Corner **5**
Enrico's **16**
Gira Polli **2**
Gold Mountain **15**
The Gold Spike **8**
Golden Boy Pizza **10**

Great Eastern **22**
House of Nanking **19**
Hunan Home's **20**
Il Pollaio **6**
L'Osteria del Forno **7**
Mario's Bohemian
Cigar Store **4**
Mo's Gourmet
Burgers **13**
North Beach Pizza **11**

Oriental Pearl **23**
Pasta Pomodoro **3**
R&G Lounge **24**
Sam Wo **22**
San Francisco Art
Institute Café **1**
Sodini's Green Valley
Restaurant **12**
The Stinking Rose **14**
Tommaso's **17**

spicy braised prawns, all served by spiffy waiters wearing white shirts and black bow ties. The roomy, spotless restaurant is so obscurely located on the second floor of a business complex that it must rely almost exclusively on repeat and word-of-mouth clientele; but the word must be spreading, because it's usually packed. Unlike most other restaurants in Chinatown, dim sum is ordered via a menu, which isn't as fun but guarantees freshness (the steaming baskets of shrimp and scallop dumplings are excellent). Prices are slightly higher than average, but are most definitely worth the extra money.

788 Clay St. (between Kearny St. and Grant Ave.). ℭ 415/433-1817. Main courses $8.25–$9.50. AE, DC, DISC, MC, V. Daily 11am–3pm and 5–9:30pm. Bus: 15, 30, 41, or 45.

R&G Lounge 🞳🞳 CHINESE/DIM SUM   It's tempting to take your chances and duck into any of the exotic restaurants in Chinatown, but if you want a sure thing, go directly to the two-story R&G Lounge. During lunch, both recently modernized floors are packed with hungry neighborhood workers who go straight for the $5.50 rice-plate specials. Even then, you can order from the dinner menu, which features legendary deep-fried salt-and-pepper crab (a little too greasy and rich for my taste); and delicious chicken with black-bean sauce. A personal favorite is melt-in-your-mouth R&G Special Beef, which explodes with the tangy flavor of the accompanying sauce. I was less excited by the tired chicken salad, house specialty noodles, and bland spring rolls. But that was just fine since I saved room for generous and savory seafood in a clay pot and delicious classic roast duck.

631 Kearny St. (at Clay St.). ℭ 415/982-7877. Reservations recommended. Main courses $9–$30. AE, DC, DISC, MC, V. Mon–Thurs 11am–9:30pm; Fri 11am–10pm; Sat 11:30am–10pm; Sun 11:30am–9:30pm. Parking validated across the street at Portsmouth Square garage 24 hr. or Holiday Inn after 5pm. Bus: 1, 9AX, 9BX, or 15. Cable Car: California line.

SUPER-CHEAP EATS

Sam Wo CHINESE/DIM SUM   Very handy for late-nighters, Sam's is a total dive that's usually packed at 1am with party people trying to sober up (I've been pulling all-nighters here since I was a teen). The restaurant's two pocket-size dining rooms are located on top of each other, on the second and third floors—take the stairs past the grimy first-floor kitchen. You'll probably have to share a table, but this place is for mingling almost as much as for eating (the bossy waitresses are pure comedy). The house specialty is *jook,* known as *congee* in its native Hong Kong—a thick rice gruel flavored with fish, shrimp, chicken, beef, or pork; the best is Sampan, made with rice and seafood. Try sweet-and-sour pork rice, wonton soup with duck, or a roast-pork/rice-noodle roll. More traditional fried noodles and rice plates are available, too, but I always end up ordering the same thing: tomato beef with noodles and house special chow mein.

813 Washington St. (by Grant Ave.). ℭ 415/982-0596. Reservations not accepted. Main courses $3.50–$6. No credit cards. Mon–Sat 11am–3am. Open Sun 11am–9:30pm in summer and on holidays. Bus: 9x, 15, 30, or 45.

7 North Beach

Caffè Macaroni 🞳🞳 ITALIAN   You wouldn't know it from the looks (or name) of it, but this tiny, funky restaurant on busy Columbus Avenue is one of the best southern Italian restaurants in the city. It looks as though it can hold only two customers at a time, and if you don't duck your head when entering the upstairs dining room, you might as well ask for one lump or two. Fortunately, the kitchen also packs a wallop, dishing out a large variety of antipasti and excellent pastas. The spinach-and-cheese ravioli with wild-mushroom sauce and the gnocchi are outstanding. The owners and staff are always vivacious and friendly, and young ladies in particular will enjoy the attentions of the charming Italian men manning the counter.

124 Columbus Ave. (at Jackson St.). ℭ **415/956-9737.** www.caffemacaroni.com. Reservations accepted. Main courses $9–$18. No credit cards. Tues–Sat 5–10pm. Closed last week of Dec–first week of Jan. Bus: 15 or 41.

Caffè Sport ℱ ITALIAN   People either love or hate this stodgy, garlic-smelling Sicilian eatery. Cluttered with hanging hams, fishnets, decorative plates, dolls, mirrors, and over 2 decades' worth of dust, Caffè Sport was once a culinary landmark. Now it's better known for its surly staff and eclectic ambience than for its good—though cream- and butter-heavy—food. Still, the Southern Italian fare is served up with hearty portions of tongue-in-cheek attitude along with huge garlic-laden pasta dishes. Lunch is tame in comparison to dinner, when the Sport is mobbed and lively, and strangers might be packed together family style. Disregard the menu and accept the waiter's "suggestions." Whatever arrives—whether calamari, mussels, shrimp in tomato-garlic sauce, or pasta in pesto sauce—it's bound to be *bene*. Bring a huge appetite, but above all, don't be late if you have a reservation.

574 Green St. (between Grant and Columbus aves.). ℭ **415/981-1251.** Reservations recommended. Main courses $15–$30. No credit cards. Tues–Thurs 5–10:30pm, Fri–Sat noon–2:30pm and 5–10:30pm. Bus: 15, 30, 41, or 45.

Capp's Corner ℱ 𝒱alue ITALIAN   Capp's is a place of givens: It's a given that high-spirited regulars are hunched over the bar and that you'll be served huge portions of straightforward Italian fare at low prices in a raucous atmosphere that prevails until closing. The waitresses are usually brusque and bossy, but always with a wink. Long tables are set up for family-style dining: bread, soup, salad, choice of around 20 classic main dishes (herb-roasted leg of lamb, spaghetti with meatballs, osso buco with polenta, fettuccine with prawns and white-wine sauce), and dessert—all for $15 to $17 or so per person, around $10 for kids. You might have to wait a while for a table, but if you want fun and authentic old-school dining without pomp or huge prices, you'll find the wait worthwhile.

1600 Powell St. (at Green St.). ℭ **415/989-2589.** www.cappscorner.com. Reservations accepted. Complete dinners $15–$17. AE, DC, MC, V. Daily 11:30am–2:30pm; Sun–Thurs 4:30–10:30pm; Fri–Sat 4:30–11pm. Bus: 15, 30, or 41.

Enrico's ℱ CALIFORNIA   Enrico's is the most fun sidewalk-restaurant/supper-club destination on North Beach's Broadway strip. Anyone with an appreciation for live jazz (featured nightly), late-night noshing, and people-watching from the outdoor patio will be quite content spending an alfresco evening under the heat lamps here. (However, the best view of the band is from inside.) I tend to drop by and snack on wine and addictive deep-fried olives or pizza Margherita and move on. But when I linger for dinner, entrees are usually satisfying and range from roasted chicken under a brick with mashed potatoes to flat-iron steak or butternut-squash ravioli. The best part? No cover charge.

504 Broadway (at Kearny St.). ℭ **415/982-6223.** www.enricossidewalkcafe.com. Reservations recommended. Main courses $7–$12 lunch, $11–$23 dinner. AE, MC, V. Sun–Thurs 11:30am–11pm; Fri–Sat 11:30am–midnight; bar daily 11:30am–1:30am or earlier depending on patronage. Valet parking (dinner only) $10. Bus: 9X, 12, or 15.

Gira Polli ℱ 𝒱alue ITALIAN   I used to live 3 blocks from Gira Polli, and man, do I miss it! Whenever I'd rent a video, I'd drop by here for the Gira Polli special: a foil-lined bag filled with half a wood-fired, crispy-skinned, herb-infused chicken (their unique Italian rotisserie roasts 126 chickens at a time), Palermo potatoes, a fresh garden salad, perfectly cooked vegetables, and a soft roll—all for under $10 if purchased before 6:30pm. Next, I'd nab a bottle of good, cheap wine from the liquor store next door, take my goodies home, disconnect the phone, and chow down in front of the TV. Seating in this shoebox-size cafe is a joke during the rush; a better bet is to order your meal to go and have a picnic lunch at Washington Square right across the street.

659 Union St. (at Columbus Ave.). (© 415/434-4472. Main courses $7.95–$14. AE, MC, V. Daily 4:30–9:30pm. Bus: 15, 30, 39, 41, or 45.

The Gold Spike ITALIAN   This dusty, dark, funky, cavelike restaurant has endured a love-hate relationship with San Francisco since 1920. (Food critics Don and Betty Martin hit the nail on the head when they described it as "a pioneer museum that exploded.") Thousands of yellowing business cards plaster the walls alongside war memorabilia, stuffed moose heads, and an endless array of knickknacks that have accumulated since the place opened. Dinner consists mainly of Italian-American standards such as osso buco and veal parmigiana, served family style or a la carte at small booths opposite the bar. Recommended dishes are the eggplant Parmesan, chicken Marsala, and Italian pot roast, served either a la carte or as part of a six-course dinner for a few extra dollars. A "Crab Cioppino Feed" is held every night during crab season (winter). Is the food good? Not particularly, but it's filling and fairly inexpensive, and the ambience is undeniably unique.

527 Columbus Ave. (between Green and Union sts.). (© 415/421-4591. Reservations accepted for parties of 6 or more. Main courses $10–$20. AE, DISC, MC, V. Mon–Tues and Thurs 5–10:30pm; Fri and Sat 5–11pm; Sun 3–10pm. Bus: 15, 30, or 41. Cable Car: Powell-Mason line.

Il Pollaio ★ *(Value* ITALIAN   Friendly, affordable, and consistently terrific chicken is the winning combination at Il Pollaio (my girlfriend is addicted to this place). Seat yourself in the tiny triangle-shaped dining room, order, and salivate until your fresh-from-the-grill chicken arrives—perfectly seasoned with a secret recipe of herbs and Italian spices, and so moist it practically falls off the bone. Each meal comes with a choice of salad or fries. If you're not in the mood for chicken, you can opt for rabbit, lamb, pork chop, Italian sausage, or a pretty good hamburger. On a sunny day, get your goods to-go and picnic across the street at Washington Square. FYI, *il pollaio* means "chicken coop" in Italian.

555 Columbus Ave. (between Green and Union sts.). (© 415/362-7727. Reservations not accepted. Main courses $8–$15. DISC, MC, V. Mon–Sat 11:30am–9pm. Bus: 15, 30, 39, 41, or 45. Cable car: Powell-Mason line.

L'Osteria del Forno ★★ ITALIAN/PIZZA   L'Osteria del Forno might be only slightly larger than a walk-in closet, but it's one of the top three authentic Italian restaurants in North Beach. Peer in the window facing Columbus Avenue, and you'll probably see two Italian women with their hair up, sweating from the heat of the brick-lined oven, which cranks out the best focaccia (and focaccia sandwiches) in the city. There's no pomp or circumstance here: Locals come strictly to eat. The menu features a variety of superb pizzas, salads, soups, and fresh pastas, plus a good selection of daily specials (pray for the roast pork braised in milk), which includes a roast of the day, pasta, and ravioli. Small baskets of warm focaccia keep you going until the arrival of the entrees, which should always be accompanied by a glass of Italian red. Good news for folks on the go: You can get pizza by the slice.

519 Columbus Ave. (between Green and Union sts.). (© 415/982-1124. Reservations not accepted. Sandwiches $6–$7, pizzas $10–$18, main courses $6–$14. No credit cards. Sun–Mon and Wed–Thurs 11:30am–10pm; Fri–Sat 11:30am–10:30pm. Bus: 15, 30, 41, or 45.

Mario's Bohemian Cigar Store *Finds* ITALIAN   Across the street from Washington Square is one of North Beach's most popular neighborhood hangouts. The century-old bar—small, well worn, and perpetually busy—is best known for its focaccia sandwiches, including meatball and eggplant. Wash it down with an excellent cappuccino or a house Campari as you watch the tourists stroll by. And no, they do not sell cigars.

566 Columbus Ave. (at Union St.). © **415/362-0536.** Sandwiches $7.75–$8.50. MC, V. Daily 10am–11pm. Closed Dec 24–25 and Jan 1. Bus: 15, 30, 41, or 45.

Mo's Gourmet Burgers *Kids* AMERICAN/BURGERS   This simple diner offers a straightforward but winning combination: big, thick, grilled patties of fresh-ground, best-quality, center-cut chuck; fresh french fries; and choice of cabbage slaw, sautéed garlic mushrooms, or beans and rice. Voilà! You've got the city's burger of choice (Zuni Café's is a contender, but at almost twice the price—p. 133). The other food—spicy chicken sandwich; steak with veggies, garlic bread, and potatoes; and token veggie dishes—is also up to snuff, but it's that messy, memorable burger that keeps the carnivores captivated (the sinisterly sweet shakes are fantastic, too). Bargain-diners will appreciate prices, with burgers ranging from $5.95 for a classic to $8.75 for an "Alpine" burger with cheese, sautéed mushrooms, and fries. Entrees start at $9 for a roasted half-chicken with three sides and top out at $14 for New York steak. The classic breakfast menu is also a bargain. A second location at SoMa's Yerba Buena Gardens, 772 Folsom St., between Third and Fourth streets (© **415/957-3779**), is open Monday from 10am to 5pm, Tuesday through Friday from 10am to 8pm, Saturday from 9am to 8pm, and Sunday from 9am to 5pm. It features breakfast and burgers.

1322 Grant Ave. (between Vallejo and Green sts.). © **415/788-3779.** Main courses $5–$14. MC, V. Sun–Thurs 11am–10:30pm; Fri–Sat 11am–11:30pm; breakfast daily 9am–2pm. Bus: 9X, 15, 30, 39, 41, or 45.

North Beach Pizza * ITALIAN/PIZZA   Whenever I order a North Beach pizza I'm always disappointed by the measly amount of toppings. Then I eat the entire damn thing in one sitting. There's something about that uniquely gooey whole-milk mozzarella and hand-spun dough with thick, chewy edges that's so addictive it's been the most awarded and widely beloved pizza in the city for 2 decades. You *can* get a better pizza in the city—Pauline's has them beat—but not in North Beach, not via free delivery throughout the city, and not at 2:30am on Sunday when you're drunk, stoned, and starving. Either create your own pizza from their list of 20 fresh ingredients (the sausage with black olives is great), or choose from the house's 10 specialties such as the San Francisco Special—clams, garlic, cheese, and one brutal case of halitosis. There are numerous satellite NBPs throughout the city offering fast, free delivery until the wee hours. *Tip:* The lunch special, daily from 11am to 4pm, gets you an individual 8-incher for under $5.

1499 Grant St. (at Union St.). © **415/433-2444.** www.northbeachpizza.com. Main courses $9–$21. AE, DC, DISC, MC, V. Mon–Thurs 11am–1am and Sun; Fri–Sat 11am–3am. Cable car: Powell-Mason line. Bus: 15, 30, 41, or 45.

Pasta Pomodoro ITALIAN   If you're looking for a good, cheap meal in North Beach—or anywhere else in town, for that matter—this San Francisco chain can't be beat. There can be a short wait for a table, but after you're seated, you'll be surprised at how promptly you're served. Every dish is fresh and sizable and, best of all, costs a third of what you'd pay elsewhere. Winners include spaghetti *frutti di mare* made with calamari, mussels, scallops, tomato, garlic, and wine; and smoked rigatoni, with roast chicken, sun-dried tomatoes, cream, mushrooms, and Parmesan—both under $8. When I don't feel like cooking, I often stop here for angel-hair pasta with tomato and basil and a decadent spinach salad with candied walnuts and bleu cheese. The tiramisu is huge, delicious, and cheap, too. There are seven other locations, including 2304 Market St., at 16th St. (© **415/558-8123**); 3611 California St., between Spruce St. and Parker Ave. (© **415/831-0900**); and 816 Irving St., between Ninth and 10th sts. (© **415/566-0900**).

655 Union St. (at Columbus Ave.). © 415/399-0300. www.pastapomodoro.com. Reservations not accepted. Main courses $6–$12. AE, MC, V. Sun–Thurs 11am–10:30pm; Fri–Sat 11am–11pm. Bus: 15, 30, 41, or 45. Cable car: Powell-Mason line.

Sodini's Green Valley Restaurant ITALIAN Sodini's is everything you would expect from a classic Italian restaurant in North Beach—a family-owned and operated business run by a friendly, vivacious staff that serves hearty Italian classics on tables topped with wax-encrusted chianti bottle candles while the Chairman of the Board (Francis Albert Sinatra, of course!) croons love songs in the background. There's usually a wait for a table; fortunately, the bar is a great place to hang out and shoot the breeze with the friendly bartender (most likely one of the owners) and get a little North Beach history lesson. The clientele is a mix of locals and tourists, all getting hungrier by the minute as the aroma of garlic and fresh basil wafts from the kitchen. The large wood-fired pizzas are very good and worth moving that belt one more notch, but their best dish is the light and tender gnocchi. Regardless of what you order, you won't leave hungry or unhappy.

510 Green St. (at Grant St.). © 415/291-0499. Main courses $10–$23. MC, V. Daily 5–10pm. Bus: 15, 30, 41, or 45. Cable car: Powell-Mason line.

The Stinking Rose ITALIAN Garlic is the "flower" from which this restaurant gets its name. From soup to ice cream, the supposedly healthful herb is a star ingredient in almost every dish. ("We season our garlic with food," exclaims the menu.) From a gourmet point of view, the Stinking Rose is unremarkable. Pizzas, pastas, and meats smothered in simple, overpowering sauces are tasty, but they're memorable only for their singular garlicky intensity. That said, this is a fun place; the restaurant's lively atmosphere and odoriferous aroma combine for good entertainment. The best dishes include iron-skillet–roasted mussels with garlic sauce; smoked mozzarella, garlic, and tomato pizza; salt-roasted tiger prawns with garlic parsley glaze; and 40-clove garlic chicken (served with garlic mashed potatoes, of course). *Tip:* Don't go here before a date.

325 Columbus Ave. (between Vallejo and Broadway). © 415/781-7673. www.thestinkingrose.com. Reservations recommended. Main courses $13–$30. AE, DC, DISC, MC, V. Sun–Thurs 11am–11pm; Fri–Sat 11am–midnight. Bus: 15, 30, 41, or 45.

Tommaso's *Kids* ITALIAN From the street, Tommaso's looks wholly unappealing—a drab, windowless brown facade sandwiched between sex shops. Then why are people always waiting in line to get in? Because everyone knows that Tommaso's, which opened in 1935, bakes one of San Francisco's best traditional-style pizzas. The center of attention in the downstairs dining room is the chef, who continuously tosses huge hunks of garlic and mozzarella onto pizzas before sliding them into the oak-burning brick oven. Nineteen different toppings make pizza the dish of choice, even though Italian classics such as veal Marsala, chicken cacciatore, superb lasagna, and wonderful calzones are also available. Tommaso's also offers half-bottles of house wines, homemade manicotti, and good Italian coffee. If you can overlook the seedy surroundings, this fun, boisterous restaurant is a great place to take the family.

1042 Kearny St. (at Broadway). ✆ **415/398-9696.** www.tommasosnorthbeach.com. Reservations not accepted. Pasta and pizza $14–$24, main courses $11–$18. AE, DC, DISC, MC, V. Tues–Sat 5–10:30pm; Sun 4–9:30pm. Closed Dec 15–Jan 15. Bus: 15 or 41.

SUPER-CHEAP EATS

Golden Boy Pizza ✮ *Value* ITALIAN/PIZZA   Pass by Golden Boy when the bars are hopping in North Beach and you'll find a crowd of inebriated sots savoring steamy slices of wondrously gooey pizza. But you don't have to be bombed to enjoy the big, doughy squares of Italian-style pizzas, each enticingly placed in the front windows (the aroma alone is deadly). Locals have flocked here for years to fill up on one of the cheapest and cheesiest meals in town. Expect to take your feast to go on busy nights, as there are only a few bar seats inside.

542 Green St. (between Stockton St. and Grant Ave.). ✆ **415/982-9738.** Pizza slice $2.50–$3.50. No credit cards. Sun–Thurs 11:30am–11pm; Fri–Sat 11:30am–2am. Bus: 15, 30, 45, 39, or 41.

San Francisco Art Institute Café ✮ *Finds* AMERICAN   Never in a million years would you stumble upon the Art Institute Café by accident (unless you happen to be wandering around the top floor of San Francisco's oldest and largest art school). One of the best-kept secrets in San Francisco, this cafe offers fresh, affordable cafe standards for in-the-know residents and visitors as well as Art Institute students: a wide array of hearty breakfast dishes, fresh salads, sandwiches on homemade bread, daily ethnically inspired specials, and anything with caffeine in it—all priced at or under $6. The view, which extends from Alcatraz Island to Coit Tower and beyond, is so phenomenal that the exterior served as the outside of Sigourney Weaver's ridiculously chic apartment in the movie *Copycat.* The cafe itself boasts an open kitchen, sleek aluminum tables, and weekly rotating student art shows. A large courtyard with cement tables (and the same Hollywood view) is the perfect spot for an alfresco lunch high above the tourist fray.

800 Chestnut St. (at Jones and Leavenworth sts.). ✆ **415/749-4567.** Main courses $3–$6. No credit cards. Fall–spring Mon–Thurs 8am–5pm; Fri 8am–4pm; Limited hours during summer. Bus: 49 or 30. Cable car: Powell-Hyde or Powell-Mason line.

8 Fisherman's Wharf

Cafe Pescatore ✮ ITALIAN   This cozy trattoria is one of the better bets in Fisherman's Wharf. Two walls of sliding glass doors offer pseudo-sidewalk seating when the weather's warm, although heavy vehicular traffic can detract from the alfresco experience. All the classics are well represented here: crisp Caesar salad; fried calamari; bruschetta; cioppino; pastas; chicken Marsala; and veal medallions with mushrooms, caramelized onions, sage, and veal sauce. The consensus is to order anything that's cooked in the open kitchen's wood-fired oven, such as pizza (Margherita), roasts (sea bass with pine-nut crust, sun-dried tomato pesto, and roasted veggies), or panini (lunch only; grilled chicken or grilled eggplant). By the way, they serve darned good breakfasts, too.

2455 Mason St. (at North Point St., adjoining the Tuscan Inn). ✆ **415/561-1111.** www.cafepescatore.com. Reservations recommended. Main courses $6–$12 breakfast, $8.50–$17 lunch and dinner. AE, DC, DISC, MC, V. Daily 7am–10pm. Bus: 15, 39, or 42. Cable car: Powell-Mason line. Streetcar: F.

Fog City Diner ✮ AMERICAN   The Fog City Diner gets a lot of mixed reviews among locals for service and food, but I've always had a satisfying experience dining here. The restaurant looks like a genuine American metallic diner—but only from the outside. Inside, dark polished woods, inspired lighting, and a well-stocked raw bar tell you this is no hash-slinger. Here dressed-up diner dishes include $11 gourmet burgers with house-made pickles, huge salads, "warm breads," soups, sandwiches, cioppino, macaroni and Gouda cheese, and pork chops. Fancier fish and meat meals include grilled catches of the day and thick-cut steaks. Light eaters can make a meal out of the long list of "small plates," which include crab cakes and quesadillas with asparagus and leek. They've recently opened for weekend brunch as well. The food is fine, but if your heart is set on coming here, do so at lunch—you'll be better off elsewhere if you want a special dinner.

1300 Battery St. (at the Embarcadero). ✆ **415/982-2000**. www.fogcitydiner.com. Reservations recommended. Main courses $11–$22. DC, DISC, MC, V. Mon–Thurs 11am–10pm; Fri 11am–11pm; Sat 10:30am–11pm; Sun 10:30am–9pm. Bus: 42.

Hard Rock Cafe *Kids* AMERICAN   I hate to plug chains, and this loud, rock-nostalgia-laden place would be no exception if: 1) I knew tourists were no longer interested in it; and 2) it didn't serve a fine burger and overall decent heaping plates of food at such moderate prices. For many, the real draw—more than 20 years past the time when it was hip to wear the restaurant's logo—is the merchandise shop, but a shopper's gotta eat. The friendly menu offers burgers, fajitas, baby back ribs, grilled fish, chicken, salads, and sandwiches, the munching of which tend to be muffled by blaring music. Although it's nothing unique to San Francisco, the Hard Rock is a fine place to bring the kids and grab a bite.

PIER 39. ✆ **415/956-2013**. www.hardrock.com. Reservations accepted for groups of 25 or more. Main courses $8–$23. AE, DC, DISC, MC, V. Sun–Thurs 11am–11pm; Fri–Sat 11am–midnight. Validated parking for 1 hr. during lunch and 2 hr. after 6pm at PIER 39 lot. Bus: 10, 15, or 47. Streetcar: F.

Lou's Pier 47 CAJUN/SEAFOOD/STEAK   This popular restaurant and blues club is one of the few establishments on Fisherman's Wharf that locals will admit they've been to at least once. The bottom floor consists of a bar and bistro-style dining room, while the upstairs hosts blues bands every night of the week, with the occasional Motown, country, and R&B act thrown in for variety. Lunch and dinner items range from a variety of Cajun classics such as gumbo ya ya, jambalaya, and shrimp Creole to baby back ribs, steamed Dungeness crab, blackened swordfish, and New York steak. There's a lengthy starters menu if you just want to nosh on a Jamaica jerk salad, Louisiana crawfish bowl, or "peel-'n'-eat" shrimp. ***Budget tip:*** The Saturday blues show from noon to 3pm is free.

300 Jefferson St. (near Pier 47). ✆ **415/771-5687**. www.louspier47.com. Reservations recommended. Main courses $11–$18. AE, DC, MC, V. Daily 11am–11pm (club remains open until 2am). Bus: 32. Cable car: Powell-Hyde line.

SUPER-CHEAP EATS

Boudin Sourdough Bakery & Café DELI   If your only taste of the crusted, tangy loaf known as sourdough has been store-bought kind outside the Bay Area, you've never really experienced this legendary bread. Though locals will argue that smaller bakeries such as East Bay's Acme and Semifreddi are better breadmasters, Boudin (bo-DEEN) has been baking sourdough breads in San Francisco for than 150 years (that, and sandwiches so hearty that it takes two hands to tame them). Bakery outposts are scattered throughout town and offer similar menus: turkey, ham, tuna, and roast beef sandwiches; salads; clam chowder; and other simple fare. At the massive new Fisherman's Wharf location (see review on p. 147) you can buy some fresh loaves to go along with your chowderboat. (Buy it fresh on the day you're leaving if you want to take some home with you.) There are dozens of locations throughout the city, including 2890 Taylor St., at Jefferson Street (© 415/776-1849), and in the basement at Macy's downtown, at O'Farrell and Stockton streets (© 415/296-4740).

(Kids The Best of San Francisco's Family-Friendly Restaurants

Andalé Taqueria (p. 128)   So casual, so inexpensive, and offering lots of options, you can feed the whole clan here—and fit them comfortably in the dining room or on the patio.

Beach Chalet Brewery & Restaurant (p. 138)   You can relax and enjoy house-made beers and snacks while the kids peer at the ocean through picture windows or check out the Beach Chalet historic displays downstairs.

Brandy Ho's Hunan Food (p. 115)   So long as the kids like Chinese food, they're welcome in this bustling, casual dining room.

Dottie's True Blue Café (p. 104)   This is a cramped, casual breakfast spot with lots of items to tempt the tots.

Eliza's (p. 132)   Serving some of the most flavorful and vibrant California-influenced Chinese food in town, Eliza's is fun for the whole family. Parents will love the quality of the cuisine and the casual surroundings that make it okay for the kids to really get into their meal. Kids will also get a kick out of the whimsical art-glass around the dining room.

Ella's (p. 127)   Provided your kids are patient enough to wait in the ever-growing line for the best breakfast in town, they'll be thrilled with the offerings in this bright, cheery, and bustling Pacific Heights restaurant—especially when they get their huge stack of pancakes.

Gold Mountain (p. 115)   Chinese families head here every weekend to gather around large round tables and indulge in dim sum small-plate feasts. Decor is minimal, which makes the folks feel that much better when the soy sauce hits the plate or a few bites of rice hit the floor.

Hard Rock Cafe (p. 124)   You know the drill: Loud music, pseudo hip environs, and kid-friendly fare.

Mo's Gourmet Burgers (p. 121)   Perfect for everyone, it's got killer burgers and a very low-key atmosphere.

Mel's Drive-In (p. 128)   A 1950s-style diner with all the trappings (think shakes, burgers, fries, and 25¢ jukeboxes), this family-friendly spot gives tots crayons and coloring-book pages.

Pasta Pomodoro (p. 121)   Cheap, fast, and informal is the perfect recipe for a tasty Italian dining experience.

Tommaso's (p. 122)   You can satisfy the kids' (and your) pizza cravings at this small North Beach joint, which is known to serve the best brick-oven baked pies in town in a very casual, cramped, and old-school authentic atmosphere.

156 Jefferson St. (between Mason and Taylor sts.). ℂ 415/928-1849. www.boudinbakery.com. Sandwiches, soups, salads $5–$6. AE, MC, V. Mon–Thurs 7:30am–9pm; Fri–Sun 7:30am–10pm. Bus: 15, 32, 39, 42, or 82X. Cable car: Powell-Mason line.

WORTH A SPLURGE

Forbes Island ⭐ (Moments) FRENCH   Been there and done that in every San Francisco dining room? Then it's time for Forbes Island, a wonderfully ridiculous floating restaurant disguised as an island (complete with a lighthouse and real 40-ft. palm trees) and unknown to even most locals. The idea's kitschy, but the execution's actually quite wonderful. Here's how it works: Arrive at the dock next to PIER 39, call the restaurant via the courtesy phone, climb aboard its pontoon boat that takes you on a 4-minute journey to the "island" located 75 feet from the city's famed sea lions, and descend into the island's bowels to find a surprisingly classy, Tudorlike wood-paneled dining room. Warmed by a fireplace and amused by fish swimming past the portholes (yes, the dining room is a wee bit underwater), guests dine on surprisingly well-prepared classic French food such as decadent ragout of wild mushrooms, toasted brioche, and soft goat cheese or roasted half-rack of lamb with herb brioche crust and tomato lamb *jus*. A recently added "Sea Lion" room boasts the closest view you'll ever get of the creatures. ***But be warned:*** The menu is very limited, the wine list features basic big-name producers without listing the vintage, and the "island" does gently rock (landlubbers need not apply or should take Dramamine 2 hr. beforehand). ***One annoyance:*** There's a mandatory $3 shuttle fee since the only other way to get here is to swim.

Water shuttle is just left of PIER 39. ℂ **415/951-4900.** www.forbesisland.com. Reservations recommended. Main courses $24–$34. AE, MC, V, DC. Wed–Sun arrive between 5–10pm. Validated parking at PIER 39 garage $8 for up to 6 hr.

9 Marina District/Cow Hollow

If you find yourself in this neck of the woods around lunchtime, you might opt for a picnic at the Marina Green, a popular recreational park with fantastic front-row bay views. The **Marina Safeway,** 15 Marina Blvd. (ℂ **415/563-4946**), is the perfect place to pick up fresh-baked breads, gourmet cheeses, and other foodstuffs (including fresh cracked crab when in season). It's open 24 hours.

Ace Wasabi's Rock 'n' Roll Sushi ⭐⭐ JAPANESE/SUSHI   What differentiates this Marina hot spot from the usual sushi spots around town are the unique combinations, the varied menu, and the young, hip atmosphere. The innovative rolls are a nice change for those bored with traditional styles, but don't worry if someone in your party isn't a raw fish fan: There are also plenty of non-seafood and cooked items on the menu. Don't miss the rainbow "Three Amigos" roll, or the "Scorpion Roll" with crunchy rock shrimp, scallops, and caramelized pecans wrapped with mango and avocado. The service, like the surroundings, is jovial.

3339 Steiner St. (at Chestnut St.). ℂ 415/567-4903. www.acewasabissushi.com. Reservations not accepted. Sushi $4–$14. AE, MC, V. Mon–Thurs 5:30–10:30pm; Fri–Sat 5:30–11pm; Sun 5–10pm. Bus: 30.

Balboa Café ⭐ AMERICAN   Back in the 1980s, the Balboa Café was San Francisco's main "meet market," filled each week with the young and the restless. Though things bottomed out in the early 1990s, the wheel is turning once again for this trendy, stylish Cow Hollow hangout. You'll probably be forced to mingle with the Marina "pretty people" crowd at the bar until a table frees up. The limited menu offers some upscale options, such as Cabernet-braised short ribs with mashed potatoes and roasted root vegetables, but it's the Balboa burgers and Caesar salads that get the most requests.

3199 Fillmore St. (at Greenwich St.). ℂ 415/921-3944. Reservations for 6 or more only. Main courses $8–$12 lunch, $8–$22 dinner, $7.50–$10 weekend brunch. AE, MC, V. Mon–Wed 11:30am–10pm; Thurs–Fri 11:30am–11pm; Sat 10am–11pm; Sun 10am–10pm; bar daily til 2am. Valet parking after 6pm for $13. Bus: 22.

Betelnut ⚶ SOUTHEAST ASIAN   While San Francisco is teeming with Asian restaurants, few offer the posh, fashionable dining environment of this restaurant on upscale Union Street. As the menu explains, the restaurant is themed after Pejui Wu, a traditional Asian beer house offering local brews and savory dishes. But with the bamboo paneling, red Formica countertops, and low-hanging lamps, the place feels less like an authentic harbor restaurant and more like a set out of Madonna's movie *Shanghai Surprise.* Still, the atmosphere is en vogue, with dimly lit booths, ringside seating overlooking the bustling stir-fry chefs, sidewalk tables (weather permitting), and body-to-body flirting at the cramped but festive bar. Starters include sashimi and tasty salt-and-pepper whole gulf prawns; main courses offer wok-seared Mongolian beef and Singapore chile crab (seasonal). Whatever you do, order their heavenly signature dessert: a mouthwatering tapioca pudding with sweet red adzuki beans.

2030 Union St. (at Buchanan St.). ℂ 415/929-8855. Reservations recommended. Main courses $9–$16. DC, DISC, MC, V. Sun–Thurs 11:30am–11pm; Fri–Sat 11:30am–midnight. Bus: 22, 41, or 45.

E'Angelo Restaurant ⚶ ITALIAN   Back when I was barely making enough to cover my rent, I would often treat myself to a night out at E'Angelo. All the pastas and pizzas cost less than $13; the atmosphere is casual and fun; tables are cozy-cramped; and the Italian staff is friendly. For me, the combination made not only for a hearty meal, but for an opportunity to mingle with San Francisco: to live a little, eavesdrop on neighbors' conversations, and perhaps even run into local celebrities such as Robin Williams with his family. While years have passed, not much has changed at this traditional Italian hot spot: The place still won't take reservations or credit cards, but it does serve decent portions of pastas, veal, lamb, chicken, and fish; a carafe of red or white wine for about 18 bucks (thrifty by-the-bottle prices, too); and one heck of a rich eggplant parmigiana. And unlike those at most of the neighboring restaurants, desserts are dirt cheap.

2234 Chestnut St. (between Pierce and Scott sts.). ℂ 415/567-6164. Reservations not accepted. Main courses $13–$17. No credit cards. Tues–Sun 5–10pm. Bus: 22, 30, 30X.

Ella's ⚶⚶ ᴋids AMERICAN/BREAKFAST   Well known throughout town as the undisputed king of breakfasts, this restaurant's acclaim means you're likely to wait to get in—up to an hour on weekends. But midweek and in the wee hours of morning, it's possible to slide onto a counter or table seat in the colorful split dining room and lose yourself in outstanding and obscenely generous servings of chicken hash, crisped to perfection and served with eggs any way you like them, with fluffy buttermilk biscuits. Pancakes, omelets, and the short list of other breakfast essentials are equally revered. Alas, service can be woefully slow, but at least the buspersons are quick to fill coffee cups. Come lunchtime, solid entrees like salads, chicken potpie, and grilled salmon with mashed potatoes remind you what's great about good old American cooking.

500 Presidio Ave. (at California St.). ℂ 415/441-5669. www.ellassanfrancisco.com. Reservations accepted for lunch. Main courses $5.50–$10 breakfast, $6–$12 lunch. AE, DISC, MC, V. Mon–Fri 7am–5pm; Sat–Sun 8:30am–2pm. Bus: 1, 3, or 43.

Isa ★★ FRENCH   Luke Sung, who trained with some of the best French chefs in the city, has captured my and many locals' hearts by creating the kind of menu us foodies dream of: a smattering of small dishes that allow you to try numerous items in one sitting. It's a good thing the menu, considered "French tapas," offers small portions at reasonable prices. After all, it's asking a lot to make a diner choose between mushroom ragout and seared foie gras with caramelized apples, potato-wrapped sea bass in brown butter, and rack of lamb. Here, a party of two can choose all of these plus one or two more and not be rolled out the door afterward. Adding to the allure is the warm boutique dining environment—50 seats scattered amid a small dining room in the front, and a large tented and heated patio out back that sets the mood with a warm yellow glow. Take a peek at the "kitchen," a shoebox of a cooking space, to appreciate Sung's accomplishments that much more. Cocktailers, have your predinner drink elsewhere: Isa serves beer and wine only.

3324 Steiner St. (between Lombard and Chestnut sts.). ℂ 415/567-9588. www.isarestaurant.com. Reservations recommended. Main courses $9–$16. MC, V. Mon–Thurs 5:30–10pm; Fri–Sat 5:30–10:30pm. Bus: 22, 28, 30, 30X, 43, or 76.

Mel's Drive-In ★ *Kids* AMERICAN   Sure, it's contrived, touristy, and nowhere near healthy, but when you get that urge for a chocolate shake and banana cream pie at the stroke of midnight—or when you want to entertain the kids—no other place in the city comes through like Mel's Drive-in. Modeled after a classic 1950s diner, right down to the jukebox at each table, Mel's harkens back to the halcyon days when cholesterol and fried foods didn't jab your guilty conscience with every greasy, wonderful bite. Too bad the prices don't reflect the '50s; a burger with fries and a Coke costs about $9.50.

There's another Mel's at 3355 Geary St., at Stanyan Street (ℂ **415/387-2244**); it's open from 6am to 1am Sunday through Thursday and 6am to 3am Friday and Saturday. Additional locations, at 1050 Van Ness (ℂ **415/292-6857**), and at 801 Mission St (ℂ **415/227-4477**), are open Sunday through Thursday 6am to 3am and Friday and Saturday 6am to 4am.

2165 Lombard St. (at Fillmore St.). ℂ 415/921-3039. www.melsdrive-in.com. Main courses $6.50–$12 breakfast, $7–$10 lunch, $8–$15 dinner. MC, V. Sun–Wed 6am–2am; Thurs 6am–3am; Fri–Sat 24 hr. Bus: 22, 30, or 43.

SUPER-CHEAP EATS

Andalé Taqueria ★★ *Kids* MEXICAN   Andalé (Spanish for "hurry up") offers incredible high-end fast food for the health-conscious and the just plain hungry. As the long menu explains, this small California chain prides itself on its fresh ingredients and low-cal options. Lard, preservatives, and canned items are eschewed; Andalé favors salad dressings made with double virgin olive oil, whole vegetarian beans (not refried), skinless chicken, salsas and *aguas frescas* made from fresh fruits and veggies, and mesquite-grilled meats. Add the location (on a sunny shopping stretch), sophisticated decor, full bar, and check-me-out patio seating (complete with corner fireplace), and it's no wonder the good-looking, fitness-fanatic Marina District considers this place home. Cafeteria-style service keeps prices low. *Bargain tips:* No one can complain about a quarter of a mesquite-roasted chicken with potatoes, salsa, and tortillas for $6.75. If you want to go traditional, stick with the giant burritos or the fantastic $2.95 tacos—a nibbler's dream.

2150 Chestnut St. (between Steiner and Pierce sts.). ℂ **415/749-0506**. Reservations not accepted. Most dishes $4.25–$11. MC, V. Mon–Thurs and Sun 11am–10pm (11am–9pm in the winter); Fri–Sat 11am–10:30pm. Bus: 22, 28, 30, 30X, 43, 76, or 82X.

Barney's Gourmet Hamburgers ⚐ *Kids* AMERICAN/HAMBURGERS   If you're on a perpetual quest for the best burger in America, a mandatory stop is Barney's Gourmet Hamburgers. Once you get past all the framed awards for the Bay Area's best burger, you're bombarded by a mind-boggling menu of beef, chicken, turkey, and vegetarian burgers to choose from, as well as sandwiches and salads. The ultimate combo is a humungous basket of fries (enough for a party of three), a one-third-pound burger, and thick shake. Popular versions are the California Burger with jack cheese, bacon, ortega chiles, and sour cream, or the Popeye Burger made with chicken, sautéed spinach and feta cheese. Be sure to dine alfresco in the hidden courtyard in back.

3344 Steiner St. (between Chestnut and Lombard sts.). ⓒ 415/563-0307. www.barneysrestaurant.com. Main courses $5–$8. No credit cards. Mon–Thurs 11am–9:30pm; Fri–Sat 11am–10pm; Sun 11am–9pm. Bus: 30.

The Grove ⚐ CAFE   The Grove is the kind of place you go just to hang out and enjoy the fact that you're in San Francisco. That the heaping salads, lasagna, pasta, sandwiches, and daily specials are wholesome is an added bonus. It's the easy-going vibe that's the real attraction: the old, large, family-style tables along the scuffed hardwood floors; huge, open windows where inside diners scope those at the sidewalk seats; a casual, attractive, sociable crowd; and Nina Simone or some fabulous blues CD playing overhead. It's the perfect place to read the newspaper, meet up with friends, or sip an enormous cup of coffee, a glass of wine, or a beer. A second Pacific Heights location is at 2016 Fillmore St., between California and Pine streets (ⓒ **415/474-1419**).

2250 Chestnut St. (between Scott and Pierce sts.). ⓒ **415/474-4843.** Most main courses $6–$7. MC, V. Mon–Fri 7am–11pm; Sat–Sun 8am–11pm. Bus: 22, 28, 30, 30X, 43, 76, or 82X.

Home Plate ⚐ *Finds* BREAKFAST   Dollar for dollar, Home Plate just may be the best breakfast place in San Francisco. Many Marina residents kick off their hectic weekends by carbo-loading here on big piles of buttermilk pancakes and waffles smothered with fresh fruit, or hefty omelets stuffed with everything from apple wood–smoked ham to spinach. You'll always start off with a coveted plate of freshly baked scones, best eaten with a bit of butter and a dab of jam. Be sure to look over the daily specials scrawled on the little green chalkboard before you order. And as every fan of this tiny cafe knows, it's best to call ahead and ask to have your name put on the waiting list before you slide into Home Plate.

2274 Lombard St. (at Pierce St.). ⓒ **415/922-HOME.** Main courses $3.95–$7. DC, DISC, MC, V. Daily 7am–4pm. Bus: 28, 30, 43, or 76.

Pluto's ⚐ *Value* CALIFORNIA   Catering to the Marina District's DINK (double income, no kids) crowd, Pluto's combines assembly-line efficiency with high quality. The result is cheap, fresh fare: huge salads with a dozen choices of toppings; oven-roasted poultry and grilled meats (the flank steak is great); sandwiches; and a wide array of sides like crispy garlic potato rings, seasonal veggies, and barbecued chicken wings. Pluto's serves teas, sodas, bottled brews, and Napa wines as well as homemade desserts. The ordering system is bewildering to newcomers; grab a checklist, and then hand it to the servers who check off your order and relay it to the cashier. Seating is limited during the rush, but the turnover is fairly fast. A second location is at 627 Irving St., at Eighth Avenue (ⓒ **415/753-8867**).

3258 Scott St. (at Chestnut St.). ⓒ **415/7-PLUTOS.** www.plutosfreshfood.com. Reservations not accepted. Main courses $3.50–$5.75. MC, V. Mon–Fri 11am–10pm; Sat–Sun 10:30am–10pm. Bus: 28, 30, or 76.

WORTH A SPLURGE

A16 ★★ ITALIAN   This sleek, casual, and wonderfully lively spot featuring Neapolitan-style pizza and cuisine from the region of Campania has been white-hot since its 2004 opening. Named after the motorway that traverses the region, the divided space boasts a full bar up front, a larger dining area and open kitchen in the back, and a wall of wines in between. But its secret weapon is chef Christophe Hille who whips up outstanding appetizers, pizza, and entrees with aplomb. Even if you must have the insanely good braised pork breast with olives, herbs, and caramelized chestnuts to yourself, start by sharing dried fava beans with fennel salad and tuna conserva with braised dandelion greens and crunchy breadcrumbs. Add to that the sommelier Shelley Lindgren, who guides diners through the exciting wine list featuring 40 wines by the half-glass, glass, and carafe, and you've got one of San Francisco's best and busiest restaurants

2355 Chestnut St. (between Divisadero and Scott sts.). *(C)* **415/771-2216.** www.a16sf.com. Reservations recommended. Main courses $8–$13 lunch, $14–$20 dinner. AE, DC, MC, V. Wed–Fri 11:30am–2:30pm; Sun–Thurs 5–10pm; Fri–Sat 5–11pm. Bus: 22, 30, or 30X.

10 Pacific Heights

Chez Nous ★★ FRENCH   Diners get crammed into the 45-seat dining area of this bright, cheery, small, and bustling cafelike dining room, but the French tapas are so delicious and affordable, no one seems to care. Indeed, this friendly and fast-paced neighborhood haunt has become a blueprint for other restaurants that understand the allure of small plates. But Chez Nous stands out as more than a petite-portion trendsetter. The clincher is that most of its Mediterranean dishes taste so clean and fresh you can't wait to come back and dine here again. Start with the soup, whatever it is; don't skip tasty french fries with *harissa* (Tunisian hot sauce) aioli; savor the lamb chops with lavender sea salt; and save room for their famed dessert, the minicustard-cakelike *canneles de Bordeaux*.

1911 Fillmore St. (between Pine and Bush sts.). *(C)* **415/441-8044.** Reservations recommended. Small plates $5–$12. AE, MC, V. Daily 11:30am–2:45pm and 5:30–10pm (Fri–Sat until 11pm). Bus: 22, 41, or 45.

SUPER-CHEAP EATS

La Méditerranée ★ *Value* MEDITERRANEAN   With an upscale-cafe ambience and quality food, La Méditerranée has long warranted its reputation as one of the quainter inexpensive restaurants on upper Fillmore. Here you'll find freshly prepared traditional Mediterranean food that's worlds apart from the Euro-eclectic fare many restaurants now call "Mediterranean." Baba ghanouj, tabbouleh, dolmas, and hummus start out the menu. More important, the menu offers one very tasty chicken Cilicia, a phyllo-dough dish that's hand-rolled and baked with cinnamony spices, almonds, chickpeas, and raisins; also good is zesty chicken pomegranate drumsticks on a bed of rice. Both come with green salad, potato salad, or soup for around $9.25. Ground lamb dishes, quiches, and Middle Eastern combo plates round out the very affordable menu, and wine comes by the glass and in half- or full liters. A second location is at 288 Noe St., at Market Street (*(C)* **415/431-7210**).

2210 Fillmore St. (at Sacramento St.). *(C)* **415/921-2956.** www.cafelamed.com. Main courses $7–$10 lunch, $8–$12 dinner. AE, MC, V. Sun–Thurs 11am–10pm; Fri–Sat 11am–11pm. Bus: 1, 3, or 22.

WORTH A SPLURGE

Cafe Kati ★★ *Finds* CALIFORNIA/EAST-WEST FUSION   Chef Kirk Webber works small wonders in an even smaller kitchen at this diminutive yet distinctive and romantic restaurant off Fillmore Street. The menu highlights California-style dishes spiced with dashes of Asia and Italy and presented in high form, such as the signature Caesar salad sculpted into a towering monument of romaine; or the "dragon roll" of crispy prawns, *shiso* (Japanese basil), avocado, and cucumber wrapped with smoked salmon and seasoned with wasabi vinaigrette. The seasonally changing menu offers such cross-cultural creations as miso-glazed black bass in *dashi* (broth); *udon* (noodles); Shanghai bok choy; tempura kabocha squash and *tagarashi* (a Japanese spice blend); or marinated skirt steak with crème fraîche whipped potatoes, crispy Vidalia onion rings, and port-wine sauce. When making a reservation, request a table in the front room.

1963 Sutter St. (between Fillmore and Webster sts.). ✆ **415/775-7313**. www.cafekati.com. Reservations recommended. Main courses $19–$26. AE, MC, V. Tues–Sun 5:30–10pm. Validated parking. Bus: 2, 3, or 22.

11 Japantown

Isobune ✦ SUSHI   Unless you arrive early, there's almost always a short wait to be seated around Isobune's enormous oval sushi bar. But once you're situated, the culinary adventure begins. Right before your eyes, plate after plate of sushi passes by on circling tugboats floating in a minuscule canal that encircles the sushi bar (your kids will be endlessly fascinated). If you see something you like, just grab it off the boat and enjoy; the service staff will tally up the damages at the end. (They can tell how much you've eaten by the number of empty plates.) It's not the best sushi in town, but it's relatively cheap, you get to see it before you eat it, and the atmosphere is fun.

In the Japan Center, 1737 Post St. ✆ **415/563-1030**. Sushi $1.20–$2.95 each. MC, V. Daily 11:30am–10pm. Bus: 2, 3, 4, 22, or 38.

Mifune *Value* JAPANESE   Mifune has been serving traditional Japanese food for 15 years and has a steady clientele of folks who are happy with the fare, and ecstatic about the prices. Slide into one of the Japanese-style booths and order the house specialty, a homemade udon and soba noodles dinner. The *donburi* dishes and tempura dinner are popular as well.

In the Japan Center, 1737 Post St. ✆ **415/922-0337**. Main courses $4–$17. AE, DC, DISC, MC, V. Daily 11am–10pm. Bus: 2, 3, 4, 22, or 38.

Neecha Thai ✦ THAI   I've been coming here for many years for very simple reasons: The food's consistently good, the ambience homey, the prices low, and I once lived down the street. In 1999, the old, dark decor was replaced by a brighter but not-quite-harmonious modern style (unfortunately, they kept the ugly fake-brick paneling). The fare is standard but well-prepared Thai, with over 70 choices, including satay; salads; lemon grass soup; coconut-milk curries; and exotic meat, chicken, seafood, and vegetable dishes—and yes, the ever-popular pad Thai, too. My favorite dishes here are the shrimp in red curry and the salmon wrapped in banana leaf.

2100 Sutter St. (at Steiner St.). ✆ **415/922-9419**. Reservations accepted only for large parties. Most dishes $5–$8. AE, MC, V. Mon–Fri 11am–3pm; daily 5–10pm. Bus: 2, 4, or 38.

Sanppo *Value* JAPANESE   This simple, unpretentious restaurant located across from the Japan Center serves standard Japanese fare at a great price. You may be asked to share one of the few tables that surround a square counter in the small dining room, but at these prices, it's worth it. Lunch items range from fresh, thick-cut sashimi to teriyaki, tempura, beef donburi, and *gyoza* (dumplings filled with savory meat and herbs). Lunches and dinners all include miso soup, rice, and pickled vegetables. Combination dishes, including tempura, sashimi, and gyoza, or tempura and teriyaki, are also available.

1702 Post St. (at Laguna St.). ☎ **415/346-3486.** Reservations not accepted. Main courses $6–$15; combination dishes $10–$17. MC, V. Mon–Thurs 11:30am–midnight; Fri–Sat 11:30am–1pm; Sun noon–10pm. Bus: 2, 3, 4, or 38.

12 Civic Center & Environs

Eliza's ⓐⓐ ⓥⓐⓛⓤⓔ ⓚⓘⓓⓢ CHINESE/DIM SUM   Eliza's is one of my favorite restaurants—I eat here whenever I'm in the 'hood. Despite the curiously colorful design of modern architecture, whimsy, and glass art, this perennially packed neighborhood haunt serves some of the freshest, best-tasting Chinese-American food in town. Unlike most comparable options, here the atmosphere (albeit unintentionally funky) and presentation parallel the food. The fresh soups, salads, seafood, pork, chicken, duck, and such specials as spicy eggplant are outstanding and are served on beautiful Italian plates. I often come at midday and order the wonderful kung pao chicken lunch special (available weekdays only): a mixture of tender chicken, peanuts, chile peppers, subtle hot sauce, and perfectly crunchy vegetables. It's one of more than 20 main-course choices that come with rice and soup for around $6. For dinner, the sea bass with black-bean sauce is hugely recommended. The place is usually busy every night, so prepare to stand in line.

2877 California St. (at Broderick St.). ☎ **415/621-4819.** Reservations not accepted. Main courses $4.50–$5.15 lunch, $5.25–$9 dinner. MC, V ($10 minimum). Mon–Fri 11am–3pm and 5–9:45pm; Sat–Sun 4:30–9:45pm. Bus: 6, 7, 21, 66, or 71.

Frjtz Fries ⓐ BELGIAN   This funky-artsy "Belgian fries, crepes, and DJ/Art teahouse" features killer, fat french fries with a barrage of exotic dipping sauces as well as fine sandwiches and salads. Grab a bag of the addictively crisp and thick fried potatoes—perhaps with chipotle rémoulade or balsamic mayo—or swerve toward less lardy options such as a sweet or savory crepe—ranging from Nutella, banana, and whipped cream to grilled rosemary chicken and Swiss cheese—a big, leafy salad, or a chunky focaccia sandwich packed with roasted peppers, red onions, pesto mayo, grilled eggplant, and melted Gorgonzola. Wash it down with Belgian ale.

579 Hayes St. (at Laguna St.). ☎ **415/864-7654.** www.frjtzfries.com. Reservations not accepted. Fries $3–$4.50, crepes $5–$8, sandwiches $7–$8.25. AE, DC, DISC, MC, V. Mon–Thurs 9am–10pm; Fri 9am–midnight; Sat 10am–midnight; Sun 10am–9pm. Bus: 21.

Tommy's Joynt ⓥⓐⓛⓤⓔ ⓚⓘⓓⓢ AMERICAN   With its colorful mural exterior, it's hard to miss Tommy's Joynt, a 58-year-old haven for cholesterol-be-damned hold-outs from America's halcyon days and a late-night favorite for those in search of a cheap and hearty meal. The restaurant's exterior is tame in comparison to the interior, which looks like a Buffalo Bill museum that imploded: a wild collage of stuffed birds, a mounted buffalo head, an ancient piano, rusty firearms, fading prints, a beer-guzzling lion, and Santa Claus masks. The hofbrau-style (think German tavern) buffet offers a cornucopia of rib-clinging a la carte dishes such as their signature buffalo stew (via a buffalo ranch in Wyoming), which resides under heat lamps among the stainless steel trays of turkeys, hams, sloppy joes, oxtails, corned beef, meatballs, mashed potatoes, and other classics. There's also a slew of seating on two levels, almost 100 varieties of beer, and a most interesting clientele of almost exclusively 50-something, pre-cardiac-arrest males (some of whom have been coming to the "Joynt" for more than forty

Finds **Hidden Treasures**

They're on the way to nowhere, but it would be a crime to ignore San Francisco's unique, destination restaurants. If you're not familiar with the streets of San Francisco, be sure to call first to get directions; otherwise, you'll spend more time driving than dining.

Thanh Long *Æ*, 4101 Judah St. (at 46th Ave.; ℂ **415/665-1146**; www. anfamily.com; streetcar: N), an out-of-the-way Sunset District Vietnamese standout known for excellent roasted crab and addictive garlic noodles, was at one time a well-guarded San Francisco secret. Since the owners, the An family, have become rather famous for their aforementioned signature dishes now that they're served in sister restaurants Crustacean in L.A., Vegas, and S.F., suffice it to say, the crab's out of the bag. But this location is still far enough on the outskirts of the city to keep it from becoming too overcrowded. The restaurant is more visually pleasing than most Southeast Asian outposts (white tablecloths, tastefully exotic decor), but the extra glitz is reflected in the prices of luxury dishes (main courses run from $14–$34) such as charbroiled tiger prawns with those famed garlic noodles and steamed sea bass with scallions and ginger sauce. On the plus side, unlike the cheaper options around town, there's a full bar here, too, serving fun cocktails such as the Hanoi Sunset—an intoxicating mixture of Chambord tequila and peach schnapps. Reservations are recommended. Thanh Long is open Sunday and Tuesday through Thursday from 4:30 to 9:30pm, open Friday and Saturday from 4:30 to 10:30pm, and is closed on Mondays.

Little Star Pizza *ÆÆ*, 846 Divisadero St. (at McCallister St.; ℂ **415/441-1118**; www.littlestarpizza.com; bus 5 or 24), may be on a dreary strip of busy Divisadero Street and feel like a bohemian speakeasy with its dark colored walls, low ceilings, and jukebox, but this joint is cranking out the best pizza in town. You're likely to have to wait for a seat at one of the well-spaced tables and you may have to strain to chat over the music and dining din, but there's little I wouldn't endure for one of Little Star's deep dish cornmeal-crust pizzas ($10–$21). Rather than inches of dough, these pies are thin and crisp with high sides that coddle fillings such as chicken, tomatoes, artichoke hearts, red bell peppers, sausage, and feta. These babies take about 20 minutes to bake, which is a great excuse to order chicken wings and a glass of wine for the wait. The place serves dinner daily from 5 to 10pm and offers happy hour drink specials between 4:30 and 6:30pm and 10 to 11:30pm.

years). It's all good stuff in a 'merican kind of way, the kind of place you take grand-pappy when he's in town just to show him that San Francisco's not entirely sissy.

1101 Geary Blvd. (at Van Ness Ave.). ℂ **415/775-4216**. www.tommysjoynt.com. Reservations not accepted. Main courses $4–$7. No credit cards. Daily 10am–2am. Bus: 2, 3, 4, or 38.

WORTH A SPLURGE

Zuni Café *ÆÆÆ* *Finds* MEDITERRANEAN   Zuni Café embodies the best of San Francisco dining: Its clientele spans young hipsters and gorgeous gays and lesbians as well as the everyday foodie; its cuisine is consistently outstanding; and the atmosphere is electric. Its expanse of windows overlooking Market Street gives the place a sense of space despite the fact that it's always packed. For the full effect, stand at the bustling, copper-topped bar and order a glass of wine and a few oysters from the oyster menu (a dozen or so varieties are on hand at all times). Then, because *of course* you made advance reservations, take your seat in the stylish exposed-brick two-level maze of little dining rooms or on the outdoor patio. Then do what we all do: Splurge on chef Judy Rodgers's Mediterranean-influenced menu. Although the changing menu always includes meat (such as hanger steak), fish (grilled or braised in the kitchen's brick oven), and pasta (tagliatelle with nettles, applewood-smoked bacon, butter, and Parmesan), it's almost sinful not to order her brick-oven roasted chicken for two with Tuscan-style bread salad. I rarely pass up the polenta with mascarpone and a proper Caesar salad. But then again, if you're there for lunch or after 10pm, the hamburger on grilled rosemary focaccia bread is a strong contender for the city's best. Whatever you decide, be sure to order a stack of shoestring potatoes.

1658 Market St. (at Franklin St.). ✆ 415/552-2522. Reservations recommended. Main courses $10–$19 lunch, $15–$29 dinner. AE, MC, V. Tues–Sat 11:30am–midnight; Sun 11am–11pm. Valet parking $8 (dinner only). Bus: 6, 7, or 71. Streetcar: All Market St. streetcars.

13 Haight-Ashbury

Cha Cha Cha ★★ (Value CARIBBEAN   This is one of my all-time favorite places to get festive, but it's not for everybody. Cha Cha Cha is not a meal, it's an experience. Put your name on the mile-long list, crowd into the minuscule bar, and sip sangria while you wait (try not to spill when you get bumped by all the young, attractive patrons who are also waiting). When you do finally get seated (it usually takes at least an hour), you'll dine in a loud—and I mean *loud*—dining room with Santería altars, banana trees, and plastic tropical tablecloths. The best thing to do is order from the tapas menu and share the dishes family-style. Fried calamari, fried new potatoes, Cajun shrimp, and mussels in saffron broth are all bursting with flavor and accompanied by rich, luscious sauces—whatever you choose, you can't go wrong. This is the kind of place where you take friends in a partying mood, let your hair down, and make an evening of it. If you want all the flavor without the festivities, come during lunch. Their second, larger location, in the Mission District, at 2327 Mission St., between 19th and 20th streets (✆ **415/648-0504**), is open for dinner only and has a full bar specializing in mojitos.

1801 Haight St. (at Shrader St.). (✆ **415/386-7670**. www.cha3.com. Reservations not accepted. Tapas $5–$9, main courses $12–$15. MC, V. Daily 11:30am–4pm; Sun–Thurs 5–11pm; Fri–Sat 5–11:30pm. Bus: 6, 7, or 71. Streetcar: N.

Citrus Club ★ NOODLES   When you're dining on a budget the cheapest, healthiest, and most satisfying two things to eat in San Francisco are burritos and noodles. Citrus Club does noodles. Large, heaping bowls of thick Asian noodles, served hot in bone-warming broth or cool, minty, and refreshing. In typical Upper Haight fashion, the Club has a sort of cheap-Polynesian-chic feel—love those Vietnamese straw hat lamps—a young, hip staff and clientele, and omnipresent world beat rhythms. Most items on the menu are unlike anything you've seen before, so take my advice and walk around the two dining rooms to see what looks good before ordering. A refreshing starter is the citrus salad made with mixed greens, mint, fried noodles, and a tangy citrus vinaigrette. Popular cold noodle selections are the spicy lime and coconut, and the orange-mint. For hot noodles, try the marmalade shrimp or sweet chile-glazed tofu and greens. If you're in a party mood, order a sake margarita; otherwise, a big pot of ginger tea goes well with any of the noodle dishes.

1790 Haight St. (at Shrader St.). ✆ 415/387-6366. Main courses $6–$10. MC, V. Mon–Thurs and Sun 11:30am–10pm; Fri–Sat 11:30am–11pm. Bus: 6, 7, 66, 71, or 73. Streetcar: N.

Kan Zaman ✿ *finds* MIDDLE EASTERN   An evening dining at Kan Zaman is one of those quintessential Haight-Ashbury experiences that you can't wait to tell your friends about back home. As you pass through glass-beaded curtains, you're led by the hostess to knee-high tables under a billowed canopy tent. Shoes removed, you sit cross-legged with your friends in cushioned comfort. The most adventurous of your group requests an *argeeleh*, a large hookah pipe filled with fruity honey or apricot tobacco. Reluctantly at first, everyone simultaneously sips the sweet smoke from the cobra-like tendrils emanating from the hookah, and then dinner arrives—inexpensive platters offering a variety of classic Middle Eastern cuisine: smoky baba ghanouj, kibbe (cracked wheat with spiced lamb) meat pies, Casablanca beef couscous, spicy hummus with pita bread, succulent lamb and chicken kabobs. The spiced wine is starting to take effect, just in time for the beautiful, sensuous belly dancers who glide across the dining room, mesmerizing the rapt audience with their seemingly impossible gyrations. The evening ends, the bill arrives: $17 each. Perfect. *Note:* Belly dancing starts at 9pm Thursday though Saturday only.

1793 Haight St. (at Shrader St.). ✆ 415/751-9656. Main courses $4–$14. MC, V. Mon–Thu 5pm–midnight; Fri 5pm–2am; Sat noon–2am; Sun noon–midnight. Streetcar: N. Bus: 6, 7, 66, 71, or 73.

RNM ✿ AMERICAN   Lower Haight is hardly known for glamour, and that's just what makes this ultra swanky restaurant such a pleasant surprise. Beyond the full-length silver mesh curtain is a deliciously glitzy diversion that looks more like it belongs in New York City rather than this funky 'hood. Warmly lit with dark-wood floors and tables, a cool full bar, and lounge mezzanine, it's the perfect setting for an equally appealing Italian- and French-inspired American tapas-style menu by chef Justine Miner, who sharpened her culinary skills and knives at San Francisco's Postrio, Café Kati, and Globe. Anticipate tasty appetizers such as ahi tuna tartare with waffle chips, quail egg, and microgreens; the charcuterie plate; and caramelized onion and wild-mushroom pizza with fontina cheese and truffle oil and entrees such as porcini-crusted day boat scallops on a purée of artichokes with shiitake mushroom ragout and a salad of mache greens and watermelon radishes with Meyer lemon vinaigrette; and pan roasted rib-eye steak with pancetta-wrapped red Irish potatoes, wild nettles, Oakville Ranch cabernet butter, and shaved black Himalayan truffles.

598 Haight St. (at Steiner St.). ✆ 415/551-7900. www.rnmrestaurant.com. Reservations recommended. Small plates and pizza $7–$14, main courses $12–$22. AE, MC, V. Tues–Thurs 5:30–10pm; Fri–Sat 5:30–11pm. Closed Sun–Mon. Bus: 7 or 22.

Thep Phanom ✿✿ THAI   It's the combination of fresh ingredients; the perfect lively balance of salty, sweet, hot, and sour flavors; and the attractive and atmospheric surroundings that usually fall short at other ethnic restaurants that make this place special. Those who like to play it safe will be more than happy with the likes of pad thai and coconut-lemongrass soup, but it's advisable to divert from the usual suspects for house specialties such as *Crying tiger* (beef salad with garlic dressing), prawns with eggplant and crisped basil, and *ped swan*—duck with a delicate honey sauce served over spinach. The Haight location usually attracts the young and alternative, but the restaurant's reputation brings in a truly diverse San Francisco crowd. As for the neighborhood: Don't leave anything even remotely valuable in your car.

400 Waller St. (at Fillmore St.). ✆ 415/431-2526. www.thepphanom.com. Reservations recommended. Main courses $9–$13. AE, DC, DISC, MC, V. Daily 5:30–10:30pm. Bus: 6, 7, 22, 66, or 71.

SUPER-CHEAP EATS

Crepes on Cole CREPES   If you're in the Cole Valley or Haight-Ashbury area and you're looking for a hearty, healthy, and very affordable meal, consider a crepe (yes, a crepe). These paper-thin, egg-based pancakes, filled with a wide variety of ingredients, can be served as a main course or a dessert. You can either build your own crepe from the wide variety of fillings, or order from choices such as the Florentine crepe made with cheddar cheese, onions, spinach, and cottage cheese, or the Mediterranean crepe with cheddar, onion, eggplant, pesto, tomato, and roasted peppers. All options, including the less-celebrated omelets, come with a heaping pile of house potatoes. You can also order one of the simple sandwiches, bagels, or an enormous Caesar salad, all for under $8.

100 Carl St. (at Cole St.). ✆ 415/664-1800. Reservations not accepted. Main courses $6–$8. No credit cards. Sun–Thurs 7am–11pm; Fri–Sat 7am–midnight. Bus: 6, 7, 66, or 71. Streetcar: N.

Zona Rosa ✿ MEXICAN   This is a great place to stop and get a cheap (and healthy) bite. The most popular items are the burritos, which are made to order and include your choice of beans (refried, whole pinto, or black), meats (the carnitas is great), or vegetarian ingredients. You can sit on a stool at the window and watch the Haight Street freaks strolling by, relax at one of five colorful interior tables, or take it to go and head to Golden Gate Park (just 2 blocks away). Zona Rosa is one of the best burrito shops around.

1797 Haight St. (at Shrader St.). ✆ 415/668-7717. Reservations not accepted. Burritos $5.50–$7.50. No credit cards. Daily 11am–10:30pm. Bus: 6, 7, 66, 71, or 73. Streetcar: N.

14 Richmond District

Burma Superstar ✿✿ *Value* BURMESE   Despite its gratuitous name, this basic dining room garners true superstar status by offering exceptional Burmese food at rock-bottom prices. Unfortunately, the allure of the tealeaf salad, clay-pot chicken curry, and sweet-tangy sesame beef is one of the city's worst-kept secrets. Add to that a no-reservations policy and you can count on waiting in line for up to an hour. (FYI, parties of two are seated more quickly than larger groups, and it's less crowded at lunch). On the bright side, you can pencil your cellphone number onto the waiting list and browse the Clement Street shops until you receive a call.

309 Clement St. (at 4th Ave.). ✆ 415/387-2147. www.burmasuperstar.com. Reservations not accepted. Main courses $8–$16. MC, V. Mon–Thurs and Sun 11am–9:30pm; Fri–Sat 11am–10pm. Bus 2, 4, 38, or 44.

Kabuto A&S ✿✿ JAPANESE/SUSHI   In a town overflowing with seafood and pretentious taste buds, you'd think it would be easier to find great sushi. The truth is, finding an outstanding sushi restaurant in San Francisco is more challenging than spotting a parking space in Nob Hill. Chopsticking these fish-and-rice delicacies is one of the most joyous and adventurous ways to dine, and Kabuto is one of the best (and most expensive) places to do it. Chef Sachio Kojima, who presides over the small, crowded sushi bar (which moved into an even tinier space across the street from its old location in 2003), constructs each dish with smooth, lightning-fast movements known only to master chefs. If you're big on wasabi, ask for the stronger stuff Kojima serves on request.

5121 Geary Blvd. (at 16th Ave.). © **415/752-5652.** www.kabutosushi.com. Reservations not accepted. Sushi $2–$10, small plates $5–$12, main courses $15–$20. MC, V. Tues–Sat 5:30–10:30pm. Bus: 38.

Khan Toke Thai House &&& *Value* THAI   Khan Toke Thai is so traditional you're asked to remove your shoes before being seated. Popular for special occasions, this Richmond District fixture is easily the prettiest Thai restaurant in the city; lavishly carved teak interiors evoke the ambience of a Thai temple.

To start, order the *tom yam gong* soup of lemon grass, shrimp, mushroom, tomato, and cilantro. Follow with such well-flavored dishes as ground pork with fresh ginger, green onion, peanuts, and lemon juice; prawns with hot chiles, mint leaves, lime juice, lemon grass, and onions; or chicken with cashews, crispy chiles, and onions. For a real treat, have the deep-fried pompano topped with sautéed ginger, onions, peppers, pickled garlic, and yellow-bean sauce; or deep-fried red snapper with "three-flavors" sauce and basil leaves. A complete dinner, including appetizer, soup, salad, two main courses, dessert, and coffee, is a great value.

5937 Geary Blvd. (between 23rd and 24th aves.). © **415/668-6654.** Reservations recommended Fri–Sat for parties of 3 or more. Main courses $6–$13, fixed-price dinner $20. AE, MC, V. Daily 5–10pm. Bus: 38.

Straits Café & SINGAPOREAN   Straits Café is what I like to call "adventure dining," because you never quite know what kind of food you're going to get. Burlap palm trees, pastel-painted trompe l'oeil houses, faux balconies, and clotheslines strung across the walls evoke a surreal image of a Singaporean village in the Richmond District. The cuisine, however, is the real thing. Among chef Chris Yeo's spicy Malaysian-Indian-Chinese offerings are *murtabak* (stuffed Indian bread), chile crab, basil chicken, *nonya daging rendang* (beef simmered in lime leaves), *ikan pangang* (banana leaf-wrapped barbecued salmon with chile paste), and, hottest of all, his green curry (prawns, scallops, and mussels simmered in a jalapeno-based curry). For dessert, try the sago pudding. Just like most Asian restaurants, the plates here are meant to be enjoyed family style.

3300 Geary Blvd. (at Parker St.). © **415/668-1783.** www.straitsrestaurants.com. Reservations recommended. Main courses $10–$27. AE, DC, MC, V. Mon–Thurs noon–2:30pm and 5:30–10pm; Fri–Sat noon–11pm; Sun noon–10pm. Bus: 2, 3, 4, or 38.

Ton Kiang &&& *Finds* CHINESE/DIM SUM   Ton Kiang is the number one place in the city to have dim sum (served daily). Wait in line (which is out the door 11am–1:30pm), get a table on the first or second floor, and get ready to say yes to dozens of delicacies, which are brought to the table for your approval. From stuffed crab claws, roast Beijing duck, and a gazillion dumpling selections (including scallop and vegetable, shrimp, and beef) to the delicious and hard-to-find *doa miu* (snow pea sprouts flash-sautéed with garlic and peanut oil), shark-fin soup, and a mesmerizing mango pudding, every tray of morsels coming from the kitchen is an absolute delight. Though it's hard to get past the dim sum, which is served all day every day, the full menu of Hakka cuisine is worth investigation as well—fresh and flavorful soups; an array of seafood, beef, and chicken; and clay-pot specialties. This is definitely one of my favorite places to do lunch, and it happens to have an unusually friendly staff.

5821 Geary Blvd. (between 22nd and 23rd aves.). © **415/387-8273.** www.tonkiang.net. Reservations accepted for parties of 8 or more. Dim sum $2–$5.50, main courses $8.50–$14. AE, DISC, DC, MC, V. Mon–Thurs 10am–10pm; Fri 10am–10:30pm; Sat 9:30am–10:30pm; Sun 9am–10pm. Bus: 38.

WORTH A SPLURGE

Aziza 🌟🌟 MOROCCAN   If you're looking for something really different—or a festive spot for a large party—head deep into the Avenues for an exotic taste of Morocco. Chef-owner Mourad Lahlou creates an excellent dining experience through colorful and distinctly Moroccan surroundings and his modern but still authentic take on the food of his homeland. In any of the three opulently adorned dining rooms (front room features private booths, the middle room is more formal, and the back has lower seating and a Moroccan lounge feel) you can indulge in the very affordable five-course tasting menu ($39) or individual treats such as kumquat-enriched lamb shank, saffron Cornish hen with preserved lemon and olives, or lavender honey-braised squab. Finish off with my favorite dessert: rhubarb *galette* with rose- and geranium-scented crème frâiche, vanilla aspic, and rhubarb consommé.

5800 Geary Blvd. (at 22nd Ave.). © **415/752-2222.** www.aziza-sf.com. Reservations recommended. Main courses $10–$20, 5-course menu $39. MC, V. Wed–Mon 5:30–10:30pm. Valet parking: $8 weekdays, $10 weekends. Bus: 29 or 38.

15 Sunset District

Beach Chalet Brewery & Restaurant 🌟 *Kids* AMERICAN   This is the most modern ocean-side restaurant in town, with commanding views of the Pacific Ocean (fog permitting). The Chalet occupies the upper floor of a historic public lounge that originally opened in 1900, but has been overhauled regularly since then. Today, the main floor's wonderful restored WPA frescoes and historical displays on the area are enough to lure tourists and locals, but there's nothing historic about the bright and cheery restaurant, which does the trick when you're in the 'hood, but is not a destination in itself. In fact, a great beer selection and live music have been the primary nighttime draws of late.

Dinner is pricey, and the view disappears with the sun, so come for breakfast or lunch when you can eat your hamburger, buttermilk fried calamari, or grilled Atlantic salmon with one of the best vistas around. After dinner, it's a more local thing, especially on Tuesday and Friday evenings when live bands accompany the cocktails and house-brewed ales and root beer. *Note:* Be careful getting into the parking lot (accessible only from the northbound side of the highway)—it's a quick, sandy turn.

⟨Value⟩ Low-Price Noshing Near Golden Gate Park

There are no restaurants other than museum cafes in Golden Gate Park, but that doesn't mean your choices are limited to the hot-dog cart. In the newly chic neighborhood of Inner Sunset, there are a handful of excellent restaurants, all of which are open for lunch, are very moderately priced, and are a block outside of the park along Ninth Avenue. One of our favorites is **Park Chow** 🌟🌟, 1240 Ninth Ave., between Lincoln and Irving (© **415/665-9912**). Its rambling wood-frame house and roof garden are a casual venue for Italian-inspired eclectic fare such as burgers, Asian noodles, grills, and roasts—all at bargain prices for such high-quality dining. Brunch goes until 2:30pm on weekends. In addition, some of the city's best sushi, sashimi, and Japanese fare is served at bare-bones traditional **Ebisu** 🌟🌟, 1283 Ninth Ave., between Lincoln and Irving (© **415/566-1770;** www.ebisusushi.com), a neighborhood favorite for more than 2 decades.

In early 2004, owners Lara and Greg Truppelli added the adjoining **Park Chalet** restaurant to the Beach Chalet. The 3,000-square-foot glass-enclosed extension behind the original landmark building offers more casual fare—with entrees ranging from $11 to $23—including cioppino and pizza with radicchio and pancetta. Other reasons to come? Retractable glass walls reveal Golden Gate Park's landmark Dutch windmill, a fireplace warms the room on chillier evenings, and live music is performed Thursday through Sunday evenings. The restaurant opens at 11am daily and, like the Beach Chalet, has varying closing times so call ahead.

1000 Great Hwy. (at west end of Golden Gate Park, near Fulton St.). ⓒ 415/386-8439. www.beachchalet.com. Reservations recommended. Main courses $8–$17 breakfast, $11–$27 lunch and dinner. AE, MC, V. Daily 9am–midnight (however, hours change frequently based on business and seasons, so call ahead). Bus: 18, 31, or 38. Streetcar: N.

SUPER-CHEAP EATS

Yum Yum Fish ⓖ *Value* SUSHI   Sure, Yum Yum Fish smells like a fish market, but that's only because it *is* a fish market. But those-in-the-know also come here for the freshest inexpensive sushi in the city, served at a little counter in the back and eaten at a folding table with two garage-sale/giveaway chairs. How inexpensive? The seven-piece inari combo (California, tofu, and mixed veggie) runs about $12 at most sushi restaurants—here, it's $4. If you want to be the life of the next potluck party, order the $40 party platter, which comes loaded with various rolls and nigiri. The staff here is super friendly, and once you get used to the smell, you're bound to stay awhile, stuffing yourself on top-notch sushi.

2181 Irving St. (between 22nd and 23rd aves.). ⓒ 415/566-6433. Main courses $6–$20. DISC, MC, V. Tues–Sun 10:30am–7:30pm. Bus: 71.

16 The Castro

Café Flore CALIFORNIA   Because of its large and lively patio overlooking a busy section of Market Street intersection, Café Flore is the top sunny-day meet-me-for-coffee spot within the Castro community. Local wits refer to it as a place where body piercing is encouraged but not mandatory, although this kind of exhibitionism tends to be more prevalent in the evening rather than during the day. And the food's as good as the people-watching. Many of the menu items are composed of mostly organic ingredients, and include a succulent version of roasted chicken over rice, Neiman Ranch hamburgers, soups, salads, and pastas. Breeders are welcome, and breakfast is served until 3pm.

2298 Market St. (at Noe St.). ⓒ 415/621-8579. Reservations not accepted. American breakfast $5.95; main courses $4.50–$10. MC, V. Sun–Thurs 7am–11:30pm; Fri–Sat 7am–midnight. Streetcar: F.

Caffé Luna Piena ⓖ CALIFORNIA/MEDITERRANEAN   This is one of the Castro's warmest dining environments. The room stretches back to the lush outdoor dining garden (yes, there are heat lamps and smoking is permitted). The fare is contemporary California during the day and Mediterranean, Italian, and French at night with daytime basics like soups, salads, and sandwiches (with a choice of garlic fries, green salad, or coleslaw). Dinner features such dishes as steak frites, New York steak, and penne pasta with house-made spicy sausage. Counter diners can watch chefs at work in the partially open kitchen. If you come for Saturday or Sunday brunch, reserve in advance or be prepared to wait in a long line. The menu includes poached eggs and smoked salmon atop an English muffin smothered in hollandaise sauce; French toast with fruit compote and mascarpone cream; and other breakfast treats.

558 Castro St. (between 18th and 19th sts.). ✆ **415/621-2566**. Reservations recommended. Main courses $6–$15 brunch and lunch, $10–$20 dinner. AE, MC, V. Mon–Thurs 9am–9pm; Fri–Sat 9am–10pm. Bus: 24, 33, 35, or 37. Streetcar: K, L, or M.

Chow ★★ *Value* AMERICAN   Chow claims to serve American cuisine, but the management must be thinking of today's America, because the menu is not exactly meatloaf and apple pie. And that's just fine for eclectic and cost-conscious diners. After all, what's not to like about starting with a Cobb salad before moving on to Thai-style noodles with steak, chicken, peanuts, and spicy lime-chile garlic broth, or lin-guine with clams? Better yet, everything except the fish of the day costs under $15, especially the budget-wise daily sandwich specials, which range from meatball with mozzarella (Sun) to grilled tuna with Asian-style slaw, pickled ginger, and a wasabi mayonnaise (Mon); both come with salad, soup, or fries. While the food and prices alone would be a good argument for coming here, beer on tap, a great inexpensive wine selection, and the fun, tavernlike environment clinch the deal. A second loca-tion, **Park Chow,** is at 1240 Ninth Ave. (✆ **415/665-9912**). You can't make reserva-tions unless you've got a party of eight or more, but if you're headed their way, you can call ahead to place your name on the wait list (recommended).

215 Church St. (near Market St.). ✆ **415/552-2469**. Reservations not accepted. Main courses $7–$15. MC, V, DISC. Mon–Thurs 11am–11pm; Fri 11am–midnight; Sat 10am–midnight; Sun 10am–11pm. Bus: 8, 22 or 37. Streetcar: F, J, K, L, or M.

Firewood Café ★★ *Value* AMERICAN/ITALIAN   One of the sharpest rooms in the neighborhood, the colorful Firewood put its money in the essentials and eliminated extra overhead. There are no waiters or waitresses; everyone orders at the counter and then relaxes at the single family-style table, at one of the small tables facing the huge street-side windows, or in the cheery back dining room. Management didn't skimp on the cozy-chic atmosphere and inspired but limited menu: The fresh salads come with a choice of three "fixin's," ranging from caramelized onions to spiced walnuts, and three gourmet dressing options. Then there are the pastas—three tortellini selections, such as roasted chicken and mortadella—and gourmet pizzas. Or how about herb-roasted half or whole chicken ($7.50 or $14, respectively) with roasted new potatoes? Wines cost $4.50 to $5.50 by the glass and a reasonable $18 to $21 per bottle. Draft and bottled beers are also available, and desserts top off at $3.25. (Thank goodness someone real-ized that $7 for an after-dinner treat borders on ridiculous.)

4248 18th St. (at Diamond St.). ✆ **415/252-0999**. www.firewoodcafe.com. Main courses $6.50–$14. MC, V. Mon–Thurs 11am–10:30pm; Fri–Sat 11am–11pm. Bus: 8, 33, 35, or 37. Streetcar: F, K, L, or M.

Nippon Sushi *Value* SUSHI   The lack of exterior signage inspired the locals to call this small, plain sushi restaurant "No Name." But even with its intentionally low pro-file, for over 10 years the tiny room has had a line out the door. What's the big deal? Since its beginnings it's been one of the cheapest sushi houses in town. How cheap? Try a vegetable roll for $2.05, a California roll for $3.60, or a melt-in-your-mouth tekka maki for $3.40. It ain't the best in town by far, but for the price, you can't beat it. *Note:* It has fewer than 30 seats, so be prepared to wait for a table, and don't expect to wash your fish down with sake or beer—Nippon has no liquor license.

314 Church St. (at 15th St.). No phone. Reservations not accepted. Sushi $2.05–$4.15 apiece. No credit cards. Mon–Sat noon–10pm. Bus: 8, 22, or 37.

Finds **Seaside Dining, Dancing & Drinking**

If you're lucky enough to be in San Francisco on one of those rare hot days, then don't waste those fleeting sunny moments lunching inside. Call for directions and head to **The Ramp** *&*, a favorite bayside hangout among in-the-know locals. The fare is of the basic pub grub variety—burgers, sandwiches, salads, and soups from $8 to $13—but the rustic boatyard environment and patio seating make this a relaxing place to dine in the sun. In summer, the place really rocks when live bands perform (4:30–7:30pm Fri–Sun Apr–Oct) and when tanned, cocktailing singles prowl the area. It's open for lunch Monday through Thursday from 11am to 3:30pm and Friday 11am to 4pm, and for brunch Saturday and Sunday from 8:30am to 4pm. The bar is open Monday through Friday from 11am to 8pm, Friday and Saturday from 8:30am to 8pm. From April to October, outdoor barbecue is offered Saturday and Sunday from 4 to 8pm; on non-barbecue days, appetizers are featured daily from 5:30 to 8pm. Take bus no. 22 or 48, or just ask the cabbie to take you to The Ramp, 855 China Basin St., at the end of Mariposa Street (*©* **415/621-2378**).

SUPER-CHEAP EATS

Marcello's Pizza PIZZA   Marcello's isn't a fancy place, just a traditional pizza joint with a couple of tables, tasty pizza by the slice, and a few other basic dishes like burgers, salads, and calzones. Weekend nights there's a line out the door of drunk and/or stoned Castro Street partyers with the late-night munchies.

420 Castro St. (at Market St.). *©* **415/863-3900**. Reservations not accepted. Pizza slices $2.25–$3; pies $11–$26. No credit cards. Sun–Thurs 11am–1am; Fri–Sat 11am–2am. Streetcar: K, L, or M.

WORTH THE SPLURGE

Mecca *&* *Finds* AMERICAN   In 1996, Mecca entered the scene in a decadent swirl of chocolate-brown velvet, stainless steel, cement, and brown Naugahyde. It's an industrial-chic supper club that makes you want to order a martini just so you'll match the ambience. The eclectic city clientele (with a heavy dash of same-sex couples) mingles at the oval centerpiece bar. A night here promises a live DJ spinning hot grooves (or live entertainment on Monday) and a fine American meal prepared by chef Stephen Barber and served at tables tucked into several nooks. Menu options include such classic starters as oysters on the half shell, seared ahi tuna, and wood-oven-roasted pork tenderloin. The food is very good, but it's that only-in–San Francisco vibe that makes this place the smokin' hot spot in the Castro. *Budget tip:* Every night from 5 to 7pm you can order unlimited $1 oysters in the bar & lounge.

2029 Market St. (between 14th and Church sts.). *©* **415/621-7000**. www.sfmecca.com. Reservations recommended. Main courses $15–$29. AE, DC, MC, V. Sunday and Tues–Thurs 5–11pm; Fri–Sat 5–midnight; bar remains open later. Valet parking $8. Bus: 8, 22, 24, or 37. Streetcar: F, K, L, or M.

17 Mission District

Delfina *&& Value* ITALIAN   Unpretentious warehouse-chic atmosphere, reasonable prices, and chef/co-owner Craig Stoll's ultrafresh seasonal Italian cuisine have made this family-owned restaurant one of the city's most cherished. Stoll, who was one of

Food & Wine's Best New Chefs in 2001, changes the menu daily, while his wife Annie works the front of the house (when she's not being a mom). Standards include Niman Ranch flat-iron steak with french fries, and roasted chicken with Yukon Gold mashed potatoes and royal trumpet mushrooms. The winter menu might include slow-roasted pork shoulder or gnocchi with squash and chestnuts, while spring indulgences can include sand dabs with frisée, fingerling potatoes, and lemon-caper butter, or lamb with polenta and sweet peas. Trust me—order the buttermilk *panna cotta* (custard) if it's available. ***A plus:*** A few tables and counter seating are reserved for walk-in diners. Delfina also has a heated and covered patio that's used mid-March through November. Cocktail alert: Wine and beer only are served here.

3621 18th St. (between Dolores and Guererro sts.). ℭ **415/552-4055.** Reservations recommended. Main courses $13–$22. MC, V. Sun–Thurs 5:30–10pm; Fri–Sat 5:30–11pm. Parking lot at 18th and Valencia sts. next to Sharin's Appliances, $8. Bus: 26 or 33. Streetcar: J.

Levende Lounge ✭✭ CALIFORNIA/AMERICAN   With brick walls, brown leather couches and banquettes, and an all-around warehouse-chic vibe, the city's hottest new cocktail spot for the young single set is also a damn fine place to eat, provided you either come early or enjoy noshing while revelers crowd the bar, flirt, and groove to the DJ's mixes. Their ace in the culinary hole is 29-year-old chef Jamie Lauren who was nominated by the *San Francisco Chronicle* as one of 10 rising star chefs in 2005. Her small-plate fare is so pristine and balanced I'm curious how long she'll be in the house before landing a more cuisine-focused gig. (I'd call first to confirm if you care about food as much as atmosphere.) Hopefully she'll stay put long enough for you to drop in and experience her beautifully balanced frisée salad with baby leek vinaigrette, bacon, and a fried quail egg; mini lamb burgers; slow-cooked baby back ribs; duck confit tacos with dried cherry mole; and diver scallops with fantastic early spring succotash. Dessert, though fine, isn't special.

1710 Mission St. (at Duboce St.). ℭ **415/864-5585.** www.levendelounge.com. Reservations recommended. Tapas $8–$18. AE, MC, V. Dinner served Tues–Fri 5–11pm; Sat 6–11pm (bar open Tues–Sat until 2am); Sun brunch 11am–4pm. Valet parking Wed–Sat only; street parking available. Bus: 14, 33, or 49.

Pauline's ✭✭ PIZZA   Housed in a cheery yellow double-decker building that stands out like a beacon in a somewhat seedy neighborhood, Pauline's does only three things—pizzas, salads, and desserts—but it does them better than most restaurants in the city. It's worth running the gauntlet of panhandlers for a slice of Louisiana Andouille pizza topped with Andouille sausage, bell peppers, and fontina cheese. Other gourmet toppings include chicken sausage, French goat cheese, roasted eggplant, Danish fontina cheese, and *tasso* (spiced pork shoulder). The salads are equally amazing: certified organic, handpicked by California growers, and topped with fresh and dried herbs (including edible flowers) from Pauline's own gardens in Berkeley. Don't forget to leave room for the house-made ice cream and sorbets or chocolate mousse and butterscotch pudding. The wine list offers a smart selection of low-priced wines, where Star Canyon Vineyards, yet another of the owners' pursuits, will be showcased. Yes, prices are a bit steep (small pizzas start at $11), but what a paltry price to pay for perfection.

260 Valencia St. (between 14th St. and Duboce Ave.). ℭ **415/552-2050.** Reservations accepted for parties of 8 or more. Main courses $12–$25. MC, V. Tues–Sat 5–10pm. Bus: 14, 26, or 49.

Mission District Dining

Delfina **6**
Foreign Cinema **7**
Levende Lounge **9**
Pauline's **1**
Puerto Alegre Restaurant **5**
Saigon Saigon **8**
Tacquerias La Cumbre **4**
Ti Couz **2**
Truly Mediterranean **3**

Saigon Saigon VIETNAMESE   Low prices, an eclectic Mission District clientele, and seating for large parties make this neighborhood restaurant a fine option for a satisfying—if not exactly memorable—meal. The menu features a variety of salads, soups, fowl, meats, seafood, and rice dishes, most of which are accompanied by very fresh veggies. Two recommended dishes are the black-pepper catfish and the crispy duck in basil sauce. The 3-course fixed price menu is an especially good deal—you'll get an appetizer, entree, and dessert for only $15. *Tip:* If you're famished, avoid ordering the seafood (other options come in larger portions), and if you arrive late, be sure to ask when the kitchen closes (I wasn't able to order dessert on my last visit).

1132 Valencia St. (between 22nd and 23rd sts.). ✆ **415/206-9635.** Reservations accepted only for large parties. Main courses $7–$9. AE, MC, V. Mon–Sat 5:30–10pm. Bus: 14, 26, or 49.

Ti Couz ✸ CREPES   At Ti Couz (say "Tee Cooz"), one of the most architecturally stylish and popular restaurants in the Mission, the headliner is simple: the delicate, paper-thin crepe. More than 30 choices of fillings make for infinite expertly executed combinations. The menu advises you how to enjoy these wraps: Order a light crepe as an appetizer, a heftier one as a main course, and a drippingly sweet one for dessert. Recommended combinations are listed, but you can build your own from the 15 main-course selections (such as smoked salmon, mushrooms, sausage, ham, scallops, and onions) and 15 dessert options (caramel, fruit, chocolate, Nutella, and more). Soups and salads are equally stellar; the seafood salad, for example, is a delicious and generous compilation of shrimp, scallops, and ahi tuna with veggies and five kinds of lettuce. Cider served in ceramic bowls, beer, and a full bar complement the cuisine.

3108 16th St. (at Valencia St.). ✆ **415/252-7373.** Reservations not accepted. Crepes $2–$11. MC, V. Mon 11am–10pm; Tues–Thurs 5–11pm; Sat 10am–11pm; Sun 10am–10pm. BART: 16th and Mission. Bus: 14, 22, 26, 33, 49, or 53.

SUPER-CHEAP EATS

Puerto Alegre Restaurant MEXICAN   This would hardly be a popular spot were it not for two critical factors: Pitchers of margaritas are a mere $11, and the dive-restaurant prices come with a more festive and intimate atmosphere than other Mexican restaurants in the 'hood. This is not a place for wolfing down a quick burrito; this is the kind of joint where you gather with friends, suck back a few slushy 'ritas, and get loose amid the plastic-covered seats and tables. And you order a burrito or combination plate not because it's the best in town but because it's *good enough* and dirt cheap, and because you're bound to get hammered if you don't soak up that tequila with something.

546 Valencia St. (between 16th and 17th sts.). ✆ **415/255-8201.** Reservations accepted only for parties of 5 or more. Main courses $3.85–$6.35. DC, MC, V. Mon 11am–10pm; Tues–Sun 11am–11pm. BART: Mission. Bus: 14, 22, 33, 49, or 53.

Taquerias La Cumbre ✸✸ MEXICAN   If San Francisco commissioned a flag honoring its favorite food, we'd probably all be waving a banner of the Golden Gate Bridge bolstering a giant burrito—that's how much I love the mammoth tortilla-wrapped meals. Taquerias La Cumbre has been around forever and still retains its "Best Burrito" title, each deftly constructed using fresh pork, steak, chicken, or vegetables, plus cheese, beans, rice, salsa, and maybe a dash of guacamole or sour cream. The fact that it's served in a cafeteria-like brick-lined room with overly shellacked tables featuring a woman with overflowing cleavage makes it taste even better.

515 Valencia St. (between 16th and 17th sts.). ℂ **415/863-8205**. Reservations not accepted. Tacos and burritos $3.50–$6.50; dinner plates $5–$7. No credit cards. Mon–Sat 11am–9pm; Sun noon–9pm. BART: Mission. Bus: 14, 22, 33, 49, or 53.

Truly Mediterranean *Value* MEDITERRANEAN   Hankering for tasty, fresh traditional Mediterranean food, but only have a few bucks to spare? Well, wind your way to this Mission District shack of a restaurant. With four stools, a small countertop, and two sidewalk tables, the place is about as charming (and as crowded) as a Muni bus. But the falafels, kabobs, baba ghanouj, and stuffed pitas are worth the trip. You can't go wrong with the combo plate: falafel, hummus, baba, tabbouleh, cucumber salad, dolmas, feta cheese, onions, tahini sauce, and pita bread (whew!)—all for $6.95.

3109 16th St. (at Valencia St.). ℂ **415/252-7482**. www.trulymed.com. Main courses $3.50–$6.75. DISC, MC, V. Mon–Thurs 11am–11pm; Fri–Sat 11am–midnight; Sun 11am–10pm. BART: Mission. Bus: 14, 22, 33, 49, or 53.

WORTH A SPLURGE

Foreign Cinema 🐾🐾 MEDITERRANEAN   This place is so chic that it's hard to believe it's a San Francisco restaurant, and it's so well hidden on Mission Street that it eludes me every time I seek the valet. An indoor seat here is a lovely place to watch San Francisco's most fashionable. Outdoors (heated, partially covered, but still chilly), the enormous foreign (and occasionally American) film showing on the side of an adjoining building steals the show. (Although the primary purpose of dining here is not to watch the film, it's still a bummer for those facing away from it.) Husband-and-wife team John Clark and Gayle Pirie create a fine Mediterranean menu. Snackers like me find solace in the oyster bar, a devilish *brandade* (fish purée) gratin, and the cheese selections. Heartier eaters can opt for roasted half-chicken with golden chanterelle and red mustard-green risotto; or grilled natural rib-eye with Tuscan-style beans and rosemary-fried peppercorn sauce. Truth be told, even if the food weren't good, I'd come here: It's just that cool. If you have to wait for your table, consider stepping next door to the adjoining bar, Lazslo's.

2534 Mission St. (between 21st and 22nd sts.). ℂ **415/648-7600**. www.foreigncinema.com. Reservations recommended. Main courses $14–$25. AE, MC, V. Sun–Wed 6–10pm; Thurs–Sat 6–11pm; Sat–Sun brunch 11am–5pm. Valet parking $8. Bus: 14, 14L, or 49.

8

Exploring San Francisco

Okay—so you've finally made it to San Francisco, checked into your hotel room, had lunch, and are ready to hit the town. You don't have a ton of cash, so you're pretty much limited to walking and looking around, right? Wrong. San Francisco may be one of the most expensive places in the world to live, but when it comes to seeing the city's sights and playing with all of its toys, you can have a ball for only a few dollars a day. Case in point: Of our favorite things to do in and around the city (see "Frommer's Favorite [& Mostly Free] San Francisco Experiences" in chapter 1), eleven are free, one costs $5, and the other options are less than $16. Not bad.

But wait, there's more. Listed below are dozens and dozens of cool places and activities to see and experience—from mind-broadening Sunday sermons to romantic rowboats for rent in Golden Gate Park—all of which have been given our stamp of approval. Stick with our recommendations and you're guaranteed an awesome stay in San Francisco at very little expense.

1 San Francisco's Top Attractions

Alcatraz Island ✸✸✸ *Kids* Visible from Fisherman's Wharf, Alcatraz Island (aka "The Rock") has seen a checkered history. Juan Manuel Ayala was the first European to discover it in 1775 and named it after the many pelicans that nested on the island. From the 1850s to 1933, when the army vacated the island, it served as a military post, protecting the bay's shoreline. In 1934, the government converted the buildings of the military outpost into a maximum-security prison. Given the sheer cliffs, treacherous tides and currents, and frigid water temperatures, it was believed to be a totally escape-proof prison. Among the famous gangsters who occupied cell blocks A through D were Al Capone, Robert Stroud, the so-called Birdman of Alcatraz (because he was an expert in ornithological diseases), Machine Gun Kelly, and Alvin Karpis. It cost a fortune to keep them imprisoned here because all supplies, including water, had to be shipped in. In 1963, after an apparent escape in which no bodies were recovered, the government closed the prison. In 1969, a group of Native Americans chartered a boat to the island to symbolically reclaim the island for the Indian people. They occupied the island until 1971, the longest occupation of a federal facility by Native Americans to this day, when they were forcibly removed by the U.S. government. The next year the island became part of the Golden Gate National Recreation Area. The wildlife that was driven away during the military and prison years has begun to return—the black-crested night heron and other seabirds are nesting here again—and a new trail passes through the island's nature areas. Tours, including an audio tour of the prison block and a slide show, are given by the park's rangers, who entertain guests with interesting anecdotes.

Allow about 2½ hours for the round-trip boat ride and the tour. Wear comfortable shoes (the National Park Service notes that there are a lot of hills to climb on the tour) and take a heavy sweater or windbreaker, because even when the sun's out, it's cold out there. You should also consider bringing snacks and drinks with you if you think you'll want them. While there is a beverage and snack bar on the ferry, the options are extremely limited and expensive, and once you get onto The Rock all you can buy is water. The excursion to Alcatraz is popular and space is limited, so purchase tickets as far in advance as possible. **Blue & Gold Fleet** (© **415/705-5555;** www.blueandgold fleet.com) operates the tour; they accept American Express, MasterCard, and Visa. You can also buy tickets in advance from the Blue & Gold ticket office on Pier 41. Alcatraz night tours are also available and are a more intimate and wonderfully spooky experience.

For those who want to get a closer look at Alcatraz without going ashore, two boat-tour operators offer short circumnavigations of the island (see "Self-Guided & Organized Tours," on p. 182, for complete information).

Pier 41, near Fisherman's Wharf. © 415/773-1188 (info only). Admission (includes ferry trip and audio tour) $16 adults with headset, $12 without; $15 seniors 62 and older with headset, $9.75 without; $11 children ages 5–11 with headset, $8.25 without. Night tours cost $24 adults; $21 seniors 62 and older; $14 children ages 5–11. Winter daily 9:30am–2:15pm; summer daily 9:30am–4:15pm. Ferries depart 15 and 45 min. after the hour. Arrive at least 20 min. before sailing time. Night tours leave Thurs–Sun at 4:20 and 5:10pm. Cable car: Take the Powell-Mason line to the last stop and walk up to the wharf.

Boudin at the Wharf 🐟   After more than 30 years of being an inconspicuous bread shop in the heart of Fisherman's Wharf, the Boudin Bakery has been super-sized. The new, ultra-modern, 26,000-square-foot baking emporium is nearly half a block long, housing not only their signature demonstration bakery but also a museum, gourmet marketplace, cafe, espresso bar, and restaurant. The Boudin (pronounced bo-*deen*) family has been baking sourdough French bread in San Francisco since the Gold Rush, using the same simple recipe and "mother dough" for more than 150 years. About 3,000 loaves a day are baked within the glass-walled bakery; visitors can watch the entire process from a 30-foot observation window along Jefferson Street or from a catwalk suspended directly over the bakery (it's quite entertaining, actually). You'll smell

Money-Saving "Go Card"

If you're planning on visiting many of San Francisco's major tourist attractions, it might behoove you to purchase a Go San Francisco Card at www.GoCard USA.com (© **800/887-9103**). Cardholders get unlimited pre-paid entry to about 45 attractions in the city and Bay Area, including museums, walking tours, bike rentals, sightseeing tours, and Six Flags Marine World. Each card comes with a free full-color guidebook that describes each attraction, as well as maps and itinerary ideas, traveler tips, and key telephone numbers. The Go Cards are smart-technology enabled, which means they operate by calendar day and are activated the first time they are swiped, so you'll want to start your touring early in the morning to get the most value. Prices range from $49 for one adult for 1 day, with lower costs per day for multi-day cards and children's cards. In addition, some stores and restaurants offer discounts of up to 20% to Go San Francisco Card holders, and a Wine Country Explorer version is available as well. The Go Cards are so new that I haven't tried one yet, but if you do, report back to me and let me know if it helped save you money.

Major San Francisco Sights

0   1 mi

0   1 km

PACIFIC OCEAN

Golden Gate Bridge ①

②

101

1

Crissy

GOLDEN GATE NATIONAL RECREATIONAL AREA

THE PRESIDIO ③

Lincoln Blvd.

Arguello Blvd.

1

Baker Beach ↗

China Beach ↗

Lake St.

California St.

Clement St.

Geary Blvd.

Park Presidio Blvd.

Arguello Blvd.

LINCOLN PARK ④

Point Lobos Ave.

43rd Ave.

36th Ave.

34th Ave.

30th Ave.

25th Ave.

10th Ave.

8th Ave.

6th Ave.

RICHMOND DISTRICT

⑤

Fulton St.

1

⑦

John F. Kennedy Dr.

⑧

GOLDEN GATE PARK

Lincoln Way

Great Highway

46th Ave.

Sunset Blvd.

Irving St.

Judah St.

25th Ave.

19th Ave.

Irving St.

Judah St.

9th Ave.

7th Ave.

Parnassus Ave.

Ocean Beach ↗ ↓ ⑥

SUNSET DISTRICT

Alamo Square Historic District **24**

Alcatraz Island **36**

Aquarium of the Bay **11**

Asian Art Museum **32**

Cable Car Museum **19**

California Palace of the Legion of Honor **4**

The Cannery **12**

California Academy of Sciences **31**

City Hall **33**

Cliff House **5**

Coit Tower **16**

Conservatory of Flowers **7**

de Young Museum **8**

Exploratorium/ Palace of Fine Arts **9**

Farmer's Market **18**

Ferry Building Marketplace **18**

Fort Point **2**

Ghirardelli Square **13**

Glide Memorial United Methodist Church **25**

Golden Gate Bridge **1**

Grace Cathedral **21**

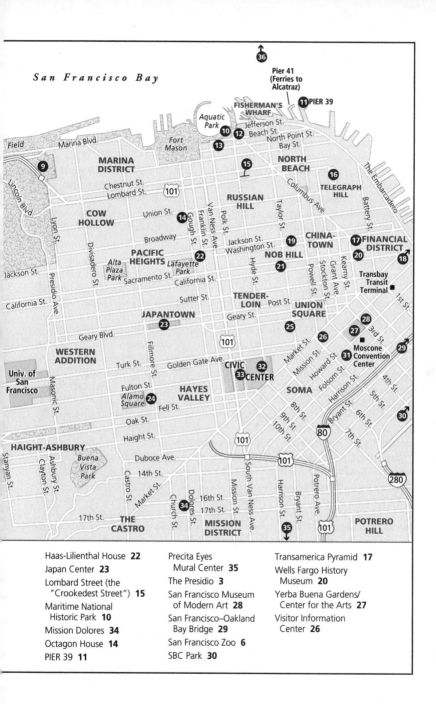

San Francisco Bay

Pier 41 (Ferries to Alcatraz)

FISHERMAN'S WHARF
PIER 39 **11**

Aquatic Park **10**
Jefferson St.
Beach St. **12**
North Point St.
Bay St. **13**

Fort Mason

Field
Marina Blvd. **9**

MARINA DISTRICT
Chestnut St.
Lombard St. 101

NORTH BEACH
15
16
TELEGRAPH HILL
Columbus Ave.
The Embarcadero

COW HOLLOW
Union St. **14**
Van Ness Ave.
Polk St.
Franklin St.
Gough St.

RUSSIAN HILL
Taylor St.

Lincoln Blvd.
Lyon St.

Broadway

PACIFIC HEIGHTS
Alta Plaza Park
Lafayette Park **22**
Sacramento St.
California St.

Jackson St.
Washington St. **19**
CHINA-TOWN
Kearny St.
Grant Ave.
Stockton St.
Powell St.

FINANCIAL DISTRICT **17**
20
18

NOB HILL **21**
Hyde St.

Transbay Transit Terminal

Jackson St.

California St.
Presidio Ave.

Sutter St.
TENDER-LOIN
Post St.
UNION SQUARE

1st St.

JAPANTOWN **23**
Geary Blvd.
Fillmore St.
Geary St.
25
26
27
28
3rd St.
29

WESTERN ADDITION
Turk St.
Golden Gate Ave.
101

CIVIC **33** CENTER **32**
Market St.
Mission St.
Howard St.
Moscone Convention Center **31**
Folsom St.

Univ. of San Francisco
Masonic Ave.

Fulton St.
HAYES VALLEY
Alamo Square **24**
Fell St.
Oak St.

SOMA
8th St.
9th St.
10th St.
Bryant St.
Harrison St.
4th St.
5th St.
6th St.
7th St.
30

Haight St.
101
80

HAIGHT-ASHBURY
Buena Vista Park
Stanyan St.
Ashbury St.
Clayton St.

Duboce Ave.
14th St.
Castro St.
Market St.
Church St.
Dolores St.
16th St.
17th St.
34
Mission St.
South Van Ness Ave.
Harrison St.
Bryant St.
Potrero Ave.
101
280

17th St.
THE CASTRO
MISSION DISTRICT
35

POTRERO HILL

36

Haas-Lilienthal House **22**	Precita Eyes Mural Center **35**	Transamerica Pyramid **17**
Japan Center **23**	The Presidio **3**	Wells Fargo History Museum **20**
Lombard Street (the "Crookedest Street") **15**	San Francisco Museum of Modern Art **28**	Yerba Buena Gardens/ Center for the Arts **27**
Maritime National Historic Park **10**	San Francisco–Oakland Bay Bridge **29**	Visitor Information Center **26**
Mission Dolores **34**	San Francisco Zoo **6**	
Octagon House **14**	SBC Park **30**	
PIER 39 **11**		

it before you see it, as the heavenly aroma emanating from the bread ovens is purposely blasted down onto the sidewalk.

The best time to arrive is in the morning when the demo bakery is in full swing. Watch (and smell) the action along Jefferson street, then when your appetite is stoked, head to the cafe for an inexpensive breakfast of sourdough French toast or their Bread Bowl Scrambler filled with eggs, bacon, cheddar, onions, and bell peppers. After breakfast, spend some time browsing the museum and marketplace. On the upper level is Bistro Boudin, a full-service restaurant serving lunch, dinner, and weekend brunch, and there's usually a jazz band playing on Friday and Saturday from 7 to 11pm. Tours of the bakery are available by appointment only. *Tip:* If the line at the cafe is too long, walk across the parking lot to the octagon-shaped building, which serves the same items—Boudin chowder bowls, salads, pizzas—in a serve-yourself setting.

160 Jefferson St. (between Taylor and Mason sts.). ℂ **415/928-1849.** www.boudinbakery.com. Bakery/cafe/market-place open daily 10am–7pm. Bistro open Sun–Thurs 11:30am–10pm, Fri–Sat 11:30am–10:30pm. Bus: 30, 47. Streetcar: F to Hyde St.

Cable Cars ★★★ (Moments (Kids   Although they may not be San Francisco's most practical means of transportation, cable cars are certainly the best loved and are a must-experience when visiting the city. Designated official historic landmarks by the National Park Service in 1964, they clank up and down the city's steep hills like mobile museum pieces, tirelessly hauling thousands of tourists each day to nowhere in particular.

London-born engineer Andrew Hallidie invented San Francisco's cable cars in 1869. He got the idea by serendipity. As the story goes, Hallidie was watching a team of overworked horses haul a heavily laden carriage up a steep San Francisco slope. As he watched, one horse slipped and the car rolled back, dragging the other tired beasts with it. At that moment, Hallidie resolved that he would invent a mechanical contraption to replace such horses, and just 4 years later, in 1873, the first cable car made its maiden run from the top of Clay Street. Promptly ridiculed as "Hallidie's Folly," the cars were slow to gain acceptance. One early onlooker voiced the general opinion by exclaiming, "I don't believe it—the damned thing works!"

Even today, many visitors have difficulty believing that these vehicles, which have no engines, actually work. The cars, each weighing about 6 tons, run along a steel cable, enclosed under the street in a center rail. You can't see the cable unless you peer straight down into the crack, but you'll hear its characteristic clickity-clanking sound whenever you're nearby. The cars move when the gripper (not the driver) pulls back a lever that closes a pincerlike "grip" on the cable. The speed of the car, therefore, is determined by the speed of the cable, which is a constant 9½ mph—never more, never less.

The two types of cable cars in use hold a maximum of 90 and 100 passengers, and the limits are rigidly enforced. The best views are from the outer running boards, where you have to hold on tightly when taking curves.

Hallidie's cable cars have been imitated and used throughout the world, but all have been replaced by more efficient means of transportation. San Francisco planned to do so, too, but the proposal met with so much opposition that the cable cars' perpetuation was actually written into the city charter in 1955. The mandate cannot be revoked without the approval of a majority of the city's voters—a distant and doubtful prospect.

San Francisco's three existing cable car lines form the world's only surviving system of cable cars, which you can experience for yourself should you choose to wait in the

Fisherman's Wharf Area Sights

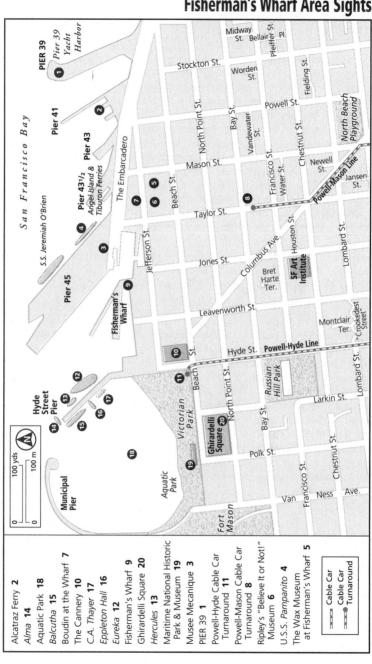

San Francisco Bay

PIER 39 Yacht Harbor

Midway St. Bellair St. Pfeiffer Pl.

Stockton St.

Worden St.

PIER 39

Pier 41

Powell St.

North Point St.

Bay St.

Vandewater St.

Fielding St.

North Beach Playground

Powell-Mason Line

Pier 43½ Pier 43

Mason St.

Francisco St.

Water St.

Chestnut St.

Newell St.

Jansen St.

Pier 43½

Angel Island & Tiburon Ferries

The Embarcadero

Beach St.

Taylor St.

Houston St.

Lombard St.

San Francisco Bay

S.S. Jeremiah O'Brien

Jefferson St.

Jones St.

Columbus Ave.

SF Art Institute

Bret Harte Ter.

Pier 45

Leavenworth St.

Montclair Ter.

"Crookedest Street"

Lombard St.

Fisherman's Wharf

Hyde St.

Powell-Hyde Line

Chestnut St.

Beach St.

North Point St.

Russian Hill Park

Larkin St.

Hyde Street Pier

Victorian Park

Ghirardelli Square

Bay St.

North Point St.

Polk St.

Municipal Pier

Aquatic Park

Fort Mason

Francisco St.

Van Ness Ave.

Chestnut St.

0   100 yds
0   100 m

Alcatraz Ferry 2
Alma 14
Aquatic Park 18
Balcutha 15
Boudin at the Wharf 7
The Cannery 10
C.A. Thayer 17
Eppleton Hall 16
Eureka 12
Fisherman's Wharf 9
Ghirardelli Square 20
Hercules 13
Maritime National Historic Park & Museum 19
Musee Mecanique 3
PIER 39 1
Powell-Hyde Cable Car Turnaround 11
Powell-Mason Cable Car Turnaround 8
Ripley's "Believe It or Not!" Museum 6
U.S.S. Pampanito 4
The Wax Museum at Fisherman's Wharf 5

Cable Car
Cable Car Turnaround

San Francisco Segway Tours

So new on the San Francisco scene that even the locals haven't figured out where they're coming from, Segway Human Transporters are those weird-looking upright scooters you've probably seen on TV. The two-wheeled transporter is an ingenious electric-powered transportation device that uses gyroscopes to emulate human balance. After the free 40-minute lesson, riding a Segway becomes intuitive: lean forward, go forward; lean back, go back; stand up, stop. Simple. The **San Francisco Electric Tour Company** offers Segway-powered tours of the San Francisco waterfront daily, starting from Fisherman's Wharf and heading out all the way to the Marina Green. It's the closest you'll come to being a celebrity (*everyone* checks you out), and very fun. *Note:* You have to be at least 12 years old to join the tour, and the cost is $65 per person. For more information log onto their website at www.sfelectrictour.com or call ☎ 415/474-3130.

endless boarding line (up to a 2-hr. wait in summer). For more information on riding them, see "Getting Around," in chapter 5, p. 63.

Powell-Hyde and Powell-Mason lines begin at the base of Powell and Market sts.; California St. line begins at the foot of Market St. $5 per ride.

The Cannery *(Overrated*   The Cannery was built by Del Monte in 1907 as was world's largest fruit-canning plant. It was converted into a mall in the 1960s and now contains 30-plus shops, a ceramic studio and gallery, and several restaurants, including **Jack's Cannery Bar** (☎ 415/931-6400), one of the few places in the city where you can sample Anchor Steam Brewery's "Old Foghorn Barleywine Style Ale" on draft (wickedly good). Vendors' stalls and sidewalk cafes occupy the courtyard amid a grove of century-old olive trees, and weather permitting, street performers are usually out in force, entertaining tourists. *Note:* This is a tourist destination that many locals avoid. Shops are open daily at 10am and Sunday at 11am except for Christmas and Thanksgiving, which are optional business days. Hours of operation vary according to the season and are extended each summer. Restaurants generally open at 11:30am.

2801 Leavenworth St. (between Beach and Jefferson sts.). ☎ 415/771-3112. www.thecannery.com. Bus: 30, 47. Streetcar: F to Hyde St.

Coit Tower *(★★*   In a city known for its great views and vantage points, Coit Tower is one of the best. Located atop Telegraph Hill, just east of North Beach, the round, stone tower offers panoramic views of the city and the bay. Completed in 1933, the tower is the legacy of Lillie Hitchcock Coit, a wealthy eccentric who left San Francisco a $125,000 bequest "for the purpose of adding beauty to the city I have always loved" and as a memorial to its volunteer firemen. She had been saved from a fire as a child and held the city's firefighters in particularly high esteem.

Inside the base of the tower are impressive murals titled *Life in California* and *1934*, which were completed under the WPA during the New Deal. They are the work of more than 25 artists, many of whom had studied under Mexican muralist Diego Rivera.

The only bummer: The narrow street leading to the tower is often clogged with tourist traffic. If you can, find a parking spot in North Beach and hoof it.

Telegraph Hill. ☎ 415/362-0808. www.coittower.org. Admission is free to enter; to go to the top $3.75 adults, $2.50 seniors, $1.50 children ages 6–12. Daily 10am–6:30pm. Bus: 39 (Coit).

Farmers' Market *Finds*   If you're heading to The Ferry Building Marketplace or just happen to be in the area at the right time, make a point of visiting the Farmers' Market, which is held in the alfresco areas in front of and behind the marketplace several days per week. This is where San Francisco foodies and many of the best local chefs peruse alfresco stands hawking the finest Northern California fruits, vegetables, breads, dairy, flowers, and readymade snacks by a few local restaurants. You'll be amazed at the variety and quality, and the crowded scene itself is something to behold. You can also pick up locally made vinegars and oils here—they make wonderful gifts. Drop by on Saturday from 10am to 2pm for the "Shop with the Chef" excursion, which is led by a local chef who interviews a local farmer and does a demo.

The Embarcadero, at Market St. © 415/291-3276. www.cuesa.org. Apr–Nov Sat 8am–2pm; Tues, Thurs, and Sun 10am–2pm; Dec–Mar Tues 10am–2pm and Sat 8am–2pm. BART: Embarcadero. Bus: 2, 7, 12, 14, 21, 66, or 71. Streetcar: F.

Ferry Building Marketplace *Finds*   There's no better way to enjoy a San Francisco morning than strolling this gourmet marketplace in the newly renovated Ferry Building and snacking your way through breakfast or lunch. Tasty tenants, open daily, include many of the best of Northern California's gourmet bounty: Cowgirl Creamery's Artisan Cheese Shop, Recchiuti Confections (amazing!), Scharffen Berger Chocolate, Acme breads, Wine Country's gourmet diner Taylor's Refresher, famed Vietnamese restaurant The Slanted Door, and myriad other restaurants, eateries, and wine bars. Check out the Imperial Tea Court where you'll be taught the traditional Chinese way to steep and sip your tea; buy cooking items at the Sur La Table shop; grab a bite and savor the bayfront views from in- and outdoor tables; or browse the farmers' market when it's up and running (see above). Whatever you do, you'll be doing it with a swarm of San Franciscans who can't get enough of this place.

The Embarcadero, at Market St. © 415/693-0996. www.ferrybuildingmarketplace.com. Most stores open daily 10am–6pm; restaurant hours vary. BART: Embarcadero. Bus: 2, 7, 12, 14, 21, 66, or 71. Streetcar: F.

Fisherman's Wharf *Overrated*   Few cities in America are as adept at wholesaling their historical sites as San Francisco, which has converted Fisherman's Wharf into one of the most popular tourist attractions in the world. Unless you come really early in the morning, however, you won't find any traces of the traditional waterfront life that once existed here—the only fishing going on at Fisherman's Wharf these days is for tourists' dollars.

Moments **Italian-Style Saturday Sing-Along**

If you haven't completely fallen in love with San Francisco yet, then show up at **Caffè Trieste** in the North Beach on most Saturdays between 1 and 5pm. That's when the stringed instruments are tuned up, the chairs are scooted against the walls, and locals entertain the crowd with their lively version of Italian operas and heartwarming folk songs. Everybody's so high on caffeine that it quickly becomes one big happy party and the highlight of everyone's vacation (even locals get a kick out of it). This family-owned corner institution is one of San Francisco's most beloved cafes—a Beat Generation hangout that's been around since 1956 serving locally roasted Italian coffee. You'll find it at 601 Vallejo St. at Grant Ave. (© **415/392-6739**; www.caffetrieste.com), next to the row of motorcycles. Call to confirm the show's on.

Funky Favorites at Fisherman's Wharf

The following sights, clustered on or near Fisherman's Wharf, are great fun for kids, adults, and kitsch-lovers of all ages. By bus, take no. 15, 30, 32, 39, 42, or 82X; by streetcar, take the F-line; to reach the area by cable car, take the Powell-Mason line to the last stop and walk to the wharf. If you're arriving by car, park on adjacent streets or on the wharf between Taylor and Jones streets. Take your parking ticket with you so you can have it validated.

The popular battle-scarred World War II fleet submarine **USS** *Pampanito,* Pier 45, Fisherman's Wharf (© 415/775-1943), saw plenty of action in the Pacific. It has been completely restored, and visitors are free to crawl around inside. Admission, which includes an audio tour, is $9 for those ages 13 to 61, $5 for seniors 62 and older, $4 for children ages 6 to 12, and free for children younger than 6; the family pass (two adults, up to four kids) costs $20. The *Pampanito* is open 9am to 6pm Sunday through Thursday, 9am to 8pm Friday and Saturday from mid-October to May 23. From May 24 to mid-October, 9am to 8pm daily, except Wednesdays 9am to 6pm.

Also on Pier 45, the Musée Mécanique (p. 160) is worth a look.

Ripley's Believe It or Not! Museum, 175 Jefferson St. (© 415/771-6188; www.ripleysf.com), has drawn curious spectators through its doors for over 30 years. Inside, you'll experience the extraordinary world of improbabilities: a $1/3$-scale matchstick cable car, a shrunken human torso once owned by Ernest Hemingway, a dinosaur made from car bumpers, a walk through a kaleidoscope tunnel, and video displays and illusions. Robert LeRoy Ripley's infamous arsenal may lead you to ponder whether truth is, in fact, stranger than fiction. Admission is $13 for adults, $10 for seniors older than 60, $7.95 for children ages 5 to 12, free for children younger than 5. The museum is open Sunday through Thursday from 10am to 10pm, until midnight on Friday and Saturday.

Conceived and executed in the Madame Tussaud mold, San Francisco's **The Wax Museum at Fisherman's Wharf,** 145 Jefferson St. (© 800/439-4305), has long been a kitschy harborside tourist trap. In 1998, with the closing of the adjoining Haunted Goldmine, the museum underwent a $20-million teardown, renovation, and expansion. It re-opened in June 2000 as a huge complex that includes the Rainforest Café, with walk-through aquariums. (Not any less of a tourist trap, mind you—only a newer, slicker one.) The overhaul spiffed up the museum's 252 lifelike figures, including Britney Spears, Marilyn Monroe, John Wayne, former President George Bush and current president George W. Bush, Giants baseball star Barry Bonds, rap singer Eminem, and "Feared Leaders" such as Fidel Castro. The Chamber of Horrors features Dracula, Frankenstein, and a werewolf, along with bloody victims hanging from meat hooks. Admission is $13 for adults, $10 for seniors 62 and older, $6.95 for children ages 5 to 17, and free for children younger than 5. Discount group rates are available and are arranged via telephone or the website, www.waxmuseum.com, which also offers a $3 discount coupon for individual guests. The complex is open Monday through Friday from 10am to 9pm, Saturday and Sunday from 9am to 9pm.

Originally called Meigg's Wharf, this bustling strip of waterfront got its present moniker from generations of fishers who used to base their boats here. Today, the bay has become so polluted with toxins that bright yellow placards warn against eating fish from the waters. A small fleet of fewer than 30 fishing boats still set out from here, but basically, Fisherman's Wharf has been converted into one long shopping mall that stretches from Ghirardelli Square at the west end to PIER 39 at the east.

Accommodating a total of 350 boats, two marinas flank PIER 39 and house the Blue & Gold bay sightseeing fleet. In recent years, some 600 California sea lions have taken up residence on the adjacent floating docks. Until they abandon their new playground, which seems more and more unlikely, these playful, noisy creatures (some nights you can hear them all the way from Washington Square) are one of the best free attractions on the wharf. Docent-led programs, offered at PIER 39 on weekends from 11am to 5pm, teach visitors about the range, habitat, and adaptability of the California sea lion.

Some people love Fisherman's Wharf; others can't get far enough away from it. Most agree that, for better or for worse, it has to be seen at least once in your lifetime.

At Taylor St. and Embarcadero. © 415/956-3493. www.fishermanswharf.org. Bus: 15, 30, 32, 39, 42, or 82X. Cable car: Powell-Mason line (get off at the last stop). Streetcar: F. If you're arriving by car, park on adjacent streets or on the wharf between Taylor and Jones sts. for $16 per day, $8 with validation.

Ghirardelli Square   This National Historic Landmark property dates from 1864, when it served as a factory making Civil War uniforms, but it's best known as the former chocolate and spice factory of Domingo Ghirardelli (pronounced "Gear-a-*deli*"), who purchased it in 1984. The factory has since been converted into an unimpressive three-level mall containing 34-plus stores and 11 dining establishments. Scheduled street performers entertain regularly in the West Plaza and fountain area. Incidentally, the Ghirardelli Chocolate Company still makes chocolate, but its

---

GoCar Tours of San Francisco

If the thought of walking up and down San Francisco's brutally steep streets has you sweating already, considering renting a talking GoCar instead. The tiny yellow three-wheeled convertible cars are easy and fun to drive—every time I see one of these things the people riding in them are grinning from ear to ear—and they're cleverly guided by a talking GPS (Global Positioning System), which means that the car always knows where you are, even if you don't. The most popular computer-guided tour is a two-hour loop around the Fisherman's Wharf area, out to the Marina District, through Golden Gate Park, and down Lombard Street. As you drive, the talking car tells you where to turn and what landmarks you're passing. Even if you stop to check something out, as soon as you turn your GoCar back on, the tour picks up where it left off. Or you can just cruise around wherever you want (but not across the Golden Gate Bridge). There's a lockable trunk for your things, and the small size makes parking a breeze. You can rent a GoCar from 1 hour (about $40) to a full day. You'll have to wear a helmet, and you must at least be a licensed driver 18 years of age. The GoCar rental shop is at 2715 Hyde St., between Beach and North Point streets at Fisherman's Wharf. For more information call © **800/91-GoCar** or © **415/441-5695,** or log onto their website at www.gocarsf.com.

(Value   **Cheap Thrills: My Favorite Things to See & Do for Free (or Almost) in San Francisco**

- **Riding Bicycles from Fisherman's Wharf to Sam's in Tiburon.** My all-time favorite way of enjoying a sunny San Francisco day is riding my bike to Sam's Anchor Cafe in Tiburon (p. 248). It's a beautiful and often exhilarating ride that takes you over the Golden Gate Bridge, through the heart of Sausalito, along the scenic North Bay bike path, and ends at the best outdoor cafe in the Bay Area. The best part is, after your margaritas, you can take the passenger ferry across the bay to Fisherman's Wharf—right back to where you started. Blazing Saddles bike rental company at Fisherman's Wharf provides free bike maps showing the way from the wharf to Sam's, as well as pre-paid ferry passes (p. 186).

- **Singing at Glide's Sunday Morning Celebration.** Every Sunday at 9 and 11am a 140-member choir accompanied by a blues-style band raises some serious roof at the nondemoninational Glide Memorial Church. It's one of the most high-energy, hand-clapping, joy-inspiring events you'll ever attend as Reverend Cecil Williams raises everyone's spirits with uplifting sermons and songs about hope and love. Locals Sharon Stone and Robin Williams are regular attendees; even Bill Clinton and Oprah Winfrey are fans. See p. 178 for more info.

- **Riding the Outdoor Elevators at the Westin St. Francis Hotel,** 335 Powell St., at Union Square. Your heart may skip a beat as you race skyward at 1,000 feet per minute. The view, as you'd expect, is dazzling, and you don't have to be a guest at the Westin to take a ride. Almost as thrilling is the glass elevator at the **Fairmont Hotel,** 950 Mason St., at California Street. The finale is a 360-degree view–the best in the city–from the Crown Room restaurant and lounge.

- **Skating Golden Gate Park on a Weekend Day.** If you've never tried in-line skating before, there's no better place to learn than on the wide, flat street through Golden Gate Park, which is closed to vehicles on weekends. **Skates on Haight,** 1818 Haight St., near Stanyan Street (© 415/752-8375; www.skatesonhaight.com), is the best place to rent in-line skates, and it's only 1 block from the park. Protective wrist guards and kneepads are included in the cost (about $9 per hour for in-line or conventional

factory is in a lower-rent district in the East Bay. Still, if you have a sweet tooth, you won't be disappointed at the mall's fantastic (and expensive) old-fashioned soda fountain, which is open until midnight.

900 North Point St. (between Polk and Larkin sts.). © 415/775-5500. Stores generally open daily 10am–9pm in summer; Sun–Fri 10am–6pm, Sat 10am–9pm rest of year. Parking $4 per hour (1 hr. free with purchase and validation, max. $16). Cable car: Take Powell-Hyde line to last stop and walk west on Beach Street to the square.

Golden Gate Bridge *Kids*   The year 2006 marks the 70th birthday of possibly the most beautiful, and certainly the most photographed, bridge in the world.

skates). A major credit card and ID are required for rentals. The shop is open daily from 10am to 6pm.

- **Riding on the Powell-Hyde Cable Car.** It's the most fun you can have in San Francisco for only $5. Start on Market Street, then hang on to the brass rail for dear life as you whiz through the city's steep streets to Fisherman's Wharf.

- **Catching Air in Your Car.** Relive *Bullit* or *The Streets of San Francisco* as you careen down the center lane of Gough Street between Ellis and Eddy streets, screaming out "Whooooeee!" as you feel the pull of gravity leave you momentarily, followed by the thump of the car suspension bottoming out. Wimpier folks can settle for the steepest street in San Francisco: Filbert Street, between Leavenworth and Hyde streets.

- **Climbing the Filbert Street Steps.** San Francisco is a city of stairs, and the crème de la crème of steps is on Filbert Street between Sansome Street and the east side of Telegraph Hill. The terrain is so steep here that Filbert Street becomes Filbert Steps, a 377-step descent that wends its way through flower gardens and some of the city's oldest and most varied housing. It's a beautiful walk down, and great exercise going up.

- **Enjoying a Coke-on-the-Rocks at the Marriott Hotel's Atrium Lobby Lounge.** It takes a few stiff sodas to get the nerve to peer 40 stories straight down from the Marriott's Atrium Lounge, 777 Market St., at Grant Avenue, where the only thing between you and the pavement is a single pane of glass.

- **Strolling Haight Street Between Stanyan and Masonic Streets.** The San Francisco Zoo pales in comparison to some of the wildlife you'll see along lower Haight Street (don't worry, they won't bite). You'll also find plenty of colorful characters on Castro Street between Market and 19th streets.

- **Pondering the Mission District Murals.** You could easily spend a day in the Mission admiring the hundreds of vibrant murals emblazoned on the garages, fences, and doorways on Balmy Street, an alley between 24th and 25th streets. If you want to take a guided tour, see "Precita Eyes Mural Arts Center" on p. 171 for more info.

Often half-veiled by the city's trademark rolling fog, San Francisco's Golden Gate Bridge spans tidal currents, ocean waves, and battering winds to connect the City by the Bay with the Redwood Empire to the north.

With its gracefully swung single span, spidery bracing cables, and zooming twin towers, the bridge looks more like a work of abstract art than one of the 20th century's greatest practical engineering feats. Construction was completed in May 1937 at the then-colossal cost of $35 million.

The almost 1¾-mile bridge (longer if you factor in the approach), which reaches a height of 746 feet above the water, is awesome to cross. Traffic usually moves quickly, however, so crossing by car won't give you too much time to see the sights. If you drive from the city, park in the lot at the foot of the bridge on the city side and make the crossing by foot. Back in your car, continue to Marin's Vista Point, at the bridge's northern end. Look back and you'll be rewarded with one of the greatest views of San Francisco.

Millions of pedestrians walk or bike across the bridge each year, gazing up at the tall red towers, out at the vistas of San Francisco and Marin County, and down into the stacks of oceangoing liners. You can walk out onto the span from either end, but be prepared—it's usually windy and cold, and the bridge vibrates. Still, walking even a short distance is one of the best ways to experience the immense scale of the structure.

Hwy. 101 N. www.goldengatebridge.org. $5 cash toll collected when driving south. Bridge-bound Golden Gate Transit buses (© **415/923-2000**) depart every 30 min. during the day for Marin County, starting from the Transbay Terminal (Mission and First sts.) and stopping at Market and Seventh sts., at the Civic Center, and along Van Ness Ave. and Lombard St.

Lombard Street ⚔ *Overrated*   Known (erroneously) as the "crookedest street in the world," this whimsically winding block of Lombard Street in Russian Hill draws thousands of visitors each year (much to the chagrin of neighborhood residents, most of whom would prefer to block off the street to tourists). The angle of the street is so steep that the road has to snake back and forth to make a descent possible. The brick-lined street zigzags around the residences' bright flower gardens, which explode with color during warmer months. This short stretch of Lombard Street is one-way, downhill, and fun to drive. Take the curves slowly and in low gear, and expect a wait during the weekend. Save your film for the bottom where, if you're lucky, you can find a parking space and take a few snapshots of the silly spectacle. You can also take staircases (without curves) up or down on either side of the street. In truth, most locals don't understand what the fuss is all about. I'm guessing the draw is the combination of a classic, unusually steep San Francisco street and a great photo op. *FYI:* Vermont Street, between 20th and 22nd streets in Potrero Hill, is even more crooked, but not nearly as picturesque.

Between Hyde and Leavenworth sts. Bus: 30.

SBC Park ⚔⚔ *Moments*   If you're a baseball fan, you'll definitely want to schedule a visit to the magnificent SBC Park, home of the San Francisco Giants and hailed as one of the finest ballparks in America. From April through October, a sell-out crowd of 40,800 fans pack the $319-million ballpark for nearly every game—which has a smaller, more intimate feel than 3Com Park (where the 49ers play) and prime views of San Francisco Bay—and root for their National League Giants.

During the Major League season, tickets to the game are usually hard to come by (and expensive when you find them), but you can try to join the Bleacher Bums by purchasing one of the 500 bleacher-seat tickets sold every day before the game. They make you work for it, however: You have to show up at the ballpark 4 hours early to get a lottery number, then come back 2 hours before the game to get your tickets (maximum four per person). The upside is that the tickets are only $8.50 to $10.

If you can't even get bleacher sets, you can always join the "knothole gang" at the Portwalk (located behind right field) to catch a free glimpse of the game through cutout portholes into the ballpark. In the spirit of sharing, Portwalk peekers are encouraged to take in only an inning or two before giving way to fellow fans.

One guaranteed way to get into the ballpark is to take a **guided tour of SBC Park** and go behind the scenes where you'll see the press box, the dugout, the visitor's clubhouse, a luxury suite, and more. All tours run daily at 10:30am and 12:30pm. Ticket prices are $10 for adults, $5 for kids age 12 and younger. There are no tours on game days, and limited tours on the day of night games. To buy tickets online log onto www.sfgiants.com, then click on "SBC Park" and "Ballpark Tours" from the drop-down list. You can also buy tour tickets at any Giants Dugout Store or Tickets.com outlet. For more tour information call ℂ **415/972-2400.**

At the southeast corner of SoMa at the south end of the Embarcadero (bounded by King, 2nd, and 3rd sts.). ℂ **415/972-2000.** www.sfgiants.com. Bus: 10, 15, 30, 45, and 47. Streetcar: N.

PIER 39 *(Overrated*   PIER 39 is a multilevel waterfront complex a few blocks east of Fisherman's Wharf. Constructed on an abandoned cargo pier, it is, ostensibly, a re-creation of a turn-of-the-20th-century street scene, but don't expect a slice of old-time maritime life here: Today, PIER 39 is a busy mall allegedly welcoming 11 million visitors per year. It has more than 110 stores, 11 bay-view restaurants, a two-tiered Venetian carousel, a Hard Rock Cafe, and a "Riptide" arcade for the kids. And everything here is slanted toward helping you part with your travel dollars. This is *the* place that locals love to hate. That said, it does have a few perks: absolutely beautiful natural surroundings and bay views, fresh sea air, and hundreds of sunbathing sea lions (about 600 in peak season) lounging along its neighboring docks.

On the waterfront at the Embarcadero and Beach St. ℂ **415/705-5500.** www.pier39.com. Shops open daily 10:30am–8:30pm, with extended weekend hours during summer. Bus: 32.

2 Other Attractions

For information on museums in Golden Gate Park, see the "Golden Gate Park" section, beginning on p. 171.

Aquarium of the Bay *(Overrated*   This $38-million, 1-million-gallon marine attraction filled with sharks, stingrays, and more transports visitors through clear acrylic tunnels via a moving footpath. Frankly, however, it's overrated and overpriced, and I recommend you skip it.

The Embarcadero at Beach St. ℂ **888/SEA-DIVE** or 415/623-5333. www.aquariumofthebay.com. Aquarium admission $14 adults, $7.50 seniors and children ages 3–11, free for children under 3. Family (2 adults, 2 children) package $34. Behind-the-scenes tour $25 per person, including admission to the aquarium. Mon–Thurs 10am–6pm; Fri–Sun 10am–7pm; summer hours 9am–8pm daily. Streetcar: F.

Asian Art Museum ✪   Previously in Golden Gate Park and reopened in what was once the Civic Center's Beaux Arts–style central library, San Francisco's Asian Art Museum is one of the Western world's largest museums devoted to Asian art. Its collection boasts more than 15,000 art objects, such as world-class sculptures, paintings, bronzes, ceramics, and jade items, spanning 6,000 years of history and regions of south Asia, west Asia, Southeast Asia, the Himalayas, China, Korea, and Japan. Inside you'll find 40,000 square feet of gallery space showcasing 2,500 objects at any given time. Add temporary exhibitions, live demonstrations, learning activities, cafe Asia, and a store, and you've got one very good reason to head to the Civic Center.

200 Larkin St. (between Fulton and McAllister sts.). ℂ **415/581-3500.** www.asianart.org. Admission $10 adults, $7 seniors 65 and older, $6 youths ages 12–17, free for children under 12, $5 flat rate for all after 5pm Thurs. Free 1st Tues of the month. Tues–Wed and Fri–Sun 10am–5pm; Thurs 10am–9pm. Bus: Bus: All Market St. buses. Streetcar: Civic Center.

Cable Car Museum _Value_ _Kids_   If you've ever wondered how cable cars work, this nifty museum explains (and demonstrates) it all. Yes, this is a museum, but the Cable Car Museum is no stuffed shirt. It's the living powerhouse, repair shop, and storage place of the cable car system and is in full operation. Built for the Ferries and Cliff House Railway in 1887, the building underwent an $18-million reconstruction in the 1980s to restore its original gaslight-era look, install an amazing spectators' gallery, and add a museum of San Francisco transit history.

The exposed machinery, which pulls the cables under San Francisco's streets, looks like a Rube Goldberg invention. Stand in the mezzanine gallery and become mesmerized by the massive groaning and vibrating winches as they thread the cable that hauls the cars through a huge figure-eight and back into the system using slack-absorbing tension wheels. For a better view, move to the lower-level viewing room, where you can see the massive pulleys and gears operating underground.

Also on display here is one of the first grip cars developed by Andrew S. Hallidie, operated for the first time on Clay Street on August 2, 1873. Other displays include an antique grip car and trailer that operated on Pacific Avenue until 1929, and dozens of exact-scale models of cars used on the various city lines. There's also a shop where you can buy a variety of cable car gifts. You can see the whole museum in about 45 minutes.

1201 Mason St. (at Washington St.). ℂ 415/474-1887. www.cablecarmuseum.org. Free admission. Apr–Sept daily 10am–6pm; Oct–Mar daily 10am–5pm. Closed Thanksgiving, Christmas, and New Year's Day. Cable car: Both Powell St. lines.

California Academy of Sciences _Kids_   Originally clustered around the Music Concourse in Golden Gate Park (in multiple buildings) and intending to return there around 2008 after a complete rebuild, this duo of outstanding museums is poorly represented in its temporary home near Moscone West and the Yerba Buena Gardens and Center for the Arts. You'll find a small selection of **Steinhart Aquarium**'s sealife here, including seahorses, turtles, snakes, and poison dart frogs as well as a two-story 20,000-gallon living coral reef featuring Yellow Tangs, sea stars, and a giant clam. Kids love the "touch tide pool" where they can get their mitts on live sea life and the African Penguin feeding show, which happens daily at 11am and 3:30pm.

Finds **San Francisco's Old-Fashioned Arcade Museum**

"Fun for all ages" isn't a trite expression when describing San Francisco's **Musée Mécanique,** a truly unique penny arcade museum containing one of the largest privately owned collections of antique coin-operated mechanical musical instruments in the world—160 machines dating back from the 1880s through the present (and they still work!). You can pay Grand-Ma Fortune Teller a quarter to see what she has to say about your future, or watch little kids cower in fear as Laughing "Fat Lady" Sal gives her infamous cackle of a greeting. Other yesteryear seaside resort games include antique movie machines, 19th-century music boxes, old-school strength testers, and mechanical cranes. The museum is located at Pier 45 at the end of Taylor Street at Fisherman's Wharf. It's open Monday through Friday from 11am to 7pm and Saturday and Sunday from 10am to 8pm. Admission is free (ℂ 415/346-2000).

Yerba Buena Gardens

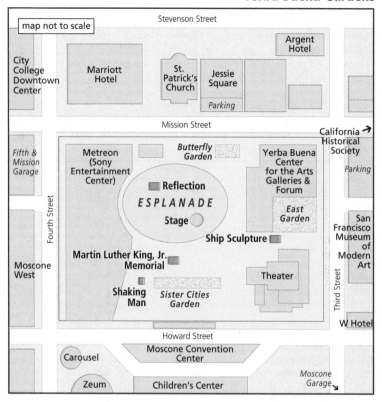

A truncated version of the **Natural History Museum** has also been transplanted here with changing exhibits, a new exhibit on California, and some of its permanent displays, including Snake Alley, where terrestrial snakes reside; and ScienceNOW, which presents a frequently changing display of Academy research, breaking science news, and expeditions around the globe. Kids 5 and under like the Nature Nest, an education center with hands-on learning activities.

Families should look into the Academy's calendar of events, which includes fun kid-friendly festivities, such as face painting, storytelling, animal origami, and exhibit-related stories and demonstrations. That having been said, I can't wait for these spectacular museums to reopen in their rightful spaces in the park: Their truncated versions don't offer nearly as much entertainment for the money as their complete collections in their original locations.

875 Howard St. (between 4th and 5th sts.). ✆ **415/321-8000** for recorded information. www.calacademy.org. Admission $7 adults; $4.50 seniors 65 and older, students with ID, and youth ages 12–17; $2 children ages 4–11; free for children under 4. Free on 1st Wed of the month. Daily 10am–5pm. BART: Powell St. Bus: 14, 15, 30, or 45. Street-car: J, K, L, or M to Montgomery.

California Palace of the Legion of Honor 🐾🐾 Designed as a memorial to California's World War I casualties, this neoclassical structure is an exact replica of the

Everything Old is New Again

After closing for several years, San Francisco's oldest museum, the **de Young Museum**, 50 Hagiwara Tea Garden Dr. (© **415/682-2481**; www.thinker.org), reopened in its new state-of-the-art facility in Golden Gate Park in October 2005. Its vast collections include American paintings, decorative arts and crafts, and arts from Africa, Oceania, and the Americas, as well as Western and non-Western textiles. Along with visit-worthy exhibitions, the de Young is also beloved for its educational arts programs for both children and adults. Admission fees are $10 for adults, $7 for seniors 62 and older, with ID, $6 for children 13 to 17, and free for children 12 and under.

Legion of Honor Palace in Paris, right down to the inscription HONNEUR ET PATRIE above the portal.

The Legion of Honor reopened in late 1995, after a 2-year, $35-million renovation and seismic upgrading. The exterior's grassy expanses, cliff-side paths, and incredible view of the Golden Gate and downtown make this an absolute must-visit attraction before you even get in the door. The inside is equally impressive. The museum's permanent collection covers 4,000 years of art and includes paintings, sculpture, and decorative arts from Europe, as well as international tapestries, prints, and drawings. The chronological display of 4,000 years of ancient and European art includes one of the world's finest collections of Rodin sculptures. The sunlight Legion Café offers indoor and outdoor seating at moderate prices.

In Lincoln Park (34th Ave. and Clement St.). © **415/750-3600**, or 415/863-3330 (recorded information). www.thinker.org. Admission $8 adults, $6 seniors 65 and older, $5 youths ages 12–17, free for children under 12. Fees may be higher for special exhibitions. Free to all on Tues. Tues–Sun 9:30am–5pm. Bus: 18.

The Exploratorium 𝄐𝄐 *Kids*   *Scientific American* magazine rated the Exploratorium "the best science museum in the world"—pretty heady stuff for this exciting hands-on science fair. The Exploratorium is not a fancy place (it's more like a block-long warehouse), but it is substance, not style, that matters here. Inside you'll find hundreds of exhibits that explore everything from giant-bubble blowing to Einstein's theory of relativity. It's like a mad scientist's penny arcade, an educational fun house, and an experimental laboratory, all rolled into one. Touch a tornado, shape a glowing electrical current, finger-paint using a computer, or take a sensory journey in total darkness in the Tactile Dome ($3 extra, call to make advance reservations)—you could spend all day here and still not see everything. Every exhibit at the Exploratorium is designed to be interactive, educational, safe, and, most important, fun. And don't think it's just for kids; parents inevitably end up being the most reluctant to leave. On the way out, be sure to stop in the wonderful gift store, which is chock-full of affordable brain candy.

The museum is in the Marina District at the beautiful **Palace of Fine Arts** 𝄐𝄐, the only building left standing from the Panama-Pacific Exposition of 1915. The adjoining park and lagoon—the perfect place for an afternoon picnic—are home to ducks, swans, seagulls, and grouchy geese, so bring bread.

3601 Lyon St., in the Palace of Fine Arts (at Marina Blvd.). © **415/563-7337**, or 415/561-0360 (recorded information). www.exploratorium.edu. Admission $12 adults; $9.50 seniors, youth ages 13–17, visitors with disabilities, and college students with ID; $8 children ages 4–12; free for children under 4. Free to all 1st Wed of each month. Groups of 10 or more must make advance reservations. AE, MC, V. Tues–Sun 10am–5pm. Closed Mon except MLK, Jr., Day, Presidents' Day, Memorial Day, and Labor Day. Free parking. Bus: 28, 30, or Golden Gate Transit.

Haas-Lilienthal House   Of the city's many gingerbread Victorians, this handsome Queen Anne house is one of the most flamboyant. The 1886 structure features all the architectural frills of the period, including dormer windows, flying cupolas, ornate trim, and a winsome turret. The elaborately styled house is now a museum, its rooms fully furnished with period pieces. The Foundation for San Francisco's Architectural Heritage maintains the house and offers docent-led 1-hour tours (the only way to see the house), which start every 20 to 30 minutes.

2007 Franklin St. (at Washington St.). ✆ 415/441-3004. 1-hr. guided tour $8 adults, $5 seniors and children ages 12 and under. Wed and Sat noon–3pm; Sun 11am–4pm. Bus: 1, 12, 19, 27, 47, or 49. Cable car: California St. line.

Maritime National Historical Park *Finds* *Kids*   Shaped like an Art Deco ship, the Maritime Museum is filled with sailing, whaling, and fishing lore. Remarkably good exhibits include intricate model craft and scrimshaw. The collection of shipwreck photographs and historic marine scenes includes an 1851 snapshot of hundreds of abandoned ships, deserted en masse by crews dashing off to participate in the gold rush. Beautifully carved, brightly painted wooden figureheads from old windjammers line the walls. Two blocks east, at the park's Hyde Street Pier, are several historic ships, now moored and open to the public.

The *Balclutha,* one of the last surviving square-riggers and the handsomest vessel in San Francisco Bay, was built in Glasgow, Scotland, in 1886 and carried grain from California at a near-record speed of 300 miles a day. The ship is now completely restored.

The 1890 *Eureka* still carries a cargo of nostalgia for San Franciscans. It was the last of 50 paddle-wheel ferries that regularly plied the bay; it made its final trip in 1957. Restored to its original splendor at the height of the ferryboat era, the side-wheeler is loaded with deck cargo, including antique cars and trucks. The black-hulled, three-masted *C. A. Thayer,* built in 1895, was crafted for the lumber trade and carried logs felled in the Pacific Northwest to the carpentry shops of California. *Note:* At presstime, the ship was undergoing a restoration that is due for completion in 2006.

Other historic ships docked here include the tiny two-masted *Alma,* one of the last scow schooners to bring hay to the horses of San Francisco; the *Hercules,* a huge 1907 oceangoing steam tug; and the *Eppleton Hall,* a side-wheel tugboat built in England in 1914 to operate on London's River Thames. At the pier's small-boat shop, visitors can follow the restoration progress of historic boats from the museum's collection. It's behind the maritime bookstore on your right as you approach the ships.

At the foot of Polk St. (near Fisherman's Wharf). ✆ 415/561-7100. www.nps.gov/safr. Museum free. Tickets to board ships $5, free for children under 16. Museum daily 10am–5pm. Ships on Hyde St. Pier open Memorial Day–Oct 15 daily 9:30am–5:30pm; Oct 16 to day before Memorial Day daily 9:30am–5pm. Bus: 19, 30, or 47. Cable car: Powell-Hyde St. line to the last stop.

Octagon House   This unusual, eight-sided, cupola-topped house dates from 1861 and is maintained by the National Society of Colonial Dames of America. Architecture buffs take note: the architectural features are extraordinary, and from the second floor it is possible to look up into the cupola, which is illuminated at night. In the small museum, you'll find Early American furniture, portraits, silver, looking glasses, and English and Chinese ceramics. There are also some historic documents, including signatures of 54 of the 56 signers of the Declaration of Independence. Even if you're not able to visit the inside, this strange structure is worth a look from the outside.

2645 Gough St. (at Union St.). (✆ 415/441-7512. Free admission; donation suggested. Feb–Dec 2nd Sun and 2nd and 4th Thurs of each month noon–3pm. Tours by appointment are the only way to see the house. Closed Jan and holidays. Bus: 41 or 45.

San Francisco Museum of Modern Art (SFMOMA) 🎬 Swiss architect Mario Botta, in association with Hellmuth, Obata, and Kassabaum, designed this $65-million museum, which has made SoMa one of the more popular areas to visit, for tourists and residents alike. The museum's permanent collection consists of more than 26,000 works, including close to 5,000 paintings and sculptures by artists such as Henri Matisse, Jackson Pollock, and Willem de Kooning. Other artists represented are Diego Rivera, Georgia O'Keeffe, Paul Klee, the Fauvists, and exceptional holdings of Richard Diebenkorn. MOMA was one of the first museums to recognize photography as a major art form; its extensive collection includes more than 12,000 photographs by such notables as Ansel Adams, Alfred Stieglitz, Edward Weston, and Henri Cartier-Bresson. Unfortunately, few works are on display at one time, and for the money, the experience can be disappointing—especially compared to the finer museums of New York. However, this is about as good as it gets in our boutique city, so take it or leave it. Docent-led tours take place daily. Times are posted at the admission desk. Phone or check MOMA's website for current details of upcoming special events and exhibitions.

The **Caffè Museo,** to the right of the museum entrance, offers very good–quality fresh soups, sandwiches, and salads. And don't miss the **MuseumStore,** which carries a wonderful array of books and trinkets: It's one of the best shops in town.

151 Third St. (2 blocks south of Market St., across from Yerba Buena Gardens). (✆ 415/357-4000. www.sfmoma.org. Admission $10 adults, $7 seniors, $6 students over 12 with ID, free for children 12 and under. Half-price for all Thurs 6–9pm; free to all 1st Tues of each month. Thurs 11am–8:45pm; Fri–Tues 11am–5:45pm. Closed Wed and major holidays. Bus: 15, 30, or 45. Streetcar: J, K, L, or M to Montgomery.

San Francisco Zoo (& Children's Zoo) 🅺ids Located between the Pacific Ocean and Lake Merced, in the southwest corner of the city, the San Francisco Zoo isn't even remotely as stellar as many other cities' zoos because it's not particularly well organized, is ever lacking in funds, and seems generally tired. Though it ain't heaven, it's all we've got, so read on and decide for yourself whether it's worth the trip.

Founded at its present site adjacent to the ocean in 1929, the zoo is spread over 125 acres, with 100 acres currently developed and housing 950 mammals, birds, reptiles, amphibians, and invertebrates. Exhibit highlights include the new Lipman Family Lemur Forest, a forest setting for five endangered species of lemurs from Madagascar that features interactive components for the visitor; Gorilla World, a tranquil setting for a family group of western lowland gorillas; Koala Crossing, which connects to the Australian WalkAbout exhibit with its kangaroos, wallaroos, and emus; Penguin Island, home to a large breeding colony of Magellanic Penguins; the Feline Conservation Center, a wooded sanctuary and breeding facility for endangered snow leopards and other small cats; and the Primate Discovery Center, home to rare and endangered monkeys. In the South American Tropical Forest building, a large green anaconda can be found as well as other South American reptile and bird species. Puente al Sur (Bridge to the South) has a pair of giant anteaters and some capybaras. The Lion House is home to rare Sumatran and Siberian tigers and African lions. You can see the big cats fed every day at 2pm (except Mon, when you are less likely to see them since

Free Culture

To beef up attendance and give indigent folk like us travel writers a break, almost all of San Francisco's art galleries and museums are open free to the public 1 day of the week or month (or both), and several never charge admission. Use the following list to plan your week around the museums' free-day schedules; refer to the individual attractions listings in this chapter for more information on each museum

First Tuesday
- California Palace of the Legion of Honor (p. 161)
- Center for the Arts at Yerba Buena Gardens (p. 166)
- San Francisco Museum of Modern Art (SFMOMA, see p. 164)
- Asian Art Museum (p. 159)

First Wednesday
- Exploratorium (p. 162)
- California Academy of Sciences (p. 160)

Always Free
- Cable Car Museum (p. 160)
- Maritime National Historical Park and Museum (there's a fee to board ships) (p. 163)
- Musée Mécanique (p. 160)
- Wells Fargo History Museum (p. 166)
- Glide Memorial United Methodist Church (p. 178)

they like to hang out in secluded areas when they're not eating). African Savanna, the latest exhibit (opened in mid-2004), is a 3-acre mixed-species habitat with giraffes, zebras, antelope, and birds.

The 6-acre Children's Zoo offers kids, and their families, opportunities for close-up encounters with domestic rare breeds of goats, sheep, ponies, and horses in the Family Farm. Touch and feel small mammals, reptiles, and amphibians along the Nature Trail (open Memorial Day to Labor Day), and gaze at eagles and hawks stationed on Hawk Hill. Visitors can see the inner-workings of the Koret Animal Resource Center, a thriving facility that houses the animals used in the educational outreach programs, and visit the incredible Insect Zoo. One of the Children's Zoo's most popular exhibits is the Meerkat and Prairie Dog exhibit, where kids can crawl through tunnels and play in sand, just like these two amazing burrowing species.

Don't miss the Little Puffer miniature steam train, which takes passengers around a ⅓-mile track, and the historic Dentzel Carousel (both $2 per ride).

Sloat Blvd. and 47th Ave. and Great Hwy. (✆ 415/753-7080. www.sfzoo.org. Admission to main zoo and Children's Zoo $8 residents, $11 nonresidents for adults; $4.50 residents, $8 nonresidents for seniors 65 and over and youth ages 12–17; $2.50 for residents, $5 nonresident for children ages 3–11; free for children under 3 when accompanied by an adult; $1 discount with valid Muni transfer. Free to all 1st Wed of each month, except $2 fee for Children's Zoo. Carousel $2. Main zoo daily 10am–5pm. Children's Zoo Mon–Fri 11am–4pm, weekends and summer 10:30am–4:30pm. Streetcar: L from downtown Market St. to the end of the line.

Wells Fargo History Museum   Wells Fargo, one of California's largest banks, got its start in the Wild West. Its history museum, at the bank's head office, houses hundreds of genuine relics from the company's whip-and-six-shooter days, including pistols, photographs, early banking articles, posters, a stagecoach, and mining equipment.

420 Montgomery St. (at California St.). ℭ 415/396-2619. www.wellsfargohistory.com. Free admission. Mon–Fri 9am–5pm. Closed bank holidays. BART: Montgomery St. Bus: Any to Market St. Cable car: California St. line.

Yerba Buena Gardens/Center for the Arts ✹ *Finds* *Kids*   The Yerba Buena Center, which opened in 1993, is the city's cultural facility, similar to New York's Lincoln Center, but far more fun on the outside. It stands on top of the northern extension of the underground Moscone Convention Center. The center's two buildings present music, theater, dance, and visual arts. James Stewart Polshek designed the 755-seat theater, and Fumihiko Maki designed the Galleries and Arts Forum, which features three galleries and a space designed especially for dance. Cutting-edge computer art, multimedia shows, contemporary exhibitions, and performances occupy the center's high-tech galleries.

More commonly explored is the 5-acre **Yerba Buena Gardens** (ℭ 415/543-1718), a great place to relax in the grass on a sunny day and check out several artworks. The most dramatic outdoor piece is an emotional mixed-media memorial to Martin Luther King, Jr. Created by sculptor Houston Conwill, poet Estella Majozo, and architect Joseph de Pace, it features 12 panels, each inscribed with quotations from King, sheltered behind a 50-foot-high waterfall. For most, this pastoral patch is a brief stopover to the surrounding attractions (see below). Since 2004, the gardens have hosted seasonal free **outdoor festivals** held on varied dates from May through October. It's definitely worth discovering whether you can catch one of these, as performances include dance, music, poetry, and more by the San Francisco Ballet, Opera, Symphony, and others; see www.ybgf.org for details.

On the periphery of Yerba Buena Gardens are a number of worthy individually operated excursions. In the Children's Center, **Zeum** (ℭ 415/777-2800) includes a cafe, interactive cultural center, bowling lanes (ℭ 415/820-3540), ice-skating rink (ℭ 415/777-3727), fabulous 1906 carousel (ℭ 415/247-6500), and interactive play and learning garden (ℭ 415/247-6500). Sony's **Metreon Entertainment Center** (ℭ 415/369-6000; www.metreon.com) is a 350,000-square-foot complex housing great movie theaters, an IMAX theater, a "Taste of San Francisco" food court with decent fare, an arcade, and shops, including the only Sony store in the U.S. completely devoted to the PlayStation (big with boys of all ages), and a Jelly Belly jellybean shop. The **California Historical Society** (ℭ 415/357-1848), home to a research library and a publicly accessible California photography and fine arts collection, rests at 678 Mission St.

701 Mission St. ℭ 415/978-ARTS (box office). www.ybca.org. Admission for gallery $6 adults, $3 seniors, teachers, and students. Free to all 1st Tues of each month. Free for seniors and students with ID every Thurs. Tues, Wed, Sun noon–5pm; Thurs–Sat noon–8pm. Bus: 5, 9, 14, 15, 30, or 45. Streetcar: J, K, L, M, N to Powell or Montgomery.

3 Neighborhoods Worth a Visit

To really get to know San Francisco, break out of the downtown and Fisherman's Wharf areas to explore the city's ethnically and culturally diverse neighborhoods. Walk the streets, browse the shops, grab a bite at a local restaurant—you'll find that San Francisco's beauty and charm are around every corner, not just at the popular tourist

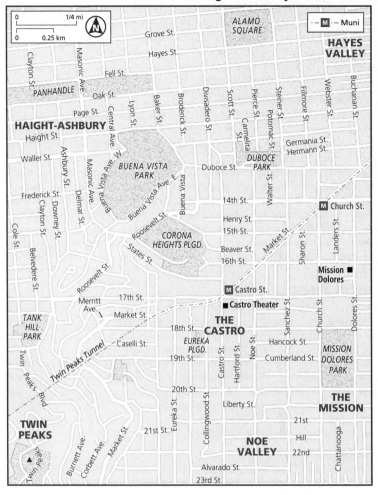

destinations. ***Note:*** For information on Fisherman's Wharf, see its entry under "San Francisco's Top Attractions," on p. 153. For information on San Francisco neighborhoods and districts that aren't discussed here, see "Neighborhoods in Brief," in chapter 5, beginning on p. 60.

NOB HILL

When the cable car started operating in 1873, this hill became the city's exclusive residential area. Newly wealthy residents who had struck it rich in the gold rush (and were known by names such as the "Big Four" and the "Comstock Bonanza kings") built their mansions here, but they were almost all destroyed by the 1906 earthquake and fire. The only two surviving buildings are the Flood Mansion, which serves today as the **Pacific Union Club,** and the **Fairmont Hotel,** which was under construction when the earthquake struck and was damaged but not destroyed. Today, the burned-out sites of former mansions hold the city's luxury hotels—the **Mark Hopkins,** the **Stanford Court,** the **Huntington,** and the spectacular **Grace Cathedral,** which stands on the Crocker mansion site. Nob Hill is worth a visit if only to stroll around **Huntington Park,** attend a Sunday service at the cathedral, or ooh and aah your way around the Fairmont's spectacular lobby.

SOUTH OF MARKET (SoMA)

From Market Street to Townsend Street and the Embarcadero to Division Street, SoMa has become the city's newest cultural and multimedia center. The process started when alternative clubs began opening in the old warehouses in the area nearly a decade ago. A wave of entrepreneurs followed, seeking to start new businesses in what was once an extremely low-rent area compared to the neighboring Financial District. Today, gentrification and high rents hold sway, spurred by a building boom that started with the **Moscone Convention Center** and continued with the **Yerba Buena Center for the Arts** and **Yerba Buena Gardens,** the **San Francisco Museum of Modern Art (SFMOMA),** the **Four Seasons Hotel,** and the **Metreon Entertainment Center.** Other institutions, businesses, and museums regularly move into the area. A substantial portion of the city's nightlife takes place in warehouse spaces throughout the district.

NORTH BEACH 🐦🐦🐦

In the late 1800s, an enormous influx of Italian immigrants to North Beach firmly established this aromatic area as San Francisco's "Little Italy." Dozens of Italian restaurants and coffeehouses continue to flourish in what is still the center of the city's Italian community. Walk down **Columbus Avenue** on any given morning, and you're bound to be bombarded by the wonderful aromas of roasting coffee and savory pasta sauces. Although there are some interesting shops and bookstores in the area, it's the dozens of eclectic little cafes, delis, and bakeries that give North Beach its Italian-bohemian character. For more perspective on this neighborhood, follow the detailed walking tour in chapter 9 (beginning on p. 197) or sign up for a guided Javawalk with coffee nut Elaine Sosa (see "Walking Tours," on p. 183 in this chapter).

CHINATOWN 🐦🐦

The first of the Chinese immigrants came to San Francisco in the early 1800s to work as servants. By 1851, 25,000 Chinese people were working in California, and most had settled in San Francisco's Chinatown. Fleeing famine and the Opium Wars, they had come seeking the good fortune promised by the "Gold Mountain" of California, and hoped to return with wealth to their families in China. For the majority, the reality of life in California did not live up to the promise. First employed as workers in the gold mines during the gold rush, they later built the railroads, working as little more than slaves and facing constant prejudice. Yet the community, segregated in the Chinatown ghetto, thrived. Growing prejudice led to the Chinese Exclusion Act of 1882, which halted all Chinese immigration for 10 years and severely limited it thereafter (the Chinese Exclusion Act was not repealed until 1943). Chinese people were also denied the opportunity to buy homes outside the Chinatown ghetto until the 1950s.

Today, San Francisco has one of the largest communities of Chinese people in the United States. More than 80,000 people live in Chinatown, but the majority of Chinese people have moved out into newer areas like the Richmond and Sunset districts.

Although frequented by tourists, the area continues to cater to Chinese shoppers, who crowd the vegetable and herb markets, restaurants, and shops. Tradition runs deep here, and if you're lucky, you might hear women mixing mah-jongg tiles as they play the centuries-old game. (*Be warned:* You're likely to hear lots of spitting around here, too—it seems to be part of local tradition.)

The gateway at Grant Avenue and Bush Street marks the entry to Chinatown. The heart of the neighborhood is Portsmouth Square, where you'll find locals playing board games (often gambling) or just sitting quietly.

On Waverly Place, a street where the Chinese celebratory colors of red, yellow, and green are much in evidence, you'll find three **Chinese temples:** Jeng Sen (Buddhist and Taoist) at no. 146, Tien Hou (Buddhist) at no. 125, and Norras (Buddhist) at no. 109. If you enter, do so quietly so that you do not disturb those in prayer.

A block west of Grant Avenue, **Stockton Street,** from 1000 to 1200, is the community's main shopping street, lined with grocers, fishmongers, tea sellers, herbalists, noodle parlors, and restaurants. Here, too, is the Buddhist Kong Chow Temple, at no. 855, above the Chinatown post office. Explore at your leisure. A Chinatown walking tour is outlined in chapter 9, beginning on p. 190.

JAPANTOWN

More than 12,000 citizens of Japanese descent (1.4% of the city's population) live in San Francisco, or Soko, as the Japanese who first emigrated here often called it. Initially, they settled in Chinatown and south of Market along Stevenson and Jessie streets from Fourth to Seventh streets. After the earthquake in 1906, SoMa became a light industrial and warehouse area, and the largest Japanese concentration took root in the Western Addition between Van Ness Avenue and Fillmore Street, the site of today's Japantown. By 1940, it covered 30 blocks.

In 1913, the Alien Land Law was passed, depriving Japanese Americans of the right to buy land. From 1924 to 1952, the United States banned Japanese immigration. During World War II, the U.S. government froze Japanese bank accounts, interned community leaders, and removed 112,000 Japanese Americans—two-thirds of them citizens—to camps in California, Utah, and Idaho. Japantown was emptied of Japanese people, and war workers took their place. Upon their release in 1945, the Japanese found their old neighborhood occupied. Most of them resettled in the Richmond and Sunset districts; some returned to Japantown, but it had shrunk to a mere 6 or so blocks. Today, the community's notable sights include the **Buddhist Church of San Francisco,** 1881 Pine St. (at Octavia St.); the **Konko Church of San Francisco,** 1909 Bush St. (at Laguna St.); the **Sokoji-Soto Zen Buddhist Temple,** 1691 Laguna St. (at Sutter St.); **Nihonmachi Mall,** 1700 block of Buchanan Street between Sutter and Post streets, which contains two steel fountains by Ruth Asawa; and the **Japan Center,** an Asian-oriented shopping mall occupying 3 square blocks bounded by Post, Geary, Laguna, and Fillmore streets. At its center stands the five-tiered **Peace Pagoda,** designed by world-famous Japanese architect Yoshiro Taniguchi "to convey the friendship and goodwill of the Japanese to the people of the United States." Surrounding the pagoda, through a network of arcades, squares, and bridges, you can explore dozens of shops and showrooms featuring everything from TVs and tansu chests to pearls, bonsai (dwarf trees), and kimonos. **Kabuki Springs & Spa** (see the "Bargain Bathing of the Mind & Body" box on p. 170) is the center's most famous tenant. But locals also head to its numerous restaurants, teahouses, shops, and multiplex movie theater.

There's often live entertainment in this neighborhood on summer weekends, including Japanese music and dance performances, tea ceremonies, flower-arranging demonstrations, and martial-arts presentations. The **Japan Center** (② **415/922-6776**) is open daily from 10am to midnight, although most shops close much earlier. To get there, take bus no. 2, 3, or 4 (exit at Buchanan and Sutter sts.) or no. 22 or 38 (exit at the northeast corner of Geary Blvd. and Fillmore St.).

HAIGHT-ASHBURY

Few of San Francisco's neighborhoods are as varied—or as famous—as Haight-Ashbury. Walk along Haight Street, and you'll encounter everything from drug-dazed drifters begging for change to an armada of the city's funky-trendy shops, clubs, and cafes. Turn anywhere off Haight, and instantly you're among the clean-cut, young urban professionals who can afford the steep rents in this hip 'hood. The result is an interesting mix of well-to-do and we'll-screw-you aging flower children, former Dead-heads, homeless people, and throngs of tourists who try not to stare as they wander through this most human of zoos. Some find it depressing, others find it fascinating, but everyone agrees that it ain't what it was in the free-lovin' psychedelic Summer of Love. Is it still worth a visit? Not if you are here for a day or two, but it's certainly worth an excursion on longer trips, if only to enjoy a cone of Cherry Garcia at the now-famous Ben & Jerry's Ice Cream Store on the corner of Haight and Ashbury streets, and then to wander and gawk at the area's intentional freaks.

THE CASTRO

Castro Street, between Market and 18th streets, is the center of the city's gay community as well as a lovely neighborhood teeming with shops, restaurants, bars, and other institutions that cater to the area's colorful residents. Among the landmarks are **Harvey Milk Plaza** and the **Castro Theatre,** a 1930s movie palace with a Wurlitzer. The gay community began to move here in the late 1960s and early 1970s from a neighborhood called Polk Gulch, which still has a number of gay-oriented bars and stores. Castro is one of the liveliest streets in the city and the perfect place to shop for gifts and revel in free-spiritedness.

Finds Bargain Bathing of the Mind & Body

Kabuki Springs & Spa, 1750 Geary Blvd., at Fillmore Street (② **415/922-6000;** www.kabukisprings.com), the Japan Center's most famous tenant, was once a traditional Japanese bathhouse. The Joie de Vivre hotel group bought and renovated it in 1999, however, and it's now more of an upscale pan-Asian spa with a focus on wellness. The deluxe deep ceramic communal tubs, sauna, and steam room stay open until 10pm and only cost $16 to $20 per person (Tues is the only coed day—other days of the week switch between men-only and women-only). The bath salts, chilled cucumber face cloths, and tea are complimentary. If you want to splurge on your body, the spa offers an array of massages (the shiatsu is incredible) and ayurvedic treatments, body scrubs, wraps, and facials, which start at about $55. *Note:* A photo ID is required.

THE MISSION DISTRICT

Once inhabited almost entirely by Irish immigrants, the Mission District is now the center of the city's Latino community as well as a mecca for young, hip residents. It's an oblong area stretching roughly from 14th to 30th streets between Potrero Avenue on the east and Dolores on the west. Many of the city's finest Victorians still stand in the outer areas, although most seem strangely out of place in the lower-income neighborhoods. The heart of the community lies along 24th Street between Van Ness and Potrero, where dozens of excellent ethnic restaurants, bakeries, bars, and specialty stores attract people from all over the city. The area surrounding 16th Street and Valencia is a hotbed for impressive—and often impressively cheap—restaurants and bars catering to the city's hip crowd. The Mission District at night doesn't feel like the safest place (although in terms of creepiness, the Tenderloin, a few blocks off Union Square, beats the Mission by far), and walking around the area should be done with caution, but it's usually quite safe during the day and is highly recommended.

For an even better insight into the community, go to the **Precita Eyes Mural Arts Center,** 2981 24th St., between Harrison and Alabama streets (© **415/285-2287;** www.precitaeyes.org), and take one of the 1½- to 2-hour tours conducted on Saturdays and Sundays at 11am and 1:30pm, where you'll see 60 murals in an 8-block walk. The 11am tour costs $10 for adults, $8 for students with ID, $5 for seniors, and $2 for children under 18; the 1:30pm tour, which is half an hour longer and includes a slide show, costs $12 for adults, $8 for students with ID, $5 for seniors and children under 18. Every year during Mural Awareness Month (usually May), tours are given daily. All but the Saturday-morning tour (call for starting place) leave from the center's 24th Street location (© **415/285-2287**).

Other signs of cultural life in the neighborhood are progressive theaters such as Theater Rhinoceros and Theater Artaud. At 16th Street and Dolores is the Mission San Francisco de Assisi, better known as **Mission Dolores** (p. 178). It's the city's oldest surviving building and the district's namesake.

4 Golden Gate Park ★★★

Everybody and everything loves **Golden Gate Park**—people, dogs, birds, frogs, turtles, and even bison (check out the Buffalo Paddock). Literally, everything feels unified here in San Francisco's enormous arboreal front yard, but this great city landmark wasn't always a favorite place to convene. It was conceived in the 1860s and 1870s and took its current shape in the 1880s and 1890s, thanks to the skill and effort of John McLaren, a Scot who arrived in 1887 and began landscaping the park.

Totaling 1,017 acres, the park is a narrow strip that stretches inland from the Pacific coast. No one had thought about the challenge the sand dunes and wind would present to any landscape artist. McLaren developed a new strain of grass called "sea bent," which he had planted to hold the sandy soil along the Firth of Forth, and he used it to anchor the soil here, too. He also built the two windmills that stand on the western edge of the park to pump water for irrigation. Every year the ocean eroded the western fringe of the park, and ultimately he solved this problem, too. It took him 40 years to build a natural wall, putting out bundles of sticks that the tides covered with sand. Under his brilliant eye, the park took shape.

Today's Golden Gate Park is a truly magical place. Spend a sunny day stretched out on the grass along JFK Drive, have a good read in the Shakespeare Garden, or stroll

Golden Gate Park

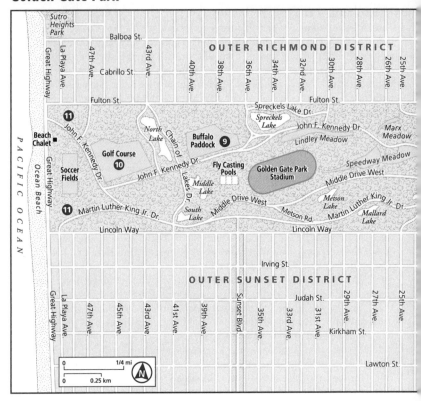

around Stow Lake, and you, too, will understand the allure. It's an interactive botanical symphony, and everyone is invited to play in the orchestra.

The park consists of hundreds of gardens and attractions connected by wooded paths and paved roads. While many worthy sites are clearly visible, there are infinite hidden treasures, so pick up information at **McLaren Lodge and Park Headquarters** (at Stanyan St. and Fell St.; © **415/831-2700**) if you want to find the more hidden spots. It's open daily and offers park maps for $3. Of the dozens of special gardens in the park, the most recognized are **McLaren Memorial Rhododendron Dell, The Rose Garden, Strybing Arboretum,** and, at the western edge of the park, a springtime array of thousands of tulips and daffodils around the **Dutch windmills.**

In addition to the highlights described in this section, the park contains lots of recreational facilities: a music concourse; tennis courts; baseball, soccer, and polo fields; a golf course; and fly-casting pools. The Strawberry Hill boathouse handles boat rentals. The park is also the home of two major museums: the **California Academy of Sciences** (currently relocated to SoMa during renovations; see listing on p. 160) and the **M. H. de Young Memorial Museum** (© **415/750-3600** or 415/863-3330), which moved to 50 Tea Garden Drive within the park in 2005 and features art of the Americas.

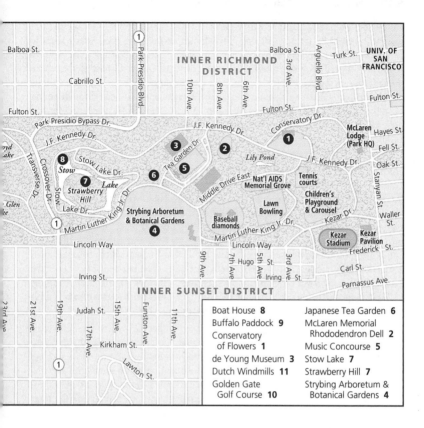

Boat House **8**	Japanese Tea Garden **6**
Buffalo Paddock **9**	McLaren Memorial
Conservatory	Rhododendron Dell **2**
of Flowers **1**	Music Concourse **5**
de Young Museum **3**	Stow Lake **7**
Dutch Windmills **11**	Strawberry Hill **7**
Golden Gate	Strybing Arboretum &
Golf Course **10**	Botanical Gardens **4**

For further information, call the **San Francisco Visitor Information Center** at ℂ **415/283-0177.** Enter the park at Kezar Drive, an extension of Fell Street; bus riders can take no. 5, 6, 7, 16AX, 16BX, 66, or 71.

MUSEUMS INSIDE THE PARK

In 2004, the California Academy of Sciences, which includes the Steinhart Aquarium, the Natural History Museum, and the Planetarium, moved from the park to a temporary location in downtown San Francisco to begin a 4-year renovation on its Golden Gate Park location. Limited aquarium and natural history exhibits are displayed in the temporary digs, but alas, the Planetarium did not relocate. See p. 160 for the temporary museums' details.

PARK HIGHLIGHTS

CONSERVATORY OF FLOWERS ✸✸ Built in 1879, this glorious Victorian glass structure is the oldest public conservatory in the western hemisphere. After a bad storm in 1995 and delayed renovations, the conservatory was closed and visitors were only able to imagine what wondrous displays existed within the striking glass assemblage. Thankfully, a $25-million renovation, including a $4-million exhibit upgrade, was completed in 2003, and now you can check out the rare tropical flora of the

Congo, the Philippines, and beyond within the stunning structure. It doesn't take long to visit, but make a point of staying a while; outside there are good sunny spots for people-watching as well as paths leading to impressive gardens begging to be explored. If you're around during summer and fall, don't miss the Dahlia Garden to the right of the entrance in the center of what was once a carriage roundabout—it's an explosion of colorful Dr. Seuss–like blooms. The conservatory is open Tuesday through Sunday from 9am to 4:30pm and is closed Mondays. Admission is $5 for adults; $3 for children 12 to 17 years of age, seniors, and students with ID; $1.50 for children ages 5 to 11 and free for children under 4 and for all visitors the first Tuesday of the month. For more information, visit www.conservatoryofflowers.org or call ℂ **415/666-7001.**

JAPANESE TEA GARDEN   John McLaren, the man who began landscaping Golden Gate Park, hired Makoto Hagiwara, a wealthy Japanese landscape designer, to further develop this garden originally created for the 1894 Midwinter Exposition. It's a quiet place with cherry trees, shrubs, and bonsai crisscrossed by winding paths and high-arched bridges over pools of water. Focal points and places for contemplation include the massive bronze Buddha (cast in Japan in 1790 and donated by the Gump family), the Buddhist wooden pagoda, and the Drum Bridge, which, reflected in the water, looks as though it completes a circle. The garden is open daily November through February from 8:30am to 5pm (teahouse 10am–4:30pm), March through October from 8:30am to 6pm (teahouse 10am–5:30pm). For **information** on admission, call ℂ **415/752-4227.** For the **teahouse,** call ℂ **415/752-1171.**

STRAWBERRY HILL/STOW LAKE   Rent a paddleboat or rowboat and cruise around the circular Stow Lake as painters create still lifes, joggers pass along the grassy shoreline, ducks waddle around waiting to be fed, and turtles bathe on rocks and logs. Strawberry Hill, the 430-foot-high artificial island and highest point in the park that lies at the center of Stow Lake, is a perfect picnic spot; it boasts a bird's-eye view of San Francisco and the bay. It also has a waterfall and peace pagoda. For the **boathouse,** call ℂ **415/752-0347.** Boat rentals are available daily from 10am to 4pm, weather permitting; four-passenger rowboats go for $13 per hour, and four-person paddleboats run $17 per hour; fees are cash-only.

STRYBING ARBORETUM & BOTANICAL GARDENS   Seven thousand plant species grow here, among them some ancient plants in a special "primitive garden," rare species, and a grove of California redwoods. Docent tours begin at 1:30pm daily, with an additional 10:30am tour on weekends. Strybing is open Monday through Friday from 8am to 4:30pm, and Saturday, Sunday, and holidays from 10am to 5pm. Admission is free. For more information, call ℂ **415/661-1316** or visit www.strybing.org.

5 The Presidio & Golden Gate National Recreation Area
THE PRESIDIO

In October 1994, the Presidio passed from the U.S. Army to the National Park Service and became one of a handful of urban national parks that combines historical, architectural, and natural elements in one giant arboreal expanse. (It also contains a previously private golf course and a home for George Lucas's production company.) The 1,491-acre area incorporates a variety of terrain—coastal scrub, dunes, and prairie grasslands—that shelter many rare plants and more than 200 species of birds, some of which nest here.

This military outpost has a 220-year history, from its founding in September 1776 by the Spanish under José Joaquin Moraga to its closure in 1994. From 1822 to 1846, the property was in Mexican hands.

During the war with Mexico, U.S. forces occupied the fort, and in 1848, when California became part of the Union, it was formally transferred to the United States. When San Francisco suddenly became an important urban area during the gold rush, the U.S. government installed battalions of soldiers and built Fort Point to protect the entry to the harbor. It expanded the post during the Civil War and during the Indian Wars of the 1870s and 1880s. By the 1890s, the Presidio was no longer a frontier post but a major base for U.S. expansion into the Pacific. During the war with Spain in 1898, thousands of troops camped here in tent cities awaiting shipment to the Philippines, and the Army General Hospital treated the sick and wounded. By 1905, 12 coastal defense batteries were built along the headlands. In 1914, troops under the command of Gen. John Pershing left here to pursue Pancho Villa and his men. The Presidio expanded during the 1920s, when Crissy Army Airfield (the first airfield on the West Coast) was established, but the major action was seen during World War II, after the attack on Pearl Harbor. Soldiers dug foxholes along nearby beaches, and the Presidio became the headquarters for the Western Defense Command. Some 1.75 million men were shipped out from nearby Fort Mason to fight in the Pacific; many returned to the Presidio's hospital, whose capacity peaked 1 year at 72,000 patients. In the 1950s, the Presidio served as the headquarters for the Sixth U.S. Army and a missile defense post, but its role slowly shrank. In 1972, it was included in new legislation establishing the Golden Gate National Recreation Area; in 1989, the Pentagon decided to close the post and transfer it to the National Park Service.

Today, the area encompasses more than 470 historic buildings, a scenic golf course, a national cemetery, 22 hiking trails (to be doubled over the next decade), and a variety of terrain and natural habitats. The National Park Service offers walking and biking tours around the Presidio (reservations are suggested) as well as a free shuttle "PresidioGo." For more information, call the **Presidio Visitors Center** at ✆ **415/561-4323.** Take bus no. 28, 45, 76, or 82X to get there.

GOLDEN GATE NATIONAL RECREATION AREA

The largest urban park in the world, GGNRA makes New York's Central Park look like a putting green, covering three counties along 28 miles of stunning, condo-free shoreline. Run by the National Park Service, the Recreation Area wraps around the northern and western edges of the city, and just about all of it is open to the public with no access fees. The Muni bus system provides transportation to the more popular sites, including Aquatic Park, Cliff House, Fort Mason, and Ocean Beach. For more information, contact the **National Park Service** (✆ **415/561-4700**). For more information on particular sites, see the "Getting Outside" section, later in this chapter.

Here is a brief rundown of the salient features of the park's peninsula section, starting at the northern section and moving westward around the coastline:

Aquatic Park, adjacent to the Hyde Street Pier, has a small swimming beach, although it's not that appealing (and darned cold). Far more entertaining is a visit to the ship-shaped museum across the lawn that's part of the Maritime National Historical Park (see p. 163 for more information).

Fort Mason Center, from Bay Street to the shoreline, consists of several buildings and piers used during World War II. Today they hold a variety of museums, theaters, shops, and organizations, and Greens vegetarian restaurant, which affords views of the

The Presidio & Golden Gate National Recreation Area

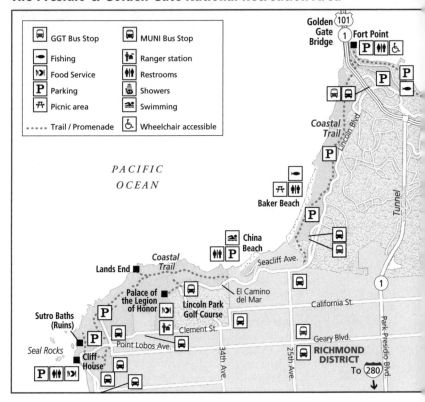

Golden Gate Bridge. For information about Fort Mason events, call © **415/441-3400.** The park headquarters is also at Fort Mason.

Farther west along the bay at the northern end of Laguna Street is **Marina Green,** a favorite local spot for kite-flying, jogging, and walking along the Promenade. The St. Francis Yacht Club is also here. Next comes the 3½-mile paved **Golden Gate Promenade** ⚓, San Francisco's best and most scenic biking, jogging, and walking path. It runs along the shore past **Crissy Field** (be sure to stop and watch the gonzo windsurfers and kites surfers, who catch major wind here, and admire the newly restored marshlands) and ends at Fort Point under the Golden Gate Bridge.

Fort Point ⚓ (© **415/556-1693**) was built in 1853 to 1861 to protect the narrow entrance to the harbor. It was designed to house 500 soldiers manning 126 muzzle-loading cannons. By 1900, the fort's soldiers and obsolete guns had been removed, but the formidable brick edifice remains. Fort Point is open Friday through Sunday only from 10am to 5pm, and guided tours and cannon demonstrations are given at the site once or twice a day on open days, depending on the time of year.

Lincoln Boulevard sweeps around the western edge of the bay to **Baker Beach,** where the waves roll ashore—a fine spot for sunbathing, walking, or fishing. Hikers can follow the **Coastal Trail** from Fort Point along this part of the coastline all the way to Lands End. A short distance from Baker Beach, **China Beach** is a small cove

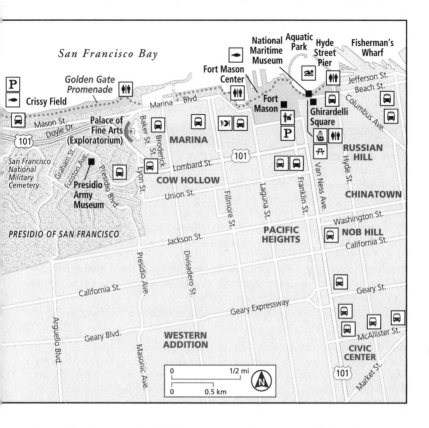

where swimming is permitted. Changing rooms, showers, a sun deck, and restrooms are available. A little farther around the coast is **Lands End** , looking out to Pyramid Rock. A lower and an upper trail offer hiking amid windswept cypresses and pines on the cliffs above the Pacific.

Still farther along the coast lie **Point Lobos,** the **Sutro Baths,** and **Cliff House** . Cliff House (www.cliffhouse.com), which just underwent major renovations, has been serving refreshments to visitors since 1863. It's famed for its views of Seal Rocks (a colony of sea lions and many marine birds) and the Pacific Ocean. Immediately northeast of Cliff House you'll find traces of the once-grand Sutro Baths, a swimming facility that was a major summer attraction accommodating up to 24,000 people until it burned down in 1966. (Alas, my favorite Cliff House attraction, the **Musée Mécanique** , an arcade featuring antique games, moved to temporary digs at Pier 45; call ⓒ **415/ 346-2000** or visit http://museemecanique.org.)

A little farther inland at the western end of California Street is **Lincoln Park,** which contains a golf course and the spectacular California Palace of the Legion of Honor museum (p. 161). At the southern end of Ocean Beach, 4 miles down the coast, is another area of the park around Fort Funston (ⓒ **415/561-4700**), where there's an easy loop trail across the cliffs. Here you can watch hang gliders take advantage of the high cliffs and strong winds.

Farther south along Route 280, **Sweeney Ridge** affords sweeping views of the coastline from the many trails that crisscross its 1,000 acres. From here the expedition led by Don Gaspar de Portolá first saw San Francisco Bay in 1769. It's in Pacifica; take Sneath Lane off Route 35 (Skyline Blvd.) in San Bruno.

The GGNRA extends into Marin County, where it encompasses the Marin Headlands, Muir Woods National Monument, and the Olema Valley behind the Point Reyes National Seashore. See chapter 12 for information on those areas' highlights.

6 Religious Buildings Worth Checking Out

Glide Memorial United Methodist Church *Moments*   There would be nothing special about this Tenderloin-area church if it weren't for its exhilarating lively sermons and accompanying gospel choir. Reverend Cecil Williams's enthusiastic and uplifting preaching and singing with the homeless and poor people of the neighborhood has attracted nationwide fame over the past 30-plus years. In 1994, during the pastor's 30th-anniversary celebration, singers Angela Bofill and Bobby McFerrin joined comedian Robin Williams, author Maya Angelou, and talk-show queen Oprah Winfrey to honor him publicly. Cecil Williams now shares pastor duties with Douglas Fitch, alternating presiding over the nondogmatic, fun Sunday services in front of a diverse audience that crosses all socioeconomic boundaries. Be sure to arrive a little early to get a first-floor seat (the balcony's view is limited).

330 Ellis St. (at Taylor St). © **415/674-6000.** www.glide.org. Services Sun at 9 and 11am. BART: Powell. Bus: 27. Streetcar: J, K, L, M, N to Powell.

Grace Cathedral   Although this Nob Hill cathedral, designed by architect Lewis P. Hobart, appears to be made of stone, it is in fact constructed of reinforced concrete, beaten to achieve a stonelike effect. Construction began on the site of the Crocker mansion in 1928 but was not completed until 1964. Among the more interesting features of the building are its stained-glass windows, particularly those by the French Loire studios and Charles Counick, depicting such modern figures as Thurgood Marshall, Robert Frost, and Albert Einstein; the replicas of Ghiberti's bronze *Doors of Paradise* at the east end; the series of religious murals completed in the 1940s by Polish artist John de Rosen; and the 44-bell carillon. Along with its magical ambience, Grace lifts spirits with services, musical performances (including organ recitals on many Sun), and its weekly Forum (Sun 9:30–10:30am except summer and major holidays), where guests lead discussions about spirituality in modern times and have community dialogues on social issues.

1100 California St. (between Taylor and Jones sts.). © **415/749-6300.** www.gracecathedral.org. Bus: 1.

Mission Dolores   San Francisco's oldest standing structure, the Mission San Francisco de Assisi (aka Mission Dolores), has withstood the test of time, as well as two major earthquakes, relatively intact. In 1776, at the behest of Franciscan missionary Junípero Serra, Father Francisco Palou came to the Bay Area to found the sixth in a series of missions that dotted the California coastline. From these humble beginnings grew what was to become San Francisco. The mission's small, simple chapel, built solidly by Native Americans who were converted to Christianity, is a curious mixture of native construction methods and Spanish-colonial style. A statue of Father Serra stands in the mission garden, although the portrait looks somewhat more contemplative, and less energetic, than he must have been in real life. A 45-minute audio tour costs $5; otherwise, admission is $3 for adults and $2 for children.

16th St. (at Dolores St.). © **415/621-8203.** $5 adults, $3 children 5 to 18; children under 5 free. Student discounts available. Daily 8am–noon, 1–4pm; Good Friday 9am–noon. Closed Thanksgiving, Easter, Christmas. Bus: 14, 26, or 33 to Church and 16th sts. Streetcar: J.

7 Architectural Highlights

MUST-SEES FOR ARCHITECTURE BUFFS

ALAMO SQUARE HISTORIC DISTRICT   San Francisco's collection of Victorian houses, known as **Painted Ladies,** is one of the city's most famous assets. Most of the 14,000 extant structures date from the second half of the 19th century and are private residences. Spread throughout the city, many have been beautifully restored and ornately painted. The small area bordered by Divisadero Street on the west, Golden Gate Avenue on the north, Webster Street on the east, and Fell Street on the south—about 10 blocks west of the Civic Center—has one of the city's greatest concentrations of Painted Ladies. One of the most famous views of San Francisco—seen on postcards and posters all around the city—depicts sharp-edged Financial District skyscrapers behind a row of Victorians. This fantastic juxtaposition can be seen from Alamo Square, in the historic district, at Fulton and Steiner streets.

CITY HALL & CIVIC CENTER   Built between 1913 and 1915, City Hall, located in the Civic Center District, is part of this "City Beautiful" complex done in the Beaux Arts style. The dome rises to a height of 308 feet on the exterior and is ornamented with oculi and topped by a lantern. The interior rotunda soars 112 feet and is finished in oak, marble, and limestone, with a monumental marble staircase leading to the second floor. No doubt you saw it on TV during early 2004, when much of the hoopla surrounding the short-lived and controversial gay marriage proceedings was depicted on the front steps. (Remember Rosie O'Donnell emerging from this very building after getting married to her girlfriend?)

OTHER ARCHITECTURAL HIGHLIGHTS

San Francisco is a center of many architecturally striking sights. This section concentrates on a few highlights.

The Union Square and Financial District areas have a number of buildings worth checking out. One is the former **Circle Gallery,** 140 Maiden Lane. Now a gallery housing Folk Art International, Xanadu Tribal Arts, and Boretti Amber & Design, it's the only building in the city designed by Frank Lloyd Wright (in 1948). The gallery was the prototype for the Guggenheim's seashell-shaped circular gallery space, even though it was meant to serve as a retail space for V. C. Morris, a purveyor of glass and crystal. Note the arresting exterior, a solid wall with a circular entryway to the left. Maiden Lane is just off Union Square between Geary and Post streets.

The **Hallidie Building,** 130–150 Sutter St., designed by Willis Polk in 1917, is an ideal example of a glass-curtain building. The vast glass facade is miraculously suspended between the two cast-iron cornices. The fire escapes that course down each side of the building complete the proscenium-like theatrical effect.

Two prominent pieces of San Francisco's skyline are in the Financial District. The **TransAmerica Pyramid,** 600 Montgomery St., between Clay and Washington streets, is one of the tallest structures in San Francisco. This corporate headquarters was completed in 1972, stands 48 stories tall, and is capped by a 212-foot spire. The former **Bank of America World Headquarters,** 555 California St., was designed by Wurster,

Bernardi, and Emmons with Skidmore, Owings, and Merrill. This carnelian-marble-covered building dates from 1969. Its 52 stories are topped by a panoramic restaurant and bar, the Carnelian Room (p. 231). The focal point of the building's formal plaza is an abstract black granite sculpture, known locally as the "Banker's Heart," designed by Japanese architect Masayuki Nagare.

The **Medical Dental Building,** 450 Sutter St., is a steel-frame structure beautifully clad in terra cotta. It was designed by Miller and Pflueger in 1929. The entrance and the window frames are elaborately ornamented with Mayan relief work; the lobby ceiling is similarly decorated with gilding. Note the ornate elevators.

At the foot of Market Street you will find the **Ferry Building.** Built between 1895 and 1903, it served as the city's major transportation hub before the Golden Gate and Bay bridges were built; some 170 ferries docked here daily unloading Bay Area commuters until the 1930s. The tower that soars above the building was inspired by the Campanile of Venice and the Cathedral Tower in Seville. Plans are afoot to restore the building to its former glory by opening the soaring galleries to the sky again. If you

Kids Especially for Kids

The following San Francisco attractions have appeal to kids of all ages:

- Alcatraz Island (p. 146)
- Cable Car Museum (p. 160)
- Cable cars (p. 150)
- California Academy of Sciences, including Steinhart Aquarium (p. 160)
- The Exploratorium (p. 162)
- Golden Gate Bridge (p. 156)
- Golden Gate Park, including the Children's Playground, Bison Paddock, and Japanese Tea Garden (p. 171)
- Maritime Museum (Maritime National Historical Park) and the historic ships anchored at Hyde Pier (p. 163)
- The Metreon Entertainment Center (p. 166)
- The San Francisco Zoo (p. 164)

In addition to the sights listed above, a number of playgrounds are of particular interest to kids. One of the most enormous, fun playgrounds for kids is in **Golden Gate Park.** Apartment buildings surround the **Cow Hollow Playground,** Baker Street between Greenwich and Filbert streets, on three of four sides. The landscaped playground features a bi-level play area fitted with well-conceived, colorful play structures, including a tunnel, slides, swings, and a miniature cable car. **Huntington Park,** Taylor Street between Sacramento and California streets, sits atop Nob Hill. This tiny play area contains several small structures particularly well suited to children under 5. **Julius Kahn Playground,** West Pacific Avenue at Spruce Street, is a popular playground inside San Francisco's great Presidio Park. Larger play structures and forested surroundings make this area attractive to children and adults alike.

stop by the Ferry Building, you might also want to go to **Rincon Center,** 99 Mission St., to see the WPA murals painted by the Russian artist Refregier in the post office.

Several important buildings are on or near Nob Hill. The **Flood Mansion,** 1000 California St., at Mason Street, was built between 1885 and 1886 for James Clair Flood. Thanks to the Comstock Lode, Flood rose from being bartender to one of the city's wealthiest men. He established the Nevada bank that later merged with Wells Fargo. The house cost $1.5 million to build at the time; the fence alone cost $30,000. It was designed by Augustus Laver and modified by Willis Polk after the 1906 earthquake to accommodate the Pacific Union Club. Unfortunately, you can't go inside: The building is now a private school.

Built by George Applegarth in 1913 for sugar magnate Adolph Spreckels, the **Spreckels Mansion,** 2080 Washington St., is currently home to romance novelist Danielle Steel (don't even try to get in to see her!). The extraordinary building has rounded-arch French doors on the first and second floors and curved balconies on the second floor. Inside, the original house featured an indoor pool in the basement, Adamesque fireplaces, and a circular Pompeian room with a fountain.

Finally, one of San Francisco's most ingenious architectural accomplishments is the **San Francisco–Oakland Bay Bridge.** Although it's visually less appealing than the nearby Golden Gate Bridge (except at night when it's lit up), the Bay Bridge is in many ways more spectacular. The silvery giant that links San Francisco with Oakland is one of the world's longest steel bridges (8¼ miles). It opened in 1936, 6 months before the Golden Gate. Each of its two decks contains five automobile lanes. The Bay Bridge is not a single bridge at all, but a superbly dovetailed series of spans joined mid-bay, at Yerba Buena Island, by one of the world's largest (in diameter) tunnels. To the west of Yerba Buena, the bridge is actually two separate suspension bridges, joined at a central anchorage. East of the island is a 1,400-foot cantilever span, followed by a succession of truss bridges. And it looks even more complex than it sounds. You can drive across the bridge (the toll is $3, paid westbound), or you can catch a bus at the Transbay Terminal (Mission at First St.) and ride to downtown Oakland.

8 Self-Guided & Organized Tours

THE 49-MILE SCENIC DRIVE 😿😿

The self-guided, 49-mile drive is one easy way to orient yourself and to grasp the beauty of San Francisco and its extraordinary location. It's also a flat-out stunning and very worthy excursion. Beginning in the city, it follows a rough circle around the bay and passes virtually all the best-known sights, from Chinatown to the Golden Gate Bridge, Ocean Beach, Seal Rocks, Golden Gate Park, and Twin Peaks. Originally designed for the benefit of visitors to San Francisco's 1939 and 1940 Golden Gate International Exposition, the route is marked by blue-and-white seagull signs. Although it makes an excellent half-day tour, this mini excursion can easily take longer if you decide, for example, to stop to walk across the Golden Gate Bridge or to have tea in Golden Gate Park's Japanese Tea Garden.

The San Francisco **Visitor Information Center,** at Powell and Market streets (p. 17), distributes free route maps, which are handy since a few of the Scenic Drive marker signs are missing. Try to avoid the downtown area during the weekday rush hours from 7 to 9am and 4 to 6pm.

A BART TOUR

One of the world's best commuter systems, **Bay Area Rapid Transit (BART)** runs along 104 miles of rail, linking 43 stations between San Francisco, Millbrae, and the East Bay. Under the bay, BART runs through one of the longest underwater transit tubes in the world. This link opened in September 1974, 2 years behind schedule and 6 months after the general manager resigned under fire. The train cars are 70 feet long and were designed to represent the latest word in public transport luxury. More than 3 decades later, they no longer seem futuristic, but they're still attractively modern, with carpeted floors, tinted picture windows, air-conditioning, and recessed lighting. The trains can hit a top speed of 80 mph; a computerized control system monitors and adjusts their speed.

The people who run BART think so highly of their trains and stations that they sell a $4.40 **"Excursion Ticket,"** which allows you, in effect, to "sightsee" the BART system, or basically ride it. "Tour" the entire system as much as you like for up to 3 hours; you must exit at the station where you entered (if you get out anywhere else along the line, the gate instantly computes the normal fare). For more information, call © **415/ 989-BART** or visit www.bart.gov.

BOAT TOURS

One of the best ways to look at San Francisco is from a boat bobbing on the bay. There are several cruises to choose from, and many of them start from Fisherman's Wharf.

Blue & Gold Fleet, PIER 39, Fisherman's Wharf (© **415/773-1188;** www.blue andgoldfleet.com), tours the bay year-round in a sleek, 350-passenger sightseeing boat, complete with food and beverage facilities. The fully narrated, 1-hour cruise passes beneath the Golden Gate Bridge and comes within yards of Alcatraz Island. Don a jacket, bring the camera, and make sure it's a clear day for the best bay cruise. Frequent daily departures from PIER 39's West Marina begin at 10:45am on week-days and 10am on weekends and holidays during winter and 10am daily during sum-mer. Tickets cost $20 for adults, $16 for seniors over 62 and juniors ages 12 to 18, and $12 for children ages 5 to 11; children under 5 are admitted free. There's a $2.25 charge for ordering tickets by phone; discounts are available online at www.blueand goldfleet.com.

The **Red & White Fleet,** Pier 43½ (© **415/447-0597;** www.redandwhite.com), offers daily "Bay Cruises" tours that leave from Pier 43½. The tour boats cruise along the city waterfront, beneath the Golden Gate Bridge, past Angel Island, and around Alcatraz and are narrated in eight languages. Prices are $21 for adults, $17 for seniors and teens ages 12 to 17, and $13 for children ages 5 to 11. Discounts are available through online purchase.

BUS TOURS

Gray Line (© **800/826-0202** or 415/434-8687; www.sanfranciscosightseeing.com) is San Francisco's largest bus-tour operator. It offers several itineraries daily. Free pickup and return are available between centrally located hotels and departure loca-tions. Reservations are required for most tours, and keep in mind that those available in French, German, Spanish, Italian, Japanese, and Korean depart at 9am only.

WALKING TOURS

Javawalk is a 2-hour walking tour by self-described "coffeehouse lizard" Elaine Sosa. As the name suggests, it's loosely a coffee walking tour through North Beach, but there's a lot more going on than drinking cups of brew. Javawalk also serves up a good share of historical and architectural trivia, offering something for everyone. The best part of the tour may be the camaraderie that develops among the participants. Sosa keeps the excursion interactive and fun, and it's obvious she knows a profusion of tales and trivia about the history of coffee and its North Beach roots. It's a guaranteed good time, particularly if you're addicted to caffeine. Javawalk is offered Saturday at 10am and Sunday through Friday for private parties of 6 or more by appointment only. The price is $20 per person, $10 for kids under 12. For information and reservations, call © **415/673-WALK;** or visit www.javawalk.com.

Cruisin' the Castro (© **415/255-1821;** www.webcastro.com/castrotour) is an informative historical tour of San Francisco's most famous gay quarter, which will give you new insight into the contribution of the gay community to the city's political maturity, growth, and beauty. Trevor Hailey, who was involved in the development of the Castro in the 1970s, conducts the tours. She knew Harvey Milk, the first openly gay politician elected to office in the United States: You'll learn about Milk's rise from shopkeeper to city supervisor and visit Harvey Milk Plaza, where marches, rallies, and protests begin. In addition, you'll explore the Castro Theatre, a memorial honoring gays who perished in the Holocaust, and side streets lined with beautifully restored Victorians, as well as the plethora of community-oriented stores in the Castro whose owners Hailey knows personally. Tours run Tuesday through Saturday from 10am to 2pm May through November and begin at Harvey Milk Plaza, atop the Castro Street

Muni station. The cost includes lunch at a Castro area restaurant. Reservations are required. The tour, with lunch, costs $45 for adults and $40 for seniors over 62; the price for children is flexible depending on their age.

On the **Haight-Ashbury Flower Power Walking Tour** (© 415/863-1621), you explore hippie haunts with Pam and Bruce Brennan ("the Hippy Gourmet"—see www.hippygourmet.com). You'll revisit in 2½ short hours the Grateful Dead's crash pad, Janis Joplin's house, and other reminders of the Summer of Love. Tours begin at 9:30am on Tuesdays and Saturdays. The cost is $15 per person (cash only). Reservations are required and the tour starts at the corner of Stanyan and Waller streets.

San Francisco's Chinatown is always fascinating, but for many visitors with limited time it's hard to know where to search out the "nontouristy" shops, restaurants, and historical spots in this microcosm of Chinese culture. **Wok Wiz Chinatown Walking Tours & Cooking Center,** 654 Commercial St., between Kearny and Montgomery streets (© **650/355-9657;** www.wokwiz.com), founded over 2 decades ago by author and cooking instructor Shirley Fong-Torres, is the answer. The Wok Wiz tours take you into Chinatown's nooks and crannies. Most guides are Chinese, speak fluent Cantonese or Mandarin, and are intimately acquainted with the neighborhood's alleys and small enterprises, as well as Chinatown's history, folklore, culture, and food. Tours are conducted daily from 10am to 1:30pm and include dim sum. There's also a less expensive tour that does not include lunch. The walk is easy, as well as fun and fascinating. Groups are generally held to a maximum of 15, and reservations are essential. Prices (including lunch) are $40 for adults and $35 for children under 11; without lunch, prices are $28 and $23, respectively.

The very gregarious and entertaining tour owner Shirley Fong-Torres also operates an **I Can't Believe I Ate My Way Through Chinatown** tour. It starts with breakfast, moves to a wok shop, and stops for nibbles at a vegetarian restaurant and dim sum, and at a marketplace before taking a break for a sumptuous authentic Cantonese luncheon. It's offered on most Saturdays and costs $75 per person, food included. The **Walk & Wok** tour includes shopping for food in Chinatown, and then cooking (and eating) it together at Shirley's Cooking Center (most Sat; $100 per person). Shirley also offers a nighttime tour, which includes dinner and starts at $65 per person; the price goes up depending on what you want to eat.

Jay Gifford, founder of the **Victorian Homes Historical Walking Tour** (© 415/ 252-9485; www.victorianwalk.com) and a San Francisco resident for 2 decades, communicates his enthusiasm and love of San Francisco throughout this highly entertaining walking tour. The 2½-hour daily tour, at a very leisurely pace, starts in the lobby of the Westin St. Francis hotel and incorporates a wealth of knowledge about San Francisco's Victorian architecture and the city's history—particularly the periods before and after the great earthquake and fire of 1906. You'll stroll through Japantown, Pacific Heights, and Cow Hollow. In the process, you'll see more than 200 meticulously restored Victorians, including the sites where *Mrs. Doubtfire* and *Party of Five* were filmed. Jay's guests often find that they are the only ones on the quiet neighborhood streets, where tour buses are forbidden. The tour ends with a trolley bus ride back to Union Square, passing through North Beach and Chinatown. Tours, which start at Union Square at 11am, are offered daily April through December and Thursday through Monday from January through March and cost $20 per person.

9 Outdoor Pursuits

Half the fun in San Francisco takes place outdoors. If you're not in the mood to trek it, there are other things to do that allow you to enjoy the surroundings.

BALLOONING   Although you must drive 1 hour to get to the tour site, hot-air ballooning guarantees you great views of the Wine Country. **Adventures Aloft,** P.O. Box 2500, Vintage 1870, Yountville, CA 94599 (② **800/944-4408** or 707/944-4408; www.nvaloft.com), is Napa Valley's oldest hot-air balloon company, staffed with full-time professional pilots. Groups are small, and each flight lasts about an hour. The cost of $205 per person ($170 ages 6–17) includes a postadventure champagne brunch and a framed "first-flight" certificate. Flights launch daily at sunrise (weather permitting).

BEACHES   For beach information, call the San Francisco Visitor Information Center at ② **415/283-0177.** Most days it's too chilly to hang out at the beach, but when the fog evaporates and the wind dies down, one of the best ways to spend the day is ocean side in the city. On any truly hot day, thousands flock to the beach to worship the sun, build sandcastles, and throw the ball around. Without a wet suit, swimming is a fiercely cold endeavor and is not recommended. In any case, dip at your own risk—there are no lifeguards on duty and San Francisco's waters are cold and have strong undertows. On the South Bay, **Baker Beach** is ideal for picnicking, sunning, walking, or fishing against the backdrop of the Golden Gate (though pollution makes your catch not necessarily worthy of eating).

Ocean Beach, at the end of Golden Gate Park, on the westernmost side of the city, is San Francisco's largest beach—4 miles long. Just offshore, at the northern end of the beach, in front of Cliff House, are the jagged Seal Rocks, inhabited by various shorebirds and a large colony of barking sea lions (bring binoculars for a close-up view). To the left, Kelly's Cove is one of the more challenging surf spots in town. Ocean Beach is ideal for strolling or sunning, but don't swim here—tides are tricky, and each year bathers drown in the rough surf.

Stop by Ocean Beach bus terminal at the corner of Cabrillo and La Playa to learn about San Francisco's playful history in local artist Ray Beldner's whimsically historical sculpture garden. Then hike up the hill to explore Cliff House and the ruins of the Sutro Baths. These baths, once able to accommodate 24,000 bathers, were lost to fire in 1966.

BIKING   The San Francisco Parks and Recreation Department maintains two city-designated bike routes. One winds 7½ miles through Golden Gate Park to Lake Merced; the other traverses the city, starting in the south, and continues over the Golden Gate Bridge. These routes are not dedicated to bicyclists, so you'll need to exercise caution to avoid crashing into pedestrians or getting creamed by a taxi. Helmets are recommended for adults and required by law for kids under 18. A bike map is available from the San Francisco Visitor Information Center, at Powell and Mason streets for $3 (see "Visitor Information," in chapter 5), and from bicycle shops all around town.

Ocean Beach has a public walk- and bikeway that stretches along five waterfront blocks of the Great Highway between Noriega and Santiago streets. It's an easy ride from Cliff House or Golden Gate Park.

For touring Golden Gate Park, contact **Avenue Cyclery,** 756 Stanyan St., at Waller Street, in the Haight (② **415/387-3155**), which rents bikes for $7 per hour or $28 per day. It's open daily, April through September from 10am to 7pm and October through March from 10am to 6pm. For cruising Fisherman's Wharf and the Golden Gate Bridge, your best bet is **Blazing Saddles** (© **415/202-8888;** www.blazingsaddles. com), which has five locations around Fisherman's Wharf. Bikes rent for $7 per hour or $28 per day, including maps, locks, and helmets; tandem bikes are available as well for $11 per hour or $48 per day.

BOATING   At the **Golden Gate Park Boat House** on Stow Lake, the park's largest body of water, you can rent a rowboat or pedal boat by the hour and steer over to Strawberry Hill, a large, round island in the middle of the lake, for lunch. There's usually a line on weekends. The boathouse is open daily from 10am to 4pm, weather permitting.

Cass Marina, 1702 Bridgeway, Sausalito; P.O. Box 643; Sausalito, CA 94966 (© **800/472-4595** or 415/332-6789; www.cassmarina.com), is a certified sailing school that rents sailboats measuring 22 to 35 feet. Sail to the Golden Gate Bridge on your own or with a licensed skipper. In addition, large sailing yachts leave from Sausalito on a regularly scheduled basis. Call or check the website for schedules, prices, and availability of sailboats. The marina is open Wednesday through Monday from 9am to sunset.

CITY STAIR CLIMBING ☛☛   Many health clubs have stair-climbing machines and step classes, but in San Francisco, you need only go outside. The following city stair climbs will give you not only a good workout, but seriously stunning neighborhood, city, and bay views as well.

Filbert Street Steps, between Sansome Street and Telegraph Hill, are a particular challenge. Scaling the sheer eastern face of Telegraph Hill, this 377-step climb winds through verdant flower gardens and charming 19th-century cottages. Napier Lane, a narrow, wooden plank walkway, leads to Montgomery Street. Turn right and follow the path to the end of the cul-de-sac, where another stairway continues to Telegraph's panoramic summit.

The **Lyon Street Steps,** between Green Street and Broadway, were built in 1916. This historic stairway street contains four steep sets of stairs totaling 288 steps. Begin at Green Street and climb all the way up, past manicured hedges and flower gardens, to an iron gate that opens into the Presidio. A block east, on Baker Street, another set of 369 steps descends to Green Street.

FISHING   Berkeley Marina Sports Center, 225 University Ave., Berkeley (© **510/ 849-2727;** www.berkeleysportfishing.com), makes daily trips for ling cod, rock fish, and many other types of game fish year-round, and it makes trips for salmon runs April through October. Fishing equipment is available; the cost, including boat ride and bait, is $70 per person. Reservations are required, as are licenses for adults. One-day licenses can be purchased for $11 before departure. Find out the latest on the season by contacting their hot line at © **510/486-8300.** Excursions run daily from 6am to 4pm. Fish are cleaned, filleted, and bagged on the return trip for a small fee (free for salmon fishing).

GOLF   San Francisco has a few beautiful golf courses. One of the most lavish is the **Presidio Golf Course** (© **415/561-4664;** www.presidiogolf.com). Greens fees are $50 until 12:30pm for residents Monday through Thursday and $96 for nonresidents; rates drop to $40 until 2pm, then $26 for the rest of the day for residents and nonresidents. Friday though Sunday rates are $96 for residents and $108 for nonresidents from 8am to 11am; from 11am to 12:30pm, the cost is $60 for residents, and after

Tips **Telephone for Tee Time**

The City and County of San Francisco maintains an **Automated Tee Time and Golf Information Line** (© 415/750-4653), with a menu of detailed information on the city's five public courses—tee times, fees, directions, and more. You can reserve a tee time, get directions to the courses, and obtain information on the hours of operation, greens fees, and lessons.

---

that it's $50 for everyone until 2pm and for the rest of the day $26. Carts are mandatory and included. There are also two decent municipal courses in town.

The 9-hole **Golden Gate Park Course,** 47th Avenue and Fulton Street (© 415/751-8987; www.goldengateparkgolf.com), charges greens fees of $13 per person Monday through Thursday, $18 Friday through Sunday. The 1,357-yard course is par 27. All holes are par 3, tightly set, and well trapped with small greens. The course is a little weathered in spots, but it's casual, fun, and inexpensive. It's open daily at 6:30am.

The 18-hole **Lincoln Park Golf Course,** 34th Avenue and Clement Street (© 415/221-9911), charges greens fees of $31 per person Monday through Thursday, $35 Friday through Sunday, with rates decreasing after 2pm in summer, 1pm in winter. It's San Francisco's prettiest municipal course, with terrific views and fairways lined with Monterey cypress and pine trees. The 5,181-yard layout plays to par 68, and the 17th hole has a glistening ocean view. This is the oldest course in the city and one of the oldest in the West. It's open daily at daybreak.

A good place for a tune-up is the **Mission Bay Golf Center,** Sixth Street at Channel Street (© 415/431-7888). San Francisco's most popular driving range is an impeccably maintained 7-acre facility that consists of a double-decker steel and concrete arc containing 66 covered practice bays. The grass landing area extends 300 yards, has nine target greens, and is lit for evening use. There's a putting green and a chipping and bunker practice area. The center is open Monday from 11:30am to 11pm, Tuesday through Sunday from 7am to 11pm. A bucket of balls costs $8, and the last bucket is sold at 10pm. To get here from downtown San Francisco, take Seventh Street south to Channel Street and turn right.

HANDBALL   The city's best handball courts are in Golden Gate Park, opposite Seventh Avenue, south of Middle Drive East. Courts are available free, on a first-come, first-served basis.

PARKS   In addition to **Golden Gate Park** and the **Golden Gate National Recreation Area** (p. 171 and 174 respectively), San Francisco boasts more than 2,000 acres of parkland, most of which is perfect for picnicking or throwing around a Frisbee.

Smaller city parks include **Buena Vista Park** (Haight St. between Baker and Central sts.), which affords fine views of the Golden Gate Bridge and the area around it and is also a favored lounging ground for gay lovers; **Ina Coolbrith Park** (Taylor St. between Vallejo and Green sts.), offering views of the Bay Bridge and Alcatraz; and **Sigmund Stern Grove** (19th Ave. and Sloat Blvd.) in the Sunset District, which is the site of a famous free summer music festival.

One of my personal favorites is **Lincoln Park,** a 270-acre green on the northwestern side of the city at Clement Street and 34th Avenue. The California Palace of the Legion of Honor is here (p. 161), as is a scenic 18-hole municipal golf course (see

"Golf," above). But the best things about this park are the 200-foot cliffs that overlook the Golden Gate Bridge and San Francisco Bay. To get to the park, take bus no. 38 from Union Square to 33rd and Geary streets, then walk a few blocks.

RUNNING   The **Bay to Breakers Foot Race** ⚓ (© **415/359-2800;** www.baytobreakers.com) is an annual 7½-mile run from downtown to Ocean Beach. About 80,000 entrants take part in it, one of San Francisco's trademark events. Costumed participants and hordes of spectators add to the fun. The event, sponsored by the *San Francisco Examiner* and Albertson's supermarket chain, is held on the third Sunday of May. Great **jogging paths** include the entire expanse of Golden Gate Park, the shoreline along the Marina, and the Embarcadero.

The *San Francisco Chronicle* **Marathon** takes place annually in the middle of July. For more information, call © **415/284-9653** or visit www.runsfm.com.

TENNIS   The **San Francisco Parks and Recreation Department** (© **415/753-7001**) maintains more than 100 courts throughout the city. Almost all are available free, on a first-come, first-served basis. The exceptions are the 21 courts in **Golden Gate Park,** which cost $4 for 90 minutes during weekdays and $6 on weekends. Courts should be reserved for weekend play by calling © **415/831-6301** on Wednesday from 4 to 6pm, Thursday and Friday from 9am to 11:30am. For midweek reservations, call © **415/753-7001.**

WALKING & HIKING   The **Golden Gate National Recreation Area** offers plenty of opportunities. One incredible walk (or bike ride) is along the Golden Gate Promenade, from Aquatic Park to the Golden Gate Bridge. The 3.5-mile paved trail heads along the northern edge of the Presidio out to Fort Point, passing the marina, Crissy Field's new restored wetlands, a small beach, and plenty of athletic locals. You can also hike the Coastal Trail all the way from the Fort Point area to Cliff House. The park service maintains several other trails in the city. For more information or to pick up a map of the Golden Gate National Recreation Area, stop by the park service headquarters at Fort Mason at the north end of Laguna Street (© **415/561-4700**).

Although most people drive to this spectacular vantage point, a more rejuvenating way to experience **Twin Peaks** is to walk up from the back roads of U.C. Medical Center (off Parnassus) or from either of the two roads that lead to the top (off Woodside or Clarendon aves.). The best time to trek is early morning, when the city is quiet, the air is crisp, and sightseers haven't crowded the parking lot. Keep an eye out for cars, however, because there's no real hiking trail, and be sure to walk beyond the lot and up to the highest vantage point.

10 Spectator Sports

The Bay Area's sports scene includes several major professional franchises. Check the local newspapers' sports sections for daily listings of local events.

MAJOR LEAGUE BASEBALL

The **San Francisco Giants** ⚓ play at the new and absolutely stunning **SBC Park,** Third and King streets (© **415/972-2000;** www.sfgiants.com), in the China Basin section of SoMa. From April to October, 41,503 fans fill the seats here to root for the National League Giants. The unobstructed bay vistas take in bobbing boats beyond the outfield at this recently completed ballpark. Tickets are hard to come by, but you can try to track them down through **Tickets.com** (© **510/762-2277;** www.tickets.com).

The American League's **Oakland Athletics** play across the bay at the McAfee Coliseum, at the Hegenberger Road exit from I-880, Oakland (© **510/430-8020**). The stadium holds close to 50,000 spectators and is accessible through BART's Coliseum station. Tickets are available from the Coliseum Box Office or by phone through **Tickets.com** (© **510/762-2277**; www.tickets.com).

PRO BASKETBALL

The **Golden State Warriors** of the NBA play at the McAfee Coliseum, at the Hegenberger Road exit from I-880, Oakland (© **510/986-2200**; www.nba.com/warriors). The Warriors play in The Arena in Oakland, a 19,200-seat facility. The season runs November through April, and most games start at 7:30pm. Tickets are available at the arena and by phone through **Tickets.com** (© **510/762-2277**).

PRO FOOTBALL

The **San Francisco 49ers** (www.sf49ers.com) play at Monster Park/Candlestick Park, Giants Drive and Gilman Avenue, on Sundays August through December; kickoff is usually at 1pm. Tickets sell out early in the season but are available at higher prices through ticket agents beforehand and from "scalpers" (illegal ticket-sellers who are usually at the gates). Ask your hotel concierge for the best way to track down tickets.

The 49ers' archenemies, the **Oakland Raiders** (www.ofma.com), play at the McAfee Stadium, off the 880 freeway (Nimitz). Call © **800/949-2626** for ticket information.

COLLEGE FOOTBALL

The **University of California Golden Bears** play at Haas Pavilion, University of California, Berkeley (© **800/GO-BEARS** or 510/642-3277; www.calbears.com), on the university campus across the bay. Tickets are usually available at game time. Phone for schedules and information.

HORSE RACING

Ten miles northeast of San Francisco is scenic **Golden Gate Fields,** Gilman Street off I-80, Albany (© **510/559-7300**; www.goldengatefields.com). It schedules thoroughbred racing from early November through March. The track is on the seashore. Call for admission prices and post times. **Bay Meadows,** 2600 S. Delaware St., off U.S. 101, San Mateo (© **650/574-7223**; www.baymeadows.com), is a thoroughbred track on the peninsula about 20 miles south of downtown San Francisco. Call for admission prices and post times.

9

City Strolls

Despite a handful of killer hills, San Francisco is best explored on foot. In this chapter, you'll find suggestions for introductory walks in two of the city's many great neighborhoods. For more extensive city walks, check out *Frommer's Memorable Walks in San Francisco* (Wiley Publishing, Inc.).

An additional budget tip: Free neighborhood tours are offered by the volunteer guides at **City Guides,** a nonprofit affiliate of the San Francisco Library. Call (C) **415/ 557-4266** for tour schedules, or log onto

their website at www.sfcityguides.org. You can also pick up a self-guided tour at any San Francisco Public Library or the **San Francisco Visitor Information Center,** on the lower level of Hallidie Plaza, 900 Market St., at Powell Street ((C) **415/391- 2000**). Better yet, download free walking tours from the **San Francisco Convention & Visitors Bureau** website at www.sf visitor.org/visitorinfo/html/walkpdfs.html. Guided walking tours of North Beach, Union Square, Pacific Heights, Fisherman's Wharf, and Chinatown are available.

WALKING TOUR 1	CHINATOWN: HISTORY, CULTURE, DIM SUM & THEN SOME

Start:	Corner of Grant Avenue and Bush Street.
Public Transportation:	Bus no. 2, 3, 4, 9X, 15, 30, 38, 45, or 76.
Finish:	Commercial Street between Montgomery and Kearny streets.
Time:	2 hours, not including museum or shopping stops.
Best Times:	Daylight hours, when there's the most action.
Worst Times:	Too early or too late, because shops are closed and no one is milling around.
Hills That Could Kill:	None.

This tiny section of San Francisco, bounded loosely by Broadway and by Stockton, Kearny, and Bush streets, is said to harbor one of the largest Chinese populations outside Asia. Daily proof is the crowds of Chinese residents who flock to the herbal stores, vegetable markets, restaurants, and businesses. Chinatown also marks the spot where the city began its development in the mid-1800s. On this walk, you'll learn why Chinatown remains intriguing to all who wind through its narrow, crowded streets, and how its origins are responsible for the city as we know it.

To begin the tour, make your way to the corner of Bush Street and Grant Avenue, four blocks from Union Square and all the downtown buses, where you can't miss the Chinatown Gateway Arch.

❶ Chinatown Gateway Arch
Traditional Chinese villages have ceremonial gates like this one. A lot less formal than those in China, this gate was built

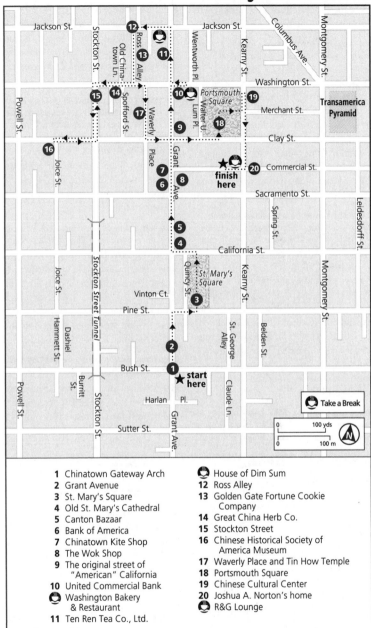

1 Chinatown Gateway Arch
2 Grant Avenue
3 St. Mary's Square
4 Old St. Mary's Cathedral
5 Canton Bazaar
6 Bank of America
7 Chinatown Kite Shop
8 The Wok Shop
9 The original street of "American" California
10 United Commercial Bank
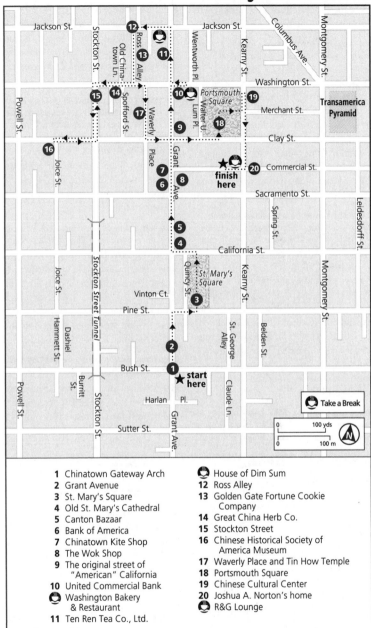 Washington Bakery & Restaurant
11 Ten Ren Tea Co., Ltd.

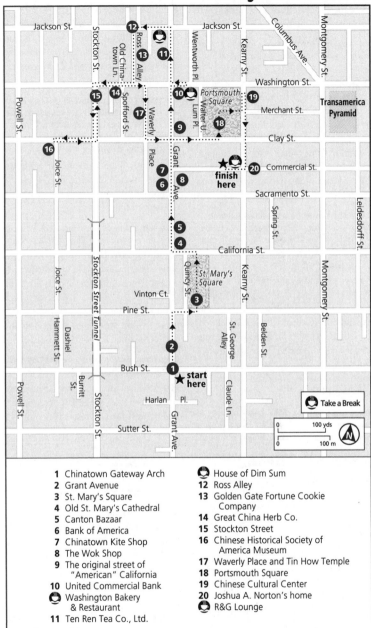 House of Dim Sum
12 Ross Alley
13 Golden Gate Fortune Cookie Company
14 Great China Herb Co.
15 Stockton Street
16 Chinese Historical Society of America Museum
17 Waverly Place and Tin How Temple
18 Portsmouth Square
19 Chinese Cultural Center
20 Joshua A. Norton's home
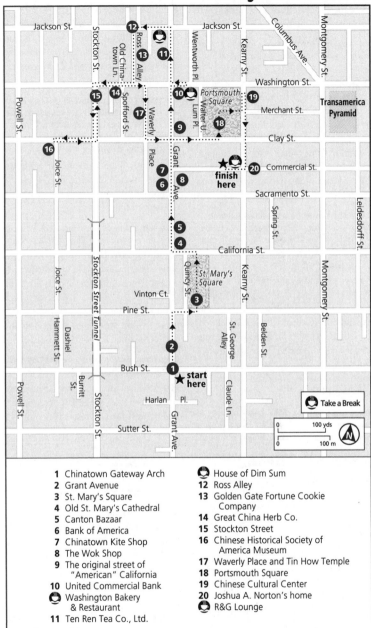 R&G Lounge

more for the benefit of the tourist industry than anything else.

Once you cross the threshold, you'll be at the
beginning of Chinatown's portion of Grant
Avenue.

➋ Grant Avenue

This is a mecca for tourists who wander
in and out of gift shops that offer a variety of unnecessary junk interspersed with
quality imports. You'll also find decent
restaurants and grocery stores frequented
by Chinese residents, ranging from children to the oldest living people you've
ever seen.

Tear yourself away from the shops and turn
right at the corner of Pine Street. Cross to the
other side of Pine, and on your left you'll come
to St. Mary's Square.

➌ St. Mary's Square

Here you'll find a huge metal-and-granite
statue of Dr. Sun Yat-sen, the founder of
the Republic of China. A native of
Guangdong (Canton) Province, Sun Yat-
sen led the rebellion that ended the reign
of the Qing Dynasty. Note also the second monument in the square, which
honors Chinese-American victims of
both World Wars.

Walk to the other end of the square, toward Cali-
fornia Street, turn left, cross California Street at
Grant Street, and you'll be standing in front of
Old St. Mary's Cathedral.

➍ Old St. Mary's Cathedral

The first Catholic cathedral in San Francisco and the site of the Chinese community's first English-language school, St.
Mary's was built primarily by Chinese
laborers and dedicated on Christmas Day
1854.

Step inside to find a written history of
the church and turn-of-the-20th-century
photos of San Francisco.

Upon leaving the church, take a right and walk
to the corner of Grant Avenue and California
Street, and then go right on Grant. Here you'll
find a shop called Canton Bazaar.

➎ Canton Bazaar

Of the knickknack and import shops lining Grant Avenue, this is one of the most
popular. It's located at 616 Grant Ave.
and boasts an array of kitschy souvenirs
and trinkets.

Continue in the same direction on Grant Avenue,
and cross Sacramento Street to the northwest
corner of Sacramento and Grant. You'll be at the
doorstep of the Bank of America.

➏ Bank of America

This bank is an example of traditional
Chinese architectural style. Notice the
dragons subtly portrayed on many parts
of the building.

Head in the same direction (north) on Grant, and
a few doors down is the Chinatown Kite Shop.

➐ Chinatown Kite Shop

This store, located at 717 Grant Ave., has
an assortment of flying objects, including
attractive fish kites, nylon or cotton
windsock kites, hand-painted Chinese
paper kites, wood-and-paper biplanes,
and pentagonal kites.

Cross Grant, and you'll arrive at The Wok Shop.

➑ The Wok Shop

Here's where you can purchase just about
any cleaver, wok, cookbook, or vessel you
might need for Chinese-style cooking in
your own kitchen. It's located at 718
Grant Ave.

When you come out of The Wok Shop, go right.
Walk past Commercial Street, and you'll arrive
at the corner of Grant Avenue and Clay Street;
cross Clay, and you'll be standing on the original
street of "American" California.

➒ Original Street of "American" California

Here, an English seaman named William
Richardson set up the first tent in 1835,
making it the first place that an Anglo set
up base in California.

Continue north on Grant to Washington Street.
Turn right, and at 743 Washington St. you will
be standing in front of the United Commercial
Bank.

⑩ United Commercial Bank

This building boasts the oldest (from 1909) Asian-style edifice in Chinatown. The three-tiered temple-style building once housed the China Telephone Exchange, known as "China-5" until 1945.

You're probably thirsty by now, so follow Washington Street a few doors down (east); on your right-hand side you will come upon 733 Washington St. and the Washington Bakery & Restaurant.

TAKE A BREAK
There's no need to have a full meal at **Washington Bakery & Restaurant** (✆ 415/397-3232)—service can be abrupt. Do stop in, however, for a little potable adventure: snow red beans with ice cream. The sugary-sweet drink mixed with whole beans and ice cream is not something you're likely to have tried elsewhere, and it happens to be quite tasty. Whatever you do, don't fill up—a few blocks away, some wonderfully fresh dim sum awaits you.

Head back to Grant Avenue, cross Washington Street, cross Grant, and follow the west side of Grant 1 block to Ten Ren Tea Co., Ltd.

⑪ Ten Ren Tea Co., Ltd.

In this amazing shop at 949 Grant Ave. (see p. 211 for more info), you can sample a freshly brewed tea variety and check out the dozens of drawers and canisters labeled with more than 40 kinds of tea. Like Washington Bakery, Ten Ren offers unusual drinks worth trying: delightful hot or iced milk teas containing giant blobs of jelly or tapioca. Try black tea or green tea and enjoy the outstanding flavors and the giant balls of tapioca slipping around in your mouth.

Leave Ten Ren, make a left, and when you reach Jackson Street, make another left. On the left side, at 735 Jackson St., through the storefront window, you'll notice stacks of steaming wooden baskets and a Chinese cook. You've reached your snacking destination.

TAKE A BREAK
The **House of Dim Sum** (✆ 415/399-0888) is nothing fancy, to be sure, but the dumplings are fresh, cheap, and delicious, and owners Cindy and Ben Yee are friendly, which is a plus in this sometimes abrupt community. Order at the counter: chive and shrimp dumplings; shark-fin dumplings; sweet buns; turnip cake; or sweet rice with chicken wrapped in a lotus leaf. Unless the three tables downstairs and more upstairs are taken, it's best to sit at one to enjoy your feast. (Last time I ate here it cost $7.58 for two people, drinks included!)

As you leave the House of Dim Sum, turn left so you're heading west on Jackson, and promptly make a left onto Ross Alley.

⑫ Ross Alley

As you walk along this narrow street, just one of the many alleyways that crisscrossed Chinatown to accommodate the many immigrants who jammed into the neighborhood, it's not difficult to believe that this block once was rife with gambling dens.

As you follow the alley south, on the left side of the street you'll encounter the Golden Gate Fortune Cookie Company.

⑬ Golden Gate Fortune Cookie Company

Located at 56 Ross Alley (see p. 211 for more info), this store is little more than a tiny place where three women sit at a conveyer belt, folding messages into warm cookies as the manager invariably calls out to tourists, beckoning them to buy a big bag of the fortune-telling treats.

You can purchase regular fortunes, unfolded flat cookies without fortunes, or, if you bring your own fortunes, custom cookies (I often do this when I'm having dinner parties) at around $6 for 50 cookies—a very cheap way to impress your friends! Or, of course, you can just take a peek and move on.

As you exit the alley, cross Washington Street, take a right heading west on Washington, and you're in front of the Great China Herb Co.

⑭ Great China Herb Co.

For centuries, the Chinese have come to shops like this one, at 857 Washington St., which are full of exotic herbs, roots, and other natural substances. They buy what they believe will cure all types of ailments and ensure good health and long life. Thankfully, unlike owners in many similar area shops, Mr. and Mrs. Ho speak English, so you will not be met with a blank stare when you inquire what exactly is in each box, bag, or jar arranged along dozens of shelves. It is important to note that you should not use Chinese herbs without the guidance of a knowledgeable source such as an herb doctor. They may be natural, but they also can be quite powerful and are potentially harmful if misused.

Take a left upon leaving the store and walk to Stockton Street.

⑮ Stockton Street

The section of Stockton Street between Broadway and Sacramento Street is where most of the residents of Chinatown do their daily shopping.

One noteworthy part of this area's history is **Cameron House** (actually up the hill at 920 Sacramento St., near Stockton St.), which was named after Donaldina Cameron (1869–1968). Called Lo Mo, or "the Mother," by the Chinese, she spent her life trying to free Chinese women who came to America in hopes of marrying well but who found themselves forced into prostitution and slavery. Today, the house still helps women free themselves from domestic violence.

A good stop if you're in the market for some jewelry is **Jade Galore** (1000 Stockton St. at Washington St.). Though the employees aren't exactly warm and fuzzy, they've got the goods. In addition to purveying jade jewelry, the store does a fair trade in diamonds.

After browsing at Jade Galore, you might want to wander up Stockton Street to absorb the atmosphere and street life of this less-tourist-oriented Chinese community before doubling back to Washington Street. At 1068 Stockton St. you'll find **AA Bakery & Café,** an extremely colorful bakery with Golden Gate Bridge–shaped cakes, bright green and pink snacks, moon cakes, and a flow of Chinese diners catching up over pastries. Another fun place at which to peek is **Gourmet Delight B.B.Q.,** at 1045 Stockton St., where barbecued duck and pork are supplemented by steamed pigs' feet and chicken feet. Everything's to go here, so if you grab a snack, don't forget napkins. Head farther north along the street and you'll see live fish and fowl awaiting their fate as the day's dinner.

Meander south on Stockton Street to Clay Street and turn west (right) onto Clay. Continue to 965 Clay St. Make sure you arrive Tuesday through Friday between noon and 5pm or Saturday or Sunday between noon and 4pm. You've arrived at 965 Clay St.

⑯ Chinese Historical Society of America Museum

Founded in 1963, this museum (*©* **415/ 391-1188;** www.chsa.org) has a small but fascinating collection that illuminates the role of Chinese immigrants in American history, particularly in San Francisco and the rest of California.

The interesting artifacts on display include a shrimp-cleaning machine; 19th-century clothing and slippers of the Chinese pioneers; Chinese herbs and scales; historic hand-carved and painted shop signs; and a series of photographs that document the development of Chinese culture in America.

The goal of this organization is not only to "study, record, acquire, and preserve all suitable artifacts and such cultural items as manuscripts, books, and works of art . . . which have a bearing on the history of the Chinese living in the

United States of America," but also to "promote the contributions that Chinese Americans living in this country have made to the United States of America." It's an admirable and much-needed effort, considering what little recognition and appreciation the Chinese have received throughout American history.

The museum is open Tuesday through Friday from noon to 5pm and Saturday and Sunday from noon to 4pm. Admission is $3 adults, $2 for college students with ID and seniors, and $1 for kids ages 6 to 17.

Retrace your steps, heading east on Clay Street back toward Grant Avenue. Turn left onto Waverly Place.

⑰ Waverly Place

Also known as "The Street of Painted Balconies," Waverly Place is probably Chinatown's most popular side street or alleyway because of its painted balconies and colorful architectural details—a sort of Chinese-style New Orleans street. You can admire the architecture only from the ground, because most of the buildings are private family associations or temples.

One temple you can visit (but make sure it's open before you climb the long, narrow stairway) is the **Tin How Temple,** at 125 Waverly Place. Accessible via the stairway three floors up, this incense-laden sanctuary, decorated in traditional black, red, and gold lacquered wood, is a house of worship for Chinese Buddhists, who come here to pray, meditate, and send offerings to their ancestors and to Tin How, the Queen of the Heavens and Goddess of the Seven Seas. There are no scheduled services, but you are welcome to visit. Just remember to quietly respect those who are here to pray, and try to be as unobtrusive as possible. It is customary to give a donation or buy a bundle of incense during your visit.

Once you've finished exploring Waverly Place, walk east on Clay Street, past Grant Avenue, and continue until you come upon the block-wide urban playground that is also the most important site in San Francisco's history.

⑱ Portsmouth Square

This very spot was the center of the region's first township, which was called Yerba Buena before it was renamed San Francisco in 1847. Around 1846, before any semblance of a city had taken shape, this plaza lay at the foot of the bay's eastern shoreline. There were fewer than 50 non–Native American residents in the settlement, there were no substantial buildings to speak of, and the few boats that pulled into the cove did so less than a block from where you're sitting.

In 1846, when California was claimed as a U.S. territory, the marines who landed here named the square after their ship, the USS *Portsmouth*. (Today, a bronze plaque marks the spot where they raised the U.S. flag.)

Yerba Buena remained a modest township until the gold rush of 1849 when, over the next 2 years, the population grew from under 1,000 to over 19,000, as gold seekers from around the world made their way here.

When the square became too crowded, long wharves were constructed to support new buildings above the bay. Eventually, the entire area became landfill. That was almost 150 years ago, but today the square still serves as an important meeting place for neighborhood Chinese—a sort of communal outdoor living room.

Throughout the day, the square is heavily trafficked by children and—in large part—by elderly men, who gamble over Chinese cards. If you arrive early in the morning, you might come across people practicing tai chi.

It is said that Robert Louis Stevenson used to love to sit on a bench here and watch life go by. (At the northeast corner of the square, you'll find a monument to his memory, consisting of a model of the *Hispañola*, the ship in Stevenson's novel *Treasure Island*, and an excerpt from his "Christmas Sermon.")

Once you've had your fill of the square, exit to the east, at Kearny Street. Directly across the street, at 750 Kearny St., is the Holiday Inn. Cross the street, enter the hotel, and take the elevator to the third floor, where you'll find the Chinese Culture Center.

⑲ Chinese Culture Center

This center is oriented toward both tourists and the community, offering interesting display cases of Chinese art, and a gallery with rotating exhibits of Asian art and writings. The center is open Tuesday through Saturday from 10am to 4pm.

When you leave the Holiday Inn, take a left on Kearny and go 3 short blocks to Commercial Street. Take a left onto Commercial and note that Joshua A. Horton was a resident of the street you are standing on.

⑳ Joshua A. Norton's Home

Norton, the self-proclaimed "Emperor of the United States and Protector of Mexico," used to walk around the streets in an old brass-buttoned military uniform, sporting a hat with a "dusty plume." He lived in a fantasy world, and San Franciscans humored him at every turn.

Norton was born around 1815 in the British Isles and sailed as a young man to South Africa, where he served as a colonial rifleman. He came to San Francisco in 1849 with $40,000 and proceeded to double and triple his fortune in real estate. Unfortunately for him, he next chose to go into the rice business. While Norton was busy cornering the market and forcing prices up, several ships loaded with rice arrived unexpectedly in San Francisco's harbor. The rice market was suddenly flooded, and Norton was forced into bankruptcy. He left San Francisco for about 3 years and must have experienced a breakdown (or revelation) of

some sort, for upon his return, Norton thought he was an emperor.

Instead of ostracizing him, however, San Franciscans embraced him as their own homegrown lunatic and gave him free meals.

When Emperor Norton died in 1880 (while sleeping at the corner of California St. and Grant Ave.) approximately 10,000 people passed by his coffin, which was bought with money raised at the Pacific Union Club, and more than 30,000 people participated in the funeral procession. Today you won't see a trace of his character, but it's fun to imagine him cruising the street.

From here, if you've still got an appetite, you should go directly to 631 Kearny St. (at Clay St.), home of the R&G Lounge.

TAKE A BREAK
The **R&G Lounge** (© 415/982-7877) is a sure thing for tasty $5 rice-plate specials, chicken with black-bean sauce, and gorgeously tender and tangy R&G Special Beef.

Otherwise, you might want to backtrack on Commercial Street to Grant Avenue, take a left, and follow Grant back to Bush Street, the entrance to Chinatown. You'll be at the beginning of the Union Square area, where you can catch any number of buses (especially on Market St.) or cable cars or do a little shopping. Or you might backtrack to Grant, take a right (north), and follow Grant to the end. You'll be at Broadway and Columbus, the beginning of North Beach, where you can venture onward for our North Beach tour (see below).

Start:	Intersection of Montgomery Street, Columbus Avenue, and Washington Street.
Public Transportation:	Bus no. 10, 12, 15, 30X, or 41.
Finish:	Washington Square.
Time:	3 hours, including a stop for lunch.
Best Times:	Monday through Saturday between 11am and 4pm.
Worst Times:	Sunday, when shops are closed.
Hills That Could Kill:	The Montgomery Street hill from Broadway to Vallejo Street; otherwise, this is an easy walk.

Along with Chinatown, North Beach is one of the city's oldest neighborhoods. Origi-nally the Latin Quarter, it became the city's Italian district when Italian immigrants moved "uphill" in the early 1870s, crossing Broadway from the Jackson Square area and settling in. They quickly established restaurants, cafes, bakeries, and other busi-nesses familiar to them from their homeland. The "Beat Generation" helped put North Beach on the map, with the likes of Jack Kerouac and Allen Ginsberg holding court in the area's cafes during the 1950s. Although most of the original Beat poets are gone, their spirit lives on in North Beach, which is still a haven for bohemian artists and writers. The neighborhood, thankfully, retains its Italian village feel; it's a place where residents from all walks of life enjoy taking time for conversation over pastries and frothy cappuccinos.

If there's one landmark you can't miss, it's the familiar building on the corner of Montgomery Street and Columbus Avenue, the TransAmerica Pyramid (take bus 15, 30X, or 41 to get there).

❶ TransAmerica Pyramid

Noted for its spire (which rises 212 ft. above the top floor) and its "wings" (which begin at the 29th floor and stop at the spire), this pyramid is San Francisco's tallest building and a hallmark of the sky-line. You might want to take a peek at one of the rotating art exhibits in the lobby or go around to the right and into ¹/₂-acre Redwood Park, which is part of the TransAmerica Center.

The TransAmerica Pyramid occupies part of the 600 block of Montgomery Street, which once held a historic building called the Montgomery Block.

❷ The Montgomery Block

Originally four stories high, the Mont-gomery Block was the tallest building in the West when it was built in 1853. San Franciscans called it "Halleck's Folly"

because it was built on a raft of redwood logs that had been bolted together and floated at the edge of the ocean (which was right at Montgomery St. at that time). The building was demolished in 1959 but is fondly remembered for its historic importance as the power center of the city. Its tenants included artists and writers of all kinds, among them Jack London, George Sterling, Ambrose Bierce, Bret Harte, and Mark Twain. This is a picturesque area, but there's no partic-ular spot to direct you to. It's worth look-ing around, however, if only for the block's historical importance.

From the southeast corner of Montgomery and Washington streets, look across Washington to the corner of Columbus Avenue, and you'll see the original TransAmerica Building, located at 4 Columbus Ave.

❸ Original TransAmerica Building

The original TransAmerica Building is a Beaux Arts flatiron-shaped building cov-ered in terra cotta; it was also the home of

Sanwa Bank and Fugazi Bank. Built for the Banco Populare Italiano Operaia Fugazi in 1909, it was originally a two-story building and gained a third floor in 1916. In 1928, Fugazi merged his bank with the Bank of America, which was started by A. P. Giannini, who also created the TransAmerica Corporation. The building now houses a Church of Scientology.

Cross Washington Street and continue north on Montgomery Street to no. 730, the Golden Era Building.

❹ Golden Era Building

Erected around 1852, this building is named after the literary magazine, Golden Era, which was published here. Some of the young writers who worked on the magazine were known as "The Bohemians"; they included Samuel Clemens (aka Mark Twain) and Bret Harte (who began as a typesetter here). Backtrack a few dozen feet and stop for a minute to admire the exterior of the annex, at no. 722 (marked by a faded black-and-white striped awning but currently under renovation). The Belli Annex, as it is currently known, is registered as a historic landmark.

Continue north on Washington Street, and take the first right onto Jackson Street. Continue until you hit the 400 block of Jackson Square.

❺ 400 Block of Jackson Square

Here's where you'll find some of the only commercial buildings to survive the 1906 earthquake and fire. The building at no. 415 Jackson (ca. 1853) served as headquarters for the Ghirardelli Chocolate Company from 1855 to 1894. The Hotaling Building (no. 451) was built in 1866 and features pediments and quoins of cast iron applied over the brick walls. At no. 441 is another of the buildings that survived the disaster of 1906. Constructed between 1850 and 1852 with ship masts for interior supporting columns, it served as the French Consulate from 1865 to 1876.

Cross the street, and backtrack on Jackson Street. Continue toward the intersection of Columbus Avenue and Jackson Street. Turn right on Columbus and look across the street for the small triangular building at the junction of Kearny Street and Columbus Avenue, Columbus Tower (aka the Sentinel Building).

❻ Columbus Tower

If you walk a little farther, and then turn around and look back down Columbus, you'll be able to get a better look at Columbus Tower. The flat-iron beauty, a building shaped to a triangular site, went up between 1905 and 1907. Movie director and producer Francis Ford Coppola bought and restored it in the mid-1970s; it is now home to his film production company, American Zoetrope Studios. The building's cafe showcases all things Niebaum-Coppola (as in Coppola's winery)—including olive oil, Parmesan cheese, and wine. It's a great place to stop for a glass of wine, an espresso, or a thin-crusted pizza snack. This is one of the few pre–1906 earthquake buildings left in the city center.

Across the street from Columbus Tower on Columbus Avenue is 140 Columbus Ave.

❼ 140 Columbus Ave.

Once home to the performance venue known as the Purple Onion, this place has seen many famous headliners, often before they were famous. Phyllis Diller, who's now so big that she's famous for something as simple as her laugh, was still struggling when she played a 2-week engagement here in the late 1950s.

Continue north on Columbus, and then turn right on Pacific Avenue. After you cross Montgomery Street, you'll find brick-lined Osgood Place on the left. A registered historic landmark, it is one of the few quiet—and car-free—little alleyways left in the city. Stroll up Osgood and go left on Broadway to 1010 Montgomery St. (at Broadway).

❽ 1010 Montgomery St.

This is where Allen Ginsberg lived when he wrote his legendary poem, "Howl," first performed on October 13, 1955, in a

Walking Tour 2: North Beach

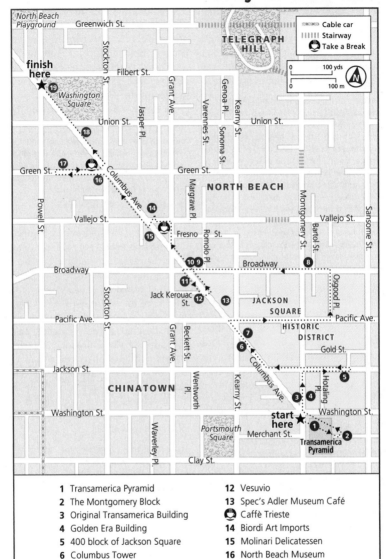

Legend:
- ▭▭▭ Cable car
- ||||| Stairway
- 🅑 Take a Break

0 — 100 yds
0 — 100 m

North Beach Playground

Greenwich St.

TELEGRAPH HILL

finish here ★ ⑲

Washington Square

Filbert St.

Stockton St.

Grant Ave.

Jasper Pl.

Genoa Pl.

Varennes St.

Kearny St.

Sonoma St.

Union St. ⑱

Union St.

⑰ 🅑 ⑯

Green St.

Columbus Ave.

Green St.

Margrave Pl.

NORTH BEACH

⑭

Powell St.

Vallejo St.

⑮ 🅑

Fresno St.

Romolo Pl.

Vallejo St.

Montgomery St.

Bartol St.

Sansome St.

Broadway

⑩ ⑨

Broadway

⑧

⑪

Jack Kerouac St.

⑫ ⑬

JACKSON SQUARE

Osgood Pl.

Pacific Ave.

Stockton St.

Grant Ave.

Beckett St.

HISTORIC DISTRICT

Pacific Ave.

⑦

Gold St.

⑥

Jackson St.

CHINATOWN

Wentworth Pl.

Kearny St.

Columbus Ave.

③ ④

Hotaling Pl.

⑤

Washington St.

Washington St.

start here ★ ①

② ▲

Portsmouth Square

Waverley Pl.

Merchant St.

Transamerica Pyramid

Clay St.

---

1 Transamerica Pyramid	**12** Vesuvio
2 The Montgomery Block	**13** Spec's Adler Museum Café
3 Original Transamerica Building	🅑 Caffè Trieste
4 Golden Era Building	**14** Biordi Art Imports
5 400 block of Jackson Square	**15** Molinari Delicatessen
6 Columbus Tower	**16** North Beach Museum
7 140 Columbus Avenue	**17** Club Fugazi
8 1010 Montgomery Street	🅑 O'Reilly's Irish Pub
9 hungry i	**18** Mario's Bohemian Cigar Store
10 Former site of the Condor Club	**19** Washington Square
11 City Lights Bookstore	

converted auto-repair shop at the corner of Fillmore and Union streets. By the time Ginsberg finished reading, he was crying and the audience was going wild. Jack Kerouac proclaimed, "Ginsberg, this poem will make you famous in San Francisco."

Continue along Broadway toward Columbus Avenue. This stretch of Broadway is San Francisco's answer to New York's Times Square, complete with strip clubs and peep shows that are being pushed aside by restaurants, clubs, and an endless crowd of visitors. It's among the most sought-after locations in the city as more and more profitable restaurants and clubs spring up. Keep walking west on Broadway, and on the right side of the street, you'll come to Black Oak Books, 540 Broadway. It sells new and used discount books and is worth a quick trip inside for a good, cheap read. A few dozen yards farther up Broadway is the current location of the hungry i.

❾ hungry i

Now a seedy strip club (at 546 Broadway), the original hungry i (at 599 Jackson St., which is under construction for senior housing) was owned and operated by the vociferous "Big Daddy" Nordstrom. If you had been here while Enrico Banducci (also of Enrico's restaurant) was in charge, you would have found only a plain room with an exposed brick wall and director's chairs around small tables. A who's who of nightclub entertainers fortified their careers at the original hungry i, including Lenny Bruce, Billie Holiday (who first sang "Strange Fruit" there), Bill Cosby, Richard Pryor, Woody Allen, and Barbra Streisand.

At the corner of Broadway and Columbus Avenue, you will see the former site of the Condor Club.

❿ Former Site of the Condor Club

The Condor Club was located at 300 Columbus Ave.; this is where Carol Doda scandalously bared her breasts and danced topless for the first time in 1964. Note the bronze plaque claiming the Condor Club as BIRTHPLACE OF THE WORLD'S FIRST TOPLESS & BOTTOMLESS

ENTERTAINMENT. Go inside what is now the Condor Sports Bar and have a look at the framed newspaper clippings that hang around the dining room. From the elevated back room, you can see Doda's old dressing room and, on the floor below, an outline of the piano that would descend from the second floor with her atop it.

When you leave the Condor Sports Bar, cross to the south side of Broadway. Note the mural of jazz musicians painted on the entire side of the building directly across Columbus Avenue. Diagonally across the intersection from the Condor Sports Bar is the City Lights bookstore.

⓫ City Lights Booksellers & Publishers

Founded in 1953 and owned by one of the first Beat poets to arrive in San Francisco, Lawrence Ferlinghetti, City Lights is now a city landmark and literary mecca. Located at 261 Columbus Ave., it's one of the last of the Beat-era hangouts in operation. An active participant in the Beat movement, Ferlinghetti established his shop as a meeting place where writers and bibliophiles could (and still do) attend poetry readings and other events. A vibrant part of the literary scene, the well-stocked bookshop prides itself on its collection of art, poetry, and political paperbacks.

Upon exiting City Lights bookstore, turn right, cross aptly named Jack Kerouac Street, and stop by Vesuvio, the bar on your right.

⓬ Vesuvio

Because of its proximity to City Lights bookstore, Vesuvio became a favorite hangout of the Beats. Dylan Thomas used to drink here, as did Jack Kerouac, Ferlinghetti, and Ginsberg. Even today, Vesuvio, which opened in 1949, maintains its original bohemian atmosphere. The bar is located at 255 Columbus Ave. (at Jack Kerouac St.) and dates from 1913. It is an excellent example of pressed-tin architecture.

Facing Vesuvio across Columbus Avenue is another favorite spot of the Beat Generation:

⑬ Spec's Adler Museum Café

Located at 12 Saroyan Place, this is one of the city's funkiest bars, a small, dimly lit watering hole with ceiling-hung maritime flags and exposed brick walls crammed with memorabilia. Within the bar is a minimuseum that consists of a few glass cases filled with mementos brought by seamen who frequented the pub from the '40s and onward.

From here, walk back up Columbus across Broadway to Grant Avenue. Turn right on Grant, and continue until you come to Vallejo Street. At 601 Vallejo St. (at Grant Ave.) is Caffè Trieste.

TAKE A BREAK
Yet another favorite spot of the Beats and founded by Gianni Giotta in 1956, **Caffè Trieste** (✆ **415/392-6739**) is still run by family members. The quintessential San Francisco coffeehouse, Trieste features opera on the jukebox, and the real thing, performed by the Giottas, on Saturday afternoons. Any day of the week is a good one to stop in for a cappuccino or espresso—the beans are roasted right next door.

Go left out of Caffè Trieste onto Vallejo Street, turn right on Columbus Avenue, and bump into the loveliest shop in all of North Beach, Biordi Art Imports, located at 412 Columbus Ave.

⑭ Biordi Art Imports

This store has carried imported hand-painted majolica pottery from the hill towns of central Italy for more than 50 years. Some of the colorful patterns date from the 14th century. Biordi hand-picks its artisans, and its catalog includes biographies of those who are currently represented.

Across Columbus Avenue, at the corner of Vallejo Street, is the Molinari Delicatessen.

⑮ Molinari Delicatessen

This deli, located at 373 Columbus Ave., has been selling its pungent, air-dried salamis since 1896. Ravioli and tortellini are made in the back of the shop, but it's the mouthwatering selection of cold salads, cheeses, and marinades up front that captures the attention of most folks. Each Italian sub is big enough for two hearty appetites.

Walk north to the lively intersection of Columbus, Green, and Stockton, and look for the U.S. Bank at 1435 Stockton St. On the second floor of the bank, you'll find the North Beach Museum.

⑯ North Beach Museum

The North Beach Museum displays historical artifacts that tell the story of North Beach, Chinatown, and Fisherman's Wharf. Just before you enter the museum, you'll find a framed, handwritten poem by Lawrence Ferlinghetti that captures his impressions of this primarily Italian neighborhood. After you pass through the glass doors, you'll see many photographs of some of the first Chinese and Italian immigrants, as well as pictures of San Francisco after the 1906 earthquake. You can visit the museum any time the bank is open (unfortunately, it's closed on weekends), and admission is free.

Now backtrack toward Columbus Avenue, and go left on Green Street to Club Fugazi, at 678 Green St.

⑰ Club Fugazi

It doesn't look like much from the outside, but Fugazi Hall was donated to the city (and more important, the North Beach area) by John Fugazi, the founder of the Italian bank that was taken over by A. P. Giannini and turned into the original TransAmerica Corporation. For many years, Fugazi Hall has been staging the zany and whimsical musical revue *Beach Blanket Babylon*. The show evolved from Steve Silver's Rent-a-Freak service, which consisted of a group of partygoers who would attend parties dressed as any number of characters in outrageous costumes. The fun caught on and soon became *Beach Blanket Babylon*.

If you love comedy, you'll love this show. We don't want to spoil it for you by telling you what it's about, but if you get tickets and they're in an unreserved-seat section, you should arrive fairly early because you'll be seated around small cocktail tables on a first-come, first-served basis. (Two sections have reserved seating, four don't, and all of them frequently sell out weeks in advance; however, sometimes it is possible to get tickets at the last minute on weekdays.) You'll want to be as close to the stage as possible. This supercharged show (see p. 222 for more information) is definitely worth the price of admission.

 TAKE A BREAK
Head back the way you came on Green Street. Before you get to Columbus Avenue, you'll see **O'Reilly's Irish Pub** (622 Green St.; ☎ 415/989-6222), a homey watering hole that dishes out good, hearty Irish food and a fine selection of beers (including Guinness, of course) that are best enjoyed at one of the sidewalk tables. The mural of Irish authors peering from the back wall is always a conversation piece. (How many can you name?)

As you come out of O'Reilly's, turn left, cross to the east side of the street, and then take a left onto Columbus. Proceed 1 block northwest to Mario's Bohemian Cigar Store.

⑱ Mario's Bohemian Cigar Store

Located at 566 Columbus Ave., across the street from Washington Square, this is one of North Beach's most popular neighborhood hangouts. No, it does not sell cigars, but the cramped and casual space overlooking Washington Square does sell killer focaccia sandwiches and coffee drinks.

Our next stop, directly across Union Street, is Washington Square.

⑲ Washington Square

This is one of the oldest parks in the city. The land was designated a public park in 1847 and has undergone many changes since then. Its current landscaping dates from 1955. You'll notice **Saints Peter and Paul Church** (the religious center for the neighborhood's Italian community) on the northwest end. Take a few moments to go inside and check out the traditional Italian interior. Note that this is the church in which baseball great Joe DiMaggio married his first wife, Dorothy Arnold. He wasn't allowed to marry Marilyn Monroe here because he had been divorced. He married Monroe at City Hall and came here for publicity photos.

Today, the park is a pleasant place in which to soak up the sun, read a book, or chat with a retired Italian octogenarian who has seen the city grow and change.

From here, you can see the famous Coit Tower at the top of Telegraph Hill to the northwest. If you'd like to get back to your starting point at Columbus and Montgomery streets, walk south (away from the water) on Columbus.

10

Shopping

Like its population, San Francisco's shopping scene is incredibly diverse. Every style, era, fetish, and financial status is represented here—not in big, homogenous shopping malls, but in hundreds of boutiques and secondhand stores scattered throughout the city. Whether it's a Chanel knockoff or Chinese herbal medicine you're looking for, San Francisco's got

it. Just pick a shopping neighborhood and give yourself a spending budget, and you're sure to end up with at least a few affordable take-home treasures. For those of you who travel cheaply so you can indulge yourself at the stores, we've also included a few of San Francisco's more costly but noteworthy shops, as well as the best of the discount-shopping scene.

1 The Shopping Scene
MAJOR SHOPPING AREAS
San Francisco has many shopping areas, but the following places are where you'll find most of the action.

UNION SQUARE & ENVIRONS   San Francisco's most congested and popular shopping mecca is centered on Union Square and bordered by Bush, Taylor, Market, and Montgomery streets. Most of the big department stores and many high-end specialty shops are here. Be sure to venture to Grant Avenue, Post and Sutter streets, and Maiden Lane. This area is a hub for public transportation; all Market Street and several other buses run here, as do the Powell-Hyde and Powell-Mason cable car lines. You can also take the Muni streetcar to the Powell Street station.

CHINATOWN   When you pass through the gate to Chinatown on Grant Avenue, say goodbye to the world of fashion and hello to a swarm of cheap tourist shops selling everything from linen and jade to plastic toys and $2 slippers. But that's not all Chinatown has to offer. The real gems are tucked away on side streets or are small, one-person shops selling Chinese herbs, original art, and jewelry. Grant Avenue is the area's main thoroughfare, and the side streets between Bush Street and Columbus Avenue are full of restaurants, markets, and eclectic shops. Stockton Street is best for grocery shopping (including live fowl and fish). Walking is the way to get around, because traffic through this area is slow at best and parking is next to impossible. Most stores in Chinatown are open daily from 10am to 10pm. Take bus no. 1, 9X, 15, 30, 41, or 45.

UNION STREET   Union Street, from Fillmore Street to Van Ness Avenue, caters to the upper-middle-class crowd. It's a great place to stroll, window-shop the plethora of boutiques, try the cafes and restaurants, and watch the beautiful people parade by. Take bus no. 22, 41, 45, 47, 49, or 76.

/ _Tips_   **Just the Facts: Hours, Taxes & Shipping**

Store hours are generally Monday through Saturday from 10am to 6pm and Sunday from noon to 5pm. Most department stores stay open later, as do shops around Fisherman's Wharf, the most heavily visited (by tourists) area.

Sales tax in San Francisco is 8.5%, which is added on at the register for all goods and services purchased. If you live out of state and buy an expensive item, you might want to have the store ship it home for you. You'll have to pay for shipping, but you'll escape paying the sales tax.

Most of the city's shops can wrap your purchase and **ship** it anywhere in the world. If they can't, you can send it yourself, either through **UPS** (© 800/742-5877), **FedEx** (© 800/463-3339), or the U.S. Postal Service (see "Fast Facts: San Francisco," in chapter 5).

CHESTNUT STREET   Parallel and a few blocks north, Chestnut is a younger version of Union Street. It holds endless shopping and dining choices, and an ever-tanned, superfit population of postgraduate singles who hang around cafes and scope each other out. Take bus no. 22, 28, 30, 43, or 76.

FILLMORE STREET   Some of the best shopping in town is packed into 5 blocks of Fillmore Street in Pacific Heights. From Jackson to Sutter streets, Fillmore is the perfect place to grab a bite and peruse the high-priced boutiques, crafts shops, and incredible housewares stores. (Don't miss Zinc Details; p. 215.) Take bus no. 1, 2, 3, 4, 12, 22, or 24.

HAIGHT STREET   Green hair, spiked hair, no hair, or mohair—even the hippies look conservative next to Haight Street's dramatic fashion freaks. The shopping in the 6 blocks of upper Haight Street between Central Avenue and Stanyan Street reflects its clientele. It offers everything from incense and European and American street styles to furniture and antique clothing. Bus nos. 6, 7, 66, and 71 run the length of Haight Street, and nos. 33 and 43 run through upper Haight Street. The Muni streetcar N line stops at Waller Street and Cole Street.

SOMA   Although this area isn't suitable for strolling, you'll find almost all the discount shopping in warehouse spaces south of Market. You can pick up a discount-shopping guide at most major hotels. Many bus lines pass through this area, including the 45, 30, and 15.

HAYES VALLEY   It's not the prettiest area in town, with some of the shadier housing projects a few blocks away. But while most neighborhoods cater to more conservative or trendy shoppers, lower Hayes Street, between Octavia and Gough streets, celebrates anything vintage, chic, artistic, or downright funky. With new shops opening frequently, it's definitely the most interesting new shopping area in town, with furniture and glass stores, thrift shops, trendy shoe stores, and men's and women's clothiers. You can find lots of great antiques shops south on Octavia and on nearby Market Street. Take bus no. 16AX, 16BX, or 21.

FISHERMAN'S WHARF & ENVIRONS _Overrated_   The tourist-oriented malls along Jefferson Street include hundreds of shops, restaurants, and attractions. Among them are Ghirardelli Square, PIER 39, The Cannery, and The Anchorage (see "Shopping Centers & Complexes," on p. 216), all reachable via the F cable car line on bus 30, 32, or 42.

2 Shopping A to Z

ANTIQUES

Jackson Square, a historic district just north of the Financial District's Embarcadero Center, is the place to go for the top names in fine furniture and fine art. You can find a number of Asian-art dealers here. More than a dozen dealers on the 2 blocks between Columbus and Sansome streets specialize in European furnishings from the 17th to the 19th centuries. Most shops here are open Monday through Friday from 9am to 5pm and Saturday from 11am to 4pm.

Bonhams & Butterfield   This renowned auction house holds preview weekends for upcoming auctions of furnishings, silver, antiques, art, and jewelry. Call for auction schedules. 220 San Bruno Ave. (at 16th St.). ℂ **800/223-2854** or 415/861-7500. www.bodhams. com/us.

Fumiki Fine Asian Arts   Come here for a beautiful collection of antique Japanese Imari, Korean and Japanese *tansus* (clothing chests), and Asian-style home accouterments. The extensive collection of Asian art and antiques includes Japanese baskets and Chinese artifacts and embroidery. 272 Sutter St. (at Grant St.). ℂ **415/362-6677.** www. fumiki.com.

Therien & Co.   For the best in Scandinavian, French, and eastern European antiques, head beyond SoMa's design center to this boutique, where you can find the real thing or antique replicas, as well as made-to-order furniture from their neighboring custom furniture shop. 411 Vermont St. (at 17th St.). ℂ **415/956-8850.** www.theiren.com.

ART

The San Francisco Gallery Guide, a comprehensive, bimonthly publication listing the city's current shows, is available free by mail. Send a self-addressed, stamped envelope to San Francisco Bay Area Gallery Guide, 1369 Fulton St., San Francisco, CA 94117 (ℂ **415/921-1600**); or pick one up at the San Francisco Visitor Information Center at 900 Market St. Most of the city's major art galleries are clustered downtown in the Union Square area.

Atelier Dore   Atelier Dore features American and European paintings from the 19th and 20th centuries. The store is open to everyone Tuesday through Saturday, but is closed on Sundays and open by appointment only on Mondays. 771 Bush St. (between Mason and Powell sts.). ℂ **415/391-2423.**

Catharine Clark Gallery ✦ *Value*   Catharine Clark's is a different kind of gallery experience. While many galleries focus on established artists and out-of-this-world prices, Catharine's exhibits highlight works by up-and-coming contemporary as well as established artists (mainly from California). It nurtures beginning collectors by offering a purchasing plan that's almost unheard of in the art business. You can buy a piece on layaway and take up to a year to pay for it—interest free! Prices here make art a realistic purchase for almost everyone for a change, but serious collectors also frequent the shows because Clark has such a keen eye for talent. Shows change every 6 weeks. 49 Geary St. (between Kearny and Grant sts.), 2nd floor. ℂ **415/399-1439.** www.cclarkgallery.com.

Fraenkel Gallery   This photography gallery features works by contemporary American and European artists. Excellent shows change every 2 months. Closed Sunday and Monday. 49 Geary St. (between Grant Ave. and Kearny St.), 4th floor. ℂ **415/981-2661.** www.fraenkelgallery.com.

Hang *Value*   Check out this amazingly affordable gallery for attractive pieces by yet-to-be-discovered Bay Area artists. The staff is friendly and helpful, and the gallery is designed to cater to new and seasoned collectors who appreciate original art at down-to-earth prices. 556 Sutter St. © 415/434-4264. www.hangart.com.

Images of the North   The highlight here is one of the most extensive collections of Canadian and Alaskan Inuit art in the United States. There's also a small collection of Native American masks and jewelry. Open Tuesday through Saturday and by appointment. 2036 Union St. (at Buchanan St.). © 415/673-1273. www.imagesnorth.com.

Meyerovich Gallery   Paintings, sculptures, and works on paper here are by modern and contemporary masters, including Chagall, Matisse, Miró, and Picasso. Meyerovich's new Contemporary Gallery, across the hall, features works by Lichtenstein, Stella, Frankenthaler, Dine, and Hockney. Closed Sunday. 251 Post St. (at Stockton St.), 4th floor. © 415/421-7171. www.meyerovich.com.

The Simmons Gallery   Formerly the Eleanor Austerer Gallery, this place is still where you'll find limited-edition graphics by modern masters like Braque, Matisse, Miró, Picasso, Calder, Chagall, and Hockney, as well as original works by European and American contemporary artists. The gallery, in a beautiful old building near Union Square, is closed on Sunday. 565 Sutter St. (between Powell and Mason sts.). © 415/986-2244. www.thesimmonsgallery.com.

Value **Discount Shopping**

Although well off the tourist beat, San Francisco has several factory outlet stores selling overstocked and discontinued fashions at bargain prices. Most outlet shops are located south of Market Street in the city's warehouse-cum–high tech district known as SoMa, so you can visit several of them in one fell swoop.

Jeremys, 2 South Park, between Bryant and Brannan streets at Second St. (© 415/882-4929; www.jeremys.com), is a serious SoMa mecca for fashion hounds thanks to the store's wide array of top designer fashions, from shoes to suits, at rock-bottom prices. There are no cheap knockoffs here, just good men's and women's clothes and accessories that the owner scoops up from major retailers who are either updating their merchandise or discarding returns.

As its name hints, the **Burlington Coat Factory,** 899 Howard St., at Fifth Street (© 415/495-7234; www.coat.com), has hundreds of coats—from cheapies to designer—as well as men's and women's clothing, shoes, and accessories. But the best deal is the home section, where designer bedding, bath, and housewares go for a fraction of their normal retail prices.

San Francisco's branch of Loehmann's, 222 Sutter St., between Kearny Street and Grant Avenue (© 415/982-3215; www.loehmanns.com), caters to a sophisticated white-collar crowd, so you won't find as much tacky fashion as you might at more suburban locations of this discount designer chain. Many women swear this place has the ultimate in professional clothing at bargain prices.

BODY PRODUCTS

Showroom by In Fiore *(Finds)*   I'm totally addicted to In Fiore—a high-end line of body balms, oils, perfumes, and facial serums—so I was especially thrilled when San Francisco–based founder Julie Elliott opened her by-appointment-only shop in what she calls the "Tender-Nob" (on the border of Nob Hill and the Tenderloin near Union Square). Come here to check out her whole line, as well as limited-edition balms, and see why celebrities like Julia Roberts and Meg Ryan are fans. Open Tuesday through Saturday and by appointment only. 868 Post St. (between Leavenworth and Hyde sts.). © 415/ 840-1726. www.infiore.net.

BOOKS

In addition to the listings below, there's a **Barnes & Noble** superstore at 2550 Taylor St., between Bay and North Point streets, near Fisherman's Wharf (© **415/292-6762**) and a four-storied **Borders** at 400 Post St., at Union Square (© **415/399-1633**).

Book Passage   If you're moseying through the Ferry Building Marketplace, drop into this cozy independent that emphasizes (for tourists and locals alike) local travel, boating on the Bay, food, cooking, sustainable agriculture and ecology, fiction, culinary and regional history and literature, and photo and gift books about the Bay Area. The store also hosts lots of author events: Check their website for details. Ferry Building Marketplace (at the Embarcadero and Market St.). © 415/835-1020. www.bookpassage.com.

The Booksmith   Haight Street's best selection of new books is in this large, well-maintained shop. It carries all the top titles, along with works from smaller presses, and more than 1,000 different magazines. 1644 Haight St. (between Clayton and Cole sts.). © 800/493-7323 or 415/863-8688. www.booksmith.com

Builders Booksource San Francisco   This independently owned shop in an old factory building in Ghirardelli Square specializes in architecture, design, construction, and home and garden and has a fine selection of exotic and limited-edition books on design and culture, but also offers a nicely edited selection of classic cookbooks and children's books. Ghirardelli Square, 900 North Point St. (at Larkin St.). © 415/440-5773. www. buildersbooksource-sf.com.

City Lights Booksellers & Publishers *(Finds)*   Brooding literary types browse this famous bookstore owned by Lawrence Ferlinghetti, the renowned Beat Generation poet. The three-level bookshop prides itself on a comprehensive collection of art, poetry, and political paperbacks, as well as more mainstream books. Open daily until midnight. 261 Columbus Ave. (at Broadway). © 415/362-8193. www.citylights.com.

A Clean, Well-Lighted Place for Books *(Finds)*   This independent store has good new fiction and nonfiction sections, and specializes in music, art, mystery, and cookbooks. The store is well known for its author readings and events. For a calendar of events, call or check the website. 601 Van Ness Ave. (between Turk St. and Golden Gate Ave.). © 415/441-6670. www.bookstore.com.

Green Apple Books *(Finds)*   The local favorite for used books, Green Apple is crammed with titles—more than 60,000 new and 100,000 used books and DVDs. Its extended sections in psychology, cooking, art, and history; collection of modern first editions; and rare graphic comics are superseded only by the staff's superlative service. 506 Clement St. (at Sixth Ave.). © 415/387-2272. www.greenapplebooks.com.

William Stout Architectural Books *(Finds)*   Step inside this shrine to all things architectural, and even if you think you're not interested in exquisite bathrooms,

Southern California's modern homes, or great gardens, you can't help but bury yourself in the thousands of design books. Their recent expansion into a second level means that if they don't have what you're looking for, it probably doesn't exist. 804 Montgomery St. (at Jackson St.). ℂ 415/391-6757. www.stoutbooks.com.

CHINA, SILVER & GLASS

Gump's *(Finds* Founded over a century ago, Gump's offers gifts and treasures ranging from Asian antiquities to contemporary art glass and exquisite jade and pearl jewelry. Many items are made specifically for the store. Gump's also has one of the city's most revered holiday window displays and is a huge wedding registry destination. Unfortunately, my personal wedding registry experience was a bumpy one at best, requiring a lot of calls to customer service to remedy "mistakes," and the staff, in general, can act very affected. 135 Post St. (between Kearny St. and Grant Ave.). ℂ 415/982-1616. www.gumps.com.

CRAFTS

The Canton Bazaar Amid a wide variety of handicrafts, here you'll find an excellent selection of rosewood and carved furniture, cloisonné enamelware, porcelain, carved jade, embroideries, jewelry, and antiques from mainland China. Open daily until 10pm. 616 Grant Ave. (between Sacramento and California sts.). ℂ 415/362-5750. www.canton bazaar.com.

The New Unique Company Primarily a calligraphy- and watercolor-supplies store, this shop also has a good assortment of books on these topics. In addition, there's a wide selection of carved stones for use as seals on letters and documents. Should you want a special design or group of initials, the store will carve seals to order. 838 Grant Ave. (between Clay and Washington sts.). ℂ 415/981-2036.

DEPARTMENT STORES (DOWNTOWN)

Macy's The seven-story Macy's West features contemporary fashions for women, juniors, and children, plus jewelry, fragrances, cosmetics, and accessories. The sixth floor offers a "hospitality suite" where visitors can leave their coats and packages, grab a cup of coffee, or find out more about the city from the concierge. The top floors contain home furnishings, and the Cellar sells kitchenware and gourmet foods. You'll even find a Boudin Cafe (though the food is not as good compared to their food at other locations) and a Wolfgang Puck Cafe on the premises. Across the street, Macy's East has five floors of men's fashions, including the largest Men's Polo by Ralph Lauren shop in the country. 170 O'Farrell St. (between Stockton and O'Farrell sts.) ℂ 415/397-3333. www.macys.com.

Neiman Marcus Some call this Texas-based chain "Needless Mark-ups." But even those who can't afford the best of everything can't deny that the men's and women's clothes, precious gems, and conservative formalwear are some of the most glamorous in town. The Rotunda Restaurant, located on the 4th floor, is a beautiful, relaxing place for lunch and afternoon tea that was renovated in 2004 to the tune of $1 million. The whole store will have received a face-lift by late 2006. 150 Stockton St. (between Geary and O'Farrell sts.). ℂ 415/362-3900. www.neimanmarcus.com.

Nordstrom Renowned for its personalized service, this is the largest branch of the Seattle-based fashion department-store chain. Nordstrom occupies the top five floors of the San Francisco Shopping Centre (see "Shopping Centers & Complexes," on p. 216) and is the mall's primary anchor. Equally devoted to women's and men's fashions, the store has one of the best shoe selections in the city and thousands of suits in stock. The Bistro, on the fourth floor, has a panoramic view and is ideal for an inexpensive lunch or light snack. Nordstrom Spa, on the fifth floor, is the perfect place to relax after a hectic day of bargain hunting. In the San Francisco Shopping Centre, 865 Market St. (between 4th and 5th sts.). ✆ 415/243-8500. www.nordstrom.com.

FABRICS

Britex Fabrics   A San Francisco institution since 1952 and newly renovated, Britex offers an absurd amount and variety of fabrics, not to mention a selection of more than 30,000 buttons. Closed Sundays. 146 Geary St. (between Stockton and Grant sts.). ✆ 415/392-2910. www.britexfabrics.com.

FASHION

See also "Vintage Clothing," later in this section.

UNISEX

At presstime, the Swedish-owned budget chain H&M was due to open their first West Coast store on Powell Street in Union Square in November of 2005. Check their website, www.hm.com, for details.

A B fits   Now in Union Square as well as North Beach, this is the place to pop in for jeans to fit all shapes, styles, and sizes as well as smart and sassy contemporary wear for gals and guys on the go. The snugly fitting stock with over 100 styles of jeans and pants ranges from Chip and Pepper, Earnest Sewn, Edwin, Notify, and Rogan, to chic wear from the likes of Twelfth Street by Cynthia Vincent, Ya-Ya, and Twinkle by Wenlan. There's another location in North Beach at 1519 Grant Ave. (at Union and Filbert sts.) with the same phone number. 40 Grant Ave. (between O'Farrell and Geary sts.). ✆ 415/982-5726. www.abfits.com.

American Rag Cie *(Finds*   Fashionistas flock to this find, on an unlikely stretch of busy Van Ness, for vintage and new duds sure to make you look street-swank. Check it out for everything from Juicy Couture to Paul & Joe and European vintage and modern masters such as Diesel or Marc Jacobs. 1305 Van Ness Ave. (at Sutter St.). ✆ 415/474-5214.

Gap   You know the look—jeans, khakis, sweatshirts, T-shirts, denim jackets. You've gotta hand it to them: Gap provides a mix-and-match backbone for men's and women's wardrobes, giving the casual look a spin of cool. Wait for sales, and you can clean up. There are locations throughout the city, but the company's flagship store in Union Square is the place to go. 890 Market St. (at Powell St.). ✆ 415/788-5909. www.gap.com.

MAC *(Finds*   No, we're not talking cosmetics. The more-modern-than-corporate stock at this hip and hidden shop just combined its men's and women's fashion meccas in a new space next door to pastry pit stop Citizen Cake. Drop in for imported tailored suits and women's separates in new and intriguing fabrics as well as gorgeous ties, vibrant sweaters, and a few choice home accouterments. Lines include Belgium's Dries Van Noten and Martin Margiela, New York's John Bartlett, and local sweater sweetheart Laurie B. The best part? Prices are more reasonable than many of the trendy clothing stores in the area. 387 Grove St. (at Gough St.). ✆ 415/863-3011. www.maccosmetics.com.

Niketown   As you'd expect, inside the doors here it's Nike's world, offering everything the Nike merchandising team could create. It's not a factory outlet, so most items are priced the same as other retail outlets, but the numerous "closeout" stands throughout the store offer great bargains. 278 Post St. (at Stockton St.). ℂ **415/392-6453.** www.niketown.com.

Wilkes Bashford *(Finds)* Wilkes Bashford is worth a peek through the window, but don't enter the boutique unless if you're feeling Trumpish—it's one of the most expensive (and best-known) clothing stores in the city. In its 3-plus decades in business, the boutique has garnered a reputation for stocking only the finest clothes in the world (which can often be seen on ex-Mayor Willie Brown and current Mayor Gavin Newsom, who do their suit shopping here). Most fashions come from Italy and France; they include women's designer sportswear and couture and men's Kiton and Brioni suits (at $2,500 and up, they're considered the most expensive suits in the world). Note that the store is closed on Sundays. 375 Sutter St. (at Stockton St.). ℂ **415/986-4380.** www.wilkesbashford.com.

MEN'S FASHIONS

All American Boy Long known for setting the mainstream style for gay men, All American Boy is the quintessential Castro clothing shop. 463 Castro St. (between Market and 18th sts.). ℂ **415/861-0444.**

Brooks Brothers In San Francisco, this bulwark of tradition is 1 block east of Union Square. Brooks Brothers introduced the button-down collar and single-handedly changed the standard of the well-dressed businessman. The multilevel shop also sells traditional casual wear, including sportswear, sweaters, and shirts. 150 Post St. (at Grant Ave.). ℂ **415/397-4500.** www.brooksbrothers.com.

Cable Car Clothiers Dapper men head to this fashion institution for traditional attire, such as three-button suits with natural shoulders, Aquascutum coats, McGeorge sweaters, and Atkinson ties. Closed Sundays. 200 Bush St. (at Sansome St.). ℂ **415/397-4740.** www.cablecarclothiers.com.

Citizen Clothing The Castro has some of America's best men's casual clothing stores, and this is one of them. Stylish (but not faddish) pants, tops, and accessories are in stock here. Its sister store, Body, located at 450 Castro St. (between 17th and 18th sts.), carries men's sportswear. 536 Castro St. (between 18th and 19th sts.). ℂ **415/575-3560.**

WOMEN'S FASHIONS

The Chanel Boutique Ever fashionable and expensive, Chanel is appropriately located on Maiden Lane, the quaint downtown side street where the most exclusive stores and spas cluster. You'll find here what you'd expect from Chanel: clothing, accessories, scents, cosmetics, and jewelry. Of course it's all outrageously priced, but it makes for fun Union Square window shopping. 155 Maiden Lane (between Stockton St. and Grant Ave.). ℂ **415/981-1550.** www.chanel.com.

emily lee More mature fashionistas head to the quaint shopping street of Laurel Village, a block-long strip mall of shops that includes emily lee, for everything from elegant to artsy-designer garb that tends to be stylish, sensible, and loose-fitting. Designers include the likes of Blanque, Eileen Fisher, Flax, Ivan Grundahl, and Three Dots. 3509 California St. (at Locust St.). ℂ **415/751-3443.**

RAG *(★★ Finds)* If you want to add some truly unique San Francisco designs to your closet, head to RAG, or Residents Apparel Gallery, a co-op shop where around 55 local emerging designers showcase their latest creations. Prices are great, fashions are forward, young, and hip, and if you grab a few pieces, no one at home's going to be able to copy your look. 541 Octavia St. (at Hayes St.). ℂ **415/621-7718.** www.ragsf.com.

CHILDREN'S FASHIONS

In addition to the below, Gap Kids is a reliable choice (there are stores throughout the city; visit www.gapkids.com.)

Minis   Christine Pajunen, who used to design for Banana Republic, opened this children's clothing store to sell her own creations. Every piece, from shirts to pants and dresses, is made from natural fibers. Every outfit perfectly coordinates with everything else in the store. In 2004, Minis expanded the store so that it now includes baby gear, including functional and versatile strollers and cribs. Minis also offers educational and creative toys and books with matching dolls as well as maternity wear. 2278 Union St. (between Steiner and Fillmore sts.). ℂ 415/567-9537. www.minis-sf.com.

FOOD

Boulangerie *(Finds*   A bit of Paris on Pine Street, this true-blue bakery sells authentically French creations, from delicious and slightly sour French country wheat bread to rustic-style desserts, including the locally famous *cannele de Bordeaux,* custard baked in a copper mold. And if you're looking for a place to eat Boulangerie bread and pastries, visit their cafes—**Boulange de Polk,** at 2310 Polk St. near Green Street (ℂ 415/345-1107), or **Boulange de Cole,** at 1000 Cole St. at Parnassas Street (ℂ 415/242-2442). Closed Mondays. 2325 Pine St. (at Fillmore St.). ℂ 415/440-0356, ext. 204. www.baybread.com.

Cowgirl Creamery *(Finds*   San Francisco is fanatical about cheese, and much of the local enthusiasm can be attributed to the women behind Cowgirl Creamery, located in the Ferry Building but still imparting the simple little neighborhood shop feel and carrying nothing other than excellent small-production local and imported cheeses along with a few other snacks. Ferry Building Plaza, no. 17. ℂ 415/362-9354. www.cowgirl creamery.com.

Golden Gate Fortune Cookies Co. ℛ   This tiny, touristy factory sells fortune cookies hot off the press. You can purchase them in small bags or in bulk, and you can even bring in your own messages and watch them be folded into fresh cookies before your eyes. Even if you're not buying, stop in to see how these sugary treats are made (although the staff can get pushy for you to buy). Open daily until 8:30pm. 56 Ross Alley (between Washington and Jackson sts.). ℂ 415/781-3956.

Joseph Schmidt Confections *(Finds*   Here, chocolate takes the shape of exquisite sculptural masterpieces—such as long-stemmed tulips and heart-shaped boxes—that are so beautiful, you'll be hesitant to bite the head off your adorable panda bear. Once you do, however, you'll know why this is the most popular—and reasonably priced—chocolatier in town. Closed Sundays. 3489 16th St. (at Sanchez St.). ℂ 800/861-8682 or 415/861-8682. www.jospehsmithconfections.com.

Ten Ren Tea Co., Ltd ℛ *(Finds*   At the Ten Ren Tea Co. shop, you will be offered a steaming cup of tea when you walk in the door. In addition to a selection of almost 50 traditional and herbal teas, the company stocks a collection of cold tea drinks and tea-related paraphernalia, such as pots, cups, and infusers. If you can't make up your mind, take home a mail-order form. The shop is open daily from 9am to 9pm. 949 Grant Ave. (between Washington and Jackson sts.). ℂ 415/362-0656. www.tentea.com.

GIFTS

Art of China   Amid a wide variety of collectibles, this shop features exquisite, hand-carved Chinese figurines. You'll also find a lovely assortment of ivory beads, bracelets,

---

Finds **Amazing Grazing**

There's no better way to enjoy a sunny San Francisco morning than by strolling the **Ferry Plaza Farmers' Market** and snacking your way through breakfast on some of America's finest organic produce. While poking among the 100 stalls crammed with Northern California fruit, vegetable, bread, shellfish, and dairy items, you're bound to bump elbows with the dozens of Bay Area chefs (such as Alice Waters) who do their shopping here. The enthusiastic vendors are always willing to educate visitors about the benefits of organic produce, and often provide free samples. It's a unique opportunity for city dwellers to buy freshly picked organic produce directly from small family-operated farms.

On Saturdays, the market offers a **Shop with the Chef** *𝒢* program in which a guest restaurant chef browses the market for ingredients, then conducts a free cooking class at 10:30am (with free samples of what he or she makes). Several local restaurants, such as North Beach's Rose Pistola, also have food stalls promoting their organic cuisine, so skip breakfast the morning you visit. You can also pick up locally made vinegars and oils, which make wonderful gifts.

The Farmers' Market takes place year-round, rain or shine, every Saturday and Sunday from 8am to 2pm, Tuesdays from 10am to 2pm, and Thursdays from 3 to 7pm at the **Ferry Building,** on the Embarcadero at the foot of Market Street (about a 15-min. walk from Fisherman's Wharf). Call *𝒞* **415/353-5650** for more information or log onto www.ferryplazafarmersmarket.com.

---

necklaces, and earrings. Pink-quartz dogs, jade figurines, porcelain vases, cache pots, and blue-and-white barrels suitable for use as table bases are just some of the many items stocked here. 839–843 Grant Ave. (between Clay and Washington sts.). *𝒞* **415/981-1602.** www.artsofchinasf.com.

Babushka   Located near Fisherman's Wharf, adjacent to the Anchorage mall, Babushka sells only Russian products, most of which are wooden nesting dolls. 333 Jefferson St. (at Leavenworth St.). *𝒞* **415/673-6740.**

Cost Plus World Market   At the Fisherman's Wharf cable car turntable, Cost Plus is a vast warehouse crammed to the rafters with Chinese baskets, Indian camel bells, Malaysian batik scarves, and innumerable other items from Algeria to Zanzibar. More than 20,000 items from 50 nations, imported directly from their country of origin, pack this well-priced warehouse. There's also a decent wine shop here. It's open Monday through Saturday from 9am to 9pm and Sunday from 10am to 8pm. Validated parking with a purchase of $10 or more is available underneath the store. 2552 Taylor St. (between North Point and Bay sts.). *𝒞* **415/928-6200.** www.worldmarket.com.

Dandelion *𝒢𝒢 Finds*   Tucked in an out-of-the-way location in SoMa is the most wonderful collection of gifts, collectibles, and furnishings. There's something for every taste and budget here, from an excellent collection of teapots, decorative dishes, and gourmet foods to silver, books, cards, and picture frames. Don't miss the Zenlike second floor, with its peaceful furnishings in Indian, Japanese, and Western styles. The store is closed Sunday and Monday except during November and December, when it's open daily. Hours are 10am to 6pm. 55 Potrero Ave. (at Alameda St.). © 415/436-9500. www.tampopo.com.

Distractions   This is the best of the Haight Street shops selling underground-rave wear, street fashion, and electronica CDs. You'll find pipes, toys, and stickers liberally mixed with lots of cool stuff to look at. 1552 Haight St. (between Ashbury and Clayton sts.). © 415/252-8751.

Flax   If you're the type of person who goes into an art store for a special pencil and comes out $300 later, don't go near this shop. Flax has everything you can think of in art and design supplies, an amazing collection of blank bound books, children's art supplies, frames, calendars—you name it. There's a gift for every type of person here, especially you. If you can't stop by, call for a mail-order catalog. 1699 Market St. (at Valencia and Gough sts.). © 415/552-2355. www.flaxart.com.

Good Vibrations &   A laypersons' sex-toy, book, and video emporium, Good Vibrations is a women-owned, worker-owned cooperative. Unlike most sex shops, it's not a back-alley business, but a straightforward shop with healthy, open attitudes about human sexuality. It also has a vibrator museum. 603 Valencia St. (at 17th St.). © 415/522-5460 or 800/BUY-VIBE (for mail order). www.goodvibes.com. A second location is at 1620 Polk St. (at Sacramento St.), © 415/345-0400, and a third is at 2504 San Pablo Ave., Berkeley (© 510/841-8987).

Kati Koos   Need a little humor in your life? Previously called Smile, this store specializes in whimsical art, furniture, clothing, jewelry, and American crafts guaranteed to make you grin. Closed Sundays. 500 Sutter St. (between Powell and Mason sts.). © 415/362-3437. www.katikoos.com.

SFMOMA MuseumStore *finds*   With an array of artistic cards, books, jewelry, housewares, furniture, knickknacks, and creative tokens of San Francisco, it's virtually impossible not to find something here you'll consider a must-have. (Check out the fog globe, a San Franciscan version on the snow globe.) Aside from being one of the locals' favorite shops, it offers far more tasteful mementos than most Fisherman's Wharf options. Open late (until 9:30pm) on Thursday nights. 151 Third St. (2 blocks south of Market St., across from Yerba Buena Gardens). © 415/357-4035. www.sfmoma.org.

HOUSEWARES/FURNISHINGS

Alabaster *finds*   Any interior designer who knows Biedermeier from Bauhaus knows that this Hayes Valley shop sets local home accessories trends with its collection of high-end must-haves. After a recent expansion, they increased their selection of everything from lighting—antique and modern Alabaster fixtures, Fortuny silk shades, Venetian glass chandeliers—to other home accessories, including one-of-a-kind antiques, body products from Florence, and more. 597 Hayes St. (at Laguna St.). © 415/558-0482. www.alabastersf.com.

Alessi   Italian designer Alberto Alessi, who's known for his whimsical and colorful kitchen-utensil designs, such as his ever-popular spiderlike lemon squeezer, opened a flagship store here. Drop by for everything from gorgeous stainless-steel double boilers to corkscrews shaped like maidens. 424 Sutter St. (at Stockton St.). © 415/434-0403. www.alessi.com.

Big Pagoda Company   When I need to buy a stylish friend a gift, I head to this downtown Asian-influenced design shop for cool, unique, and contemporary finds.

Within the bi-level boutique, East meets West and old meets new in the form of anything from an antique Chinese scholar's chair to a new wave table that hints at Ming or Mondrian. Its furniture and glass art is hardly cheap (a Tibetan antique dragonhead goes for $30,000), but you can get fabulous designer martini glasses at $15 a pop. Open Monday through Saturday 10am to 6pm. 310 Sutter St. (at Grant St.). ✆ 415/296-8881. www.bigpagoda.com.

Biordi Art Imports *(Finds* Whether you want to decorate your dinner table, color your kitchen, or liven up the living room, Biordi's Italian majolica pottery is the most exquisite and unusual way to do it. The owner has been importing these hand-painted collectibles for 59 years, and every piece is a showstopper. Call for a catalog. They'll ship anywhere. Closed Sundays. 412 Columbus Ave. (at Vallejo St.). ✆ 415/392-8096. www.biordi.com.

Diptyque If the idea of spending $40 on a candle makes you laugh, this isn't the place for you. But if you're the type willing to throw down good money to scentualize your living space, don't skip this French shop offering dozens of spectacular flaming fragrances. I'm such a fan that every time I went to Paris I'd weigh down my luggage with these 50-hour burners. (Before the horrible exchange rate, that is.) But now I can scoop them up in my own backyard. They also make great gifts. 171 Maiden Lane (near Stockton St.). ✆ 415/402-0600. www.diptyqueusa.com.

Limn For the latest in Europe's trendsetting and ultramodern furniture and lighting, go straight to local SoMa celebrity Limn, which also showcases artworks in its adjoining gallery. 290 Townsend St. (at Fourth St.). ✆ 415/543-5466. www.limn.com.

Nest *(Finds* Don't come into Fillmore's cutest French interiors store without your credit cards. Nest carries adorable throws, handmade quilts, must-have slippers and sleepwear, and a number of other things you never knew you needed until now. 2300 Fillmore St. (at Clay St.). ✆ 415/292-6199.

Propeller *(Finds* This airy skylight-lit shop is a must-stop for lovers of the latest in übermodern furniture and home accessories. Owner/designer Lorn Dittfeld handpicks pieces by emerging designers from as far away as Sweden, Italy, and Canada as well as a plethora of national newbies. Drop in to lounge on the hippest sofas; grab pretty and practical gifts like ultracool magnetic spice racks; or adorn your home with Bev Hisey's throws and graphic pillows, diamond-cut wood tables by William Earle, or hand-tufted graphic rugs by Angela Adams. 555 Hayes St. (between Laguna and Octavia sts.). ✆ 415/701-7767. www.propeller-sf.com.

Sue Fisher King *(Finds* For the ultimate in everything on the traditional side for the tabletop, bedroom, and beyond, head to this exclusive neighborhood boutique known by the society set as the only place to shop. It's filled with items like exquisite table linens, cashmere blankets, towels, china, silver flatware, and more. Closed Sundays. 3067 Sacramento St. (at Baker St.). ✆ 415/922-7276. www.suefisherking.com.

Sur La Table Cooks should bee-line it to this Union Square shop specializing in all things culinary. Its two floors are packed to the rafters with pricey but stylish high-quality pots and pans, utensils, tabletop items, books, and more, coupled with an extremely helpful and knowledgeable staff. 77 Maiden Lane (at Grant St.). ✆ 415/732-7900. www.surlatable.com.

The Wok Shop ✦ This shop has every conceivable implement for Chinese cooking, including woks, brushes, cleavers, circular chopping blocks, dishes, oyster knives, bamboo steamers, and strainers. It also sells a wide range of kitchen utensils, baskets, handmade linens from China, and aprons. 718 Grant Ave. (at Clay St.). © **415/989-3797** or 888/780-7171 for mail order. www.wokshop.com.

Zinc Details *Finds*   This contemporary furniture and knickknack shop has received accolades everywhere from *Elle Decor Japan* to *Metropolitan Home* to *InStyle* for its amazing collection of glass vases, pendant lights, ceramics from all over the world, and furniture from local craftsmen. A portion of these true works of art are made specifically for the store. 1905 Fillmore St. (between Bush and Pine sts.). © **415/776-2100**. www.zincdetails.com.

JEWELRY

Dianne's Old & New Estates   Many of the city's single women shop for their engagement rings from this fantastic little shop featuring top-of-the-line antique jewelry—pendants, diamond rings, necklaces, bracelets, and pearls. If you decide to spring for a special gift, check out the collection of platinum wedding and engagement rings and vintage watches. Don't worry if you can't afford it now—the shop offers 1-year interest-free layaway. Better yet, if you buy a ring, they'll send you off with a thank-you bottle of celebration bubbly. 2181A Union St. (at Fillmore St.). © **888/346-7525** or 415/346-7525. www.diannesestatejewelry.com.

Pearl & Jade Empire   The Pearl & Jade Empire has been importing jewelry from all over the world since 1957. It specializes in unusual pearls and jade and offers restringing on the premises as well as boasting a collection of amber from the Baltic Sea. Depending on the quality and size of the stone, you can pick up some beautiful mementos here for under $20. 427 Post St. (between Powell and Mason sts.). © **415/362-0606**. www.pearlempire.com.

Tiffany & Co.   Even if you don't have lots of cash with which to buy an exquisite bauble that comes in Tiffany's famous light-blue box, enjoy this renowned store a la Audrey Hepburn in *Breakfast at Tiffany's*. The designer collection features Paloma Picasso, Jean Schlumberger, and Elsa Peretti in both silver and 18-karat gold, and there's an extensive gift collection in sterling, china, and crystal. 350 Post St. (at Powell St.). © **415/781-7000**. www.tiffany.com.

Union Street Goldsmith   A showcase for Bay Area goldsmiths, this exquisite shop sells a contemporary collection of fine custom-designed jewelry in platinum and all karats of gold. Many pieces emphasize colored stones. 1909 Union St. (at Laguna St.). © **415/776-8048**. www.unionstreetgoldsmith.com.

MUSIC

Recycled Records *Finds*   Easily one of the best used-record stores in the city, this loud shop in the Haight has cases of used "classic" rock LPs, sheet music, and tour programs. It's open 10am to 8pm daily. 1377 Haight St. (between Central and Masonic sts.). © **415/626-4075**. www.recycled-records.com.

Streetlight Records   Overstuffed with used music in all three formats, this place is best known for its records and excellent CD collection. It also carries new and used DVDs and computer games. Rock music is cheap, and the money-back guarantee guards against defects. 3979 24th St. (between Noe and Sanchez sts.). © **415/282-3550**. www.streetlight records.com. There's a second location at 2350 Market St., between Castro and Noe streets (© **415/282-8000**). www.streetlightrecords.com.

Virgin Megastore   With thousands of CDs, including an impressive collection of imports, videos, DVDs, a multimedia department, a cafe, and related books, this enormous Union Square store can make any music-lover blow his or her entire vacation fund. It's open Sunday through Thursday from 10am to 11pm and Friday and Saturday from 10am to midnight. 2 Stockton St. (at Market St.). ℂ 415/397-4525. www.virginmega.com.

SHOES

Gimme Shoes   The staff is funky-fashion snobby, the prices are steep, and the European shoes and accessories are utterly chic. Additional locations are at 416 Hayes St. (ℂ **415/864-0691**) and 50 Grant Ave. (ℂ **415/434-9242**). 2358 Fillmore St. (at Washington St.). ℂ 415/441-3040. www.gimmeshoes.com.

Kenneth Cole   This trendy shop carries high-fashion footwear for men and women. There is also an innovative collection of handbags and small leather goods and accessories. Other shops are at 2078 Union St., at Webster Street (ℂ **415/346-2161**) and 166 Grant St., at Post Street (ℂ **415/981-2653**). 865 Market St. (in the San Francisco Shopping Centre). ℂ 415/227-4536. www.kennethcole.com.

SHOPPING CENTERS & COMPLEXES

The Anchorage   This touristy waterfront mall has close to 50 stores that offer everything from music boxes to home furnishings; street performers entertain during open hours. This is not a stop for staples, but more for tourist trinkets. 2800 Leavenworth St. (between Beach and Jefferson sts. on Fisherman's Wharf). ℂ 415/775-6000.

The Cannery at Del Monte Square   This attractive complex was built in 1907 as a Del Monte fruit-canning plant and converted to a mall in the 1960s. It contains 30 plus unimpressive shops, a ceramic studio and gallery, and several restaurants including **Jack's Cannery Bar** (ℂ 415/931-6400). I'd recommend skipping The Cannery completely, except for **The Oakville Grocery** (2801 Leavenworth St.; ℂ 415/614-1600; open daily from 9am to 7pm), which carries artisanal food and wine from Northern California, including fresh-daily salads, sandwiches, and wood-fired pizzas that are perfect for lunch. 2801 Leavenworth St. (between Beach and Jefferson sts.). ℂ 415/771-3112. www.delmontesquare.com.

Crocker Galleria   Modeled after Milan's Galleria Vittorio Emanuele, this glass-domed, three-level pavilion, about 3 blocks east of Union Square, features around 40 high-end shops with expensive and classic designer creations. Fashions include Aricie lingerie, Gianni Versace, and Polo/Ralph Lauren. Closed Sundays. 50 Post St. (at Kearny St.). ℂ 415/393-1505. www.shopatgalleria.com.

Ghirardelli Square   This former chocolate factory is one of the city's quaintest shopping malls and most popular landmarks. It dates from 1864, when it served as a factory making Civil War uniforms, but it's best known as the former chocolate and spice factory of Domingo Ghirardelli (say "Gear-a-*deli*"). A clock tower, an exact replica of the one at France's Château de Blois, crowns the complex. Inside the tower, on the mall's plaza level, is the fun Ghirardelli soda fountain. It still makes and sells small amounts of chocolate, but the big draw is the old-fashioned ice-cream parlor. (Got a late-night craving? The place stays open until midnight on Fri and Sat.) A free map and guide to the mall is available from the information booth in the center courtyard. If you're coming to shop, think again: It's pretty lame in that department, but you can dine decently at Ana Mandara. Main plaza shops' and restaurants' hours are 10am to 6pm Sunday through Thursday and 10am to 9pm Friday and Saturday, with extended hours during the summer. (Incidentally, the Ghirardelli Chocolate Company still makes chocolate in the East Bay.) 900 North Point St. (at Polk St.). ℂ 415/775-5500. www.ghirardellisq.com.

PIER 39 *Overrated*   The automated information line reminds callers not to forget to bring your Discover credit card (their "preferred card," but not the only one accepted) to this bayside tourist trap, which also happens to have stunning views. To residents, that pretty much wraps up PIER 39—an expensive spot where out-of-towners go to waste money on worthless souvenirs and greasy fast food. For vacationers, though, PIER 39 does have some redeeming qualities—fresh crab (in season), playful sea lions, phenomenal views, and plenty of fun for the kids. If you want to get to know the real San Francisco, skip the cheesy T-shirt shops and limit your time here to one afternoon, if at all. Fisherman's Wharf (at Beach St. and the Embarcadero) www.pier39.com.

Westfield San Francisco Centre   Opened in 1988, this $140-million complex is one of the few vertical malls (multilevel rather than sprawling) in the United States. Its most attractive features are the four-story spiral escalators that circle up to Nordstrom (p. 208) and the nine-story atrium covered by a retractable skylight. More than 65 specialty shops include Abercrombie & Fitch, Ann Taylor, bebe, Benetton, Footlocker, J. Crew, and Victoria's Secret. In 2006, the center will expand to include a Bloomingdale's department store and a Century movie theatre. If you want one-stop shopping, this is as good as it gets. 865 Market St. (at Fifth St.). ℂ 415/495-5656. www.westfield.com.

TOYS

The Chinatown Kite Shop   This shop's playful assortment of flying objects includes attractive fish kites, windsocks, hand-painted Chinese paper kites, wood-and-paper biplanes, pentagonal kites, and do-it-yourself kite kits, all of which make great souvenirs or decorations. Computer-designed stunt kites have two or four control lines to manipulate loops and dives. Open daily from 10am to 8pm. 717 Grant Ave. (between Clay and Sacramento sts.). ℂ 415/391-8217. www.chinatownkite.com.

TRAVEL GOODS

Flight 001   Jetsetters zoom into this space-shuttle–like showroom for hip travel accessories. Check out the sleek luggage, "security friendly" manicure sets, and other mid-air must-haves. 525 Hayes St. (between Laguna and Octavia sts.). ℂ 415/487-1001. www.flight001.com.

VINTAGE CLOTHING

Aardvark's   One of San Francisco's largest secondhand clothing dealers, Aardvark's has seemingly endless racks of shirts, pants, dresses, skirts, and hats from the past 30 years. It's open daily from 11am to 7pm. 1501 Haight St. (at Ashbury St.). ℂ 415/621-3141.

Buffalo Exchange   This large and newly expanded storefront on upper Haight Street is crammed with racks of antique and new fashions from the 1960s, 1970s, and 1980s. It stocks everything from suits and dresses to neckties, hats, handbags, and jewelry. Buffalo Exchange anticipates some of the hottest new street fashions. A second shop is at 1210 Valencia St., at 24th Street (ℂ 415/647-8332). 1555 Haight St. (between Clayton and Ashbury sts.). ℂ 415/431-7733. www.buffaloexchange.com.

Good Byes ★★ *Finds*   One of the best new- and used-clothes stores in San Francisco, Good Byes carries only high-quality clothing and accessories, including an exceptional selection of men's fashions at unbelievably low prices (for example, $350 preowned shoes for $35). Women's wear is in a separate boutique across the street. 3464 and 3483 Sacramento St. (between Laurel and Walnut sts.). ℂ 415/346-6388. www.goodbyesf.com.

La Rosa   On a street packed with vintage-clothing shops, this is one of the more upscale options. It features a selection of high-quality, dry-cleaned secondhand goods.

Formal suits and dresses are its specialty, but you'll also find sport coats, slacks, and shoes. The more moderately priced sister store, **Held Over,** is located at 1543 Haight St., near Ashbury (© **415/864-0818**), and their discount store, **Clothes Contact,** is located at 473 Valencia St., at 16th Street (© **415/621-3212**). 1711 Haight St. (at Cole St.). © 415/668-3744.

WINE & SAKE

True Sake   Amid woven sea grass flooring, colorful backlit displays, and a so-hip Hayes Valley location are more than 140 varieties of sake ranging from an $8 300ml bottle of Ohyama to an $180 720ml bottle of Kotsuziami Rojohanaari. Owner Beau Timken (who is on hand to describe each wine), says the Rojohanarri is available at no other retail store in the U.S. 560 Hayes St. (between Laguna and Octavia sts.). © 415/355-9555.

Wine Club San Francisco *(Value)*   The Wine Club is a discount warehouse that offers bargain prices on more than 1,200 domestic and foreign wines. Bottles cost between $4 and $1,100. 953 Harrison St. (between Fifth and Sixth sts.). © 415/512-9086.

11

San Francisco After Dark

For a city with fewer than a million inhabitants, San Francisco boasts an impressive after-dark scene. Dozens of piano bars and top-notch lounges augment a lively dance-club culture, and skyscraper lounges offer dazzling city views. The city's arts scene is also extraordinary: The opera is justifiably world renowned, the ballet is on its toes, the Asian Art Museum has settled into its Civic Center digs, and theaters are high in both quantity and quality. In short, there's always something going on, so get out there.

For up-to-date nightlife information, turn to the *San Francisco Weekly* (www.sfweekly.com) and the *San Francisco Bay Guardian* (www.sfbg.com), both of which run comprehensive listings. They are available free at bars and restaurants and from street-corner boxes all around the city. *Where* (www.wheresf.com), a free tourist-oriented monthly, also lists programs and performance times; it's available in most of the city's finer hotels. The Sunday edition of the *San Francisco Chronicle* features a "Datebook" section, printed on pink paper, with information on and listings of the week's events. If you have Internet access, it's a good idea to check out www.citysearch.com or www.sfstation.com for the latest in bars, clubs, and events. And if you want to secure seats at a hot-ticket event, either buy well in advance or contact the concierge of your hotel and see if they can't swing something for you.

Typically, cover charges at most clubs and rooftop lounges range from $5 to $10; if it's anything over that, you're probably paying too much. Note that most clubs waive cover charges during the week, but overall you should expect to spend at least $20 on admission and a few drinks. Opera, symphony, ballet, and major theatrical tickets are usually pricey, ranging from $25 to $140; but if you can wait until the night of the performance, you may be able to get in for half-price (see "Getting Tickets" below).

For information on local theater, check out www.bayareatheatre.org. For information on major league baseball, pro basketball, pro and college football, and horse racing, see the "Spectator Sports" section of chapter 8, beginning on p. 188.

And don't forget that bars close at 2am, so you'll need to get an early start if you want a full night on the town here.

GETTING TICKETS **Tix Bay Area** (℡ 415/433-7827; www.tixbayarea.org) sells half-price tickets to theater, dance, and music performances on the day of the show only; tickets for Sunday and Monday events, if available, are sold on Saturday and Sunday. Tix Bay Area also sells advance, full-price tickets for most performance halls, sporting events, concerts, and clubs. Tickets are sold only in person and not over the phone or via the Web. To find out which shows they are selling half-price tickets for, call their info line or check out their website. A service charge, ranging from $1.75 to $5, is levied on each ticket depending on its price. You can pay with cash, traveler's checks, Visa, MasterCard, American Express, or Discover Card with photo ID.

Tix, located on Powell Street between Geary and Post streets, is open Tuesday through Thursday from 11am to 6pm, Friday from 11am to 7pm, Saturday from 10am to 7pm, and Sunday from 10am to 3pm. *Note:* Half-price tickets go on sale at 11am.

You can also get tickets to most theater and dance events through **City Box Office,** 180 Redwood St., Suite 100, between Golden Gate and McAllister streets off Van Ness Avenue (© **415/392-4400;** www.city

boxoffice.com). MasterCard and Visa are accepted.

Tickets.com (© **415/478-2277** or 510/762-2277; www.tickets.com) sells computer-generated tickets (with a hefty service charge of $3–$19 convenience fee per ticket) to concerts, sporting events, plays, and special events. **Ticketmaster** (© **415/421-TIXS;** www.ticketmaster. com) also offers advance ticket purchases (also with a service charge).

1 The Performing Arts

Special concerts and performances take place in San Francisco year-round. **San Francisco Performances,** 500 Sutter St., Suite 710 (© **415/398-6449;** www.performances. org), has brought acclaimed artists to the Bay Area for 25 years. Shows run the gamut from chamber music to dance to jazz. Performances are held at several venues, including the Herbst Theater and the Center for the Performing Arts at Yerba Buena Center. The season runs from late September to June. Tickets cost from $12 to $60 and are available through **City Box Office** (© **415/392-2545**) or through the San Francisco Performances website.

CLASSICAL MUSIC

Philharmonia Baroque Orchestra   This early music orchestra performs in San Francisco and all around the Bay Area. The season lasts September through April. Performing in Herbst Theater, 401 Van Ness Ave. © 415/392-4400 (box office) or 415/252-1288 (administrative offices). www.philharmonia.org. Tickets $28–$62.

San Francisco Symphony 👁👁   Founded in 1911, the internationally respected San Francisco Symphony has long been an important part of the city's cultural life under such legendary conductors as Pierre Monteux and Seiji Ozawa. In 1995, Michael Tilson Thomas took over from Herbert Blomstedt; he has led the orchestra to new heights and crafted an exciting repertoire of classical and modern music. The season runs September through June. Summer symphony activities include a Summer Festival and a Summer in the City series. Tickets are very hard to come by, but if you're desperate, you can usually pick up a few outside the hall the night of the concert. Also, the box office occasionally has a few last minute tickets. Performing at Davies Symphony Hall, 201 Van Ness Ave. (at Grove St.). © 415/864-6000 (box office). www.sfsymphony.org. Tickets $12–$103.

DANCE

In addition to the local companies, top traveling troupes like the Joffrey Ballet and the American Ballet Theatre make regular appearances in San Francisco. Primary modern dance spaces include the **Cowell Theater,** at Fort Mason Center, Marina Boulevard at Buchanan Street (© **415/345-7575**), and the **ODC Theatre,** 3153 17th St., at Shotwell Street in the Mission District (© **415/863-9834**). Check the local papers for schedules or contact the theater box offices for more information.

San Francisco Ballet   Founded in 1933, the San Francisco Ballet is the oldest professional ballet company in the United States and is regarded as one of the country's

> ### (*Value*) **Free Opera**
>
> Every year, the **San Francisco Opera** stages a number of free performances. A free performance of Opera in the Park launches the season in September, followed by occasional free performances throughout the city as part of the Brown Bag Opera program. Schedule details can be found on the company's website at **www.sfopera.com**.

finest. It performs an eclectic repertoire of full-length, neoclassical, and contemporary ballets. The 2006 Repertory Season runs February through May; the company performs *The Nutcracker* in late November through most of December. The San Francisco Ballet Orchestra accompanies most performances. War Memorial Opera House, 301 Van Ness Ave. (at Grove St.). (℃) 415/865-2000 for tickets and information. www.sfballet.org. Tickets $10–$165. Student rush tickets $15; standing room $10 (cash only for both).

OPERA

Besides San Francisco's major opera company, you might also check out the amusing **Pocket Opera,** 469 Bryant St. (℃ 415/972-8930; www.pocketopera.org). From early March to mid-July, the comic company stages farcical performances of well-known operas in English. The staging is intimate and informal, without lavish costumes and sets. The cast ranges from 3 to 16 players, supported by a chamber orchestra. The rich repertoire includes such works as *Don Giovanni, The Barber of Seville,* and over 80 other operas. Performances are primarily on Sundays at 2pm though there are occasionally shows on Saturdays. Call the box office for complete information, location (which varies), and show times. Tickets cost from $15 (students) to $30.

San Francisco Opera   The San Francisco Opera was the second municipal opera in the United States and is one of the city's cultural icons. Brilliantly balanced casts may feature celebrated stars like Frederica Von Stade and Plácido Domingo along with promising newcomers and regular members, in productions that range from traditional to avant-garde. All productions have English supertitles. The season starts in September, lasts 14 weeks, takes a break for a few months, and then picks up again in June and July. During the interim winter period, future opera stars are featured in showcases and recitals. Performances are held most evenings, except Monday, with matinees on Sundays. Tickets go on sale as early as June for subscribers and August for the general public, and the best seats sell out quickly. Unless Domingo is in town, some less coveted seats are usually available until curtain time. War Memorial Opera House, 301 Van Ness Ave. (at Grove St.). (℃) 415/864-3330 (box office). www.sfopera.com. Tickets $24–$235; student rush tickets $15; standing room $10 (cash only for both).

THEATER

American Conservatory Theater (A.C.T.) 🛠🛠 *Finds*   The Tony Award–winning American Conservatory Theater made its debut in 1967 and quickly established itself as the city's premier resident theater group and one of the nation's best. The A.C.T. season runs September through July and features both classic and experimental works. A.C.T. recently returned to its home, the fabulous **Geary Theater** (1910), a national historic landmark, after the theater sustained severe damage in the 1989 earthquake and closed for renovations. Now it is fully refurbished and modernized to such an extent that it's regarded as one of America's finest performance spaces. Performing at the Geary Theater, 415 Geary St. (at Mason St.). © **415/749-2ACT.** www.act-sf.org. Tickets $11–$68.

Eureka Theatre Company   Eureka produces contemporary plays September through June, and performances are usually Wednesday through Sunday. 215 Jackson St. (between Battery and Front sts.). © **415/788-7469.** www.eurekatheatre.org or www.tickets.com. Tickets $17–$30; discounts for students and seniors.

Lorraine Hansberry Theatre   San Francisco's top African-American theater group performs in a 300-seat theater off the lobby of the Sheehan Hotel, near Mason Street. It mounts special adaptations from literature along with contemporary dramas, classics, and music. 2006 marks the theater's 25th anniversary and with it will likely come some special performances. Phone for dates and programs. Performing at 620 Sutter St. (at Mason St.). © **415/474-8800.** www.lhtsf.org. Tickets $25–$32.

The Magic Theatre   The highly acclaimed Magic Theatre is a major West Coast company dedicated to presenting the works of new plays; over the years it has nurtured the talents of such luminaries as Sam Shepard and Jon Robin Baitz. Shepard's Pulitzer Prize–winning play *Buried Child* had its premiere here, as did *Body Familiar* by Joe Goode. The season usually runs October through June; performances are held Tuesday through Sunday. An added perk: They just redecorated the lobby in 2005 and added new seats in one of the theaters. Performing at Building D, Fort Mason Center, Marina Boulevard (at Buchanan St.). © **415/441-8822.** www.magictheatre.org. Tickets $20–$38; discounts for students, educators, and seniors.

Theatre Rhinoceros   Founded in 1977, this was America's first (and remains its foremost) theater ensemble devoted solely to works addressing gay, lesbian, bisexual, and transgender issues. The company presents main-stage shows and studio productions of new and classic works each year. 2926 16th St. © **415/861-5079.** www.therhino.org. Tickets $15–$35. The theater is 1 block east of the 16th Street/Mission BART station.

2 Comedy & Cabaret

BATS Improv *Finds*   Combining improvisation with competition, BATS operates an improvisational tournament in which four-actor teams compete against each other, taking on hilarious suggestions from the audience. There are also long-form shows throughout the year with improvisations of movies, musicals, and even Shakespeare. The audience supplies a title for the performers and the plot, characters and dialogue are all made up right there on the spot. Shows are Friday through Sunday at 8pm. Reservations can only be made through their website. Remaining tickets are sold at the box office the night of the show. Performing at Bayfront Theatre at the Fort Mason Center, Building B, no. 350, 3rd floor. © **415/474-8935.** www.improv.org. Tickets $8–$15.

Beach Blanket Babylon *★★★ Moments*   A San Francisco tradition, *Beach Blanket Babylon* evolved from Steve Silver's Rent-a-Freak service—a group of party-givers extraordinaire who hired themselves out as a "cast of characters" complete with fabulous costumes and sets, props, and gags. After their act caught on, it moved into the Savoy-Tivoli, a North Beach bar. By 1974, the audience had grown too large for the facility, and *Beach Blanket* has been at the 400-seat Club Fugazi ever since. The show is a comedic musical send-up that is best known for outrageous costumes and oversize headdresses. It's been playing for 32 years, and almost every performance sells out. The show is updated often enough that locals still attend. Those under 21 are welcome at

Sunday matinees, when no alcohol is served; photo ID is required for evening performances. Write for weekend tickets at least 3 weeks in advance, or get them through their website or by calling their box office. *Note:* There are only 44 tickets per show with assigned seating. All other tickets are within specific sections depending on price, but seating is first-come, first-seated within that section. Performances are Wednesday and Thursday at 8pm, Friday and Saturday at 7 and 10pm, and Sunday at 1 and 4pm. At Club Fugazi, Beach Blanket Babylon Boulevard, 678 Green St. (between Powell St. and Columbus Ave.). ℂ 415/421-4222. www.beachblanketbabylon.com. Tickets $25–$75.

Cobb's Comedy Club   Cobb's features such national headliners as Joe Rogan, Brian Regan, and Jake Johannsen. There is comedy Wednesday through Sunday, including a 15-comedian All-Pro Wednesday showcase (a 3-hr. marathon). Cobb's is open to those 18 and older, and occasionally to kids ages 16 and 17 when accompanied by a parent or legal guardian (call ahead). Shows are held Wednesday, Thursday, and Sunday at 8pm, Friday and Saturday at 8 and 10:15pm. 915 Columbus Ave. (at Lombard St.). ℂ 415/928-4320. www.cobbscomedy.com. Cover $15–$30. 2-beverage minimum.

Punch Line Comedy Club   Adjacent to the Embarcadero One office building, this is the largest comedy nightclub in the city. Three-person shows with top national and local talent are featured here Tuesday through Saturday. Showcase night is Sunday, when 15 comics take the mic. There's an all-star showcase or a special event on Monday. Shows are Tuesday through Thursday and Sunday at 9pm, Friday and Saturday at 9 and 11pm. 444 Battery St. (between Washington and Clay sts.), plaza level. ℂ 415/397-4337 or 415/397-7573 for recorded information. www.punchlinecomedyclub.com. Cover $5 Mon; $7.50 Sun; $10–$25 Tues–Sat. 2-drink minimum.

3 The Club & Music Scene

The greatest legacy from the 1960s is the city's continued tradition of live entertainment and music, which explains the great variety of clubs and music enjoyed by San Francisco. The hippest dance places are South of Market Street (SoMa), in former warehouses; the artsy bohemian scene centers are in the Mission; and the most popular cafe culture is still in North Beach.

Drink prices at most bars, clubs, and cafes range from about $3.50 to $9, unless otherwise noted. Most San Francisco nightclubs are open daily, from around 8pm till 2 pm. I've noted exceptions below.

Note: The club and music scene is always changing, often outdating recommendations before the ink can dry on a page. Most of the venues below are promoted as different clubs on various nights of the week, each with its own look, sound, and style. Discount passes and club announcements are often available at clothing stores and other shops along upper Haight Street.

Tips **Club-Hopping Tour**

If you prefer to let someone else take the lead (and the driver's seat) for a night out, contact **3 Babes and a Bus** (ℂ **800/414-0158**; www.threebabes.com). The nightclub tour company (the head babe is a stockbroker by day) will take you and a gaggle of 20- to 40-something partyers (mostly single women) out on the town, skipping lines and cover charges, for $35 per person.

DANCE CLUBS

Although a lot of clubs allow dancing, the following are the places to go if all you want to do is shake your groove thang.

The EndUp This unique party space with a huge heated outdoor deck (with waterfall and fountain), indoor fireplace, and eclectic clientele has always thrown some of the most kickin' parties in town. There's a different theme every night: Thursday's Wind Up offers up a variety of house DJs; Fag Friday is just what it sounds like, plus lots of throw-down dancing; and The EndUp is ever-popular with the sleepless dance-all-day crowd that comes here after the other clubs close (it's open Sat morning from 6am–noon and then nonstop from Sat night around 10pm until Sun night/Mon morning at 4am). Call to confirm nights—offerings change from time to time. 401 Sixth St. (at Harrison St.). © 415/357-0827. www.theendup.com. Cover $5–$15.

The Factory The maze of rooms and nonstop barrage of house, funk, lounge vibes, salsa, and club classics attract swarms of young urbanites (read: 21- to 25-year-olds) here looking to rave it up. Management tries to eliminate the riffraff by enforcing a dress code (collared shirts and boots for men and no sports caps). Open Saturday only 9:30pm–3:30am. 525 Harrison St. (at First St.). © 415/339-8686. Cover $20.

Nickie's Bar-be-cue Don't show up here for dinner—the only hot thing you'll find is the small, crowded dance floor. But don't let that stop you from checking it out—Nickie's is a sure thing. Here the old-school hits are in full force, casually dressed young dancers lose all their inhibitions, and the crowd consists of all types of friendly San Franciscans. This place is perpetually hot, so dress accordingly; you can always cool down with a pint from the wine-and-beer bar. Keep in mind that lower Haight is on the periphery of a shady neighborhood, so don't make your car look tempting, and stay alert as you walk through the area. Closed on Sundays. 460 Haight St. (between Fillmore and Webster sts.). © 415/621-6508. www.nickies.com. Cover $5.

Paradise Lounge Labyrinthine Paradise features three dance floors simultaneously vibrating to different beats ranging from house and R&B to hip-hop and occasional live events. Smaller auxiliary spaces host private parties or rentable tables. The crowd ranges from everyday party people to more upscale folks. Open Thursday through Saturday only. Dress code enforced. 1501 Folsom St. (at 11th St.). © 415/621-1911. www.paradise lounge.com. Cover $5–$20.

Ruby Skye Downtown's most glamorous and gigantic nightspot is all aglitter thanks to a dramatic renovation and the addition of killer light and sound systems within the 1890s Victorian playhouse previously known as The Stage Door. Inside, hundreds of partyers boogie on the ballroom floor to house music, mingle on the mezzanine and around the three bars, and puff freely in the smoking room while DJs or live music bring down the dancing house Thursdays through Saturdays. Big spenders should book the VIP lounge, which offers glitzy, bird's-eye views of the whole club scene. 420 Mason St. (between Geary and Post sts.). © 415/693-0777. www.rubyskye.com. Cover $20–$25.

JAZZ & LATIN CLUBS

Cafe du Nord ⟲ *(Finds* Although it's been around since 1907, this basement supper club is rightfully self-proclaimed as the place for a "slightly lurid indie pop scene set in a beautiful old speakeasy." It's also where you'll find an eclectic (and usually younger generation) crowd that flocks here to linger at the front room's 40-foot mahogany bar or dine on the likes of phylo-wrapped prawns with romesco sauce or sip cocktails at

Tips **Scope-a-Scene**

The local newspapers won't direct you to the city's underground club scene, nor will they advise you which of the dozens of clubs are truly hot. To get clued in, check out reviews from the clubbers themselves at www.sfstation.com. The far more commercial **Club Line** (© **415/339-8686**; www.sfclubs.com) offers up-to-date schedules for the city's larger dance venues.

the back room tables—while listening to live rock and singer/songwriter music. *Note:* If Lavay Smith and Her Red Hot Skillet Lickers or Ledici are in the house, definitely don't miss them. 2170 Market St. (at Sanchez St.). © **415/861-5016**. www.cafedunord.com. Cover $5–$15.

Jazz at Pearl's *®* One of the best jazz venues in the city. See "Supper Clubs" below.

Rasselas Large, casual, and comfortable with couches and small tables, this is a favorite spot for local jazz, blues, soul, and R&B combos. The adjacent restaurant serves Ethiopian cuisine in a Bedouin tent. Menu items range from $4 to $14. 1534 Fillmore St. (at Geary Blvd.). © **415/567-5010**. www.rasselasjazzclub.com. 2-drink minimum. Cover $7 Fri–Sat.

A RETRO CLUB

Club Deluxe *(Finds* Long before the 1940s trend hit the city circa *Swingers,* Deluxe and its fedora-wearing clientele had been celebrating the bygone era for years. Fortunately, even with all the retro hype, the vibe here hasn't changed. Expect an eclectic mix of throwbacks and generic San Franciscans in the intimate bar and adjoining lounge, and live jazz or swing most nights. Although many regulars dress the part, there's no attitude here, so come as you like. 1511 Haight St. (at Ashbury St.). © **415/552-6949**. Cover $3–$10. www.clubdeluxesf.com.

ROCK & BLUES CLUBS

In addition to the following listings, see "Dance Clubs," below, for (usually) live, danceable rock.

Biscuits and Blues *®* With a crisp, blow-your-eardrums-out sound system, New Orleans–speakeasy (albeit commercial) appeal, and a nightly lineup of live entertainment, there's no better place to muse the blues than this basement-cum-nightclub. During performances, covers range, but there's a daily happy hour from 5 to 7pm, when there's usually recorded music, drink specials, and inexpensive snacks. Dinner is served nightly in their new quieter restaurant (entrees $15–$20), which opens at 5:30pm. Their namesake—moist, flaky biscuits—are served in the bar and dining room. 401 Mason (at Geary St.). © **415/292-2583**. www.biscuitsandblues.com. Cover (during performances) $5–$20.

The Boom Boom Room *® (Finds* The late John Lee Hooker and his partner Alex Andreas bought this Western Addition club several years back and used Hooker's star power to pull in some of the best blues bands in the country (even the Stones showed up for an unannounced jam session). Though it changed focus and is now a roots music oriented club, it's still a fun, dark, small, cramped, and steamy joint where you can hear good live tunes—ranging from New Orleans funk, soul, and new wave to drum 'n' bass, electronica, house, and more—6 nights a week until 2am. If you're going to The Fillmore (see below) to see a band, stop by here first for a drink and come back after your show for more great music. The neighborhood's a bit rough, so be sure to park in the underground lot across the street. 1601 Fillmore St. (at Geary Blvd.). ℂ 415/ 673-8000. www.boomboomblues.com. Cover varies from free to $15.

Bottom of the Hill ⓥ𝑎𝑙𝑢𝑒   Voted one of the best places to hear live rock in the city by the *San Francisco Bay Guardian,* this popular neighborhood club attracts an eclectic crowd ranging from rockers to real-estate salespeople. The main attraction is live music every night, but the club also offers pretty good burgers and a bar menu, outdoor seating on the back patio, and an awesome barbecue on Sundays from April through August from 4 to 7pm. Happy hour runs Wednesdays to Fridays from 4 to 7pm. 1233 17th St. (at Missouri St.). ℂ 415/621-4455. www.bottomofthehill.com. Cover $6–$12.

Empire Plush Room ⓕinds   San Francisco is woefully short on cabaret and jazz venues, but thanks to the Plush Room, there's still one swank little boutique establishment that lures national talent on stage. Check out their schedule and perhaps you'll get to catch a burlesque show or locals such as Paula West, Wesla Whitfield, Faith Winthrop, Jacqui Naylor, or others doing their classic and under-celebrated thing. Come thirsty: There's a two-drink minimum. In the York Hotel, 940 Sutter St. (between Hyde and Leavenworth sts.). ℂ 415/885-2800. www.empireplushroom.com. Tickets $20–$55. 2 drink minimum.

The Fillmore ⓕ   Made famous by promoter Bill Graham in the 1960s, the Fillmore showcases big names in a moderately sized standing room only space. Check listings in papers, call the theater, or visit their website for information on upcoming events. And if you make it to a show, check out the fabulous collection of vintage concert posters chronicling the hall's history. 1805 Geary Blvd. (at Fillmore St.). ℂ 415/346-6000. www. thefillmore.com. Tickets $17–$45.

Grant & Green Saloon   The atmosphere at this historic North Beach dive bar is not that special, but the local bands (live music usually on weekends only) are pretty good and the space is an all-around good place to let your hair down. 1371 Grant Ave. (at Green St.). ℂ 415/693-9565. www.grantandgreen.com.

Lou's Pier 47 Club   You won't find many locals in the place, but Lou's happens to be good, old-fashioned fun. It's a casual spot where you can let your hair down with

---

Ⓣ*ips* Local Talent

Want to see the best of local jazz, cabaret, or blues performers? Check the *San Francisco Chronicle*'s Sunday "Datebook" to see if the following artists are in the house. Better yet, buy their CDs and take San Francisco's music scene home with you:

- **Faith Winthrop,** a veteran cabaret diva with a velvet voice and heartfelt delivery.
- **Ledisi,** a young local blues singer with a penchant for scatting and smoky, deep, soulful self-written tunes.
- **Jacqui Naylor,** a seductive young talent with a love for standards and reinventing a phrase with her own modern twist.
- **Lavay Smith & Her Red Hot Skillet Lickers**—swing hasn't swung this hard since it was invented.

Cajun seafood (downstairs) and live blues bands (upstairs). A vacation attitude makes the place one of the more, um, jovial spots near the wharf. There's a $3 to $5 cover for bands that play between 4 and 7 or 8pm and a $5 to $10 cover for bands that play between 8 or 9pm and midnight or 1am. 300 Jefferson St. (at Jones St.). © **415/771-5687.** www.louspier47.com. Cover $3–$10.

Pier 23   If there's one good-time destination that's an anchor for San Francisco's party people, it's the Embarcadero's Pier 23. Part ramshackle patio spot and part dance floor with a heavy dash of dive bar, here it's all about fun for a startlingly diverse clientele. The well-worn box of a restaurant with tented patio is a prime sunny-day social spot for white collars, but on weekends, it's a straight-up people zoo where every age and persuasion coexists more peacefully than the cast in a McDonald's commercial. Expect to dance shoulder-to-shoulder to 1980s hits and leave with the contagious feel-good vibe. Pier 23, at the Embarcadero (at Battery St.). © **415/362-5125.** www.pier23cafe.com. Cover $5–$8 during performances.

The Saloon   An authentic gold rush survivor, this North Beach dive is the oldest bar in the city. Popular with both bikers and daytime pinstripers, it schedules live blues nightly and afternoons Friday through Sunday. 1232 Grant Ave. (at Columbus St.). © **415/ 989-7666.** Cover $5–$10 Fri–Sat.

Slim's   Co-owned by musician Boz Scaggs, this glitzy restaurant and bar serves California cuisine and seats 200, but it's usually standing room only during almost nightly shows ranging from performers of homegrown rock, jazz, blues, and alternative music. An added bonus for the musically inclined family: All ages are always welcome. Call or check their website for a schedule; hot bands sell out in advance. 333 11th St. (at Folsom St.). © **415/522-0333.** www.slims-sf.com. Cover free to $30.

SUPPER CLUBS

If you can eat dinner, listen to live music, and dance (or at least wiggle in your chair) in the same room, it's a supper club—those are our criteria here.

Harry Denton's Starlight Room 👁👁 *Moments*   Come to this celestial high-rise cocktail lounge and nightclub, where tourists and locals watch the sunset at dusk and groove to live '70s, '80s, Motown covers, and jazz and funk Friday through Tuesday nights; live Salsa on Thursday nights; or the DJs' hip-hop and Top-40 tunes after dark on Wednesdays. The room is classic 1930s San Francisco, with red-velvet banquettes, chandeliers, and fabulous views. But what really attracts flocks of all ages is a night of Harry Denton–style fun, which usually includes plenty of drinking and unrestrained dancing. The full bar stocks a decent collection of single-malt Scotches and champagnes, and you can snack from the pricey Starlight appetizer menu (make a reservation to guarantee a table and you'll also have a place to rest your weary dancing-dogs). Early evening is more relaxed, but come the weekend, this place gets loose. *Tip:* Come dressed for success (no casual jeans, open-toed shoes for men, or sneakers), or you'll be turned away at the door. Atop the Sir Francis Drake hotel, 450 Powell St., 21st floor. © **415/395-8595.** www.harrydenton.com. Cover $10 Wed after 7pm; $10 Thurs–Fri after 8pm; $15 Sat after 8pm.

Jazz at Pearl's   A change of ownership in 2003 converted one of the best jazz venues in the city into one of the best supper clubs. Voted Top 30 Club Worldwide by *Condé Nast Travel Magazine* in 2005, Jazz at Pearl's combines Spanish and French cuisine with great live music. Doors open at 7pm, first show starts at 8:30pm with a second at 10:30pm. 256 Columbus Ave. (at Broadway). © **415/291-8255.** www.jazzatpearls.com. Tickets $10–$75.

Julie's Supper Club   Julie's is a longtime standby for cocktails and late dining in a groovy setting. The vibe in both rooms is very 1950s cartoon, with a space-age Jetsons appeal and good-looking singles on the prowl. The food is hit-or-miss, but the atmosphere is definitely a winner—casual and playful—and it comes with a little interesting history: This building is one location where the Symbionese Liberation Army held Patty Hearst hostage in the 1970s. Menu items range from $6 to $20 and happy hour, Wednesday through Saturday from 5pm to 7:30pm, includes free snacks and discounted drinks. 1123 Folsom St. (at Seventh St.). © 415/861-0707. www.juliessupperclub.com.

4 The Bar Scene

Finding your idea of a comfortable bar has a lot to do with picking a neighborhood filled with your kind of people and investigating that area. There are hundreds of bars throughout San Francisco, and although many are obscurely located and can't be classified by their neighborhood, the following is a general description of what you'll find, and where:

- **Chestnut and Union Street** bars attract a post-collegiate crowd.
- Young alternatives frequent **Mission District** haunts.
- **Upper Haight** caters to eclectic neighborhood cocktailers.
- **Lower Haight** is skate- and snowboarder grungy.
- Tourists mix with theatergoers and thirsty businesspeople in **downtown** pubs.
- **North Beach** serves all types.
- **The Castro** caters to gay locals and tourists.
- **SoMa** offers an eclectic mix.

The following is a list of a few of San Francisco's most interesting bars. Unless otherwise noted, these bars do not have cover charges. Also, most San Francisco bars are open daily, from around 6pm and stay open till 2 pm. I've noted exceptions below.

Buena Vista Café *(Moments)*   "Did you have an Irish coffee at the Buena Vista?" The myth is that the Irish coffee was invented at the Buena Vista, but the real story is that this popular wharf cafe was the first bar in the country to serve Irish coffee after a local journalist came back from a trip and described the drink to the bartender. Since then, the bar has poured more of these pick-me-up drinks than any other bar in the world, and ordering one has become a San Francisco must-do. Fact is, it's entertaining just to watch the venerable tenders pour up to 10 whiskey-laden coffees at a time (a rather messy event). The cafe is in a prime tourist spot along the wharf, so plan on waiting for a stool or table to free up. And don't worry if you need a little snack to soak up the booze—they serve food here, too. 2765 Hyde St. (at Beach St.). © 415/474-5044. www.thebuenavista.com.

Edinburgh Castle   Since 1958, this legendary Scottish pub has been known for unusual British ales on tap and the best selection of single-malt Scotches in the city. The huge pub is decorated with horse brasses, steel helmets, and an authentic Ballantine caber (a long wooden pole) used in the annual Scottish games. Fish and chips and other traditional foods are available until 11pm. 950 Geary St. (between Polk and Larkin sts.). © 415/885-4074. www.castlenews.com.

Li Po Cocktail Lounge *(Finds)*   A dim, divey, slightly spooky Chinese bar that was once an opium den, Li Po's alluring character stems from its mishmash clutter of dusty Asian furnishings and mementos, including an unbelievably huge ancient rice-paper

---

Tips **Smoke it Outside**

California forbids smoking in bars, restaurants, hotel lobbies, and public areas of any kind. Some bars break the rules. Others ask their guests to step out-side. Either way, don't count on lighting up inside any public place. Establish-ment owners are quick to enforce the rule because they can be fined if patrons disobey.

---

lantern hanging from the ceiling and a glittery golden shrine to Buddha behind the bar. The bartenders love to creep out patrons with tales of opium junkies haunting the joint. 916 Grant Ave. (between Washington and Jackson sts.). ✆ 415/982-0072.

Matrix Fillmore   Closetlike booths with privacy curtains and side tables in shapes of "S," "E," and "X" spell out that this remains one of the young and yuppies' hottest singles scenes despite its dramatic detour from its previous life as the Pierce Street Annex. Those already spoken for can still appreciate the slick lounge atmosphere of candlelight, dark woods and walls, flatscreen TVs, and free-standing centerpiece fire-place with its Lincoln Log–like mantel—not to mention bar snacks like ahi tuna cones and smoked chicken quesadillas. Though it's a martini and mojito crowd, the bar also offers 15 wines by the glass and a large by-the-bottle selection including cult classics like Dalla Valle. Drinks range from $7 to $10. 3138 Fillmore St. (between Greenwich and Fil-bert sts.). ✆ 415/563-4180. www.plumpjack.com/pjmatrix.

Perry's   If you read *Tales of the City,* you already know that this bar and restaurant has a colorful history as a pickup place for Pacific Heights and Marina singles. Although the times are not as wild today, locals still come to casually check out the happenings at the dark mahogany bar. A separate dining room offers breakfast, lunch, dinner, and weekend brunch. It's a good place for hamburgers, simple fish dishes, and pasta. Menu items range from $6 to $22. 1944 Union St. (at Laguna St.). ✆ 415/922-9022. www.perrysunionst.citysearch.com.

Pied Piper Bar   The huge Pied Piper mural by Edwardian illustrator Maxfield Par-rish steals the show at this historic mahogany bar, where high stakes were once won and lost on the roll of the dice. Happy hour Wednesday through Friday features a complimentary buffet and 75¢ oysters on Fridays. In the Palace Hotel, 2 New Montgomery (at Market St.). ✆ 415/512-1111.

The Red Room   Ultramodern, small, and deliciously dim, this lounge reflects no other color but ruby red. It's a sexy place to sip the latest cocktail. In the Commodore Hotel, 827 Sutter St. (at Jones St.). ✆ 415/346-7666.

The Redwood Room   Hotelier Ian Schrager renovated this historic Art Deco room flanked in redwood paneling and illuminated with beautiful sconces in 2001. It retains its gorgeous redwood interior made from a single 2,000-year-old tree, but the vibe is definitely updated to attract swinging singles, the tragically hip, and posers who mix, mingle, and seem to have a pretty fab and glamorous time here despite steep drink prices ($9–$15). In the Clift Hotel, 495 Geary St. ✆ 415/775-4700.

Spec's *Finds*   The location of Spec's—Saroyan Place, a tiny alley at 250 Columbus Ave.—makes it less of a walk-in bar and more of a lively local hangout. Its funky decor—maritime flags hang from the ceiling; posters, photos, and oddities line the exposed-brick walls—gives it a character that intrigues every visitor. A "museum," displayed under glass, contains memorabilia and items brought back by seamen who drop in between voyages. The clientele is funky enough to keep you preoccupied while you drink a beer. 12 Saroyan Place (at 250 Columbus Ave.). ℂ 415/421-4112.

The Tonga Room & Hurricane Bar 𝒦 *Finds* It's kitschy as all get out, but there's no denying the goofy Polynesian pleasures of the Fairmont Hotel's tropical oasis. Drop in and join the crowds for an umbrella drink, a simulated thunderstorm and downpour, and a heavy dose of whimsy that escapes most San Francisco establishments. If you're on a budget, you'll definitely want to stop by for the weekday happy hour from 5 to 7pm, when you can stuff your face at the all-you-can-eat bar-grub buffet (chicken wings, chow mein, pot stickers) for $7 and the cost of one drink. Settle in and you'll catch live Top-40 music after 8pm Wednesday through Saturday. In the Fairmont Hotel, 950 Mason St. (at California St.). ℂ 415/772-5278. www.tongaroom.com. Cover $3–$5 Wed–Sat.

Toronado Lower Haight isn't exactly a charming street, but there's plenty of nightlife here, catering to an artistic/grungy/skateboarding 20-something crowd. While Toronado definitely draws in the young'uns, its 50-plus microbrews on tap and 100 bottled beers also entice a more eclectic clientele in search of beer heaven. The brooding atmosphere matches the surroundings: an aluminum bar, a few tall tables, dark lighting, and a back room packed with tables and chairs. Happy hour runs 11:30am to 6pm everyday with $1 off draft beers. 547 Haight St. (at Fillmore St.). ℂ 415/863-2276. www.toronado.com.

Tosca *Finds* Open Tuesday through Sunday from 5pm to 2am, Tosca is a low-key and large popular watering hole for local politicos, writers, media types, incognito visiting celebrities, such as Johnny Depp or Nicholas Cage, and similar cognoscenti of unassuming classic characters. Equipped with dim lights, red leather booths, and high ceilings, it's everything you'd expect an old North Beach legend to be. 242 Columbus Ave. (between Broadway and Pacific Ave.). ℂ 415/986-9651.

Vesuvio 𝒦 Situated along Jack Kerouac Alley, across from the famed City Lights bookstore, this renowned literary beatnik hangout is packed to the second-floor rafters with neighborhood writers, artists, songsters, wannabes, and everyone else ranging from longshoremen and cab drivers to businesspeople, all of whom come for the laid-back atmosphere. The convivial space is two stories of cocktail tables, complemented by a changing exhibition of local art. In addition to drinks, Vesuvio features an espresso machine. No credit cards. 255 Columbus Ave. (at Broadway). ℂ 415/362-3370. www.vesuvio.com.

BREWPUBS

Gordon Biersch Brewery Restaurant Gordon Biersch Brewery is San Francisco's largest brew restaurant, serving decent food and tasty beer to an attractive crowd of mingling professionals. There are always several beers to choose from, ranging from light to dark. Menu items run $9.50 to $20. (See p. 111 for more information.) 2 Harrison St. (on the Embarcadero). ℂ 415/243-8246. www.gordonbiersch.com.

San Francisco Brewing Company Surprisingly low key for an alehouse, this cozy brewpub serves its creations with burgers, fries, grilled chicken breast, and the like. The bar is one of the city's few remaining old saloons (ca. 1907), aglow with stained-glass windows, tile floors, a skylit ceiling, beveled glass, and a mahogany bar. A massive overhead fan runs the full length of the bar—a bizarre contraption crafted from brass and palm fronds. The handmade copper brew kettle is visible from the street.

Most evenings the place is packed with everyday folks enjoying music, darts, chess, backgammon, cards, dice and, of course, beer. Menu items range from $3.70—curiously, for edamame (soybeans)—to $20 for a full rack of baby back ribs with all the fixings. The happy-hour special, an 8½-ounce microbrew beer for a dollar (or a pint for $2.50), is offered daily from 4 to 6pm and midnight to 1am. 155 Columbus Ave. (at Pacific St.). ℂ 415/434-3344. www.sfbrewing.com.

ThirstyBear Brewing Company   Nine superb, handcrafted varieties of brew are always on tap at this stylish high-ceilinged brick edifice. Good Spanish food is served here, too. Pool tables and dartboards are upstairs, and live flamenco can be heard on Sunday nights. 661 Howard St. (1 block east of the Moscone Center). ℂ 415/974-0905. www.thirstybear.com.

COCKTAILS WITH A VIEW

See "Supper Clubs," above, for a full review of **Harry Denton's Starlight Room.** Unless otherwise noted, these establishments have no cover charge.

Carnelian Room   On the 52nd floor of the Bank of America Building, the Carnelian Room offers uninterrupted views of the city. From a window-front table you feel as though you can reach out, pluck up the TransAmerica Pyramid, and stir your martini with it. In addition to cocktails, the restaurant serves a three-course meal ($45 per person) as well as a la carte items ($22–$50 for main entrees). Jackets are required and ties for men are optional, but encouraged. *Note:* The restaurant has one of the most extensive wine lists in the city—1,600 selections, to be exact. 555 California St., in the Bank of America Building (between Kearny and Montgomery sts.). ℂ 415/433-7500. www.carnelianroom.com.

Finds   **Midnight (or Midday) Mochas**

If you happen to be wandering around North Beach past your bedtime and need your caffeine fix, seek out these two cafes. They offer not only excellent espresso, but also a glimpse back at the days of the beatniks, when nothing was as crucial as a strong cup of coffee, a good smoke, and a stimulating environment.

Doing the North Beach thing is little more than hanging out in a sophisticated but relaxed atmosphere over a well-made cappuccino. You can do it at **Caffè Greco,** 423 Columbus Ave., between Green and Vallejo streets (ℂ 415/397-6261), and grab a bite, too—until midnight. The affordable cafe fare includes beer and wine as well as a good selection of coffees, focaccia sandwiches, and desserts (try the gelato or homemade tiramisu).

Caffè Trieste, 601 Vallejo St., at Grant Avenue (ℂ 415/392-6739; www. caffetrieste.com), is one of San Francisco's most beloved cafes—very downhome Italian, with espresso drinks, wine, pizza, and pastries at indoor and outdoor seating. Opera is always on the jukebox, unless it's Saturday afternoon, when the family and their friends break out in arias during an operatic performance from 2 to 5pm every other Saturday. Another perk: They offer access to free Wi-Fi with purchase, but you'll have to bring your own laptop. Check 'em out until 10pm Sunday through Thursday and midnight on Friday and Saturday.

Cityscape   When you sit under the glass roof and sip a drink here, it's as though you're sitting out under the stars and enjoying views of the bay. Dinner, focusing on California cuisine, is available (though not destination worthy), and there's dancing to a DJ's picks nightly from 10:30pm. The mirrored columns and floor-to-ceiling windows help create an elegant and romantic ambience. *FYI:* They also offer a live jazz champagne brunch on Sundays from 10am to 2pm. Hilton San Francisco, Tower I, 333 O'Farrell St. (at Mason St.), 46th floor. ℰ 415/923-5002. Cover $10 Fri and Sat nights.

Equinox   Though locals don't frequent this Fi-Di (Financial District) place, it's very popular with tourists. The hook? The 17-story Hyatt's rooftop restaurant has a revolving floor that gives each table a 360-degree panoramic view of the city every 45 minutes. In addition to cocktails, the Equinox serves dinner daily. In the Hyatt Regency Hotel, 5 Embarcadero Center. ℰ 415/788-1234.

Top of the Mark *(Moments)*   This is one of the most famous cocktail lounges in the world, and for good reason—the spectacular glass-walled room features an unparalleled 19th-floor view. During World War II, Pacific-bound servicemen toasted their goodbyes to the States here. While less dramatic today than they were back then, evenings spent here are still sentimental, thanks to the romantic atmosphere. Live bands play throughout the week; Jazz on Tuesdays starts at 7pm; Salsa on Wednesdays begins at 9pm; and a dance band playing everything from 50s through contemporary music happens Fridays and Saturdays starting at 9pm. Drinks range from $7 to $10. A $59 three-course fixed-price sunset dinner is served Friday and Saturday at 7:30pm. Sunday brunch, served from 10am to 2pm, costs $59 for adults and includes a glass of champagne; for children 4 to 12, the brunch is $30. In the Mark Hopkins Inter-Continental, 1 Nob Hill (California and Mason sts.). ℰ 415/616-6916. Cover $5–$10.

DESTINATION BARS WITH DJ GROOVES

Bambuddha Lounge *(Finds)*   The hottest place for the young and the trendy to feast, flirt, or just be fabulous is this restaurant/bar adjoining the funky-cool Phoenix Hotel. With a 20-foot reclining Buddha on the roof, ultramodern San Francisco–meets–Southeast Asian decor (including waterfalls in the dining room and outdoor poolside cocktail lounge and *salas,* Balinese-style outdoor lounge areas by an outdoor pool), very affordable and above-average Southeast Asian cuisine served late into the evening and topping out at $22, and a state-of-the-art sound system streaming ambient, down-tempo, soul, funk, and house music, this is the "it" joint of the moment. 601 Eddy St. (at Larkin St.). ℰ 415/885-5088. www.bambuddhalounge.com. Cover $5–$10 Thurs–Sat.

The Bliss Bar   Surprisingly trendy for sleepy family-oriented Noe Valley, this small, stylish, and friendly bar is a great place to stop for a varied mix of locals, colorful cocktail concoctions, and a DJ spinning at the front window from 9pm to 2am every night except Monday. If it's open, take your cocktail into the too-cool back Blue Room. And if you're on a budget, stop by from 4:30 to 7pm when martinis—lemon drops, cosmos, watermelon cosmos, and apple martinis—are $4. 4026 24th St. (between Noe and Castro sts.) ℰ 415/826-6200. www.blissbarsf.com.

Levende Lounge *(★)*   A fusion of fine dining and cocktails, 2004's hottest Mission addition was recently voted best bar for singles, romance, bar food, and received a slew of other accolades by CitySearch.com, while its chef Jamie Lauren was chosen as one of the city's Rising Star Chefs of 2005 by the *San Francisco Chronicle.* Drop in early for a meal of California-style tapas (small plates) in a more standard dinner setting amidst exposed brick walls and cozy lighting. Later, tables are traded for lounge furnishings for late-night noshing and grooving. Tip: Some nights have covers charges, but you can avoid the fee with a dinner reservation, and food is served until 11pm. 1710 Mission St. (at Duboce St.). ✆ 415/864-5585. www.levendesf.com.

The Monkey Club Casual and tucked away in a quiet section of the Mission, this hip locals bar (think 20s through 30s) is an ever fun and rather red spot to park on plush and comfy couches backed by giant picture windows; nibble on decent and inexpensive appetizers; and down stiff drinks while a DJ spins grooving house, jazz, and world music Wednesday through Sunday. 2730 21st St. (at Bryant St.). ✆ 415/647-6546.

Wish Bar Flirtation, fun, and a very attractive staff await at this somewhat mellow, narrow bar in the popular night crawler area around 11th and Folsom streets. Swathed in burgundy and black with exposed cinderblock walls and cement floors, all's aglow a la candlelight and red-shaded sconces. With a bar in the front, DJ spinning upbeat lounge music in the back, and seating—including cushy leather couches—in between, it's often packed with a surprisingly diverse (albeit youthful) crowd and ever filled with eye candy. 1539 Folsom St. (between 11th and 12th sts.). ✆ 415/278-9474. www.wishsf.com.

A SPORTS BAR

Greens Sports Bar If you think San Francisco sports fans aren't as enthusiastic as those on the East Coast, try to get a seat at Green's during a 49ers game. It's a classic old sports bar, with lots of polished dark wood and windows that open onto Polk Street, but it's loaded with modern appliances (including two large-screen televisions and 18 smaller ones) and modern partyers (read: the mid-20s and -30s set). With 18 beers on tap, a pool table, and a happy hour Monday through Friday from 4pm to 7pm, there are reasons to cheer here even when the home team's got a day off. 2239 Polk St. (at Green St.). ✆ 415/775-4287.

WINE & CHAMPAGNE BARS

The Bubble Lounge Toasting the town is a nightly event at this two-level champagne bar. With 300 champagnes and sparkling wines, about 30 by the glass, brick walls, couches, and velvet curtains, there's plenty of pop in this fizzy lounge. 714 Montgomery St. (between Washington and Jackson sts.). ✆ 415/434-4204. www.bubblelounge.com.

Eos If you're in the Financial District, head for the London Wine Bar (see below). If you're around the Civic Center, make it Hayes and Vine (see below). For anything west of these two, your top choice should be Eos, a highly successful restaurant in Cole Valley (near the Haight), with an adjoining wine bar where you can sip from the huge by-the-glass selection or choose a bottle from some 200 vintages from around the world. 901 Cole St. (at Carl St.). ✆ 415/566-3063. www.eossf.com.

First Crush If you're staying downtown and want to sip through regional specialties, stop by this wine-centric restaurant and bar. Amidst a sleek and stylish interior, an eclectic clientele noshes on reasonably priced "progressive American cuisine" paired, if desired, with an outstanding selection of California wines. But plenty of people drop in simply to sample wine—especially since there are around three dozen excellent choices for filling your glass and the joint serves until 11pm (until midnight Thurs–Sat; closed Tues). 101 Cyril Magnin St. (aka Fifth St., just north of Market St., at Ellis St.). ✆ 415/982-7874. www.firstcrush.com.

London Wine Bar This British-style wine bar and store is a popular after-work hangout for Financial District suits. It's more of a place to drink and chat, however, than one in which to admire fine wines. Usually 50 wines, mostly from California, are open at any given time and 800 are available by the bottle. It's a great venue for sampling local Napa Valley wines before you buy. 415 Sansome St. (between Sacramento and Clay sts.). © 415/788-4811.

Nectar Wine Lounge   Catering to the Marina's young and beautiful, this ultra-hip place to sip—and snack—pours an exciting and well-edited wine selection (plus 800 choices by the bottle) along with creative small plates (pairings optional). Industrial-slick decor includes cube chairs, a long bar, and lounge areas that are often packed with 20- through 40-somethings. 3330 Steiner St. (at Chestnut St.). © 415/345-1377. www.nectarwinelounge.com.

5 Gay & Lesbian Bars & Clubs

Just like straight establishments, gay and lesbian bars and clubs target varied clienteles. Whether you're into leather or Lycra, business or bondage, in San Francisco, there's gay nightlife just for you.

Check the free weeklies, the *San Francisco Bay Guardian* and *San Francisco Weekly*, for listings of events and happenings around town. The *Bay Area Reporter* is a gay paper with comprehensive listings, including a weekly community calendar. All these papers are free and distributed weekly on Wednesday or Thursday. They can be found stacked at the corners of 18th and Castro streets and Ninth and Harrison streets, as well as in bars, bookshops, and other stores around town. There are also a number of gay and lesbian guides to San Francisco. See "Gay & Lesbian Travelers," in chapter 2, beginning on p. 27, for further details and helpful information. Also check out the rather homely, but very informative site titled "Queer Things to Do in the San Francisco Bay Area" at www.io.com/~larrybob/sanfran.html for a plethora of gay happenings.

Listed below are some of the city's most established mainstream gay hangouts.

The Café *(Finds)*   When this place first got jumping, it was the only predominantly lesbian dance club on Saturday nights in the city. Once the guys found out how much fun the girls were having, however, they joined the party. Today, it's a happening mixed gay and lesbian scene with three bars, two pool tables, a steamy, free-spirited dance floor, and a small, heated patio and balcony where smoking and schmoozing is allowed. A perk: They open at 4pm weekdays and 3pm weekends. 2367 Market St. (at Castro St.). © 415/861-3846. www.cafesf.com.

The Cinch Saloon   Among the popular attributes of this cruisy neighborhood bar are the outdoor patio and progressive music by DJs after 9pm (except for Mon and Tues). San Francisco 49ers fans also sometimes gather here for televised games. Decorated in a Southwestern theme ("down home in Arizona"), the bar attracts a mixed crowd of gays, lesbians (now that there are almost no exclusively lesbian bars left in San Francisco), and gay-friendly straights. There's a happy hour on Mondays from 4pm until closing. 1723 Polk St. (near Washington St.). © 415/776-4162. www.thecinch.com.

Detour   Right in the heart of gay San Francisco, this bar attracts a young, often hot crowd of boys, with its low lighting and throbbing house music. Chain-link fences seem to hold in the action while a live DJ spins a web of popular hits nightly. Half-price drinks are available nightly until 8pm. 2348 Market St. (near Castro St.). © 415/861-6053.

The Eagle   One of the city's most traditional Levi's 'n' leather bars, The Eagle boasts a heated outdoor patio (where smoking is permitted), a happy hour (Mon–Fri from

4–8pm), live bands every Thursday at 9pm, and a popular Sunday-afternoon beer fest from 3 to 6pm. 398 12th St. (at Harrison St.). ℂ 415/626-0880. www.sfeagle.com.

The EndUp It's a different nightclub every night of the week, but regardless of who's throwing the party, the place is always jumping to the tunes blasted by DJs. There are two pool tables, a fireplace, an outdoor patio and, on the dance floor, a mob of gyrating souls. Some nights are straight, so call ahead. (See p. 224 for more information.) 401 Sixth St. (at Harrison St.). ℂ 415/357-0827. www.theendup.com. Cover $5–$15.

Kimo's This neighborhood bar in the seedier gay section of town is a friendly oasis, decorated with plants and pictures. The bar provides a relaxing venue for chatting, drinking, and quiet cruising and livens up with punk rock bands nightly upstairs. 1351 Polk St. (at Pine St.). ℂ 415/885-4535. Cover $5–$10 for live music.

Lone Star Saloon Expect lesbians and a heavier, furrier motorcycle crowd (both men and women) here most every night. The Thursday-night and Saturday and Sunday afternoon beer busts on the patio are especially popular and cost $7 to $9 per person. 1354 Harrison St. (between 9th and 10th sts.). ℂ 415/863-9999.

Metro This bar provides the gay community with high-energy music and the best view of the Castro District from its large balcony. The bar seems to attract people of all ages who enjoy the friendliness of the bartenders and the highly charged, cruising atmosphere. There's a Spanish restaurant on the premises if you get hungry. 3600 16th St. (at Market St.). ℂ 415/703-9750.

The Mint Karaoke Lounge This is a gay and lesbian karaoke bar—sprinkled with a heavy dash of straight folks on weekends—where you can sing show tunes every night. Along with song, you'll encounter a mixed 20- to 40-something crowd that combines cocktails with do-it-yourself cabaret. Want to eat and listen at the same time? Feel free to bring in the Japanese food from the attached restaurant. Sashimi goes for about $7, main entrees $8, and sushi combo plates are about $11. 1942 Market St. (at Laguna St.). ℂ 415/626-4726. www.themint.net. 2-drink minimum.

The Stud The Stud, which has been around for almost 40 years, is one of the most successful gay establishments in town. The interior has an antiques-shop look. Music is a balanced mix of old and new, and nights vary from cabaret to oldies to disco punk. Check their website in advance for the evening's offerings. Drink prices range from $3 to $8. Happy hour runs Monday through Saturday 5 to 9pm with $1 off well drinks. 399 Ninth St. (at Harrison St.). ℂ 415/863-6623 or ℂ 415/252-STUD event info line. www.studsf.com. Cover free–$9.

Twin Peaks Tavern Right at the intersection of Castro, 17th, and Market streets is one of the Castro's most famous (at 40 years old) gay hangouts. It caters to an older crowd but often has a mixture of patrons and claims to be the first gay bar in America. Because of its relatively small size and desirable location, the place becomes fairly crowded and convivial by 8pm, earlier than many neighboring bars. 401 Castro St. (at 17th and Market sts.). ℂ 415/864-9470.

6 Film

The **San Francisco International Film Festival** (ℂ 415/561-5000; www.sffs.org), held at the end of April, is one of America's oldest film festivals. Entries include new films by beginning and established directors. Call or surf ahead for a schedule or information, and check out their website for more information on purchasing tickets, which are relatively inexpensive.

If you're not here in time for the festival, don't despair. The classic, independent, and mainstream cinemas in San Francisco are every bit as good as the city's other cultural offerings.

REPERTORY CINEMAS

Castro Theatre 🏕🏕 *(Finds)*   Built in 1922, the beautiful Castro Theatre is known for its screenings of classics and for its Wurlitzer organ, which is played before each evening show. There's a different feature almost nightly, and more often than not it's a double feature. They also play host to a number of festivals throughout the year. Bargain matinees are usually offered on Wednesday, Saturday, Sunday, and holidays. Phone or visit their website for schedules, prices, and show times. 429 Castro St. (near Market St.). ⓒ 415/621-6120. www.castrotheatresf.com.

Red Vic   The worker-owned Red Vic movie collective originated in the neighboring Victorian building that gave it its name. The theater specializes in independent releases and premieres and contemporary cult hits, and situates its patrons among an array of couches. Prices are $7 for adults ($5 for matinees) and $4 for seniors and kids ages 12 and younger. Tickets go on sale 20 minutes before each show. Phone for schedules and show times or look around the city for printouts. 1727 Haight St. (between Cole and Shrader sts.). ⓒ 415/668-3994. www.redvicmoviehouse.com.

Roxie   The Roxie consistently screens the best new alternative films anywhere. The low-budget contemporary features are largely devoid of Hollywood candy coating; many are West Coast premieres. Films change weekly and sometimes more often. Phone for schedules, prices, and show times. 3117 16th St. (at Valencia St.). ⓒ 415/863-1087. www.roxie.com.

12

Side Trips from San Francisco

The City by the Bay is, without question, captivating, but don't let it ensnare you to the point of ignoring its environs. The surrounding areas contain a multitude of natural spectacles such as Mount Tamalpais and Muir Woods; scenic communities like Tiburon and Sausalito; and great cities such as up-and-coming Oakland and its youth-oriented next-door neighbor, Berkeley.

Most of the attractions at these destinations are free or very inexpensive. Hiking will cost you only calories, and strolling the shorelines and boutique-filled streets doesn't cost a thing (until you invariably slap down your credit card for a bayside lunch or souvenir).

From San Francisco, you can reach any of these points in an hour or less by car. Public transportation options are also listed throughout the chapter. Another option is to hitch a ride with **San Francisco Sightseeing** (© 415/434-8687; www.sanfranciscosightseeing.com), which runs regularly scheduled bus tours to neighboring towns and the countryside. Half-day trips to Muir Woods and Sausalito, and full-day trips to Napa and Sonoma are available, as are excursions to Yosemite and the Monterey Peninsula. Phone for prices and schedules.

See the inside back cover of this book for a map of the Bay area.

1 Berkeley

10 miles NE of San Francisco

Berkeley is famous as the home of the University of California at Berkeley, which is world-renowned for its academic standards, 18 Nobel Prize winners (seven are active staff), and protests that led to the most famous student riots in U.S. history. Today, there's still hippie idealism in the air, but the radicals have aged; the 1960s are present only in tie-dye and paraphernalia shops. The biggest change the town is facing is yuppification; as San Francisco's rent and property prices soar out of the range of the average person's budget, everyone with less than a small fortune is seeking shelter elsewhere, and Berkeley is one of the top picks (although Oakland is quickly becoming a favorite, too). Berkeley is a charming town teeming with all types of people, a beautiful campus, vast parks, great shopping, and some incredible restaurants.

ESSENTIALS

The Berkeley **Bay Area Rapid Transit (BART)** station is 2 blocks from the university. The fare from San Francisco is less than $4.

If you are coming **by car** from San Francisco, take the Bay Bridge (go during the evening commute, and you'll think Los Angeles traffic is a breeze). Follow I-80 east to the University Avenue exit, and follow University until you hit the campus. Parking is tight, so either leave your car at the Sather Gate parking lot at Telegraph Avenue and Durant Street, or expect to fight for a spot.

WHAT TO SEE & DO

Hanging out is the preferred Berkeley pastime, and the best place to do it is **Telegraph Avenue,** the street that leads to the campus's southern entrance. Most of the action lies between Bancroft Way and Dwight Way, where coffeehouses, restaurants, shops, great book and record stores, and crafts booths (vendors selling everything from T-shirts and jewelry to I Ching and tarot-card readings pack the avenue) swarm with life. Pretend you're a local: Plant yourself at a cafe, sip a latte, and ponder something intellectual, or survey the town's unique residents.

Bibliophiles must stop at **Cody's Books,** 2454 Telegraph Ave. (© **510/845-7852;** www.codysbooks.com), to peruse its gargantuan selection of titles, independent-press books, and magazines. If used and antiquarian books are your thing, stop by **Moe's Books,** 2476 Telegraph Ave. (© **510/849-2087;** www.moesbooks.com). After exploring four floors of new, used, and out-of-print books, you're unlikely to leave empty-handed.

UC BERKELEY CAMPUS

The University of California at Berkeley (www.berkeley.edu) campus is worth a stroll. It's a beautiful old place with plenty of woodsy paths, architecturally noteworthy buildings and, of course, 33,000 students, many of them scurrying to and from classes. Among the architectural highlights of the campus are a number of buildings by Bernard Maybeck, Bakewell and Brown, and John Galen Howard.

Contact the **Visitor Information Center,** 101 University Hall, 2200 University Ave., at Oxford Street (© **510/642-5215;** www.berkeley.edu/visitors), to join a free 90-minute campus tour. Tours are available year-round Monday through Saturday at 10am and Sunday at 1pm. Weekday tours depart from the Visitor's Center and weekend tours start from Sather Bell Tower in the middle of campus. Additional tours are available March 15 through April 30 at 1pm Monday through Friday. $25 electric cart tours are available year-round with advance reservations; no tours are given from mid-December to mid-January. Or stop by the office and pick up a self-guided walking-tour brochure or a free Berkeley map. *Note:* The information center is closed on weekends, but you can find the latest information on their website.

The university's southern, main entrance is at the northern end of Telegraph Avenue, at Bancroft Way. Walk through the entrance into Sproul Plaza, and when school is in session, you'll encounter the gamut of Berkeley's inhabitants: colorful street people, rambling political zealots, chanting Hare Krishnas, and ambitious students. You might be lucky enough to stumble upon some impromptu musicians or a heated, and possibly absurd, debate. There's always something going on here, so stretch out on the grass for a few minutes and take in the Berkeley vibe. You'll also find the student union, complete with a bookstore, cafes, and an information desk on the second floor where you can pick up the student newspaper (also found in dispensers throughout campus).

For viewing more traditional art forms, there are some noteworthy museums, too. The **Lawrence Hall of Science** ⚘ (east of campus on Centennial Dr., just above the Botanical Gardens; © **510/642-5132;** www.lawrencehallofscience.org) offers hands-on science exploration, is open daily from 10am to 5pm, and is a wonderful place to watch the sunset. Admission is $8.50 for adults; $6.50 for seniors, students, and children ages 5 to 18; $4.50 for children ages 3 or 4; free for kids younger than 3. The

Berkeley

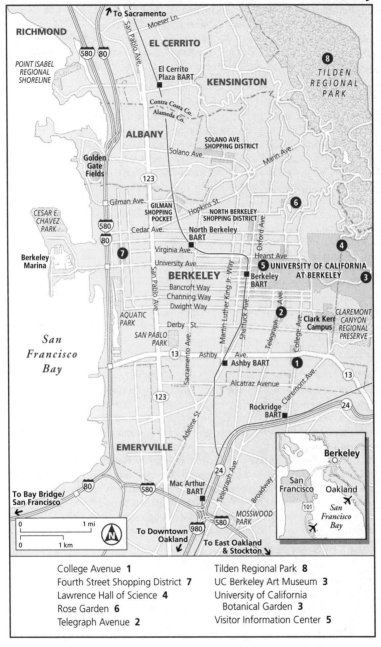

To Sacramento
Moeser Ln.

RICHMOND

EL CERRITO

POINT ISABEL
REGIONAL
SHORELINE

El Cerrito
Plaza BART

KENSINGTON

8

TILDEN
REGIONAL
PARK

Contra Costa Co.
Alameda Co.

ALBANY

Golden
Gate
Fields

Solano Ave.

SOLANO AVE
SHOPPING DISTRICT

Marin Ave.

CESAR E.
CHAVEZ
PARK

123

Gilman Ave.

GILMAN
SHOPPING
POCKET

Hopkins St.

NORTH BERKELEY
SHOPPING DISTRICT

6

Cedar Ave.

North Berkeley
BART

Berkeley
Marina

580

80

7

Virginia Ave.

University Ave.

San Pablo Ave.

Hearst Ave.

5 UNIVERSITY OF CALIFORNIA
AT BERKELEY

4

3

BERKELEY

Bancroft Way

Channing Way

Dwight Way

Berkeley
BART

Martin Luther King Jr. Way

Shattuck Ave.

Oxford St.

2

Telegraph Ave.

College Ave.

Clark Kerr
Campus

CLAREMONT
CANYON
REGIONAL
PRESERVE

AQUATIC
PARK

Derby St.

SAN PABLO
PARK

Sacramento Ave.

13

Ashby Ave.

San
Francisco
Bay

Ashby BART

Alcatraz Avenue

1

Claremont Ave.

13

123

Adeline St.

Rockridge
BART

24

EMERYVILLE

Mac Arthur
BART

24

To Bay Bridge/
San Francisco

80

580

Telegraph Ave.

Broadway

MOSSWOOD
PARK

980

580

To Downtown
Oakland

To East Oakland
& Stockton

0   1 mi

0   1 km

N

Berkeley

San
Francisco

Oakland

101

San
Francisco
Bay

College Avenue **1**
Fourth Street Shopping District **7**
Lawrence Hall of Science **4**
Rose Garden **6**
Telegraph Avenue **2**

Tilden Regional Park **8**
UC Berkeley Art Museum **3**
University of California
   Botanical Garden **3**
Visitor Information Center **5**

UC Berkeley Art Museum ⓡ (2626 Bancroft Way, between College and Telegraph aves.; ⓒ **510/642-0808**) is open Wednesday through Sunday from 11am to 5pm. Admission is $8 for adults; $5 for seniors, students, visitors with disabilities, and children ages 12 to 17; free for kids younger than 12 and UC students. This museum contains a substantial collection of Hans Hofmann paintings, a sculpture garden, and the Pacific Film Archive.

PARKS

Unbeknownst to many travelers, Berkeley has some of the most extensive and beautiful parks around. If you want to wear out the kids or enjoy hiking, swimming, sniffing roses, or just getting a breath of California air, jump in your car and make your way to **Tilden Regional Park** ⓡ. On the way, stop at the colorful terraced **Rose Garden** ⓡ, in north Berkeley on Euclid Avenue between Bay View and Eunice Street. Then head high into the Berkeley hills to Tilden, where you'll find plenty of flora and fauna, hiking trails, an old steam train and merry-go-round, a farm and nature area for kids, and a chilly tree-encircled lake. By air-conditioned public transit, bus lines 65 and 67 skirt the edge of the park on weekdays and go all the way to the Tilden Visitors Center on Saturdays and Sundays. Call ⓒ **510/562-PARK** or see www.ebparks. org for further information.

Note: You'll want to avoid People's Park, which has played an interesting part in Berkeley activism but offers little in the way of attractions.

Another worthy nature excursion is **The University of California Botanical Garden** (ⓒ **510/643-2755;** http://botanicalgarden.berkeley.edu), which features a vast collection of herbage ranging from cacti to redwoods. It's on campus in Strawberry Canyon on Centennial Drive. Unfortunately no public bus can take you directly there, so driving is the way to go. Call for directions.

SHOPPING

If you're itching to exercise your credit cards, head to one of two places. **College Avenue** from Dwight Way to the Oakland border overflows with eclectic boutiques, antiques shops, and restaurants. The other option is **Fourth Street,** in west Berkeley, 2 blocks north of the University Avenue exit. This shopping strip is the perfect place to go on a sunny morning. Grab a cup of java, read the paper at a patio table, then hit the **Crate & Barrel Outlet,** 1785 Fourth St., between Hearst and Virginia (ⓒ **510/ 528-5500**). Prices are 30% to 70% off retail. It's open daily from 10am to 6pm. This area also boasts small, wonderful stores crammed with imported and locally made housewares. Nearby is **REI,** the Bay Area's favorite outdoors outfitter, 1338 San Pablo Ave., near Gilman Street (ⓒ **510/527-4140**). It's open Monday through Friday 10am to 9pm, Saturday from 10am to 8pm, and Sunday from 10am to 7pm.

GREAT DEALS ON DINING

East Bay dining is a relaxed alternative to the city's gourmet scene. There are plenty of ambitious Berkeley restaurants and, unlike San Francisco, plenty of parking off-campus.

If you want to dine student-style, eat on campus Monday through Friday. Buy something at a sidewalk stand or in the building directly behind the Student Union. The least expensive food is available downstairs in the **Cafeteria,** on Lower Sproul Plaza. There's also the **Bear's Lair Pub and Coffee House,** the **Terrace,** and the **Golden Bear Restaurant.** All the university eateries have both indoor and outdoor seating. Telegraph Avenue has an array of small, ethnic restaurants, cafes, and sandwich shops. Follow the students: If the place is crowded, it's either good, super cheap, or both.

Finds Sweet Sensations at Berkeley's Chocolate Factory

If you haven't had chocolate nibs, you haven't lived—at least that's what choco-holics are likely to discover upon visiting **Scharffen Berger Chocolate Maker,** California's runaway-success chocolatier that opened its factory and retail-shop doors in Berkeley in mid-2001. Within the brick building, visitors can not only taste the nibs (crunchy roasted and shelled cocoa beans), but also see how the famous chocolate company uses vintage European equipment during regularly scheduled free tours (call or visit their website to reserve a spot as spaces are limited). And let's not forget there are plenty of tasty products, from candy bars to cocoa powder to chocolate sauce, available in the retail shop (© **510/ 981-4066**). You can also have lunch or dinner at their neighboring Café Cacao. The factory is located at 914 Heinz Ave., Berkeley (© **510/981-4050;** www. scharffenberger.com). From I-80 East take the Ashby Avenue exit, turn left on Seventh Street, and turn right on Heinz.

Blue Nile ✿ ETHIOPIAN   As soon as you step into the dining room filled with African paintings and sounds, you'll know you're in for a different kind of dining experience. Blue Nile offers a rare opportunity to sample flavorful Ethiopian special-ties such as *doro wat* (a spiced stew of beef, lamb, or chicken, served with a fluffy crepe *injera* [bread]) or *gomen wat* (mustard greens sautéed in cream) with no utensils other than your fingers. Sure, you could convince the waitstaff to drum up a fork or two, but why? No appetizers are served, but meals come with a small salad. Be sure to order the honey wine—it's unlike anything you've ever tasted.

2525 Telegraph Ave. © **510/540-6777.** Reservations required Fri and Sat. Main courses $8.75–$9.95. MC, V. Tues–Sat 11:30–10pm, Sun 5–10pm.

Cafe Fanny ✿✿ FRENCH/ITALIAN   Alice Waters's (of Chez Panisse fame) cafe is one of those local must-do East Bay breakfast traditions. Grab the morning paper, put on your Birkenstocks, and head here to wait in line for a simple yet masterfully pre-pared stand-up French breakfast. The menu offers such items as a soft-boiled farm egg with levain toast (toast from naturally leavened bread) and house jam, buckwheat crepes with jam, and an assortment of sweet pastries. Lunch is more of a Mediter-ranean experience featuring seasonal selections. Two of my favorite sandwiches are the baked ham and watercress on focaccia, or grilled chicken breast wrapped in prosciutto, sage, and aioli on an Acme bread. There's also a selection of pizzettas, salads, and soup. Eat inside at the stand-up food bar (one bench), or outside (virtually in the parking lot) at one of the cafe tables.

1603 San Pablo Ave. (at Cedar St.). © **510/524-5447.** Most breakfast items $7; lunch $7–$12. MC, V. Mon–Fri 7am–3pm; Sat 8am–4pm; Sun 8am–3pm. Breakfast is served until 11am except for Sun when it's an all-day thing. Closed major holidays.

Cafe Rouge ✿ MEDITERRANEAN   After cooking at San Francisco's renowned Zuni Cafe for 10 years, chef-owner Marsha McBride launched her own restaurant, a sort of Zuni East. She brought former staff members and some of the restaurant's fla-vor with her, and now her sparse, loftlike dining room serves salads, rotisserie chicken with oil and thyme, steaks, and homemade sausages. East Bay carnivores are especially happy with the burger—like Zuni's, it's top-notch—and the Niman Ranch hot dog with cabbage relish and potato chips is a steal at $6.50. During warm days, outdoor dining overlooking the shopping square is ideal.

1782 Fourth St. (between Delaware and Hearst). ✆ 510/525-1440. www.caferouge.net. Reservations recommended. Main courses $6.50–$24. MC, V. Tues–Thurs and Sun 11:30am–9:30pm (limited menu available 3–5:30pm); Tues–Sat 3–4:30pm (with interim menu bar menu available), Fri–Sat 11:30am–10:30pm (limited menu available 3–5:30pm). Lunch only on Monday (11:30am–3pm).

O Chamé 𝓇𝓇 JAPANESE   Spare and plain in its decor, with ocher-colored walls etched with patterns, this spot has a meditative air to complement the traditional, experimental, and very fresh and clean Japanese-inspired cuisine. The menu, which changes daily, offers meal-in-a-bowl dishes ($9–$13) that allow a choice of soba or udon noodles in a clear soup with a variety of toppings—from shrimp and wakame seaweed to beef with burdock root and carrot. Appetizers include a flavorful melding of grilled shiitake mushrooms, as well as portobello mushrooms and green-onion pancakes. Their main entree selection always includes delicious roasted salmon, but you can also easily fill up on an inexpensive bowl of soba or udon noodles with fresh, wholesome fixings (think roasted oysters, sea bass, and tofu skins).

1830 Fourth St. (near Hearst). ✆ 510-841-8783. Reservations recommended for Fri–Sat dinner. Main courses $9–$19. AE, MC, V. Mon–Sat 11:30am–3pm; Mon–Thurs 5:30–9pm; Fri–Sat 5:30–9:30pm.

2 Oakland

10 miles E of San Francisco

Although it's less than a dozen miles from San Francisco, Oakland is worlds apart from its sister city across the bay. Originally little more than a cluster of ranches and farms, Oakland exploded in size and stature practically overnight, when the last mile of transcontinental railroad track was laid down. Major shipping ports soon followed and, to this day, Oakland remains one of the busiest industrial ports on the West Coast.

The price for economic success, however, is Oakland's lowbrow reputation as a predominantly working-class city; it is forever in the shadow of chic San Francisco. However, as the City by the Bay has become crowded and expensive in the past few years, Oakland has experienced a rush of new residents and businesses. As a result, Oaktown is in a renaissance, and its future continues to look brighter and brighter.

Rent a sailboat on Lake Merritt, stroll along the waterfront, explore the fantastic Oakland Museum: They're all great reasons to hop the bay and spend a fog-free day exploring one of California's largest and most ethnically diverse cities.

ESSENTIALS

BART connects San Francisco and Oakland through one of the longest underwater transit tunnels in the world. Fares range from $2 to $4, depending on your station of origin; children under 5 ride free. BART trains operate Monday through Friday from 4am to midnight, Saturday from 6am to midnight, and Sunday from 8am to midnight. Exit at the 12th Street station for downtown Oakland.

By car from San Francisco, take I-80 across the San Francisco–Oakland Bay Bridge and follow signs to downtown Oakland. Exit at Grand Avenue South for the Lake Merritt area.

For a calendar of events in Oakland, contact the **Oakland Convention and Visitors Bureau,** 463 11th St., Oakland, CA 94607 (✆ **510/839-9000;** www.oaklandcvb.com). The city also sponsors free guided tours, including African-American Heritage and downtown tours held Wednesdays and Saturdays May through October; call ℂ **510/238-3234** or visit www.oaklandnet.com/walkingtours for details.

Downtown Oakland lies between Grand Avenue on the north, I-980 on the west, Inner Harbor on the south, and Lake Merritt on the east. Between these landmarks are three BART stations (12th St., 19th St., and Lake Merritt), City Hall, the Oakland Museum, Jack London Square, and several other sights.

WHAT TO SEE & DO

Lake Merritt is Oakland's primary tourist attraction, along with Jack London Square (see below). Three and a half miles in circumference, the tidal lagoon was bridged and dammed in the 1860s and is now a wildlife refuge that is home to flocks of migrating ducks, herons, and geese. The 122-acre **Lakeside Park,** a popular place to picnic, feed the ducks, and escape the fog, surrounds the lake on three sides. At the **Municipal Boathouse** ⟨ (ℂ **510/238-2196**), in Lakeside Park along the north shore, you can rent sailboats, rowboats, pedal boats, canoes, or kayaks for $6 to $12 per hour (cash only). Or you can take an hour-long gondola ride with **Gondola Servizio** (ℂ **510/663-6603;** www.gondolaservizio.com). Experienced gondoliers will serenade you as you glide across the lake; the cost ranges from $45 to $225 for two depending on the time and gondola style.

Another site worth visiting is Oakland's **Paramount Theatre** ⟨, 2025 Broadway (ℂ **510/893-2300;** www.paramounttheatre.com), an outstanding National Historic Landmark and example of Art Deco architecture and decor. Built in 1931 and authentically restored in 1973, it's the city's main performing-arts center, hosting big-name performers like Smokey Robinson and Alicia Keys. Guided tours of the 3,000-seat theater are given the first and third Saturday morning of each month, excluding holidays. No reservations are necessary; just show up at 10am at the box office entrance on 21st Street at Broadway. The tour lasts 2 hours, cameras are allowed, and admission is $1.

If you take pleasure in strolling sailboat-filled wharves or are a die-hard fan of Jack London, you might enjoy a visit to **Jack London Square** ⟨ (ℂ **866/295-9853;** http://jacklondonsquare.com). Though as of 2005, it's undergoing a five- to 10-year $300 million site-by-site renovation and expansion, so for now, Oakland's only patently tourist area remains a relatively low-key version of San Francisco's Fisherman's Wharf, and shamelessly plays up the fact that Jack London spent most of his youth along the waterfront. The square fronts the harbor, housing a tourist-tacky complex of boutiques and eateries that are about as far from the "call of the wild" as you can get, as well as a more locals-friendly farmers market year-round on Sundays from 10am to 2pm and May through October on Wednesdays from 10am to 2pm. Most shops are open Monday through Sunday from 10am to 7pm (some restaurants stay open later). One of the best options is live jazz at **Yoshi's World Class Jazz House & Japanese Restaurant** ⟨, 510 Embarcadero West (ℂ **510/238-9200;** www.yoshis.com), which serves some fine sushi in its adjoining restaurant. In the center of the square is a small, reconstructed Yukon cabin in which Jack London lived while prospecting in the Klondike during the gold rush of 1897.

In the middle of Jack London Square you'll find a more authentic memorial, **Heinold's First and Last Chance Saloon** (ℂ **510/839-6761**), a funky, friendly little bar and historic landmark that's worth a visit. This is where London did some of his writing and most of his drinking; the corner table he used has remained exactly as it was nearly a century ago. Jack London Square is at Broadway and Embarcadero. Take

I-880 to Broadway, turn south, and drive to the end. Or you can ride BART to 12th Street station, then walk south along Broadway (about half a mile); a free shuttle runs from there Monday through Friday from 11am to 2pm. Or take bus no. 72R or 72M to the foot of Broadway.

Oakland Museum of California ✠ Two blocks south of Lake Merritt, the Oakland Museum of California incorporates just about everything you'd want to know about the state and its people, history, culture, geology, art, environment, and ecology. Inside a low, modern building set among sweeping gardens and terraces, it's actually three museums in one: exhibitions of works by California artists from Bierstadt to Diebenkorn; collections of historic artifacts, from Pomo Indian basketry to Country Joe McDonald's guitar; and re-creations of California habitats from the coast to the Sierra Mountains. The museum holds major shows of California artists and exhibitions dedicated to major California movements. Recent exhibits included "Aftershock: Personal Stories from the '06 Quake and Fire," and "Baseball as America," which showcases artifacts and photos of the nation's favorite sport. The museum also frequently shows photography from its huge collections.

Forty-five-minute guided tours leave from the gallery information desks on request or by appointment. There's a fine cafe, a **gallery** (♁ **510/834-2296**) that sells works by California artists, and a book and gift shop. The cafe is open Wednesday through Saturday from 10:30am to 4:30pm, Sunday from 1:30 to 4:30pm.

1000 Oak St. (at 10th St.). ♁ **888/625-6873,** or 510/238-2200 for recorded information. www.museumca.org. Admission $8 adults; $5 students and seniors; free for children under 6. 2nd Sun of the month is free. Wed–Sat 10am–5pm; Sun noon–5pm; open until 9pm 1st Fri of the month. Closed Jan 1, July 4, Thanksgiving, Dec 25. BART: Lake Merritt station; walk 1 block north. From I-880 north, take the Oak St. exit; the museum is 5 blocks east. Or take I-580 to I-980 and exit at the Jackson St. ramp.

GREAT DEALS ON DINING

À Côté ✠✠ FRENCH TAPAS   I've always been a huge fan on the superb Mediterranean-inspired small plates at this loud, festive, and warmly lit joint. A "no reservations" policy means there's usually a long wait during prime dining hours, but once seated you can join locals in a nosh fest featuring the likes of Croque monsieur; pommes frites with aioli; wood-oven cooked mussels in Pernod; and grilled pork tenderloin with creamy polenta, traviso cheese, and pancetta—and wash it down with Belgium ales, perky cocktails, or excellent by-the-glass or -bottle selections from the great wine list. *Note:* The heated and covered outdoor seating area tends to be quieter.

5478 College Ave. (at Taft Ave.). ♁ **510/655-6469.** www.citron-acote.com. Reservations not accepted except for parties of 10 or more. Small plates $5–$14. MC, V. Sun–Tues 5:30–10pm; Wed–Thurs 5:30–11pm; Fri–Sat 5:30pm–midnight.

Caffe 817 ✠ ITALIAN   After a career as an electrical engineer, Alessandro Rossi decided to go into the restaurant business, and Oakland residents have been ever so grateful for his decision. Rossi hired local craftspeople to fashion the avant-garde furnishings for his high-ceilinged space, yet despite its fashionable decor, the menu is very modestly priced (particularly considering the quality of ingredients, all of which are organically grown). Pastries and cappuccino are the mainstays in the morning, and simple salads, Italian sandwiches (favorites are the grilled mozzarella with artichokes and prosciutto with herb butter and pears), and freshly made soups and stews are on the midday menu. Trust me: You'll wish this cafe was in your neighborhood.

817 Washington St. (between Eighth and Ninth sts.). ♁ **510/271-7965.** www.cafe817.com. Main courses $5–$8.75. AE, MC, V. Mon–Fri 7:30am–3pm; Sat 8:30am–3pm.

Oliveto Cafe ☆☆☆ ITALIAN   Paul Bertolli, former chef at the world-renowned Chez Panisse restaurant, jumped ship to open one of the top Italian cafes in the Bay Area (and certainly the best in Oakland). Local workers pile in at lunchtime for wood-fired pizzas, house-made pastas, simple salads, flame-broiled rotisserie, and sandwiches served in the lower-level cafe (the upstairs restaurant is more elegant but the menu is far more expensive). The Arista (classic Italian pork with garlic and rosemary and pork *jus*) is insanely good, and no one does fried calamari, onion rings, and lemon slices better than Oliveto. *Tip:* There's free parking in the lot at the rear of the Market Hall building.

Rockridge Market Hall, 5655 College Ave. (off the northeast end of Broadway at Shafter/Keith St., across from the Rockridge BART station). ℂ 510/547-5356. www.oliveto.com. Reservations recommended for restaurant. Main courses cafe $2.50–$12 breakfast, $4–$8 lunch, $12–$15 dinner; restaurant $11–$15 lunch, $16–$30 dinner. AE, DC, MC, V. Mon 7am–9pm; Tues–Fri 7am–10pm; Sat 8am–10pm; Sun 8am–9pm.

3 Angel Island & Tiburon

8 miles N of San Francisco

A federal and state wildlife refuge, Angel Island is the largest of San Francisco Bay's three islets (the others are Alcatraz and Yerba Buena). The island has been, at various times, a prison, a quarantine station for immigrants, a missile base, and even a favorite site for duels. Nowadays, most visitors are content with picnicking on the large green lawn that fronts the docking area; loaded with the appropriate recreational supplies, they claim a barbecue pit, plop their fannies down on the lush green grass, and while away an afternoon free of phones, televisions, and traffic. Hiking, mountain biking, and guided tram tours are other popular activities here.

Tiburon, situated on a peninsula of the same name, looks like a cross between a fishing village and a Hollywood Western set—imagine San Francisco reduced to toy dimensions. The seacoast town rambles over a series of green hills and ends up at a spindly, multicolored pier on the waterfront, like a Fisherman's Wharf in miniature. In reality, it's an extremely plush patch of yacht-club suburbia, as you'll see by the marine craft and the homes of their owners. Ramshackle, color-splashed old frame houses line Main Street, sheltering chic boutiques, souvenir stores, antiques shops, and art galleries. Other roads are narrow, winding, and hilly and lead up to dramatically situated homes. The view from here of San Francisco's skyline and the islands in the bay is a good enough reason to pay the precious price to live here.

While there is a hotel in Tiburon, I wouldn't recommend staying there: It's a 1-block town, and the hotel is very expensive. There are no hotels on Angel Island. Both destinations are better as day trips.

ESSENTIALS

Ferries of the **Blue & Gold Fleet** (ℂ **415/705-5555;** www.blueandgoldfleet.com) from Pier 41 (Fisherman's Wharf) travel to both Angel Island and Tiburon. Boats run on a seasonal schedule; phone or look online for departure information. The round-trip adult fare is $12 to Angel Island, $6.50 for kids ages 6 to 11, and free for kids younger than 6. The fare includes state park fees. Tickets to Tiburon are $7.25 each way for adults, $4 for kids ages 6 to 11, and free for kids younger than 5. Tickets are available at Pier 41 or over the phone.

By car from San Francisco, take U.S. 101 to the Tiburon/Highway 131 exit, then follow Tiburon Boulevard all the way downtown, a 40-minute drive from San Francisco.

Catch the **Tiburon–Angel Island Ferry** (© 415/435-2131; www.angelislandferry. com) to Angel Island from the dock at Tiburon Boulevard and Main Street. The 15-minute round-trip costs $10 for adults, $7.50 for children ages 5 to 11, and $1 for bikes. One child under 4 is admitted free with each paying adult. Tickets can only be purchased when boarding. Boats run on a seasonal schedule, but usually depart hourly from 10am to 4pm. Call ahead or look online for departure information.

WHAT TO SEE & DO ON ANGEL ISLAND

Passengers disembark from the ferry at **Ayala Cove,** a small marina abutting a huge lawn area equipped with tables, benches, barbecue pits, and restrooms. Also at Ayala Cove are a small store, gift shop, cafe (with surprisingly good grub), and an overpriced mountain-bike rental shop.

Angel Island's 12 miles of hiking and mountain-bike trails include the **Perimeter Road,** a partly paved path that circles the island. It winds past disused troop barracks, former gun emplacements, and other military buildings; several turnoffs lead to the top of Mount Livermore, 776 feet above the bay. Sometimes referred to as the "Ellis Island of the West," Angel Island was used as a holding area for detained Chinese immigrants awaiting admission papers from 1910 to 1940. You can still see faded Chinese characters on the walls of the barracks where the immigrants were held. During the warmer months you can camp at a limited number of reserved sites; call **Reserve America** at © 800/444-7275 and ask about environmental campgrounds at Angel Island. For more information about the island, call **Angel Island** at © 415/435-3522 or visit www.angelisland.org.

Guided **sea-kayak tours** ℛ are also available. The all-day trips, which include a catered lunch, combine the thrill of paddling stable two- or three-person kayaks with an informative, naturalist-led tour around the island (conditions permitting). All equipment is provided, kids are welcome, and no experience is necessary. Rates run about $110 per person. A shorter trip takes 2½ hours and costs $75 per person. For more information, call **Sea Trek** (© 415/332-8494; www.seatrekkayak.com).

The 1-hour **Angel Island Tram Tour** (© 415/897-0715; www.angelisland.com) costs $13 for adults, $11 for seniors, $7.50 for children ages 6 to 12, and is free for children younger than 6; schedules vary depending on the time of year, though they generally do not run during winter. It's the lazy man's (or woman's) way to check out the island's flora and fauna, though the reason most come here is to trek around—on foot.

WHAT TO SEE & DO IN TIBURON

The main thing to do in touristy, but pretty and very tiny, Tiburon is to stroll along the waterfront, pop into the stores, and spend an easy $50 on drinks and appetizers before heading back to the city. For a taste of the Wine Country, stop at **Windsor Vineyards,** 72 Main St. (© 800/214-9463 or 415/435-3113; www.windsorvineyards.com)—its Victorian tasting room dates from 1888. Twenty or more choices are available for a free tasting. Wine accessories and gifts—glasses, cork pullers, carry packs (which hold six bottles), gourmet sauces, posters, and maps—are also available. Ask about personalized labels for your selections. The shop is open Sunday through Thursday from 10am to 6pm, Friday and Saturday from 10am to 7pm.

WHERE TO DINE IN TIBURON

Guaymas MEXICAN   Guaymas offers authentic Mexican regional cuisine and a spectacular panoramic view of San Francisco and the bay. In good weather, the two heated outdoor patios are almost always packed with diners soaking in the sun and

Marin Headlands

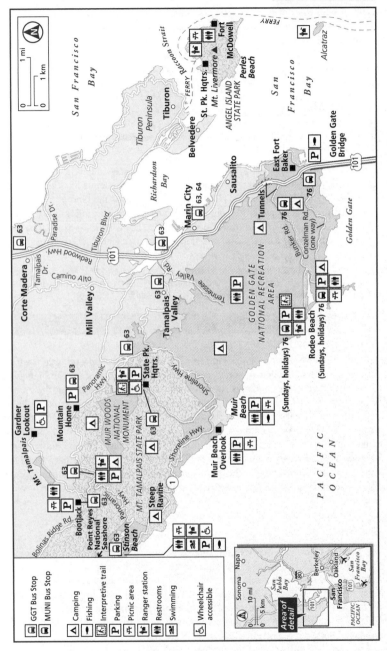

scene. Inside, colorful Mexican artwork brightens the beige walls. Should you feel chilled, to the rear of the dining room is a beehive-shaped adobe fireplace.

Guaymas is named after a fishing village on Mexico's Sea of Cortez, and both the town and the restaurant are famous for their *camarones* (giant shrimp). The restaurant also features ceviche, handmade tamales, and charcoal-grilled beef, seafood, and fowl. In addition to a good selection of California and Central American wines, the restaurant offers an exceptional variety of tequilas and Mexican beers.

5 Main St. ☎ 415/435-6300. www.guaymas.com. Reservations recommended. Main courses $13–$23. AE, DC, DISC, MC, V. Mon–Thurs 11:30am–10pm; Fri–Sat 11:30am–11pm; Sun 10:30am–10pm. Ferry: Walk about 10 paces straight from the landing. From U.S. 101, exit at Tiburon/Hwy. 131; follow Tiburon Blvd. 5 miles and turn right onto Main St. Restaurant is behind the bakery.

Sam's Anchor Café *(Finds* SEAFOOD   Summer Sundays are liveliest in Tiburon, when weekend boaters tie up at the docks of waterside restaurants like this one, and good-time cyclists pedal from the city to relax here. Sam's is the kind of place where you and your cronies can take off your shoes and have a fun, relaxing time eating burgers and drinking margaritas outside on the pier. The fare is typical—sandwiches, salads, and such—but the quality and selection are inconsequential: beers, burgers, and a designated driver are all you really need.

27 Main St. ☎ 415/435-4527. www.samscafe.com. Main courses $9–$13 brunch, $9–$21 lunch, $15–$24 dinner. AE, DC, DISC, MC, V. Mon–Fri 11am–10pm; Sat–Sun 9:30am–10pm. Ferry: Steps from the landing. From U.S. 101, exit at Tiburon/Hwy. 131; follow Tiburon Blvd. 4 miles and turn right onto Main St.

4 Sausalito

5 miles N of San Francisco

Just off the northern end of the Golden Gate Bridge is the eclectic little town of Sausalito, a slightly bohemian, nonchalant, studiedly quaint adjunct to San Francisco. With fewer than 8,000 residents, Sausalito feels rather like St. Tropez on the French Riviera—minus the starlets and the social rat race. It has its quota of paper millionaires, but they rub their permanently suntanned shoulders with a good number of hard-up artists, struggling authors, shipyard workers, and fishers. Next to the swank restaurants, plush bars, and antiques shops and galleries, you'll see hamburger joints, beer parlors, and secondhand bookstores. Sausalito's main strip is Bridgeway, which runs along the water. Those in the know make a quick detour to Caledonia Street, 1 block inland; not only is it less congested, but it also has a far better selection of inexpensive cafes and shops. Since the town is all along the waterfront and only stretches a few blocks, it is easy to find your way around.

ESSENTIALS

The **Golden Gate Ferry Service** fleet, Ferry Building (☎ **415/923-2000;** www.golden gateferry.org), operates between the San Francisco Ferry Building, at the foot of Market Street, and downtown Sausalito. Service is frequent, running at reasonable intervals every day of the year except New Year's Day, Thanksgiving, and Christmas Day. Phone for an exact schedule. The ride takes a half-hour, and one-way fares are $6.15 for adults and $4.60 for kids ages 6 to 12. Seniors and passengers with disabilities ride for $3.05; children 5 and younger ride free. Family rates are available on weekends.

Ferries of the **Blue & Gold Fleet** (☎ **415/705-5555;** www.blueandgoldfleet.com) leave from Pier 41 (Fisherman's Wharf); the one-way cost is $7.25 for adults, $4 for kids ages 5 to 11. Boats run on a seasonal schedule; phone for departure information.

By car from San Francisco, take U.S. 101 north, then take the first right after the Golden Gate Bridge (Alexander exit). Alexander becomes Bridgeway in Sausalito.

WHAT TO SEE & DO

Above all else, Sausalito has scenery and sunshine, for once you cross the Golden Gate Bridge, you're out of the San Francisco fog patch and under blue California sky (we hope). Houses cover the town's steep hills, overlooking a forest of masts on the waters below. Most of the tourist action, which is almost singularly limited to window-shopping and eating, takes place at sea level on Bridgeway.

Sausalito is a mecca for shoppers seeking handmade, original, and offbeat clothes and footwear, as well as arts and crafts. Many of the town's shops are in the alleys, malls, and second-floor boutiques reached by steep, narrow staircases on and off Bridgeway. Caledonia Street, which runs parallel to Bridgeway 1 block inland, is home to more shops.

Bay Model Visitors Center *Kids*   The U.S. Army Corps of Engineers once used this high-tech, 1½-acre model of San Francisco's bay and delta to resolve problems and observe the impact of changes in water flow. Today, the model is strictly for educational purposes and reproduces (in scale) the rise and fall of tides and the flows and currents of water. There's a 10-minute film, self-guided and audio tours ($3 donation requested), and a 1-hour tour (free; book a reservation), but the most interesting time to visit is when the model is in operation, so call ahead.

2100 Bridgeway. © 415/332-3871. www.spn.usace.army.mil/bmvc. Free admission. Labor Day to Memorial Day (winter hours) Tues–Sat 9am–4pm; Memorial Day to Labor Day (summer hours). Tues–Fri 9am–4pm, Sat–Sun and holidays 10am–5pm.

WHERE TO DINE

Hamburgers BURGERS   Like the name says, the specialty at this tiny, narrow cafe is juicy flame-broiled hamburgers, arguably Marin County's best. Look for the rotating grill in the window off Bridgeway, and then stand in line and salivate with the rest. Chicken burgers are a slightly healthier option. Order a side of fries, grab a bunch of napkins, and head to the park across the street.

737 Bridgeway. © 415/332-9471. Sandwiches $5.50–$6.50. No credit cards. Daily 11am–5pm. From U.S. 101 north, take the 1st right after the Golden Gate Bridge (Alexander exit); Alexander becomes Bridgeway in Sausalito.

Moments A Picnic Lunch, Sausalito Style

If the crowds are too much or the prices too steep at Sausalito's bayside restaurants, grab a bite to go for an impromptu picnic in the park fronting the marina. It's one of the best and most romantic ways to spend a warm, sunny day in Sausalito. The best source for some inexpensive eats a la carte is the European-style **Venice Gourmet Delicatessen** *&* at 625 Bridgeway, located right on the waterfront just south of the ferry landing. This venerable deli has all the makings for a superb picnic: wines, cheeses, fruits, stuffed vine leaves, salads, quiche, delicious sandwiches (made to order on sourdough bread), and fresh-baked pastries. It's open daily from 9am to 6pm (© **415/332-3544**; www.venice gourmet.com).

Horizons ♣ SEAFOOD/AMERICAN   Eventually every San Franciscan ends up at Horizons to meet a friend for Sunday bloody marys. Built in 1898 by the San Francisco Yacht Club, it's not much to look at from the outside, but it gets better as you head past the 1960s-era dark-wood interior toward the waterside terrace. On warm days it's worth the wait for alfresco seating if only to watch sailboats glide past San Francisco's distant skyline. The food here can't touch the view, but it's well portioned and satisfying enough. Seafood dishes are the main items, including steamed clams and mussels, freshly shucked oysters, and a variety of seafood pastas. In fine Marin tradition, Horizons has an "herb tea and espresso" bar.

558 Bridgeway. Ⓡ 415/331-3232. www.horizonssausalito.com. Reservations accepted weekdays only. Main courses $9–$22; salads and sandwiches $6–$11. AE, MC, V. Mon–Fri 11:30am–9pm; Sat 10:30am–10pm; Sun 4–9pm. Valet parking $4.

---

5 Muir Woods, Mount Tamalpais & Stinson Beach

12 miles N of the Golden Gate Bridge

While the rest of Marin County's redwood forests were being devoured to feed San Francisco's turn-of-the-20th-century building spree, Muir Woods, in a remote ravine on the flanks of Mount Tamalpais, escaped destruction in favor of easier pickings.

MUIR WOODS

Although the magnificent California redwoods have been successfully transplanted to five continents, their homeland is a 500-mile strip along the mountainous coast of southwestern Oregon and Northern California. The coast redwood, or *Sequoia sempervirens,* is the tallest tree in the immediate region; the largest known specimen in the Redwood National Forest towers 368 feet. It has an even larger relative, the *Sequoiadendron giganteum* of the California Sierra Nevada, but the coastal variety is stunning enough. Soaring toward the sky like a wooden cathedral, Muir Woods is unlike any other forest in the world and an experience you won't soon forget.

Granted, Muir Woods is tiny compared to the Redwood National Forest farther north, but you can still get a pretty good idea of what it must have been like when these giants dominated the entire coastal region. What is truly amazing is that they exist a mere 6 miles (as the crow flies) from San Francisco—close enough, unfortunately, that tour buses arrive in droves on the weekends. You can avoid the masses by hiking up the **Ocean View Trail** and returning on the **Fern Creek Trail.** The moderately challenging hike shows off the woods' best sides and leaves the lazy-butts behind.

To reach Muir Woods from San Francisco, cross the Golden Gate Bridge heading north on Highway 101, take the Stinson Beach/Highway 1 exit heading west, and follow the signs (and the traffic). The park is open daily from 8am to sunset, and the admission fee is $3 per person 16 and older. There's also a small gift shop, educational displays, and ranger talks. For more information, call the **Muir Woods information line** (Ⓡ **415/388-2595**) or visit www.visitmuirwoods.com.

If you don't have a car, you can book a bus trip with the **Red & White Fleet** (Ⓡ **800/229-2784** or 415/447-0597; www.redandwhite.com), which takes you straight to Muir Woods and makes a short stop in Sausalito on the way back. The 3½-hour tour runs twice daily at 9am and 2pm and costs $39 for adults, $20 for children ages 5 though 11; free for kids younger than 5. Call for information and departure times.

MOUNT TAMALPAIS

The birthplace of mountain biking, Mount Tam—as the locals call it—is the Bay Area's favorite outdoor playground and the most dominant mountain in the region. Most every local has his or her secret trail and scenic overlook, as well as an opinion on the raging debate between mountain bikers and hikers (a touchy subject). The main trails—mostly fire roads—see a lot of foot and bicycle traffic on weekends, particularly on clear, sunny days when you can see a hundred miles in all directions, from the foothills of the Sierra to the western horizon. It's a great place to escape from the city for a leisurely hike and to soak in breathtaking views of the bay.

To get to Mount Tamalpais **by car,** cross the Golden Gate Bridge heading north on Highway 101, and take the Stinson Beach/Highway 1 exit. Follow the signs up the shoreline highway for about 2½ miles, turn onto Pantoll Road, and continue for about a mile to Ridgecrest Boulevard. Ridgecrest winds to a parking lot below East Peak. From there, it's a 15-minute hike up to the top.

STINSON BEACH

One of the most popular beaches in Northern California, this 3-mile-wide stretch of sand at the western foot of Mount Tamalpais is packed with Bay Area residents (and their dogs) on those rare fog-free summer weekends. Granted, it lacks the hard bodies and soft golden sand of Southern California, but it still makes for an enjoyable day trip via the scenic drive on Calif. 1. Although swimming is allowed and lifeguards are on duty from May to mid-September, notices about riptides (and the cold water) usually discourage beachgoers from venturing too far into the water. Adjoining the beach is the small town of Stinson Beach, where you can have an enjoyable alfresco lunch at the numerous cafes along Calif. 1.

To reach Stinson Beach from San Francisco, cross the Golden Gate Bridge heading north on U.S. 101, take the Stinson Beach/Calif. 1 exit heading west, and follow the signs (it's a 20-mile trip that's full of curves). The beach is open daily from 9am to 10pm, and there's no charge for admission. For more information, contact the Stinson Beach ranger and lifeguard station at ✆ **415/868-0942.**

6 Point Reyes National Seashore

35 miles NW of San Francisco

The National Seashore system was created to protect rural and undeveloped stretches of the coast from the pressures brought by soaring real-estate values and increasing population. Nowhere is the success of the system more evident than at Point Reyes. Residents of the surrounding towns—Inverness, Point Reyes Station, and Olema—have steadfastly resisted runaway development. You won't find any strip malls or fast-food joints here, just laid-back coastal towns with cafes and country inns, where gentle living prevails.

Although the peninsula's people and wildlife live in harmony above the ground, the situation beneath the soil is much more volatile. The infamous San Andreas Fault separates Point Reyes—the northernmost landmass on the Pacific Plate—from the rest of California, which rests on the North American Plate. Point Reyes is making its way toward Alaska at a rate of about 2 inches per year, but at times it has moved much faster. In 1906, Point Reyes jumped north almost 20 feet in an instant, leveling San Francisco and jolting the rest of the state. The half-mile Earthquake Trail, near the Bear Valley Visitor Center, illustrates this geological drama with a loop through an area torn by the slipping fault. Shattered fences, rifts in the ground, and a barn knocked off its foundation by the quake illustrate how alive the earth is. If that doesn't convince you, a seismograph in the visitor center will.

ESSENTIALS

Point Reyes is only 30 miles northwest of San Francisco, but it takes at least 90 minutes to reach **by car** (it's all the small towns, not the topography, that slow you down). The easiest route is Sir Francis Drake Boulevard from Highway 101 south of San Rafael; it takes its bloody time getting to Point Reyes, but it does so without any detours. For a much longer but more scenic route, take the Stinson Beach/Highway 1 exit off Highway 101 just south of Sausalito and follow Highway 1 north.

As soon as you arrive at Point Reyes, stop at the **Bear Valley Visitor Center** (© **415/464-5100;** www.nps.gov/pore) on Bear Valley Road (look for the small sign just north of Olema on Hwy. 1) and pick up a free Point Reyes trail map. The rangers are extremely friendly and helpful and can answer any questions about the National Seashore. Be sure to check out the great natural-history and cultural displays while you're there. The center is open weekdays from 9am to 5pm, weekends and holidays from 8am to 5pm. Entrance to the park is free. **Camping** is $15 per site per night up to 6 people, and permits are required. All the sites range from a 1.4 to 5.5 mile hike in from the nearest trail head. Reservations can be made up to 3 months in advance by calling © **415/663-8054** Monday through Friday from 9am to 2pm.

WHAT TO SEE & DO

When headed to any part of the Point Reyes coast, expect to spend the day surrounded by nature at its finest; however, bear in mind that as beautiful as the wilderness can be, it's also untamable. The bone-chilling waters in these areas are not only home to a vast array of sea life, including sharks, but are unpredictable and dangerous. There are no lifeguards on duty, and swimming is strongly discouraged because of the waves and rip tides. Pets are not permitted on any of the area's trails. However, if you are looking for a place to swim, consider heading towards Tomales Bay during the summer months.

By far the most popular—and crowded—attraction at Point Reyes National Seashore is the venerable **Point Reyes Lighthouse** ✸ (© **415/669-1534**), at the westernmost tip of Point Reyes. Even if you plan to forgo the 308 steps to the lighthouse itself (sorry—no strollers or wheelchairs), the area is still worth a visit. The dramatic scenery includes thousands of common murres and prides of sea lions that bask on the rocks far below (binoculars come in handy). It's open Thursday through Monday from 10am to 4:30pm and admission is free.

The lighthouse is also the top spot on the California coast from which to observe **gray whales** as they make their southward and northward migrations along the coast January through April. The annual round-trip is 10,000 miles—one of the longest mammal migrations known. The whales head south in January and return north in March. There's never a guarantee that you will see a whale, but it's best to come during clear, calm weather. *Note:* If you plan to drive to the lighthouse to whale-watch, arrive early because parking is limited. If possible, come on a weekday. On a weekend or holiday from January through the beginning of April, it's wise to park at the Drake's Beach Visitor Center and take the shuttle bus (weather permitting) to the lighthouse and on to Chimney Rock to watch elephant seals; the shuttle bus runs from around New Year's Day to the beginning of April and costs $5 for adults, free for children

---

⟨Tips **Whale Sightings**

Rangers suggest that during the whales' southern migration (Jan), you should go to the lighthouse for the best view. During their northern migration (Mar), you can see 'em from any of the area's beaches.

---

younger than 16. Dress warmly when you come here—it's often quite cold and windy—and bring binoculars.

Whale watching is far from the only activity at the Point Reyes National Seashore. On weekend afternoons or daily during the summer months, many different tours are offered: You can walk along the Bear Valley Trail, spotting the wildlife at the ocean's edge; see the waterfowl at Alamere Falls; explore tide pools; view some of North America's most beautiful ducks in the wetlands of Limantour; hike to the promontory overlooking Chimney Rock to see the sea lions, harbor seals, elephant seals, and seabirds; or take a guided walk along the San Andreas Fault to observe the epicenter of the 1906 earthquake and learn about the regional geology. And this is just a sampling. Tours vary seasonally; for the most up-to-date details, call the **Bear Valley Visitors Center** (© **415/464-5100**) or visit the National Park Service's website (www.nps.gov/pore) where you can also get a lay of the land and more details, including area maps, in the "Plan Your Visit" section of the site. *Note:* Many tours are suitable for travelers with disabilities.

Some of the park's best—and least crowded—highlights can be approached only on foot. They include **Alamere Falls,** a freshwater stream that cascades down a 40-foot bluff onto Wildcat Beach, and **Tomales Point Trail,** which passes through the Tule Elk Reserve, a protected haven for roaming herds of Tule Elk that once numbered in the thousands. Hiking most of the trails usually ends up being an all-day outing, however, so it's best to split a 2-day trip into a "by car" day and a "by foot" day.

If you're into bird-watching, you'll definitely want to visit the **Point Reyes Bird Observatory** (© **415/868-1221**), one of the few full-time ornithological research stations in the United States. It's at the southeast end of the park on Mesa Road. This is where ornithologists keep an eye on more than 400 feathered species. Admission to the visitor center and nature trail is free, and visitors are welcome to observe the tricky process of catching and banding the birds. The observatory is open daily from 15 minutes after sunrise to sunset. Banding hours vary; contact them (© **415/868-0655;** www.prbo.org) for exact times.

One of my favorite things to do in Point Reyes is paddle through placid Tomales Bay, a haven for migrating birds and marine mammals. **Blue Waters Kayaking** 𝕮 (© **415/663-1743;** www.bwkayak.com) organizes kayak trips, including 3-hour morning or sunset outings, oyster tours, day trips, and longer excursions. Instruction, private groups and classes, clinics, and boat delivery are available, and all ages and levels are welcome. Prices for tours start at $65. Rentals begin at $35 for one person, $60 for two. Don't worry—the kayaks are very stable, and there are no waves to contend with. There are two launching points: One is on Highway 1 at the Marshall Boatworks in Marshall, 8 miles north of Point Reyes Station and the other is on Sir Francis Drake Boulevard, in Inverness, 5 miles east of Point Reyes Station. Blue Waters is open daily April to October from 9am to 5pm and by appointment.

WHERE TO STAY

Inns of Marin, P.O. Box 547, Point Reyes Station, CA 94956 (© **800/887-2880** or 415/663-2000), is a free service that can help you find accommodations ranging from one-room cottages to inns to complete vacation homes. Many places have a 2-night minimum, but at slow times they might make an exception. The service can also refer you to restaurants, hiking trails, and area attractions.

Bear Valley Inn Bed & Breakfast 𝒢   This two-story 1919 farmhouse has survived everything from a major earthquake to a recent forest fire, which is lucky for you because you'll be hard-pressed to find a better B&B for the price in Point Reyes. Loaded with charm, down to the profusion of flowers and vines outside and comfy chairs fronting a toasty-warm woodstove inside, it's in a great location, too, with two good restaurants within walking distance and the entire national seashore at your doorstep. One of the units is a private cottage with two futon couches in the living area, suitable for children.

88 Bear Valley Rd., Olema, CA 94950. © **415/663-1777.** www.bearvinn.com. 4 units. $110–$135 double; $140–$185 cottage. Rates include breakfast. AE, DISC, MC, V. *In room:* A/C, TV, free Wi-Fi, kitchen (in cottage), coffeemaker (in some units), hair dryer, iron.

Motel Inverness 𝑲𝒊𝒅𝒔   Finding an inexpensive place to stay in Point Reyes is next to impossible, because hoity-toity B&Bs reign supreme. There is, however, one exception—Motel Inverness, a homey, well-maintained lodging fronting Tomales Bay. For the outdoor adventurer who plans to spend as little time indoors as possible, it's the perfect place to hole up. (Those seeking romance should dig a little deeper into their pockets and opt for Manka's; see above.) Each of the guest rooms, with the exception of one twin-bed option, has queen-size beds and skylights. Attached to the hotel is a giant great room, complete with fireplace and pool table to distract the kids; parents

---

Finds   Johnson Drake's Oyster Farm

If you want to escape the crowds and enjoy some man-made entertainment, head to **Johnson Drake's Oyster Farm.** Located on the edge of Drakes Estero (a large saltwater lagoon on the Point Reyes peninsula that produces nearly 20% of California's commercial oyster yield), **Johnson Drake's Oyster Farm** didn't look like much—a cluster of trailer homes, shacks, and oyster tanks surrounded by huge piles of oyster shells—until a change in ownership in 2005. The new owners are in the midst of restoring the historic buildings, adding visitor-friendly areas that allow you to watch the oyster-farming process, and doing general clean-up, so that the delicious fresh-out-of-the-water oysters dipped in Johnson's special sauce will come with more atmospheric flavor, too. They even added picnic tables and barbeques (supplies available) so you can enjoy your recently purchased bivalves right then and there, with Johnson's special sauce. Johnson Drake's (© **415/669-1149**) is off Sir Francis Drake Boulevard, about 6 miles west(ish) of Inverness. It's open daily 8am to 4:30pm.

Finds Steep Ravine Environmental Cabins

How's this for a great deal? For only $75 you and four of your friends can stay the night in a rustic redwood cabin that's perched on a bluff overlooking the ocean with access to hiking trails and a small, secluded beach. Mount Tamalpais State Park rents 10 bare-bones cabins that were once the private retreats of Bay Area politicians. The cabins, all of which have gorgeous ocean views, are now available to those who are stubborn enough to get a reservation and who don't mind bringing their own sleeping bags and lantern. Wood-burning stoves, platform beds, running water, and outhouses are provided, but there's no electricity, and firewood costs extra. Each cabin sleeps up to five, but only one car per cabin is allowed. The cabins are located off Highway 1, a mile south of Stinson Beach; look for a paved turnout and a brown metal sign. The cabins are very popular, so be sure to reserve one as far in advance as possible (you can book them up to 7 months prior). For reservations call ✆ **800/444-7275** or reserve online at www.reserveamerica.com. For more information, call Mount Tamalpais State Park at ✆ **415/388-2070.**

can relax and children can play on the back lawn overlooking the bay, bird sanctuary, and rolling green hills beyond. The two-bedroom suite, which has a king-size bed and a kitchenette, is ideal for families, as is the Dacha cottage, which is on the water and boasts three bedrooms, a living/dining room, large sitting room, and deck with Tomales Bay views. *Note:* The motel is nonsmoking.

12718 Sir Francis Drake Blvd., Inverness, CA 94937. ✆ **888/669-6909** or 415/669-1081. www.motelinverness.com 8 units. $99–$175 double; $400–$500 suite. MC, V. Free parking. **Amenities:** Lodge with kitchenette, pool table, and TV. *In room:* TV, coffeemaker, kitchen and Jacuzzi (in some).

SUPER-CHEAP SLEEPS

Point Reyes Hostel *Kids*   Located deep within Point Reyes National Seashore, this beautiful old ranch-style complex has 44 dormitory-style accommodations, including one room that's reserved for families (though at least one child must be 5 years old or younger). There are also two common rooms, each warmed by wood-burning stoves on chilly nights, as well as a fully equipped kitchen, barbecue (BYO charcoal), and patio. If you don't mind sharing your sleeping quarters with strangers, this is a deal that can't be beat. Reservations (and earplugs) are strongly recommended.

Off Limantour Rd. (P.O. Box 247), Point Reyes Station, CA 94956. ✆ **415/663-8811.** www.norcalhostels.org. 44 bunks, 1 private unit. $16 per adult, $9 per child under 17 with parents. MC, V. Free parking. Reception hours 7:30–10am and 4:30–9:30pm daily. **Amenities:** Kitchen, outdoor barbecue. *In room:* No phone.

WHERE TO DINE

Station House Café *&&* AMERICAN   For more than 2 decades, the Station House Café has been a favorite pit stop for Bay Areans headed to and from Point Reyes. It's a friendly, low-key place with an open kitchen, an outdoor garden dining area (key on sunny days), and live music on weekend nights. Breakfast dishes include a Hangtown omelet with local oysters and bacon, and eggs with creamed spinach and mashed-potato pancakes. Lunch and dinner specials might include fettuccine with fresh local mussels steamed in white-wine-and-butter sauce or two-cheese polenta served with fresh spinach sauté and grilled garlic-buttered tomato—all made from local produce, seafood, and organically raised Niman Ranch beef. The cafe has an extensive list of fine California wines and local as well as imported beers.

Main St., Point Reyes Station. ✆ **415/663-1515**. www.stationhousecafe.com. Reservations recommended. Breakfast $4.50–$8.50; main courses $7–$11 lunch, $9–$25 dinner. DISC, MC, V. Sun–Tues and Thurs 8am–9pm; Fri–Sat 8am–10pm.

Taqueria La Quinta *Value* MEXICAN Fresh, fast, good, and cheap: What more could you ask for in a restaurant? Taqueria La Quinta has been one of my favorite lunch stops in downtown Point Reyes for years. A huge selection of Mexican-American dishes are posted above the counter. My favorite is chile verde in a spicy tomatillo sauce with a side of handmade corn tortillas. Those in the know inquire about the seafood specials. Since it's all self-serve, you can skip the tip, but watch out for the salsa—that sucker's *hot*.

11285 Calif. 1 (at Third and Main sts.), Point Reyes Station. ✆ **415/663-8868**. Main courses $5–$9. No credit cards. Wed–Mon 11:30am–7:30pm.

The Wine Country

Even if you're having the time of your life in downtown San Francisco, I highly recommend at least a quick jaunt to the Wine Country, an hour or so north by car. Amid the mountains dipping into grapevine-trellised valleys, you'll experience an entirely different Northern California: fresh country air, mustard-flower-draped hillsides in spring, hot weather during summer, some of the world's finest wineries, incredible restaurants, green cow-studded pastures, and virtually nothing to do but overindulge. With eating, drinking, and lounging the encouraged attractions, there's virtually no better definition of a vacation than a few days here.

To decide which of the Wine Country's two distinct valleys (Napa and Sonoma) you prefer to visit, you need to consider their differences: The most obvious is size—Napa Valley dwarfs Sonoma Valley in population, number of wineries, and sheer volume of tourism (and traffic). Napa is definitely the more commercial of the two, with many more wineries and spas to choose from, and a superior selection of restaurants, hotels, and quintessential Wine Country activities, like

hot-air ballooning. Furthermore, if your goal is to really learn about the world of winemaking, Napa Valley should be your choice. World-class wineries such as Sterling and Robert Mondavi offer the most interesting and edifying wine tours in North America, if not the world (although Sonoma's Benziger Winery does give them a run for their money).

Meanwhile, Sonoma Valley is the answer for those who are in the less-is-more camp. Napa Valley's neighbor has fewer wineries (about 35), fewer big hotels and restaurants, and a less commercial feel. As a result, there are fewer crowds on the low-key country roads; more down-home charm in the country communities, B&Bs, and little family-run restaurants; and, in general, more opportunities for intimate pastoral experiences. For more on Sonoma Valley's offerings (as spectacular as Napa Valley's but more low-key), see the "Sonoma Valley" section.

If you're planning a more extensive trip to the area, consult *Frommer's Portable California Wine Country* (Wiley Publishing, Inc.).

1 Napa Valley

Just 55 miles north of San Francisco, the city of Napa and its neighboring towns have an overall tourist and big-business feel. You'll see plenty of rolling hills, flora and fauna, and vast stretches of vineyards, but they come hand-in-hand with upscale restaurants, designer discount outlets, rows of hotels and, in summer, traffic clustered more tightly than the grapes hanging heavy on the vine. Even with hordes of visitors year-round, Napa is still pretty sleepy, focusing on daytime attractions (wine, outdoor activities, and spas) and, of course, food. Nightlife is very limited, but after indulging all day, most visitors are ready to turn in early anyway.

Tips   **Reservations at Wineries**

Plenty of wineries' doors are open to everyone between 10am and 4:30pm. Most wineries that require reservations for visits do so because of local permit laws. It's always best to call ahead if you have your heart set on visiting a certain winery. A few wineries limit the number of guests to create a more intimate experience. In many cases, however, they'll be just as happy to see you if you arrive unannounced.

Although the name "Napa Valley" seems sprawling, the actual area is relatively condensed and only 35 miles long. You can venture from the town of Napa all the way to Calistoga in half an hour (traffic permitting).

ESSENTIALS

GETTING THERE   From San Francisco, cross the Golden Gate Bridge and continue north on U.S. 101. Turn east on California Highway 37, turn left onto the 12/121 turn-off and follow it through the Carneros District to Highway 29, the main road through the Wine Country. Head north on 29. Downtown Napa is a few minutes ahead, while Yountville, Oakville, Rutherford, St. Helena, and Calistoga are farther along.

Highway 29 (the St. Helena Hwy.) runs the length of Napa Valley. You really can't get lost—there's just one north-south road, on which most of the wineries, hotels, shops, and restaurants are located. The other main thoroughfare, which parallels Highway 29, is the Silverado Trail. You'll find lots of great wineries here, too.

VISITOR INFORMATION   Once you're in Napa Valley, you can stop at the **Napa Valley Conference & Visitors Bureau,** 1310 Town Center Mall, Napa, CA 94559 (*©* **707/226-7459;** www.napavalley.org). It offers a $10 package that includes *The Napa Valley Guide,* a bunch of brochures, a map, and a "Four Perfect Days in The Wine Country" itinerary. If you don't want to pay for the official publications, point your browser to www.napavalley.org, the NVCVB's official site, which has lots of the same information for free.

TOURING THE NAPA VALLEY & WINERIES

Napa Valley claims more than 37,000 acres of vineyards, making it the most densely planted wine-growing region in the United States. The venture from one end to the other is easy; you can drive it in around half an hour (but expect it to take closer to 50 min. during high season, Apr–Nov). With nearly 300 wineries tucked into the nooks and crannies surrounding Highway 29 and the Silverado Trail—almost all of which offer tastings and sales—it's worthwhile to research which wineries you'd like to visit before you hit the wine trails. If you'd like a map outlining the details around all of the region's wineries, you can grab one from the visitor center or see *Frommer's Portable California Wine Country.*

Conveniently, most of the large wineries—as well as most of the hotels, shops, and restaurants—are along a single road, Highway 29. It starts at the mouth of the Napa River, near the north end of San Francisco Bay, and continues north to Calistoga and the northern limits of the grape-growing region. When planning your tour, keep in mind that most wineries are closed on major holidays.

The Wine Country

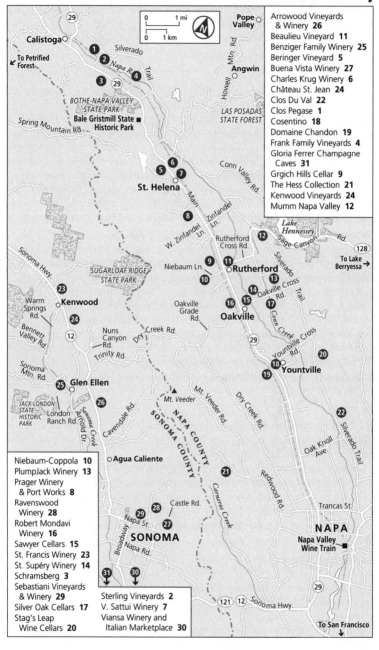

Calistoga

To Petrified Forest

Silverado Trail

Napa Rd.

BOTHE-NAPA VALLEY STATE PARK

Spring Mountain Rd.

Bale Gristmill State Historic Park ■

St. Helena

W. Zinfandel Ln.

Zinfandel Ln.

Sonoma Hwy.

SUGARLOAF RIDGE STATE PARK

Warm Springs Rd.

Kenwood

Bennett Valley Rd.

Sonoma Mtn. Rd.

Glen Ellen

JACK LONDON STATE HISTORIC PARK

London Ranch Rd.

Nuns Canyon Rd.

Trinity Rd.

Dry Creek Rd.

Oakville Grade Rd.

Niebaum Ln.

Rutherford Cross Rd.

Rutherford

Oakville

Oakville Cross Rd.

Conn Creek Rd.

Yountville Cross Rd.

Yountville

Conn Valley Rd.

Lake Hennessey

Sage Canyon Rd.

To Lake Berryessa →

128

Silverado Trail

Pope Valley

Angwin

Howell Mtn. Rd.

LAS POSADAS STATE FOREST

Cavendale Rd.

Mt. Veeder

Mt. Veeder Rd.

NAPA COUNTY

SONOMA COUNTY

Dry Creek Rd.

Redwood Rd.

Oak Knoll Ave.

Silverado Trail

Trancas St.

NAPA

Napa Valley Wine Train ■

Agua Caliente

Castle Rd.

Napa St.

SONOMA

Napa Rd.

Broadway

Carneros Creek

121

12

Sonoma Hwy.

29

To San Francisco ↓

Arrowood Vineyards & Winery **26**
Beaulieu Vineyard **11**
Benziger Family Winery **25**
Beringer Vineyard **5**
Buena Vista Winery **27**
Charles Krug Winery **6**
Château St. Jean **24**
Clos Du Val **22**
Clos Pegase **1**
Cosentino **18**
Domaine Chandon **19**
Frank Family Vineyards **4**
Gloria Ferrer Champagne Caves **31**
Grgich Hills Cellar **9**
The Hess Collection **21**
Kenwood Vineyards **24**
Mumm Napa Valley **12**

Niebaum-Coppola **10**
PlumpJack Winery **13**
Prager Winery & Port Works **8**
Ravenswood Winery **28**
Robert Mondavi Winery **16**
Sawyer Cellars **15**
St. Francis Winery **23**
St. Supéry Winery **14**
Schramsberg **3**
Sebastiani Vineyards & Winery **29**
Silver Oak Cellars **17**
Stag's Leap Wine Cellars **20**

Sterling Vineyards **2**
V. Sattui Winery **7**
Viansa Winery and Italian Marketplace **30**

All of the Napa Valley establishments in this chapter—every town, winery, hotel, and restaurant—is organized below from south to north, beginning in the city of Napa, and can be reached from the main thoroughfare of Highway 29.

NAPA

55 miles N of San Francisco

The city of Napa serves as the commercial center of the Wine Country and the gateway to Napa Valley—hence the high-speed freeway that whips you right past it and on to the "tourist" towns of St. Helena and Calistoga. However, if you veer off the highway, you'll be surprised to discover a small but burgeoning community of nearly 73,000 residents with the most cosmopolitan (if you can call it that) atmosphere in the county—and some of the most affordable accommodations in the valley. It's in the process of gentrification, thanks to (relatively) affordable housing, a charming old-fashioned downtown, and ongoing additions of new restaurants. Heading north on either Highway 29 or the Silverado Trail leads you to Napa's wineries and the more quintessential Wine Country atmosphere of vineyards and wide-open country views.

The Hess Collection *★★ Finds* Tucked into the hillside of rural Mount Veeder, one of the region's sexiest wineries brings art and wine together like no other destination in the valley. Swiss art collector Donald Hess is behind the 1978 transformation of the Christian Brothers' 1903 property into a winery-art gallery exhibiting huge, colorful works by the likes of Frank Stella, Francis Bacon, and the latest addition, an Anselm Kiefer. A free self-guided tour leads you through the collection and the winemaking facilities. Equally alluring is the picturesque courtyard and exceptionally tasteful gift shop. For $5, you can sample the current cabernet and chardonnay and one other featured wine. For bottles, current-release prices start at $10 and top off at around $90. *The only downside:* Staff can be cold and stuffy.

4411 Redwood Rd., Napa. ✆ 707/255-1144. www.hesscollection.com. Daily 10am–4pm, except some holidays. From Hwy. 29 north, exit at Redwood Rd. west, and follow Redwood Rd. for 6½ miles.

Clos Du Val Outside French and American flags mark the entrance to the ivy-covered building and well-manicured rose garden. Inside, you'll experience a friendly, small-business atmosphere along with a matter-of-fact tasting room pouring California wines made in subtler French-style.

Cabernet makes up 70% of the winery's production, but other varietals include chardonnay, pinot noir, and merlot. There's a $5 tasting charge (refunded with purchase) for about four wines, which may include a library selection or two. Lovely picnic facilities and free access to the lawn game *petanque* are available.

5330 Silverado Trail (north of Oak Knoll Ave.), Napa. ✆ 707/259-2200. Daily 10am–5pm. Tours by appointment only.

Stag's Leap Wine Cellars Founded in 1972, Stag's Leap shocked the oenological world in 1976 when its 1973 cabernet won first place over French wines in a Parisian blind tasting. Visit the charmingly landscaped, unfussy winery and its very cramped "tasting room" where, for $10 per person, you can judge the four to six current releases; or you can fork over up to $30 for estate samples. A 1-hour tour and tasting runs through everything from the vineyard and production facilities to the ultra-swank $5-million wine caves (used to store and age wine), which premiered in mid-2001.

5766 Silverado Trail, Napa. ✆ 707/944-2020. www.cask23.com. Daily 10am–4:30pm. Tours by appointment only. From Hwy. 29, go east on Trancas St. or Oak Knoll Ave., then north to the cellars.

YOUNTVILLE
70 miles N of San Francisco

Yountville (pop. 2,916) was founded by the first white American to settle in the valley, George Calvert Yount. While it lacks the small-town charm of neighboring St. Helena and Calistoga—primarily because its main street, though filling up with hotels, restaurants, and shops, doesn't feel like a center—it's still a great starting point for valley exploration. It's home to a handful of excellent wineries and inns and a small stretch of fab restaurants, including the world-renowned French Laundry.

Domaine Chandon *Kids Finds*   Founded in 1973 by French champagne house Moët et Chandon, the valley's most renowned sparkling winemaker rises to the grand occasion with truly elegant grounds and atmosphere. Here manicured gardens showcase locally made sculpture, and guests linger—their glasses fizzing with bubbly—under the patio's umbrella shade. In the restaurant, diners indulge in a somewhat formal French-inspired meal (there's a more casual menu at lunchtime). If you can pull yourself away from the Salon's bubbly (sold in tastings for $9–$14), the comprehensive tour of the facilities is interesting, very informative, and friendly. There's also a boutique. *Note:* The restaurant, which is closed on Tuesday and Wednesday and has even more restricted winter hours, usually requires reservations.

1 California Dr. (at Hwy. 29), Yountville. (C) **707/944-2280**. www.chandon.com. Daily 10am–6pm; hours vary by season, so call to confirm. Call for free tour schedules.

Cosentino   Known for its friendly, laid-back atmosphere and vast selection of wines, Cosentino's tasting room is a great stop for anyone interested in covering a lot of wine-tasting ground under one roof. Pay $5 to taste ($10 for reserve wines) among 40 wines from their portfolio, with prices ranging from $12 to $100 (and yes, you get to keep the glass). There's lots of entertainment value at the long copper-top bar as well. Join the wine club for free tastings and 25% off purchases.

7415 St. Helena Hwy. (Hwy. 29), Yountville. (C) **707/944-1220**. www.cosentinowinery.com. Daily 10am–5pm (until 5:30pm during daylight saving time).

OAKVILLE
68 miles N of San Francisco

Driving farther north on Highway 29 brings you to Oakville, most easily recognized by Oakville Cross Road.

PlumpJack Winery   If most wineries are like a Brooks Brothers suit, PlumpJack stands out as the Todd Oldham of wine tasting: chic, colorful, a little wild, and popular with a young, hip crowd as well as a growing number of aficionados. Like the

---

Tips **Napa Valley Traffic**

Travel the Silverado Trail as often as possible to avoid California Highway 29's traffic. It runs parallel to and about 2 miles east of Highway 29. You get there from the city of Napa or by taking any of the "crossroads" from Highway 29. Crossroads are not well signposted, but they're clearly defined on most maps. Avoid passing through Main Street in St. Helena during high season. Although a wintertime ride from Napa to Calistoga can take 30 minutes, in summer you can expect the trek to take closer to 50 minutes.

Value Wine-Shopping Wisdom

Before you buy wine from the wineries, be sure to check out the local wine shops. More often than not, prices in the shops are usually better, and they're likely to stock that buttery chardonnay or fat cabernet that you tasted earlier in the day. In Napa, head to St. Helena, where both **Dean & DeLuca Market,** 607 S. Main St. (© **707/967-9980;** www.deandeluca.com), and **Safeway** supermarket, 1026 Hunt Ave. (© **707/963-3833**), have enormous wine selections. In fact, Safeway offers some of the best deals and selections in the entire Wine Country. In Sonoma, your best bet is the **Wine Exchange of Sonoma,** on the plaza at 452 First St. E. (© **800/938-1794** or **707/938-1794;** www.wineexsonoma.com), which carries more than 700 domestic wines (some at steep discounts) and has a tasting bar run by a savvy staff.

franchise's PlumpJack San Francisco restaurants and wine shop, and Lake Tahoe resort, this playfully medieval winery is a welcome diversion from the same old same old. With Getty bucks behind what was once Villa Mt. Eden winery, the budget covers far more than just atmosphere: There's some serious winemaking going on here, too. For $5 you can sample the cabernet, merlot, and chardonnay. Alas, there are no tours or picnic spots.

620 Oakville Cross Rd. (just west of the Silverado Trail), Oakville. © **707/945-1220.** www.plumpjack.com. Daily 10am–4pm.

Robert Mondavi Winery ★ *(Finds)*   At mission-style Mondavi, computers control almost every variable in the winemaking process—it's fascinating to watch, especially since Mondavi gives the most comprehensive tours in the valley. Basic jaunts, which cost $20 and last about an hour and fifteen minutes, take you through the vineyards—complete with examples of varietals—and through their newest winemaking facilities. Ask the guides anything; they know a heck of a lot. After the tour, you taste the results of all this attention to detail in selected current wines. If you're really into learning more about wine, ask about their myriad in-depth tours, such as the $50 "essence tasting," which explores the flavor profiles of wine by sniff-comparing varietals alongside the scents of fresh fruits, spices, and nuts. In summer, the winery also schedules some great outdoor concerts; previous performers included Buena Vista Social Club and Chaka Kahn. Call about upcoming events.

7801 St. Helena Hwy. (Hwy. 29), Oakville. © **800/MONDAVI** or 707/226-1395. www.robertmondaviwinery.com. Daily 10am–4pm, till 5 in summer. Reservations recommended for guided tour; book 1 week ahead, especially for weekend tours.

RUTHERFORD
3 miles N of Oakville

If you so much as blink after Oakville, you're likely to overlook Rutherford, the next small town that borders on St. Helena. Each town in Napa Valley has its share of spectacular wineries, but you won't see most of them while driving along Highway 29.

Sawyer Cellars *(Finds)*   The most attractive thing about Sawyer, aside from its clean and tasty wines, is its dedication to extremely high quality wine while it maintains a humble, accommodating attitude. Step into the simple restored 1920s barn to see what I mean. Whatever you ask, the tasting-room host will answer. Whatever your request, they do their best to accommodate it. Want to picnic on the back patio overlooking the vineyards? Be their guest. Like to participate in a crush? Come on over and get your hands dirty. Reserve their charming wine library for a private luncheon? Pay a minimal fee and make yourself at home. Here you can tour the property on a little tram or learn more about winemaker Brad Warner, who spent 30 years at Mondavi before embarking on this exclusive endeavor. Plunk down $5 to taste delicious estate-made wines: sauvignon blanc, merlot, cabernet sauvignon, and Meritage ($16–$46 for current releases), which some argue are worth twice the price. With a total production of only 4,200 cases and a friendly attitude, this winery is a rare treat.

8350 St. Helena Hwy. (Hwy. 29), Rutherford. © **707/963-1980**. www.sawyercellars.com. Daily 10am–5pm. Tasting and tours by appointment.

St. Supéry Winery *Kids*   The outside looks like a modern corporate office building, but inside you'll find a functional, welcoming winery that encourages first-time tasters to learn more about oenology. On the self-guided tour, you can wander through the demonstration vineyard, where you'll learn about growing techniques. Inside, kids gravitate toward coloring books and "SmellaVision," an interactive display that teaches you how to identify different wine ingredients. Adjoining it is the Atkinson House, which chronicles more than 100 years of winemaking history during public tours at 1pm and 3pm. For $10, you'll get lifetime tasting privileges and a tour, which includes samples of four wines, which hopefully includes their excellent and very well-priced sauvignon blanc. Even the prices make visitors feel at home: Bottles start at $19, although the tag on their high-end bordeaux red blend is $50.

8440 St. Helena Hwy. (Hwy. 29), Rutherford. © **800/942-0809** or 707/963-4507. www.stsupery.com. Daily 10am–5pm (until 5:30pm during summer). Daily tours at 1pm and 3pm $10.

Niebaum-Coppola   Hollywood meets Napa Valley at Francis Ford Coppola's historic Inglenook Vineyards, now known as Niebaum-Coppola (*Nee*-bom *Coh*-pa-la). Outside the spectacular 1880s ivy-draped stone winery and grounds are historic grandeur. Inside, you'll find one giant wine bar and retail center downstairs and, upstairs, displays from Coppola's films, memorabilia, from Academy Awards to trinkets from *The Godfather* and *Bram Stoker's Dracula*. Wine, food, and gift items dominate the cavernous tasting area, where wines such as an estate-grown blend, cabernet Franc, merlot, zinfandel made from organically grown grapes are sampled four wines for $15 (price includes a souvenir glass). Bottles range from around $19 to more than $100. Multiple daily tours include the Historic Tour, Vineyard Experience, Rubicon Winery, and more. *Tip:* Drop by, snoop around on your own, and spend the cash you save from skipping the tour on one more bottle for your vacation collection. Basic tours are $25.

1991 St. Helena Hwy. (Hwy. 29), Rutherford. © **707/968-1100**. www.niebaum-coppola.com. Sept–May daily 10am–5pm; June–Aug Sun–Thurs 10am–5pm and Fri–Sat 10am–6pm. Tours daily.

Beaulieu Vineyard   Bordeaux native Georges de Latour founded the third-oldest continuously operating winery in Napa Valley in 1900. With the help of legendary oenologist André Tchelistcheff, he produced world-class, award-winning wines that have been served by every president of the United States since Franklin D. Roosevelt. The brick-and-redwood tasting room isn't much to look at, but with Beaulieu's (*Bowl*-you) stellar reputation, it has no need to visually impress. Appellation tastings cost $5, and a variety of bottles sell for under $20. The recently remodeled Reserve Tasting Room offers a "flight" of five reserve wines to taste for $25, but if you want to take a bottle to go, it may cost upward of $100.

1960 St. Helena Hwy. (Hwy. 29), Rutherford. © **707/967-5230**. www.bvwines.com. Daily 10am–5pm.

Grgich Hills Cellar   Croatian émigré Miljenko (Mike) Grgich (*Grr*-gitch) made his presence known to the world when his 1973 Château Montelena chardonnay bested the top French white burgundies at the famous 1976 Paris tasting. Since then, the master vintner teamed up with Austin Hills (of the Hills Brothers coffee fortune) and started this extremely successful and respected winery featuring estate grown wines from organically and biodynamically farmed vineyards.

The ivy-covered stucco building isn't much to behold, and the tasting room is even less appealing, but people don't come here for the scenery: As you might expect, Grgich's chardonnays are legendary—and priced accordingly. The smart buys are the outstanding zinfandel and cabernet sauvignon, which cost around $28 and $50, respectively. The winery also produces a fantastic fumé blanc for $21 a bottle. Before you leave, be sure to poke your head into the barrel-aging room and inhale the divine aroma. Tastings cost $5 (which includes the glass). No picnic facilities are available.

1829 St. Helena Hwy. (Hwy. 29, north of Rutherford Cross Rd.), Rutherford. © **707/963-2784**. www.grgich.com. Daily 9:30am–4:30pm. $10 tours by appointment only, Mon–Fri 11am and 2pm; Sat–Sun 11am and 1:30pm.

Mumm Napa Valley   At first glance, Mumm, housed in a big redwood barn, looks almost humble. Once you're through the front door, however, you'll know that they mean business—big business. Just beyond the extensive gift shop (filled with all sorts of namesake mementos) is the tasting room, where you can purchase sparkling wine by the glass ($5–$8), three-wine flights ($8–$25), or the bottle ($16–$70), and appreciate breathtaking vineyard and mountain views on the open patio. You can also take a 45-minute free educational tour and stroll the impressive photography gallery, which features a permanent Ansel Adams collection and ever-changing photography exhibits. Sorry, there's no food or picnicking here.

8445 Silverado Trail (just south of Rutherford Cross Rd.), Rutherford. © **800/686-6272** or 707/942-3434. www.mummnapa.com. Daily 10am–5pm. Tours offered every hour daily 10am–3pm.

ST. HELENA
73 miles N of San Francisco

Located 17 miles north of Napa on Highway 29, this former Seventh-Day Adventist village maintains a pseudo–Old West feel while catering to upscale shoppers with deep pockets—hence Vanderbilt and Company, purveyor of fine housewares, at 1429 Main St. St. Helena is a quiet, attractive little town, where you'll find a slew of beautiful old homes and first-rate restaurants and accommodations.

V. Sattui Winery ⊛ *Kids* *Finds*   So what if it's touristy and crowded? This enormous winery is also a fun picnic-party stop thanks to a huge gourmet deli and grassy expanse. It's especially great for families since you can fill up on wine, pâté, and cheese samples without ever reaching for your pocketbook, while the kids romp around the grounds. The gourmet store stocks more than 200 cheeses, sandwich meats, exotic salads, and desserts such as white-chocolate cheesecake. (It would be an easy place to graze were it not for the continuous mob scene at the counter.) Meanwhile, the extensive wine offerings flow at the long wine bar in the back. Wines aren't distributed, so if you taste something you simply must have, buy it. (A case purchase will get you membership into their private cellar and its less crowded, private tasting room.) Wine prices start at around $9, with many in the $16 neighborhood; reserves top out at around $75. *Note:* To use the picnic area, you must buy food and wine here.

1111 White Lane (at Hwy. 29), St. Helena. © 707/963-7774. www.vsattui.com. Winter daily 9am–5pm; summer daily 9am–6pm.

Prager Winery & Port Works *(Finds* If you want a real down-home, off-the-beaten-track experience, Prager's can't be beat. Turn the corner from Sutter Home winery and roll into the small gravel parking lot; you're on the right track, but when you pull open the creaky old wooden door to this shack of a wine-tasting room, you'll begin to wonder. Don't turn back! Pass the oak barrels, and you'll quickly come upon the clapboard tasting room, made homey with a big Oriental rug and a Prager family host. Fork over $10 (includes a complimentary glass), and they'll pour you samples of late-harvest Johannesburg Riesling and the tawny port (which costs $45–$65 per bottle). Also available is "Prager Chocolate Drizzle," a chocolate liqueur that tops ice creams and other desserts. If you're looking for a special gift, consider their bottles, which can be custom etched in the design of your choice for around $75, plus the cost of the wine.

1281 Lewelling Lane (just west of Hwy. 29, behind Sutter Home), St. Helena. © 800/969-PORT or 707/963-7678. www.pragerport.com. Daily 10:30am–4:30pm.

Beringer Vineyards *(Finds* You won't find a personal experience at this tourist-heavy stop. But you will find a regal 1876 estate founded by brothers Jacob and Frederick and hand-dug tunnels in the hillside. The oldest continuously operating winery in Napa Valley, Beringer managed to stay open even during Prohibition by making "sacramental" wines. White zinfandel is the winery's most popular seller, but plenty of other varietals are available to enjoy. Tastings of current vintages ($5–$16) are conducted in new facilities, where there's also a large selection of bottles for less than $20. Reserve wines are available for tasting in the remarkable Rhine House and tours range from the $5 standard or $18 historical to the $30 1½-hour vintage legacy tour.

2000 Main St. (Hwy. 29), St. Helena. © 707/963-7115. www.beringer.com. Winter daily 10am–5pm (last tour 3:30pm, last tasting 4:30pm); summer 10am–6pm (last tour 3:30pm, last tasting 5:30pm).

Charles Krug Winery Founded in 1861, Krug was the first winery built in the valley. The family of Peter Mondavi (yes, Robert is his brother) owns it today. It's worth paying your respects here by dropping $5 to sip current releases, $8 to sample reserves. On the grounds are picnic facilities with umbrella-shaded tables overlooking vineyards or the wine cellar.

2800 Main St. (St. Helena Hwy.), St. Helena. © 707/963-5057. www.charleskrug.com. Daily 10:30am–5pm.

CALISTOGA
81 miles N of San Francisco

Calistoga, the last tourist town in Napa Valley, got its name from Sam Brannan, entrepreneur extraordinaire and California's first millionaire. After making a bundle supplying miners during the gold rush, he went on to take advantage of the natural geothermal springs at the north end of the valley by building a hotel and spa here in 1859. Flubbing up a speech, in which he compared this natural California wonder to New York State's Saratoga Springs resort town, he serendipitously coined the name "Calistoga," and it stuck. Today, this small, simple resort town, with 5,225 residents and an old-time main street (no building along the 6-block stretch is more than two stories high), is popular with city folk who come here to unwind. Calistoga is a great place to relax and indulge in mineral waters, mud baths, Jacuzzis, massages and, of course, wine. The vibe is more casual—and a little groovier—than you find in neighboring towns to the south.

Frank Family Vineyards ⓡ *Finds*   "Wine dudes" Dennis, Tim, Jeff, Grant, and Pat will do practically anything to maintain their rightfully self-proclaimed reputation as the "friendliest winery in the valley." In recent years the name may have changed from Kornell Champagne Cellars to Frank-Rombauer to Frank Family, but the vibe's remained constant; it's all about down-home, friendly fun. No muss, no fuss, no intimidation factor. At Frank Family, you're part of their family—no joke. They'll greet you like a long-lost relative and serve you all the bubbly you want (three to four varieties: blanc de blanc, blanc de noir, reserve, rouge, at $20–$70 a bottle). Still-wine lovers can slip into the equally casual back room to sample chardonnay and a very well received cabernet sauvignon. Behind the tasting room is a choice picnic area, situated under the oaks and overlooking the vineyards.

1091 Larkmead Lane (just off the Silverado Trail), Calistoga. ⓒ **707/942-0859**. Daily 10am–5pm.

Schramsberg ⓡⓡ *Finds*   This 217-acre champagne estate, a landmark once frequented by Robert Louis Stevenson, has a wonderful old-world feel and is one of the valley's all-time best places to explore. Schramsberg is the label that presidents serve when toasting dignitaries from around the globe, and there's plenty of historic memorabilia in the front room to prove it. But the real mystique begins when you enter the champagne caves, which wind 2 miles (reputedly the longest in North America) and were partly hand-carved by Chinese laborers in the 1800s. The caves have an authentic Tom Sawyer ambience, complete with dangling cobwebs and seemingly endless passageways; you can't help but feel you're on an adventure. The comprehensive, unintimidating tour ends in a charming tasting room, where you'll sit around a big table and sample four surprisingly varied selections of bubbly. Tastings are a bit dear ($20 per person), but it's money well spent. Note that tastings are offered only to those who take the free tour, and you must reserve in advance.

1400 Schramsberg Rd. (off Hwy. 29), Calistoga. ⓒ **707/942-2414**. www.schramsberg.com. Daily 10am–4pm. Tours and tastings by appointment only.

Sterling Vineyards ⓡ *Kids* *Finds*   No, you don't need climbing shoes to reach this dazzling white Mediterranean-style winery, perched 300 feet up on a rocky knoll. Just fork over $15 ($10 for kids—including a goodie bag) and take the aerial tram, which offers stunning bucolic views along the way. Once you're back on land, follow the self-guided tour (one of the most comprehensive in the Wine Country) of the winemaking process. Wine tastings of four varietals in the panoramic tasting room are included in the tram fare, but more sophisticated sips—limited releases or reserve flights—will set you back anywhere from $3 to $25, respectively. Expect to pay anywhere from $14 to $75 for a souvenir bottle ($20 is the average).

1111 Dunaweal Lane (off Hwy. 29, just south of downtown Calistoga), Calistoga. ⓒ **707/942-3344**. www.sterling vineyards.com. Daily 10:30am–4:30pm.

Clos Pegase ⓡ *Finds*   Renowned architect Michael Graves designed this incredible oasis, which integrates art, 20,000 square feet of aging caves, and a luxurious hilltop private home. Viewing the art is as much the point as tasting the wines—which, by the way, don't come cheap: Prices range from $13 for the 2000 Vin Gris merlot to as much as $75 for the 1998 Hommage Artist Series Reserve, an extremely limited blend

Tips   **The Ins & Outs of Shipping Wine Home**

Because of absurd and forever fluctuating "reciprocity laws"—which supposedly protect the business of the country's wine distributors—wine shipping is limited by regulations that vary in each of the 50 states. Shipping rules also vary from winery to winery.

If you happen to live in a reciprocal state and the winery you're buying from offers shipping, you're in luck. You buy and pay the postage, and the winery sends your purchase for you. It's as simple as that. If that winery doesn't ship, it can most likely give you an easy solution.

If you live in a nonreciprocal state, the winery might still have shipping advice for you, so definitely ask. Some refuse to ship at all; others are more than accommodating. Be cautious of wineries that tell you they can ship to nonreciprocal states, and make sure you get a firm commitment. If they can't help you, ask them who can. Everyone knows how to get around these rules.

You may face the challenge of finding a shipping company yourself. If that's the case, keep in mind that it's technically illegal to box your own wine and send it to a nonreciprocal state; the shipper could lose its license, and you could lose your wine. If you do get stuck shipping illegally (not that we're recommending you do that), you might want to package your wine in an unassuming box and head to a post office, UPS, or other shipping company outside the Wine Country area. It's less obvious that you're shipping wine from Vallejo or San Francisco than from Napa Valley.

Napa Valley Shipping Companies
The UPS Store, at 3212 Jefferson St. in the Grape Yard Shopping Center (© **707/259-1398**), claims to pack and ship anything anywhere. Rates for a case of wine were quoted at approximately $25 for ground shipping to Los Angeles and $64 to New York.

St. Helena Mailing Center, 1241 Adams St., at Highway 29, St. Helena (© **707/963-2686**), says they will pack and ship to reciprocal states within the U.S. Rates for pre-wrapped shipments are around $30 per case for ground delivery to Los Angeles, $92 to New York.

Sonoma Valley Shipping Companies
Mail Boxes Etc., 19229 Sonoma Hwy., at Verano Street, Sonoma (© **707/935-3438**), has a lot of experience with shipping wine. It claims it will ship your wine to any state. Prices vary from $22 to Los Angeles to as much as $73 to the East Coast and $140 to Hawaii and Alaska.

The **Wine Exchange of Sonoma,** 452 First St. E., between East Napa and East Spain streets, Sonoma (© **707/938-1794**), will ship your wine, but there's a catch: You must buy an amount of any wine at the store that is equal to the amount of wine that you're shipping home (the prices here are quite competitive). Shipping rates range from $20 to Los Angeles to $50 to the East Coast.

of the winery's finest lots of cabernet sauvignon and merlot. Tasting current releases cost $5 for three whites and $10 for five reds. The grounds at Clos Pegase (Clo Pey-*goss*) feature an impressive sculpture garden as well as scenic picnic spots.

1060 Dunaweal Lane (off Hwy. 29 or the Silverado Trail), Calistoga. (€) **707/942-4981.** www.clospegase.com. Daily 10:30am–5pm. Tours daily at 11am and 2pm.

BEYOND THE WINERIES: WHAT TO SEE & DO IN NAPA VALLEY
NAPA/ST. HELENA

If you have plenty of time and a penchant for Victorian architecture, seek out the **Napa Valley Conference & Visitors Bureau,** 1310 Napa Town Center, off First Street (€ **707/226-7459;** www.napavalley.com), which offers $2 self-guided walking tours of the town's historic buildings.

A MUSEUM   **Copia: The American Center for Wine, Food & the Arts,** at 500 First St. (€ **707/259-1600;** www.copia.org), opened at the end of 2001 with a mission to explore how wine and food influence our culture. This $50-million multifaceted facility, which was spearheaded by Robert Mondavi, tackles the topic in a myriad of ways, including visual arts a la rotating exhibits, vast organic vegetable and herb gardens, fun culinary demonstrations, basic wine classes, concerts, and opportunities to dine and drink on the premises. There's not a ton to look at, but kids will get a kick out of identifying candy bars through pictures, while connoisseurs might pay extra to slip into seasonal cooking demos by famous chefs. Drop by the cafe for gourmet picnic items or the neighboring gift shop for food-related finds, but skip the so-so adjoining restaurant. Also, drop by Tuesday morning from April through November for the outdoor farmers market and check out their Monday night summer concert series for great, affordable alfresco entertainment.

(*Finds* Enjoying Art & Nature

Anyone with an appreciation for art absolutely must visit the **di Rosa Preserve.** Rene and Veronica di Rosa collected contemporary American art for more than 40 years and then converted their 215 acres of prime property into a monument to Northern California's regional art and nature. Veronica has passed on, but Rene still carries the torch through his world-renowned collection featuring 2,000 works in all media, by more than 900 Greater Bay Area artists. The di Rosas' treasures are on display practically everywhere—along the shores of the property's 35-acre lake and in each nook and cranny of their 125-year-old winery-turned-residence, adjoining building, two newer galleries, and gardens. With hundreds of surrounding acres of rolling hills (protected under the Napa County Land Trust), this place is a must-see for both art and nature lovers. It's at 5200 Carneros Hwy. (Hwy. 121/12); look for the gate. Each tour lasts 2 to 2½ hours, has a maximum of 25 guests, and costs $12 per person on weekdays, $15 on Saturday (10am tour is free every Wed). Reservations recommended. Call € **707/226-5991** to make reservations. Open Tuesday to Friday 9:30am to 3pm and Saturday by appointment. www.dirosapreserve.org

---

Tips Sip Tip

You can cheaply sip your way through downtown Napa without ever getting behind the wheel with the new "Taste Napa Downtown" wine card. For a mere $15, you get 10¢ tasting privileges at 10 local wine-centric watering holes and tasting rooms, all of which are within walking distance of each other. Plus you'll get 10% discounts at tasting rooms and free admission to Copia. It's available at the **Napa Valley Conference & Visitors Bureau,** 1310 Napa Town Center, off First St. (© **707/226-7459**) and Copia (see above). Learn more at **www.napa downtown.com**.

Copia admission is $13 for adults, $10 for seniors 62 and over, $7.50 for students of any age, $5 for young adults ages 13 to 20, and free for children 13 and younger. The center is open Wednesday through Monday from 10am to 5pm. The restaurant stays open until 9:30pm from Thursday through Sunday. Wednesday admissions are half-price for Napa and Sonoma residents.

SHOPPING   Shopaholics should make a beeline to the **Napa Premium Outlets** (© 707/226-9876; www.premiumoutlets.com), where Barneys New York can inspire even a jaded local to take the First Street exit off Highway 29 and brave the crowds. Unfortunately, Barneys now carries only cheap outlet-store stuff, but, you'll find multiple places to part with your money, including TSE (killer cashmere at basement prices), Banana Republic, Calvin Klein, Nine West, Benetton, Jones New York, BCBG, more fashion shops, a few kitchenware shops, a food court, and a decent (but expensive) sushi restaurant. Shops are open Monday through Saturday from 10am to 8pm and Sunday from 10am to 6pm. Call for seasonal hours.

In Yountville, it's worth peeking into **Mosswood Collection,** 6550 Washington St. (© 707/944-8151), for Elizabeth Lampe's selection of pretty, perky hand-painted martini glasses, wall tapestries, and fabulous customizable food-and-wine etchings. You'll also find antique corkscrews, garden art, tabletop items, children's toys, and a great selection of ribbons. Open daily 10am to 5pm.

St. Helena's Main Street ✦ is the best place to go if you're suffering serious retail withdrawal. Here you'll find trendy fashions at **Pearl,** 1428 Main St. (© 707-963-3236), Jimmy Choo shoes at **Footcandy,** 1239 Main St. (© 707/963-2040), chic pet gifts at **Fideaux,** 1312 Main St. (© 707/967-9935), custom-embroidered French linens at **Jan de Luz,** 1219 Main St. (© 707/963-1550), estate jewelry at **Patina,** 1342 Main St. (© 707/963-5445), and European home accessories, sample holiday table settings, and free gift-wrapping at **Vanderbilt and Company,** 1429 Main St. (© 707/963-1010).

Most stores are open from 10am to 5pm Monday through Sunday; Main Street is between Pope Street and Pine Street.

Shopaholics should also take the sharp turn off Highway 29, 2 miles north of downtown St. Helena to the **St. Helena Premier Outlets** (© 707/963-7282; www.st helenapremieroutlets.com). Featured designers include Escada, Coach, Tumi, and Movado. The stores are open daily from 10am to 6pm.

One last favorite stop: **Napa Valley Olive Oil Manufacturing Company** (© 707/963-4173), 835 Charter Oak Ave., at the end of the road behind Tra Vigne restaurant. This tiny market presses and bottles its own oils and sells them at a fraction of the price you'll pay elsewhere. In addition, it has an extensive selection of Italian cooking ingredients, imported snacks, great deals on dried mushrooms, and a picnic table in the parking lot. You'll love the age-old method for totaling the bill, which you simply must find out for yourself.

HORSEBACK RIDING If you like horses and venturing through cool, misty forests, then $90 will seem like a bargain for a 2-hour ride with a friendly tour guide and owner, Midori, from the **Napa Valley Trailrides and Sonoma Cattle Company,** P.O. Box 6883, Napa, CA 94581 (© **707/255-2900;** www.napavalleytrailrides.com). After a lesson in the basics of horse handling at the stable, you'll be led on a leisurely stroll. The price includes photos and refreshments. The ride goes through beautiful Skyline Park in Napa.

SPA-ING IT If the Wine Country's slow pace and tranquil vistas aren't soothing enough for you, the region's diverse selection of spas can massage, bathe, wrap, and steam you into an overly pampered pulp. Should you choose to indulge, do so toward the end of your stay—when you've wined and dined to the point where you have only enough energy left to make it to and from the spa.

Compared to the cosmopolitan-chic day spas of the Fairmount Sonoma Mission Inn and Health Spa Napa Valley (St. Helena), which isn't much more than a gym and a spa, **White Sulphur Springs Retreat & Spa** ⊛, 3100 White Sulphur Springs Rd. (© **707/963-4361;** www.whitesulphursprings.com), offers a more spiritual day of cleansing and pampering. Yes, you will encounter massages, aromatherapy treatments, seaweed or mineral mud wraps, and a pool and Jacuzzi for guests' use. But the most blissful benefits at this funky-chic spot come from the surrounding acres of redwoods, streams, grassy fields, and wooded groves. Massages ($80 for 50 min.; $50 for 25 min.) are given in the homey spa building or outside, amid the redwoods.

BIKING The quieter northern end of the valley is an ideal place to rent a bicycle and ride the Silverado Trail. **St. Helena Cyclery,** 1156 Main St. (© **707/963-7736**), rents bikes for $7 per hour or $30 a day, including a rear rack, helmet, lock, and bag in which you can pack a picnic.

NIGHTLIFE The whole valley has little in the way of after-dinner entertainment, which leaves revelers with little choice but to turn to **1351 Lounge,** 1351 Main St. (© **707/963-1969**), a renovated stone-walled former bank complete with a shiny vault. Here locals and visitors settle around cocktail tables or at the old mahogany bar for cocktails and entertainment ranging from open-mic night to live rock, blues, or funk.

CALISTOGA

BICYCLING Cycling enthusiasts can rent bikes from **Getaway Adventures BHK** (© **800/499-BIKE** or 707/568-3040; www.getawayadventures.com). Full-day group tours cost $115 per person, include lunch and a visit to four or five wineries or $105 per person for private groups of 6 or more. Bike rental without a tour costs $28 per day plus a $20 delivery fee (for up to 20 bikes), though you can pick bikes up free of charge. You can also inquire about the company's kayaking and hiking tours.

MUD BATHS The one thing you should do while you're in Calistoga is what people have been doing here for the past 150 years: Take a mud bath. The natural baths contain local volcanic ash, imported peat, and naturally boiling mineral hot-springs water, mulled together to produce a thick mud that simmers at a temperature of about 104°F (40°C).

Indulge yourself at any of these Calistoga spas: **Dr. Wilkinson's Hot Springs,** 1507 Lincoln Ave. (© 707/942-4102); **Golden Haven Hot Springs Spa,** 1713 Lake St. (© 707/942-6793); **Calistoga Spa Hot Springs,** 1006 Washington St. (© 707/942-6269); **Calistoga Village Inn & Spa,** 1880 Lincoln Ave. (© 707/942-0991); **Indian Springs Resort,** 1712 Lincoln Ave. (© 707/942-4913); or **Roman Spa Motel,** 1300 Washington St. (© 707/942-4441).

NATURAL WONDERS   Old Faithful Geyser of California, 1299 Tubbs Lane (© **707/942-6463;** www.oldfaithfulgeyser.com), is one of only three "old faithful" geysers in the world. It's been blowing off steam at regular intervals for as long as anyone can remember. The 350°F (176°C) water spews at a height of about 40 to 60 feet every 40 minutes, day and night. The performance lasts about 3 minutes, and you can bring a picnic lunch to munch on between spews. An exhibit hall, gift shop, and snack bar are open every day. Admission is $8 for adults, $7 for seniors, $3 for children ages 6 to 12, free for children younger than 6. The geyser is open daily from 9am to 6pm (to 5pm in winter). To get there, follow the signs from downtown Calistoga; it's between Highway 29 and Calif. 128.

You won't see thousands of trees turned into stone, but you'll still find many interesting petrified specimens at the **Petrified Forest,** 4100 Petrified Forest Rd. (© **707/942-6667;** www.petrifiedforest.org). Volcanic ash blanketed this area after an eruption near Mount St. Helena 3 million years ago. You'll find redwoods that have turned to rock through the slow infiltration of silicas and other minerals, a ¼-mile walking trail, museum, discovery shop, and picnic grounds. Admission is $6 for adults, $5 for seniors and juniors ages 11 to 17, $3 for children ages 6 to 11, free for children younger than 6. The forest is open daily from 9am to 7pm (to 5pm in winter). Heading north from Calistoga on Calif. 128, turn left onto Petrified Forest Road, just past Lincoln Street.

AFFORDABLE PLACES TO STAY IN THE NAPA VALLEY

Because the Napa Valley's towns are in such close proximity, it doesn't much matter which town you use as a base. Hotels in this entire region are generally expensive, so don't expect much bang for your buck. When planning your trip, keep in mind that during the high season—between June and November—hotels are usually at their most expensive and sell out completely on weekends; many have a 2-night minimum. Always ask about discounts, particularly during mid-week, when most hotels drop their rates by as much as 30%. Off season, you have far better bargaining power and may be able to get a room at almost half the summer rate. It also helps to plan well in advance, since bargains are always snatched up quickly.

If you need help organizing your Wine Country vacation, contact an agency. **Bed & Breakfast Inns of Napa Valley** (© **707/944-4444**), an association of B&Bs, provides descriptions and makes reservations. **Napa Valley Reservations Unlimited** (© **800/251-NAPA** or 707/252-1985; www.napavalleyreservations.com) is also a source for booking everything from hot-air balloon rides to guided wine-tasting tours.

NAPA

Chablis Inn ✿   There's no way around it: If you want to sleep cheaply in a town where the *average* room rate tops $200 per night in high season, you're destined for a motel. Look on the bright side: Because your room is likely to be little more than a crash pad after a day of eating and drinking, a clean bed and a remote control are all you'll really need anyway. And Chablis offers much more than that. All of the motel-style rooms are superclean, and some even boast kitchenettes or whirlpool tubs. Guests have access to a heated outdoor pool and hot tub.

3360 Solano Ave., Napa, CA 94558. (C) **707/257-1944**. Fax 707/226-6862. www.chablisinn.com. 34 units. May to mid-Nov $99–$165 double; mid-Nov to Apr $79–$150 double. AE, DC, DISC, MC, V. **Amenities:** Heated outdoor pool; Jacuzzi. *In room:* A/C, satellite TV, dataport (in some rooms), kitchenette (in some rooms), fridge, coffeemaker, hair dryer.

Napa Valley Redwood Inn   This no-frills lodging offers an excellent location—close to Highway 29—and simple, clean, and comfortable rooms. It's the perfect place to stay if you want to save money and plan on spending most of the day and evening touring the Wine Country anyway. Local calls are free, and guests can enjoy the complimentary continental breakfast and the small heated pool on the premises. *Note:* The bathrooms have showers only.

3380 Solano Ave., Napa, CA 94558. (C) **877/872-6272** or 707/257-6111. Fax 707/252-2702. www.napavalley redwoodinn.com. 58 units. $67–$150 double. Rates include continental breakfast. AE, DISC, MC, V. Pets accepted for $10 fee. From Hwy. 29 north, turn left onto the Redwood Rd. turnoff and go 1 block to Solano Ave.; then turn left and go a half block to the motel. **Amenities:** Outdoor pool. *In room:* A/C, dataport, fridge.

Wine Valley Lodge ✿ *Value*   Dollar for dollar, the Wine Valley Lodge offers a great deal. At the south end of town in a quiet residential neighborhood, the mission-style motel is extremely well kept and accessible, just a short drive from Highway 29 and the wineries to the north. The reasonably priced two-bedroom deluxe units are great for families.

200 S. Coombs St. (between First and Imola sts.), Napa, CA 94559. (C) **800/696-7911** or 707/224-7911. www.wine valleylodge.com. 54 units. $89–$124 double; $150–$165 deluxe. AE, DC, DISC, MC, V. **Amenities:** Heated outdoor pool (closed during the winter). *In room:* A/C, TV.

YOUNTVILLE

Maison Fleurie ✿✿   It's impossible not to enjoy your stay at Maison Fleurie. One of the prettiest garden-set B&Bs in the Wine Country, it's comprised of a trio of beautiful 1873 brick-and-fieldstone buildings overlaid with ivy. The main house—a charming Provençal replica with thick brick walls, terra-cotta tile, and paned windows—holds seven rooms; the rest are in the old bakery building and the carriage house. Some feature private balconies, patios, sitting areas, Jacuzzi tubs, and fireplaces. An above-par breakfast is served in the quaint little dining room; afterward, you're welcome to wander the landscaped grounds or hit the wine-tasting trail, returning in time for afternoon hors d'oeuvres and wine.

6529 Yount St. (between Washington St. and Yountville Cross Rd.), Yountville, CA 94599. (C) **800/788-0369** or 707/ 944-2056. Fax 707/944-9342. www.maisonfleurienapa.com. 13 units. $120–$285 double. Rates include full breakfast and afternoon hors d'oeuvres. AE, DC, DISC, MC, V. **Amenities:** Heated outdoor pool; Jacuzzi; complimentary bikes. *In room:* A/C, TV, dataport, hair dryer, iron.

Napa Valley Railway Inn ✿   This is a favorite place to stay in the Wine Country. Why? Because it's inexpensive and it's cute as all get-out. Looking hokey as heck from the outside, the Railway Inn consists of two rows of sun-bleached cabooses and rail cars sitting on a stretch of Yountville's original track and connected by a covered wooden walkway. Things get considerably better when you enter your private caboose or car, especially since they're redecorating each one as this book goes to press. Each is sumptuously appointed, with comfy love seat, king- or queen-size brass bed and tiled bathroom. The coups de grâce are the bay windows and skylights, which let in plenty of California sunshine. Adjacent to the inn is Yountville's main shopping complex.

6503 Washington St., Yountville, CA 94599. © **707/944-2000.** 9 units. $90–$170 double. AE, MC, V. *In room:* A/C, TV, coffeemaker, hair dryer (upon request).

ST. HELENA

El Bonita Motel ℛ *Kids* *Value*   This 1930s Art Deco motel is a bit too close to Highway 29 for comfort, but the 2½ acres of beautifully landscaped gardens behind the building (away from the road) help even the score. The rooms, while small and nothing fancy (think motel basic), are spotlessly clean and decorated with newer furnishings and kitchenettes; some have a whirlpool bathtub. It ain't heaven, but it is cheap for St. Helena.

195 Main St. (at El Bonita Ave.), St. Helena, CA 94574. © **800/541-3284** or 707/963-3216. Fax 707/963-8838. www.elbonita.com. 41 units. $89–$259 double. Rates include continental breakfast. AE, DC, DISC, MC, V. **Amenities:** Heated outdoor pool; spa; Jacuzzi; free Internet access in lobby. *In room:* A/C, TV, free wireless Internet access, fridge, coffeemaker, hair dryer, iron, microwave.

White Sulphur Springs Retreat & Spa ℛ   If your idea of the ultimate vacation is a cozy cabin on 45 acres, paradise is a short, winding drive away from downtown St. Helena. Established in 1852, Sulphur Springs claims to be the oldest resort in California. The property holds a creek, a waterfall, a naturally heated sulfur hot spring, and redwood, madrone, and fir trees. Guests stay in different-size creek-side cabins (which were renovated in 1998 and 1999), the inn, or the Carriage House. The cabins are decorated with simple but homey furnishings; cabin no. 9 has two queen-size beds and a kitchenette. From here you can take a dip in the natural hot sulfur spring; lounge by the large unheated outdoor pool; sit under a tree and watch for deer, fox, raccoon, spotted owl, or woodpecker; or schedule a day of massage (they're fantastic!), aromatherapy, and other spa treatments in their spa. *Note:* No RVs are allowed, and all rooms are nonsmoking. Call well in advance; the resort is often rented by large groups.

3100 White Sulphur Springs Rd., St. Helena, CA 94574. © **800/593-8873** in California, or 707/963-8588. Fax 707/ 963-2890. www.whitesulphursprings.com. 37 units, 14 with shared bathroom; 9 cottages. Carriage House (shared bathroom) $95–$120, small creek-side cottages $170–$190, large cottages $185–$200, cottage no. 9 $190–$210. Rates include continental breakfast. 2-night minimum stay on weekends Apr–Oct and all holidays. AE, DC, DISC, MC, V. **Amenities:** Outdoor pool; soaking pool; full-service spa; Jacuzzi; free Internet access in hospitality room. *In room:* A/C (in some rooms), fridge, hair dryer, iron (in large cottage).

CALISTOGA

Calistoga Spa Hot Springs ℛ *Kids* *Value*   Very few hotels in the Wine Country cater specifically to families with children, which is why I recommend Calistoga Spa Hot Springs if you're bringing the little ones: They classify themselves as a family resort and are very accommodating to visitors of all ages. In any case, it's a great bargain, offering unpretentious yet comfortable rooms, as well as a plethora of spa facilities. All of Calistoga's best shops and restaurants are within easy walking distance, and you can even whip up your own grub at the barbecue grills near the large pool and patio area.

1006 Washington St. (at Gerrard St.), Calistoga, CA 94515. © **866/822-5772** or 707/942-6269. www.calistogaspa. com. 57 units. Winter $104–185 double, summer $127–185 double. MC, V. **Amenities:** 3 heated outdoor pools; kids' wading pool; health club; spa. *In room:* A/C, TV, kitchenette, fridge, coffeemaker, hair dryer, iron.

Dr. Wilkinson's Hot Springs Resort ☞   This spa/"resort," located in the heart of Calistoga, is one of the best deals in Napa Valley. The rooms range from attractive Victorian-style accommodations to modern, cozy, recently renovated guest rooms in the main 1950s-style motel. All rooms are spiffier than most in the area's other hotels, with surprisingly tasteful textiles and basic motel-style accouterments. Larger rooms have refrigerators and/or kitchens. Facilities, which are the highlight of a Calistoga visit, include three mineral-water pools (two outdoor and one indoor), a Jacuzzi, a steam room, and mud baths. All kinds of body treatments are available in the spa, including famed mud baths, steams, and massage—all of which I highly recommend. Be sure to inquire about their excellent midweek packages and their new, fantastic facial held in your very own facial cottage

1507 Lincoln Ave. (Hwy. 29, between Fairway and Stevenson aves.), Calistoga, CA 94515. ✆ 707/942-4102. www.drwilkinson.com. 42 units. $109–$199 double. Weekly discounts and packages available. AE, MC, V. **Amenities:** 3 mineral-water pools; spa; Jacuzzi, steam room; massage; mud bath. *In room:* A/C, TV, dataport, kitchen (in some rooms), fridge (in some rooms), coffeemaker, hair dryer.

Euro Spa & Inn ☞☞   In a quiet residential section of Calistoga, this small European-style inn and spa provides a level of solitude and privacy that few other spas can match. The horseshoe-shaped inn consists of 13 stucco bungalows, a spa center, and an outdoor patio, where a light breakfast and snacks are served. The rooms, although small, are pleasantly decorated in Pottery Barn decor, whirlpool tubs, decks, gas wood stoves, and kitchenettes. Spa treatments range from clay baths and foot reflexology to mini-facials.

1202 Pine St. (at Myrtle), Calistoga, CA 94515. ✆ 707/942-6829. Fax 707/942-1138. 13 units. $119–$229 double. Rates include deluxe continental breakfast. Off-season and midweek package discounts available. AE, DC, DISC, MC, V. **Amenities:** Outdoor heated pool; Jacuzzi. *In room:* A/C, TV, free wireless Internet access (in most rooms), kitchenette, hair dryer, iron, robes.

GREAT DEALS ON DINING IN THE NAPA VALLEY
NAPA

Alexis Baking Company ☞ BAKERY/CAFE   Alexis (aka ABC) is a quaint, casual stop for residents and in-the-know tourists. On weekend mornings—especially Sunday, which is when you'll find me devouring their out-of-this-world Sunday-only huevos rancheros—the line stretches out the door. Once you order (from the counter during the week and at the table on weekends) and find a seat, you can relax and enjoy the coffeehouse atmosphere. Start your day with spectacular pastries, coffee drinks, and breakfast goodies like pumpkin pancakes with sautéed pears. Lunch also bustles with locals who come for simple, fresh fare like grilled hamburgers with Gorgonzola; grilled-chicken Caesar salad; roast lamb sandwich with minted mayo and roasted shallots on rosemary bread; and lentil bulgur orzo salad. (Sorry fries lovers; you won't find any here.) Desserts run the gamut; during the holidays, they include a moist and magical steamed persimmon pudding. Oh, and the pastry counter's cookies and cakes beg you to take something for the road.

1517 Third St. (between Main and Jefferson sts.), Napa. ✆ 707/258-1827. Main courses $5–$10 breakfast, $7–$10 lunch. MC, V. Mon–Fri 6:30am–4pm; Sat 7:30am–3pm; Sun 8am–2pm.

Bistro Don Giovanni ☞☞☞ (Value) REGIONAL ITALIAN   Donna and Giovanni Scala—who launched Scala's Bistro in San Francisco—own this bright, bustling, and cheery Italian restaurant, which also happens to be one of my favorite restaurants in Napa Valley. Fare prepared by chef/partner Scott Warner highlights quality ingredients and California flair and never disappoints, especially when it comes to the thin-crusted pizzas and house-made pastas. Every time I grab a menu, I can't get past the salad of beets and *haricots verts* or the pasta with duck Bolognese. On the rare occasion that I do, I am equally smitten with outstanding classic pizza Margherita fresh from the wood-burning oven, seared wild salmon filet perched atop a tower of buttermilk mashed potatoes, and steak frites. Even though portions are generous, there's always room for tiramisu. Alfresco dining in the vineyards is available—and highly recommended on a warm, sunny day. Come midwinter, I prefer dining at the bar.

4110 Howard Lane (at St. Helena Hwy.), Napa. ℂ **707/224-3300.** Reservations recommended. Main courses $12–$24. AE, DC, DISC, MC, V. Sun–Thurs 11:30am–10pm; Fri–Sat 11:30am–11pm.

The Boon Fly Café ℱ AMERICAN   Along the rural Carneros highway is a great bargain dining option: the Boon Fly Café, the gourmet roadhouse fronting the Carneros Inn. The slick and inviting interior is modern barn style complete with a corrugated metal watershedlike pizza oven and light, airy surroundings with dark wood tables and floors. The food similarly balances rustic and chic with fancy renditions of comfort classics like killer beer-battered onion rings; thin-crust pizza; great Cobb salad; omelets; pancakes; and roasted half chicken with bacon, roasted potatoes, sautéed mushrooms, and chicken stock and white wine reduction. With prices topping out in the mid-teens, it's almost cheaper to eat here than dine at home. An added bonus: If you're passing by and in a hurry, they offer to-go items like donut holes and breakfast sandwiches.

4048 Sonoma Highway/121 (near Old Sonoma Road), Napa. ℂ **707/299-4900.** Main courses $4–$9 breakfast, $15–$25 lunch and dinner. AE, DC, DISC, MC, V. Daily 7am–10pm.

Ristorante Allegria ℱ NORTHERN ITALIAN   When all I really want is a quality dinner at everyday prices, I go directly to this local spot housed downtown in a beautiful historic bank. High ceilings, faux-finished walls, mood lighting, an accordion player on Wednesdays, and a sectioned-off full bar create an excellent atmosphere, the staff is very friendly, and you won't find a more perfectly prepared grilled salmon over Yukon gold potatoes, and baby spinach hash topped with lemon-caper aioli. They also make a generous Caesar salad, offer plenty of antipasti and pastas (the latter of which are not nearly as good as Don Giovanni), and offer the likes of filet mignon with garlic-mashed potatoes and Gorgonzola compound butter to satisfy red-meat lovers. You won't get the vineyard view "wine country" dining experience—or its corresponding high prices—here, but sometimes, that's exactly what the diner ordered. One last perk: You can pay $10 to bring and drink your own bottle of wine and they waive the fee if you order a bottle from the list as well.

1026 First St. (at Main St.), Napa. ℂ **707/254-8006.** www.ristoranteallegria.com. Most main courses $9–$16 lunch, $11–$18 dinner. AE, MC, V. Mon–Thurs 11am–2:30pm (lunch) and 5–10pm (dinner); Fri–Sun 10am–11pm.

Villa Corona ℱ MEXICAN   The best Mexican food in town is served in this bright, funky, and colorful restaurant hidden in the southwest corner of a strip mall behind an unmemorable sports bar and restaurant. The winning plan here is simple: Order and pay at the counter, sit at either a plastic-covered table or at one of the few sidewalk seats, and wait for the huge burritos, enchiladas, and chimichangas to be delivered to your table. Those with pork preferences shouldn't miss the carnitas, which are abundantly flavorful and juicy. My personal favorites are hard-shell tacos or chicken enchiladas with light savory red sauce, a generous side of beans, and rice.

Don't expect to wash down your menudo, or anything else for that matter, with a margarita. The place serves only beer and wine. Don't hesitate to come for a hearty breakfast, too. Excellent *chilaquiles* (eggs scrambled with salsa and tortilla) and huevos rancheros are part of the package.

3614 Bel Aire Plaza (on Trancas St.), Napa. ℂ **707/257-8685**. Main courses $6–10. MC, V. Tues–Fri 9am–9pm; Sat 8am–9pm; Sun 8am–8pm.

ZuZu ✪✪ TAPAS   A local place to the core, ZuZu lures neighborhood regulars with a no-reservation policy, a friendly cramped wine and beer bar, and very affordable Mediterranean small plates, which are meant to be shared. The comfortable, warm, and not remotely corporate atmosphere extends from the environment to the food, which includes sizzling mini skillets of tangy and fantastic paella, addictive prawns with requisite Pimento bread-dipping sauce, light and delicate sea scallop ceviche salad, and Moroccan barbecued lamb chops with a sweet-and-spicy sauce. Desserts aren't as fab, but with a bottle of wine and tastier plates than you can possibly devour, who cares?

829 Main St., Napa. ℂ **707/224-8555**. Reservations not accepted. Tapas $3–$13. MC, V. Mon–Thurs 11:30am–10pm; Fri 11:30am–midnight; Sat 4pm–midnight; Sun 4–9pm.

YOUNTVILLE
Bouchon Bakery ✪ FRENCH BAKERY   In the summer of 2003, famed French Laundry chef Thomas Keller opened this adorable authentic French bakery next door to his restaurant Bouchon (see above). As bakeries go it ain't cheap, but that doesn't stop locals and visitors from lining up amid the pretty green-mosaic-tiled storefront for the outstanding bread baked twice daily, paper-wrapped panini, killer treats (think éclairs, cookies, tarts, and more), coffee drinks, classic sandwiches, and near-perfect pastry. Grab it to go or snack at one of the garden tables, which overlook Yountville's main drag.

6528 Washington St. (between Jefferson and Yount sts.). ℂ **707/944-2253**. Pastries and sandwiches $2.25–$7. MC, V. Daily 7am–7pm.

Piatti ✪ ITALIAN/CALIFORNIA   This local favorite—the first (and best) of a swiftly growing Northern California chain—is known for serving good, fresh, and reasonably priced food in a rustic Italian-style setting. On the menu the classics are covered—from antipasti and *insalata* (salad) to pasta, oven-baked pizza, and nightly house specialties. For the perfect meal, start with a salad of morning-cut field greens mixed with white corn and Napa Valley strawberry crostini, accompanied by a bowl of spaghetti squash and sweet-potato soup. Although there's a wide array of superb pastas and pizzas, it's the wood oven–roasted duck—basted with sweet huckleberry sauce and served with grilled polenta and braised greens—that brings back the regulars. There are far fancier and more intimate restaurants in the valley, but none where you can fill up on such outstanding fare at these prices. Piatti also offers patio dining year-round, weather permitting.

6480 Washington St. (corner of Oak Circle). ℂ **707/944-2070**. Reservations recommended. Main courses $10–$22. AE, DC, MC, V. Daily 11:30am–9pm.

ST. HELENA
The Cantinetta at Tra Vigne ✪✪ *Value* WINE BAR/ITALIAN DELI   Regardless of where else I dine while in the valley, I always make a point of stopping at Tra Vigne's Italian-style deli and wine bar for a glass of wine and a snack at their sun-filled courtyard. Part cafe, part gourmet shop, it's a casual place with a few tables, a counter, a

gorgeous garden seating, and one of the best selection of wines by the glass in Northern California—there are more than 110. The focaccias, pasta salads, and pastries are outstanding, and the *boconcini per wini* ("little bites for wine") such as house-smoked salmon with lemon asparagus are just $2.50 per plate. There's also a selection of cookies and other sweets, flavored oils (free tastings), and an array of gourmet food items, many of which are made in-house. You can also get great picnic foods to go. The Cantinetta is the ultimate lifesaver when crowds are gathered elsewhere in town and I'm starving. Despite its popularity there's virtually never a line here and you can devour your feast in the same famed courtyard as diners at the much pricier Tra Vigne restaurant.

At Tra Vigne Restaurant, 1050 Charter Oak Ave. (C) 707/963-8888. www.travignerestaurant.com. Main courses $6–$7. DC, DISC, MC, V. Mon–Fri 11:30am–6pm, Sat–Sun 11:30am–9pm.

Tips Where to Stock Up for a Gourmet Picnic

You can easily plan your whole trip around restaurant reservations, but gather one of the world's best gourmet picnics, and the valley's your oyster.

One of the finest gourmet-food stores in the Wine Country, if not all of California, is the **Oakville Grocery Co.**, 7856 St. Helena Hwy., at Oakville Cross Road, Oakville ((C) 707/944-8802). You can put together the provisions for a memorable picnic or, with at least 24-hours' notice, the staff can prepare a picnic basket for you. The store, with its small-town vibe and claustrophobia-inducing crowds, can be quite an experience. You'll find shelves crammed with the best breads and choicest cheeses in the northern Bay Area, as well as pâtés, cold cuts, crackers, top-quality olive oils, fresh foie gras (domestic and French, seasonal), smoked Norwegian salmon, fresh caviar (Beluga, Sevruga, Osetra) and, of course, an exceptional selection of California wines. The store is open daily from 9am to 6pm. There's also an espresso bar tucked in the corner (open Mon–Fri 7am–6pm; Sat–Sun 8am–6pm), offering lunch items, a complete deli, and house-baked pastries.

Another of my favorite places to fill a picnic basket is New York's version of a swank European marketplace, **Dean & DeLuca**, 607 S. St. Helena Hwy. (Hwy. 29), north of Zinfandel Lane and south of Sulphur Springs Road, St. Helena ((C) 707/967-9980; www.deananddeluca.com). The ultimate in gourmet grocery stores is more like a world's fair of foods, where everything is beautifully displayed and often painfully pricey. As you pace the barn-wood plank floors, you'll stumble upon more high-end edibles than you've probably ever seen under one roof. They include local organic produce (delivered daily); 200 domestic and imported cheeses (with an on-site aging room to ensure proper ripeness); shelves and shelves of tapenades, pastas, oils, hand-packed dried herbs and spices, chocolates, sauces, cookware, and housewares; an espresso bar; one hell of a bakery section; and more. Along the back wall, you can watch the professional chefs prepare gourmet takeout, including salads, rotisserie meats, and sautéed vegetables. You can also snag a pricey bottle from the wine section's 1,200-label collection. The store is open daily from 9am to 7pm (the espresso bar is open Mon–Sat at 7:30am and Sun at 9am).

Pizzeria Tra Vigne ⓡ *Kids* *Value* ITALIAN   After spending a week in Wine Country, I usually can't stand the thought of another decadent wine and foie gras meal. That's when I race here for a $5.95 chopped salad, a welcome respite from gluttonous excess. Families and locals come here for another reason: Although the menu is limited, it's a total winner for anyone in search of freshly prepared, wholesome food at atypically cheap Wine Country prices. A Caesar salad, for example, costs a mere $5.95. "Pia-dine"—pizzas folded like a soft taco—are the house specialty and come filled with such delights as fresh rock shrimp, Crescenza cheese sauce, scallions, and deep fried lemons. Pizzas are of the build-your-own variety, with gourmet toppings like sautéed mush-rooms, fennel sausage, baby spinach, sun-dried tomatoes, and homemade pepperoni. The 14 respectable local wines come by the glass starting at a toast-worthy $5, or $18 per bottle. Dessert, at less than $4 a pop for gelato or biscotti, or $6 for tiramisu, is an overall sweet deal. Kids especially like the pool table and big-screen TV.

At the Inn at Southbridge, 1016 Main St., St. Helena. ⓒ **707/967-9999**. www.pizzeriatravigne.com. Pastas $8–$11; pizzas $9–$17. DC, DISC, MC, V. Daily 11:30am–8:30pm (Fri–Sat until 9:30pm).

Taylor's Automatic Refresher DINER   Yet another winner to slip from sublime status to buyer beware, this gourmet roadside burger shack built in 1949 still draws huge lines of tourists who love the notion of ordering at the counter and feasting alfresco. But the last few meals I had there left me knowing the $80 I coughed up for lunch for five would have been better spent at Oakville Grocery's deli. The burger, onion rings, and fries were mediocre at best, the iceberg salad was unwieldy, and only the shake left me satisfied. (How hard is it to make a great shake, after all?) Perhaps it's that the owners now have a closer eye on their San Francisco outpost, which is great, by the way. No matter. It's still the only casual burger joint in St. Helena (espe-cially considering it offers ahi tuna burgers and various tacos and salads) and its ever-bustling status proves everyone knows it.

933 Main St., St Helena. ⓒ **707/963-3486**. www.taylorsrefresher.com. Main courses $4–$13. AE, MC, V. Daily 11am–8pm, til 9pm in summer.

Wine Spectator Greystone Restaurant ⓡ CALIFORNIA   The trick to dining at Greystone on a budget (and without reservations) is to snack at the bar and save the big meals for elsewhere. Even if you spend a bit more than planned, it's worth it: this place offers a visual and culinary feast that's unparalleled in the area, if not the state. The room is an enormous stone-walled former winery, but the festive decor and heavenly aromas warm the space up. Cooking islands—complete with scurrying chefs, steaming pots, and rotating chicken—provide edible entertainment. The tastings (appetizer) menu fea-tures dishes inspired by fresh, seasonal ingredients such as grilled mahimahi with aspara-gus salad, oven-roasted chicken breast with mashed potatoes, and Dungeness crab salad with avocado and grapefruit sauce. If you're in the mood to splurge, order the Flights of Fancy for $14 to $25, which allows you to sample three 3-ounce pours of local wines such as white Rhone, pinot, or zinfandel. While the food is serious, the atmosphere is playful—casual enough that you'll feel comfortable in jeans or shorts.

At the Culinary Institute of America at Greystone, 2555 Main St., St. Helena. ⓒ **707/967-1010**. Reservations rec-ommended. Temptations $9; main courses $17–$29. AE, DC, MC, V. Daily 11:15am–10pm.

CALISTOGA
Palisades Market ⓡⓡDELI/MARKET   Trust me, sandwiches as delicious as those served at this adorable, old-fashioned gourmet market are an absolute rarity and

a sure-fire addiction. Drop in for wine, juice, soda, cheese, tamales, green salads, lasagna, crab cakes, soup, picnic items, and every kind of treat you can think of, but under no circumstances should you skip the sandwiches, which range from pesto, turkey, provolone, lettuce, and tomatoes on sun-dried tomato focaccia to ham, Gruyère cheese, onions, lettuce, mayo, and Dijon mustard on a baguette. Call 2 days in advance and Palisades will box a lunch for you; $16 will get you a sandwich, salad, fruit, cookie, and utensils.

1506 Lincoln Ave., Calistoga. ℂ **707/942-9549.** Sandwiches $4.95–$7.95. AE, MC, V. Sun–Wed 7:30am–6pm; Thurs–Sat 7:30am–7pm.

Wappo Bar & Bistro GLOBAL   One of the best alfresco dining venues in the Wine Country is under Wappo's jasmine-and-grapevine–covered arbor. Unfortunately, food and service are a very distant second. But much can be forgiven when the wine's flowing and you're surrounded by pastoral splendor. The menu offers a global selection, from tandoori chicken to roast rabbit with gnocchi and mustard cream sauce. Desserts of choice are black-bottom coconut cream pie and strawberry rhubarb pie.

1226B Washington St. (off Lincoln Ave.), Calistoga. ℂ **707/942-4712.** www.wappobar.com. Main courses $9–$14 lunch, $14–$25 dinner. AE, MC, V. Wed–Mon 11:30am–2:30pm and 6–9:30pm.

2 Sonoma Valley

A pastoral contrast to Napa, Sonoma manages to maintain a backcountry ambience, thanks to its far lower density of wineries, restaurants, and hotels. Small, family-owned wineries are Sonoma's mainstay; tastings are low-key and come with plenty of friendly banter with the winemakers. Basically, this is the valley to target if your ideal vacation includes visiting a handful of wineries along quiet woodsy roads, avoiding shopping outlets and Napa's high-end glitz, and simply enjoying the laid-back country atmosphere.

The valley is some 17 miles long and 7 miles wide, and it's bordered by two mountain ranges: the Mayacamas to the east and the Sonomas to the west. Unlike in Napa Valley, you won't find palatial wineries with million-dollar art collections, aerial trams, and Hollywood ego trips (read: Niebaum-Coppola). Rather, the Sonoma Valley offers a refreshing dose of reality, where modestly sized wineries are integrated into the community. If Napa Valley feels like a fantasyland, where everything exists to service the almighty grape and the visitors it attracts, then the Sonoma Valley is its antithesis, an unpretentious gaggle of ordinary towns, ranches, and wineries that welcome tourists but don't necessarily rely on them. The result is a chance to experience what Napa Valley must have been like long before the Seagrams and Moët et Chandons of the world turned the Wine Country into a major tourist destination.

As in Napa, you can pick up *Wine Country Review* throughout Sonoma. It gives you the most up-to-date information on wineries and related area events.

ESSENTIALS

GETTING THERE   From San Francisco, cross the Golden Gate Bridge and stay on U.S. 101 North. Exit at Highway 37; after 10 miles, turn north onto Highway 121. After another 10 miles, turn north onto Highway 12 (Broadway), which takes you directly into the town of Sonoma.

VISITOR INFORMATION   While you're in Sonoma, stop by the **Sonoma Valley Visitors Bureau,** 453 First St. E. (ℂ **707/996-1090;** www.sonomavalley.com). It's open daily from 9am to 6pm. An additional **Visitors Bureau** is a few miles south of the square at 25200 Arnold Dr. (Hwy. 121), at the entrance to Viansa Winery (© 707/935-4747); it's open daily from 9am to 5pm and to 6pm in summer.

If you prefer advance information from the bureau, you can contact the Sonoma Valley Visitors Bureau to order the free *Sonoma Valley Visitors Guide,* which lists almost every lodge, winery, and restaurant in the valley.

TOURING THE SONOMA VALLEY & WINERIES

Sonoma Valley is currently home to about 35 wineries (including California's first winery, Buena Vista, founded in 1857) and 13,000 acres of vineyards. It produces roughly 25 types of wines, totaling more than 5 million cases a year. Unlike the rigidly structured tours at many of Napa Valley's corporate-owned wineries, on the Sonoma side of the Mayacamas Mountains, tastings are usually low-key and tours are free.

The towns and wineries covered below are organized geographically from south to north, starting at the intersection of Highway 37 and Highway 121 in the Carneros District and ending in Kenwood. The wineries tend to be a little more spread out here than they are in Napa Valley, but they're easy to find. Still, it's best to decide which wineries you're most interested in and devise a touring strategy before you set out, so you don't do too much backtracking.

I've reviewed some of my favorite Sonoma Valley wineries here—more than enough to keep you busy tasting wine for a long weekend. If you'd like a complete list of local wineries, be sure to pick up one of the free guides available at the Sonoma Valley Visitors Bureau (see "Visitor Information," above).

For a map of the wineries below, please see "The Wine Country" map on p. 259.

THE CARNEROS DISTRICT

As you approach the Wine Country from the south, you must first pass through the Carneros District, a cool, windswept region that borders the San Pablo Bay and marks the entrance to both the Napa and Sonoma valleys. Until the latter part of the 20th century, this mixture of marsh, sloughs, and rolling hills was mainly used as sheep pasture (*carneros* means "sheep" in Spanish). However, after experimental plantings yielded slow-growing, high-quality grapes—particularly chardonnay and pinot noir—several Napa and Sonoma wineries expanded their plantings here. They eventually established the Carneros District as an American Viticultural Appellation, a legally defined wine-grape growing area. Although about a dozen wineries are spread throughout the region, there are no major towns or attractions—just plenty of gorgeous scenery as you cruise along Highway 121, the major junction between Napa and Sonoma.

Viansa Winery and Italian Marketplace ⊛ *Finds* The first major winery you'll encounter as you enter Sonoma Valley from the south, this sprawling Tuscan-style villa perches atop a knoll overlooking the entire lower valley. Viansa is the brainchild of Sam and Vicki Sebastiani, who left the family dynasty to create their own temple to food and wine. (*Viansa* is a contraction of "Vicki and Sam.") Here you'll find a large room crammed with a cornucopia of high-quality mustards, olive oils, pastas, salads, breads, desserts, Italian tableware, cookbooks, and wine-related gifts as well as tasting opportunities.

The winery, which does an extensive mail-order business through The Tuscan Club, has established a favorable reputation for its Italian varietals. Tastings, which cost $5 to $20 per person, are offered at the east and west end of the marketplace, and the self-guided tour includes a trip through the underground barrel-aging cellar adorned with colorful hand-painted murals. Guided tours, held at 11am and 2pm, will set you back $5.

Viansa is also one of the few wineries in Sonoma Valley that sells deli items—the focaccia sandwiches are delicious. You can dine alfresco under the grape trellis while you admire the bucolic view.

25200 Arnold Dr. (Hwy. 121), Sonoma. © **800/995-4740** or 707/935-4700. www.viansa.com. Daily 10am–5pm. Free daily self-guided tours. Guided tours daily 11am and 2pm for $5.

Gloria Ferrer Champagne Caves 🕏 *Finds*   When you have had it up to here with chardonnays and pinots, it's time to pay a visit to Gloria Ferrer, the grande dame of the Wine Country's sparkling-wine producers. Who's Gloria? She's the wife of José Ferrer, whose family has made sparkling wine for 5 centuries. The family business, Freixenet, is the largest producer of sparkling wine in the world; Cordon Negro is its most popular brand. That equals big bucks, and certainly a good chunk went into building this palatial estate. Glimmering like Oz high atop a gently sloping hill, it overlooks the verdant Carneros District. On a sunny day, you really must enjoy a glass of dry brut while soaking in the magnificent views here.

If you're unfamiliar with the term *méthode champenoise,* be sure to take the free 30-minute tour of the fermenting tanks, bottling line, and caves brimming with racks of yeast-laden bottles. Afterward, retire to the elegant tasting room, order a glass of one of 7 sparkling wines ($4–$10 a glass) or tastes of their 8 still wines ($2–$3 per taste), find an empty chair on the veranda, and say, "Ahhh. *This* is the life." There are picnic tables, but it's usually too windy for comfort, and you must buy a bottle (from around $18–$40) or a glass of sparkling wine to reserve a table.

23555 Carneros Hwy. (Hwy. 121), Sonoma. © **707/996-7256**. www.gloriaferrer.com. Daily 10am–5:15pm. Free tours daily; call day of visit to confirm schedule.

SONOMA

At the northern boundary of the Carneros District along Highway 12 is the centerpiece of Sonoma Valley. The midsize town of Sonoma owes much of its appeal to Mexican general Mariano Guadalupe Vallejo, who fashioned this pleasant, slow-paced community after a typical Mexican village—right down to its central plaza, Sonoma's geographical and commercial center. The plaza sits at the top of a T formed by Broadway (Hwy. 12) and Napa Street. Most of the surrounding streets form a grid pattern around this axis, making Sonoma easy to negotiate. The plaza's Bear Flag Monument marks the spot where the crude Bear Flag was raised in 1846, signaling the end of Mexican rule; the symbol was later adopted by the state of California and placed on its flag. The 8-acre park at the center of the plaza, complete with two ponds populated by ducks and geese, is perfect for an afternoon siesta in the cool shade.

Buena Vista Winery   Count Agoston Haraszthy, the Hungarian émigré who is universally regarded as the father of California's wine industry, founded this historic winery in 1857. A close friend of General Vallejo, Haraszthy returned from Europe in 1861 with 100,000 of the finest vine cuttings, which he made available to all growers. Although Buena Vista's winemaking now takes place at an ultramodern facility in the Carneros District, the winery maintains a tasting room inside the restored 1862 Press House. The beautiful stone-crafted room brims with wines, wine-related gifts, and accessories.

Tastings are $5 for four wines, $10 for a flight of three library wines. You can take the self-guided tour any time during operating hours; a "Historical Tour and Tasting,"

Tips A Garden Detour

Garden lovers should pull over for a $9 gander at the latest downtown Sonoma addition, the **Cornerstone Festival of Gardens,** 23570 Arnold Dr., Sonoma (*(C)* 707/933-3010; www.cornerstonegardens.com; children under 12 are free). Modeled in part after the International Garden festival at Chaumont-sur-Loire in France's Loire Valley and the Grand Metis in Quebec, Canada, the 9-acre property is the first gallery-style garden exhibit in the United States and includes a series of 15 ever-changing gardens designed by famed landscape architects and designers. If you get inspired, you can load up on loot here that will help your own garden grow—from furniture and gifts to plants, garden art, and books. The gardens are open Tuesday through Sunday 10am to 5pm, Monday noon to 4pm.

---

offered daily at 11am and 2pm, details the life and times of Count Haraszthy and includes a viticultural tour and wine and food pairing. If you drop by on a Saturday you can also opt for the $35 wine and cheese tasting. After tasting, grab your favorite bottle, a selection of cheeses from the Sonoma Cheese Factory, salami, bread, and spreads (all available in the tasting room), and plant yourself at one of the many picnic tables in the lush, verdant setting.

18000 Old Winery Rd. (off E. Napa St., slightly northeast of downtown), Sonoma. *(C)* **800/926-1266** or 707/265-1472. www.buenavistawinery.com. Nov–May daily 10am–5pm, June–Oct daily 10am–5:30pm.

Sebastiani Vineyards & Winery   The name Sebastiani is practically synonymous with Sonoma. What started in 1904, when Samuele Sebastiani began producing his first wines, has in three generations grown into a small empire, producing some 200,000 cases a year. After a few years of seismic retrofitting, a face-lift, and a temporary tasting room, the original 1904 winery is now open to the public with more extensive educational tours ($5 per person), an 80-foot S-shaped tasting bar, and lots of shopping opportunities in the gift shop. In the contemporary tasting room's minimuseum area you can see the winery's original turn-of-the-20th-century crusher and press, as well as the world's largest collection of oak-barrel carvings, crafted by bygone local artist Earle Brown. If it's merely wine that interests you, you can sample an extensive selection of wines ranging from a complimentary selection to $18 for a flight of their fancy stuff, the latter of which includes a keepsake glass. Bottle prices are reasonable, ranging from $13 to $75. A picnic area adjoins the cellars; a far more scenic spot is across the parking lot in Sebastiani's Cherryblock Vineyards.

389 Fourth St. E., Sonoma. *(C)* **800/888-5532** or 707/933-3200. www.sebastiani.com. Daily 10am–5pm. $5 educational tours: winter daily 11am and 3pm; summer 11am, 1pm, and 3pm.

Ravenswood Winery   Compared to old heavies like Sebastiani and Buena Vista, Ravenswood is a relative newcomer to the Sonoma wine scene. Nevertheless, it quickly established itself as the sine qua non of zinfandel, the versatile red grape that's known in these parts for being big, ripe, juicy, and powerful. The first winery in the United States to focus primarily on zins, which make up about three-quarters of its 700,000-case production, Ravenswood underscores zins' zest with their motto, "No Wimpy Wines." But they also produce merlot, cabernet sauvignon, Rhone varietals, and a small amount of chardonnay.

The winery is smartly designed—recessed into the hillside to protect its treasures from the simmering summers. Tours ($10 per person) follow the winemaking process from grape to glass, and include a visit to the aromatic oak-barrel aging rooms. You're welcome to bring your own picnic basket to any of the tables, but if you're coming on the weekend from Memorial Day to Labor Day, consider joining one of their famously fun barbecues (call for details). Regardless, tastings are $5 for four wines, but the fee is refundable with a purchase.

18701 Gehricke Rd. (off Lovall Valley Rd.), Sonoma. (C) **888/NO-WIMPY** or 707/933-2332. www.ravenswood-wine. com. Labor Day–Memorial Day 10am–4:30pm; Memorial Day–Labor Day 10am–5pm. $10 tours by reservation only at 10:30am.

GLEN ELLEN

About 7 miles north of Sonoma on Highway 12 is the town of Glen Ellen. Although just a fraction of the size of Sonoma, Glen Ellen is home to several of the valley's finest wineries, restaurants, and inns. Aside from the addition of a few new restaurants, this charming town hasn't changed much since the days when Jack London settled on his Beauty Ranch, about a mile west. Other than the wineries, you'll find few real signs of commercialism; the shops and restaurants, along one main winding lane, cater to a small, local clientele—that is, until the summer tourist season begins and traffic nearly triples on the weekends. If you haven't decided where you want to set up camp during your visit to the Wine Country, I highly recommend this lovable little rural region.

Arrowood Vineyards & Winery   Richard Arrowood had already established a reputation as a master winemaker at Château St. Jean when he and his wife, Alis Demers Arrowood, set out on their own in 1986. Their picturesque winery stands on a gently rising hillside lined with perfectly manicured vineyards. Tastings take place in the Hospitality House, the newer of Arrowood's two stately gray-and-white buildings. They're fashioned after New England farmhouses, complete with wraparound

---

Moments Touring the Sonoma Valley by Bike

Sonoma and its neighboring towns are so small, close together, and relatively flat that it's not difficult to get around on two wheels. In fact, if you're in no great hurry, there's no better way to tour the Sonoma Valley than by bicycle, even though there are no great bike routes (it's all along the road for the most part). You can rent a bike from the **Goodtime Bicycle Company** (⌖ ((C) **888/525-0453** or 707/938-0453; www.goodtimetouring.com). The staff will happily point you to easy bike trails, or you can take an organized excursion to Kenwood-area wineries, south Sonoma wineries, or even northern Sonoma's Russian River and Dry Creek areas. Rentals cost $25 a day, and include helmets, locks, everything else you'll need, and delivery and pick-up to and from local hotels.

Mountain bikes, helmets, and locks are also available for rent from **Sonoma Valley Cyclery**, 20093 Broadway, Sonoma ((C) **707/935-3377**), for $35 a day. Hybrid bikes (better for casual wine-tasting cruisers) are $25 per day, helmet and lock included.

porches. Richard's focus is on making world-class wine with minimal intervention, and his results are impressive: More than one of his current releases has scored over 90 points in *Wine Spectator.* Mind you, excellence doesn't come cheap: a taste here is $5 or $10 for four limited-production wines, but if you're curious about what near-perfection tastes like, it's well worth it. *Note:* No picnic facilities are available here.

14347 Sonoma Hwy. (Hwy. 12), Glen Ellen. © 707/935-2600. www.arrowoodvineyards.com. Daily 10am–4:30pm. $15 tours by appointment only, daily at 10:30am and 2:30pm.

Benziger Family Winery *Finds*   A visit here confirms that this is indeed a family winery. At any given time, two generations of Benzigers (*Ben*-zigger) may be running around tending to chores, and they instantly make you feel as if you're part of the clan. The pastoral, user-friendly property features an exceptional self-guided tour of the certified biodynamic winery, gardens, and a spacious tasting room staffed by amiable folks. The $10 45-minute tram tour, pulled by a beefy tractor, is both informative and fun. It winds through the estate vineyards and into caves, and ends with a tasting. *Tip:* Tram tickets—a hot item in the summer—are available on a first-come, first-served basis, so either arrive early or stop by in the morning to pick up afternoon tickets.

Tastings of the standard-release wines are $5. Tastes including several limited-production wines or reserve or estate wines cost $10. The winery offers several scenic picnic spots.

1883 London Ranch Rd. (off Arnold Dr., on the way to Jack London State Historic Park), Glen Ellen. © 800/989-8890 or 707/935-3000. www.benziger.com. Tasting room daily 10am–5pm. Tram tours daily (weather permitting) $10 adults and $5 children at 11:30am, noon, 12:30, 1:30, 2:30, and 3:30pm.

KENWOOD

A few miles north of Glen Ellen, along Highway 12, is the tiny town of Kenwood, the valley's northernmost outpost. Although Kenwood Vineyards' wines are well known throughout the United States, the town itself consists of little more than a few restaurants, wineries, and modest homes on the wooded hillsides. The nearest lodging, the luxurious Kenwood Inn & Spa, is about a mile south of the vineyards. Kenwood makes for a pleasant day trip—a tour of Château St. Jean (see below), dinner at Kenwood Restaurant—from Glen Ellen or Sonoma.

Kenwood Vineyards   Kenwood's history dates from 1906, when the Pagani brothers made their living selling wine straight from the barrel and into the jug. In 1970 the Lee family bought the property and dumped a ton of money into converting the aging winery into a modern, high-production facility (most of it cleverly concealed in the original barnlike buildings). Since then, Kenwood has earned a solid reputation for consistent quality with each of its varietals: cabernet sauvignon, chardonnay, zinfandel, pinot noir, merlot and, most popular, sauvignon blanc—a crisp, light wine with hints of melon.

Although the winery looks rather modest in size, its output is staggering: nearly 500,000 cases of ultra-premium wines fermented in steel tanks and French and American oak barrels. Popular with collectors is winemaker Michael Lee's Artist Series cabernet sauvignon, a limited production from the winery's best vineyards, featuring labels with original artwork by renowned artists. The tasting room, housed in one of the old barns, offers complimentary tastes, $2 to $5 tastings of private reserve wines, and gift items for purchase. *FYI:* The Lees no longer own the winery.

9592 Sonoma Hwy. (Hwy. 12), Kenwood. © 707/833-5891. www.kenwoodvineyards.com. Daily 10am–4:30pm. No tours.

Château St. Jean ⭐ *(Finds)*   Château St. Jean is notable for its exceptionally beautiful buildings, expansive landscaped grounds, and gourmet marketlike tasting room.
Among California wineries, it's a pioneer in vineyard designation—the procedure of
making wine from, and naming it for, a single vineyard. A private drive takes you to
what was once a 250-acre country retreat built in 1920; a well-manicured lawn overlooking the meticulously maintained vineyards is now a picnic area, complete with a
fountain and picnic tables. In the huge tasting room—where there's also a charcuterie
shop and plenty of housewares for sale—you can sample Château St. Jean's wide array
of wines. They range from chardonnays and cabernet sauvignon to fumé blanc, merlot, Johannesburg riesling, and gewürztraminer. Tastings are $5 per person; $10 per
person for reserve wines.

8555 Sonoma Hwy. (Calif. 12), Kenwood. ℂ 800/543-7572 or 707/833-4134. www.chateaustjean.com. Tasting daily
10am–5pm. Free tours 11am and 3pm. At the foot of Sugarloaf Ridge, just north of Kenwood and east of Hwy. 12.

St. Francis Winery   Although St. Francis Winery makes a commendable chardonnay, zinfandel, and cabernet sauvignon, they're best known for their highly coveted
merlot. Winemaker Tom Mackey, a former high-school English teacher from San
Francisco, has been hailed as the "Master of Merlot" by *Wine Spectator* for his uncanny
ability to craft the finest merlot in California.

If you've visited this winery and haven't been here in a while, don't follow your
memory to the front door. In 2001, St. Francis moved a little farther north to digs
bordering on the Santa Rosa County line. The original property was planted in 1910
as part of a wedding gift to Alice Kunde (scion of the local Kunde family) and christened St. Francis of Assisi in 1971 when Joe Martin and Lloyd Canton—two white-
collar executives turned vintners—completed their long-awaited dream winery. Today,
the winery still owns the property, but there's new history in the making at their much
larger facilities, which include a tasting room and upscale gift shop. Tastings are $10
for four current releases. The $20 for reserve tasting is paired with food, served in the
private reserve tasting room, and requires an appointment. Now that St. Francis is
planning more special activities, it's worthwhile to call or check their website for their
calendar of events.

100 Pythian Rd. (Calif.12/Sonoma Hwy.), Santa Rosa (at the Kenwood border). ℂ 800/543-7713 or 707/833-4666.
www.stfranciswinery.com. Daily 10am–5pm.

WHERE TO STAY IN SONOMA VALLEY

Keep in mind that during the peak season and on weekends, most B&Bs and hotels
require a minimum 2-night stay. Of course, that's assuming you can find a vacancy;
make reservations as far in advance as possible. If you are having trouble finding a room,
call the **Sonoma Valley Visitors Bureau** (ℂ 707/996-1090; www.sonomavalley.
com). The staff will try to refer you to a lodging that has a room to spare but won't make
reservations for you. Another option is the **Bed and Breakfast Association of Sonoma
Valley** (ℂ 800/969-4667), which can refer you to a B&B that belongs to the association. You can also find updated information on their website, **www.sonomabb.com**.
Keep in mind, however, that most B&B rates *start* at well over $100.

SONOMA
Best Western Sonoma Valley Inn *(Kids)*   There are just two reasons to stay here: (1)
It's the only place left with a vacancy, or (2) you're bringing the kids along. Otherwise,
unless you don't mind staying in a rather drab room with thin walls and small bathrooms,

you're probably going to be a little disappointed. Kids, on the other hand, will love this place: There's plenty of room to run around, plus a large heated outdoor pool, gazebo-covered spa, and sauna to play in. The rooms *do* come with a lot of perks, such as continental breakfast delivered to your room each morning, a gift bottle of white Sonoma Valley wine (chilling in the fridge), and satellite TV with HBO. Most rooms have either a balcony or a deck overlooking the inner courtyard. The inn is also in a good location, just a block from Sonoma's plaza.

550 Second St. W. (1 block from the plaza), Sonoma, CA 95476. ✆ 800/334-5784 or 707/938-9200. Fax 707/938-0935. www.sonomavalleyinn.com. 80 units. $114–$361 double. Rates include continental breakfast. AE, DC, DISC, MC, V. **Amenities:** Heated outdoor pool; health club; Jacuzzi; sauna; steam room; free wireless Internet access in lobby. *In room:* A/C, TV, dataport, fridge, coffeemaker, hair dryer, iron.

El Pueblo Inn *Value*   Located on Sonoma's main east-west street, 8 blocks from the center of town, this isn't Sonoma's fanciest hotel, but it offers some of the best-priced accommodations around and doesn't require a 2-day minimum. Family owned and operated since 1958, the guest rooms here are pleasant enough, with post-and-beam construction, exposed brick walls, light-wood furniture, and tub/shower combos in every bathroom. We especially like the heavy curtains that block the sunlight and let you sleep off that wine hangover. A coffee machine should be a comfort to early risers, and an outdoor heated pool—surrounded by wisteria, hyacinths, and palms—will cool you off in hot weather. Reservations should be made at least a month in advance for the spring and summer months.

896 W. Napa St., Sonoma, CA 95476. ✆ 800/900-8844 or 707/996-3651. www.elpebloinn.com. 38 units. May–Dec $115–$255 double; Jan–Apr $90–$185 double. AE, DISC, MC, V. **Amenities:** Outdoor pool; nearby golf course; whirlpool spa; bike rental. *In room:* A/C, TV/VCR, dataport, fridge, coffeemaker, hair dryer, iron.

Sonoma Chalet *✦*   If you like country rustic with a dash of the eclectic, you'll like the Sonoma Chalet. This is one of the few accommodations in Sonoma that's truly secluded; it's on the outskirts of town, in a peaceful country setting overlooking a 200-acre ranch. The accommodations, housed in a Swiss-style farmhouse and several cottages, are all individually decorated by someone with an eye for color and a concern for comfort. They all have claw-foot tubs, beds covered with country quilts, comfortable furnishings, and private decks; some have woodstoves or fireplaces. The two least expensive rooms (about $110 per night) share a bathroom, while the cottages offer the most privacy. A breakfast of fruit, yogurt, pastries, and cereal is served either in the country kitchen or in your room. After a long day of wine tasting, the outdoor hot tub looks mighty inviting.

18935 Fifth St. W., Sonoma, CA 95476. ✆ 800/938-3129 or 707/938-3129. www.sonomachalet.com. 3 units (2 with shared bathroom), 1 suite, 3 cottages. Apr–Oct $110–$235 double; Nov–Mar $110–$225 double; suite $170–$190; cottages $185–$225. Rates include continental breakfast. AE, MC, V. **Amenities:** Outdoor hot tub. *In Room:* No phone.

Sonoma Hotel *✦✦*   This cute little historic hotel on Sonoma's tree-lined town plaza emphasizes 19th-century elegance and comfort. Built in 1880 by German immigrant Henry Weyl, it has attractive guest rooms decorated in early California style, with French country furnishings, wood and iron beds, and pine armoires. In a bow to modern luxuries, recent additions include private bathrooms, cable TV, phones with dataports, and (this is crucial) air-conditioning. Perks include fresh coffee and pastries in the morning and wine in the evening. The lovely restaurant, The Girl & the Fig serves California-French cuisine.

110 W. Spain St., Sonoma, CA 95476. (C) **800/468-6016** or 707/996-2996. Fax 707/996-7014. www.sonomahotel.com. 16 units. Winter $95–$195 double; summer $110–$245 double. 2-night minimum required for summer weekends. Rates include continental breakfast and evening wine. AE, DC, MC, V. **Amenities:** Restaurant. *In room:* A/C, TV, dataport.

Victorian Garden Inn 🟅🟅 Here, proprietor Donna Lewis runs what is easily the cutest B&B in Sonoma Valley. A small picket fence, a wall of trees, and an acre of gardens enclose an adorable Victorian garden brimming with violets, roses, camellias, and peonies, all shaded under flowering fruit trees. It's truly a marvelous sight in the springtime. The guest units—three in the century-old water tower and one in the main building (an 1870s Greek Revival farmhouse), as well as a cottage—continue the Victorian theme, with white wicker furniture, floral prints, padded armchairs, and claw-foot tubs. The most popular units are the Top o' the Tower and the Woodcutter's Cottage. Each has its own entrance and a garden view; the cottage boasts a sofa and armchairs set in front of the fireplace. After a hard day of wine tasting, spend the afternoon cooling off in the pool or on the shaded wraparound porch, enjoying a mellow merlot while soaking in the sweet garden smells. *New parents, take note:* The property recommends you leave young tots behind.

316 E. Napa St., Sonoma, CA 95476. (C) **800/543-5339** or 707/996-5339. Fax 707/996-1689. www.victoriangarden inn.com. 3 units, 1 cottage. $139–$259 double. Rates include continental breakfast. AE, DC, MC, V. **Amenities:** Outdoor pool; hot tub; concierge; business center; free Internet access in business center; laundry service. *In room:* A/C, fireplace (in some rooms).

GLEN ELLEN

Beltane Ranch 🟅 *Finds* The word *ranch* conjures up a big ole' two-story house in the middle of hundreds of rolling acres, the kind of place where you laze away the day in a hammock watching the grass grow or pitching horseshoes in the garden. Well, friend, you can have all that and more at the well-located Beltane Ranch, a century-old buttercup-yellow manor that's been everything from a bunkhouse to a brothel to a turkey farm. You simply can't help but feel your tensions ease away as you prop your feet up on the shady wraparound porch overlooking the quiet vineyards, sipping a cool chardonnay while reading *Lonesome Dove* for the third time. Each room is uniquely decorated with American and European antiques; all have sitting areas and separate entrances. A big and creative country breakfast is served in the garden or on the porch overlooking the vineyards. For exercise, you can play tennis on the private court or hike the trails meandering through the 105-acre estate. The staff here is knowledgeable and helpful. *Tip:* Request one of the upstairs rooms, which have the best views.

11775 Sonoma Hwy./Hwy. 12. (P.O. Box 395) Glen Ellen, CA 95442. (C) **707/996-6501**. www.beltaneranch.com. 5 units, 1 cottage. $140–$190 double; $220 cottage. Rates include full breakfast. No credit cards; personal checks accepted. **Amenities:** Tennis court. *In room:* No phone.

WHERE TO DINE IN SONOMA
SONOMA

Basque Boulangerie Café 🟅 *Value* BAKERY/DELI If you're the type that prefers a light morning meal and strong coffee, stand in line with the locals at the Basque Boulangerie Café, the most popular gathering spot in the Sonoma Valley. Most everything—sourdough Basque breads, pastries, quiche, soups, salads, desserts, sandwiches—is made in-house, and made well. Daily lunch specials, such as a grilled veggie sandwich with smoked mozzarella cheese, are listed on the chalkboard out front. Seating is scarce, and if you can score a sidewalk table on a sunny day, consider yourself one lucky person. A popular option is ordering to go and eating in the shady plaza across the street. The cafe sells wine by the glass, as well as a wonderful cinnamon bread by the loaf—ideal for making French toast.

460 First St. E., Sonoma. ⓒ **707/935-7687.** Menu items $3–$7. No credit cards. Daily 7am–6pm.

Black Bear Diner *Kids* DINER   When you're craving a classic Americana breakfast with all the cholesterol and the fixin's (perhaps to counterbalance that wine hangover), make a beeline for this old-fashioned diner. First, it's fun with its over-the-top bear paraphernalia, gazette-style menu listing local news from 1961 and every possible diner favorite, and absurdly friendly waitstaff. Second, it's darned cheap. Third, helpings are huge. What more could you want? Kids get a kick out of coloring books, old-timers reminisce over Sinatra playing on the jukebox, and everyone leaves stuffed on omelets, scrambles, and pancakes. Lunch and dinner feature steak sandwiches, salads, and comfort food faves like barbecued pork ribs, Cobb salad, fish and chips, and burgers—they grind their own beef. But unless you like old-school run-of-the-mill diner fare, your best bet is to dine elsewhere. That said, you can load up here on the cheap, especially since dinners come with salad or soup, bread, and two sides. Seniors can order from a specially priced menu.

201 West Napa St. (at Second St.), Sonoma. ⓒ **707/935-6800.** Main courses $5–$8.50 breakfast, $5.50–$17 lunch and dinner. AE, DISC, MC, V. Sun–Thurs 6am–10pm; Fri–Sat 6am–midnight.

Della Santina's *𝕬𝕬* TUSCAN   For those of you who just can't swallow another expensive, chichi California meal, follow the locals to this friendly, traditional Italian restaurant. How traditional? Ask father-and-son team Dan and Robert: When I last dined here, they pointed out Signora Santina's hand-embroidered linen doilies as they proudly told me about her Tuscan recipes. (Heck, even the dining room looks like an old-fashioned, elegant Italian living room.) And their pride is merited: Every dish my party tried was refreshingly authentic and well flavored, without overbearing sauces or one *hint* of California pretentiousness. Be sure to start with traditional antipasti, especially sliced mozzarella and tomatoes, or delicious white beans. The nine pasta dishes are, again, wonderfully authentic (gnocchi lovers, rejoice!). The spit-roasted meat dishes are a local favorite (although I found them a bit overcooked); for those who can't choose between chicken, pork, turkey, rabbit, or duck, there's a selection that offers a choice of three. Don't worry about breaking your bank on a bottle of wine, because many choices here go for under $40. Portions are huge, but be sure to save room for a wonderful dessert.

133 E. Napa St. (just east of the square), Sonoma. ⓒ **707/935-0576.** Reservations recommended. Main courses $10–$20. AE, DISC, MC, V. Daily 11:30am–3pm and 5–9:30pm.

Maya *𝕬𝕬* MEXICAN   Gourmet Mexican might be the best way to describe the food at this lively grill and rotisserie restaurant on the southeast corner of Sonoma's plaza. We're not talking top-shelf enchiladas here—rather, it's a winning combination of traditional Yucatán dishes prepared with ultrafresh ingredients. Take salmon, for instance: a thick cut of fresh salmon, perfectly cooked and matched with pasilla pesto, chervil and tarragon risotto, and a medley of root vegetables. The commendable *Maya pollo rostizado*—a spit-roasted half chicken with a Yucatán spice rub—could easily feed two. Yes, you're probably going to pay a bit more than you planned to pay for Mexican food, but it's worth the extra few dollars. You're likely to enjoy the faux Mayan village ambience as well: desert earth tones with bright splashes of colorful art and thick, hand-carved wood furnishings. The only caveat is the *muy fuerte* noise level, but order a couple of fantastic margaritas on the rocks, and you'll soon be in fiesta mode yourself.

101 E. Napa St., Sonoma. © **707/935-3500**. www.mayarestaurant.com. Reservations recommended. Main courses $9–$20. MC, V. Mon–Thurs 11:45am–9:30pm; Fri–Sat 11:45am–10:30pm; Sun 4–9pm.

Rin's Thai ⊛ THAI   When valley residents or visitors get a hankering for Pad Thai, curry chicken, or *tom yam* (classic spicy soup), they head to this adorable little restaurant just off Sonoma Plaza. The atmosphere itself—contemporary, sparse yet warm environs within an old house—is welcoming and the staff is extremely accommodating. After you settle into one of the well-spaced tables within or on the outside patio (weather permitting), go for your favorites—from satay with peanut sauce and cucumber salad to superb *gai kraprao* (minced chicken, chiles, basil, and garlic sauce) or char-broiled vegetables or ribs with chile-garlic dipping sauce. They've got it all covered, including that oh-so-sweet Thai iced tea, fried bananas with coconut ice cream, and fresh mango with sticky rice (seasonal).

139 E. Napa St. (just east of the plaza), Sonoma. © **707/938-1462**. www.rinsthai.com. Reservations recommended. Main courses $7.50–$9.25 lunch; $8.25–$11 dinner. MC, V. Sun–Thurs 11:30am–9:00pm; Fri–Sat 11:30am–9:30pm.

KENWOOD

Café Citti ⊛ *(Value* ITALIAN   If you're this far north into the Wine Country, then you're probably doing some serious wine tasting. If that's the case, then you don't want to spend half the day at a fancy, high-priced restaurant. What you need is Café Citti (*cheat*-ee), a roadside do-it-yourself Italian trattoria that is both good and cheap. There's no menu; you order from the menu board displayed above the open kitchen. Afterwards you scramble for a table (the ones on the patio, shaded by umbrellas, are the best on warm afternoons), and a server will bring your meal. It's all hearty, home-cooked Italian. Standout dishes are the green-bean salad, tangy Caesar salad, focaccia sandwiches, and roasted rotisserie chicken. The freshly made pastas come with a variety of sauces; my favorite is the ravioli in basil cream sauce. Wine is available by the bottle, and the espresso is plenty strong. Everything is available to go, which makes Café Citti an excellent resource for picnic supplies.

9049 Sonoma Hwy., Kenwood. © **707/833-2690**. Main courses $6–$9.50. MC, V. Lunch daily 11am–3:30pm; dinner Sun–Thurs 5–8:30pm, Fri–Sat 5–9pm.

Appendix:
San Francisco in Depth

Born as an out-of-the-way backwater of colonial Spain and blessed with a harbor that would have been the envy of any of the great cities of Europe, San Francisco boasts a story as varied as the millions of people who have passed through its Golden Gate.

1 History 101

THE AGE OF DISCOVERY

After Columbus "discovered" the New World in 1492, legends of the fertile land were discussed in the universities and taverns of Europe, even though no one quite understood where the mythical land was. (Some evidence of arrivals in California by Chinese merchants hundreds of years before Columbus's landing has been unearthed, although few scholars are willing to draw definite conclusions.) The first documented visit by a European to Northern California was by the Portuguese explorer Juan Rodriguez Cabrillo, who circumnavigated the southern tip of South America up the western coast of North America as far north as the Russian River in 1542. Nearly 40 years later, in 1579, Sir Francis Drake landed on the Northern California coast, stopping for a time to repair his ships and to claim the territory for Queen Elizabeth of England. Another Portuguese, Sebastian Cermeño, "discovered" Punta de los Reyes (King's Point) in the mid-1590s. All three adventurers completely missed the narrow entrance to San Francisco Bay, either because it was shrouded in fog or, more likely, because they simply weren't looking for it. Believe it or not, the bay's entrance is nearly impossible to see from the ocean.

Two more centuries passed before a European actually saw the bay that would later extend Spain's influence over much of the American West. Gaspar de Portolá, a soldier sent from Spain to meddle in a rather ugly conflict between the Jesuits and the Franciscans, accidentally stumbled upon the bay in 1769, en route to somewhere else. He stoically plodded on to his original destination, Monterey Bay, more than 100 miles to the south. Juan Ayala actually sailed into San Francisco Bay 6 years later while on a mapping expedition for the Spanish and immediately realized the enormous strategic importance of his find.

Colonization quickly followed. Juan Bautista de Anza and around 30 Spanish-speaking families marched through the deserts from Sonora, Mexico, arriving after many hardships at the northern tip of modern-day San Francisco in June 1776. They immediately claimed the peninsula for Spain. (Their claim of allegiance to Spain occurred only about a week before the 13 English-speaking colonies of North America's eastern seaboard declared their independence from Britain.) Their headquarters was an adobe fortress, the Presidio, built on the site of today's park with the same name. The settlers' church, a mile to the south, was the first of five Spanish missions later developed around the edges of San Francisco Bay. Although the name of the church was officially *Nuestra Señora de Dolores,* it was dedicated to St. Francis of Assisi and nicknamed San Francisco by the Franciscan priests. Later, the name applied to the entire bay.

In 1821, Mexico broke away from Spain, secularized the Spanish missions, and abandoned all interest in the natives. Freed of Spanish restrictions, California's ports suddenly opened to trade. The region around San Francisco Bay supplied large amounts of hides and tallow for transport around Cape Horn to the tanneries and factories of New England and New York. The prospects for prosperity persuaded an English-born sailor, William Richardson, to jump ship in 1822 and settle on the site of what is now San Francisco. To impress the commandant of the Presidio, whose daughter he loved, Richardson converted to Catholicism and established the beginnings of what would soon became a thriving trading post and colony. Richardson named his trading post Yerba Buena (or "good herb") because of a species of wild mint that grew there, near the site of today's Montgomery Street. (The city's original name was recalled with great mirth 120 years later during San Francisco's hippie era.) He conducted a profitable hide-trading business and eventually became harbormaster and the city's first merchant prince. By 1839, the place was a veritable town, with a mostly English-speaking populace and a saloon of dubious virtue.

Throughout the 19th century, armed hostilities between English-speaking settlers from the eastern seaboard and the Spanish-speaking colonies of Spain and Mexico erupted in places as widely scattered as Texas, Puerto Rico, and along the frequently shifting U.S.–Mexico border. In 1846, a group of U.S. Marines from the warship *Portsmouth* seized the sleepy main plaza of Yerba Buena, ran the U.S. flag up a pole, and declared California an American territory. The Presidio (occupied by about a dozen Mexican soldiers) surrendered without a fuss. The first move made by the new, mostly Yankee citizenry was to officially adopt the name of the bay as the name of their town.

THE GOLD RUSH

The year 1848 was one of the most pivotal in European history, with unrest sweeping through Europe, horrendous poverty in Ireland, and widespread disillusionment about hopes for prosperity throughout Europe and the East Coast of the United States. Stories about the golden port of San Francisco and the agrarian wealth of the American West filtered slowly east, attracting slow-moving groups of settlers. Ex-sailor Richard Henry Dana extolled the virtues of California in his best-selling novel, *Two Years Before the Mast,* and helped fire the public's imagination about

Dateline

- **1542** Juan Rodriguez Cabrillo sails up the California coast.
- **1579** Sir Francis Drake lands near San Francisco, missing the entrance to the bay.
- **1769** Members of the Spanish expedition led by Gaspar de Portolá become the first Europeans to see San Francisco Bay.

- **1775** The *San Carlos* is the first European ship to sail into San Francisco Bay.
- **1776** Captain Juan Bautista de Anza establishes a presidio (military fort); San Francisco de Asis Mission opens.
- **1821** Mexico wins independence from Spain and annexes California.
- **1835** The town of Yerba Buena develops around the port; the United States tries

unsuccessfully to purchase San Francisco Bay from Mexico.
- **1846–48** War between the United States and Mexico.
- **1847** Americans annex Yerba Buena and rename it San Francisco.
- **1848** Gold is discovered in Coloma, near Sacramento.
- **1849** In the year of the Gold Rush, San Francisco's population swells from under 1,000 to 26,000.

the territory's bounty, particularly that of the Bay Area.

The first overland party crossed the Sierra and arrived in California in 1841. San Francisco grew steadily, reaching a population of approximately 900 by April 1848, but nothing hinted at the population explosion that was to follow. Historian Barry Parr has referred to the California Gold Rush as the most extraordinary event to ever befall an American city in peacetime. Even without the lure of gold, San Francisco's winning combination of raw materials, healthful climate, and freedom would eventually have attracted thousands of settlers. But the gleam of the soft metal is said to have compressed 50 years of normal growth into less than 6 months. In 1848, the year gold was discovered, the population of San Francisco jumped from under 1,000 to 26,000. As many as 100,000 more passed through San Francisco in the space of less than a year on their way to the hinterlands where the gold was rumored to be.

If not for the discovery of some small particles of gold at a sawmill that he owned, Swiss-born John Augustus Sutter would have left a far less flamboyant legacy. Despite Sutter's wish to keep the discovery quiet, his employee, John Marshall, leaked word of the discovery to friends. It eventually appeared in local papers, and smart investors on the East Coast took immediate heed. The rush did not start, however, until Sam Brannan, a Mormon preacher and famous charlatan, ran through the streets of San Francisco shouting, "Gold! Gold in the American River!" (Brannan, incidentally, bought up all the harborfront real estate he could and cornered the market on shovels, pick-axes, and canned food just before making the announcement that was heard around the world.)

A world on the brink of change responded almost frantically. The Gold Rush was on. Shop owners hung GONE TO THE DIGGINGS signs in their windows. Flotillas of ships set sail from ports throughout Europe, South America, Australia, and the East Coast, sometimes nearly sinking with the weight of mining equipment. Townspeople from the Midwest headed overland, and the social structure of a nation was transformed almost overnight. Not since the Crusades of the Middle Ages had so many people mobilized in so short a time. Daily business stopped; ships arrived in San Francisco and their crews almost immediately deserted. News of the gold strike spread like a plague through every discontented hamlet in the known world.

Although other settlements were closer to the gold strike, San Francisco was the famous name and, therefore, where the gold diggers disembarked. Tent cities

- **1851** Lawlessness becomes acute; attempts are made to curb it.
- **1869** The transcontinental railroad reaches San Francisco.
- **1873** Andrew S. Hallidie invents the cable car.
- **1906** The Great Earthquake strikes, and the resulting fire levels the city.
- **1915** The Panama-Pacific International Exposition celebrates San Francisco's

restoration and the completion of the Panama Canal.
- **1936** The Bay Bridge is built.
- **1937** The Golden Gate Bridge is completed.
- **1945** The United Nations' Charter is drafted in San Francisco and adopted by representatives of 50 countries.
- **1950** The Beat Generation moves into the bars and cafes of North Beach.

- **1967** A free concert in Golden Gate Park attracts 20,000 people, ushering in the Summer of Love and the hippie era.
- **1974** BART's high-speed transit system opens the tunnel linking San Francisco with the East Bay.
- **1978** Harvey Milk, a city supervisor and America's first openly gay politician, is assassinated, along with

sprang up, and demand for virtually everything skyrocketed. Although some miners actually found gold, smart merchants quickly discovered more enduring business in servicing the needs of the thousands of miners who arrived ill-equipped and ignorant of the lay of the land. Prices soared. Miners, faced with staggeringly inflated prices for goods and services, barely turned a profit after expenses. Most prospectors failed, many died of hardship, and others committed suicide at the alarming rate of 1,000 a year. Yet despite the tragedies, graft, and vice associated with the Gold Rush, within mere months San Francisco was forever transformed from a tranquil Spanish settlement into a roaring, boisterous boomtown.

BOOMTOWN FEVER

By 1855, most of California's surface gold had already been panned out, leaving only the richer but deeper veins of ore, which individual miners couldn't retrieve without massive capital investments. Despite that, San Francisco had evolved into a vast commercial magnet, sucking into its warehouses and banks the staggering riches that overworked newcomers had dragged, ripped, and distilled from the rocks, fields, and forests of western North America.

Investment funds poured into more than mining, however. Speculation on the newly established San Francisco stock exchange could make or destroy an investor in a single day, and several noteworthy writers (including Mark Twain) were among the young men forever influenced by the boomtown spirit. The American Civil War left California firmly in the Union camp, ready, willing, and able to receive hordes of disillusioned soldiers fed up with the internecine warmongering of the eastern seaboard. In 1869, the transcontinental railway linked the eastern and western coasts of the United States, ensuring the fortunes of the barons who controlled it. The railways shifted economic power bases, however, as cheap manufactured goods from the East undercut the costly articles that sailed or steamed around the tip of South America. The "Big Four"—iron-willed capitalists Leland Stanford, Mark Hopkins, Collis P. Huntington, and Charles Crocker—almost completely controlled ownership of the newly formed Central Pacific and Southern Pacific railroads, and their ruthlessness was legendary. (Much of the bone-crushing railway labor was done by low-paid Chinese newcomers, most of whom arrived in overcrowded ships at San Francisco ports.) As the 19th century came to a close, civil unrest became more frequent as the monopolistic grip of the railways and

Mayor George Moscone, by political rival Dan White.

- **1989** An earthquake registering 7.1 on the Richter scale hits San Francisco just before a World Series baseball game, as 100 million people watch on TV; the city quickly rebuilds.
- **1991** Fire rages through the Berkeley and Oakland hills, destroying 2,800 homes.

- **1996** Former Assembly Speaker Willie Brown elected mayor of San Francisco.
- **2001** The dot-com craze comes to a crashing end; thousands are laid off. A major electricity shortage results in rolling blackouts throughout California.
- **2003** The recall effort that unseats Governor Gray Davis, and replaces him with actor Arnold Schwarzenegger puts

California in the national spotlight.

- **2004** Mayor Newsome's permission of gay marriages garners national attention before it's quashed by governmental higher ups.
- **2005** San Francisco is one of the first major U.S. cities to offer housing and assistance to victims of Hurricane Katrina.

robber barons became more obvious. Adding to the discontent were the uncounted thousands of Chinese immigrants who fled starvation and unrest in Asia at rates rivaling those of the Italians, Poles, Irish, and British.

During the 1870s, the flood of profits from the Comstock Lode in western Nevada diminished to a trickle, a cycle of droughts wiped out part of California's agricultural bounty, and local industry struggled to survive against the flood of manufactured goods coming by rail from well-established East Coast and Midwest factories. Often, discontented workers blamed their woes on the now-unwanted hordes of Chinese workers, who by preference and for mutual protection had congregated in teeming all-Asian communities.

Despite these downward cycles, the city enjoyed other bouts of prosperity around the turn of the century, thanks to the Klondike gold rush in Alaska and the Spanish-American War. Long accustomed to making a buck off gold fever, San Francisco managed to position itself as a point of embarkation for supplies bound for Alaska. Also during this time, the Bank of America emerged; it eventually grew into the largest bank in the world. Founded in North Beach in 1904, the bank was the brainchild of Italian-born A. P. Giannini, who later funded part of the construction for a bridge that many critics said was preposterous: the Golden Gate.

THE GREAT FIRE

On the morning of April 18, 1906, San Francisco changed for all time. The city has never experienced an earthquake as destructive as the one that hit at 5:13am (scientists estimate its strength at 8.1 on the Richter scale). All but a handful of the city's 400,000 inhabitants lay fast asleep when the ground went into a series of convulsions. As one eyewitness put it, "The earth was shaking . . . It was undulating, rolling like an ocean breaker." The quake

ruptured every water main in the city and simultaneously started a chain of fires that rapidly fused into one gigantic conflagration. The fire brigades were helpless, and for 3 days San Francisco burned.

Militia troops finally stopped the flames from advancing by dynamiting entire city blocks, but not before more than 28,000 buildings lay in ruins. Minor tremors lasted another 3 days. The final damage stretched across a path of destruction 450 miles long and 50 miles wide. In all, 497 city blocks, or about one-third of the city, was razed. As Jack London wrote in a heartbreaking newspaper dispatch, "The city of San Francisco is no more." The earthquake and subsequent fire so decisively changed the city that post-1906 San Francisco bears little resemblance to the town before the quake. Out of the ashes rose a bigger, healthier, and more beautiful town, although latter-day urbanologists regret that the rebuilding that followed the San Francisco earthquake did not follow a more enlightened plan. So eager was the city to rebuild, that the old, somewhat unimaginative gridiron plan was reinstated, despite the opportunities for more daring visions that the quake's aftermath afforded.

In 1915, in celebration of the opening of the Panama Canal and to prove to the world that San Francisco was restored to its full glory, the city was host to the Panama-Pacific International Exhibition, a world's fair that exposed hundreds of thousands of visitors to the city's unique charms. The frenzy of boosterism, however, reached its peak during the years just before World War I, when investments and civic pride might have reached an all-time high. Despite Prohibition, speakeasies in and around the city did a thriving business, and building sprees were as high-blown and lavish as the profits on the San Francisco stock exchange.

WORLD WAR II

The Japanese attack on Pearl Harbor on December 7, 1941, mobilized the United

States into a massive war machine, with many shipyards strategically positioned along the Pacific Coast, including San Francisco. Within less than a year, several shipyards were producing up to one new warship per day, employing hundreds of thousands of people working around the clock. (The largest, Kaiser Shipyards in Richmond, employed more than 100,000 workers.) In search of work and the excitement of life away from their villages and cornfields, workers flooded into the city from virtually everywhere, forcing an enormous boom in housing. Hundreds found themselves separated from their small towns for the first time in their lives and reveled in their newfound freedom.

After the hostilities ended, many soldiers remembered San Francisco as the site of their finest hours and returned to live there permanently. The economic prosperity of the postwar years enabled massive enlargements of the city, including freeways, housing developments, a booming financial district, and pockets of counterculture enthusiasts, such as the beatniks, gays, and hippies.

THE 1950s: THE BEATS

San Francisco's reputation as a rollicking place where anything goes dates from the Barbary Coast days in the 1800s when gang warfare, prostitution, gambling, and drinking were major pursuits, and citizens took law and order into their own hands. Its more modern role as a catalyst for social change and the avant-garde began in the 1950s. A group of young writers, philosophers, and poets challenged the materialism and conformity of American society by embracing anarchy and Eastern philosophy, expressing their notions in poetry. They adopted a uniform of jeans, sweater, sandals, and beret, called themselves "Beats," and hung out in North Beach, where rents were low and cheap wine was plentiful. *San Francisco Chronicle* columnist Herb Caen, to whom they

were totally alien, dubbed them "beatniks" in his column.

Allen Ginsberg, Gregory Corso, and Jack Kerouac had begun writing at Columbia University in New York, but it wasn't until they came west and hooked up with Lawrence Ferlinghetti, Kenneth Rexroth, Gary Snyder, and others that the movement gained national attention. The bible of the Beats was Ginsberg's "Howl," which he first read at the Six Gallery on October 13, 1955. By the time he finished reading, Ginsberg was crying, the audience was chanting, and his fellow poets were announcing the arrival of an epic bard. Ferlinghetti published "Howl," which was deemed obscene, in 1956. A trial followed, but the court found that the book had redeeming social value, reaffirming the right of free expression. The other major work, Jack Kerouac's *On the Road,* was published in 1957 and instantly became a bestseller. (He had written it as one long paragraph in 20 days in 1951.) The freedom and sense of possibility the book conveyed became the bellwether for a generation.

While the Beats gave poetry readings and generated controversy, two clubs in North Beach were making waves, notably the "hungry i" and the Purple Onion, where everyone who was anyone or became anyone on the entertainment scene appeared. Mort Sahl, Dick Gregory, Lenny Bruce, Barbra Streisand, and Woody Allen all worked there. Maya Angelou appeared as a singer and dancer at the Purple Onion. The cafes of North Beach—the Black Cat, Vesuvio's, Caffè Trieste, Caffè Tosca, and Enrico's Sidewalk Cafe—were the center of bohemian life in the '50s. When the tour buses started rolling in, rents went up, and Broadway became a sex-club strip in the early 1960s. Thus ended an era, and the Beats moved on. The alternative scene shifted to Berkeley and the Haight.

THE 1960s: THE HAIGHT

The torch of freedom passed from the Beats and North Beach to the hippies and Haight-Ashbury, but it was a radically different torch. The hippies replaced the Beats' angst, anarchy, negativism, nihilism, alcohol, and poetry with love, communes, openness, drugs, rock music, and a back-to-nature philosophy. Although the scent of marijuana wafted everywhere—on the streets, in the cafes, in Golden Gate Park—the real drugs of choice were LSD (a tab of good acid cost $5) and other hallucinogenics. Timothy Leary experimented with its effects and exhorted youth to "turn on, tune in, and drop out." Instead of hanging out in coffeehouses, the hippies went to concerts at the Fillmore or the Avalon Ballroom to dance. The first Family Dog Rock 'n' Roll Dance and Concert, "A Tribute to Dr. Strange," was at the Longshoreman's Hall in 1965. It featured Jefferson Airplane, the Marbles, the Great Society, and the Charlatans. At the event, the first major happening of the 1960s, Ginsberg led a snake dance through the crowd. In January 1966, Longshoreman's Hall was the site of the 3-day Trips Festival, organized by rock promoter Bill Graham. The climax came with Ken Kesey and the Merry Pranksters Acid Test show, which used five movie screens, psychedelic visions, and the sounds of the Grateful Dead and Big Brother and the Holding Company. The "be-in" followed in the summer of 1966 at the polo grounds in Golden Gate Park, when an estimated 20,000 heard Jefferson Airplane perform and Ginsberg chant, while Hell's Angels acted as unofficial police. During the Summer of Love in 1967, thousands of young people streamed into the city in search of drugs and sex.

The '60s Haight scene was very different from the '50s Beat scene. The hippies were much younger than the Beats had been, constituting the first youth movement to take over the nation. (They also became the first generation of young, independent, and moneyed consumers to be courted by corporations.) Ultimately, the Haight and the hippie movement deteriorated from love and flowers into drugs and crime, drawing a fringe of crazies like Charles Manson and leaving only a legacy of sex, drugs, violence, and consumerism. As early as October 1967, the "Diggers," an anarchist, guerilla street-theater group, who had opened a free shop and soup kitchen in the Haight, symbolically buried the dream in a clay casket in Buena Vista Park.

The end of the Vietnam War and the resignation of President Nixon took the edge off politics. The last fling of the mentality that had driven the 1960s occurred in 1974, when the Symbionese Liberation Army kidnapped newspaper heiress Patty Hearst from her Berkeley apartment and took her on a bank-robbing spree before surrendering in San Francisco.

THE 1970s: GAY RIGHTS

The homosexual community in San Francisco developed at the end of World War II, when thousands of military personnel returned to the U.S. via San Francisco. Many returning vets who were homosexuals decided to stay in the city. A gay community grew up along Polk Street between Sutter and California. Later, the larger community moved into the Castro, where it remains today.

The gay political-protest movement is usually dated from the 1969 Stonewall raid in Greenwich Village. Although the political movement started in New York, California had already given birth to two major organizations for gay rights: the Mattachine Society, founded in 1951 by Harry Hay in Los Angeles, and the Daughters of Bilitis, a lesbian organization founded in 1955 in San Francisco.

After Stonewall, the Committee for Homosexual Freedom was created in the spring of 1969 in San Francisco; a Gay Liberation Front chapter was organized at

Berkeley. In the fall of 1969, Robert Patterson, a columnist for the *San Francisco Examiner*, referred to homosexuals as "semi-males," "drag darlings," and "women who aren't exactly women." On October 31 at noon, a group began a peaceful picket of the *Examiner*. Peace reigned until someone threw a bag of printer's ink from an *Examiner* window. Someone wrote "F*** the Examiner" on the wall, and the police moved in to clear the crowd, clubbing as they went. The remaining picketers retreated to Glide Methodist Church, and then marched on City Hall. Unfortunately, the mayor was away. Unable to air their grievances, they started a sit-in that lasted until 5pm, when they were ordered to leave. Most did, but three remained and were arrested.

Later that year, at an anti-Thanksgiving rally, gays protested against several national and local businesses: Western and Delta airlines (the former for firing lesbian stewardesses, the latter for refusing to sell a ticket to a young man wearing a Gay Power button); and radio station KFOG, for its anti-homosexual broadcasting; and some local gay bars for exploitation. On May 14, 1970, a group of gay and women's liberationists invaded the convention of the American Psychiatric Association in San Francisco to protest the reading of a paper on aversion therapy for homosexuals, forcing the meeting to adjourn.

The rage against intolerance was appearing on all fronts. At the National Gay Liberation conference in August 1970 in the city, Charles Thorp, chairman of the San Francisco State Liberation Front, called for militancy and issued a challenge to come out with a rallying cry of "Blatant is beautiful." He also argued for the use of what he felt was the more positive, celebratory term "gay" instead of "homosexual," and decried the fact that homosexuals were kept in their place at the three Bs: the bars, the beaches, and the baths. As the movement grew in size and power, debates on strategy and tactics occurred, most dramatically between those who wanted to withdraw into separate ghettos and those who wanted to enter mainstream society. The most extreme proposal was made in California by Don Jackson, who proposed establishing a gay territory in California's Alpine County, about 10 miles south of Lake Tahoe. It would have had a totally gay administration, civil service, university, museum—everything. The residents of Alpine County were not pleased with the proposal. But before the situation turned really ugly, Jackson's idea was abandoned because of lack of support in the gay community. In the end, the movement concentrated on integration and civil rights, not separatism. Gays would elect politicians who were sympathetic to their cause and celebrate their new identity by establishing National Gay Celebration Day and Gay Pride Week, the first of which was celebrated in June 1970, when 1,000 to 2,000 marched in New York, 1,000 in Los Angeles, and a few hundred in San Francisco.

By the mid-1970s, the gay community craved a more central role in city politics. Harvey Milk, owner of a camera store in the Castro, decided to run for the Board of Supervisors. He won, becoming the first openly gay person to hold a major public office in the city. He and liberal Mayor George Moscone developed a gay rights agenda, but in 1978 both were killed by former Supervisor Dan White, who shot them after Moscone refused his request for reinstatement. White, a former police officer, had consistently opposed the more liberal policies of Milk and Moscone. At his trial, White successfully pleaded temporary insanity caused by additives in his fast-food diet. The media dubbed it the "Twinkie defense," but the murder charges against White were reduced to manslaughter. On that day, angry and grieving, the gay community rioted, overturning and burning police cars in a night of rage. To this day, a candlelight memorial parade is held on November 27. Milk's martyrdom was both a political and a practical inspiration to gay candidates across the country.

The emphasis in the gay movement shifted abruptly in the 1980s, when the AIDS epidemic struck the community. AIDS has had a dramatic impact on the Castro. While it's still a thriving and lively community, it's no longer the constant party it once was. The hedonistic lifestyle that had played out in the discos, bars, baths, and streets changed as the seriousness of the epidemic sunk in and the number of deaths increased. Political efforts have shifted away from enfranchisement and toward demanding money for social services and research money to deal with the AIDS crisis. The gay community has developed its own organizations, such as Project Inform and Gay Men's Health Crisis, to publicize information about the disease, available treatments, and safe sex. New cases of AIDS in the gay community are on the decline in San Francisco, but it remains a serious problem.

THE 1980s: THE BIG ONE, PART TWO

The 1980s may have arrived in San Francisco with a whimper (compared to previous generations), but they went out with quite a bang. At 5:04pm on Tuesday, October 17, 1989, as more than 62,000 fans filled Candlestick Park for the third game of the World Series—and the Bay Area commute moved into its heaviest flow—a magnitude 7.1 earthquake struck. Within the next 20 seconds, 63 lives were lost, $10 billion in damage occurred, and the entire Bay Area community was reminded of its humble insignificance. Centered about 60 miles south of San Francisco in the Forest of Nisene Marks, the deadly temblor was felt as far away as San Diego and Nevada.

Although scientists had predicted an earthquake would hit on this section of the San Andreas Fault, certain structures built to withstand such an earthquake failed miserably. The most catastrophic event was the collapse of the elevated Cypress Street section of Interstate 880 in Oakland, where the upper level of the freeway pancaked the lower level, crushing everything with such force that cars were reduced to inches-high blocks of metal. Other heavily damaged structures included the San Francisco–Oakland Bay Bridge, shut down for months when a section of the roadbed collapsed; San Francisco's Marina District, where several multimillion-dollar homes collapsed on their weak, shifting bases of landfill and sand; and the Pacific Garden Mall in Santa Cruz, which was devastated.

President George H.W. Bush declared the seven hardest-hit counties a disaster area; at least 3,700 people were reported injured and more than 12,000 were displaced. More than 18,000 homes were damaged and 963 others destroyed. Although fire raged in the city and water supply systems were damaged, the major fires in the Marina District were brought under control within 3 hours, mostly through the heroic efforts of San Francisco's firefighters.

After the rubble finally settled, it was unanimously agreed that San Francisco and the Bay Area had pulled through miraculously well. After the quake, a feeling of *esprit de corps* swept the city as neighbors helped each other rebuild and donations poured in from all over the world. Although over a decade has passed, San Francisco still feels the effects of the quake, most noticeably during rush hour as commuters take a variety of detours to circumvent freeways that were damaged or destroyed and are still under construction.

THE 1990s: THE NEW GOLD RUSH

During the 1990s, the nationwide recession influenced the beginning of the decade, while the quiet rumblings of the

SAN FRANCISCO TODAY 299

new frontier in Silicon Valley escaped much notice. By the middle of the decade, San Francisco and the surrounding areas were the site of a new kind of gold rush—the birth of Internet industry.

Not unlike the gold fever of the 1800s, people flocked to the western shores to strike it rich—and they did. In 1999, the local media reported that each day, 64 Bay Area residents were gaining millionaire status. Long before the last year of the millennium, real estate prices went into the stratosphere, and the city's gentrification financially squeezed out many of those residents who didn't mean big business (read: many of the alternative types, elderly, and minorities who made the city colorful).

New business popped up everywhere—especially in the SoMa area, where startup companies jammed warehouse spaces to the rafters.

The new millennium was christened with bubbly in hand, foie gras and caviar on the linen tablecloth, and seemingly everyone in the money. New restaurants charging $35 per entree were all the rage, hotels were renovated, the new bayfront ballpark was packed, and stock-market tips were as plentiful as new million-dollar SoMa condos and high-rises. Though there were whispers of a stock market correction, San Franciscans were too busy raking in the dough and working and playing hard to heed the writing on the wall.

2 San Francisco Today

At the turn of the millennium, some didn't want to think that San Francisco's second Gold Rush was destined to dry up. The initial fallout in the market and the instability of overly funded dot-com companies was inevitable; everyone cashing in on the new economy knew the situation was too good to last. Venture capitalists began holding onto their funding, rather than doling it out to anyone with business plan and a ".com" suffix. The scale was finally balancing, with brick-and-mortar companies re-establishing dominance over the newcomers surfing the bandwidth bandwagon. Dot-com obituaries and mass layoffs grew longer and grimmer; as this book goes to press, thousands of Bay Area employees from all walks of high-tech life are still searching for jobs.

But even the darkest clouds have a silver lining. The dot-com bomb has led to a welcomed rise in vacancies and declines in rent (though it's still outrageous) as the droves of itinerant gold diggers hitched up and moved out. And since the terrorist attacks on September 11, 2001, we've

even surprised ourselves at how patriotic we can be in the face of adversity. Every citizen was knocked senseless by the evil deeds of religious fanatics, but we quickly fought back to regain our civic pride and enviable California lifestyle.

But just when things were getting back to normal, along came the 2003 recall effort to oust Governor Gray Davis, launching California politics into the international news limelight as Arnold "The Terminator" Schwarzenegger campaigned successfully to unseat the unpopular Davis. This was followed by more national headlines as our neophyte Mayor Gavin Newsom unleashed a political and legal tempest when he ordered the city clerk to issue marriage licenses to same-sex couples in 2004. Despite all the political hubbub, it's safe to say that San Francisco's future is looking optimistic. The past couple of years have given us a much-needed reality check and a chance to step back, look at where we've come from, and move forward at a more reasonable speed to where we'd like to go.

Index

See also Accommodations and Restaurant indexes, below.

GENERAL INDEX

AAA (American Automobile Association), 15, 20, 36, 47
AA Bakery & Café, 194
Aardvark's, 217
AARP, 28
A B fits, 209
Access-Able Travel Source, 27
Access America, 25
Accessible Journeys, 27
Accommodations, 73–97. See also Accommodations Index
　best, 9–10
　chains, 75
　family-friendly, 80
　money-saving tips and discounts, 16–17
　Napa Valley, 271–274
　parking, 16, 83
　Point Reyes, 254–255
　price categories, 74
　reservation services, 74
　Sonoma Valley, 285–287
　surfing for, 30–32
　tipping, 51
　what's new in, 1
A Clean, Well-Lighted Place for Books, 207
Addresses, finding, 60
A Different Light Bookstore, 28
Adventures Aloft, 185
AIDSinfo, 40
Airfares, money-saving tips, and discounts on, 14–15, 35
　for international visitors, 45
Airlines, 33–34, 46
Airports, 32–33
　security procedures, 34–35
Air Tickets Direct, 35
Alabaster, 213
A La Carte, A La Park, 23
Alamere Falls, 253
Alamo, 27, 47, 67
Alaska Airlines, 33
Alcatraz Island, 4, 54, 146–147

Alessi, 213
All American Boy, 210
American Airlines, 33
American Airlines Vacations, 36
American Automobile Association (AAA), 15, 20, 36, 47
American Conservatory Theater (A.C.T.), 221–222
American Express, 69–70
　traveler's checks, 19–20
American Foundation for the Blind (AFB), 27
American Rag Cie, 209
America West Airlines, 33
Amoco Motor Club, 15, 36
Amtrak, 36
The Anchorage, 216
Angel Island, 245–246
Angel Island Tram Tour, 246
Antiques, 205
A-One Rent-A-Car, 15
Aquarium of the Bay, 159
Aquatic Park, 175
Architectural highlights, 179–182
Area codes, 70
Arrowood Vineyards & Winery (Glen Ellen), 283–284
Art galleries, 205–206
　Oakland, 244
Art of China, 211–212
Artspan Open Studios, 24
Asian Art Museum, 159
Atelier Dore, 205
ATMs (automated teller machines), 19, 44
Atrium Lobby Lounge, Marriott Hotel's, 157
Australia
　customs regulations, 42
　embassy and consulate, 48
　passport information, 41
　visa information, 40
Avenue Cyclery, 185–186
Avis, 27, 47, 67
Ayala Cove (Angel Island), 246

Babushka, 212
Baker Beach, 176, 185
Balboa Café, 56
Balclutha, 163
Ballooning, 185
Bambuddha Lounge, 3, 232
Bank of America, 192
Bank of America World Headquarters, 179–180
Barnes & Noble, 207
Bars, 228–234
　gay and lesbian, 234–235
BART (Bay Area Rapid Transit), 67
　to/from airports, 32, 33
　Berkeley, 237
　Oakland, 33, 242
　tour, 182
Baseball, 5, 188–189
Basketball, 189
BATS Improv, 222
Bay Area Reporter, 28, 234
Bay Meadows, 189
Bay Model Visitors Center (Sausalito), 249
Bayporter Express, 33
Bay to Breakers Foot Race, 22, 188
Beach Blanket Babylon, 201, 222–223
Beaches, 185
Bear Valley Visitors Center (Point Reyes), 252, 253
The beats, 200, 201, 295
Beaulieu Vineyard (Rutherford), 263–264
Bed & Breakfast Inns of Napa Valley, 271
Bed and breakfasts (B&Bs), 16
Belden Place, 108
Benziger Family Winery (Glen Ellen), 284
Beringer Vineyards (St. Helena), 265
Berkeley, 237–242
Berkeley Marina Sports Center, 186

Bicycling, 57, 58, 156, 185–186, 270
  Mount Tamalpais, 251
  Napa Valley, 270
  Sonoma Valley, 283
BiddingForTravel, 30
Big Pagoda Company, 213–214
Biordi Art Imports, 201, 214
Bird-watching, Point Reyes, 253
Biscuits and Blues, 225
Blazing Saddles, 57, 186
The Bliss Bar, 232
Blue & Gold Fleet, 69, 147
  Angel Island and Tiburon, 245
  cruises, 183
  Sausalito, 248
Blue Waters Kayaking, 253
Boating, 186. *See also* Kayaking
Boat tours, 182–183
Bonhams & Butterfield, 205
Book Passage, 207
Books, recommended, 37–38
The Booksmith, 207
Bookstores, 207–208
  Berkeley, 238
The Boom Boom Room, 225–226
Borders, 207
Bottom of the Hill, 226
Bouchon Bakery (Yountville), 3
Boudin at the Wharf, 2, 147
Boulange de Cole, 211
Boulange de Polk, 211
Boulangerie, 211
Brainwash, 71
Brewpubs, 230–231
Britex Fabrics, 209
Brooks Brothers, 210
The Bubble Lounge, 233
Bucket shops, 14, 35
Buddhist Church of San Francisco, 169
Budget car rentals, 27, 47, 67
Buena Vista Café, 54, 58, 228
Buena Vista Park, 187
Buena Vista Winery (Sonoma), 281–282
Buffalo Exchange, 217
Builders Booksource San Francisco, 207
Burlington Coat Factory, 206
Buses, 66
Business hours, 47, 70
Bus tours, 183
  Muir Woods, 250
Bus travel, 46

Cabaret, 222–223
Cable Car Clothiers, 210
Cable Car Museum, 160
Cable cars, 8, 52, 54, 63, 66, 150, 152
The Café, 234
Cafe du Nord, 224–225
Caffè Greco, 55, 231
Calendar of events, 21–25
California Academy of Sciences, 160–161, 172
California Historical Society, 166
California Palace of the Legion of Honor, 161–162
Calistoga, 265–266, 268
  accommodations, 273–274
  bicycling, 270
  mud baths, 270–271
  restaurants, 278–279
Calistoga Spa Hot Springs, 271
Calistoga Village Inn & Spa, 271
CalTrain, 36
Cameron House, 194
Camping, Point Reyes, 252
Canada
  customs regulations, 42
  embassy of, 48
  health insurance, 43
  passport information, 41
The Cannery at Del Monte Square, 152, 216
The Canton Bazaar, 192, 208
Carnaval, 22
Carnelian Room, 231–232
The Carneros District, 280–281
Car rentals, 47, 67–68
  for disabled travelers, 27
  money-saving tips, 15
Car travel, 35–36, 46–47, 67
  driving safety, 45
Cass Marina, 186
The Castro, 5, 63
  accommodations, 95–96
  restaurants, 139–141
  sights and attractions, 170
Castro Street Fair, 24
Castro Theatre, 236
Catharine Clark Gallery, 205
C. A. Thayer, 163
The Chanel Boutique, 210
Charles Krug Winery (St. Helena), 265
Charter flights, 14–15
Château St. Jean (Kenwood), 285
Cherry Blossom Festival, 21
Chestnut Street, shopping, 204

Children, families with
  Children's Zoo, 165
  information and resources, 29
  shopping, 211, 217
  sights and attractions, 180
China Beach, 176–177
Chinatown, 4–5, 54, 61
  restaurants, 115–118
  shopping, 203
  sights and attractions, 168–169
  walking tours
    guided, 184
    self-guided, 190–196
Chinatown Gateway Arch, 190, 192
The Chinatown Kite Shop, 192, 217
Chinese Chamber of Commerce, 59
Chinese Culture Center, 196
Chinese Historical Society of America Museum, 194–195
Chinese New Year, 21
Chowhound, 31
The Cinch Saloon, 234
Cinco de Mayo Celebration, 21–22
Cinemas, 235–236
Circle Gallery, 179
Citizen Clothing, 210
City Box Office, 220
City Guides, 190
City Hall, 179
City Lights Booksellers & Publishers, 38, 200, 207
CityPass, 16, 18, 66
Cityscape, 232
Civic Center, 62, 179
  accommodations, 93–94
  restaurants, 132–134
Classical music, 220
Cliff House, 177
Climate, 20–21
Clos Du Val (Napa), 260
Clos Pegase (Calistoga), 266, 268
Clothes Contact, 218
Club and music scene, 223–228
  gay and lesbian, 234–235
Club Deluxe, 225
Club Fugazi, 201
Club Line, 225
Coastal Trail, 8, 176
Cobb's Comedy Club, 223
Cody's Books (Berkeley), 238
Coit Tower, 152
College Avenue (Berkeley), 240

Columbus Avenue, 168
No. 140, 198
Columbus Tower, 198
Comedy clubs, 222–223
Condor Club, former site of, 200–201
Condor Sports Bar, 200
Conservatory of Flowers, 173–174
Consolidators, 14, 35
Consulates, 48
Continental Airlines, 33
Continental Airlines Vacations, 36
Copia: The American Center for Wine, Food & the Arts (Napa), 268–269
Copy Central, 71
Cornerstone Festival of Gardens (Sonoma), 282
Cosentino (Yountville), 261
Cost Plus World Market, 212
Cowell Theater, 220
Cowgirl Creamery, 211
Cow Hollow, 62
accommodations, 89–92
restaurants, 126–130
Cow Hollow Playground, 180
Crafts, 208
Crate & Barrel Outlet (Berkeley), 240
Credit cards, 20, 44
Crissy Field, 176
Crocker Galleria, 216
Cruisin' the Castro, 183–184
Currency and currency exchange, 43
Customs regulations, 41–42

Dance clubs, 224
Dance companies, 220
Dandelion, 212–213
Daylight saving time, 51
Dean & DeLuca Market (St. Helena), 262, 277
Delta Air Lines, 33
Delta Vacations, 36
Dentists, 70
Department stores, 208–209
Detour, 234
De Young Museum, 2, 162
Dianne's Old & New Estates, 215
Dining, 98–145. See also Restaurant Index
Berkeley, 240–242
best, 10–12
by cuisine, 99–102
family-friendly, 125

money-saving tips and discounts, 17
Napa Valley, 274–279
Oakland, 244–245
Point Reyes, 255–256
Sausalito, 249–250
Sonoma Valley, 287–289
Tiburon, 246, 248
tipping, 51
what's new in, 1–2
Diptyque, 2, 214
Di Rosa Preserve (Napa), 268
Disabilities, travelers with, 26–27
Discount shopping, 206
Distractions, 213
Doctors, 70
Dollar, 67
Dollar car rentals, 47
Domaine Chandon (Yountville), 261
Drinking laws, 47–48
Driver's licenses, foreign, 40
Drugstores, 70
Dr. Wilkinson's Hot Springs (Calistoga), 271
Dutch windmills, 172

Eagle, The, 234–235
Earthquakes, 70–71
of 1906, 294
Edinburgh Castle, 228
Elderhostel, 28
Electricity, 48
The Embarcadero, 60
Embarcadero Four's Justin Herman Plaza, 109
Embassies and consulates, 48
Emergencies, 48, 71
Emily lee, 210
Empire Plush Room, 3, 226
The EndUp, 224, 235
Enrico's, 55
Enterprise car rentals, 67
Eos, 233
Equinox, 232
Eureka, 163
Eureka Theatre Company, 222
Exotic Erotic Halloween Ball, 24
Expedia, 29–31, 36
The Exploratorium, 162–163

Fabrics, 209
The Factory, 224
Fairmont Hotel & Tower, 10, 156
Families with children
Children's Zoo, 165
information and resources, 29

shopping, 211, 217
sights and attractions, 180
Family Travel Files, 29
Family Travel Forum, 29
Family Travel Network, 29
Farmers' Market, 9, 153, 212
Fashions (clothing), 209–211
vintage, 217–218
Fax machines, 50
Fern Creek Trail (Muir Woods), 250
Ferries, to/from Sausalito or Larkspur, 69, 248
Ferry Building, 180
Ferry Building Marketplace, 153
Ferry Plaza Farmers' Market, 9, 153, 212
Festivals and special events, 21–25
Fideaux (St. Helena), 269
Filbert Street Steps, 157, 186
The Fillmore, 226
Fillmore Street, shopping, 204
Fillmore Street Jazz Festival, 23–24
Film, 235–236
Film Festival, San Francisco International, 21, 235–236
Financial District, 60–61
restaurants, 108–110
First Crush, 3, 233
Fisherman's Wharf, 8, 61, 153, 155
accommodations, 88–89
restaurants, 123–126
shopping, 204
sights and attractions, 154
Fishing, 186
Flax, 213
Fleet Week, 24
Flight 001, 217
Flood Mansion, 181
FlyCheap, 35
Flying Wheels Travel, 27
Folsom Street Fair, 24
Food stores, 211
Football, 189
Footcandy (St. Helena), 269
Foreign visitors, 39–51
customs regulations, 41–42
driver's licenses, 40
entry requirements, 39–40
immigration and customs clearance, 45–46
money matters, 43–44
passports, 40–41
safety suggestions, 44–45
traveling around the U.S., 46–47
traveling to the U.S., 45–46

Fort Mason Center, 175–176
Fort Point, 176
49-mile scenic drive, 182
Fourth of July Celebration & Fireworks, 23
Fourth Street (Berkeley), 240
Fraenkel Gallery, 205
Frank Family Vineyards (Calistoga), 266
Free or almost free activities, 4–5, 8–9, 156–157
    art galleries and museums, 165
Frequent-flier clubs, 35
Friendship Line for the Elderly, 28
Fumiki Fine Asian Arts, 205

Gap, 209
Gasoline, 48
Gay and lesbian travelers, 23
    bars and clubs, 234–235
    bookstore, 28
    history, 296–298
    information and resources, 27–28
Gay Men's Health Crisis, 40
Geary Theater, 221–222
Getaway Adventures BHK (Calistoga), 270
Ghirardelli Square, 155–156, 216
Gifts, 211–213
Gimme Shoes, 216
Ginsberg, Allen, 198
Giovanni's Room, 28
Glen Ellen, 283–284
    accommodations, 287
Glide Memorial United Methodist Church, 8, 156, 178
Gloria Ferrer Champagne Caves (Sonoma), 281
GoCars, 2, 155
Golden Era Building, 198
Golden Gate Bridge, 4, 55–56, 58
    sightseeing, 156–158
Golden Gate Ferry Service, 69, 248
Golden Gate Fields, 189
Golden Gate Fortune Cookie Company, 193, 211
Golden Gate National Recreation Area (GGNRA), 175–178, 188
Golden Gate Park, 5, 8, 56, 156, 171–174, 180
    tennis courts, 188

Golden Gate Park Boat House, 186
Golden Gate Park Course, 187
Golden Gate Promenade, 176
Golden Haven Hot Springs Spa (Calistoga), 271
Golden State Warriors, 189
Gold Rush, 291–293
Golf, 186–187
Gondola Servizio (Oakland), 243
Good Byes, 217
Goodtime Bicycle Company (Sonoma), 283
Good Vibrations, 213
Gordon Biersch Brewery Restaurant, 230
Go San Francisco Card, 147
Gourmet Delight B.B.Q., 194
Grace Cathedral, 178
Grant & Green Saloon, 226
Grant Avenue, 192
Gray Line, 183
Great China Herb Co., 194
Great Fire (1906), 294
Green Apple Books, 207
Greens Sports Bar, 233
Greyhound/Trailways, 46
Grgich Hills Cellar (Rutherford), 264
Gump's, 208

Haas-Lilienthal House, 163
Haight-Ashbury, 5, 56, 63
    accommodations, 94
    in the 1960s, 296
    restaurants, 134–136
    sights and attractions, 170
Haight-Ashbury Flower Power Walking Tour, 184
Haight Street, 157
    shopping, 204
Haight Street Fair, 22
Hallidie Building, 179
Halloween, 24
Hamburgers (Sausalito), 249
Handball, 187
Hang, 206
Harrington's Bar & Grill, 21
Harry Denton's Starlight Room, 227
Hawaiian Airlines, 33
Hayes Valley, shopping, 204
Health concerns, 26
Health insurance, 25, 26
    for international visitors, 42–43
Heinold's First and Last Chance Saloon (Oakland), 243–244

Held Over, 218
Hertz, 27, 47, 67
The Hess Collection (Napa), 260
Highways, 35–36
Hiking and walking, 188
History, 290–299
HIV-positive visitors, 40
Holidays, 49
Horseback riding, Napa Valley, 270
Horse racing, 189
Hot-air ballooning, 185
Hotels, 73–97. See also Accommodations Index
    best, 9–10
    chains, 75
    family-friendly, 80
    money-saving tips and discounts, 16–17
    Napa Valley, 271–274
    parking, 16, 83
    Point Reyes, 254–255
    price categories, 74
    reservation services, 74
    Sonoma Valley, 285–287
    surfing for, 30–32
    tipping, 51
    what's new in, 1
Hotels.com, 30
Hotwire, 30, 31
Housewares and furnishings, 213–215
Hungry i, 200
Huntington Park, 180

I Can, 27
I Can't Believe I Ate My Way Through Chinatown tour, 184
Images of the North, 206
Ina Coolbrith Park, 187
Indian Springs Resort (Calistoga), 271
Inns of Marin (Point Reyes), 254
Insurance, 25–26
International Ameripass, 46
International Gay and Lesbian Travel Association (IGLTA), 28
International visitors, 39–51
    customs regulations, 41–42
    driver's licenses, 40
    entry requirements, 39–40
    immigration and customs clearance, 45–46
    money matters, 43–44
    passports, 40–41
    safety suggestions, 44–45
    traveling around the U.S., 46–47
    traveling to the U.S., 45–46

Internet access, 71
Ireland
    embassy and consulate, 48
    passport information, 41
    visa information, 40
Italian Heritage Parade, 24
Itineraries, suggested, 52–58
Itravelnet.com, 30

Jack London Square
    (Oakland), 243
Jack's Cannery Bar, 216
Jackson Square
    400 block of, 198
    shopping, 205
Jade Galore, 194
Jan de Luz (St. Helena), 269
Japan Center, 169, 170
Japanese Tea Garden, 174
Japantown, 62
    restaurants, 131–132
    sights and attractions,
    169–170
Javawalk, 183
Jazz at Pearl's, 225, 227
Jeremys, 206
JetBlue, 33
Jewelry, 215
Johnson Drake's Oyster
    Farm, 254
Joseph Schmidt Confections,
    211
Joshua A. Norton's Home, 196
Julie's Supper Club, 228
Julius Kahn Playground, 180

Kabuki Springs & Spa,
    169, 170
Kati Koos, 213
Kayaking
    Angel Island, 246
    Point Reyes, 253
Kenneth Cole, 216
Kenwood
    restaurant, 289
    wineries, 284–285
Kenwood Vineyards, 284
Kids
    Children's Zoo, 165
    information and resources, 29
    shopping, 211, 217
    sights and attractions, 180
Kimo's, 235
Kinko's, 71
Konko Church of San Francisco,
    169

Lakeside Park (Oakland), 243
Lands End, 177
Larkspur, 69
La Rosa, 217–218
Lastminute.com, 30
Laundry, 71
Lavay Smith & Her Red Hot
    Skillet Lickers, 226
Lawrence Hall of Science
    (Berkeley), 238
Ledisi, 226
Legal aid, 49
Levende Lounge, 232–233
Limn, 214
Lincoln Park, 8, 177, 187–188
Lincoln Park Golf Course, 187
Li Po Cocktail Lounge, 228–229
Liquor laws, 71
Lombard Street, 52, 54, 158
London Wine Bar, 233–234
Lone Star Saloon, 235
Lorraine Hansberry
    Theatre, 222
Lost-luggage insurance, 25–26
Lou's Pier 47 Club, 226–227
Luxor Cabs, 69
Lyon Street Steps, 186

MAC, 209
Macy's, 208
The Magic Theatre, 222
Mail, 49
Mail Boxes Etc. (Sonoma), 267
Mapquest, 31
Marathon, San Francisco
    Chronicle, 23, 188
Marina District, 55, 56, 61–62
    accommodations, 89–92
    restaurants, 126–130
Marina Green, 176
Marina Safeway, 12, 126
Marin Headlands, 5, 178
Maritime National Historical
    Park, 163
Market Street, 60
MasterCard ATM Locator, 31
MasterCard traveler's checks, 20
Matrix Fillmore, 229
McLaren Lodge and Park
    Headquarters, 172
McLaren Memorial Rhododen-
    dron Dell, 172
Medical Dental Building, 180
MedicAlert identification tag, 26
Medical insurance, 25, 26
    for international visitors, 42–43

Medical requirements for
    entry, 40
Merritt, Lake (Oakland), 243
Metreon Entertainment
    Center, 166
Metro, 235
Meyerovich Gallery, 206
M. H. de Young Memorial
    Museum, 2, 162
Minis, 211
The Mint Karaoke Lounge, 235
Mission Bay Golf Center, 187
Mission District, 62–63
    murals, 157
    restaurants, 141–145
    sights and attractions, 171
Mission Dolores, 171, 178–179
Moe's Books (Berkeley), 238
Molinari Delicatessen,
    11, 201–202
Money matters, 19–20
    for international visitors,
    43–44
Money-saving tips and
    discounts
    accommodations, 16–17,
    73–74
    airfares, 14–15
    car rentals, 15
    nightlife, 18–19
    off season, 13
    restaurants, 17
    $70 a day premise, 13
    shopping, 18
    sightseeing, 17–18
    transportation, 15–16
The Monkey Club, 3, 233
The Montgomery Block, 197
Montgomery St., No. 1010, 198
MossRehab, 27
Mosswood Collection
    (Yountville), 269
Mount Tamalpais, 251
Mount Tamalpais State Park,
    255
Movies, 235–236
Mud baths, Calistoga, 270–271
Muir Woods, 8, 250
Mumm Napa Valley (Ruther-
    ford), 264
Muni (San Francisco Municipal
    Railway), 63, 72
    discount passes, 66
Muni Access Guide, 27
Municipal Boathouse
    (Oakland), 243
Murals, 157, 171
Musée Mécanique, 160, 177
Museum of Modern Art, 8
Music stores, 215–216

Napa, 260
  accommodations, 271–273
  restaurants, 274–276
Napa Premium Outlets, 269
Napa Valley, 257–279
  accommodations, 271–274
  outdoor activities, 270–271
  restaurants, 274–279
  shopping, 269–270
  sights and attractions,
    268–269
  traveling to, 258, 261
  visitor information, 258
  wineries, 258–266, 268
Napa Valley Conference & Visitors Bureau, 258, 268, 269
Napa Valley Olive Oil Manufacturing Company, 269–270
Napa Valley Reservations Unlimited, 271
National car rentals, 47, 67
Natural History Museum, 161
Naylor, Jacqui, 226
Nectar Wine Lounge, 3, 234
Neighborhoods
  in brief, 60–63
  sights and attractions in,
    166–171
Neiman Marcus, 208
Nest, 214
Newspapers and magazines, 71
  alternative and tourist, 18
The New Unique Company, 208
New Zealand
  customs regulations, 42
  embassy and consulate, 48
  passport information, 41
  visa information, 40
Nickie's Bar-be-cue, 224
Niebaum-Coppola (Rutherford), 263
Nightlife, 219–236
  bars, 228–234
  club and music scene, 223–228
  current listings, 219
  money-saving tips and
    discounts, 18–19
  Napa Valley, 270
  performing arts, 220–222
  tickets, 219–220
  what's new in, 3
Nihonmachi Mall, 169
Niketown, 209–210
Nob Hill, 61
  accommodations, 75–84
  restaurants, 110
  sights and attractions,
    167–168

Nordstrom, 208–209
North Bay tour, 58
North Beach, 54, 61
  accommodations, 88–89
  cafes, 5
  restaurants, 118–123
  sights and attractions, 168
  walking tour, self-guided,
    197–202
  walking tours, coffee guided
    tour, 183
North Beach Festival, 22
North Beach Museum, 201
Northwest Airlines, 33
Norton, Joshua A., Home, 196
Now, Voyager, 28

Oakland, 242–245
Oakland Athletics, 189
Oakland Convention and Visitors Bureau, 242–243
Oakland International Airport, 33
Oakland Museum of California, 244
Oakland Raiders, 189
Oakville, 261–262
The Oakville Grocery, 216, 277
Ocean Beach, 185
Ocean View Trail (Muir Woods), 250
Octagon House, 163–164
ODC Theatre, 220
Old Faithful Geyser of California, 271
Old St. Mary's Cathedral, 192
OpenTable.com, 31
Opera, 221
Opera in the Park, 23
Orbitz, 29, 36
Original Street of 'American' California, 192
Original TransAmerica Building, 197–198
Outdoor activities, 185–188

Pacific Heights, 62
  accommodations, 92
  restaurants, 130–131
Package tours, 36–37
Painted Ladies, 179
The Palace Hotel, 10
Palace of Fine Arts, 162–163
Pampanito, USS, 154
Paradise Lounge, 224
Paramount Theatre (Oakland), 243

Parking, 68–69
  at hotels, 16, 83
Parks, 187–188
  Berkeley, 240
Passports (discount passes), 66
Passports (travel documents), 40–41
Patina (St. Helena), 269
Patricia Unterman's San Francisco Food Lover's Guide, 104
Peace Pagoda, 169
Pearl (St. Helena), 269
Pearl & Jade Empire, 215
Performing arts, 220–222
Perimeter Road (Angel Island), 246
Perry's, 229
Petrified Forest, 271
Petrol, 48
Philharmonia Baroque Orchestra, 220
Picnic fare, 17
  Napa Valley, 277
  Sausalito, 249
Pied Piper Bar, 229
Pier 23, 227
PIER 39, 159, 217
PlumpJack Winery (Oakville), 261–262
Pocket Opera, 221
Point Lobos, 177
Point Reyes Bird Observatory, 253
Point Reyes Lighthouse, 252
Point Reyes National Seashore, 251–256
Police, 71
Portsmouth Square, 195–196
Postage rates, 49
Post offices, 72
Powell-Hyde Cable Car, 157
Prager Winery & Port Works (St. Helena), 265
Precita Eyes Mural Arts Center, 171
Prescription medications, 26
The Presidio, 174–175
Presidio Golf Course, 186–187
Priceline, 30–32
Propeller, 214
Punch Line Comedy Club, 223

Quikbook.com, 30

RAG, 2, 210
Rainfall, average, 21
Rasselas, 225

Ravenswood Winery (Sonoma), 282–283
Recycled Records, 215
Red & White Fleet, 183, 250
The Red Room, 229
Red Vic, 236
The Redwood Room, 229
Reggae in the Park, 24
REI (Berkeley), 240
Religious buildings, 178–179
Reneson hotels, 10, 85
Reserve America, 246
Restaurants, 98–145. See also Restaurant Index
　　Berkeley, 240–242
　　best, 10–12
　　by cuisine, 99–102
　　family-friendly, 125
　　money-saving tips and discounts, 17
　　Napa Valley, 274–279
　　Oakland, 244–245
　　Point Reyes, 255–256
　　Sausalito, 249–250
　　Sonoma Valley, 287–289
　　Tiburon, 246, 248
　　tipping, 51
　　what's new in, 1–2
Richmond and Sunset Districts, 63
　　accommodations, 94–95
　　restaurants, 136–138
Rincon Center, 181
　　Food Court, 109
Ripley's Believe It or Not! Museum, 154
Robert Mondavi Winery (Oakville), 262
Roman Spa Motel (Calistoga), 271
Rose Garden (Berkeley), 240
The Rose Garden (Golden Gate Park), 172
Ross Alley, 193
Roxie, 236
Ruby Skye, 224
Running, 188
Russian Hill, 61
　　restaurants, 110
Rutherford, 262–264

Safety, 26, 72
　　for international visitors, 44–45
Safeway, 12, 126
Safeway (St. Helena), 262
Saint Francis Memorial Hospital, 70
St. Francis Winery (Santa Rosa), 285

St. Helena, 269
　　accommodations, 273
　　restaurants, 276–278
　　wineries, 264–265
St. Helena Cyclery, 270
St. Helena Mailing Center, 267
St. Helena Premier Outlets, 269
St. Mary's Square, 192
St. Patrick's Day Parade, 21
Saints Peter and Paul Church, 202
St. Supéry Winery (Rutherford), 263
The Saloon, 227
SamTrans, 33
San Francisco Ballet, 220–221
San Francisco Bay Guardian, 18, 71, 219
San Francisco Blues Festival, 23
San Francisco Brewing Company, 230–231
San Francisco Chronicle, 31, 71, 219
San Francisco Chronicle Marathon, 23, 188
San Francisco CityPass, 16, 18, 66
San Francisco Convention and Visitors Bureau, 19, 31
San Francisco Dental Office, 70
San Francisco Electric Tour Company, 2, 152
San Francisco 49ers, 189
The San Francisco Gallery Guide, 205
San Francisco Giants, 188
San Francisco International Airport (SFO), 32
　　accommodations near, 96–97
San Francisco International Film Festival, 21, 235–236
San Francisco Jazz Festival, 25
San Francisco Lesbian, Gay, Bisexual, Transgender Pride Parade & Celebration, 23
San Francisco Marathon, 23
San Francisco Museum of Modern Art (SFMOMA), 164
　　MuseumStore, 213
San Francisco–Oakland Bay Bridge, 181–182
San Francisco Opera, 221
San Francisco Performances, 220
San Francisco Reservations, 74
San Francisco Sightseeing, 237
San Francisco Symphony, 220
San Francisco Visitor Information Center, 17, 59
San Francisco Weekly, 71, 219

San Francisco Zoo (& Children's Zoo), 164–165
SATH (Society for Accessible Travel & Hospitality), 27
Sausalito, 58, 248–250
　　ferries, 69
Sausalito Art Festival, 23
Sawyer Cellars (Rutherford), 262–263
SBC Park, 5, 158–159, 188
Scharffen Berger Chocolate Maker (Berkeley), 241
Schramsberg (Calistoga), 266
Seasons, 13, 16, 20
Sea Trek, 246
Sebastiani Vineyards & Winery (Sonoma), 282
Segway-powered tours, 152
Senior Citizen Information Line, 28
Senior travelers, 28–29
SFMOMA (San Francisco Museum of Modern Art), 164
　　MuseumStore, 213
SFO Airporter buses, 32
Shipping your purchases, 204
　　wines, 267
Shoes, 216
Shopping, 203–218
　　Berkeley, 240
　　discount, 206
　　hours, 204
　　major shopping areas, 203–204
　　money-saving tips, 18
　　Napa Valley, 269–270
　　sales tax, 204
　　shipping your purchases, 204
　　what's new in, 2
Shopping centers and complexes, 216–217
Shop with the Chef program, 212
Showroom by In Fiore, 2, 207
SideStep, 29
Sights and attractions, 146–184
　　for kids, 180
　　money-saving tips and discounts, 17–18
　　new, 2
Sigmund Stern Grove, 187
The Simmons Gallery, 206
Site59.com, 30
Skates on Haight, 156
Skylink Women's Travel, 28
Slim's, 227
Smarter Travel, 30
Smith, Lavay, 226
Smoking, 72, 229

Society for Accessible Travel & Hospitality (SATH), 27
Sokoji-Soto Zen Buddhist Temple, 169
SoMa (South of Market), 62
    accommodations, 84–88
    restaurants, 110–111, 114–115
    shopping, 204
    sights and attractions, 168
Sonoma
    restaurants, 287–289
    wineries, 281–283
Sonoma Valley, 279–289
    accommodations, 285–287
    restaurants, 287–289
    traveling to, 279
    visitor information, 279–280
    wineries, 280–285
Sonoma Valley Cyclery, 283
Sonoma Valley Visitors Bureau, 279–280
Southwest Airlines, 33–34
Spas, Napa Valley, 270, 271
Special events and festivals, 21–25
Spec's, 229–230
Spec's Adler Museum Café, 201
Spectator sports, 188–189
Spreckels Mansion, 181
Stag's Leap Wine Cellars (Napa), 260
Stair climbing, 186
STA Travel, 35
Steinhart Aquarium, 160
Sterling Vineyards (Calistoga), Napa Valley, 266
Stern Grove Midsummer Music Festival, 22
Stinson Beach, 8–9, 251
Stockton Street, 169, 194
Stow Lake, 174
Strawberry Hill/Stow Lake, 174
Streetcars, 66–67
Streetlight Records, 215
Strybing Arboretum & Botanical Gardens, 172, 174
The Stud, 235
Sue Fisher King, 214
Sunset District, 63
    accommodations, 94–95
    restaurants, 136–138
SuperShuttle, 32–33
Supper clubs, 227–228
Sur La Table, 214
Sutro Baths, 177
Sweeney Ridge, 178
Sweeny, Tom, 78

Taxes, 49, 72
Taxis, 15, 69
    airport, 32
    for disabled travelers, 26–27
Telegraph Avenue (Berkeley), 238
Telegraph Hill, 61
Telephone, 49–50
    area codes, 70
Telephone directories, 50
Temperatures, average, 21
Tennis, 188
Ten Ren Tea Co., Ltd., 193, 211
Theater, 221–222
Theatre Rhinoceros, 222
Therien & Co., 205
ThirstyBear Brewing Company, 231
1351 Lounge, 270
3 Babes and a Bus, 223
Thrift stores, 18
Thrifty, 47, 67
Tiburon, 246, 248
Tiburon–Angel Island Ferry, 246
Ticketmaster, 220
Tickets.com, 220
Tiffany & Co., 215
Tilden Regional Park (Berkeley), 240
Time zones, 50, 72
Tin How Temple, 195
Tipping, 51
Toilets, 51
Tomales Point Trail, 253
The Tonga Room & Hurricane Bar, 12, 17, 230
Top of the Mark, 232
Toronado, 230
Tosca, 230
Tourist information, 19, 59
Tours
    Angel Island, 246
    club-hopping, 223
    GoCar, 155
    organized, 182–184
    package, 36–37
Train travel, 36, 46
TransAmerica Building, Original, 197–198
TransAmerica Pyramid, 179, 197
Transit information, 72
Transportation, 63
    discounts, 15–16
Travel agencies
    for gay and lesbian travelers, 28
    online, 36
    for travelers with disabilities, 27

TravelAxe, 30
Traveler, 19
Traveler's Aid International, 48
Traveler's checks, 19–20, 43
Travelex Insurance Services, 25
Travel Guard Alerts, 25
Travel Guard International, 25
Traveling Internationally with Your Kids, 29
Travel insurance, 25–26
Travel Insured International, 25
Travelocity, 29, 30, 36
Travelweb, 30
TripAdvisor, 30, 31, 36
Trip-cancellation insurance, 25
True Sake, 2, 218
Twin Peaks, 188
Twin Peaks Tavern, 235

UC Berkeley Art Museum, 240
Union Square, 52, 60
    accommodations, 75–84
    restaurants, 102–108
    shopping, 203
Union Street, shopping, 203
Union Street Art Festival, 22–23
Union Street Goldsmith, 215
United Airlines, 34
United Commercial Bank, 193
United Kingdom
    embassy and consulate, 48
    health insurance, 43
    passport information, 41
    visa information, 39
United Vacations, 36
Universal Currency Converter, 31
University of California at Berkeley, 238, 240
The University of California Botanical Garden (Berkeley), 240
University of California Golden Bears, 189
The UPS Store, 50, 267
US Airways, 34
USA Rail Pass, 46

Vanderbilt and Company (St. Helena), 269
Van Ness Avenue, 60
Venice Gourmet Delicatessen (Sausalito), 249
Vesuvio, 200, 230
Veteran's Cab, 69

Viansa Winery and Italian Marketplace (Sonoma), 280–281
Victorian Homes Historical Walking Tour, 184
Virgin Megastore, 215–216
Visa ATM Locator, 31
Visas, 39–40
Visa traveler's checks, 20
Visa Waiver Program, 39
Visitor information, 19, 59
Visitor Information Center (Berkeley), 238
Visit USA, 46
V. Sattui Winery (St. Helena), 264–265

Walgreens, 70
Walk & Wok tour, 184
Walking tours
    guided, 183–184
    self-guided, 190–202
        Chinatown, 190–196
        North Beach, 197–202
Washington Square, 202
Waverly Place, 195
The Wax Museum at Fisherman's Wharf, 154
Weather, 20–21, 72
Websites
    traveler's toolbox, 31
    travel-planning and booking, 29–32
    visitor information, 19
Wells Fargo History Museum, 166
Westfield San Francisco Centre, 217
Westin St. Francis Hotel, outdoor elevators at, 156
Whale-watching, Point Reyes, 252–253
Wheelchair accessibility, 26–27, 49, 219
Where San Francisco, 71, 219
White Sulphur Springs Retreat & Spa, 270
Wilkes Bashford, 210
William Stout Architectural Books, 207–208
Windsor Vineyards (Tiburon), 246
Wine and champagne bars, 233–234
Wine Club San Francisco, 218
Wine Country, 257–289. *See also* Napa Valley; Sonoma Valley
Wine Exchange of Sonoma, 262, 267

Wineries
    Napa Valley, 258–268
    reservations at, 258
    Sonoma Valley, 280–285
Wines and shops, 218
    shipping wine home, 267
    Wine Country, 262
Winthrop, Faith, 226
Wish Bar, 233
The Wok Shop, 192, 214–215
Wok Wiz Chinatown Walking Tours & Cooking Center, 184
World War II, 294–295
Worldwide Assistance Services, 43

Yellow Cab, 26–27, 69
Yerba Buena Gardens/Center for the Arts, 166
Yoshi's World Class Jazz House & Japanese Restaurant (Oakland), 243
Yountville
    accommodations, 272–273
    restaurants, 276
    wineries, 261

Zeum, 166
Zinc Details, 215
Zoo, 164–165

ACCOMMODATIONS

Americania, 85
The Andrews Hotel, 75
The Archbishop's Mansion, 93
Bay Bridge Inn, 84–85
Bear Valley Inn Bed & Breakfast (Point Reyes), 3, 254
Beck's Motor Lodge, 95
Beltane Ranch (Glen Ellen), 287
Best Western, 75
Best Western Sonoma Valley Inn (Sonoma), 285–286
Calistoga Spa Hot Springs, 273
Carriage Inn, 85
The Cartwright Hotel, 76
The Castillo Inn, 95
Chablis Inn (Napa), 271–272
Chelsea Motor Inn, 89
Comfort Inn, 75
Comfort Suites, 80, 96
The Cornell Hotel de France, 76
Cow Hollow Motor Inn & Suites, 80, 89
Days Inn, 75
Doubletree Hotels, 75

Dr. Wilkinson's Hot Springs Resort (Calistoga), 274
Econo Lodges, 75
Edward II Inn & Suites, 89–90
El Bonita Motel (St. Helena), 273
Elements Hotel, 1, 93
El Pueblo Inn (Sonoma), 286
Embassy Suites, 96–97
Euro Spa & Inn (Calistoga), 274
Fitzgerald Hotel Union Square, 76, 78
Flamingo Inn, 85
The Golden Gate Hotel, 10, 78
Grant Plaza Hotel, 78
The Halcyon Hotel, 9, 79, 80
Holiday Inn, 75, 97
Hostelling International San Francisco—Downtown, 84
Hostelling International San Francisco—Fisherman's Wharf, 92
Hotel Beresford, 79
Hotel Beresford Arms, 79
Hotel Bijou, 79–80
Hotel Bohème, 9, 88–89
Hotel Britton, 85
Hotel Carlton, 1, 80
Hotel Del Sol, 10, 80, 91
Hotel des Arts, 1, 9, 10, 81
Howard Johnson, 75
Inn on Castro, 95–96
La Quinta Motor Inns, 75
The Laurel Inn, 9, 91
Lombard Motor Inn, 90
Maison Fleurie (Yountville), 272
Marina Inn, 9, 90
Marina Motel, 90–91
Metro Hotel, 94
Monte Cristo Bed and Breakfast, 10, 92
The Mosser, 9, 85
Motel Capri, 91
Motel Inverness (Point Reyes), 254–255
Motel 6, 75
Napa Valley Railway Inn (Yountville), 272–273
Napa Valley Redwood Inn (Napa), 272
Nob Hill Hotel, 10, 81
Nob Hill Motor Inn, 82
Phoenix Hotel, 10, 93–94
Point Reyes Hostel, 255
The Queen Anne Hotel, 92
Ramada, 75
Red Victorian Bed, Breakfast & Art, 10, 94
Renoir Hotel, 82
Rodeway Inns, 75

San Francisco Airport North
Travelodge, 80, 97
The San Remo Hotel, 9, 88
The Savoy Hotel, 82
Seal Rock Inn, 9, 94–95
Sonoma Chalet, 286
Sonoma Hotel, 286–287
Steep Ravine Environmental
Cabins (Mount Tamalpais
State Park), 3
The Stratford Hotel, 9, 83
Super 8, 75
Travelodge, 75
24 Henry, 96
Victorian Garden Inn
(Sonoma), 287
The Wharf Inn, 10, 80, 88
White Sulphur Springs Retreat
& Spa (St. Helena), 273
The Willows Inn, 96
Wine Valley Lodge (Napa), 272
York Hotel, 84

RESTAURANTS

Ace Wasabi's Rock 'n' Roll
Sushi, 126
Alexis Baking Company (Napa),
274
Andalé Taqueria, 125, 128
AsiaSF, 11, 110–111
A16, 130
Aziza, 138
Balboa Café, 126–127
Barney's Gourmet Hamburgers,
2, 129
Basque Boulangerie Café
(Sonoma), 287–288
Beach Chalet Brewery &
Restaurant, 125, 138–139
Betelnut, 127
B44, 108
Bistro Don Giovanni (Napa),
274–275
Black Bear Diner (Sonoma),
288
Blue Nile (Berkeley), 241
Bocadillos, 1–2, 102
The Boon Fly Café (Napa), 275
Bouchon Bakery (Yountville),
276
Boudin Sourdough Bakery &
Café, 124–126
Boulevard, 11, 114–115
Brandy Ho's Hunan Food,
115, 125
Burma Superstar, 136
Cafe Bastille, 108
Café Citti (Kenwood), 289

Café Claude, 102, 104
Café de la Presse, 104
Café do Brasil, 82
Cafe Fanny (Berkeley), 241
Café Flore, 139
Cafe Kati, 130–131
Café Metropol, 104
Cafe Pescatore, 123
Cafe Rouge (Berkeley), 241–242
Cafe Tiramisu, 108
Caffe Centro, 114
Caffe 817 (Oakland), 244
Caffè Greco, 231
Caffé Luna Piena, 139–140
Caffè Macaroni, 118–119
Caffè Museo, 8
Caffè Sport, 119
Caffè Trieste, 12, 153, 201, 231
The Cantinetta at Tra Vigne
(St. Helena), 276–277
Capp's Corner, 12, 55, 119
Cha Am Thai, 111
Cha Cha Cha, 11, 56, 134
Chez Nous, 130
Chow, 140
Citrus Club, 134–135
A Côté (Oakland), 3, 244
Crepes on Cole, 10–11, 136
Delfina, 141–142
Della Santina's (Sonoma), 288
Dottie's True Blue Café, 12,
104–105, 125
E'Angelo Restaurant, 127
Ebisu, 138
Eliza's, 125, 132
Ella's, 12, 125, 127
Emporio Armani Cafe, 105
Enrico's, 119
Firewood Café, 140
Fog City Diner, 123–124
Forbes Island, 126
Foreign Cinema, 145
Frjtz Fries, 132
Gira Polli, 119–120
Golden Boy Pizza, 11, 123
Gold Mountain, 115–116, 125
The Gold Spike, 120
Gordon Biersch Brewery
Restaurant, 111
Grand Café, 12, 107
Great Eastern, 116
The Grove, 55, 129
Guaymas (Tiburon), 246, 248
Hana Zen, 105
Hard Rock Cafe, 124, 125
Home Plate, 55, 129
Horizons (Sausalito), 58, 250
House of Dim Sum, 54, 193
House of Nanking, 116

Hunan Home's, 116
Il Pollaio, 120
Isa, 56, 128
Isobune, 131
Jack's Cannery Bar, 152
Kabuto A&S, 136–137
Kan Zaman, 12, 135
Khan Toke Thai House, 137
Kokkari, 11, 109
Kuleto's, 105
La Méditerranée, 130
Levende Lounge, 2, 142
Little Star Pizza, 133
L'Osteria del Forno, 120
Lou's Pier 47, 124
Manora's, 111, 114
Marcello's Pizza, 141
Mario's Bohemian Cigar Store,
12, 54, 121, 202
Maya (Sonoma), 288–289
Mecca, 141
Mel's Drive-In, 125, 128
Mifune, 131
Mocca, 106
Mo's Gourmet Burgers,
12, 121, 125
Neecha Thai, 131
Nippon Sushi, 140
Nob Hill Café, 110
North Beach Pizza, 121
O Chamé (Berkeley), 242
Oliveto Cafe (Oakland), 245
O'Reilly's Irish Pub, 202
Oriental Pearl, 116, 118
Palisades Market (Calistoga),
278–279
Park Chalet, 139
Park Chow, 138, 140
Pasta Pomodoro, 121–122, 125
Pauline's, 11, 142
Pho Hoa, 106
Piatti (Yountville), 276
Pizzeria Tra Vigne (St. Helena),
278
Plouf, 108
Pluto's, 129
Postrio, 108
Puccini & Pinetti, 106
Puerto Alegre Restaurant, 144
The Ramp, 141
R&G Lounge, 118, 196
Rin's Thai (Sonoma), 289
Ristorante Allegria (Napa), 275
RNM, 135
Saigon Saigon, 144
Sam's Anchor Café, 58
Sam's Anchor Café (Tiburon),
248
Sam Wo, 11, 118

San Francisco Art Institute
Café, 123
Sanppo, 131–132
Sanraku, 106–107
Sears Fine Foods, 107
The Slanted Door, 109–110
Sodini's Green Valley
Restaurant, 122
Station House Café (Point
Reyes), 255–256
The Stinking Rose, 122
Straits Café, 137
Swan Oyster Depot, 11, 110

Taqueria La Quinta (Point
Reyes), 256
Taquerias La Cumbre, 11, 17,
144–145
Taylor's Automatic Refresher
(St. Helena), 278
Thanh Long, 133
Thep Phanom, 17, 135
ThirstyBear Brewing
Company, 114
Ti Couz, 11, 144
Tommaso's, 122–123, 125
Tommy's Joynt, 12, 132–133
Ton Kiang, 11, 137

Truly Mediterranean, 145
Tú Lan, 11, 114
Villa Corona (Napa), 275–276
Wappo Bar & Bistro
(Calistoga), 279
The Warming Hut, 57–58
Washington Bakery &
Restaurant, 193
Wine Spectator Greystone
Restaurant (St. Helena), 278
Yank Sing, 11, 108–109
Yum Yum Fish, 139
Zona Rosa, 136
Zuni Café, 133–134
ZuZu (Napa), 276

THE NEW TRAVELOCITY GUARANTEE

EVERYTHING YOU BOOK WILL BE RIGHT, OR WE'LL WORK WITH OUR TRAVEL PARTNERS TO MAKE IT RIGHT, RIGHT AWAY.

*To drive home the point,
we're going to use the word "right" in every single sentence.*

Let's get right to it. Right to the meat! Only Travelocity guarantees everything about your booking will be right, or we'll work with our travel partners to make it right, right away. Right on!

Here's a picture taken smack dab right in the middle of Antigua, where the guarantee also covers you.

The guarantee covers all but one of the items pictured to the right.

Now, you may be thinking, "Yeah, right, I'm so sure." That's OK; you have the right to remain skeptical. That is until we mention help is always right around the corner. Call us right off the bat, knowing that our customer service reps are there for you 24/7. Righting wrongs. Left and right.

For example, what if the ocean view you booked actually looks out at a downright ugly parking lot? You'd be right to call – we're there for you. And no one in their right mind would be pleased to learn the rental car place has closed and left them stranded. Call Travelocity and we'll help get you back on the right track.

Now if you're guessing there are some things we can't control, like the weather, well you're right. But we can help you with most things – to get all the details in righting,* visit **travelocity.com/guarantee.**

*Sorry, spelling things right is one of the few things not covered under the guarantee.

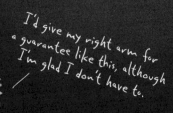

I'd give my right arm for a guarantee like this, although I'm glad I don't have to.

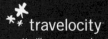

travelocity
You'll never roam alone.